[英 汉 对 照]

西方学术经典文库

经济发展理论

对利润、资本、信贷、利息和经济周期的探究

THE THEORY OF ECONOMIC DEVELOPMENT

AN INQUIRY INTO PROFITS, CAPITAL, CREDIT, INTEREST, AND THE BUSINESS CYCLE

[美] 约瑟夫·阿洛伊斯·熊彼特 著

叶 华 译

(一)

九 州 出 版 社
JIUZHOUPRESS

图书在版编目（CIP）数据

经济发展理论：对利润、资本、信贷、利息和经济周期的探究／（美）熊彼特著；叶华译．—北京：九州出版社，2006.11（2007.10 重印）

（西方学术经典文库）

ISBN 978-7-80195-553-1

Ⅰ.经…　Ⅱ.①熊…②叶…　Ⅲ.经济发展—理论研究—汉、英　Ⅳ.F201

中国版本图书馆 CIP 数据核字（2006）第 129246 号

经济发展理论：对利润、资本、信贷、利息和经济周期的探究

作　　者　［美］约瑟夫·阿洛伊斯·熊彼特
译　　者　叶　华
出　　版　九州出版社
出 版 人　徐尚定
地　　址　北京市西城区阜外大街甲 35 号（100037）
发行电话　（010）68992190/2/3/5/6
网　　址　www.jiuzhoupress.com
电子信箱　jiuzhou@jiuzhoupress.com
印　　刷　三河东方印刷厂
开　　本　630 × 970 毫米　1/16 开
印　　张　36.75
字　　数　394 千字
版　　次　2007 年 1 月第 1 版
印　　次　2007 年 10 月第 2 次印刷
书　　号　ISBN 978-7-80195-553-1/C · 104
定　　价　76.00 元（全两册）

出版说明

在西方学术思想的发展流变中，出现过很多影响深远的经典著作，这些著作穿越时空，为人们长久研读，有的甚至影响了整个人类文明的发展进程。这套《西方学术经典文库》（英汉对照本），精选了其中最有代表性的一些名著，计划达到一百部，将陆续分批出版直至全部完成。

《西方学术经典文库》由多位专家学者指导分类选目，内容涵盖哲学、文学、宗教学、政治学、经济学、社会学、人类学、心理学、法学、历史学等类，注重权威性、学术性和影响性，收录了不同国家、不同时代、不同流派的诸多名著。

《西方学术经典文库》中译本译自英文原著或其他文种的英文译本，以英汉对照的形式出版，读者可以参照原文对作品有更加客观的理解，更好地把握西方学术思想的精髓。

为加以区别，原文中的英文注释，注释号用①、②……形式表示；中文译者注释则以〔1〕、〔2〕……形式表示。至于英译本中出现的原文页码和特殊索引等问题，中文译者在“译者后记”中将予以解释、说明。另外，在英文原著中，有一些表示着重意义的斜体或大写等字体，考虑到读者可以在对照英文阅读中看到，因此在中译文中，没有照样标出，还望读者理解。

九州出版社

The Theory Of Economic Development

By *Joseph Alois Scumpeter*

English Translation By

Redvers Opie

本书根据 Harvard University Press 1934 年版本译出

CONTENTS
目　录

（一）

（二）

Preface To
The English Edition

Some of the ideas submitted in this book go back as far as 1907; all of them had been worked out by 1909, when the general framework of this analysis of the purely economic features of capitalistic society took the shape which has remained substantially unaltered ever since. The book was published for the first time, in German, in the fall of 1911. When, after it had been out of print for ten years, I consented, not without some reluctance, to a second edition, I omitted the seventh chapter, rewrote the second and the sixth, and shortened and added here and there. This was in 1926. The third German edition is merely a reprint of the second, from which also the present English version has been made.

I should be passing a very damaging verdict on what I have done and thought since the book first appeared, if I were to say that my failure to make alterations of other than expository consequence was caused by a belief that it is satisfactory in every detail. Although I do consider both the outlines-what might be termed the "vision"-and the results as correct in the main, there are many points on which I now have another opinion. To mention but one, by way of example: when the theory of the business cycle, which the reader finds in the sixth chapter, was first worked out, I took it for granted that there was a single wave-like movement, viz. that discovered by Juglar. I am convinced now that there are at least three such movements,

英文版序言

这本书所提出的某些思想可以追溯，远到1907年；到了1909年，所有这些思想和观点都已经整理有序，那时关于资本主义社会纯经济特征的这种分析的总框架已经形成，而且自此没有发生重大的改变。本书第一次出版是以德文形式，在1911年秋天。在它停止出版10年之后，当时我有些勉强地同意了印刷第二版，我删掉了第七章，重新写了第二章和第六章，并且在文章的某些地方做了缩减和增补。这是在1926年。德文的第三版仅仅是第二版的重印，现在的英文译本也是根据德文第二版翻译的。

如果说，在本书这次再版中，我除了对其评注以外没有其他任何改动，是因为我相信原书中每一个论点都是让人满意的，那我将是对本书自第一次问世以来我所做的和所想的做了一个非常有害的判断。尽管我确实认为本书的纲要——或者被称作“观点”——以及本书的结论在总体上是正确的，但是也有许多地方我现在有其他的看法。我只举一个例子来说：当经济周期理论第一次提出时，读者可以在第六章找到，我当时想当然地认为只存在一种单一的波浪式运动，也就是尤格拉所发现的那种周期。但是我现在相信至少存在三种这样的运动，

probably more, and that the most important problem which at present faces theorists of the cycle consists precisely in isolating them and in describing the phenomena incident to their interaction. But this element has not been introduced into the later editions. For books, like children, become independent beings when once they leave the parents' home. They lead their own lives, while the authors lead their own also. It will not do to interfere with those who have become strangers to the house. This book has fought its own way, and rightly or wrongly has won its place in the German literature of its time and field. It had seemed to me best to leave it undisturbed as much as possible. I should hardly have thought of an English translation but for the suggestion and encouragement of my eminent friend Professor Taussig.

For similar reasons, I have not followed the example of my great teacher Böhm-Bawerk, who with infinite care took notice of every objection or critique and embodied his own comments in his later editions. It is not any want of respect towards those who did me the honor of careful criticism of my argument that leads me to limit controversy to the minimum. I have to confess, however, that I have never come across an objection on essential points which carried conviction to my mind.

In aim and method, this book is frankly "theoretical." This is no place for a *professio fidei* on method. Perhaps I think somewhat differently now about the relation between "factual" and "theoretical" research than I did in 1911. But my conviction stands that our science cannot, any more than others, dispense with that refined common-sense which we call "theory" and which provides us with the tools for approaching both facts andpractical problems. However important may be the bearing of new masses of unanalysed, especially statistical, facts upon our theoretic apparatus – and undoubtedly

可能还更多；而且当前经济周期理论家所面临的最重要的问题是精确地把它们分开来，并描述它们之间相互作用所产生的各种现象。但是我没有在本书后来的版本中把这一要素引用进来。因为书籍就像孩子们一样，当他们一旦离开父母的家，就成为独立的人了。他们过着自己的生活，而作者也有他们自己的生活，我们不应该去干预那些离开了家成为局外的人。本书已经开拓出了它自己的路，不管是对的还是错的，它在其所处的时代和研究领域中，在德文文献中已经赢得了某种地位。对我来说，看起来最好是应尽可能地让它不受干扰。要不是由于我的受尊敬的朋友陶西格教授的建议和鼓励，我几乎就没有想到要出一个英文版本。

也由于同样的原因，我没有遵照我的伟大的导师庞巴维克的方式办事，他在他出书以后的版本中，极其细心地关注每一个反对或批评的意见，并加上他自己的评论。而我对于那些对我的论点提出仔细批评的人——这是我所荣幸的事，我却把争论限制到最低限度，这绝不是我对他们缺乏任何尊敬。然而我必须坦言，我从来没有遇到过这种情况，即一种在实质性问题上的反对意见，并且这个意见在我看来具有说服力。

很显然，就目的和方法而言，本书是“理论性”的，这里不是作为方法上的一种信仰表白的地方。关于“事实”研究和“理论”研究的关系，我想，或许我现在的想法和1911年有所不同了。但是，我仍然坚信，我们的科学，和其他任何事物一样，不能没有我们称之为“理论”的那些被提炼了的常识，这些常识为我们考察事实和实际问题提供了工具。不管新的众多的未经分析的事实，尤其是统计上的事实，对我们的理论工具的关系是多么重要——毫无疑问，

increasing wealth offactual material must continually suggest new theoretical patterns, and thereby currently and silently improve any existing theoretical structure-at any given stage *some* theoretical knowledge is a prerequisite to dealing with new facts, that is with facts not already embodied in existing theorems, If this knowledge remains rudimentary and subconscious, it may be had theory but it will not cease to be theory. I have not been able to convince myself, for example, that such questions as the source of interest are either unimportant or uninteresting. They could be made so, at all events, only by the fault of the author. I hope, however, to supply before long the detailed material which is here missing by more "realistic" studies in money and credit, interest, and cycles.

The argument of the book forms one connected whole. This is not due to any preconceived plan. When I began to work on the theories of interest and of the cycle, nearly a quarter of a century ago, I did not suspect that these subjects would link up with each other and prove closely related to entrepreneurs' profits, money, credit, and the like, in precisely the way in which the current of the argument led me. But it soon became clear that all these phenomena – and many secondary ones – were but incidents of a distinct process, and that certain simple principles which would explain them would explain also that process itself. The conclusion suggested itself that this body of theory might usefully be contrasted with the theory of equilibrium, which explicitly or implicitly always has been and still is the centre of traditional theory. I at first used the terms "statics" and "dynamics" for these two structures, but have now (in deference to Professor Frisch) definitively ceased to use them in this sense. They have been replaced by others,

随着大量事实材料不断增加，新的理论模式也必将不断地被启示，从而逐步地，静静地改进现有的任一理论结构——在任何给定的阶段，具有某些理论知识是处理新的事实的一个先决条件，因为这些事实还没有体现在现存的理论中。如果某个知识是粗浅的而且是下意识的，那么可以说它是一种坏的理论，但它仍然不失为一种理论。比如说，我至今还不能让自己确信诸如利息的来源之类的问题是既不重要也不令人感兴趣的。可以这样来看待这些问题，但无论如何，那只是由于作者的过错。但我仍然希望，通过在货币、信贷、利息以及经济周期方面的一些更加“现实”地研究，能够在不久提供详尽的资料，这些资料正是现在这里所缺乏的。

本书的论点形成一个相互联系的整体，但这并不是由于事先周密的计划。大约在 25 年前，当我开始从事利息理论和经济周期理论的研究时，我并没有怀疑这些课题将会彼此间相互联系，并与企业家的利润、货币、信贷等等类似的问题有紧密的联系，而且这些恰好在当时以论点的方式向我表现出来。但是不久就变得很清楚，所有这些现象——包括许多次要的现象——都只不过是另一个不同过程所引起的事件，而且将用来解释这些现象的那种简单的原理也会用来解释特殊过程本身。结果表明，这些理论本身对我们是很有用的，并且可以与均衡理论相对应，均衡理论不论是明显地还是含蓄地曾经总是，并且现在仍然是传统理论的核心。起初，我用了“静态”和“动态”这两个名词来表示这两种结构，但是现在（遵从弗瑞希教授），我明确地说不再使用这两个词表示这个意义。它们已经被其他的词所替代了，

which are perhaps clumsy. But I keep to the distinction, having repeatedly found it helpful in my current work. This has proved to be so even beyond the boundaries of economics, in what may be called the theory of cultural evolution, which in important points presents striking analogies with the economic theory of this book. The distinction itself has met with much adverse criticism. But is it really untrue to life or artificial to keep separate the phenomena incidental to running a firm and the phenomena incidental to creating a new one? And has it necessarily anything to do with a "mechanical analogy"? Those who have a taste for delving into the history of terms should rather, if they feel so inclined, speak of a zoological analogy; for the terms static and dynamic were, although in a different sense, introduced into economics by John Stuart Mill. Mill probably had them from Comte, who, in turn, tells us that he borrowed them from the zoologist de Blainville.

My cordial thanks are due to my friend Dr. Redvers Opie, who with unparalleled kindness undertook the arduous task of translating a text which proved very refractory to the operation. We have decided to omit the two appendices to Chapters I and III of the original, and also passages or paragraphs here and there. In some places, the exposition has been modified and a number of pages have been rewritten. As the argument itself has nowhere been altered, I think it superfluous to give a list of the changes.

JOSEPH A. SCHUMPETER
CAMBRIDGE, MASSACHUSETTS
March, 1934

可能这些替代的词看起来有些拙劣。但是我仍然坚持这种区别，因为我不断地发现它们在我现在的研究工作中有很多帮助。即使超越经济学范畴，这种情况在其他理论中已经被证实，即我们称之为文化演进的理论；这种文化演进理论，在重要的论点上，与本书的经济理论有惊人的相似之处。这种区别本身曾经遇到过敌对的批评。但是，如果把日常经营一家公司所产生的现象同新创一家公司所产生的现象区分开来，难道这样真是与现实生活不相符合，或者是人为的吗？难道它同一种"机械的类比"就一定有着某种关系吗？那些对钻研词语的历史感兴趣的人，如果他们觉得应该这样做，倒应该谈到某种动物学上的类比。因为静态和动态这两个词语是由约翰·斯图亚特·穆勒引入经济学的，虽然它们有着不同的含义。穆勒可能是从孔德那里引入的，而回过头来，孔德又告诉我们他是从动物学家德·布兰维尔那里借用来的。

我诚挚地感谢我的朋友雷德弗斯·奥佩博士，他给予了我无可比拟的帮助，承担了这样一种非常难驾驭的原文的艰苦的翻译工作。我们决定删去原版第一章和第三章的两个附录部分，以及其中的一些段落或小节。在某些地方，我们改动了一些说明性文字，好些页数也重新改写了。由于书中的论点本身没有任何改动，故我觉得做一张更改对照表是多余的。

约瑟夫·A. 熊彼特

美国，马萨诸塞州，坎布里奇

1934 年 3 月

CHAPTER Ⅰ

The Circular Flow Of Economic Life As Conditioned By Given Circumstances[1]

The social process is really one indivisible whole. Out of its great stream the classifying hand of the investigator artificially extracts economic facts. The designation of a fact as economic already involves an abstraction, the first of the many forced upon us by the technical conditions of mentally copying reality. A fact is never exclusively or purely economic; other-and often more important – aspects always exist. Nevertheless, we speak of economic facts in science just as in ordinary life, and with the same right; with the same right, too, with which we may write a history of literature even though the literature of a people is inseparably connected with all the other elements of its existence.

Social facts are, at least immediately, results of human conduct, economic facts results of economic conduct. And the latter may be defined as conduct directed towards the acquisition of goods. In this sense we also speak of an economic motive to action, of economic forces in social and economic life, and so forth. However, since we are concerned only with that economic conduct which is directed towards the acquisition of goods through exchange or production, we shall restrict the concept of it to these types of acquisition,

---

① This title is chosen with reference to an expression used by Philippovich. Cf. his Grundriss Ⅱ. Bd. , Introduction.

第一章　在给定环境条件下经济生活的循环流转[①]

社会过程事实上是一个不可分割的整体。从它巨大的洪流中,研究者用其分类之手人为地提取出经济的事实。把一个事实称作经济的事实，本身就已经包含了一种抽象过程，这种抽象是在思想上模拟现实的技术条件下，我们被迫不得不作出的许多抽象中的第一个。一个事实绝不会完全是或者纯粹是经济的，总会存在其他的——而且通常是更重要的——方面。然而，我们有同样的理由这样做：在科学中谈论经济的事实就像在日常生活中一样，我们也可以根据同样的理由来写一部文学史，尽管一个民族的文学同她生存的所有其他因素是不可分割地联系在一起的。

社会事实是（至少直接是）人们行为的结果，而经济事实是经济行为的结果。同时，经济行为可以被定义为人们为了获取物品的行为。在这个意义上，我们也可以谈行为的经济动机，谈社会和经济生活中的经济影响力，等等。然而，由于我们所研究的仅仅是那些目的在于通过交换或生产来获得物品的经济行为，因此，我们将经济行为的概念限制在这些获取行为的类型上，

---

① 这个题目是参考菲利波维奇的表述而选定的。参阅他的《概论》，第Ⅱ编,绪论。

while we shall leave that wider compass to the concepts of economic motive and economic force, because we need both of them outside the narrower field within which we shall speak of economic conduct.

The field of economic facts is thus first of all delimited by the concept of economic conduct. Everyone must, at least in part, act economically; everyone must either be an "economic subject" (Wirts - chaftssubjekt) or be dependent upon one. As soon as the members of social groups become occupationally specialised, however, we can distinguish classes of people, whose chief activity is economic conduct or business, from other classes in which the economic aspect of conduct is overshadowed by other aspects. In this case, economic life is represented by a special group of people, although all other members of society must also act economically. The activity of that group may then be said to constitute economic life, *κατ' εξοχην*, and saying this no longer implies an abstraction, in spite of all the relations of economic life in this sense to other vital manifestations of the people.

As of economic facts in general, so we speak of economic development. The explanation of it is our object here. Before we turn to our argument, we shall provide ourselves in this chapter with the necessary principles, and familiarise ourselves with certain conceptual devices, which we shall need hereafter. Besides, what follows must be provided, so to speak, with cogs to grip the wheels of received theory. The armor of methodological commentaries I renounce completely. In this connection let it only be observed that what this chapter offers is indeed part of the main body of economic theory, but in essentials requires nothing fromthe reader that needs special justification to-day. Further, since only a few of the results of theory are necessary for our purpose,

而把那更为广阔的领域留给经济动机和经济影响力这些概念，因为，在我们将要谈到的经济行为这个比较狭窄的领域之外，我们还需要经济动机和经济影响力这两个概念。

因此，经济事实这个领域首先就是被经济行为的概念所限定。每一个人都必定（至少部分的）有经济的行为，每一个人都必定要么是一个“经济主体”（“economic subject”德语译为：Wirtschaftssubjekt），要么是依附于一个经济主体。然而，一旦社会各团体的成员在职业上有了各自的分工以后，我们就能够区分两大类人：一类人他们的主要活动是经济活动或者商业活动，而另一类人他们在经济方面的行为被其他方面的行为所掩盖。在这种情况下，虽然社会所有其他成员也都必定有经济方面的行为，但经济生活却由一个特殊团体的人所代表。于是可以说，这个团体的活动构成了经济生活，这样说也就不再意味着抽象，不管从这种意义上说的经济生活与人们其他重要的表现之间的一切关系如何。

正像谈一般的经济事实一样，我们也谈经济发展。对经济发展进行解释说明是本书的目的。在提出我们的论点之前，我们在本章将给自己提出一些必要的原则，使我们自己熟悉某些概念上的设计，这些在以后我们是会用到的。而且，我们必须为以后的讨论提供一些工具，比方说诸如“嵌齿”之类的东西，以便掌握公认理论的“轮子”。我完全摒弃了方法论上的评论这个武器。关于这一点，我只想大家能够注意到，本章所说的确实是经济理论主体的一部分，但是在实质上并不要求读者具有今天为论证而必需的特殊的知识。其次，由于只有少数理论上的结论是我们论证所必需的，

I have gladly used the proffered opportunity to convey what I have to say as simply and non-technically as possible. This involves the sacrifice of absolute correctness. I have, however, decided on such a course wherever the advantages of more correct formulation lie in points which are of no further importance for us. In this connection I refer to another book of mine. ①

When we inquire shout the general forms of economic phenomena, about their uniformities, or about a key to understanding them, we *ipso facto* indicate that we wish at that moment to consider them as something to be investigated, to be sought for, as the "unknown"; and that we wish to trace them to the relatively "known," just as any science deals with its object of inquiry. When we succeed in finding a definite causal relation between two phenomena, our problem is solved if the one which plays the "causal" rŏle is non-economic. We have then accomplished what we, as economists, are capable of in the case in question, and we must give place to other disciplines. If, on the other hand, the causal factor is itself economic in nature, we must continue our explanatory efforts until we ground upon a non – economic bottom. This is true for general theory as well as for concrete cases. If I could say, for example, that the phenomenon ground – rent is founded upon differences in the qualities of land, the economic explanation would be completed. If I can trace particular price movements to political regulations of commerce, then I have done what I can as an economic theorist, because political regulations of commerce do not aim immediately at the acquisition of goods through exchange or production, and hence do not fall within our concept of purely economic facts.

---

① Das Wesen und der Hauptinhalt der theoretischen NationalÖkonomie, henceforth cited as Wesen.

我很高兴利用这次提供的机会，尽可能不用专业术语而是简单地来表达我所要说的东西，这也不免要牺牲绝对的准确性。但是，凡是当更加准确表述的好处仅存在于那些对我们没有进一步重要性之点的场合时，我都决定采用这种办法。关于这一点，我请读者参考我的另一本书。①

当我们探讨经济现象的一般形式，探讨它们的一致性，或者探讨理解经济现象的关键点时，我们在事实上表明了：在这个时候，我们希望把经济现象看做是某种“未知的事物”，看做是需要进行研究的东西，需要探索的东西；我们想要探索经济现象的本源，直到相对来说成为“已知的事物”，正像任何一门科学对待它的研究客体一样。当我们成功地发现了两种现象之间的明确的因果关系时，如果起“原因”作用的现象是非经济现象，那么我们的问题就解决了。这样，我们就完成了作为经济学家在当前问题下所能够做到的事情，以后我们必须让位于其他学科。相反，如果起“原因”作用的现象本身的性质就是经济的，那么我们就必须继续我们在解释说明方面的努力，直到我们找到非经济的基地，这对一般理论和对具体事实都是如此。例如，如果我能说，地租这一现象是由土地的质量不同引起的，那么，经济上的解释就算已经完成了。如果我能把某种特定的价格运动归结为商业的政府管制，那么，我就尽到了作为经济理论家所能尽到的责任，因为政府对商业管制的直接目的并不是通过交换或者生产去获得实物，因而它不属于我们所说的纯粹的经济事实这一概念范畴。

① 《理论政治经济学的本质和主要内容》，以下简称为《本质》。

Always we are concerned with describing the general forms of the causal links that connect economic with non-economic data. Experience teaches the possibility of this. Economic events have their logic, which every practical man knows, and which we have only consciously to formulate with precision. In doing so we shall, for the sake of simplicity, consider an isolated community; the essence of things, which alone is the concern of this book, we can see as well in this as we could in the more complicated case.

Hence we shall outline the leading characteristics of a mental picture of the economic mechanism. And, to that end, we shall primarily think of a commercially organised state, one in which private property, division of labor, and free competition prevail.

If someone who has never seen or heard of such a state were to observe that a farmer produces corn to be consumed as bread in a distant city, he would be impelled to ask how the farmer knew that this consumer wanted bread and just so much. He would assuredly be astonished to learn that the farmer did not know atall where or by whom it would be consumed. Furthermore, he could observe that all the people through whose hands the corn must go on its way to the final consumer knew nothing of the latter, with the possible exception of the ultimate sellers of bread; and even they must in general produce or buy before they know that this particular consumer will acquire it. The farmer could easily answer the question put to him: long experience,[①] in part inherited, has taught him how much to produce for his greatest advantage; experience has taught him to know the extent and intensity of the demand to be reckoned with.

---

① Cf. Wieser, Der natürliche Wert, where this point was worked out and its meaning elucidated for the first time.

我们总是从事于描述因果关系的一般形式，这些一般形式把经济数据和非经济数据联系起来。经验告诉我们这样做是可能的。每一个从事实践的人都知道，经济事件有它们的逻辑性，只不过我们需要有意识地准确地对其进行表述。我们在这样做时，为了简便起见，我们将考虑一个孤立的社会，在这个孤立的社会中，我们能够看到事物的本质。这与在比较复杂的环境下一样，而本书所要研究的就是这种事物的本质。

因此，我们将要概述心中所想像的经济机制的主要特征。为了这个目的，我们主要思考的是一个商业上有组织的国家，在这样的国家，私人财产、劳动分工和自由竞争居于主导地位。

如果一个从来没有看到过或听到过这样一个国家的人，观察到一个农民为了一个遥远的城市的面包消费而去生产谷物，他就不禁会问，这个农民是怎么知道城市的消费者需要面包并且恰好需要多少呢？当他了解到这个农民根本不知道谷物在哪儿被消费或者被谁消费时，他一定会大吃一惊。此外，他还能观察到，谷物必须经过一些人的手才能到达最终消费者那里，而所有这些人也都根本不知道最终的消费者是谁，或许只有最后的面包销售者可能知道最终的消费者。并且，甚至这些销售者在知道这个特定的面包消费者之前，他们通常也必须从事过生产或者购买面包的活动。农民很容易回答给他提出的问题：长期的经验①（部分是继承于他人的）告诉他，为了实现自己的最大利益，他应该生产多少；经验教育了他，使他懂得应当考虑需求的大小和强度。

① 参阅维塞尔的《自然价值》，在那里首次提出了这一点，并说明了它的意义。

To this quantity he adheres, as well as he can, and only gradually alters it under the pressure of circumstances.

The same holds good for other items in the farmer's calculations, whether he reckons as perfectly as a great industrialist or arrives at his decisions half unconsciously and by force of custom. He knows ordinarily, within certain limits, the prices of the things he must buy; he knows how much of his own labor he must expend (whether he values the latter according to purely economic principles, or whether he looks upon labor on his own land with quite different eyes from any other); he knows the method of cultivation – all from long experience. From experience also all the people from whom he buys know the extent and intensity of his demand. Since the circular flow of the economic periods, this most striking of all economic rhythms, goes relatively fast, and since in every economic period essentially the same thing occurs, the mechanism of the exchange economy operates with great precision. Past economic periods govern the activity of the individual – in a case like ours – not only because they have taught him sternly what he has to do, but also for another reason. During every period the farmer must live, either directly upon the physical product of the preceding period or upon what he can obtain with the proceeds of this product. All the preceding periods have, furthermore, entangled him in a net of social and economic connections which he cannot easily shake off. They have bequeathed him definite means and methods of production. All these hold him in iron fetters fast in his tracks. Here a force appears which is of considerable significance for us and which will soon engage us more closely. Yet at this juncture we shall only state that in the following analysis we shall always assume that everyone lives in each economic period on goods produced in the preceding period – which is possible if production extends into the past, or if the produce of a factor of production flows continuously.

他尽可能地维持这个数量，只是在环境的压力下才逐渐改变它。

在农民的核算中，其他物品的持有也是同样的方式，而不管他是像大工业家一样进行完全的核算，或是半自觉地并受到习惯力量的影响来作出决定。在一定的限度内，农民通常都知道他所必须购买的物品的价格，他知道自己必须付出多少劳动（不论他是按照纯粹的经济原理来估计他自己劳动的价值，还是用完全不同于任何其他人的眼光来看待他在自己土地上的劳动）；他知道耕作的方法——这些都是从长期的经验中获得的。同样也是从经验中，所有那些卖给他东西的人也都知道他的需求的大小和程度。由于经济周期的“循环流转”——这是最引人注目的，在所有的经济节奏中——进行的相对而言比较快，并且由于在每一个经济时期都发生基本上相同的事情，所以交换经济的机制以极其精确的方式运行着。过去的经济周期支配着人们的活动——和我们的情况一样——这不仅因为它们严格地告诉个人必须做些什么，而且还有另一个原因。在每一个时期，农民都必须要么直接依靠前一时期生产的物质产品而生活，要么依靠用这种产品的收入所能获得的东西而生活。此外，所有以前的时期都使他卷入了一个社会和经济的关系网，而这个关系网是他不能轻易摆脱的。它们给他留下了一定的生产资料和生产方法。所有这一切把他紧紧地束缚在他的轨道上。在这里出现了一种力量，这种力量对我们有重大的意义，不久我们将要更加仔细地研究它。但在此刻我们只需要说明，在接下来的分析里，我们将一直假定：在每一个经济时期，每一个人都是依靠前一时期生产的物品来生活——只要生产延伸到过去，或者，只要一个生产要素的产品继续不停地流动，

This is merely a simplification of the exposition.

The case of the farmer may now be generalised and somewhat refined. Let us suppose that everyone sells all his product and, in so far as he himself consumes, is his own customer, since indeed such private consumption is determined by the market price, that is indirectly by the quantity of other goods obtainable by curtailing private consumption of one's own products; and conversely that the quantity of private consumption operates on market price just as if the quantity in question actually appeared on the market. All businessmen are, therefore, in the position of the farmer. They are all at the same time buyers for the parposes of their production and consumption and sellers. In this analysis the workers may be similarly conceived, that is their services may be included in the same category with other marketable things. Now since every one of these businessmen, taken by himself, produces his product and finds his buyers on the basis of his experience, just like our farmer, the same must be true for all taken together. Apart from disturbances, which obviously may occur for all sorts of reasons, all products must be disposed of; for they will indeed only be produced with reference to empirically known market possibilities.

Let us drive this home. How much meat the butcher disposes of depends upon how much his customer the tailor will buy and at what price. That depends, however, upon the proceeds from the latter's business, these proceeds again upon the needs and the purchasing power of his customer the shoemaker, whose purchasing power again depends upon the needs and purchasing power of the people for whom he produces; and so forth, until we finally strike someone

这就是可能的。我们这样假定，只是为了把表述简单化。

现在我们就可以把上面农民的这个例子一般化，并且变得更精确一些。让我们假定：所有的人都出售他的全部产品，而当他消费自己的产品时，他就是他自己的顾客，因为这种个人消费确实是由市场价格决定的，也就是说，这是由通过削减对自己产品的个人消费从而获得的其他物品的数量来间接决定；相反，私人消费的数量是按照市场价格进行的，这就好比说，个人消费的数量实际上出现在市场上一样。所以，所有的商人都与农民一样，处于相同的地位。他们在同一时候既是消费者——为了他们的生产和消费——也是销售者。在这里的分析中，也可以同样的方式看待工人，也就是说，工人的生产服务可以和其他能够在市场上出售的东西列为同一类。现在，既然每一个商人——从他自己来看——根据他自己的经验来生产产品并且寻找各自的买主，就像我们的农民一样，那么，如果把所有的这些人放在一起来看，情况就一定完全一样了。除去一些干扰因素（由于各种各样的原因，这些干扰显然是可能发生的），所有的产品都必须被卖掉，因为它们确确实实是根据经验上所得知的市场消费的可能性而生产的。

让我们更进一步地来说明这一点。屠户能出售多少肉，取决于他的顾客，比如说裁缝，将要买多少布并且以什么价格购买来决定，可是，这又取决于后者的经营收入，这种收入又取决于后者的顾客，比如说鞋匠对商品的需求和购买力，而鞋匠的购买力又取决于他所为之生产的人们对商品的需求和购买能力；如此这样循环，直到我们最后找到一个人，

whose income derives from the sale of his goods to the butcher. This concatenation and mutual dependence of the quantities of which the economic cosmos consists are always visible, in whichever of the possible directions one may choose to move. Wherever one breaks in and wherever one turns from this point, one must always, after perhaps a great but a finite number of steps, return to the starting point. The analysis neither comes to a natural full stop nor stumbles upon a cause, that is an element which does more to determine other elements than it is by them determined.

Our picture will be more complete if we represent the act of consuming otherwise than is customary. Everyone, for instance, considers himself a consumer of bread, but not of land, services, iron, and so forth. If we consider people as consumers of these other things, however, we can see still more clearly the way taken by individual goods in the circular flow.[①] Now it is obvious that every unit of every commodity does not always travel the same road to the same consumer that its predecessor in the process of production travelled in the preceding economic period. But we may suppose that this *does* happen without altering anything essential. We can imagine that, year in and year out, every recurring employment of permanent sources of productive power endeavors to reach the same consumer. The result of the process is in any case the same as if this happened. Hence it follows that somewhere in the economic system a demand is, so to say, ready awaiting every supply, and nowhere in the system are there commodities without complements, that is other commodities in the possession of people

---

① Cf. A. Marshall (Principles, bk. VI, as well as his address, "The Old Generation of Economists and the New"), for whom this conception plays the same part.

他的收入来自于将自己的物品销售给屠户。在这个经济完整的体系中，这种数量上相互联系，相互依存的关系随处可见，正是这些构成了统一的经济体系，不论人们选择什么方向走动。不论你从哪儿进入，也不论你从一点走向哪里，可能在你走了很多步但是是确定数量的步子之后，你必定还是回到这个起点。这种分析既不会自然而然完全地停止，也不会由于某种原因——这种因素不是由其他因素决定，而是更多地决定其他因素——而走向歧途。

如果我们不是用习惯的方式来表示消费行为，那么我们的图画将会更加完整。比如说，我们每个人都认为自己是面包的消费者，而不是土地、服务、铁等等的消费者。然而，如果我们把人们看做是这些东西的消费者，我们就能够更加清楚地看到各类商品在循环流转中所采取的方式。[①] 现在很显然，每一类商品的每一单位，并不总是以它的先行者在前一个经济时期内所经历的生产过程那样经过同样的途径到达同一个消费者。但是，我们可以假定，在不改变任何实质性的东西的前提下，这种事情确实会发生。我们可以想象，年复一年地，生产力的永久源泉的每一次重复使用，都是为了到达相同的消费者。这个过程的结果也就是在任何情况下都相同，就像这种事情发生了一样。因此，我们说，在经济体系的某一处，一项需求可以说正在等待每一项供给，并且，在这个体系里，没有哪一处是只有商品而没有它的补充品，这个补充品也就是人们所持有其他商品，

① 参阅 A. 马歇尔：《原理》第Ⅵ编，以及他的演说《老一代经济学家和新一代》，对他来说，这个概念起着相同的作用。

who will exchange them under empirically determined conditions for the former goods. It follows, again from the fact that all goods find a market, that the circular flow of economic life is closed, in other words that the sellers of all commodities appear again as buyers in sufficient measure to acquire those goods which will maintain their consumption and their productive equipment in the next economic period at the level so far attained, and vice versa.

The individual household or firm acts, then, according to empirically given data and in an equally empirically determined manner. Obviously this does not mean that no changes can take place in their economic activity. The data may change, and everyone will act accordingly as soon as it is noticed. But everyone will cling as tightly as possible to habitual economic methods and only submit to the pressure of circumstances as it becomes necessary. Thus the economic system will not change capriciously on its own initiative but will be at all times connected with the preceding state of affairs. This may be called Wieser's principle of continuity. ①

If the economic system really does not change "of itself", we overlook nothing essential to our present purpose if we simply assume that it remains as it is, but we merely express in so doing a fact with ideal precision. And if we depict a downright changeless system, it is true we make an abstraction, but only for the purpose of exhibiting the essence of what actually happens. Provisionally we shall do this. It is not contrary to orthodox theory, but at the most only to the customary exposition which does not clearly

① Most recently expounded in the work on the problem of the value of money, Schriften des Vereins für Sozialpolitik, Reports of the Session of 1909.

人们将会根据从实践上确定的条件，用这些补充品来交换前面提到的该种商品。再根据所有商品都能找到市场这一事实，可以说，经济生活的循环周转就结束了，换句话说，所有商品的卖主又以买主的身份出现，他们购买充足的商品，以使他们能够按照已经达到的水平在下一个经济时期维持消费和生产装备，反之亦然。

可见，各个家庭和厂商都是按照经验给定的数据以及由经验确定的方式来决定其行为的。当然这并不是说，在他们经济活动的领域里不发生任何变化。数据可能变化，并且，每一个人一旦注意到这种变化，就会立即按照变化来行动。但是，每一个人都会尽可能地紧紧地遵从习惯的经济方法，并且只有在迫不得已的时候才屈从于环境的压力。这样，经济体系不会自行随意地发生变化，而是在任何时候都和先前存在的状态相联系。这可能就被称为“威泽尔的继续性原则”。①

如果经济体系真的不会自行变化，那么，如果我们简单地假定，它是维持原状的，我们并没有忽视任何对我们现在的目的相当重要的东西，我们这样做也只是为了用理想的精确性表达一个事实而已。如果我们描述一个彻底没有变化的系统，那么我们确实是在做一种抽象，但是其目的仅仅是为了表达实际所发生的事情的实质。我们将暂时这样做。这种做法与传统理论并不相矛盾，最多也只是与习惯的做法有些不同，习惯的说法并不能清楚

① 最近在关于货币价值问题的著作《社会政策协会论文》（1909 年会议报告）中阐述。

express our point. ①

The same result may be arrived at by another route. The total of all commodities produced and marketed in a community within an economic period may be called the social product. It is unnecessary for our purpose to go more deeply into the meaning of the concept. ②The social product does not exist as such. It is just as little the consciously aspired-to result of systematic activity as the economic system as such is an "economy" working according to a uniform plan. But it is a useful abstraction. We can imagine that the products of all individuals form a heap somewhere at the end of the economic period, which is then distributed according to certain principles. Since it involves no essential change in the facts, the assumption is so far quite permissible. We can then say that each individual throws a contribution into this great social reservoir, and later receives something from it. To each contribution there corresponds somewhere in the system a claim of another individual; the share of everyone lies ready somewhere. And since all know from experience how much they must contribute in order to get what they want, having regard to the condition that each share involves a certain contribution, the circular flow of the system is closed, and all contributions and shares must cancel out, whatever the principle according to which the distribution is made. The assumption is so far made that all the quantities concerned are empirically given.

---

① Cf. Wesen, bk. Ⅱ.

② Cf. on this point especially Adam Smith and A. Marshall. The concept is almost as old as economics and, as is well known, has an eventful past which makes it necessary to use it with caution. For connected concepts cf. also: Fisher, Capital and Income; A. Wagner, Grundlegung; and finally, Pigou, Preferential and Protective Tariffs, where great use is made of the concept "National Dividend." Note also his Economics of Welfare.

地表述我们的论点。①

通过另一个途径可以得到相同的结果。一个社会在一个经济时期内生产和消费的所有商品的总和，可以被称为社会产品。为了我们的目的，没有必要对于这个概念的意义更加深入地钻研下去。② 社会产品本身并不是作为社会产品而存在的。就像经济系统本身也不是一种按照统一计划运行的“经济”一样，社会产品不是系统活动有意识的结果。但是这是一种有用的抽象。我们可以想像：在经济周期的末期，所有个人的产品在某个地方形成一个大堆，然后按照某种原则对其进行分配。由于这个假设不包含对事实的重大改变，所以至今，它是完全可以容许的。进而，我们可以说，每一个人都对这个巨大的社会库藏做出了一种贡献，然后又从它得到一些东西。在这个体系的某一处，对每一种贡献都有着与之相应的另一个人的请求权；并且每一个人的份额都在某处随时准备着。由于每一个人从经验中都知道为了获得他们需要的东西，他们必须贡献多少（他们已经考虑到每一份额包含一定贡献这个条件）；这个系统的循环周转就结束了，所有的贡献和份额必然相互抵消，不论根据什么原则进行分配。到这里我们所做的假设是：所有相关的数量都是由经验给定的。

---

① 参阅《本质》第二章。

② 关于这一点，特别要参阅亚当·斯密和 A. 马歇尔的著作。这个概念几乎和经济学一样古老，大家都知道，它有一段丰富的过去，这使得在使用它时一定要谨慎。对于有关的概念还可以参阅费希尔的《资本与收入》；A. 瓦格纳的《奠定基础》；以及皮古的《优惠关税和保护关税》，在那里皮古大量利用了“国民总利得”这个概念。还可参阅他的《福利经济学》。

This picture may be refined, and made to yield more insight into the functioning of the economic system, by means of a well known device. We assume all this experience to be nonexistent, and reconstruct it *ab ovo*, ①as if the same people, still having the same culture, tastes, technical knowledge, and the same initial stocks of consumers' and producers' goods, ②but unaided by experience, had to find their way towards the goal of the greatest possible economic welfare by conscious and rational effort. We do not thereby imply that people would in practical life be capable of such an effort. ③We merely want to bring out the *rationale* of economic behavior irrespective of the actual psychology of the households and firms under observation. ④Neither do we aim at giving a sketch of economic history. Not how the economic process developed historically to the state in which we actually find it, but the working of its mechanism or organism at any given stage of development, is what we want to analyse.

This analysis suggests, elaborates, and uses those conceptual tools with which we are all familiar by now. Economic activity may have *any* motive, even a spiritual one, but its *meaning* is always the satisfaction of wants. Hence the fundamental importance of those concepts and propositions which we derive from the fact of wants,

---

① This method is due to Léon Walras.

② As every reader of J. B. Clark knows, it is strictly speaking necessary to consider these stocks, not in their actual shapes-as so many ploughs, pairs of boots, and so on – but as accumulated productive forces which can at any moment and without loss or friction be turned into any specific commodities wanted.

③ There is, therefore, misunderstanding in the objection so often levelled at pure theory that it assumes the hedonistic motive and perfectly rational conduct to be the only forces actually at work in economic life.

④ Psychology, to be sure, comes in later on in order to explain actual conduct and its deviations from the rat ional picture. Our argument in the following chapters turns largely upon one class of such deviations – force of habit and non-hedonistic motives. But this is another matter.

用一个大家都熟悉的方法，我们可以对这幅图画加以精炼，使这幅图画对经济系统的运转提供更加深入的认识。我们假定这种经验全不存在，必须重新构建它，① 就好像同一民族的人民，仍然有着相同的文化、嗜好、技术知识，对消费品和生产物品有着同一的最初存量，② 但是没有经验的帮助，他们必须通过自觉的合理的努力，去寻找各自的办法，以达到最大可能的经济福利这个目标。我们并不因此就认为，在现实生活中人们能够做出这种努力。③ 我们只是想要突出经济行为的理性，而不考虑所观察的各个家庭和厂商的实际心理如何。④ 我们也不想勾画出经济史的轮廓。我们分析的目的不是经济过程是如何从历史上发展到我们现在实际观察到的这样，而是在任何一个给定的发展阶段上，经济机制或经济组织是怎样运转的。

这个分析提醒我们，要详细阐述且实际应用我们现在全都熟悉的那些概念工具。经济活动可能有任何的动机，甚至是精神方面的动机，但是它的意义总是在于满足需要。因此，那些我们从需要这个事实所得出的概念和命题具有根本的重要性，

---

① 这个方法是莱昂·瓦尔拉所用的。

② 正如J. B. 克拉克的每一个读者所知的，严格说必须这样看待这些存量：不是按照它们的自然形态——如多少张犁，多少双靴子，等等——而是作为累计的生产力，它可以在任何时候没有损失地，没有摩擦地变成想要的任何特定商品。

③ 因此，对纯粹理论常常提出的反对意见不免是一种误解：说它假定享乐主义的动机和完全合理的行为是经济生活中实际起作用的唯一力量。

④ 诚然，稍后还要引用心理学，以便说明实际行为与合理图画的偏离。在以后各章中我们的讨论主要是这样的偏离：习惯的力量和非享乐主义的动机。但这是另外一回事。

foremost among which is the concept of utility and its derivative, marginal utility, or, to use a more modern term, the "coefficient of choice." We go on to state certain theorems about the distribution of resources over the range ofpossible uses, about complementariness and rivalry among goods, and rationally we deduce ratios of exchange, prices, and the old empirical "law of supply and demand." We finally arrive at a preliminary idea of a system of values and of the conditions of its equilibrium. ①

Production is, on one side, conditioned by the physical properties of material objects and natural processes. In this respect it can for economic activity, as John Rae② has observed, be only a question of observing the outcome of natural processes and making the most of them. How much of the realm of physical fact may be relevant to economics cannot be stated once for all. According to the type of theory one aims at, such things as the law of decreasing (physical) returns may mean much or little in the way of specifically economic results. There is no relation between the importance of a fact to the welfare of mankind and its importance within the explanatory endeavor of economic theory. But we may of course, as the example of Böhm-Bawerk③shows, be driven at any moment to introducing new technical facts into our apparatus. Facts of social organisation are not in the same class. Yet they stand on a par with technical facts in that they are outside the domain of economic theory, and mere "data" for it. ④

---

① I may refer here to the whole literature of the marginal utility theory and its successors.

② Cf. the edition of his work by Mixter under the title The Sociological Theory of Capital. The powerful penetration and originality of this work may still repay perusal by the modern student.

③ His law of returns increasing with the length of the period of production seems to me the one successful attempt to introduce the element of time explicitly into the equations of production.

④ For this, as for other reasons, the sharp distinction drawn by J. S. Mill between production and distribution seems to me to be less than satisfactory.

其中最重要的是效用的概念以及由效用引出的边际效用，或者，用一个更加现代化的术语，就是“选择系数”。我们继续提出某些原理，是关于资源在各种可能使用的范围内分配的原理，关于货物之间相互补充和竞争的原理，而且我们可以合理地引申出交换比率、价格和古老的源自经验的“供求法则”。最后我们达到价值体系及其均衡条件的最初的思想。①

一方面，生产是由物质客体的物质属性和自然过程决定的。在这方面，就经济活动而言，就像约翰·雷所说的，② 经济活动只是一个观察自然过程结果并加以充分利用的问题。与经济学相关的自然事实领域究竟有多少，是难以一言而尽的。根据人们所针对的理论类型，像（物质）收益递减规律这样的理论，对于具体的经济结果，可能有很大意义，也有可能没什么意义。一个有关人类福利的事实的重要性与它在经济理论中所做的解释作用的重要性之间是没有联系的。但是，像庞巴维克的例子所表明的那样③，我们也可能自然地，在任何时候都会被迫地把新技术事实引进我们的工具。关于社会组织的事实就不属于同一类。但是在经济理论领域之外，社会组织只是作为技术事实的“数据”这一点，它们处于相同的地位。④

---

① 在这里请读者参考边际效用理论及其后继者的全部文献。

② 参考米克斯特编著的《资本的社会学理论》。这一著作强大的洞察力和创见，仍值得现代学者一读。

③ 收益随着生产时期的长度而增长的规律，在我看来，似乎是把时间因素引入生产方程式的一种成功的尝试。

④ 由于这一点，也还由于其他原因，约翰·穆勒关于生产和分配的鲜明区分，在我看来，是有些不能令人满意的。

The other side of the matter, the side on which we can penetrate much more deeply into the core of production than on its physical and social side, is the concrete purpose of every act of production. The aim which the economic man pursues when he produces, and which explains why there is any production at all, puts its stampclearly on the method and volume of production. Obviously, no argument is required to prove that it must be determining for the "what" and the "why" of production within the framework of given means and objective necessities. This aim can only be the creation of useful things, of objects of consumption. In a nonexchange economy it can only be s question of utilities for consumption within the system. Every individual produces in this case directly for consumption, that is to satisfy his needs. And clearly the nature and intensity of the needs for this product are, within the practical possibilities, decisive. The given external conditions and the needs of the individual appear as the two decisive factors for the economic process, which cooperate in determining the result. Production follows needs; it is so to speak pulled after them. But exactly the same holds good *mutatis mutandis* for an exchange economy.

This second "side" of production makes it at the outset an economic problem. It must be distinguished from the purely technological problem of production. There is s contrast between them which we frequently witness in economic life in the personal opposition between the technical and the commercial manager of an enterprise. We often see changes in the productive process recommended on one side and rejected on another; for example, the engineer may recommend a new process which the commercial head rejects with the argument that it will not pay. The engineer and the businessman can both express their point of view thus: that their aim is to run the business suitably and that their judgment derives from the knowledge of this suitability. Apart from misunderstandings, lack of knowledge of facts, and so forth, the difference in judgment can only come from the fact that each has a different kind of appropriateness in view. What the businessman means when he speaks of appropriateness

事情的另一方面，相对对它的物质和社会方面进行研究而言，我们可以对生产的核心进行更为深入的探讨，这是每一个生产行为的具体目的。一个经济人在生产时所追求的目的（它解释了为什么会存在生产），给生产的方法和数量刻下了清晰的烙印。显然不用提出论据来证明：在给定的资料和客观需要的框架内，目的必然决定着生产“什么”和“为什么”生产。这个目的只能是创造有用的东西，创造消费品。在一个非交换的经济系统内，它只是在这个系统内为了消费效用的问题。在这种情况下，每个人从事生产都是为了直接消费，也就是满足他自身的需要。而对这种产品需要的性质和强度，在实际可能的范围内，显然起着决定性的作用。给定的外部条件和个人的需求，显然是经济过程的两个决定因素，两者共同决定着结果。需求决定生产，可以说生产被需求拉着走。但就一种交换经济来说，在细节已作必要修正的前提下，情形也是这样。

生产的第二个“方面”使得它一开始就是一个经济问题。它必须同生产的纯技术问题相区分。它们之间有一种对立，这种对立我们在经济生活中，常常可以从一个企业的技术经理和商业经理之间个人的对立上看到。我们常常看到，一方建议生产过程改变，而另一方拒绝；例如，工程师可能建议采用一种新的工艺，而商业部门的领导认为那将不会有收益，所以拒绝。工程师和商人都可能这样来表达他们的观点：他们的目标是恰当的管理企业，他们的判断就来自于关于这种恰当性管理的知识。除了误解、对事实不了解等等因素之外，他们判断的差异就只能来自这样的事实：每一个人对于恰当性都有不同的看法。商人所说的恰当性，

is clear. He means commercial advantage, and we can express his view thus: the resources which the provision of the machine would require could be employed elsewhere with greater advantage. The commercial director means that in a non-exchange economy the satisfaction of wants would not be increased, but on the contrary, reduced, by such an alteration in the productive process. If that is true, what meaning can the technologist's standpoint have, what kind of appropriateness has he in mind? If the satisfaction of wants is the only end of all production, then there is indeed no economic sense in having recourse to a measure which impairs it. The business leader is right in not following the engineer, provided his protest is objectively correct. We disregard the half-artistic joy in technically perfecting the productive apparatus. Actually, in practical life we observe that the technical element must submit when it collides with the economic. But that does not argue against its independent existence and significance, and the sound sense in the engineer's standpoint. For, although the economic purpose governs the technical methods as used in practice, there is good sense in making the inner logic of the methods clear without regard to practical barriers. This is best seen in an example. Suppose a steam engine in all its component parts complies with economic appropriateness. In the light of this appropriateness it is made the most of. There would then be no sense in turning it to greater account in practice by heating it more, by letting more experienced men work it, and by improving it, if this would not pay, that is if it could be foreseen that the fuel, cleverer people, improvements, and increase in raw materials would cost more than they would yield. But there is good sense in considering the conditions under which the engine could do more, and how much more, which improvements are possible with present knowledge, and so forth. For then all these measures will be worked out ready

意义是很清楚的。他指的是商业利益，我们可以这样表达他的观点：提供给机器所需要的资源如果用在其他地方，能得到更大的利益。商业部门的领导人认为：在一个非交换经济中，生产过程的改变不会增加需要的满足，相反，会减少这种满足。如果这是真的话，那么，技术人员的观点又是什么呢，他所想到的适当性又是什么样的呢？如果所有生产的唯一目的是满足需求，那么将资源用在有损它的措施上，的确就没有什么经济意义了。只要商业领导人的异议在客观上是正确的，他不听从工程师的话就是对的。我们不考虑由于技术使生产工具趋于完美而带来的半艺术性的快乐。事实上，我们在实际生活中观察到，当技术因素与经济因素发生冲突时，技术必须屈服。但这并不能否定技术的独立存在性和它的重要性，以及工程师的观点中合理的判断。因为，尽管经济目的决定着实际使用的技术方法，但是弄清楚技术方法的内在逻辑而不考虑实际障碍，还是很有意义的。这一点可以通过一个例子很好地看出来。假定一台蒸汽机在它所有的部件上都符合经济恰当性，由于这种恰当性，蒸汽机已经被充分地利用。那么，如果用对它更多地加热，让更多的有经验的人去操作它，对它加以改善等等方法使它在实际中更大限度地被利用，如果这样做并不能带来好处的话，那就没有什么意义了；也就是说，如果能够预见到燃料、更聪明的人、技术的改进以及原材料的增加，所付出的成本比得到的好处更大的话，那样做就没有意义了。但是如果考虑一下，在什么样的条件下机器能做更多的事，能多做多少，利用现有的知识能使机器进行什么样的改进等等，还是很有意义的。因为这样以来，所有这些措施就能准备好，

for the time when they become advantageous. And it is also useful to be constantly putting the ideal beside the actual so that the possibilities are passed by, not out of ignorance but on well-considered economic grounds. In short, every method of production in use at a given time bows to economic appropriateness. These methods consist of ideas not only of economic but also of physical content. The latter have their problems and a logic of their own, and consistently to think these through – first of all without considering the economic, and finally decisive factor – is the purport of technology; and in so far as the economic element does not decree otherwise, to put them into practical effect is to produce in the technological sense.

Just as in the last resort expediency governs technological as well as economic production, and the distinction between the two lies in the difference in the nature of this expediency, so a somewhat different line of thought shows us first of all a fundamental analogy and then the same distinction. Technologically as well as economically considered, production "creates" nothing in the physical sense. In both cases it can only influence or control things and processes – or "forces." We now need for what follows a concept which embraces this "utilising" and this "influencing." They include many different methods of using, and of behaving towards, goods; all kinds of locational changes, and changes in mechanical, chemical, and other processes. But it is always a question of changing the existing state of the satisfaction of our wants, of changing the reciprocal relations of things and forces, of uniting some and disconnecting others. Technologically as well as economically considered, to produce means to combine the things and forces within our reach. Every method of production signifies some such definite combination. Different methods of production can only be distinguished by the manner of the combination, that is either by the objects combined

当它们一旦变得有利时就可以付诸实施。而且，不断地把理想与实际相比较，使得那些被放弃的可能性选择不是由于无知而是根据考虑成熟的经济原理做出的，这也是很有用的。总之，在一个给定的阶段，所使用的每一个生产方法，都要遵从经济上的适当性。这些方法不仅包含经济学的思想，而且还包含物质内容的思想。但后者有它们自己的问题和逻辑，而且，通常将这些问题彻底想清楚——首先不去考虑经济因素以及最终起决定作用的因素——是根据技术的目的；只要经济因素不另作指示，将其在实践中付诸实施就是技术意义的生产。

正像归根结底还是权益之计决定着技术上的和经济上的生产，两者的区别在于这种权益之计的本质不同一样，一种稍有区别的思想路线首先向我们展现一个最根本的类似点，然后再展现一个同样的区别。从技术上以及经济上考虑，生产在物质的意义上并没有“创造出”什么东西。在两种场合下，它都仅仅能影响或者控制事物和过程——或者说“力量”。为了以后的论述，现在我们需要一个概念，它包括这个“利用”和“影响”。它们包含许多不同的利用物品以及处理物品的方法；包括各种所有位置上的变化，以及物理的、化学的和其他过程中的变化。但是要改变我们的需要得以满足的现存状况，改变事物和力量之间的相互关系，把某些事物组合起来而把另一些事物分割开来，这一直是一个问题。从技术上以及经济上考虑，生产意味着在我们所能达到的范围内结合事物和力量。每一种生产方法都意味着某种这样特定的组合。不同的生产方法只有通过组合方式的不同加以区别，也就是说，要么根据所组合的事物加以区别，

or by the relation between their quantities. Every concrete act of production embodies for us, is for us, such a combination. This concept may be extended even to transportation and so forth, in short to everything that is production in the widest sense. An enterprise as such and even the productive conditions of the whole economic system we shall also regard as "combinations." This concept plays a considerable part in our analysis.

But the economic and the technological combinations, the former concerned with existing needs and means, the latter with the basic idea of the methods, do not coincide. The objective of technological production is indeed determined by the economic system; technology only develops productive methods for goods demanded. Economic reality does not necessarily carry out the methods to their logical conclusion and with technologicalcompleteness, but subordinates the execution to economic points of view. The technological ideal, which takes no account of economic conditions, is modified. Economic logic prevails over the technological. And in consequence we see all around us in real life faulty ropes instead of steel hawsers, defective draught animals instead of show breeds, the most primitive hand labor instead of perfect machines, a clumsy money economy instead of a cheque circulation, and so forth. The economic best and the technologically perfect need not, yet very often do, diverge, not only because of ignorance and indolence but because methods which are technologically inferior may still best fit the given economic conditions.

"Production coefficients" represent the quantitative relation of production goods in a unit of product, and are therefore an essential characteristic of the combination. At this point the economic element is sharply contrasted with the technological. The economic point of view here will not only decide between two different methods of production, but even within any given method will operate upon the coefficients, since the individual means of production can to a certain extent be substituted for one another, that is deficiencies in one can be compensated for by increases in another

要么通过它们数量之间的关系进行区别。每一个具体的生产行为，都为我们展现了这样一种组合，对我们而言就是这样的组合。这个概念甚至可以延伸应用到运输等等，总之，从广义上来说可以延伸到称为生产的每一件事。这样的每一个企业，甚至是整个经济系统的生产条件，我们都可以将其看做一种“组合”。这个概念在我们的分析中起着很大的作用。

但是，经济的和技术的组合彼此并不是一致的，前者涉及现有的需要和方法，后者涉及方法的基本思想。技术生产的目的的确是由经济体制决定的，技术仅仅是为了所需要的货物发展生产方法。经济的现实并不一定把方法贯彻执行到它们的逻辑结论，并使得技术趋于完善，而只是使执行服从于经济的观点。技术的思想被修正，它不考虑经济条件。经济的逻辑胜过了技术上的逻辑。因此，我们看到，在我们周围的现实生活中，劣质绳索替代了钢缆，有缺陷的耕畜代替了比赛的良驹，最原始的手工劳动代替了完美的机器，笨拙的货币经济代替了支票流通，等等。经济上的最佳与技术上的完美不一定背道而驰，但往往是背道而驰，这不仅是因为无知和懒惰，而且还由于在技术上很低劣的方法可能仍然是最适合给定的经济条件的。

“生产系数”代表在一单位产出中的各种生产要素货物的数量关系，因此，它也表示了生产要素组合的主要特征。在这一点上，显然，经济因素与技术因素是相对立的。在这里，经济观点不仅将在两个不同的生产方法中做决定，而且，甚至在任何给定的方法中，也会考虑生产系数，因为在某种程度上，个别的生产资料能被另一种所取代，也就是说，一种资料的短缺可以通过增加另一种资料来代替，

without changing the method of production, for example a decrease in steam power by an increase in hand labor and vice versa. ①

We have characterised the process of production by the concept of combinations of productive forces. The results of these combinations are the products. Now we must define precisely what it is that is to be combined: generally speaking, all possible kinds of objects and "forces." In part they consist of products again, and only in part of objects offered by nature. Also many "natural forces" in the physical sense will assume the character of products for us, as for example in the case of electric current. They comprise partly material, partly immaterial things. Furthermore, it is frequently a matter of interpretation whether one conceives a good as product or as means. Labor, for example, is capable of being regarded as the product of goods consumed by the worker or as an original means of production. We decided for the latter alternative: for us labor is not a product. Frequently the classification of a good in one or another category depends upon the standpoint of the individual, so that the same good may be consumption good for one person and means of production for another. Likewise the character of a given good may frequently depend upon the use to which it is put. Theoretical literature, especially in earlier times, is full of the discussion of these things. We shall content ourselves with this reference. The following, however, is a more important matter.

It is usual to classify goods in "orders," according to their distance from the final act of consumption. ②Consumption goods are of the first order, goods from combinations of which consumption goods immediately originate are of the second order, and so on, in continually higher or more remote orders.

---

① These "variations" are very clearly and neatly expounded by Carver, The Distribution of Wealth.

② Cf. K. Menger's Grundsätze and Böhm-Bawerk's Positive Theorie des Kapitals.

而不改变生产方法，例如，通过增加手工劳动来补偿蒸汽动力的减少，反之亦然①。

我们通过生产力量组合这个概念已经对生产过程进行了描述。这些要素结合的结果就是产出产品。现在我们必须明确地界定什么样的要素被组合在一起：通常来说，各种所有可能的物体和“力量”。部分地说，它们也是由产品构成的，其中只有一部分物品是由自然赋予的。当然，从物质意义上说，许多“自然的力量”也为我们扮演着产品的角色，例如电流。它们所包括的，部分是物质的东西，部分是非物质的东西。此外，人们把一种物品看成是产品还是生产资料，这常常是如何解释的问题。例如，劳动可以被看做是生产的物品，它们被工人所消费，也可以被看做是原始的生产资料或生产工具。我们决定用后者：对我们来说，劳动不是产品。通常，一种物品被划分为这一类还是列为那一类，取决于个人的观点，所以，同样的物品对某个人来说可能是消费品，而对另一个人来说就可能是生产资料。同样，一个给定的物品，它的性质，常常是由它指定的用途所决定的。理论文献，尤其是早期的理论文献，充满了对这些问题的讨论。我们指出这一点，让读者去参考就足够了。而下面的问题相对来说是更重要的问题。

人们常常根据物品与最终消费行为的距离按顺序将物品分类。② 消费品排在第一位，直接产生消费品，用来生产消费品的组合中的物品居于第二位，依此类推，逐渐到更高或更远的位次。

---

① 卡弗在《财富的分配》中，非常清楚明白地解释了这些“变动”。

② 参阅 K. 门格尔的《原理》和庞巴维克的《资本的实证理论》。

It must not be forgotten that only goods ready for consumption in the hands of consumers fall in the first order and that bread at the baker's, for example, is strictly speaking only brought into the first order by combining it with the labor of the errand-boy. Goods of lower order, if not immediately the gifts of nature, always originate in a combination of goods of higher order. Although the scheme could be constructed otherwise, it is best for our purposes to rank a good in the highest of the orders in which it ever appears. Accordingly labor is, for example, a good of the highest order, because labor enters at the very beginning of all production, although it is also to be found at all other stages. In successive productive processes or combinations each good matures into a consumption good through the addition of other goods belonging to a greater or lesser number of orders; with the help of such additions it makes its way to the consumer just as a stream, helped by inflowing rivulets of water, breaks its way through the rock ever more deeply into the earth.

The fact must now be taken account of that when we look at the orders from below upwards the goods become increasingly amorphous; more and more they lose that characteristic form, those precise qualities, which predestinate them for one use and exclude them from others. The higher up we go in the orders of goods, the more they lose their specialisation, their efficacy for a particular purpose; and the wider their potential uses, the more general their meaning. We meet continually fewer distinguishable kinds of goods, and individual categories become correspondingly more embracing, as when we ascend in a system of logical concepts we come to continually fewer, ever thinner in content but ever wider in compass. The genealogical tree of goods becomes progressively thinner. This simply means that

一定要记住，只有那些已在消费者手中，为消费做准备的物品才能被排在第一位，而例如面包师手中的面包，严格地说，只有当它与送面包人的劳动结合在一起时才能被列为第一位。位次较低的物品，如果不是自然界直接给予的，那就总是由位次较高的物品相组合而产生的。尽管这种结构图可以用另一种方式构建，但为了我们的目的，最好还是按照该种物品曾经从中出现过的最高位次把它列入那个最高位次。例如劳动就是处于最高位次的货物，因为劳动在所有生产的最开始就出现了，而不管它也出现在其他任何阶段。按照生产过程或者组合的顺序，每一种物品都通过添加其他列为较高位次或者较低位次的物品而成熟为消费品；在这种添加方式的帮助下，它逐渐走到消费者面前，就像一条河流，借助于流进来的各条小溪，冲破岩石的阻挡，越来越深地在地面上形成一条大的河流。

现在必须考虑这样一个事实，即，当我们按照由低至高的顺序来看位次时，物品就逐渐变得模糊起来，没有定形；它们越来越失去自己的特征形状，即预先决定它们只作一种用途而不作其他用途的那些明确的特征。当我们沿着物品的位次顺序走得越来越高，就会发现物品越来越失去它们的专门性，即它们为达到特定目的的效能；而且它们潜在的用途越广泛，它们的意义就越普遍。我们不断遇到各种货物，它们越来越不容易被清楚地辨别，单个种类相应地变得包含越来越广，就像当我们沿着逻辑概念系统自下往上走时，我们将不断遇到这样的概念，这些概念的数目逐渐减少，内容也逐渐变得空洞，但是它们所包含的范畴将不断扩大。货物的家系图也变得越来越单薄。这仅仅说明，

the further away from consumption goods we choose our standpoint, the more numerous the goods of the first order become which descend from similar goods of higher orders. When any goods are wholly or partially combinations of similar means of production, we say they are related in production. Therefore we can say that the productive relationship of goods increases with their order.

Thus, if we ascend in the hierarchy of goods, we finally come to the ultimate elements in production for our purposes. That these ultimate elements are labor and gifts of nature or "land," the services of labor and of land, requires no further argument. ① All other goods "consist" of at least one and mostly of both of these. We can resolve all goods into "labor and land" in the sense that we can conceive all goods as bundles of the services of labor and land. On the other hand, consumption goods are a special class characterised by their capacity to be consumed. But the remaining products, that is the "produced means of production," are, on the one hand, only the embodiment of those two original production goods, on the other hand "potential" consumption goods, or better, parts of potential consumption goods. So far we have found no reason, and it will appear later that there is no reason at all, why we should see in them an independent factor of production. We "resolve them into labor and land." We can also resolve the consumption goods, and conversely conceive the original productive factors as potential consumption goods. Both views, however, are applicable only to produced means of production; for they have no separate existence.

---

① This was particularly sharply emphasised by O. Effertz. When one reflects how one-sidedly the classical economists emphasised labor, how closely this was connected with some of their results, and that really Böhm-Bawerk alone achieved complete consistency on this point, one must recognise Effertz' emphasis of the matter as actually an important service.

如果我们选择的立场离消费品越远，处于第一位的货物的数量就越来越多，它们都是由较高位次的相同货物形成的。当任何一种货物全部或者部分地是相同生产资料的组合时，我们就可以说，它们在生产上是相关联的。因此，我们可以说，货物的生产关系随着它们所处位次的提高而增加。

这样，如果我们沿着货物的层级向上走，最后我们就会走到生产的最终要素，他们将符合我们的目的。没有必要进一步论证：这些终极要素就是劳动、自然禀赋或“土地”，是劳动提供了服务，土地提供了服务。① 所有其他货物至少“包含着”两种要素中的一个，多数情况下包含两者。在某种意义上我们就可以把所有货物分解为“劳动和土地”，也就是说我们可以将所有货物看成是劳动服务和土地服务的集合体。另一方面，由于消费品具有直接供消费的特征，它们属于特殊的一类。但是，其余的产品，即“作为生产资料而生产出的产品”，一方面仅是那两个原始生产货物的体现，另一方面也是“潜在的”消费品，或者，更准确地说是潜在消费品的组成部分。至此我们没有为要在它们之中发现一种独立的生产要素找到理由，而且以后我们也会明白，根本没有这种理由。我们“把它们分解为劳动和土地”。我们也可以分解消费品，并且相应地，我们可以把原始生产要素看做是潜在的消费品。然而这两种观点都只适合于生产出的生产资料；因为它们不是独立地存在。

---

① O. 埃费尔兹特别强调地指出了这一点。当人们仔细想想古典经济学家是怎样片面地强调劳动，这一点与他们的某些结论是多么紧密的相关，而实际上，只有庞巴维克一人在这一点上达到了完全达到了一致性，人们必须承认，埃费尔兹对这件事的强调，实际上是一项重要的贡献。

The question now arises, in what relation do the two original productive factors stand to each other? Does either of the two take precedence over the other, or are their rõles essentially different? We cannot answer this from a philosophical, physical, or any other general point of view, but only from the economic. For us it is only a question of how their relation is represented for the purposes of the economic system. The answer, however, which ought to be valid in the realm of economic doctrine cannot be valid generally but only with respect to a particular construction of the theoretical system. Thus the Physiocrats, for example, answered the first question in the affirmative, and indeed favorably to land – in itself perfectly correctly. In so far as they would express by their view nothing more than the fact that labor can create no new physical matter, there is nothing to be objected against it. It is only a question of how fruitful this conception is in the economic field. Agreement with the Physiocrats on this point, for example, does not prevent our withholding our approval from their further arguments. Adam Smith also answered the same question affirmatively, but in favor of labor. This also is not false in itself; it would even be proper to take this conception as a starting point. It gives expression to the fact that the use of land demands no sacrifice in disutility from us, and if anything wereto be gained by it we might also appropriate this conception. It is true that Adam Smith clearly thought of productive powers offered by nature as free goods, and attributed the fact that they were not actually so considered in the economic system to their occupation by landowners. Clearly he thought that in a community with no private property in land, labor alone would be a factor in economic calculations. Now this is decidedly incorrect, but his point of departure in itself is not on that account untenable. Most of the classical econom ists put the labor element in the foreground

现在的问题上升为：这两种原始生产要素彼此之间是什么样的关系呢？在两者中是一个比另一个重要，还是它们的作用根本不同？我们不能从哲学的、物理学的，或者任何其他通常的观点去回答这个问题，而只有从经济的观点回答问题。对我们来说，这只是一个为了经济系统的目的如何反映它们之间的关系的问题。然而，在经济学说领域应该被认为是有效的回答，却不能是普遍有效的，而只能说按照理论体系的某个特殊的构造来说是有效的。这样，例如重农主义者回答第一个问题将是肯定的，他们确实更看重土地——这样回答本身是完全正确的。如果说他们这样回答只不过是要表明劳动不能创造出新的物质的东西，那么就没有任何反对它的余地了。这只是这样一个问题，即在经济学领域这个概念有多大用处。比如，我们赞同重农主义的这一观点，但这并不妨碍我们对他们的进一步论证持有反对意见。亚当·斯密也对这个问题做了正面回答，但是他认为劳动比土地更重要。这本身也没有错；甚至将这一概念当做一个出发点也是恰当的。它表达了这样一个事实，即土地的利用并不需要我们在非实用上作出牺牲，同时，如果我们想从土地上获得什么东西，我们也可以采用这个概念。诚然，亚当·斯密清楚地把自然界所提供的生产力量看做是自由货物，而实际上，在经济体系里土地并没有被看做是自由的，对于这一事实，亚当·斯密把其归因于地主们对土地的占有。显然他认为，在一个没有土地私有制的社会里，只有劳动才是经济核算的因素。现在这种想法肯定是不正确的，但是他的出发点本身并不因此就站不住脚。大多数古典经济学家都把劳动要素放在第一位——

above all Ricardo. They could do so, because by means of their theory of rent they eliminated land and the determination of its value. If the theory of rent were tenable, then we could certainly content ourselves with this conception. Even as independent a spirit as Rae contented himself with it, precisely because he accepted that theory of rent. Finally, a third group of writers answered our question in the negative. With these we side. For us, the deciding point is that both original productive factors are equally indispensable in production, and indeed for the same reason and in the same manner.

The second question can again be answered variously, quite independently of the answer to the first. Thus Effertz, for example, assigns an active part to labor and a passive one to land. Why he does so is quite clear. He thinks that labor is the motivating element in production, while land represents the object on which labor manifests itself. In this he is right, but his arrangement gives us no new knowledge. On the technical side, the conception of Effertz is hardly one to be adopted, but this aspect is not decisive for us. We are only concerned with the part played by the two original productive factors in the economic deliberations and dealings of individuals, and in this connection the two show up quite equally. Labor as well as land is "economised." Labor as well as land is valued, is used according to economic principles, and both receive equally economic consideration. And in neither case is there anything else involved. Since nothing else is relevant to our purposes with respect to the original factors of production, we shall put them on terms of equality. In this interpretation we agree with the other marginal utility theorists.

While we have nothing further to say about the productive factor, land, it is advisable for us to examine the other factor, labor, somewhat more closely. Passing over the differences between productive and unproductive labor, between labor used directly and

尤其是李嘉图。他们之所以能够这样做，是因为借助于他们的地租理论，他们排除了土地及其价值的决定因素。如果这个地租理论能够站得住脚，那么我们就一定能对这个概念满意。甚至像 Rae 这样有独立见解的人也对这个概念满意，恰恰是因为他接受了地租理论。最后，有第三类作家否定地回答了我们的问题。我们是站在这些人的一边的。对我们来说，起决定作用的论点是，在生产过程中，两种原始生产要素是平等的，都是必不可少的，的确这是出于同样的原因，同样的态度。

第二个问题又可以有各种不同的回答，它与第一个问题的回答没有任何关系。例如，埃费尔兹把劳动作为主动因素，把土地看做被动因素。他这样做的理由是很明显的。他认为，劳动在生产中是主动的因素，而土地则是劳动在其上表现自己的客观因素。他说的这一点是正确的，但是他的安排并没有给我们提供新的知识。在技术层面上，埃费尔兹的观点并不可取，但这一方面对我们并不起决定作用。我们仅仅关心在个人的经济思考和行为中这两种原始生产要素所起的作用，并且在这一点上，两者表现的完全一样。劳动与土地一样都是“有经济价值的”。劳动与土地都要受到评价，要根据经济原则来使用，而且两者都要得到同样的经济上的考虑。它们均不涉及什么别的事情。既然在原始生产要素方面再没有什么别的与我们的目的相关，我们就将把它们放在同等的位置上来对待。在这种解释上，我们赞同其他边际效用理论家的观点。

尽管我们对于生产要素——土地，没有什么更多的话要说，但对于另一个生产要素——劳动，我们最好还是要稍微仔细些来研究。暂且不管生产劳动和非生产劳动、直接用于生产的劳动和

indirectly in production, and, as likewise irrelevant, the distinctions between mental and manual and between skilled and unskilled labor, we must comment on two other distinctions which are significant in so far as we can start from them in order to make an observation which is essential for us . These are the distinctions between directing and directed and between independent and wage labor. What distinguishes directing and directed labor appears at first sight to be very fundamental. There are two main characteristics. In the first place directing labor stands higher in the hierarchy of the productive organism. This direction and supervision of the "executing" labor appears to lift the directing labor out of the class of other labor. While the executing labor is simply on a par with the uses of land and from the economic standpoint has absolutely the same function as these, the directing labor is clearly in a governing position in contrast to both the executing labor and the uses of land. It forms, as it were, a third productive factor. And the other characteristic separating it from directed labor appears to constitute its nature: the directing labor has something creative in that it sets itself its own ends. The distinction between independent and wage labor we can likewise trace to that between directing and directed labor. Independent labor is something peculiar precisely in so far as it possesses the function of directing labor, while for the rest it differs in no way from wage labor. If, therefore, an independent individual produces on his own account and also does executing work, then he splits, so to say, into two individuals, namely a director and a worker in the ordinary sense.

It is easy to see that the characteristic of being in a higher rank, the function of superintendence in itself, constitutes no essential economic distinction. The mere circumstance that ranks one worker above another in the industrial organisation, in a directing and superintending position, does not make his labor into something distinct. Even if

间接用于生产的劳动这些区别，以及类似的不相关的劳动，脑力劳动和体力劳动、熟练劳动和非熟练劳动的这些区别，我们必须对其他两类区别加以评论，它们如此重要是因为我们要提出一项对我们至关重要的意见，可以从它们开始。这就是领导的劳动和被领导的劳动之间的区别，独立的劳动和含有工资的劳动之间的区别。初看起来，区分领导的劳动和被领导的劳动的东西是非常根本性的东西。这里有两个主要特点。第一，领导的劳动在生产组织结构的等级中处于较高的地位。这种对“执行的”劳动的管理和监督似乎把领导的劳动从其他类的劳动中提升出来。尽管执行的劳动只不过与土地的各种用途相同，从经济的观点看，它与这些用途的职能绝对相同，但是，领导的劳动相对于执行的劳动及土地的用途，很显然，它处于支配的地位。它似乎形成了第三种生产要素。而将领导的劳动与被领导的劳动区别开来的其他特征似乎也就成为它的性质：领导的劳动有某种创造性，因为它能为自己定出目的。对于独立劳动和工资劳动的区别，我们同样可以追溯到领导劳动和被领导劳动的区别。独立劳动之所以有某种特殊的东西，正是因为它具有领导的劳动的职能，而在其他方面它与工资劳动并没有任何差别。因此，如果一个独立的个人独自进行生产，他同时也做执行的工作，那么可以说，他把自己分成两种类型的人，即一种是领导者，一种是平时所说的工人。

很容易看出，处于较高等级的特点，即监督管理职能本身，并不构成实质上的经济区别。在工业组织里仅仅依据一个工人位于另一个工人之上，即一个工人处于领导和监督的地位这一情况，并不能使他的劳动变成某种性质不同的东西。即使在这个意

the "leader" in this sense does not move a finger or contribute anything directly to production, he still performs indirect labor in the usual sense, exactly as, say, a watchman. Much more importance seems to attach to the other element, which lies in the decision about the direction, method, and quantity of production. Even if one allows that the above-mentioned higher ranking does not signify much economically – though perhaps a lot sociologically – one will still see an essential distinguishing feature in this function of making decisions.

But we see at once that the necessity of making decisions occurs in any work. No cobbler's apprentice can repair a shoe without making some resolutions and without deciding independently some questions, however small. The "what" and the "how" are taught him; but this does not relieve him of the necessity of a certain independence. When a worker from an electrical firm goes into a house to repair the lighting system, even he must decide something of the what and the how. An agent may even have to take part in decisions relative to prices, the setting of the price of his article within certain limits may be left to him – but he is nevertheless neither "leader" nor necessarily "independent." Now the director or independent owner of a business has certainly most to decide and most resolutions to make. But the what and the why are also taught him. He knows first of all the how: he has learned both the technical production and all the economic data concerned. What there is still to be decided only differs in degree from the decisions of the cobbler's apprentice. And the what is prescribed for him by demand. He sets no particular goal, but given circumstances force him to act in a definite way. Certainly the given data may change, and then it will depend upon his ability how quickly and successfully he reacts to it. But so it is in the carrying out of any work. He acts, not on the basis of the prevailing conditions of things,

义上说的“领导者”不动一个手指头，或者对生产没有任何直接的贡献，但是他仍然执行着普通意义上说的间接劳动，准确地说就好像是一个看守人一样。更重要的作用似乎可以赋予另一个因素，这一因素在于它能决定生产的方向、方法和数量。即使人们赞同上述较高等级的人在经济上没有多大重要性——虽然在社会学上或许还有他的重要性——但人们在这个做决策的职能上仍然能够看到一种实质上不同的特征。

但是我们立刻看到，在任何工作中都会出现做决策的必要性。一个修鞋匠的徒弟不作出某种决定，不独立的决定某些问题，不管大还是小，他就不能修理鞋。“做什么”和“怎样做”是教过他的，但是他必须具有某种独立性，这是不能被免除的。当一个电机公司的工人到一个家庭去修理照明系统，甚至他也必须对做什么和怎样做这样的问题作出某些决定。一个代理商可能不得不参与到有关价格方面的决策中，因为在一定范围之内可能把规定货物价格的权利委托给他——然而他既不是“领导”也不一定是“独立者”。现在一个企业的领导或者独立的所有者肯定要对大部分事情作出决定，作出决议。但是做什么和为什么这样做是已经教给他们的了。他首先知道怎样去做：他已经懂得技术的生产和有关的所有的经济数据。这里还有其他需要作出决定的，与修鞋匠的学徒所要作的决定，只有程度上的区别。而做什么已由需求事先给他规定了。他不制定具体的目标，但是给定的环境迫使他按照一定的方式去做。当然给定的数据也可能发生变化，那么他能多么迅速，多么成功地对变化做出反映，就取决于他的能力了。然而执行任何工作都是这样。他的行为并不是根据事情当前的条件，

but much more according to certain symptoms of which he has learned to take heed, especially of the tendencies immediately showing in the demand of his customers. And to these tendencies he yields step by step, so that only elements of minor significance can ordinarily be unknown to him. From this consideration, however, it follows that in so far as individuals in their economic conduct simply draw conclusions from known circumstances – and that indeed is what we are here dealing with and what economics has always dealt with – it is of no significance whether they are directing or directed. The conduct of the former is subject to the same rules as that of the latter, and to establish this regularity, to show that the apparently fortuitous is really strictly determined, is a fundamental task of economic theory.

Under our assumptions, therefore, the means of production and the productive process have in general no real leader, or rather the real leader is the consumer. The people who direct business firms only execute what is prescribed for them by wants or demand and by the given means and methods of production. Individuals have influence only in so far as they are consumers, only in so far as they express a demand. In this sense indeed every individual takes part in the direction of production, not only the one to whom the rôle of director in a business has fallen, but everyone, especially the worker in the narrowest sense. In no other sense is there a personal direction of production. The data which have governed the economic system in the past are familiar, and if they remain unchanged the system will continue in the same way. The changes which the data may undergo are not quite so familiar; but in principle the individual follows them as well as he can. He alters nothing spontaneously; he only alters what the conditions are already altering of their own accord; he removes those discrepancies between the data and his conduct which emerge if the given conditions change and people try to continue operating in the same way. Any individual can indeed act otherwise than our view assumes;

而更多的是根据某些象征，他已经学会了要关注这些象征，尤其是从他的顾客的需求中直接表现出来的趋势。他一步一步地屈从于这些趋势，所以通常只有次要的因素是他所不了解的。然而，从这方面考虑，就可以认为，只要个人在他自己的经济行为中只根据已知的环境得出结论——这也确实是我们在这里所研究的，是经济学一直在研究的——那么究竟是他们领导别人还是被领导就不重要了。前者的行为和后者的行为一样都服从于同样的规则。建立这种规则，并且表明在表面上是偶然的东西实际上是被严格定义的，这是经济理论的一项根本任务。

因此，根据我们的假设，生产资料和生产过程一般没有真正的领导者，或者更确切地说，真正的领导者是消费者。管理工商企业的人仅仅是执行由需要或需求以及给定的资料和生产方法为他们规定了的事情。个人只有在他们是消费者时，只有在他们表示需求时才会有影响。在这个意义上，每一个人确实都参与了生产管理，不仅是承担企业领导责任的人，而且每一个人，特别是在最狭窄意义上所说的工人。除此之外，个人对生产的领导没有其他任何意义。人们对过去支配经济系统的数据是熟悉的，如果这些数据保持不变，那么这个系统就会以同样的方式继续下去。人们对数据可能经历的变化并不熟悉；但是从原则上讲，个人会尽可能地追随着这些变化。他不会自发地改变任何东西；他只是改变那些环境已经正以自己的准则改变的东西；他排除数据与他的行为之间的差异，如果给定的条件发生变化，而人们仍然试图继续以同样的方式行动，就会产生这种差异。当然任何个人都可能采取与我们的观点所假设的完全不一样的方式行动；

but in so far as changes result merely from the pressure of objective necessity, any creative rôle in the economic system is absent. If the individual acts differently, then essentially different phenomena appear, as we shall see. But here we are only concerned with stating the logic inherent in economic facts.

From our assumptions it also follows that the quantity of labor is determined by the given circumstances. Here we append the consideration of a question which was left open earlier, namely the magnitude of the supply of labor existing at any time. How much a given number of men work is obviously not rigorously determined at the outset. If we assume for the moment that the best possibilities of employing the labor of all individuals are known, that there is, therefore, a strictly determined scale of such employments, then at every point on this scale the anticipated utility of every concrete employment of labor is compared with the disutility accompanying the employment. Thousands of voices from everyday life remind as that the work concerning our daily bread is a heavy burden, which one only undergoes because one must, and which one throws off if one can. From this emerges unequivocally the amount of work that a worker will perform. At the beginning of each working-day such a comparison naturally always turns out favorably to the work to be undertaken. The further one progresses, however, in the satisfaction of wants, the more the impulse to work declines and at the same time the more the quantity with which it is compared, namely the disutility of work, increases; so that the comparison becomes continually more unfavorable to the continuation of work, until the moment comes for every worker when increasing utility and increasing disutility of work balance each other. Naturally, the strength of both forces varies according to individuals and according to countries. In these variations there lies a fundamental explanatory factor in the shaping of personal and national history. But the essence of the theoretical principle

但是只要变化的产生仅仅来源于客观压力的需要，那么经济系统中的任何创造性的角色都不存在。如果每个人的行为方式不一样，那么就会出现实质上不同的现象，这是我们将要看到的。但我们在这里仅仅是想要说明经济事实的内在逻辑。

根据我们的假设也可以推断出：劳动的数量决定于给定的环境。这里我们要附加考虑一个先前留下没有回答的问题，即在任何时候劳动供给量的大小。很显然，一定数量的人做多少工作，这不是在一开始就严格确定的。如果我们暂且假定，所有雇佣个体的劳动的最佳可能性是已知的，从而就有着这种雇佣的严格确定的尺度，于是在这个尺度上的每一点，每一种具体劳动的雇佣的预期效用就可以与伴随着雇佣产生的非效用相比较。来自于日常生活的众多的声音提醒我们，涉及我们日用面包的劳动是一项沉重的负担，人们只有在不得已时才去承担，并且只要有可能人们就会将其扔掉。这里明确地显示了一个工人将要完成的工作量。在每一个工作日的开始，这种比较自然总是有利于所要承担的工作的完成。然而，如果你在想要的满足上前进得越远，对工作的动力下降得就越多，同时，它所比较的数量，就是劳动的非效用，就会增加；因此这种比较逐渐变得越来越不利于工作的继续，直到对每个工人来说，当劳动所逐渐增加的效用与逐渐增加的非效用达到彼此平衡这一时刻到来为止。当然，这两种力量的强度因人而异，也因国别而异。在这些差异中，存在一个本质的说明因素来说明个人历史和国家历史的形成。但是理论原则

is undisturbed by them. ①

The services of labor and of land are therefore simply productive powers. The measurement of the quantity of labor of any quality certainty presents difficulties, but it can be effected, just as there would be no difficulties in principle in setting up some physical measure of the services of land however complicated the matter might be in practice. Then if there were only one factor of production, if for example labor of one quality could produce all goods – which is conceivable by assuming that all gifts of nature are free goods, so that no question of economic conduct with respect to them arises – or if both factors of production worked separately, so that each produced distinct goods for itself alone, such a measurement would be all that the practical man required for his economic plans. For example, if the production of a consumption good of definite value required three units of labor and another of the same value required two, then his conduct would be determined. In reality, however, this is not so. The productive factors practically always operate together. Now if, say, three units of labor and two of land were necessary to produce one good of definite value, but two units of labor and three of land to produce another, which alternative should the producer choose? Obviously a standard is necessary to compare the two combinations; a common denominator is required. We may call this question Petty's problem. ②

① For details cf. Wesen, bks. I and II. Obviously the principle is valid only for a given outcome from effort, that is an unequivocal result, such as real wages per hour.

② Petty put this problem incidentally in his work Political Arithmetic, which also contains, as is well known, many other germs of later theoretical analysis.

的实质并不受它们的干扰。①

因此，劳动和土地的服务只是生产力量。衡量任一质量的劳动的数量肯定是存在困难的，但这是可以办到的，就像我们在原则上对土地的服务规定某种物质上的衡量不会有困难一样，而不管在实际上这件事可能是多么复杂。那么，如果只有一种生产要素，比如，如果一种质量的劳动能生产所有的货物——并且通过假定所有自然所赋予的东西为自由品，那么对它们来说就不会产生经济行为的问题，这种假定是可以设想的——或者如果两种生产要素分别起作用，因而 每一种都只为自己生产不同的产品，那么这种衡量就是从事实践的人为了他自己的经济计划所必须的。例如，如果某种确定价值的消费品的生产需要三个单位的劳动，而另一个同样价值的消费品需要两单位的劳动，那么这个生产者的行为将是确定的了。然而实际上，情况并不是这样。事实上，各种生产要素总是一道起作用。比如说，如果现在生产一种确定价值的某种货物需要三单位劳动和两单位土地，而生产另一种货物需要两单位的劳动和三单位的土地，那么生产者将如何在这两者中选择呢？显然需要一个标准来对这两种组合进行比较；需要有一个共同的标准。我们可以把这个问题称为配第的问题。②

---

① 详细说明，请参考《本质》第Ⅰ编和第Ⅱ编。显然这个原则仅对努力的一定成果有效，这是一个明确的结论，例如每小时的实际工资。

② 配第附带地将这个问题放在他的《政治算术》一书中，正如大家所知道的，这本书同样也包含着许多其他后来理论分析的根源。

The solution of it gives us the imputation theory. What the individual wishes to measure is the relative significance of quantities of his means of production. He needs a standard with the help of which to regulate his economic conduct; be needs indexes to which he can conform. In short, he requires a standard of value. But he has such a thing directly only for his consumption goods; for only these immediately satisfy his wants, the intensity of which is the basis of the meaning of his goods to him. For his stock of services of labor and land there is in the first instance no such standard, and likewise none, we may now add, for his produced means of production.

It is clear that these other goods also owe their importance merely to the fact that they likewise serve to satisfy wants. They contribute to the satisfaction of wants because they contribute to the realisation of consumption goods. Therefore they receive their value from the latter; the value of the consumption goods, as it were, radiates back to them. It is "imputed" to them, and on the basis of this imputed value they receive their place in each economic scheme. A finite expression for the total value of the stock of means of production or of one of the two original productive factors will thus not always prove possible, because such total value will very often be infinitely large. However, it is not necessary for the practical man or for theory to know this total value. It is never a question of parting with every possibility of production, that is of existence, but simply of assigning certain quantities of productive means to some end or other. An isolated individual, for example, who could not produce (or live) at all without either of the original productive factors could state no finite expression of value for either. To this extent Mill is quite

由这个问题的解决，我们得到了归属理论。生产者个体想要衡量的是他的生产资料数量的相对重要性。他必须借助于一种标准来规范自己的经济行为；他需要各种指标，依靠这些指标来做事。总之，他需要一种价值标准。但是他只是直接对他的消费品才有这些标准；因为只有这些消费品能够立即满足他的需求，这种对消费品需要的强度就是这些货物对他的意义的基础。对他的劳动服务和土地服务的储存量而言，首先就没有这种标准；我们现在还可以再补充说，对于他的被生产出来的生产资料来说，同样也没有这种标准。

很显然，这些其他货物之所以有它们的重要性；仅仅在于它们同样是为满足直接需求服务的。它们为需求的满足作出贡献，正是因为它们对消费品的实现有贡献。因此，它们从后者那里获得了自身的价值；消费品的价值，如果有，那么就好像是回射到它们身上。价值“归属于”它们，依赖这种归属的价值，在每一种经济结构中，它们获得了自己的地位。所以，要对生产资料的储存量或者对两个原始生产资料中的一个的总价值进行确切的表述，并不总是可能的，因为这种总价值常常是无限大的。然而，对于一个从事实践生产的人或者对理论来说，知道这个总价值也是没有必要的。这绝不是一个放弃每一个生产可能性的问题，也就是放弃存在性的问题，而仅仅是为达到这一目的或另一目的来安排一定量的生产资料的问题。例如，一个孤立的个体，如果他没有两种原始生产要素中的任何一个，就根本不能从事生产（或者生活），他也就不能对任何一个生产要素的价值进行确切的表述。如果从这个范围上说，穆勒认为劳动服务和土地的服务是不确定

right[1] when he says that the services of labor and of land are indefinite and incommensurable. But he is wrong when he goes on to say also that in the particular case one can never say what are the shares of "nature" and of labor in a product. Physically, indeed, the two will not allow of separation, but this also is not necessary for the purposes of the economic system. What is necessary for the latter every individual knows well enough, namely, what increase in satisfaction he owes to any small increment of each means of production. However, we shall not go more closely into the problem of the imputation theory here.[2]

In contrast to use value of consumption goods this value of production goods is "return value" (Ertragswert), or as one might also say, productivity value (Produktivitä tswert). To the marginal utility of the former corresponds the marginal productive use (Produktivitä tsgrenznutzen) of the latter, or, following the usual term, the marginal productivity; the significance of an individual unit of the services of labor or land is given by the marginal productivity of labor or land, which is therefore to be defined as the value of the least important unit of product so far produced with the help of a unit of a given stock of the services of labor or land. This value indicates the share of every individual service of labor or land in the value of the total social product, and can hence be called in a definite sense the "product" of a service of labor or land. To one not completely at home in the theory of value, these meagre statements will not convey what they ought. I refer the reader to J. B. Clark's Distribution of Wealth,

---

① Principles, ed. Ashley, p. 26.

② Cf. K. Menger, Wieser, and BÖhm-Bawerk, who first treated the problem. Cf. also Wesen, bk. II, and my Bemerkungen zum Zurechnungsproblem, Zeitschrift für Volksw., Sozialpol. und Verw. (1909). We are not concerned with the more difficult problems which arise out of the theory of marginal productivity, and need not, therefore, refer to its present, and much more correct, form.

的以及是不可衡量的,[1] 他的观点就是正确的。但是他又进一步说，在一个特定的情况下，人们绝不能对一个产品说出它的“自然”份额和劳动份额，这种说法就是错误的。诚然，从物质上说，这两者是不能划分开的，但就经济体系的目的来说，这种划分是不必要的。对于后者来说，每一个人都十分清楚地知道什么是必须的，也就是，它的满足的增加，有多少是归因于每一种生产资料的任何小量的增加。然而，在这里我们不打算对归属理论问题做更深入的研究。[2]

与消费品的使用价值相比较，生产物品的这种价值不同，它是“收益价值”，或者也可以像某些人所说的，是生产力价值。与前者的边际效用相对应的是后者的边际生产用途，或者用一个常用的术语：边际生产力；每一单位劳动服务或土地服务的重要意义是由劳动或者土地的边际生产力给定的，因此，它被定义为：借助于一单位劳动服务或土地服务的给定存量，至今所生产的最不重要的一单位产品的价值。这个价值表明了在总的社会产品的价值中，每一个别劳动服务或土地服务所占的份额，因此就能够被明确地称为某种劳动或土地服务的“产品”。对一个不完全懂得价值理论的人来说，以上这些简短的说明并不能表达它们的全部意义。这里我给读者指出一本书：J. B. 克拉克的《财富的分配》，

---

① 参见《原理》，阿什利编，第 26 页。

② 参考 K. 门格尔、维塞尔和庞巴维克，他们最先研究这个问题。还可参考《本质》第二编，以及我的《归属问题评述》，刊登在《政治经济学、社会政策和管理杂志》（1909 年）。我们不涉及由边际生产理论产生来的更复杂的问题，因此也就没必要谈现在的、更为正确的形式。

where the theory is accurately stated and its meaning elucidated,[1] and merely remark that this is the only precise meaning of the expression "product of labor" for the purposes of a purely economic treatment. In this sense alone we shall use it here. In this sense also we say that the prices of the services of land and labor in an exchange economy, that is rent and wages, are determined by the marginal productivity of land and labor, and therefore that under free competition landlord and laborer receive the product of their means of production. This theorem, which is hardly a controversial one in modern theory, is merely stated here. It will become clearer in later amplifications.

The following point is also important for us. In reality, the individual uses this value of productive means with such readiness because the consumption goods into which they ripen are empirically familiar. Since the value of the former is dependent upon that of the latter, the former must change when other consumption goods than hitherto are produced. And because we wish to disregard the existence of this given experience, and to allow it to arise before our eyes, in order to investigate its nature, we must start from the point where the individual is not yet clear about the choice between the existing possibilities of employment. Then he will first of all employ his means of production in the production of those goods which satisfy his most pressing needs, and thereafter proceed to produce for continually less urgently felt needs. Moreover, at every step he will consider what other feelings of want must go unsatisfied in consequence of the employment of production goods for the wants preferred at the moment.

---

① Misunderstandings arise especially from an inadequate comprehension of the marginal concept. Cf. on this Edgeworth's article "The Theory of Distribution," in the Quarterly Journal of Economics (1904), particularly his reply to Hobson's arguments against Clark.

在这本书中作者精确地表达了这种理论，阐述了理论的意义，[①]这里，我只想说，从一种纯粹的经济论述的目的考虑，这种描述是“劳动产品”一词的唯一精确的含义的表达。在这里我们仅仅在这个意义上使用它。也是从这种意义上我们说，在一个交换经济中，土地和劳动所提供服务的价格，即地租和工资，是由土地和劳动的边际生产力所决定的，因此在自由竞争情况下，地主和劳动者获得了他们所拥有的生产资料或者生产方式的产品。在现代理论结构中这个命题几乎是没有争议的，在这里我仅仅是提及一下。在以后展开的论述中，这个命题将会变得更加清楚。

下面这一观点对我们来说也是相当重要的。实际中，个人是这么容易地利用他所拥有的生产资料的价值，因为个人在经验上对这些生产资料所能生产出的消费品是很熟悉的。由于生产资料的价值依赖于所生产的消费品的价值，所以，当要生产迄今为止尚未生产过的消费品时，生产资料必须改变。同时由于我们希望忽视或者不顾这个给定经验的存在，并让它在我们眼前出现以便研究它的本质，所以我们必须从这一点开始，在这一点上个人对如何在现有的各种使用可能性之间作出选择还不是很清楚。于是个人将首先使用他的生产资料生产那些当前他最需要满足的物品，然后将逐步生产那些需要的迫切性不断下降的物品。此外，每走一步他都将考虑，由于为了满足当前选定的需要而使用生产的货物，那么有什么其他的需要的感觉就必然得不到满足。

① 特别由于对边际概念的理解不完全，产生了许多误解。关于这一点请参阅埃奇沃思的论文“分配理论”，载《经济学季刊》（1904 年），特别是他对霍布森反对克拉克的观点的回答。

Each step may only be taken economically provided that the satisfaction of more intensive wants is not thereby made impossible. So long as the choice is not made, the means of production will have no definite value. To each contemplated possibility of employment there will correspond a particular value of every increment. And then, which of these values will he definitely associated with any increment can only appear after the choice has been made and has stood the test of experience. The fundamental condition that a given want will not be satisfied before more intensive wants have been satisfied leads finally to the result that all goods should be so divided amongst their different possible uses that the marginal utility of each good is equal in all its uses. In this arrangement the individual has then found the arrangement which, under the given conditions and from his standpoint, is the best possible. If he so acts, then he can say that, according to his light, he has made the best of these circumstances. He will strive after this distribution of his goods and will vary every conceived or executed economic plan until it is achieved. If no experience is at hand, then he must feel his way by step to this distribution. If such experience from earlier economic periods is already available, he will try to traverse the same path. And should the conditions of which this experience is the expression change, then he will submit to the pressure of the new conditions and adapt his conduct and his valuations to them.

In all cases there is a definite method of employing every good, hence a definite satisfaction of wants, and so a utility index for the individual increments of the goods which gives expression to them. This utility index characterises the place of each increment in the individual's economy. If a new possibility of employment arises, it must be considered in the light of this value. However, if we return to the individual "acts of choice" which have been made and which result in this utility index,

只有当更迫切的需要的满足不会因当前的选择而变得不可能时，那么每一步的选择才会是经济的。只要还没有作出选择，那么生产资料的价值就是不确定的。对于每一种所考虑的使用可能性，相应地每一增量都将有一种特定的价值。那么在这些价值中哪一个与任意的增量一定有联系，这只有在作出选择之后并且经受住了经验的考验，才能显现出来。一个给定的需要在比它更迫切的需要得到满足之前是不会得到满足的，这一基本条件最终将导致这样的结果，就是所有的商品都将在它们不同的可能的用途之间进行划分，使得每一种商品的边际效用在它们所有的用途中相等。在这样的安排中，个人在给定的条件下并从他自身的观点看就找到了最好的可能的安排。如果他这样行动，那他就可以说，他已经尽其所能地充分利用了这些环境。他将努力实现他的商品的这种分配，改变每一种所考虑的和执行的经济计划，直到达到这种分配。如果没有可以借鉴的经验，那他就必须探索着一步一步地实现这种分配。如果可以从先前各经济时期已经积累的经验中获得这种经验，他就会试着遵循同样的路径。如果这种经验所要表达的条件发生变化，那么他就会因新条件的压力而屈服，并且调整自己的行为和评价以符合新的条件。

在所有的情况下，都存在着一种确定的方法使用每一种物品，因此有一个明确的需要满足，反映这种需要的商品的各自增长都有一个效用指数。这个效用指数能表明每一增长在个人经济中的地位。如果产生一种新的使用生产资料的可能性，就必须根据这个价值来考虑它。然而如果我们返回到个人的“选择行为”，这个选择行为是已经作出的并且已经实现了这个效用指数，

we find that in every case another and not this definitive utility is decisive. If I have divided a certain good amongst three possibilities of employment, I shall esteem it, when a fourth possibility arises, according to the state of satisfaction realised in the first three. For the division between these three, however, this utility is not determining, because it comes into existence only after the division has been decided on. But there finally emerges for every good a definite utility-scale, which reflects the utilities of all its uses and which gives it a definite marginal utility. For a means of production the same is given, as we have said, through its "product," or, according to Wieser's expression, through its "productive contribution."

Since all production involves a choice be tween competing possibilities and always means the renunciation of the production of other goods, the total value of the product is never a net gain, but only its surplus over the value of the product which would otherwise have been produced. The value of the latter represents a counter-argument against the chosen product and at the same time measures its strength. Here we meet the element of costs. Costs are a value phenomenon. In the final analysis what the production of a good costs the producer is those consumption goods which could otherwise be acquired with the same means of production, and which in consequence of the choice of production cannot now be produced. Therefore the outlay of means of production involves a sacrifice, in the case of labor just as in the case of other means of production. To be sure, in the case of labor there is also another condition which must be fulfilled, viz., that every expenditure of labor must result in a utility which at least compensates for the disutility attaching to that expenditure of labor. This, however, in no way alters the fact that within the limits of this condition the individual behaves towards the expenditure of labor exactly as towards the expenditure of other productive resources.

那么我们就会发现在每一种情况下，是另一种而不是这个确定的效用起决定作用。如果我已经把某种商品按照三种使用的可能性进行划分，当第四种使用的可能性出现时，我将会根据前三种已经实现了满足状态去考虑它。然而就这三种划分来看，这个效用并不起决定作用，因为效用只是在划分的决策已经作出之后才产生的，但是对每一种商品而言，最终都存在一个确定的效用尺度，这个尺度反映了该商品所有用途的效用，并且提供了这种商品的一个确定的边际效用。就一种生产资料而言，也提供了同样的东西，正如我们已经说的，通过它的“产品”，或者根据维塞尔的表述，通过它的“生产贡献”。

既然所有的生产都包含着在各种竞争的可能性之间进行选择，并且总是意味着放弃其他物品的生产，那么产品的总价值就绝不是一种净收益，而只是在减去如果可以生产出来的而实际未生产的其他产品的价值之后的余值。后者的价值代表对所选的产品的反向论据，同时也衡量了它的需求强度。在这里我们遇到了成本要素。成本是一种价值现象。在最后的分析中，对于生产者而言，生产某种产品所花费的成本就是那样一些消费品，它们本来可以通过使用相同的生产资料生产出来，而由于选择生产现在的产品不能生产出来。因此使用生产资料包含着一种牺牲，在其他生产资料方面就像和在劳动方面一样。当然，在劳动方面还有另一个条件必须满足，就是每一次劳动的支出都必须产生一种效用，这个效用至少能够弥补由于劳动支出所产生的反效用。然而，这绝不会改变这样一个事实，即在这个条件的限定内，个人选择劳动支出的行为，与他选择其他生产资料支出的行为是完全一样的。

Unsatisfied wants are, therefore, by no means without significance. Their impress is noticeable everywhere, and every productive decision must do battle with them, And the further the producer pushes production in a given direction, the harder this battle becomes; that is the more a particular want is satisfied, the less the intensity of the desire for more in the same line, hence the less the increase in satisfaction to be achieved through further production. Moreover, the sacrifice connected with production in this direction also increases simultaneously. For the means of production for this product must be withdrawn from ever more important categories of wants. The gain in value from the production in one direction becomes therefore continually smaller, and finally it vanishes. When that happens, this particular production comes to an end. Thus we can speak here of a law of decreasing returns in production. This has, however, a completely different meaning from the law of decreasing physical product, of which the validity of our proposition is independent. ①It is obvious that the economic law of increasing costs would finally operate, even if the physical proposition were not valid and even if its contrary were true. For the value of the investment to be made would eventually rise so much that the gain in utility accruing through production would vanish even if the physical amount of this investment progressively sank. If the latter were the case, obviously the condition of satisfaction of the wants of everyone would be at a higher level, but the essential phenomena would not on that account be different.

① In thus turning away from the law of physical decrease we take a decisive step away from the system of the classical economists. Cf. my essay, "Das Rentenprinzip in der Verteilungslehre," Schmoller's Jahrbuch (1906 and 1907). Further: F. X. Weiss, "Abnehmender Ertrag," in the Handwörterbuch der Staatswissenschaften.

因此，没有得到满足的需要绝不是不重要。随处可见它们的效应，每一个生产决策都必须与它们作斗争。沿着一个给定的方向，生产者将生产推得越远，这种斗争就变得越困难；也就是说，一个特定的需要越是得到满足，在同一线上想要得到更多的这一欲望的强度就会越小，因此，通过进一步生产该商品所得到的满足感的增长就越少。此外，伴随着这个方向的生产所带来的牺牲也在同时增加。因为，为生产这种产品所用的生产资料必须从越来越重要的需求类型中抽出来。从某一个方向的生产中获得的价值因此就不断变得越来越小，最终近乎消失。当这种情况发生时，这种具体的生产也就走到了尽头。所以我们在这里可以谈到一种生产中的收益递减规律。然而，这同物质生产递减规律有着完全不同的意义，我们的命题是否有效合理与物质生产递减规律是毫不相干的。[①] 显然，成本不断增长的经济规律最终会起作用，即使物质的命题没有效，不合理，即使它的反面是正确的。因为即将作出的投资的价值最终会上升很多以至于通过生产所得的效用的增加将消失，即使这种投资的物质数量不断降低。如果后者变为现实，那么很显然，每一个人的需要得到满足的条件会达到一个较高的水平，但是本质的现象不会因此而有不同。

---

① 这种背离物质递减规律，是我们远离古典经济学家体系迈出的决定性的一步。参阅我的论文《分配理论中的地租原理》，载《年鉴》，施穆勒编（1906 年和 1907 年）。还可参考怀兹的《收益递减》，载《社会科学简明词典》。

The consideration which producers actually give to the element of cost of production is therefore nothing but a way of taking account of other possibilities of employing production goods. This consideration constitutes the brake on every productive employment and a guide which every producer follows. But in practice, custom very soon crystallises it into a short handy expression of which every individual makes use, without forming it anew every time. With it the producer works in practice, adapting it to changing circumstances as the necessity arises; in it all the relations between wants and present means are expressed, in a large measure unconsciously; in it all the conditions of his life and his economic horizon are mirrored.

Costs as an expression of the value of other potential employment of means of production constitute the liability items in the social balance sheet. This is the deepest significance of the cost phenomenon. From this expression the value of producers' goods must be distinguished. For it represents the – *ex hypothesi* – higher total value of the actually created product. But at the margin of production, according to the above, both quantities are equal, because these costs rise to the height of the marginal utility of the product, therefore also of the participating combination of productive means. At this point emerges that relatively best position which is usually called the economic equilibrium,[①] and which, as long as the given data are maintained, tends to repeat itself in every period.

This has a very noteworthy consequence. It follows from it, first of all, that the last increment of every product will be produced without a gain in utility above costs. Correctly understood this is, to be sure, simply self-evident. But further, it follows that in production generally

① Cf. Wesen, bk. II.

因此，实际上生产者对生产成本要素的考虑，只不过是考虑使用生产货物的其他可能的生产方式。这种考虑构成了对每一种生产使用方式的制约，而且成为每一个生产者所遵循的准则。但在实际上，很快习惯就把它提炼成一句简短方便的表述，使每一个人都能使用它，而不必每一次都重新构造它。生产者用它在现实中工作，在必要的时候调整它以适应变化的环境；在那里，需求与现有的资料之间的所有关系都被描述了，而且大体上都是不自觉地形成的；在那里生产者的所有生活条件和他的经济地位都被反映了。

成本，作为生产资料其他潜在使用方式的价值表现形式，构成了社会总资产负债表的负债项目。这是成本现象最深刻的意义。生产者的商品的价值必须同这个概念区分开来。因为成本所代表的——根据假设——是实际创造出来的产品的更高一层的总价值。但是根据上面的叙述，在生产边际上，两者在数量上是相等的，因为这些成本上升到产品的边际效用的高度，因此也上升到参与生产资料构成的高度。在这一点上出现了相对最好的位置，通常它被称为经济均衡，[①] 只要保持给定的数据，这个均衡在每一个时期都会以自身的方式重复。

这里有一个非常值得关注的结果。在那里得到这样的结论：首先，每一产品的最后增量将在得到的效用不高于成本的情况下生产出来。如果对这句话正确的理解，就会发现它确实只是一个显然的道理。但是，进一步说，可以得到这个结论：一般而言，

---

① 参阅《本质》第Ⅱ编。

no surplus value above the value of producers' goods can be attained. Production realises only the values foreseen in the economic plan, which previously exist potentially in the values of means of production. Also in this sense, not only in the above-mentioned physical sense, production "creates" no values, that is in the course of the productive process no increase in value occurs. The future satisfaction of wants, before production has done its work, is exactly as dependent upon the possession of the necessary means of production as it is afterwards upon the possession of the product. The individual will try to avert loss of the former just as energetically as of the latter, and renounce the former only for the same compensation as for the latter.

Now the imputation process must go back to the ultimate elements of production, the services of labor and land. It cannot halt at any produced means of production, for the same argument may be repeated for each of them. Hence, no product can so far show a surplus value over the value of the services of labor and land contained in it. Just as we previously resolved produced means of production into labor and land, so we see now that they are only transitory items in the valuation process.

Hence, in an exchange economy – for the moment we anticipate a little-the prices of all products must, under free competition, be equal to the prices of the services of labor and nature embodied in them. For the same price as is obtained for the product after production must have been obtainable beforehand for the complete set of necessary means of production, because exactly as much depends upon them as upon the product. Each producer must give up his total receipts to those who supplied him with means of production, and in so far as they were again producers of some product or other, they must in their turn pass ou their receipts until finally the whole original total price falls to the purveyors of the services of labor and of nature. However, we shall return to this later.

在生产中不会得到超过生产货物的价值的剩余价值。生产只能实现在经济计划中预先安排的价值，这个价值是早先已经潜存于生产资料价值中的价值。也是在这个意义上，而不只是上面所说的物质意义，我们说生产不“创造”价值，意思是，在生产过程的进程中不会发生价值的增值。在生产完成它的工作之前，未来对需求的满足，完全取决于对必要生产资料的拥有，就像这之后完全依赖于对产品的拥有一样。个人将努力避免前者的损失，就像他努力避免后者的损失一样，他放弃前者也正像放弃后者一样只是为了得到同样的补偿。

现在归属的过程必须回到根本的生产要素上，即劳动和土地的服务。它不能停止在任何被生产出来的生产资料上，因为那样的话它们中的每一个都会重复相同的争论。因此，直到现在没有一种产品能显示它有超过它所包含的劳动和土地服务价值的剩余价值。就像我们先前把生产出来的生产资料分解为劳动和土地一样，现在我们看到，它们在价值评价过程中只是暂时的项目。

因此，在一个交换经济中——暂且我们稍微提前一点预测——在自由竞争下，所有产品的价格必须与体现在产品中的劳动服务和自然服务的价格相等。因为这个价格就是生产以后产品所得到的价格，就一整套必要生产资料来说它必须是预先可以获得的，因为依存于生产资料的恰恰与依存于产品的一样多。每一个生产者都必然将他们的总收入转让给那些为他们提供生产资料的人，而且由于这些人又是某个其他产品的生产者，他们也必然将自己的收入转让出去，直到最后整个原始总价值回到劳动和自然服务的提供者手中。不过，我们稍后将回到这个问题。

Here we come upon a second concept of cost, that of the exchange economy. The businessman considers as his coats: those sums of money which he must pay to other individuals, in order to procure his wares or means of producing them, that is his expenses of production. We complete his calculation in that we also include in costs the money value of his personal efforts. ①Then costs are in their essence price totals of the services of labor and of nature. And these price totals must always equal the receipts obtained for the products. To this extent, therefore, production must flow on essentially profitless. That the economic system in its most perfect condition should operate without profit is a paradox. If we remember the meaning of our statements, the paradox vanishes, at least in part. Of course our assertion does not mean that if it is perfectly balanced the economic system produces without result, but only that the results flow entirely to the original productive factors. As value is a symptom of our poverty, so profit is a symptom of imperfection. However, the paradox remains in part. It seems obvious that producers do as a rule receive more than wages for their labor and rent for the land they may possess. Will there not be a general rate of net profit in the sense of a surplus above costs? Competition may wash away the particular surplus profit of an industry, but it could not destroy profits common to all branches of production. But let it be assumed that producers make such a profit. Then they must value correspondingly the means of production to which they owe it. Now these are either original means of production, viz. personal efforts or natural agents, in which case we are where we were before; or else they are produced means of production,

① Personal labor services are, so to speak, "virtual expenses," as Seager appropriately said; cf. his Introduction to Economics, p. 55. Every businessman who calculates at all correctly now includes the rent of his own land in his expenses.

这里我们接触到成本的第二个概念，就是交换经济的成本。商人们把那些他必须支付给其他个人以获得商品或者获得为了生产产品所用的资料的总货币额看做是他的成本，也就是他的生产费用。为了将他的核算更完整，我们把他的个人努力的货币价值也算在成本之中。[①] 那么在本质上，成本就是劳动和自然服务的总价格之和。而且这些价格之和必然总是等于从产品中获得的收入。因此，在这个程度上，我们说生产必然在实质上没有源源不断的利润。说经济系统在其最完美的条件下不会产生利润，这是一个矛盾。可是如果我们还记得我们论述的意义，这就不是矛盾了，至少部分地不矛盾了。当然我们的论证并不意味着，如果经济系统处于完全均衡的状态，它的生产就没有结果，而只是说，生产的结果将全部流向原始生产要素。正如价值是我们贫困与否的象征一样，利润也是不完善的象征。然而矛盾仍然部分地存在着。显然，生产者一般确实获得的东西远超过他们付给劳动的工资以及他们可能拥有的土地的地租。难道就没有一个一般意义上的净利润率，即超过成本的剩余吗？竞争可能冲刷掉一个部门的个别剩余利润，但是它不会销毁所有生产部门所共有的利润。但是姑且假定生产者获得了这种利润。那么相应地他们就必须对其拥有的产生利润的生产资料进行评价。既然这些生产资料要么是原始的生产资料，即个人努力或者自然的力量，这样我们就回到我们原来的地方；要么就是被生产出来的生产资料，

① 正像西格恰当地描述的，个人劳动服务是“实际的支出”；参阅他的《经济学导论》，第55页。每一个精确核算的商人现在都把他自己的土地的地租纳为他的费用支出。

in which case these must be correspondingly more highly prized, that is the services of labor and land embodied in them must be more highly prized than other such services. That, however, is impossible, since laborers and landlords can compete very effectively with these quantities of labor and land which were previously invested. Consequently, net profit cannot exist, because the value and price of the original productive services will always absorb the value and price of the product, even if the productive process is parcelled out among ever so many independent firms. I do not want to tire the reader too much, and have put in a later place further analysis which properly belongs here. ①

This is not so opposed even to classical doctrine as it may seem to some readers. The cost theory of value and especially the Ricardian labor theory very strongly suggest the same conclusion, and some doctrinal tendencies such as the tendency to label all kinds of revenue, sometimes even interest, as wages are explained by it. If in classical times it was not expressly stated, ②it is first because the older economists were not very rigorous in recognising the consequences of their own principles, and secondly because our conclusion appears too blatantly to contradict the facts. Böhm-Bawerk was indeed the first who expressly said that the whole value of the product must in principle be divided between labor and land, if the process of production is to proceed with ideal perfection. This, of course, requires that the whole economic system be accurately adapted to the production undertaken, and that all values be appropriately adjusted to the data; that all economic schemes work harmoniously together and that nothing disturb their execution. Two circumstances, however, so Böhm-Bawerk proceeds, disturb the equilibrium between the values of the product and of the means of production again and again. The first is known under the name of friction.

---

① Cf. Chapter Ⅳ, and especially Chapter Ⅴ.

② Lotz, for example, did this, even if he turned aside from the perception in very weak fashion; see his Handbuch der Staatswissenschaftslehre. Very plain suggestions are to be found in Smith.

这样它们必然相应地被赋予更高的评价，也就是说，体现在它们身上的劳动和土地服务必然得到比其他的这种服务更高的评价。然而，那是不可能的，因为劳动者和地主能够与先前投入的劳动和土地的数量进行非常有效的竞争。因此，净利润是不会存在的，因为即使生产过程在这么多独立的企业中分割开来，原始生产性服务的价值和价格总是会吸收产品的价值和价格。我不想让读者感到太多厌倦，我把本属于应该在这里进一步分析的放在后面分析。①

这一点不像某些读者可能看到的那样，甚至与古典学说相对立。价值的成本理论，尤其是李嘉图的劳动理论，非常强烈地表明了相同的结论，某些理论趋势，比如把所有各种收入，甚至有时把利息都称为工资的这种趋势，就是用它来解释的。在古典时期如果这一点没有被明确地表达出来，② 这是因为首先年纪较长的经济学家对认可他们自己的理论的推论不是非常严格，第二是因为我们的结论似乎显得与事实过于相悖。庞巴维克确实是第一个说出这一观点的人，即如果生产过程想要在理想的状态下进行，那么产品的整个价值必须在原则上根据劳动和土地进行划分。这自然就要求整个经济系统必须精确地调整适应所从事的生产，所有的价值都必须与数据恰好相适应；而且要求所有的经济规划都一起和谐地运转，没有任何事情破坏它们的执行。然而，庞巴维克也指出，有两种环境会反反复复破坏这种产品价值与生产资料价值之间的均衡。第一个被称为摩擦。

---

① 参阅第四章，特别是第五章。

② 例如，洛茨就是这样，尽管他用非常微弱的方式回避这种直觉；参阅他的《社会科学简明辞典》。在斯密的书中可以找到非常朴实的表述。

For a thousand reasons the economic organism does not function quite promptly. Error, mishap, indolence, and so forth become, in the well known manner, a continual source of loss, but also of profit. ①

Before we pass on to the second circumstance alluded to by BÖhm-Bawerk, let us insert here a few words about two elements which are of considerable significance. The first is the element of risk. Two kinds of risk may be distinguished, the risk of the technical failure of production, in which we can include the danger of loss from acts of God, and the risk of commercial failure. In so far as these dangers are foreseen they operate immediately upon economic plans. Businessmen will either include premiums for risk in their cost accounting or they will make outlays to guard against certain dangers, or finally they will take account of – and equalise – the differences in risk between the branches of production by simply avoiding the more risky branches until the consequent increase of prices in the latter offers a compensation. ② None of these methods of evening out economic risks, in principle, creates a profit. A producer who takes precautions against risk by whatever measures – the building of dams, insurance of machinery, and so forth – certainly has an advantage in that he protects the fruit of his production, but ordinarily he also has corresponding costs. The risk – premium is no source of gain for the producer – but at the most for an insurance company, which can make an intermediary's profit from it, chiefly by combining many risks – for in the course of time it will be claimed by cases of need arising. And the compensation for greater risk is only apparently a greater return:

① Cf. Böhm-Bawerk's exposition, Positive Theorie des Kapitalzinses, 4 ed. pp. 219—316.

② Cf. Emery, quoted in my essay, "Die neuere Wirtschaftstheorie in den Vereinigten Staaten," Schmoller's Jahrbuch (1910), and Fisher, Capital and Income.

有无数的原因使得经济有机体不能十分快速地运转。错误、意外、惰性等等，以人们皆知的方式，成为损失的不断的源泉，但也是利润的源泉。①

在我们转到庞巴维克所提到的第二个环境之前，让我们在这里先插入几句关于两个相当重要的因素的话。第一个就是风险因素。有两种风险可以被区分，一种是生产技术失败的风险，这里我们可以包括由于上帝的行为而遭受损失的危险，另一个是商业失败的风险。只要这些危险可以被预测，它们就直接对经济计划起作用。商人们要么把风险的保险费包括在他们的成本会计中，要么他们将有开支以防范一定的危险，或者最后他们将考虑——均衡——生产各部门之间风险的差异，这只是为了避免风险最高的部门，直到后者因此而产生的价格增长能提供一种补偿。②这些将经济风险平衡的方法，在原则上没有一个能创造利润。一个通过任何方式，小心采取行动以防范风险的生产者——通过建筑水坝、机器保险等等——他肯定会在保护其生产成果方面得到益处，但通常他也要付出相应的成本。风险保险金对于生产者来说并不是收益的源泉——至多只是对保险公司来说是，保险公司可以从中直接获得中间利润，主要是通过把许多风险汇总起来——因为随时间的发展，当需要的情况发生时，要靠它来支付。同时，对较大的风险的补偿只在表面上是较大的收益：

---

① 参阅庞巴维克的注解，《资本利息的实证理论》第 4 版，第 219 ~ 316 页。

② 参阅埃默里，在我的引文《美国的新经济理论》中，载施穆勒的《年鉴》（1910 年）和费希尔的《资本与收入》。

it has to be multiplied by a probability coefficient, whereby its real value is again reduced – and indeed exactly by the amount of the surplus. Anyone who simply consums this surplus will atone for it in the course of events. Therefore, there is nothing in the independent rôle often attributed to the element of risk, and in the independent return which is sometimes connected with it. The matter is different, of course, if the risks are not foreseen or at any rate are not taken account of in the economic plan. Then they become on the one hand sources of temporary loss and on the other hand sources of temporary gain.

The chief source of these gains and losses – and this is the second element that I wish to consider here – is spontaneous changes in the data with which the individual is accustomed to reckon. They create new situations, adaptations to which require time. And before that can happen a great many positive or negative discrepancies between cost and receipts occur in the economic system. Adaptation always offers difficulties. The mere knowledge of the changed state of affairs is not attained in most cases with the desirable promptness. To draw conclusions from the knowledge is again a big step, which meets many obstacles in unpreparedness, the lack of means, and so on. But often perfect adaptation relative to the formerly existing products is impossible, and of course especially in the case of durable producers' goods. During the time which must elapse before they are worn out, such changes in conditions unavoidably appear, and this causes one of the peculiarities in the determination of their value which Ricardo considered in Section Ⅳ of his first chapter. Returns to them lose all connection with their costs and must be just simply accepted; their appropriate values are altered without the possibility of the corresponding supply being modified. Thus they become, in a certain sense, a special kind of returns and can rise above or fall below the price-total of the services of labor and land contained in them. They appear to the businessman in a light similar to that in which natural agents appear. We call them, with Marshall, quasi-rents.

它必须乘上一个概率系数，这样它的真实价值再一次被降低——而且正是减少了剩余的数额。任何只消费这个剩余的人，将在事情发展过程中为之付出代价。因此，经常赋予风险要素独立的角色，以及有时候赋予与风险有关的独立收益，都是没有多少意义的。当然，如果风险不是预先所料的，或者无论怎样都不是在经济计划中所考虑到的，那么情况就不同。这样，风险一方面就成为暂时损失的来源，另一方面成为暂时所得的来源。

这些所得和损失的主要源泉——这是我在这里想考虑的第二个因素——是数据的自发的变化，而这些数据是个人所习惯考虑的。这些变化创造了新的环境，而且适应它是需要时间的。在适应发生之前，成本与收入之间的大量的积极与消极的脱节在经济系统内发生了。适应总是有困难的。在多数情况下，即使对已经变化的事物的状态的知识，我们也不能像期望的那样快地得到。从知识中得出结论也是很大的一步，在没有准备，缺乏资料等等情况下，这是会遇到很多障碍的。但是相对于以前，所有产品都完全适应，往往是不可能的，而且尤其是对于耐用生产者物品更是不可能。在货物完全磨损之前，它们必须经历的时间里，环境条件的变化不可避免地会发生，这就产生了李嘉图在他书中第一章第四部分所考虑的决定它们价值的特点之一。它们的收益与它们的成本失去了所有的联系，而且只有这样接受；它们的恰当的价值被改变了，但是却不可能修改相应的供给。这样，在一定意义上，它们就变成了一种特殊的收益，而且可能高于或者低于包含在它们自身的劳动服务和土地服务的总价格中 。它们出现在商人眼中就好像自然事物出现在他的眼中一样。像马歇尔那样，我们称之为准地租。

However, Böhm-Bawerk points to a second circumstance which may alter the result of imputation and may prevent a part of the value of the product from being reflected in the services of labor and nature. This is, as is well known, the lapse of time① involved in all production except the instantaneous production of primitive efforts to maintain life. Because of it, the means of production are not merely potential consumption goods, but they are distinguished from the latter by a new essential characteristic, the distance in time which separates them from goods capable of being consumed. The means of production are *future* consumption goods and as such are worth less than consumption goods. Their value does not exhaust the value of the product.

We are here touching upon an exceedingly delicate problem. But as its importance for the argument of this book is limited we shall only ask ourselves one question here. In the normal course of an economic system in which year in and year out the process of production follows the same route and all data remain the same, would there be a systematic undervaluation of means of production as compared with products? This question subdivides into two others: abstracting from objective and personal coefficients of risk, in such an economic system can future satisfactions be systematically and generally valued at less than equal present satisfactions? And in such an economic system, quite apart from the influence of the *passing of time itself* upon valuations, can *what happens* in the course of time establish these differences in value?

An affirmative answer to the first question sounds plausible enough. Certainly the immediate handing over of some gift is more agreeable than its promise for the future.② This, however, is not the question here, but rather the valuation of a regular flow of income. If possible,

① For the element of time in economic life Böhm-Bawerk is the most important authority. W. S. Jevons and John Rae come next. For a detailed working out of the special element "time-preference," Fisher's Rate of Interest is relevant. Cf. also the treatment of the time element by A. Marshall.

② However, it may be mentioned that even this fact is also not so clear and simple; on the contrary, the reasons for it require analysis, which shall be given briefly below.

然而，庞巴维克谈到了第二种情况，这种情况可能改变归属的结果，而且可能阻止产品的一部分价值在劳动和自然的服务中表现出来。正如人们所知道的，这是在所有的生产中包含的时间的流逝，[①] 除了那种为了维持生命的原始努力的瞬间生产。因为时间的流逝，生产资料就不仅仅是潜在的消费品，而是被一种新的本质上的区别，从消费品中区分开来，即时间距离，把它们与能被消费的货物分割开来。生产资料是未来的消费品，所以价值比消费品低。它们的价值不会耗尽产品的价值。

在这里我们接触到一个非常微妙的问题。但是由于它的重要性对于本书的论述是有限的，因此我们在这里将只问我们自己一个问题。在一个经济系统正常的进程中，生产过程一年一年地遵循着相同的路线，所有的数据都保持不变，那么，生产资料与产品相比较，是否存在系统对价值的低估呢？这个问题可以分解为两个问题：除去客观的和个人的风险系数，在这样一个经济系统中，系统地和一般地评价，对未来的满足能否比对当前同样的满足更低呢？除了时间流逝本身对评价的影响外，在这个经济系统里，在时间的发展中所发生的事能否确立这些在价值上的区别？

对第一个问题的肯定回答听起来好像是很有道理的。当场给予某种礼品肯定比答应在将来某时给予更受欢迎。[②] 然而，这不是这里的问题，而是对收入的有规则波动的评价。如果可能，

---

① 在经济生活中，关于时间因素，庞巴维克是最重要的权威。其次是 W. S. 杰文斯和约翰·雷。费希尔的《利息率》一书关于“时间偏好”这一特殊因素有详细的研究。还可参阅 A. 马歇尔对时间因素的阐述。

② 然而，可以顺便提一下，即使这一事实也不是那么清楚和简单；相反，它的道理需要分析，下面将给出简略的分析。

imagine the following case. Someone enjoys a life – annuity. His wants remain absolutely constant in kind as well as in intensity throughout the rest of his life. The annuity is big and secure enough to relieve him of the necessity of creating funds for special emergencies and for the possibility of loss. He knows himself secure from responsibilities arising towards others and proof against sudden desires. No possibility of investing savings at interest exists-for if we were to grant this we should assume the element of interest beforehand and come dangerously near to circular reasoning. Now will a man in such a position esteem future instalments of his annuity less than those nearer in time? Would he – always abstracting from the personal risk of life – give up future more easily than present instalments? Obviously not, for if he did, that is if he gave up a future instalment for smaller compensation than one nearer in time, he would discover in due course that he had obtained a smaller total satisfaction than he might have done. His conduct would therefore cause him loss; it would be uneconomic. Such a course may nevertheless be taken, just as in other respects offences against the rules of economic reason frequently occur. But it is not an element of these rules themselves that they should occur.① Of course most of the exceptions which we meet with in practical life are not "offences," but are to be explained by our assumptions failing to fit the facts. However, where we find quite striking overestimation of present enjoyments, as particularly in the case of children and savages, what we have before us is merely

---

① My objection is well expressed by the most eminent living exponent of the element of underestimation of future satisfactions, Professor Fisher, when he introduces the term "impatience" for it. Irrational impatience, like error and so on, undoubtedly exists. But it is no element of the normal course of things.

让我们想像一下下面的情况。某人享有一笔终身年金，他要求在他的余生中，这笔年金的种类和购买力保持绝对不变。这笔年金数目足够大，足够安全，使他不必为防备特别紧急情况和可能遭受的损失而另创基金。他知道自己很安全，不会发生对其他人承担的义务，也不会有突发的欲望。没有按利息来投资储蓄的可能性——因为，假定如果我们有这种可能，我们就要事先假定利息因素，那么我们就会危险地接近循环推论。现在，处于这种状况的人，会不会认为他的年金的未来分期支付远不如那种在时间上更早支付的情况呢？他会——总是从个人的生命风险中跳出来——相对现在的支付，更容易地放弃未来的分期支付吗？显然不会，因为如果他确实这样做了，即如果他对放弃一次未来支付比对放弃一次在时间上较近的支付用更少的补偿，那么他会发现，到头来，他所得到的总的满足小于他可能得到的。因此，他的行为导致他的损失，这将是不经济的。然而这种行为，正像在其他方面经常发生的违背经济理性规则的行为一样，也是可能发生的。但是这种现象的发生并不是应该存在的这些规则本身的一个要素。[①] 当然，我们在现实生活中所遇到的大多数例外情况并不是“违背”，而是因为我们的假设与事实不相符合。可是，当我们发现对当前的享受估价高得惊人时，尤其是针对儿童和原始人的情况，那么摆在我们面前的就仅仅是要解

① 费希尔教授，作为在世的最杰出的对未来满足低估这一要素进行论述的人，充分地把我的反对的观点表达出来了。他引用“缺乏耐心”一词来表达这个意思。非理性的缺乏耐心，就像错误等等一样，无疑是存在的。但它不是事物正常发展过程中的要素。

a discrepancy between the economic problem to be solved and the economic outlook of the subject: children and primitive men know only instantaneous production. Future wants do not appear smaller to them; they do not see them at all. Therefore they will not stand the test of decisions which require a wider horizon. This is obvious; but ordinarily they have not to make such decisions, He who grasps the double rhythm of wants and means of satisfaction can perhaps in a particular case scorn the conclusion that a onesided displacement of either means loss of satisfaction, but he cannot reject it in principle.

But what of our second question? Cannot the process of production proceed in ways to which the assumptions of our typical case do not conform? Cannot the continuous flow of goods move sometimes more feebly, sometimes more strongly? But especially, must not the fact that a more fertile method of production demands more time affect the value of present goods, the possession of which alone makes the choice of it possible, and thus constitutes time a factor in the circular flow? The negative answer which we give to this question can easily be misunderstood and will only later acquire its full significance. I do not deny the importance of the element of time in economic life, but only look at it in a different light. The question of the *introduction* of more productive but more time-consuming processes and the question of how the time element affects it are quite distinct problems. We are not now speaking of the *introduction* of new processes, but of the circular flow which consists of given processes already in working order. And here the more fruitful method of production yields its results just as immediately as any other, no matter what the length of its period may be. A method of production will obviously only be called "more fruitful" if it gives more products than the sum of the less fruitful processes

决的经济问题和人们主观的经济观点之间的不一致：儿童和原始人只知道瞬间的生产。在他们面前，未来的需要并不是显得小一些，而是他们根本看不到这种需要。因此他们经受不住那种决策的考验，而这种决策是需要有一个更广阔的视野的。这是很显然的，但是通常他们也不需要做这样的决策。一个人如果能够把握需求以及达到满意的手段这双重要素，那么他可能在特殊的场合下会嘲笑这个结论，即任何倾向一方的替换意味着满足的损失，但是在原则上他不能否定这个结论。

但是我们的第二个问题是怎样的呢？难道生产过程不能以一种与我们的经典例子的假设不相适应的方式进行吗？难道货物的持续流动不能在有时更弱一些，在有时更强一些吗？尤其是，一个更能多产的生产方法需要更多的时间这一事实，难道不一定影响当前货物的价值——当然只有拥有这种价值才有可能选择它——从而构造时间作为循环流动的一个因素？我们对这个问题的否定回答可能很容易被误解，而且只在后来将获得它的全部意义。我并不否认在经济生活中时间要素的重要性，而只是用一种不同的眼光去看待它。引进一种生产性更强，而同时也更消耗时间的生产过程这个问题，与时间因素是如何影响它的问题，是两个截然不同的问题。我们现在并不是谈论新过程的引进问题，而是谈论由给定过程所构成的循环流转，这些给定的过程已经处于正常运转的状态中了。在这里越是有成效的生产方法，就像任何其他方法一样，立刻产生成果，不管它的时期可能有多长。显然，一种生产方法只有当它能生产比各个成效较小的生产过程的总和所提供的产品更多时，它才能被称为“更有效的”，

which can be executed in the same time by means of the same quantity of productive factors. Given the necessary quantities of labor and natural agents, production by this method will be repeated indefinitely without any exercise of choice, and the stream of products will be continuous. But even if that were not the case, there would be no underestimation of future produces. For if the productive process turned out its results in periodic intervals there would still be no waiting, because consumption could adapt itself and run on continuously and at an equal rate per unit of time, so that there would be no motive for underestimating future products.① I may quite well prize present goods more highly than future ones if their possession assures me *more* goods for the future. But I shall do this no longer and my present and future valuations must be equalised when I am assured of the richer flow of goods and my conduct has been adapted to it. "More" goods in the future are then no longer dependent upon the possession of present goods. We can also extend the example of our pensioner to this case. Suppose he has received hitherto a thousand dollars a month. Then he is offered, instead, twenty thousand dollars at the end of a year. Now, until the first year's instalment falls due the element of time may make itself felt very unpleasantly. From the time it falls due onwards, however, he will see his position improved, and indeed he will estimate this improvement by the full addition of eight thousand dollars a year, and not by a part of this sum.

① Immediately after the harvest corn is of course cheaper than later. This fact is, however, explicable by storage costs, by the actual existence of interest, and by many other circumstances, all of which change nothing in our principle.

这些较小成效的生产过程之和是在相同的时间内，用相同数量的生产要素可以执行的。当劳动和自然力量的必要数量已经给定，用这种方法的生产将会无限地重复下去，而不必进行任何选择，而且产品流也会持续下去。但是即使情况不是这样，也不会低估未来产品。因为，如果生产过程定期地生产出产品，那就仍然不会有等待的状态，因为消费能使自己适应生产，而且以同样的速度在单位时间内连续地流动，因此对未来的产品就不会有低估的倾向。① 如果持有现在的物品能保证在未来我能得到更多的物品，那我很可能会评价现在的货物比未来的货物价值更高。但是当我被确认有更丰富的商品流入，而且我的行为已经适应了这种情况，我就不再这样做，我对现在和未来的估价必然是相等的。那么未来“更多的”货物将不再依赖于对现在物品的拥有。我们也可以将我们持有年金的人的例子扩展应用到这种情况。假定他至今每月都已经得到 1000 美元。然而现在，他被提供在每年末获得 20000 美元代替先前的每月领取。那么现在，直到第一年的分期付款到期为止，时间因素本身可能让人感到很不高兴。然而从收到这次付款之后，他将看到他的情况被改善了，而且他确实会按这年全部增加额为 8000 美元来估计他的改善程度，而不只是按其中的一部分估计。

① 谷物在刚刚收获之后，肯定比将来的价格要便宜。可是，可以用储藏成本、利息的实际存在以及许多其他情况来解释这个事实，所有的这些对我们的原则都不会改变。

A similar argument applies to the element of abstinence,[①] the necessity of waiting, and so forth. And here I refer the reader especially to the exposition of Böhm-Bawerk. For us it is only necessary to formulate our position precisely. This phenomenon also cannot be simply denied out of existence. But it is much more complicated than it has the appearance of being, and it is noteworthy that its nature and its manifestations have as yet found no penetrating analysis. Here also one must distinguish the process of creating a productive apparatus from the process of operating it when once created. Whatever the rôle of abstinence in the former may be – we shall have to speak of this repeatedly, first of all in the discussion of saving in the next chapter – certainly in the latter the necessity of waiting does not recur every time a process of production is repeated. One need not "wait" for the regular returns, since one receives them as a matter of course just when they are needed. In the normal circular flow one has not periodically to withstand a temptation to instantaneous production, because one would *immediately* fare worse by succumbing. Therefore there can be no question of abstinence in the sense of non-consumption of the sources of returns, because by our assumptions there are no other sources of returns than labor and land. Could not, finally, the element of abstinence play a part in the normal circular flow, because if it is necessary to the initial creation of the productive apparatus it has to be paid for afterwards out of the regular output of production? In the first place it will appear in the course of our investigation, that abstinence plays only a very secondary part in the provision of the necessary factors; that, speaking concretely, the introduction of new methods of production requires on the whole

① The chief authors are Senior and-on the other side-Böhn-Bawerk in his Geschichte und Kritik der Kapitalzinstheorien; and most recently the American writer McVane. Cf. also the article "Abstinence" in Palgrave's Dictonary and the literature specified there. For the carelessness with which this element is often treated, Cassel, The Nature and Necessity of Interest, is typical. Our position is near to Wieser's Natürlicher Wert, and John B. Clark's Distribution of Wealth. Cf. also Wesen, bk. Ⅲ.

同样的论证也适用于节制因素，[①] 等待的必要性，等等。在这里我请读者特别参阅庞巴维克的说明。对我们来说，只需要精确地表达我们的观点。也不能简单地否定这种想像的存在。但是实际上它比所表现的外表要更复杂，而且值得注意的是，它的本质和它的外在表现还没有得到深入的分析。在这里我们必须能够把一种生产工具的创造过程从一旦把它创造出来而对它使用操作的过程中区分开来。不管在前者中节制的角色是什么样——我们将不得不反复谈到这一点，首先是在下一章讨论储蓄中——在后者中，等待的必要性肯定不会重新地出现在生产过程的每一次重复中。人们不需要“等待”经常性的收益，因为当人们需要它的时候，会很自然地得到它。在正常的循环流动中，人们不必定期地抵制即刻生产的诱惑，因为如果人们屈服，他的情况就会立即变得更坏。因此在不消耗收益源泉意义上不会发生节制的问题，因为根据我们的假定，除了劳动和土地之外没有其他可以获得收益的源泉了。最后，难道节制因素在正常的循环流动中不能起作用，因为如果它对生产工具的最初创造是必须的，那么它在以后的正规产出中就必须得到补偿？首先，在我们的进一步考察中将会发现，在对必要的生产要素的提供中，节制只起到非常次要的作用；具体地说，即新的生产方法的引用从整体上说并

① 主要的作者是西尼尔，以及庞巴维克，后者在他的《资本利息的历史及其批判》中有论述；最近还有美国的作者麦克文。也可以参阅《帕尔格雷夫辞典》中的“节制”一条以及所列举的文献。关于这一因素常常被忽视，卡塞尔的《利息的性质和必要性》是代表作。我们的观点接近维塞尔的《自然价值》和约翰·B. 克拉克的《财富的分配》。还可参阅《本质》第Ⅲ篇。

no previous accumulation of goods. And secondly, considering abstinence as an independent element of cost involves in this case counting the same item twice, as Böhm-Bawerk has shown. ① Whatever may be the nature of waiting, it is certainly not an element of the economic process which we are here considering, because the circular flow, once established, leaves no gaps between outlay or productive effort and the satisfaction of wants. Both are, following Professor Clark's conclusive expression, automatically synchronised. ②

The theory of imputation explains the values of all individual goods. It only remains to be added that the individual values are not independent, but mutually condition one another. The only exception to the rule is in the case of a commodity which cannot be replaced by another, which has only such means of production as are incapable of substitution and moreover are not employable elsewhere. Such instances are imaginable; they can occur, for example, in the case of consumption goods offered immediately by nature; but they are a negligible exception. All other quantities of goods and their values stand in a strict mutual relation. It is expressed by their relation as complements, by the possibility of alternative employment, and by the substitutive relation. Even if two goods have only a single agent of production in common, their values are still connected; for the quantities and hence the values of both goods, depending upon the cooperation of this one agent, will follow the rule of equi-marginalutility with respect to the agent of production common to both.

---

① Fisher's treatment of the same subject (Rate of Interest, pp. 43 – 51) is vitiated by his considering time discount as a primary fact the existence of which is almost self-evident.

② Clark, it is true, attributes to capital the merit of bringing about this "synchronisation." As will appear, we do not follow him in this. I emphasise once more: outlay and return are automatically synchronised with one another under the accelerating and retarding influence of profit and loss.

不需要有事先的货物积累。其次，把节制看做是成本的一个独立要素，在这种情况下意味着把同一个项目计算两次，正如庞巴维克曾经表述的。① 无论等待的性质是什么，它肯定不是我们在这里所考虑的经济过程的一个要素，因为一旦循环流动过程建立，在支出或者生产努力和需求的满足之间就不会留下任何缺口。按照克拉克教授的结论性的描述，这两者会自动地同时发生。②

归属理论解释了所有单个物品的价值。这里只是补充说明一点，个别价值并不是独立的，而是互为条件的。这个规则唯一的例外存在于这样的情况，即那种不能由另一种商品替代的商品，这种商品只有用这样的生产资料：它们不能由其他生产资料替代，而且它们也不能被用在其他地方。这样的例子是可以想像的，例如在由大自然直接提供的消费品的情况下，它们就可能发生，但它们只是一种可以忽略的例外。所有其他商品的数量及其价值都处在一种严格的相互关系中。这种关系是通过它们作为互补品的关系、交换使用的可能性以及替代关系所表达的。即使两种商品只有一个共同的生产要素，它们的价值也仍然是相互联系的，因为两种商品的数量，以及因此产生的价值，取决于这单一要素的配合，考虑到它们两者共有的生产要素，它们将遵从等边

① 费希尔对这个题目的表述（《利息率》，第 43 ~ 51 页）被认为是没有说服力的，因为他把时间贴现看做是一个基本事实，而它的存在几乎是自明之理。

② 克拉克确实把带来这种“同时发生”的功劳归于资本。接下来可以看到，对此我们并不赞同他的观点。我再一次强调，在利润和损失不断加速和阻挠的影响下，支出和收益彼此是自动地同时发生的。

It need hardly be pointed out that the productive relationship resulting from the productive factor labor in particular embraces practically all goods. The determination of the quantity of each good and hence its value is under the influence of the values of all other goods and is completely explicable only by having regard to them. Therefore we can say that the values of individual goods for everyone form a value system, the separate elements of which are mutually dependent.

In this system of values a person's whole economy is expressed, all the relations of his life, his outlook, his method of production, his wants, all his economic combinations. The individual is never equally conscious of all parts of this value system; rather at any moment the greater part of it lies beneath the threshold of consciousness. Also, when he makes decisions concerning his economic conduct he does not pay attention to all the facts given expression to in this value system, but only to certain indices ready at hand. He acts in the ordinary daily round according to general custom and experience, and in every use of a given good he starts from its value, which is given to him by experience. But the structure and nature of this experience are given in the value system. The values, as adjusted to each other, are realised by the individual year in and year out. Now this value system, as already mentioned, exhibits a very noteworthy stability. In every economic period the tendency exists to turn again into the former well-worn tracks, and to realise once more the same values. And even when this constancy is interrupted, some continuity always remains; for even if the external conditions change, it is never a question of doing something completely new, but only of adapting what was previously done to the new conditions. The value system once established and the combinations once given are always the starting point for every new economic period and have so to speak a presumption in their favor.

际效用规则。几乎没有必要指出：尤其是由劳动这一生产要素产生的生产关系，实际上包括了所有的商品。对每一种货物的数量的决定，从而对其价值的决定，都受到所有其他货物的价值的影响，所以只有考虑了这些价值之后，才能作出完全的解释。因此我们可以说，每一种货物的价值对每一个人形成一个价值体系，其中各个要素是相互依存的。

在这个价值体系里，一个人的整个经济都被表现出来，包括涉及他的生活、他的观点、他的生产方法、他的需求的所有关系，他的所有经济组合。个人绝不会对这个价值体系中的所有部分同时意识到；相反，在任何时候，很大部分倒是处于意识范围之外。而且，当他为自己的经济行为作出决策时，他并没有关注这个价值体系里所表达的所有事实，而只是关注手头现有的某些指标。在日常生活中，他根据一般的习惯和经验采取行动，对每一种商品的每次使用，他都从货物的价值开始，而这个价值是经验告诉他的。但是这种经验的结构和本质是由这个价值体系给定的。这种相互调整的价值，是通过个人一年一年地实现的。正如已经提到的，现在这个价值体系表现出一种非常值得关注的稳定性。在每一个经济时期都存在这样的趋势：价值体系又转到先前旧的轨道上，再一次实现相同的价值。即使这种连贯性被打破，某种持续性总是会保存下来；因为即使外部条件改变了，这也绝不是要做一种全新的事情的问题，而只是使先前做的事适应于新的条件。曾经建立的价值体系，以及给定的要素组合总是作为每一个新的经济时期的出发点，因此可以说总有一种对它们有利的推测。

This stability is indispensable for the economic conduct of individuals. In practice they could not, in by far the majority of the cases, do the mental labor necessary to create this experience anew. We also see, in fact, that the quantity and value of goods in past periods partly determine the quantities and values of goods in the following ones, but this alone does not explain the stability. The salient fact is obviously that these rules of behavior have stood the test of experience and that individuals are of the opinion that on the whole they cannot do better than go on acting according to them. And our analysis of the value system, the geology, as it were, of this mountain of experience, has also shown us that actually these quantities and these values of goods are explicable, given the wants and the horizons of the people, as rational consequences of the given conditions in the surrounding world.

This empirical way of acting in the individual is therefore no accident, but has a rational basis. There is one kind of economic conduct which, under given conditions, establishes the equilibrium between means on hand and wants to be satisfied in the best way possible. The value system that we have described corresponds to a position of economic equilibrium whose constituent parts cannot be altered (if all the data remain the same) without the individual's having the experience that he is worse off than before. In so far, therefore, as it is a question of adapting himself to the conditions and of simply complying with the objective necessities of the economic system without wishing to change them, one and only one particular way of acting commends itself to the individual,[①] and the results of this action will remain the same as long as the given conditions remain the same.

---

① This is universally recognised, indeed, only for the cases of free competition and unilateral monopoly in the technical sense of both words. Yet it is sufficient for our purposes. And it has been shown of late that Cournot was not wrong, after all, in holding that there are important cases of determinateness even in the field of "monopolistic competition."

对于个人的经济行为来说，这种稳定性是不可缺少的。实际中，在大多数情况下，他们不能从事那种为重新创造这种经验所必需的脑力劳动。事实上我们也看到，过去各个时期货物的数量和价值部分地决定着随后各时期货物的数量和价值，不过仅从这一点还不能解释这种稳定性。显然一个重要的事实是，这些行为规则已经经受住了经验的考验，而且每个人都认为，就整体来说，他们除了继续按照这个规则行动之外，没有什么行动比这样更好了。我们对价值体系的分析，这个价值体系就好像是这座经验之山的地质学，也向我们表明了，在人们的需求和视野给定的情况下，货物的这些数量和价值实际上可以解释为在周围环境条件给定情况下的合理的结果。

因此，这种在个人行为里的经验方式绝不是偶然的，而是有它的合理的基础。在一定条件下，有一种经济行为能够在现有的手段与可能的最好的方式所满足的需要之间建立一种均衡。我们所描述的价值体系与经济均衡的位置是相对应的，而这种经济均衡的构成部分是不能改变的（如果所有的数据保持不变），否则，个人就会感受到他的境况比以前差。因此，只要问题是使自己适应条件，而且只是服从经济系统的客观需要，而并不是期望改变它，那么对于个人来说就只有一个并且是唯一的一个行为方式采用，① 这个行为的结果将保持不变，只要给定的条件也保持不变。

---

① 当然，这只在自由竞争和单方垄断的情况下被普遍认可（这两个词都是从技术意义上说的）。然而就我们的目的来说，这已足够了。最近已经证明，库诺最终没有错，他主张：即使在“垄断竞争”领域也存在可确定性的重要实例。

Assuming the reader to be familiar with the general theory of both competitive and monopolistic exchange and prices, we may notice in passing that the ubiquitous possibility of exchange will naturally alter everyone's system of values. The fundamental theorem, according to which units of resources are distributed among possible uses so as to yield equal marginal satisfactions, will of course still hold. In an exchange economy we may express it by saying that for all households prices must be proportional to marginal utilities of consumers' goods and that for all firms prices of producers' goods must be proportional to their marginal productivities. But a new phenomenon presents itself in the fact that products will be estimated by their producers no longer according to any "value-in-use" which they might have for them, but according to the utility of those commodities which producers ultimately acquire for them. ①Everyone's scale of valuation of his products, and hence everyone's scale of valuation of the means of production he may happen to have, will be composed of the scale of valuation of the goods received in exchange or bought with the income derived from selling the services of those means of production. The most advantageous way of performing these operations will be found by experience, and every commodity or productive service will be valued accordingly.

All the innumerable exchanges which we can observe in an exchange economy in each period constitute in their totality the external form of the circular flow of economic life. The laws of exchange show us how this circular flow is explicable from given conditions, and also teach us why it does not alter so long as these conditions remain the same, and why and how it changes in adapting itself to changes in these conditions.

---

① This is what the Austrians used to call "subjective exchange value." Readers who are familiar with the history of theoretical discussions of the last fifty years will recall how this phenomenon gave rise to an indictment of circular reasoning implied, as many opponents of the Austrian theory held, in any argument which tries to explain prices of producers' goods by "utility." To-day, it would hardly be worth while to go out of our way in order to show why this objection fails.

假定读者对竞争与垄断情况下的交换和价格的一般理论是熟悉的，我们就可以顺便注意到，普遍存在的交换可能性很自然地将会改变每个人的价值体系。根据根本的原理，资源的各个单位在可能的各种用途之间分配，以产生相等的边际满足，这个根本的原理当然将仍然起作用。在交换经济中，我们可能这样表述这个根本原理：对所有的家庭来说，价格必须与消费品的边际效用成比例；同时对所有的厂商来说，产品的价格必须与它们的边际生产率成比例。但是实际中一个新的现象产生了，即生产者将不再按照对于他们来说这些产品所具有的任何“使用价值”来估计产品的价值，而是按照生产者最后所获得的产品的效用来估计。[①] 每个人对自己的产品的评价尺度，以及因此产生的每个人对他自己可能拥有的生产资料的评价尺度，将由这些商品的价值尺度构成，即用通过出售这些生产资料的服务所获得的收入来交换或者买入的商品。完成这些操作的最有利的途径是根据经验找到的，每一种商品或者生产性服务都将按此来评价。

在交换经济的每一个时期，我们所能观察到的所有无数的交换，在总体上构成了经济生活循环流动的外部形态。交换规律向我们展现了根据给定的条件，这种循环流动是怎样得到解释的；它也告诉我们，只要这些条件保持不变，为什么这种循环就不会改变，以及为了让自己适应这些条件的变化，这种循环流动为什么

① 这就是奥地利人过去称为的“主观交换价值”概念。熟悉过去50年里理论讨论的历史的读者，会回忆起这种现象如何引起了对其所包含的循环推理的控告，许多反对奥地利理论的人认为，在试图用“效用”来解释产品价格的任何论辩中，都包含着循环推理。今天，如果离开我们的论点而去说明为什么这种反对是失败的，这是不值得的。

Under the assumption of constant conditions, consumers' and producers' goods of the same kind and quantity would be produced and consumed in every successive period because of the fact that in practice people act in accordance with well-tried experience, and that in theory we regard them as acting in accordance with a knowledge of the best combination of present means under the given conditions. But there is also another connection between the successive periods because every period operates with goods which an earlier period prepared for it, and in every period goods are produced for use in the next. We shall now, to simplify the statement, express this fact by assuming that in every period only products which were produced in the previous period are consumed, and that only products which will be consumed in the following period are produced. This dovetailing of the economic periods does not change anything essential, as may easily be seen. According to it, every consumption good requires two economic periods, neither more nor less, for its completion.

Now we shall classify the exchanges which are necessary to carry out this simplified economic process in every period. First, we discard those which are carried out merely in order to hand on again whatever is so received. Theory demonstrates that such exchanges must exist in great numbers in every trading economy, yet these purely technical transactions do not interest us here. ① Then there is the exchange of the services of labor and land against consumption goods, which occurs in every trading economy. No doubt this class of exchanges embodies the bulk of the economic system's stream of goods and connects its source with its mouth. But laborer and landlord sell their productive services, which only yield their product at the end of each period, for consumption goods which are already on hand. Further, they sell their productive services for consumption goods, even though some of their services go towards the production of producers' goods.

---

① Cf. Wesen, bk. Ⅱ.

改变和是怎样改变的。在假定条件保持不变的情况下，在每一个连续的时期内，同一种类、同一数量的消费品和生产者货物就会被生产出来和被消费，因为在实际上，人们是根据经过反复证明的经验来采取行动的，而且我们认为，在理论上，他们是在给定的条件下，按照现有方法的最佳组合的知识采取行动的。但是在各个连续时期之间还有另一种联系，因为每一个时期都会使用其前一时期为它准备的物品，而且每一时期也会生产货物供下一时期使用。为了使陈述简单化，我们现在将这样表述这一事实，假定每一时期只消费上一时期生产的产品，而且只生产将在下一时期被消费的产品。这种让两个经济时期相吻合的办法不会改变任何实质性的东西，这是很容易看清楚的。根据这个假定，每一种消费品都需要两个经济时期才能完成，不多也不少。

现在，我们要对每一时期中为了执行这个简单化的经济过程所必须的交换进行分类。首先，我们把那些仅仅为了将所得的东西再转出去而执行的交换排除在外。理论表明，在每一种贸易经济中必然存在大量的这样的交换，然而在这里，我们对这些纯粹技术性的交易并不感兴趣。① 第二，在每一种贸易经济中都会发生劳动和土地的服务对消费品的交换。毫无疑问，这类交换体现了一个经济系统的商品流的绝大部分，并且连接了它的来源和出口。但是劳动者和地主是为了已在他们手中的消费品而出售他们的生产性服务，这些生产性服务只在每一时期末才产出产品。进一步说，即使他们的某些服务是用来生产生产者的商品，

① 参阅《本质》第二篇。

In every period those services of labor and land which are not already embodied in means of production to be employed in the period under consideration are exchanged for consumption goods which were completed in the previous period. Whatever in this assertion is contrary to fact serves merely to simplify the exposition and does not affect the principle. It is clear who possess the services of labor and land before this exchange. But who constitute the other party in the transaction? In whose hands, before the exchange, are the consumption goods for paying for the services? The answer is, simply those people who need the services of labor and land in this period, that is those who wish to transform the means of production produced in the previous period into consumption goods by the addition of more services of labor and land or who wish to produce new means of production. Let us assume, for simplicity's sake, that both categories do the same in all periods to be considered, that is keep on producing either consumption goods or production goods – which conforms to the principle of a trading economy with division of labor. Then we can say that those individuals who produced consumption goods in the preceding period give up a part of them in the present period to workers and landlords whose services they require for the production of new consumption goods for the following period. Those individuals who produced production goods in the preceding period and who wish to do likewise in the present will give up these production goods to the producers of consumption goods in return for those consumption goods which they want in order to acquire new productive services.

Therefore workers and landlords always exchange their productive services for present consumption goods only, whether the former are employed directly or only indirectly in the production of consumption goods. There is no necessity for them to exchange their services of labor and land for future goods or for promises of future consumption goods or to apply for any "advances" of present consumption goods. It is simply a matter of exchange, and not of credit transactions. The element of time plays no part. All products are *only* products and nothing more.

他们出售他们的生产性服务也是为了消费品。在每一时期，那些还没有包括在所观察的时期内将使用的生产资料之中的劳动和土地服务，将用来交换上一时期已经完成的消费品。这种说法中有与事实相反的东西，只是为了让说明简单化，它并不影响原则。很清楚，在这种交换之前，是谁拥有劳动和土地服务。但是在交易中谁是另一方呢？在交换之前，用来支付这些服务的消费品在谁的手中呢？答案是：在这一时期那些需要劳动和土地服务的人，也就是想把前一时期生产出来的生产资料通过追加更多的劳动和土地服务转变成消费品的人，或者是那些想生产新的生产资料的人。为了简单化，我们假定，那两类人在所考查的所有时期做相同的事情，也就是要么持续生产消费品，要么持续生产生产性货物——这是符合具有劳动分工的贸易经济的原则的。于是我们可以说，前一时期生产消费品的那些人，在本时期放弃了一部分消费品给工人和地主，因为他们为了下一时期生产新的消费品，需要工人和地主提供的服务。在前一时期生产生产性货物的人，在本期仍然想这样生产，他们将放弃一些生产性货物给生产消费品的人，这样以取得那些为了获得新的生产性服务所必需的消费品。

因此，工人和地主总是只把他们的生产性服务交换现在的消费品，不管前者是被直接使用还是在消费品的生产过程中只被间接使用。对他们来说，没有必要用他们的劳动和土地服务交换未来的货物，或者交换未来给予消费品的承诺，或者申请对现有消费品的任何“预支”。这只是一种交换，不是信用交易。时间因素不起作用。所有的产品都仅仅是产品，不包含其他的意义。

For the individual firm it is a matter of complete indifference whether it produces means of production or consumption goods. In both cases the product is paid for immediately and at its full value. The individual need not look beyond the current period, even though he always works for the next. He simply follows the dictates of demand, and the mechanism of the economic process sees to it that he also provides for the future at the same time. He is not concerned with what happens further to his products, and he would probably never begin the process of production if he had to follow it to the end. Consumption goods in particular are also only products and nothing more, products to which nothing more happens than their sale to consumers. They form in nobody's hands a "fund" for the maintenance of laborers, and so on; they serve neither directly nor indirectly further productive ends. Hence every question of the accumulation of such stocks disappears. How such a mechanism, which, once adjusted, continually maintains itself, comes into existence is another question. How it develops is a different problem from how it functions.

It follows, again, that everywhere, even in a trading economy, produced means of production are nothing but transitory items. Nowhere do we find a stock of them fulfilling any functions, as it were, in their own right. No claim on the national dividend is made by them beyond wages and rent for the services of labor and land contained in them. No element of net income attaches finally to them. No independent demand issues from them. On the contrary, in each period all the consumption goods on hand will go to the services of labor and land employed in this period; hence all incomes are absorbed under the title of wages or rent of natural agents. ①

① The first fundamental theorem of the theory of distribution lies in this statement.

对单个厂商来说，不管他是生产生产资料还是生产消费品，那是完全不相关的事。在两种场合下，产品都是立即支付并且按其全部价值支付。尽管个人总是在为下一时期工作，但是个人不必超越当前时期向外看。他只是跟从需求的指示，而他同时也在为将来提供东西，这就由经济过程的机制来管理了。他对他的产品进一步将发生的事情不关心，如果他不得不对自己的产品负责到底，他可能根本不会开始这一生产过程。尤其是消费品，它也只是产品，而不再是别的什么，它是除了销售给消费者之外不会发生更多事情的产品。它们不会在任何人手中形成“基金”来维持劳动者，等等；它们不会为进一步生产的结果提供直接或者间接的服务。因此，不存在这种存量积累的问题。这种机制，一旦得到调整就能持续地维持自身，这是如何形成的呢？这就是另一个问题了。它是怎样发展的，与它是如何起作用的，是两个不同的问题。

我们还可以推论，在任何地方，甚至在贸易经济中，生产出来的生产资料也只不过是暂时的项目。我们在哪里都找不到它们的存量，似乎它们以自身的权利执行着任何功能。除了给包含在它们之中的劳动和土地服务支付工资和地租之外，它们不能再对国民总报酬提出任何要求。最终没有任何净收入成分附加在它们身上。没有任何独立的要求产生于它们。相反，所有手头的消费品，在每一时期都将归于本期所使用的劳动和土地服务；因此，所有的收入都以工资或者自然力量的租金的名义被吸收。①

① 分配理论的第一条基本原理就存在于这个表述中。

Thus we come to the conclusion that the process of exchange between labor and land on the one side and consumption goods on the other side not only supplies the chief direction of the stream of economic life, but that under our assumptions this would be the only one. Labor and land share the whole national dividend, and there are just as many consumption goods on hand as are necessary to satisfy their effective demand, and no more. And this is in accordance with the ultimate pair of data in economics: wants and the means for their satisfaction. It is also a true picture of that part of economic reality of which we have been taking account so far. It was mutilated by theory and from it a great number of fictions and sham problems were artificially created – including the problem of what is the "fund" out of which the services of labor and land are remunerated.

The organisation of an exchange economy therefore presents itself to us in the following manner. Individual businesses appear to us now as places of production for the requirements of other people, and the output of the whole production of a nation will in the first place be "distributed" among these units. Within the latter, however, there are no other functions than that of combining the two original factors of production, and this function is performed in every period mechanically as it were, of its own accord, without requiring a personal element distinguishable from superintendence and similar things. Thus, if we suppose that the services of land are in private hands, then abstracting from monopolists there are no people with any claims upon the product except those who perform some kind of labor or place the services of land at the disposal of production. Under these conditions there is no other class of people in the economic system, in particular there is no class whose characteristic is that they *possess* produced means of production or consumption goods. We have already seen that the idea that somewhere there is an accumulated stock of such goods is absolutely false. It is chiefly evoked by the fact that very many produced means of production last through a series of economic periods.

这样我们得出结论：以劳动和土地为一方，以消费品为另一方的交换过程，不仅为经济生活的趋势提供了主要方向，而且在我们的假设条件下，这也是唯一的方向。劳动和土地分享国民报酬的全部，而且现场所拥有的消费品的数量恰好就是能够满足其有效需求所必须的那么多的消费品的数量，没有更多的。这正符合经济学中最后一对数据：需求及其满足的手段。它也正是我们一直在考虑的那部分经济现实的真实写照。它已经被理论弄得残缺不全了，其中人为地创造了大量的虚构和臆造的问题——包括什么是产生于被补偿的劳动和土地服务的“基金”这个问题。

因此，交换经济以下面的方式向我们展现了它自己。现在，单个企业是作为一个生产的地方出现在我们面前的，这个生产是为了他人的需求而进行的，而一国全部生产的产出将首先在这些组织中进行“分配”。然而，在这些企业里，除了把两种原始生产要素结合起来，就没有其他的功能了，而这一职能在每一时期似乎都是自行机械地完成的，并不需要什么个人因素，这个个人因素不同于监督以及相类似的东西。这样，如果我们假定土地的服务掌握在私人手中，那么，不考虑垄断者，除了那些从事某种劳动或者将土地服务提供给生产的人之外，就没有人能对产品有任何要求权了。在这些条件下，经济系统里就没有其他阶级的人，尤其是没有这样一个阶级，它的特征是拥有生产出来的生产资料或者消费品。我们已经知道，认为在某处有某种货物的积累存量是绝对错误的。这个观点主要是因一个事实而产生，这个事实即是，许许多多生产出来的生产资料最终要经历一系列经济时期。

However, this is not an essential element, and we alter nothing fundamental if we limit the use of such means of production to one economic period. The ides of a stock of consumption goods has not even this support; on the contrary consumption goods are generally only in the hands of retailers and consumers in the quantity necessary to meet the requirements of the moment. We find a continuous flow of goods and a continuously moving economic process, but we find no stocks which are either constant in their component parts or constantly replaced. It also makes no difference to an individual firm whether it produces consumption or production goods. In both cases it disposes of its products in the same way, receives, under the hypothesis of completely free competition, a payment corresponding to the value of its land or labor services, and nothing else. If we choose to call the manager or owner of a business "entrepreneur," then he would be an *entrepreneur faisant ni bénéfice ni perte*, ① without special function and without income of a special kind. If the possessors of produced means of production were called "capitalists," then they could only be producers, differing in nothing from other producers, and could no more than the others sell their products above the costs given by the total of wages and rents.

From the standpoint of this interpretation, therefore, we see a stream of goods being continually renewed. ② Only for a single moment is there anything like a stock of certain individual goods; moreover one can actually speak of "stocks" only in an abstract sense, namely in the sense that goods of a certain kind and quantity always appear through the mechanism of production and exchange at definite places in the economic system.

---

① A construction of Walras. It is true, however, that interest exists as an income in his equilibrium system.

② Sharply separating "funds" and "flows" and making the separation fruitful constitute one of the merits of the too little appreciated book of S. Newcomb, Principles of Political Economy. In contemporary literature the point is particularly emphasised by Fisher. The circular flow of money is nowhere more clearly described than in Newcomb, p. 316 ff.

然而，这并不是最关键的要素，如果我们把这种生产资料的使用限制在一个经济时期内，我们并没有在实质上改变什么。消费品存量的观点甚至没有这种依据；相反，消费品通常只掌握在零售商和消费者手中，它的数量只是满足当前需要的必需的数量。我们看到货物的持续流动以及经济过程的不停移动，但是我们没有发现其组成部分要么是保持不变，要么是稳定地替代的那种存量。对于一家厂商来说是生产消费品还是生产生产性货物，这是没有什么区别的。两种场合处理产品的方式是相同的，即在完全自由竞争的假设下，获得与其土地或劳动服务的价值相应的支付，没有其他东西。如果我们选择称一个企业的经理或所有者为"企业家"，那他就是一个既没有所得也不会有损失的企业家，[①] 没有特殊的职能，也没有特殊的收入。如果拥有生产出来的生产资料的人被称作"资本家"，那么他也只能是生产者，与其他的生产者没有什么区别，也同其他人一样，出售产品的价格不能高于由工资和地租总和确定的成本的数额。

因此，从这个解释的观点出发，我们看到了不断得到更新的商品流。[②] 只在瞬间似乎存在与某种个别货物存量相类似的东西；而且实际上人们只能在一种抽象的意义上谈论"存量"，也就是从某一种类和数量的货物总是通过经济系统中一定地区的生

---

① 这是瓦尔拉的用语。然而，事实上，在他的均衡体系里把利息作为一种收入而存在。

② 严格区别"基金"和"流动"，并使这种区分有意义，这是 S. 纽克姆的一本没被人们重视的书《政治经济学原理》的功劳之一。在现代文献中，费希尔特别强调这一点。没有哪本书比纽克姆在书中（第 316 页）对货币的循环流动描述得更清楚的了。

Stocks in this sense are comparable to a river-bed rather than to the water which flows through it. The stream is fed from the continually flowing springs of labor-power and land, and flows in every economic period into the reservoirs which we call income, in order there to be transformed into the satisfaction of wants. We shall not enlarge upon this, but only observe shortly that it involves accepting a definite concept of income, namely Fetter's, and excluding from its scope all those goods which are not regularly consumed. In one sense the circular flow ends at this place. In another sense, however, it does not, for consumption begets the desire to repeat it and this desire again begets economic activity. We shall be pardoned if we have not in this connection spoken of quasi-rent as we ought to have done. More serious at first sight appears to be the absence of any mention of saving. Yet this point will also be explained. In any case, saving would not play a great part in economic systems displaying no change.

The exchange value of every quantity of a commodity for every individual depends upon the value of the goods which he can procure and actually intends to procure with it. As long as the latter is undecided, this exchange value will undoubtedly fluctuate according to the possibilities conceived at the time, and likewise it will alter if the individual alters the direction of his demand. Yet, when the best employment in exchange is found for any good, the exchange value remains at one and only one definite height, given constancy in the conditions. Obviously, taken in this sense, the exchange value of any unit of one and the same commodity is different for different individuals, and indeed not only in consequence of the differences, firstly of their tastes, and secondly of their economic situations as a whole, but also thirdly, quite independently of these facts,

产和交换机制进而表现出来的这种意义，来谈论“存量”。在这个意义上所说的存量可以比作河床，而不是流经它的河水。这个流量从劳力和土地这种连续不断流动的源泉中得到补充，而且在每一经济时期它都流入我们称之为收入的水库，在那里它们被转变为需要的满足。对此我们并不做深入的解释，只是简短地做一个评述，它包括接受一种确定的收入概念，即费特的概念，而把所有那些不经常消费的货物排除在它的范围之内。从一种意义上说，循环流动在此终结。然而，从另一种意义上说，它并没有结束，因为消费产生出重复消费的欲望，而这种欲望又推动了经济行为。我们在此要请读者原谅，因为在这里我们应该谈一谈准地租，可是我们没有谈。初看起来，我们根本没有谈到储蓄，这似乎是更严重的问题。然而这一点也可以做相应的解释。无论怎样，在保持不变的经济系统里，储蓄并不起很大的作用。

对每一个人来说，一种商品的每一数量的交换价值，取决于他能用它获得的并且确实打算用它来获得的商品的价值。只要后者还没有被决定，毫无疑问，这个交换价值将随着当时所想像的可能性而波动，而且如果个人改变他需求的方向，这个交换价值也会改变。但是，当任何一种商品在交换中找到了它的最佳用途时，交换价值就会保持在一个，而且是唯一的这个确定的高度上，假定条件是保持不变的。显然，从这个意义上说，任何一个单位的同一种商品的交换价值对不同的个人是不相同的，这种差别的确不仅是因为，首先个人的嗜好不同，其次是他们的整体经济情况不同，而且还由于第三点，这一点与这些事实完全没有关系，

in consequence of differences in the goods which the individual exchanges.[①] But the relation of the quantities in which any two goods are exchanged in the market, or of their reciprocals, the price of each good, is the same for all individuals rich or poor – as we said before. That the price of every good is connected with the prices of all other goods will only become quite clear if we reduce them all to a common denominator.[②]

Let us now introduce this denominator of price and medium of exchange and let us choose gold for the rôle of "money commodity." While for our purposes we require very little of the familiar theory of exchange and hence could treat it quite briefly, we must go rather further into the theory of money. But here also we shall confine ourselves to those points which will be significant for us later, and we shall consider even them only so far as is necessary for what follows. Therefore we shall leave on one side problems which will not crop up again in this book, for example the problem of bimetallism or of the international value of money. And theories whose merits lie in directions which we shall have no opportunity of following, we shall replace without scruple by simpler or better known ones, provided they will serve us as well, even if they are in other respects much more incomplete.[③]

Experience shows that every individual values his stock of money. And in the market all these individual value-estimates lead to the establishment of a definite exchange relation between the unit of money and quantities of all other goods, in principle just as we asserted earlier of

---

① I mean: in consequence of the differences in taste and in the total economic situation, each individual values differently even the same goods which other individuals likewise exchange. But the individuals also exchange different goods.

② Cf. Wesen, bk. II.

③ The reader will find the leading features of my ideas on money and its value in "Das Sozialprodukt und die Rechenpfennige," Archiv für Sozialwissenschaft, Bd. 44 (1918). The concept of money employed there is an entirely different one.

即个人所交换的商品不同。[①] 但是在市场上被交换的任意两种商品之间的数量关系，或者它们的倒数，即每种商品的价格，对所有的个人，不管贫富，都是一样的——与我们前面说过的一样。每一种货物的价格都与所有其他货物的价格相联系，这一点将变得十分清楚，只有当我们把它们归结到一个共同的标准下时。[②]

现在让我们引入这个价格的标准和交换的媒介，并让我们选择黄金来充当“货币商品”的角色。从我们的目的出发，尽管我们对已熟悉的交换理论的需要非常少，因而对它可以说得简短一些，但是对货币理论，我们必须说得更多一些。不过在这里，我们也仅限于以后对我们有用的那些论点，而且即使对于这些论点，我们也只是在必要的限度内对这些为以后论证所必需的进行论述。因此，我们将把不会再出现在本书中的问题放在一边，例如，金银复本位制的问题或者货币的国际价值问题。有些理论，它们的价值存在于我们以后没有机会去讨论的那些方面，我们也会毫不犹豫地用更简单的或者更为人们所熟悉的理论去代替，只要它们对我们也是有用的，即使它们在其他方面有很多不完善。[③]

经验表明，每一个人都对他的货币存量估价。在市场上，所有这些个人的估价会导致在每一单位货币和所有其他商品的数量之间建立一种确定的交换关系，原则上就像我们以前说其他商品一样。

---

① 我的意思是，由于嗜好和总的经济情况不同，即使对于其他人也同样用来交换的相同的货物，每一个人的估价都是不同的。更何况个人还交换不同的商品。

② 参阅《本质》第二章。

③ 读者可以从“社会产品和计算单位”一文，载《社会科学档案》，第44卷（1918年），了解我关于货币及其价值的思想的主要特征。在那里所使用的货币概念是一个完全不同的概念。

other goods. From the competition between individuals and between possibilities of employment there issue, under given conditions, as many definite "prices" of money as there are other goods. These prices of money – an expression which is completely defined by the preceding statements and which we shall often use in what follows – are, therefore, like any other price, founded upon individual value-estimates. But upon what do these rest? The question obtrudes itself, because here in the case of money we have not the simple explanation which for any other commodity lies in the satisfaction of wants obtained by the individual from his consumption. We answer the question after Wieser: ① the use value of the material commodity of course provides the historical foundation upon which money acquires a definite exchange relation to other goods, but its value for every individual and its price on the market may and actually do move from this basis. Of course it is obvious that neither the individual marginal utility nor the price of gold as money can deviate from its individual marginal utility and its market price as a commodity. For if this happened, a continual tendency would exist to remove the difference by coining gold from the arts or by melting down gold coin. This is correct. Only it proves nothing. Because a commodity fetches the same price in two different uses it cannot be concluded that the one use determines the price and that the other simply follows it. On the contrary it is clear that both employments together form the value scale of the good

① Schriften des Vereins für Sozialpolitik. Reports of the Session of 1909. On this see Mises, Theorie des Geldes und der Umlaufsmittel, 2 ed, and earlier, Weiss, "Die moderne Tendenz in der Lehre vom Geldwert," Zeitschrift für Volksw., Sozialpol. und Verw. (1910). To Professor von Mises' book the reader may also be referred in case he should suspect that the above argument implies circular reasoning Although it does not, the author wishes to state that he would not now consider this way of introducing the element of money to be satisfactory, even within the limits of the purposes of this chapter.

在给定的条件下，从个体之间的竞争，以及各种使用的可能性之间的竞争中，产生了如同其他货物一样多的多种确定性的货币“价格”。因此，这些货币价格——这个表达已经完全由前面的叙述定义了，而且在以后我们将常常用到——像任何其他价格一样，是以个人的价值估计为基础的。但是个人的价值估计又是以什么为基础而建立的呢？这个问题是自发产生的，因为在这里，对于货币，我们没有像对任何其他商品那样做简单的解释，这种解释就在于个人通过他的消费所得到的需求的满足。我们根据维塞尔的论述对这个问题进行了回答，[①] 即，物质商品的使用价值自然提供了历史的基础，在此基础上，货币获得了与其他商品的一种确定的交换关系，但是，货币对每一个人的价值和它在市场上的价格可能而且实际上偏离了这个基础。作为货币的黄金所具有的单个边际效用和价格，都不能偏离它作为商品的个人边际效用和它的市场价格，这一点肯定是很明白的。因为，如果一旦偏离，就会出现一种通过把艺术品铸成金币，或者把金币熔化的方式来消除差异的趋势。这是正确的。不过它并不能用来证明什么。因为如果同一种商品在两种不同的用途上以同样的价格出售，我们不能说，一种用途决定了价格，而另一种用途只是跟随这个价格。与此相反，显然是两种用途一起形成了商品的价值尺度，

① 《社会政策协会文集》，1909 年大会报告。关于这一点，参阅米塞斯《货币与流通手段的理论》第二版；早一些的有怀兹的“货币价值理论的现代趋势”，载《政治经济学、社会政策和管理》杂志（1910 年）。如果读者怀疑上述论点含有循环推理，也可以看一看米塞斯教授的书。尽管它没有包含循环推理，但作者希望表明：他现在并不认为引进货币要素这一方式就令人满意，即使仅限于本章的目的。

and that its price would be different if one ceased to exist. The money commodity is in this position. It serves two different possibilities of employment, and although the marginal utilities and the prices must certainly be equal in both if the good can move freely from one to the other, yet its value is never explicable from the employment in the arts alone. This becomes especially clear if we imagine that the whole stock of money commodity is coined, which would indeed be possible. Money would even then have value and a price, but the above explanation would obviously break down. The suspension of coinage on the one hand and the prohibition of melting on the other likewise offer us examples from experience of the independent character of the value of money.

Therefore the value of money as money can be completely separated theoretically from the value of the material. To be sure, the latter is the historical source of the former. But in principle we can neglect the value of the material in explaining a concrete instance of the value of money, just as in considering the lower course of a great stream we can neglect the contribution to its volume which comes from its source. We can imagine that individuals receive, in proportion to their possession of goods, or more correctly to the latter expressed in prices, an allotted portion of units of some medium of exchange without use value, for which all goods must be disposed of in each economic period. Then this medium would be valued only as a medium of exchange. Its value *exhypothesi* can be only an exchange value. ① Every individual, as we asserted earlier of all goods produced for the market, will value this medium of exchange according to the value of the goods which he can obtain with it. Every individual will therefore value his money differently,

---

① Money will be esteemed for its exchange function. And this is obviously analogous to the function of means of production. If one conceives money simply as "bene istrumentale" (as do many Italians) the matter is clearer.

而且如果一种用途不存在了，它的价格将会不同。货币商品就处于这种位置。对货币的使用有两种不同的可能性，虽然这两种用途中的边际效用和价格肯定必须相等，如果货物能够自由地从一种用途流向另一个用途；但是仅从艺术用途是绝不能解释它的价值的。如果我们假定货币商品的全部存量是铸币，这确实也是可能的，那么前面所说的就变得格外明显了。即使在这时，货币也会有价值和价格，但是上面的解释显然就站不住脚了。一方面停止铸币，一方面禁止熔化，这同样为我们提供了经验上的例子，以说明货币价值的独立的特性。

因此，作为货币的货币价值，在理论上完全可以与物质的价值分开来。诚然，后者是前者的历史源泉。但是原则上，当我们解释货币价值的具体实例时，可以不考虑货币的物质价值，就像在考虑一条巨大的河流的下游时，我们可以忽略从它的源泉流来的水量一样。我们可以想像，个人根据他所拥有的货物的比例，或者更准确地说，他根据以价格表示的货物的比例，获得了一定数量的某种交换媒介，这种媒介没有使用价值，但是在每一经济时期所有的商品都必须换成这种交换媒介。于是，这个媒介只是作为交换媒介被定值。根据假设，它的价值只能是一种交换价值。① 就像我们前面关于为市场生产的所有商品所说的，每一个人将根据他用这种媒介所能换得的商品的价值，来评价这个交换媒介的价值。因此，每个人对他的货币的评价将是不同的；

① 货币将由于它的交换职能被评价。这显然与生产工具的职能类似。如果人们只把货币当做“最好的工具”（像许多意大利人那样），情况就会更清楚。

and even if each expresses his value estimates of other goods in money, these estimates will have a different significance from individual to individual even if they are numerically equivalent. In the market, it is true, every good will have only one price in money, and also there can be only one price of money in the market at any moment. All individuals calculate with these prices and meet on common ground at this point. But only superficially, for while equal for all, the prices have a different implication for each; they signify for each different limits to the acquisition of goods.

How is this personal exchange value of money formed, then? At this point we shall link up the theory of money with what we have just said about the flow of the economic process. We see at once that according to our conception, personal exchange value must go right back to producers' goods. We said that producers' goods are transitory items and that they involve no independent formation of value in an exchange economy. We said also that no stream of income flows to those who possess them at any time. Therefore there is no occasion here for the construction of an independent personal exchange value of money. As in the economic process, so in the money calculations of the businessman produced means of production are transitory items under our assumption. These individuals will not esteem money according to its personal exchange value, since they procure no goods for their own consumption by means of it but simply pass it on. Hence we cannot seek here for the determination of the personal exchange value of money; on the contrary the exchange value which is reflected in these transactions must originate elsewhere. Hence, only the primary stream of goods remains, only the exchange between services of labor and land on the one hand and consumption goods on the other. Solely according to the values of the consumption goods which can be obtained with money does one value one's stock of money. The exchange between money income and real income is therefore the salient point, is the place in the economic process where personal exchange value and hence the price of money is formed.

即使每个人都用货币来表达他对其他商品的估价，这种估价在不同的个体之间也会有不同的意义，即使它们在数量上相等。的确，在市场上，每种商品只有一种货币价格，而且，在市场上的任何时候也只能有一种货币价格。所有的个体都根据这个价格来计算，在这一点上，他们有着共同的立场。但这只是表面现象，因为尽管对所有的人，价格是相等的，但对每一个人来说，价格有着不同的内涵；它们表明每一个人获得商品的不同限度。

那么，这种个人的货币交换价值是怎么形成的呢？在这点上，我们将结合货币理论和我们刚才所讲的经济过程的流转来谈。根据我们的概念，我们立刻会看到，个人的交换价值必须一直回溯到生产者的货物。我们说过，生产者的货物是暂时性项目，并且在交换经济中不包含价值的任何独立形式。我们还说过，收入流任何时候不会流向那些拥有生产者货物的人。因此，在这里没有机会形成一种货币的独立的个人交换价值。就像在经济过程中，商人在计算货币时，在我们的假设下，生产出来的生产资料也是一个暂时性的项目。这些个人并不是根据货币的个人交换价值去评价货币，因为他们通过它得不到他们自身消费所需要的货物，而只是把它转让出去。因此我们不能从这里寻找货币的个人交换价值的决定因素；相反，反映在这些交换过程的交换价值必然起源于其他某处。因此，只有货物的最初流量保留下来，只有以劳动和土地服务为一方，以消费品为另一方的交换。人们只是单独根据能够用货币购买到的消费品的价值来评价自己的货币存量。因此，货币收入和真实收入之间的交换是关键点，它是经济过程中，形成个人交换价值，从而形成货币价格的地方。

The result is now easy to state: the exchange value of money for everyone depends upon the use value of the consumption goods which he can obtain for his income. The total effective demand in terms of goods in a period serves as the value scale for the units of income available in this economic process. Therefore, under given conditions, there is for every individual an unequivocally determined value scale and definite marginal utility of his stock of money. ① The absolute magnitude of this stock of money in the economic system is irrelevant. In principle a smaller total performs the same service as a larger. If we assume the existing quantity of money to be constant, then there will be the same demand for money year in and year out, and the same value of money will emerge for every individual. Money will be so distributed in the economic system that a uniform price of money emerges. This is the case when all consumption goods are disposed of and all services of labor and land paid for. The exchange between services of labor and land on the one hand and consumption goods on the other is divided into two parts: the exchange between services of labor and land and money, and that between money and consumption goods. Since the values and prices of money must be equal on the one hand to the values and prices of consumption goods and on the other hand to the values and prices of services of labor and land, ② it is clear that the essential lines of our picture are not altered by the insertion of intermediate links, that money only performs the function of a technical instrument, but adds nothing new to the phenomena. To employ a customary expression, we can say

① With a given technique of the market exchange and given habits of payment. Cf. on this Marshall's Money, Credit and Commerce or Keynes' Tract on Monetary Reform, and also Schlesinger, Theorie der Geld-und Kreditwirtschaft.

② We are considering here for simplicity's sake, I repeat, an isolated economic system, since the inclusion of international relations would complicate the exposition without contributing anything essential. Similarly we are considering an economic system in which all individuals reckon perfectly in money and are connected with each other.

现在很容易表述这个结论：货币对于每一个人的交换价值，取决于他自己的收入可能获得的消费品的使用价值。在一个时期用商品表示的总的有效需求就是这个经济过程中所使用的收入单位的价值尺度。因此，在给定条件下，对每一个人来说，关于他的货币存量都有一个明确决定的价值尺度和确定的边际效用。① 在经济系统里这一货币存量的绝对数量是互不相关的。原则上，一个较小的总数也提供了像较大的总数一样的相同的服务。如果我们假定现存的货币量固定不变，那么以后每年对货币的需求量将是一样的，同时每一个人都会面对相同的货币价值。在经济系统中货币将是这样地被分配，以形成统一的货币价格。当所有的消费品得到消费，所有的劳动和土地服务得到支付，就会出现这样的情形。以劳动和土地服务为一方，以消费品为另一方之间的交换被分成两部分：一部分是劳动和土地服务与货币之间的交换，一部分是货币与消费品之间的交换。由于货币的价值和价格一方面必须等于消费品的价值和价格，另一方面又必须等于劳动和土地服务的价值和价格，② 所以很清楚，我们图画的主线索不会因插入中间环节而变化，货币只执行技术工具的职能，对现象并不增加新的东西。用一个习惯的表达，我们可以说，

---

① 假定市场交换技术和支付习惯是给定的。关于这一点，参阅马歇尔的《货币、信用和商业》或者凯恩斯的《货币改革小议》，还可参阅施莱辛格的《货币经济和信用经济理论》。

② 为了简单化，我再重复一次，在这里我们只考虑一个独立的经济系统，因为如果包括国际关系，那么将使说明复杂化，而不会有什么实质性的帮助。同样我们所考虑的经济系统中，所有个人都完全用货币计算，而且彼此互相联系。

that money thus far represents only the cloak of economic things and nothing essential is overlooked in abstracting from it.

At first sight money appears as a general order upon different quantities of goods[①] or as we may say as "general purchasing power." Every individual regards money first of all as a means of obtaining goods in general; if he sells his services of labor or land, he sells them not for definite goods but, as it were, for goods in general. If one looks more closely, however, things take on a different aspect. For every individual values his money income really according to the goods which he actually obtains with it and not according to goods in general. When he speaks of the value of money, the range of goods he customarily purchases floats more or less plainly before his eyes. If whole classes of buyers were suddenly to change the expenditure of their incomes, then obviously the price of money and also the personal exchange value of money would undoubtedly have to change. Ordinarily, however, this does not happen. In general, a definite plan of expenditure is adhered to as being the best, and it does not change quickly. This is why, in practice, everyone can normally reckon with a constant value and price of money and he need only gradually adjust them to changed conditions. Therefore, one can also say of money what we said earlier of all other goods, namely that for every part of the existing purchasing power there lies ready somewhere in the economic system a demand for it, a supply of goods for it, and that the bulk of the money, just as the bulk of the means of production and consumption goods, goes the same way year in and year out. Here too we can assert that we change nothing essential if we imagine that every individual piece of money travels exactly the same route in every economic period.

---

① This conception is to be found as early as Berkeley. It has never been lost, and J. S. Mill more recently gave it currency. In contemporary German literature it is found chiefly in Bendixen. It contradicts neither the quantity theory, nor the cost of production nor the "balance" theory.

到现在为止货币只代表着经济事物的外壳，对它进行抽象并没有忽视实质性的东西。

初看起来，货币似乎是加在不同商品量上的一般规则，[①] 或者我们可以说是“一般购买力”。每个人首先把货币当做可以获得商品的一般手段；如果他出卖他的劳动或者土地服务，这并不是为了得到特定的货物，而好像是为了得到一般的货物。可是，如果我们更进一步观察，就会发现事情呈现出不同的状况。因为每个人确实是按照他用货币所实际购买到的商品的价值来评价他的货币收入，而不是根据一般的商品。当他谈到货币价值时，他所习惯购买的那些商品或多或少地就会清楚地浮现在他眼前。如果所有类型的购买者都突然改变他们收入的支出，那么显然，货币的价格，货币的个人交换价值无疑都将改变。然而，通常这种事情并不会发生。一般，一个明确的支出计划被认为是最好的而被坚持下来，那它就不会很快改变。这就是为什么每个人在实际中通常都能用一种固定的货币价值和价格计算，而他们必须做的只是逐渐调整它们以适应改变了的条件。因此，我们也可以用我们先前说所有其他货物的话来说货币，即，就现有购买力的每一部分来说，在经济系统的某个地方早已经存在着对它的需求，存在着对它的货物供应；而货币的大部分，就像大部分生产资料和消费品一样，年复一年走着相同的路。在这里我们也可以断言，如果我们假定每一块货币在每一个经济时期经历着完全相同的路线，

① 这个概念最早是伯克莱提出的。以后就一直存在着，最近 J. S. 穆勒把它传播开来。在现代德文文献中，这主要存在于本迪克森那里。它与数量理论、生产成本理论或者“平衡”理论都不矛盾。

This relation of real income and money income also determines the changes in the value of money. ①

We have so far considered money solely as a circulating medium. We have had in view the determination of the value of only those quantities of money which are actually used for the movement of the mass of commodities periodically. Obviously there are also in every economic system, for well known reasons, noncirculating quantities of money, and the determination of their value is not yet explained. For so far we have not learned of any employment of money which necessitates an accumulation beyond the measure that enables the individual to pay for his current purchases. To this point we must return later. We shall not go into it further here, but content ourselves with having explained the circulation and determination of the value of those quantities of money which correspond to the chief exchange transactions which we have depicted. In any case, in the normal circular flow, which we have in view here, no holding of important stocks of money for other purposes would be necessary.

We have also neglected another element. Purchasing power is employed not only to carry out the exchange of consumption goods against the services of labor and land, but also to transfer the possession of landed property itself, and furthermore purchasing power itself is transferred. We could easily take account of all these elements, but they have an essentially different significance for us from that of those which we can analyse within the framework of our present argument. We may only briefly point out that within the continually recurring economic process which we have been describing there would be little room for these things. Transfers of purchasing power as such are not necessary elements of this process. It rather flows along as it were of its own accord and in its essence makes no kind of credit transactions necessary. We have already pointed out that

① Cf. Wieser, loc. cit.

那么我们没有改变任何实质性的东西。这种实际收入和货币收入之间的关系也决定着货币价值的变化。[①]

至此，我们仅仅是把货币当做流通手段。我们所观察到的只是那些货币量的价值的确定，这些货币量实际上是用来使大量商品定期流通的。显然，在每一个经济系统里，由于众所周知的原因，还存在着不流通的货币量，它们的价值决定还没有被说明。到此为止，我们还没有学到这样的货币使用方式，它要求个人必须积累超过他当期能够支付的购买的货币。以后我们必须回到这一点。在这里，我们对此不作进一步论述，而对我们已经做的说明已很满足了，我们已说明了与我们已经描述的主要交换行为相对应的那些货币量的流通和价值决定。不管怎样，在正常的循环流动中——这是我们在这里所考虑的——没有必要为其他目的而持有重要的货币存量。

我们也忽视了另一个要素。购买力不仅被用来执行消费品对劳动和土地服务的交换，还被用来转移土地财产本身的所有权，而且，购买力本身也被转移。我们能够很容易地考虑所有这些要素，但是它们同我们在当前讨论范围内所能分析的那些要素，对于我们的意义有着实质性的不同。我们只能简略地指出，在我们一直描述的这个连续不断重复出现的经济过程中，没有地方容纳这些东西。购买力本身的转移并不是这一经济过程的必要因素。它实际上可以说是按照自己的方式在流转，在本质上，它对任何一种信用交易都是不必要的。我们已经指出，

---

① 参阅维塞尔的书。

no advances are made to laborers and landlords, but that their means of production are simply bought from them. This is not altered by the intervention of money, and an advance payment of money is no more necessary than an advance of consumption goods or means of production. Obviously we need not exclude the case in which individuals obtain purchasing power from others and transfer to them in return a part of their original productive powers, land for example. Such is the case of borrowing for purposes of consumption, to which no special interest attaches. Similarly, as we shall show below, in the case of transfers of labor and land in general, and therefore we can say that money has, in the circular flow, no other röle than that of facilitating the circulation of commodities.

It may also be added that for a similar reason we have not spoken of credit instruments. Of course not only a part but the whole of the exchange process can be settled by such credit media. It is not uninteresting even to imagine that, instead of actual metal money, only, say, bills of exchange circulate. For example, this teaches us that the assertion about an *original* necessity of money's having a commodity value does not mean that the particular money commodity must actually circulate. For indeed nothing more is necessary to put money in a fixed relation to the values of other goods than that it should be *connected* with something of definite value. The economic process could, therefore, be carried out without the intervention of metal money. Anyone who supplies services of labor and land would receive a bill for a determined amount of monetary units, then buy consumption goods with it, in order to receive again in the next period – if we adhere to our conception of the identity of the routes travelled by money periodically – the same amount of units in the shape of another bill of exchange. Assuming smooth functioning and general acceptability, such a medium of exchange fills the röle of money perfectly, and because it does, it will be valued by individuals just as metal money, and change hands at the same "prices" expressed in commodities.

没有对劳工和地主预先支付，他们的生产资料只不过是从他们那里买来的。这一点并没有因货币的介入而改变，货币的预先支付和消费品以及生产资料的预先支付一样，都是不必要的。显然我们没必要排除这种情况，即个人用转移自己的一部分原始生产力的方式作为回报，比如转移土地，而从他人那里获得购买力。为了消费而借入就是这种情况，它没有附加特别的利息。同样，就像我在下面将要说明的，劳动和土地的一般转移也是这种情况；因此我们可以说，在循环流转中，货币除了推动商品的流通之外，没有其他什么作用了。

我们还可以补充一句：由于同样的原因，我们没有谈到信用工具。当然，不仅是交换过程的一部分，而且是全部过程都可以这种信用媒介来解决。甚至这样想像：不用实际的金属货币，而只有，票据在流通，这是很有意思的。例如，这告诉我们：货币具有商品价值，主张这种原始必要性并不意味着具体的货币商品在实际中就必须流通。因为，要使货币与其他商品的价值有一种固定的关系，除非它必须与某种有明确价值的货物相联系，确实不需要别的什么了。因此，经济过程在没有金属货币的干预下仍可以运转。任何一个提供劳动和土地服务的人都会收到一张有确定货币单位数额的支票，然后用它来购买消费品，为的是在下一期再收到——如果我们坚持货币定期地经历相同的路径这一概念——有着相同数量货币单位的另一张交换票据。假定这样一种交换媒介完全履行着货币的职能，能够顺利地流通并被普遍接受；由于它能起货币的作用，所以个人对它的评价就与对金属货币的评价一样，它会以用商品表达的相同的“价格”转手流通。即使从来没有任何偿还债款

This is true even if there is never any question of redemption, but simply of a continuous process of claims to legal tender being offset against each other. There will therefore be a demand for this medium of exchange, which will under our assumptions always be met by a corresponding supply. But since we have seen that the price of the unit of metal money simply mirrors the price of consumption goods and hence of production goods, it follows that the price of our hypothetical bills of exchange will do the same. Hence they will be negotiated at their full nominal value, or, in other words, will always be at par. For no motive exists to allow a discount. This argument teaches us in a somewhat more practical manner than an earlier has already done that no interest would appear in the economic system under our assumptions, and that therefore the logic of economic things as here described does not explain the phenomenon of interest.

But apart from this, there is no reason for us to occupy ourselves further in this place with credit means of payment. If credit instruments only replace some already existing metal money, then their use will not of itself produce any new phenomena. If a particular exchange transaction is settled year in and year out by means of such credit instruments, then the latter play the same part as the corresponding amount of metal money would and there is no incentive so far to the sudden introduction of credit into the circular flow, which we should have to consider. For this reason, but also because the element of credit will later become very important for us and because we want very much to contrast this sharply with the function of money described here, we shall assume that our money circulation so far consists only of metal money[①] and indeed,

① The quantity of "metal money" in such an economic system corresponds not only to a definite price level, but also to a definite rapidity of circulation of money. If all incomes were paid yearly, then obviously a greater amount of money would be required, or all prices must be lower, than if they were paid weekly. We assume this rapidity of circulation to be constant, since we quite agree, within the

的问题，而只有对法定通货的要求权相互抵消的连续过程的问题，这种情形也是真实的。因此，对这种交换媒介就会有需求，在我们的假设下，它将总是由于有相应的供给而得到满足。但是由于我们已经看到，金属货币单位的价格只是对消费品价格的反映，从而也是对生产性货物价格的反映，那么我们就认为，我们所假设的交换票据的价格也会起同样的作用。因此，它们将以它们充分的名义价值流通，或者，换一种说法，它将总是按票面价值流通。这是由于不存在给予折扣的动机。这个论据相对于先前的论据，用更实际的方式告诉我们，在我们假设的经济系统里，没有利息出现，因此，这里所描述的经济事物的逻辑不能用来解释利息现象。

但是除了这一点，我们没有理由在这里再进一步谈信用支付工具。如果信用工具只是用来替代某种已经存在的金属货币，那么它们的使用本身将不会产生任何新的现象。如果一种特别的交换行为年年反反复复地采用这种信用工具，那么这种信用工具就和相应数量的金属货币起着相同的作用，至此仍然没有刺激要在循环流转中突然地引进信用，而这种信用是我们应该加以考虑的。由于这个原因，而且还由于信用要素在今后将变得对我们更加重要，同时因为我们非常需要对它和我们在这里所描述的货币职能作一个鲜明的对比，所以我们假定，到此为止，我们的货币流通只是由金属货币①构成的，

① 在这样一种经济系统里，“金属货币”的数量，不仅和一定的价格水平相适应，而且还和一定的货币流通速度相适应。如果所有的收入按年支付，那么显然，所需要的货币量将比按周支付所需要的货币量多，否则就需要价格更低一些。我们假定这个流通速度是固定不变的，因为在这

to simplify matters, of gold. In order to keep the two elements separate, we shall in general understand by money only metal money. And we include this concept, together with such credit instruments as do not simply replace previously existing quantities of money, in the concept of means of payment. The problem of whether "credit means of payment" are money will be dealt with later. ②

Thus, corresponding to the stream of goods there is a stream of money, the direction of which is opposite to that of the stream of goods, and the movements of which, upon the assumption that no increase of gold or any other one-sided change occurs, are only reflexes of the movement of goods. With this we have closed the description of the circular flow. For an exchange economy as a whole there is the same continuity, and under the same assumptions, the same changelessness as for a non-exchange economy – continuity and constancy not only of the processes but also of values. It would indeed be a misrepresentation of the facts to speak of social valuations. Psychic values must live in a consciousness, hence if the word is to have any meaning at all they must be by nature individual. The values with which we have to do here carry meaning not with reference to the point of view of the whole economic system but only to that of the individual. The social fact, here as in all valuations, is in the circumstance that individual values are interrelated and are not independent of each other. The totality of the

---

limits of this argument, with Wieser when he says (loc. cit., p. 522 f.) that changes in the rapidity of circulation, like the quantity of the credit means of payment, are not independent causes of changes in the price level, since they – it is better from our standpoint to say "in so far as they" – are induced by commodity movements. Cf. also Aupetit, Théorie de la monnaie; Del Vecchio, "Teoria della moneta," Giornale degli Economisti (1909).

② Cf. on the concept of "purchasing power," amongst others, Davenport, Value and Distribution.

而且简单地说是由黄金构成的。为了分开这两个要素，一般我们所理解的货币就只是金属货币。我们将把金属货币这个概念以及那些信用工具——这些信用工具不仅是替代先前存在的货币数量，都放入支付手段这个概念中。我们将在以后对“信用支付手段”是不是货币这个问题进行讨论。②

这样，与商品流量相对应的就有一个货币流量，不过它的方向与商品流量的方向相反；如果假定黄金不会增加，或者不会发生任何其他单方面的变化，那么货币流的运动只是商品流动的反映。这样我们就结束了对循环流转的描述。对于整个交换经济来说，有一个相同的持续性，并在同样的假设下，有着相同的不变性，就像对于非交换经济一样——不仅它的过程，而且它的价值，都有持续性和不变性。谈到社会评价，那确实是对事实的一种扭曲。心理的价值必然存在于潜意识中，因此，如果要赋予这个词任何意义，那么心理的价值在本质上必须是发自个人的。在这里我们所说的价值，其包含的意义，不是从整个经济系统的观点来考虑的，而是从个人的观点出发的。社会事实——在这里就像在所有的评价中一样——它处在这样的环境中，这里个别价值彼此之间是相互联系而不是各自独立的。

个论点的限制范围内，我们完全同意维塞尔的这个观点（上引书，第522页）：就像信用支付工具的数量一样，流通速度的变化并不是价格水平变化的独立的原因，因为它是由商品的运动产生的——从我们的观点最好是说“就它是由商品运动引起的而言”。也可以参考奥佩蒂的“货币理论”，德尔·韦奇奥的“货币理论”，载《经济学家杂志》（1909年）。

② 关于“购买力”的概念，在其他文献中，可以参阅达文波特的《价值与分配》。

economic relations constitutes the economic system, just as the totality of social relations constitutes society. If one may not speak of social values, there is yet a social value system, a social system of individual values. These values are interrelated similarly with the values within the individual's economy. They operate upon one another through the exchange relation so that they influence and are influenced by all the values of other individuals. ①In this social value system all the conditions of life in a country are mirrored, in particular all "combinations" are expressed in it. The sediment of the social value system is the price system. It is a unit in the same sense. To be sure, prices do not express a kind of estimate of the social value of a good. Indeed they are not at all the immediate expression of a definite value, but only the results of processes which work under the pressure of many individual valuations.

① There is general interdependence between them. Cf. Wesen, bk. II, for more extensive details on this point.

经济关系的总和构成了经济系统，就像社会关系的总和构成社会一样。如果人们不能谈社会价值，那就还有一个社会价值体系，一个个别价值的社会体系。这些价值与个体经济中的价值同样是相互联系的。它们通过交换关系互相发生作用，因此，它们影响着所有其他个人的价值，也被这些价值所影响着。[①] 在这个社会价值体系中，一个国家所有的生活条件都被反映出来，尤其是所有的“组合”都表现在其中。价格体系是社会价值系统的沉积，同时它也是一个单位。当然，价格并不表示对一种商品的社会价值的估计。的确，价格根本不是一种对价值的确定且直接的表现形式而只是在许多个人评估的压力下发生作用的各过程的结果。

① 它们之间存在着一般的相互依存关系。关于这一点可以参阅《本质》第Ⅱ编，那里有更详细的说明。

CHAPTER II

The Fundamental Phenomenon Of Economic Development

I

The social process, which rationalises[①] our life and thought, has led us away from the metaphysical treatment of social development and taught us to see the possibility of an empirical treatment; but it has done its work so imperfectly that we must be careful in dealing with the phenomenon itself, still more with the concept in which we comprehend it, and most of all with the word by which we designate the concept and whose associations might lead us astray in all manner of undesirable directions. Closely connected with the metaphysical preconception – more precisely with the ideas which grow out of metaphysical roots and become preconceptions if, neglecting unbridgeable gulfs, we make then do the work of empirical science – even if not itself such a metaphysical preconception, is every search for a "meaning" of history. The same is true of the postulate that a nation, a civilization or even the whole of mankind, must show some kind of uniform unilinear development, as even such a matter-of-fact mind as Roscher

---

① This is used here in Max Weber's sense. As the reader will see, "rational" and "empirical" here mean, if not identical, yet cognate, things. They are equally different from, and opposed to, "metaphysical," which implies going beyond the reach of both "reason" and "facts," beyond the realm, that is, of science. With some it has become a habit to use the word "rational" in much the same sense as we do "metaphysical." Hence some warning against misunderstanding may not be out of place.

第二章　经济发展的基本现象

I

理性地说明①我们的生活与思想的社会过程，已经引导我们从抽象地、超自然地对待社会发展中走出来，并教导我们看出了对其进行经验处理的可能性；但是社会过程很不完善地处理自己的任务，所以我们必须小心地对待现象本身，尤其是我们用来理解它的概念，这其中特别要小心我们用来表示这种概念的文字，文字的各种联系很可能引导我们步入歧途，走向各种不值得的方向。与先验的先入之见——更确切地说，如果我们忽略不可逾越的鸿沟，使它做经验科学的工作（尽管它本身不是这样一种先验的先入之见），那它就是产生于先验的根子并且已变成了先入之见的思想——密切关联的，就是对历史的“意义”的各种探索。认为一个民族，一种文化，甚至整个人类，一定会表现出某种一致的、直线式的发展，这种假设也是如此；甚至像罗雪尔这种有务实

① 这里用的是马克斯·韦伯的含义。读者可以看出，这里“理性的”和“经验的”含义是指同源的东西，如果不是同一事物的话。它们都与“先验的”一词不同，而且意思相反，“先验的”暗含着超出“理性”和“事实”的范围，超出科学的领域。就某些人来说，使用“理性的”一词已经成为一种习惯，这跟我们使用“先验的”一词的含义差不多。所以提醒读者以免产生误解是有必要的。

assumed and as the innumerable philosophers and theorists of history in the long brilliant line from Vico to Lamprecht took and still take for granted. Here, too, belong all kin is of evolutionary thought that centre in Darwin – at least if this means no more than reasoning by analogy – and also the psychological prejudice which consists in seeing more in motives and acts of volition than a reflex of the social process. But the evolutionary idea is now discredited in our field, especially with historians and ethnologists, for still another reason. To the reproach of unscientific and extra-scientific mysticism that now surrounds the "evolutionary" ideas, is added that of dilettantism. With all the hasty generalizations in which the word "evolution" plays a part, many of us have lost patience.

We must get away from such things. Then two facts still remain: first the fact of historical change, whereby social conditions become historical "individuals" in historical time. These changes constitute neither a circular process nor pendulum movements about a centre. The concept of social development is defined by these two circumstances, together with the other fact: that whenever we do not succeed in adequately explaining a given historical state of things from the preceding one, we do indeed recognise the existence of an unsolved but not insoluble problem. This holds good first of all for the individual case. For example, we understand Germany's internal political history in 1919 as one of the effects of the preceding war. It also holds good, however, for more general problems.

Economic development is so far simply the object of economic history, which in turn is merely a part of universal history, only separated from the rest for purposes of exposition. Because of this fundamental dependence of the economic aspect of things on everything else, it is not possible to explain *economic* change by previous *economic* conditions alone. For the economic state of a people does not emerge simply from the preceding economic conditions, but only from the preceding total situation. The expository and analytical difficulties which arise from this are very much diminished,

思想的人也这样假定，一系列才华横溢的人从维科到兰普雷希特，无数的哲学家和历史理论家过去和现在都认为这是理所当然的。以达尔文为中心的各种进化论思想——至少如果这只不过是意味着类比的推论——以及把动机和意志行为不只看成是社会过程的反映这种心理学上的偏见，这儿都属于这一类。但是，现在进化思想在我们的研究领域受到怀疑，尤其是对历史学家和人类学家来说，这是有另一个原因的。现在除了对围绕着“进化论”观点的不科学和超科学的神秘主义谴责外，还加上了对肤浅涉猎的谴责。对“进化”一词在其中所起的作用的所有仓促的一般性判断，我们当中许多人已经失去了耐心。

我们必须远离这些东西。还有两个事实留下来了，一个是历史变化的事实，由于历史的变化，在历史长河中社会条件成为历史的“个体”。这些变化既不构成循环过程，也不构成以一个中心摆动的运动。这两种情况与另一个事实限定了社会发展的概念，这个事实即是，每当我们不能根据以前的情况成功地对事物的特定的历史状态进行充分说明时，我们确实意识到有一个没有解决的、但不是不能解决的问题存在。这一点首先对于个体的情况是适用的。例如，我们理解1919年德国的国内政治史是前一次战争的影响之一。但是，对于更加一般的问题它也是适用的。

经济发展至今只不过是经济史的对象，而经济史也只不过是通史的一部分，之所以把它划分出来只是为了说明的目的。由于事物的经济方面对每一种其他事物的这种本质上的依存性，所以不能仅仅用先前的经济情况解释经济的变化。因为一个民族的经济状况并不只是产生于先前的经济情况，而是产生于以前的全部形势。由此而产生的解释上和分析上的困难被大大减少了，

practically if not in principle, by the facts which form the basis of economic interpretation of history; without being compelled to take a stand for or against this view, we can state that the economic world is relatively autonomous because it takes up such a great part of a nation's life, and forms or conditions a great part of the remainder; wherefore writing economic history by itself is obviously a different thing from writing, say, military history. To this must be added still another fact which facilitates the separate description of any of the divisions of the social process. Every sector of social life is, as it were, inhabited by a distinct set of people. The heteronomous elements generally do not affect the social process in any such sector directly as the bursting of a bomb "affects" all things which happen to be in the room in which it explodes, but only through its data and the conduct of its inhabitants; and even if an event occurs like the one suggested by our metaphor of a bursting bomb, the effects only occur in the particular garb with which those primarily concerned dress them. Therefore, just as describing the effects of the Counter Reformation upon Italian and Spanish painting always remains history of art, so describing the economic process remains economic history even where the true causation is largely non-economic.

The economic sector, again, is open to an endless variety of points of view and treatments, which one can array, for example, according to the breadth of their scope – or we might just as well say according to the degree of generalization which they imply. From an exposition of the nature of the economic life of the Niederaltaich monastery in the thirteenth century to Sombart's exposition of the development of economic life in western Europe, there runs a continuous, logically uniform thread. Such an exposition as Sombart's is theory, and indeed theory of economic development in the sense in which we intend it for the moment. But it is not economic theory in the sense in which the contents of the first chapter of this book are economic theory, which is what has been understood by "economic theory" since Ricardo's day. Economic theory in the latter sense, it is true, plays a part in a theory like Sombart's, but a wholly subordinate one: namely,

因为有构成历史的经济解释基础的那些事实，如果这些在实际中如此，而在原则上不是如此；如果不必对这个观点表示支持或者反对，我们就可以说经济世界是相对独立的，因为它在一个民族的生命中占据了这么重要的地位，并且形成或者决定着其他生活的大部分；因此，写一部经济史本身显然不同于军事史。必须在这一点上再加上另一个事实，这个事实推进了对社会过程任何一个部门的单独描述。社会的每一部分，都好像居住着一组不同特征的人们。各种有差异的要素一般并不直接影响任何一个这样的部门的社会过程，就像一颗爆炸的炸弹只对那些恰好在它爆炸的地方的所有事物产生“影响”，而也只是通过它的数据和它的居民的行为去影响；即使一个事件就像我们所说的炸弹爆炸那个比喻所表明的那样发生，它的影响也只是发生在那些有关的主要的人们所穿着的外衣上。因此，就像总是把关于基督教反革命运动对意大利和西班牙绘画的影响的描述归于艺术史一样，对经济过程的描述也总是归于经济史，即使在那里真正的原因大部分是非经济的。

经济部门又是可以用无数种观点和处理方式去研究的，例如，人们可以根据这些观点和处理方式的范围的宽度去安排——或者我们也可以说，根据它们所暗含的理论的一般程度去安排。从对13世纪尼德阿尔泰寺院的经济生活的本质的说明，到桑巴特对西欧经济生活的发展的说明，其中贯穿着一条连续不断、逻辑上一致的线索。像桑巴特的这种说明就是理论，它确实是我们此刻想要说的那种经济发展理论。但它不是本书第一章的内容所意味的那种经济理论，第一章所说的是自李嘉图时代以来人们所理解的那种“经济理论”。诚然，后者意义上的经济理论，在像桑巴特的理论中也起作用，但它完全属于一种次要的作用，也就是

where the connection of historical facts is complicated enough to necessitate methods of interpretation which go beyond the analytic powers of the man in the street, the line of thought takes the form offered by that analytical apparatus. However, where it is simply a question of making development or the historical outcome of it intelligible, of working out the elements which characterise a situation or determine an issue, economic theory in thetraditional sense contributes next to nothing. ①

① If economists, nevertheless, have always had something to say on this theme, this is only because they did not restrict themselves to economic theory, but – and whether individual events like the appearance of American gold indeed quite superficially as a rule – studied historical sociology or made assumptions about the economic future. Division of labor, the origin of private property in land, increasing control over nature, economic freedom, and legal security – these are the most important elements constituting the "economic sociology" of Adam Smith. They clearly relate to the social framework of the economic course of events, not to any immanent spontaneity of the latter. One can also consider this as Ricardo's theory of development (say in Bücher's sense), which, moreover, exhibits the line of thought which earned the characterisation of "pessimist" for him: namely the "hypothetical prognosis" that in consequence of the progressive increase of population together with the progressive exhaustion of the powers of the soil (which can according to him only temporarily be interrupted by improvements in production) a position of rest would eventually appear – to be distinguished *toto coelo* from the ideal momentary position of rest of the equilibrium of modern theory – in which the economic situation would be characterised by an hypertrophy of rent, which is something totally different from what is understood above by a theory of development, and still more different from what we shall understand by it in this book. Mill worked out the same line of thought more carefully, and also distributed color and tone differently. In essence, however, his Book IV, "Influence of the Progress of Society on Production and Distribution," is just the same thing. Even this title expresses how much "progress" is considered as something non-economic, as something rooted in the data that only "exercises an influence" upon production and distribution, In particular his treatment of improvements in the "arts of production" is strictly "static." Improvement, according to this traditional view, is something which just happens and the effects of which we have to investigate, while we have nothing to say about its occurrence *per se*. What is thereby passed over is the subject matter of this book, or rather the foundation stone of its construction. J. B. Clark (Essentials of Economic Theory), whose merit is in having consciously separated "statics" and "dynamics," saw in the dynamic elements a disturbance of the static equilibrium. This is likewise our view, and also from our standpoint an essential task is to investigate the effect of this disturbance and the new equilibrium which then emerges. But while he confines himself to this and just like Mill sees therein the meaning of dynamics, we shall first of all give a theory of these causes of disturbances in so far as they are more than mere disturbances for us and in so far as it seems to us that essential economic phenomena depend upon their appearance. In particular: two of the causes of disturbance enumerated by him (increase of capital and population) are for us, as for him, merely causes of disturbance, however important as "factors of change" they may be for another kind of problem just indicated in the text. The same is true of a third (changes in the direction of consumers' tastes) which will later be substantiated in the text. But the other two (changes in technique and in productive organisation) require special analysis and evoke something different again from disturbances in the theoretical sense. The non-recognition of this is the most important single reason for what appears unsatisfactory to us in economic theory. From this insignificant-looking source flows, as we shall see, a new conception of the economic process, which overcomes a series of fundamental difficulties and thus justifies the new statement of the problem in the text. This statement of the problem is more nearly parallel to that of Marx. For according to him there is an internal economic development and no mere adaptation of economic life to changing data. But my structure covers only a small part of his ground.

说，在历史事实之间的联系非常复杂以至有必要引用超过一般人的分析能力的解释方法的地方，思路就采用那种由分析工具提供的形式。然而，如果问题只是使发展或者发展的历史结果变成可以理解的，只是为了得出某种形势或者对某个问题的决策的要素，那么传统意义上的经济理论几乎就没有什么贡献了。①

---

① 然而，如果经济学家关于这个论题总是有一些说的内容，这只是因为他们没有把自己限制在经济理论上，而是——的确仍然是很肤浅地——去研究历史社会学或者对经济未来做假设。劳动分工、土地私有权的起源、对自然的不断增长的控制、经济自由以及法律安全——这些是构成亚当·斯密的“经济社会学”的最重要的要素。显然，它们同事件的经济进程的社会结构是相关的，而不是同经济进程的任何内在的自发性相关。人们也可以把它看成是李嘉图的发展理论（比如说毕希尔的意思）而且，它展现了一种思想路线，这个路线为他赢得了“悲观主义”的称号，即一种“假设性的预测”：由于人口的不断增长以及土地资源的不断耗尽（根据他的意思，这只能由生产的改进而暂时地被打断），最终将出现一种静止状态——这要与现代理论中理想的暂时静止的均衡状态完全区分开来——在这种状态中，经济形势将以地租的极大增加为特征，这在某种意义上与我们上面所理解的发展理论完全不同，与我们在本书中将要理解的发展理论更是不同。穆勒更加仔细地描绘了相同的思想路线，在色彩和语调的分布上也有所不同。然而在实质上，他书中的第四篇“社会进步对生产和分配的影响”正是相同的东西。即使这个标题也表明了“进步”在多大程度上被认为是非经济的，被认为是植根于只对生产和分配“发生影响”的数据之中的某种东西。尤其是他对“生产工艺”的改进的处理是严格“静态的”。根据这个传统的观点，改进只是偶然发生的事件，对于它的影响我们必须进行考察，然而对于它的产生本身，我们没有什么可以说的。因此被忽略的东西正是本书要研究的主题，或者说是本书结构的基石。

J. B. 克拉克（《经济理论要义》），他的可贵之处是有意识地区分了“静态学”和“动态学”，他看出了动态要素干扰了静态均衡。这也是我们的观点，从我们的观点出发，重要的事情也是考察这种干扰的影响，以及随后出现的新的均衡。但是尽管他把自己限制在这一点上，并且就像穆勒一样从中也看出了动态学的意义，我们首先将给这些干扰的原因提出一种理论，因为我们认为，它们不仅仅是干扰，而且我们看来，主要的经济现象也依赖于它们的出现。尤其是：在他列举的干扰原因中的两个原因（资本和人口的增加），对我们来说，也像对他来说一样，只是干扰原因，不管它们对本文刚刚提到的另一个问题，它们作为“变化因素”的重要性有多大。第三个原因（消费者偏好方向的改变）也是如此，这在以后的正文中将具体说明。但是其他两个（技术上和生产组织上的变化）需要做特别的分析，并将产生与从理论意义上说的干扰不相同的某些事情。不承认这一点，是经济理论中存在我们不能满意的东西的最重要的唯一的原因。从这个看来不重要的源泉，产生了经济过程的新概念，正如我们将要看到的，这个新概念征服了一系列基本的困难，并且验证了我们在正文中对这个问题的新表述是正确的。对问题的这个新称述与马克思的称述更接近。因为根据马克思的观点，存在一种内部的经济发展，而不只是经济生活要去适应变化的情况。不过，我的结构只包括了他所研究范围的一小部分。

We are not concerned here with a theory of development in this sense. No historical evolutionary factors will be indicated – whether individual events like the appearance of American gold production in Europe in the sixteenth century, or "more general" circumstances like changes in the mentality of economic men, in the area of the civilized world, in social organization, in political constellations, in productive technique, and so forth – nor will their effects be described for individual cases or for groups of cases. ① On the contrary, the economic theory the nature of which was sufficiently expounded to the reader in the first chapter will simply be improved for its own purposes, by building onto it. If this were also to enable this theory to perform better than hitherto its service to the other kind of theory of development, the fact would still remain that the two methods lie in different planes.

Our problem is as follows. The theory of the first chapter describes economic life from the standpoint of a "circular flow," running on in channels essentially the same year after year similar to the circulation of the blood in an animal organism. Now this circular flow and its channels do alter in time, and here we abandon the analogy with the circulation of the blood. For although the latter also changes in the course of the growth and decline of the organism, yet it only does so continuously,

---

① Therefore one of the most annoying misunderstandings that arose out of the first edition of this book was that this theory of development neglects all historical factors of change except one, namely the individuality of entrepreneurs. If my representation were intended to be as this objection assumes, it would obviously be nonsense. But it is not at all concerned with the concrete factors of change, but with the method by which these work, with the *mechanism of change*. The "entrepreneur" is merely the bearer of the mechanism of change. And I have taken account not of one factor of historical change, but of none. We have still less to do here with the factors which in particular explain the changes in the economic organisation, economic custom, and so on. This is still another problem, and although there are points at which all these methods of treatment collide, it means spoiling the fruit of all if they are not kept apart and if each is not allowed the right to grow by itself.

在这里我们不打算考虑在这种意义上的发展理论。我们既不能指出历史演进的因素——不论是个别事件，比如十六世纪在欧洲出现了美洲黄金生产，还是“更普遍”的情况，比如在经济人的心理方面，在文明世界的范围内，在社会组织里，在政治群星中，在生产技术上等方面所发生的变化；我们也不能对个别情况或者各组情况的影响进行描述。① 相反，在第一章我们已经向读者作了充分说明的经济理论——那是第一章的本质内容，它只是为了它自身的目的而需要改进，通过在原有基础上创建。如果这样做也是为了能够使这种理论比以往的理论对其他种类的发展理论更好地提供服务，那么事实仍然是，两种方法是基于不同的水平之上的。

我们的问题如下所述。第一章的理论从“循环流转”的视角描述了经济生活，这种生活年复一年基本上是按相同的路线运行——就像生物机体内的血液的循环流动一样。现在，这种循环流动及其运行的路线确实及时地发生了改变，这里我们就放弃了与血液循环相类似的类比。因为，虽然血液循环在生物有机体的成长和衰退过程中也发生变化，然而它只是循序渐进地这样做，

---

① 因此本书第一版发行以后出现的最让人烦恼的误解之一就是，这个发展理论忽视了所有历史变革因素，除了企业家的独立性之外。如果我表达的意思正如反对意见所说的，那它显然就是没有意义的。但它根本没有涉及变化因素，只是涉及这些变化因素起作用的方法，以及变化的机制。企业家只是这种机制的承担者。我不是只考虑历史变革因素，而是没有考虑任何一个这样的因素。在这里我们也没有更多地考虑、要特别解释那些在经济组织、经济传统等之中的变化因素。这是另一个问题，尽管这些方法有着相互冲突的地方，但是如果我们不把它们分开，如果不给予它们自行成长的权利，这将意味着损害所有这些方法的成果。

that is by steps which one can choose smaller than any assignable quantity, however small, and always within the same framework. Economic life experiences such changes too, but it also experiences others which do not appear continuously and which change the framework, the traditional course itself. They cannot be understood by means of any analysis of the circular flow, although they are purely economic and although their explanation is obviously among the tasks of pure theory. Now such changes and the phenomena which appear in their train are the object of our investigation. But we do not ask: what changes of this sort have actually made the modern economic system what it is? nor: what are the conditions of such changes? We only ask, and indeed in the same sense as theory always asks: how do such changes take place, and to what economic phenomena do they give rise?

The same thing may be put somewhat discreetly. The theory of the first chapter describes economic life from the standpoint of the economic system's tendency towards an equilibrium position, which tendency gives us the means of determining prices and quantities of goods, and may be described as an adaptation to data existing at any time. In contrast to the conditions of the circular flow this does not mean in itself that year after year "the same" things happen; for it only means that we conceive the several processes in the economic system as partial phenomena of the tendency towards an equilibrium position, but not necessarily towards the same one. The position of the ideal state of equilibrium in the economic system, never attained, continually "striven after" (of course not consciously), changes, because the data change. And theory is not weaponless in the face of these changes in data. It is constructed so as to be able to deal with the consequences of such changes; it has special instruments for the purpose (for example the instrument called quasi-rent). If the change occurs in the non-social data. (natural conditions) or in non-economic social data (here belong

也就是说，它变化的步伐是人们所选择的比任何一个可以分配的数量都小的步子，不管它怎么小，它总是处在同一结构中。经济生活也经历着这样的变化，但它还经历着其他的变化，这种变化不是循序渐进地表现的，它改变了结构，即改变了传统过程本身。我们不能通过对循环流转的任何分析的方法来理解它们，尽管它们是纯粹经济性的，尽管对它们的解释显然也是属于纯粹理论的任务。现在这些变化，以及由此而出现的现象，就是我们研究的对象。但是我们并不去问：在这些变化中是哪一些在实际上使得现代经济系统成为现在这个样子？也不问：这种变化的条件是什么？我们只是问，而且的确像理论上经常问的那样：这种变化是怎么发生的，它们又将产生什么经济现象？

同样的事情可以做稍微不同的说明。第一章的理论从经济体系的趋势是走向一个均衡位置的观点来描述经济生活，这种趋势给我们提供了决定商品价格和数量的工具，而且可以描述为在任何时候对现有事实的适应。与循环流转的情况对比，它本身并不意味着年复一年发生“相同的”事情；因为它只是意味着，我们把经济系统中的各个过程当做是走向均衡位置趋势的部分现象，但不一定是走向同一个均衡位置。经济系统中均衡的理想状态所处的位置，从来没有达到过，却被不断地“追寻着”（当然并不是有意识的），这个位置是变化的，因为事实在变化。而在事实的这些改变面前，理论也不是没有用武之地的。理论正是被构造得能够处理这种变化带来的后果；它是用于这一目的的特殊的工具（比如被称作“准地租”这样的工具）。如果变化出现在非社会的事实中（自然条件），或者出现在非经济的社会事实中（这里有战

the effects of war, changes in commercial, social, or economic policy), or in consumers' tastes, then to this extent no fundamental overhaul of the theoretical tools seems to be required. These tools only fail – and here this argument joins the preceding – where economic life itself changes its own data by fits and starts. The building of a railway may serve as an example. Continuous changes, which may in time, by continual adaptation through innumerable small steps, make a great department store out of a small retail business, come under the "static" analysis. But "static" analysis is not only unable to predict the consequences of discontinuous changes in the traditional way of doing things; it can neither explain the occurrence of such productive revolutions nor the phenomena which accompany them. It can only investigate the new equilibrium position after the changes have occurred. It is just this occurrence of the "revolutionary" change that is our problem, the problem of economic development in a very narrow and formal sense. The reason why we so state the problem and turn aside from traditional theory ties not so much in the fact that economic changes, especially, if not solely, in the capitalist epoch, have actually occurred thus and not by continuous adaptation, but more in their fruitfulness.①

By "development," therefore, we shall understand only such changes in economic life as are not forced upon it from without but arise by its own initiative, from within. Should it turn out that there are no such changes arising in the economic sphere itself, and that the phenomenon that we call economic development is in practice simply founded upon the fact

① The problems of capital, credit, entrepreneurial profit, intent on capital, and crises (or business cycles) are the ones in which this fruitfulness will be demonstrated here. Yet it is not thereby exhausted. For the expert theorist I point, for example, to the difficulties which surround, the problem of increasing return, the question of multiple points of intersection between supply and demand carves, and the element of time, which even Marshall's analysis has not overcome.

争的影响，商业、社会、或者经济政策的变化），或者是消费者偏好的变化，那么在这个程度上，对理论工具似乎就不需要做根本性的检修。这些工具只有在经济生活本身时起时落地变动自己的数据时才不起作用——这里的论点与前面的论点联系在一起了。铁路建设可以作为这样的一个例子。连续的变化，它们是通过无数的小步骤而形成的连续的适应，最后使一家小零售商店成长为一家大百货公司，这是以“静态的”分析为基础的。但是，“静态的”分析不仅不能对传统的行为方式中非连续性变化的结果进行预测，它还既不能解释这种生产性革命的产生，又不能说明伴随着生产性革命的现象。它只能在变化发生以后研究新的均衡位置。正是这种“革命性”的变化的出现是我们要研究的问题，即在一种非常狭窄和正式的意义上的经济发展的问题。我们为什么要这样陈述问题并且离开传统的理论，其原因与其说是经济变化实际上就是这样发生的，而不是为了连续不断的适应（尤其是，如果不完全是，在资本主义时期），还不如说是由于这种变化本身就是富有成果的。①

因此，我们将要研究的“发展”只是经济生活中的这些变化，它们不是外部强加于经济生活的，而是产生于内部，由自身引起的变化。如果在经济领域本身内并不产生这种变化，并且我们所称的经济发展的现象在实际上只是基于这样一个事实而建

① 资本、信用、企业家利润、资本利息和危机（或商业周期）问题就是这种富有成果的变化在这里所表现出来的问题。不过，并不止这些。对专门的理论家，我可以指出，比如，围绕收益递增问题、供需曲线有多个交点的问题以及时间要素问题等困难，即使是马歇尔的分析也不能克服它们。

that the data change and that the economy continuously adapts itself to them, then we should say that there is *no* economic development. By this we should mean that economic development is not a phenomenon to be explained economically, but that the economy, in itself without development, is dragged along by the changes in the surrounding world, that the causes and hence the explanation of the development must be sought outside the group of facts which are described by economic theory.

Nor will the mere growth of the economy, as shown by the growth of population and wealth, be designated here as a process of development. For it calls forth no qualitatively new phenomena, but only processes of adaptation of the same kind as the changes in the natural data. Since we wish to direct our attention to other phenomena, we shall regard such increases as Changes in data. ①

Every concrete process of development finally rests upon preceding development. But in order to see the essence of the thing dearly, we Shall abstract from this and allow the development to arise out of a position without development. Every process of development creates the prerequisites for the following. Thereby the form of the latter is altered, and things will turn out differently from what they would have been if every concrete phase of development had been compelled first to create its own conditions. However, if we wish to get at the root of the matter, we may not include in the data of our explanation elements of what is to be explained. But if we do not do this, we shall create an apparent discrepancy between fact and theory, which may constitute an important difficulty for the reader.

① We do this because these changes are small per annum and therefore do not stand in the way of the applicability of the "static" method. Nevertheless, their appearance is frequently a condition of development in our sense. But even though they often make the latter possible, yet they do not create it out of themselves.

立的，即，数据在变化，而经济则连续不断地使自己适应这种变化；那么我们应当说，没有经济发展。说到这里，我们的意思是，经济发展并不是可以从经济的方面来解释的现象，而是被它周围世界的变化拖着走，在其本身内并没有发展；发展的原因，以及由此产生的对其的解释，必须从经济理论所描述的一组事实之外的地方去找。

仅仅是经济的增长，像由人口和财富的增长所表现的，在这里并不能被看做是发展过程。因为它没有在本质上产生新的现象，而只是同一种适应过程，就像自然数据的变化一样。因为我们希望转移我们的注意力到其他的现象，因此我们把这种增长看做是数据的变化。①

每一个具体的发展过程最后都依存于以前的发展。可是为了清楚地看到事物的实质，我们将把这一点抽象掉，允许发展产生于一种没有过发展的状态。每一个发展过程为接下来的发展过程创造先决条件。因此后者的形式被改变了，事情将变得与如果在每一个发展阶段不得不首先创造自己的条件这样的情况下应该发生的状况有所不同。然而，如果我们想要找到事物的根源，我们可以在我们的解释的事实中不包括被解释的要素。但是，如果我们不这样做，我们将会在事实与理论之间造成一种明显的脱钩，这将会给读者带来重大的困难。

---

① 我们这样做是因为，这些变化每年都很小，因此并不妨碍“静态”方法的运用。然而，它们的出现常常是在我们所认为的意义上的发展的一个条件。尽管它们常常使我们所认为的发展成为可能，但是它们并不从它们自身来创造这种发展。

If I have been more successful than in the first edition in concentrating the exposition upon essentials and in guarding against misunderstandings, then further special explanations of the words "static" and "dynamic," with their innumerable meanings, are not necessary. Development in our sense is a distinct phenomenon, entirely foreign to what may be observed in the circular, flow or in the tendency towards equilibrium. It is spontaneous and discontinuous change in the channels of the flow, disturbance of equilibrium, which forever alters and displaces the equilibrium state previously existing, Our theory of development is nothing but a treatment of this phenomenon and the processes incident to it. ①

Ⅱ

These spontaneous and discontinuous changes in the channel of the circular flow and these disturbances of the centre of equilibrium appear in the sphere of industrial and commercial life, not in the sphere of the wants of the consumers of final products, Where spontaneous and discontinuous changes in consumers' tastes appear, it is a question of a sudden change in data with which the businessman must cope, hence possibly a question of a *motive* or an opportunity for other than gradual adaptations of his conduct, hut not of such other conduct itself. Therefore this case does not offer any other problems than a change in natural data or require any new method of treatment; wherefore we shall neglect

① In the first edition of this book, I called it "dynamics" But it is preferable to avoid this expression here, since it so easy leads us astray because of the associations which attach themselves to its various meanings. Better, then, to say simply what we mean: economic life changes; it changes partly because of changes in data, to which it tends to adapt itself. But this is not the only kind of economic change; there is another which is not accounted for by influence on the data from without, but which arises from within the system, and rids kind of change is the cause of so many important economic phenomena that it seem worth while to build a theory for it, and, in order to do so, to isolate it from all the other factors of change. The author begs to add another more exact definition, which he is in the habit of using: what we are about to consider is that kind of change arising from within the system *which so displaces its equilibrium point that the new one cannot be reached from the old one by infinitesimal steps.* Add successively as many mail coaches as you please, you will never get a railway thereby.

如果我已经比在第一版中更加成功地对本质性的东西的说明以及防范误解给予关注，那么进一步特别解释“静态”和“动态”这两个词以及它们数不清的含义，是不必要的。我们所指的发展是一种特殊的现象，它完全不同于我们在循环流转中或者均衡趋势中所观察到的现象。它是在流转渠道中的自发的和间断的变化，它打破了均衡，并且永远改变着和替代着先前存在的均衡状态。我们的发展理论，只不过是对这种现象以及伴随而生的过程的论述。①

Ⅱ

循环流转中的这些自发和间断的变化，以及对均衡中心的这些干扰，出现在工业和商业生活领域，而不是在消费者对最终产品的需求领域。在消费者的偏好出现自发和间断性变化的地方，那是商人必须应对的数据突然发生变化的问题，因此那可能是他的逐渐适应的行为以外的动机和机会的问题，但不是其他行为本身的问题。所以，这种情况除了自然事实的改变以外，没有提出其他任何问题，也没有要求任何其他新的处理方法；因此，我们忽略掉消费者需

① 在本书第一版中，我称为“动态学”。但在这里最好避免用这种表述，因为由它的各种不同的意思所带来的联想，很容易使我们产生错误。所以，最好只是简单地表达我们的意思：经济生活在变化，这种变化部分的是由于事实的变化，经济生活倾向于使自己适应事实的变化。但这并不是唯一的经济变化；还有另一种经济变化，它是不能用从外部对事实的影响来说明的，它是从系统内部产生的，而且这种变化是这么多重要经济现象产生的原因，所以，看上去为它建立一种理论是很值得的，并且，要这样做就得把它从所有其他变化的因素中隔离出来。作者要求加上另一个更加准确的定义，这是他习惯用的：我们所要考察的是产生于系统的那种变化，这种变化是这样替代系统均衡的，即，旧的均衡点不能通过许多无限小的步骤达到新的均衡点。不管你把多少辆邮车连续排起来，也决不会获得一条铁路。

any spontaneity of consumers' needs that may actually exist, and assume tastes as "given." This is made easy for us by the fact that the spontaneity of wants is in general small. To be sure, we must always start from the satisfaction of wants, since they are the end of all production, and the given economic situation at any time must be understood from this aspect. Yet innovations in the economic system do not as a rule take place in such a way that first new wants arise spontaneously in consumers and then the productive apparatus swings round through their pressure. We do not deny the presence of rids nexus; It is, however, the producer who as a rule initiates economic change, and consumers are educated by him if necessary; they are, as it were, taught to want new things, or things which differ in some respect or other from those which they have been in the habit of using. Therefore, while it is permissible and even necessary to consider consumers' wants as an independent and indeed the fundamental force in a theory of the circular flow, we must take a different attitude as soon as we analyze *change*.

To produce means to combine materials and, forces within our reach (cf. *supra*, Chapter I). To produce other things, or the same things by a different method, means to combine these materials and forces differently. In so far as the "new combination" may in time grow out of the old by continuous adjustment in small steps, there is certainly change, possibly growth, but neither a new phenomenon nor development in our sense. In so far as this is not the case, and the new combinations appear discontinuously, then the phenomenon characterising development emerges. For reasons of expository convenience, henceforth, we shall only mean the latter case when we speak of new combinations of productive means. Development in our sense is then defined by the carrying out of new combinations.

求的任何自发性，这可能在实际中是存在的，并且假定偏好是“给定的”。事实是，需求的自发性通常是很小的，这就使我们很容易这样做。当然，我们必须总是从需求的满足出发，因为需求是所有生产的终点，而且在任何时候特定的经济形势必须从这一点去理解。不过，经济系统中的创新通常不以下面这种方式发生，即，首先，消费者的新的需求自发地产生，然后生产工具由于自发的需求的压力而转动起来。我们不能否认这种联系方式的存在。然而，通常是生产者发起经济的变化，消费者只是在必要的时候受到生产者的启发；消费者好像是被告知去需求新的东西，或者在某些方面是不同于，甚至完全不同于他们已经习惯使用的东西。因此，尽管可以容许甚至是必要地把消费者的需求看做是循环流转理论中的一种独立的而且的确是基本的力量，但是，只要我们分析变化时，就必须立即采取一种不同的态度。

生产意味着将我们能掌握的原材料和生产要素组合起来（参阅前面第一章）。生产其他的东西，或者用不同的方法生产相同的东西，这意味着用不同的方式组合原材料和生产力量。只要“新的组合”能够通过不间断的小步骤调整，从旧组合中及时产生，那么就肯定有变化，可能也有增长，但是这既没有新现象，也没有我们所说的发展。只要情况不是这样，而且新组合是间断地出现的，那么以发展为特征的现象就出现了。以后，为了说明的方便，当我们说到生产手段的新组合时，我们就仅指后一种情况。那么，我们所说的发展就被定义为能执行新的组合。

This concept covers the following five cases: (1) The introduction of a new good – that is one with which consumers are not yet familiar – or of anew quality of a good. (2) The introduction of a new method of production, that is one not yet tested by experience in the branch of manufacture concerned, which need by no means be founded upon a discovery scientifically new, and can also exist in a new way of handling a commodity commercially. (3) The opening of a new market, that is a market into which the particular branch of manufacture of the country in question has not previously entered, , whether or not this market has existed before. (4) The conquest of a new source of supply of raw materials or half-manufactured goods, again irrespective of whether this source already exists or whether it has first to be created. (5) The carrying out of the new organisation of any industry, like the creation of a monopoly position (for example through trustification) or the breaking up of a monopoly position.

Now two things are essential for the phenomena incident to the carrying out of such new combinations, and for the understanding of the problems involved. In the first place it is not essential to the matter – though it may happen – that the new combinations should be carried out by the same people who control the productive or commercial process which is to be displaced by the new. On the contrary, new combinations are, as a rule, embodied, as it were, in new firms which generally do not arise out of the old ones but start producing beside them; to keep to the example already chosen, in general it is not the owner of stage-coaches who builds railways. This fact not only puts the discontinuity which characterizes the process we want to describe in a special light, and creates so to speak still another kind of discontinuity in addition to the one mentioned above, but it also explains important features of the course of events, Especially in a competitive economy, in which new combinations mean the competitive elimination of the old, it explains on the one hand the process by which individuals and families rise and fall economically and socially and which is peculiar to this form of organisation,

这个概念包括下面五种情况：（1）引进一种新的产品——也就是消费者当前还不熟悉的产品——或者一种产品产生某种新的特性。（2）采用一种新的生产方法，也就是当前在有关制造部门还没有通过经验检验的方法，这种方法的建立绝不需要以科学上新的发现为基础，而且它还可以在商业上处理某种产品的新方式之中存在。（3）打开一个新的市场，也就是所研究的国家的某一个制造部门以前没有进入过的市场，而不管这个市场以前是否存在。（4）征服或者控制原材料或半制成品的某种新的供给来源，而不关心这种来源是已经存在的，还是第一次被创造出来的。（5）任何一种工业执行新的组织，比如造成一种垄断地位（例如通过托拉斯化），或者打破一种垄断地位。

对于伴随着执行这种新的组合而产生的现象，以及对于理解它所涉及的问题，现在有两件事情是很重要的。首先，新的组合不一定要由控制被新过程所代替的原来的生产或商业过程的相同的人去执行，虽然这种情况也可能发生。相反，新的组合通常似乎是体现在新的企业里的，这些新的企业通常也不是从旧的企业产生的，而是在老企业旁边和它一起开始生产的。我们还是继续用我们已经选用的例子来说明，也就是说，通常并不是驿路马车的所有者建造铁路。这个事实不仅把我们想要描述的过程的非连续性特征进行了特别的说明，而且可以说，它还创造了除上面提到的那种非连续性之外的另一种非连续性（间断性），但它对事态进程的重要特征也给予了解释。尤其是在竞争性经济里，新组合意味着对旧组合通过竞争而加以消灭，一方面它解释了个人和家庭在经济上和社会上的上升和下降的过程，这是这种组织形式特有

as well as a whole series of other phenomena of the business cycle, of the mechanism of the formation of private fortunes, and so on. In a non-exchange economy, for example a socialist one, the new combinations would also frequently appear side by side with the old. But the economic consequences of this fact would be absent to some extent, and the social consequences would be wholly absent. And if the competitive economy is broken up by the growth of great combines, as is increasingly the case today in all countries, then this must become more and more true of real life, and the carrying out of new combinations must become in ever greater measure the internal concern of one and the same economic body. The difference so made is great enough to serve as the water-shed between two epochs in the social history of capitalism.

We must notice secondly, only partly in connection with this element, that whenever we are concerned with fundamental principles, we must never assume that the carrying out of new combinations takes place by employing means of production which happen to be unused. In practical life, this is very often the case. There are always unemployed workmen, unsold raw materials, unused productive capacity, and so forth. This certainly is a contributory circumstance, a favorable condition and even an incentive to the emergence of new combinations; but great unemployment is only the consequence of non-economic eventsas for example the World War-or precisely of the development which we are investigating. In neither of the two cases can its existence play a fundamental role in the explanation, and it cannot occur in a well balanced circular flow from which we start. Nor would the normal yearly increment meet the case, as it would be small in the first place, and also because it would normally be absorbed by a corresponding expansion of production within the circular flow, which, if we admit such increments, we must think of as adjusted to this rate of growth. ① As a rule

① On the whole it is much more correct to say that population grows slowly up to the possibilities of any economic environment than that it has any tendency to outgrow it and to become thereby an independent cause of change.

的，另一方面它解释了商业周期，个人财富的形成机制等整个系列的其他现象。在非交换经济中，例如在社会主义经济中，新组合也频繁地出现在旧组合的一边。但是这一事实的经济后果在某种程度上会消失，而社会后果将会完全消失。如果竞争性经济被强大的联合组织打破，就像今天在所有的国家都在不断出现的情况那样，那么在现实生活中这必将变得越来越真实，新组合的实施必然，甚至在更大的程度上，变成同一个经济实体的内部事情。这样形成的差异已经足够大以至成为资本主义社会历史中的两个时代的分界线。

第二，我们必须注意，与这个要素只有部分关系的是，无论什么时候当我们关心基本原则，我们绝不能假定新组合的实施是通过使用恰好未被使用过的生产资料来进行的。在现实生活中，这是常有的现象，社会上总是有失业的工人，未出售的原材料，未利用的生产能力等。这对于新组合的出现，当然是一个有作用的环境，一个有利的条件，甚至是一种刺激因素；但是大量的失业只是非经济事件的后果——比如说世界大战——或者恰好是我们正在研究的发展的结果。它的存在在这两种情况下都不会在我们的解释中起根本性的作用，并且它不可能出现在我们开始所说的极度平衡的循环周转中。正常年份的增长也不能应对这种情况，首先因为这种增长很小，其次还因为，增长通常会被循环流转中相应的生产扩张吸收，如果我们承认这种增加，我们就必须把相应的生产扩张当做已经调整到这个增长速度上来了。[①] 通常，

① 从整体上讲，说人口缓慢地增长到在任何环境下所能够承受的范围，比说人口增长有任何趋势超过这种可能范围从而成为产生变化的一个独立的原因，要更正确。

the new combinations must draw the necessary means of production from some old combinations – and for reasons already mentioned we shall assume that they *always* do so, in order to put in bold relief what we hold to be the essential contour line. The carrying out of new combinations means, therefore, simply the different employment of the economic system's existing supplies of productive means – which might provide a second definition of development in our sense. That rudiment of a pure economic theory of development which is implied in the traditional doctrine of the formation of capital always refers merely to saving and to the investment of the small yearly increase attributable to it. In this it asserts nothing false, but it entirely overlooks much more essential things. The slow and continuous increase in time of the national supply of productive means and of savings is obviously an important factor in explaining the course of economic history through the centuries, but it is completely overshadowed by the fact that development consists primarily in employing existing resources in a different way, in doing new things with them, irrespective of whether those resources increase or not. In the treatment of shorter epochs, moreover, this is even true in a more tangible sense. Different methods of employment, and not saving and increases in the available quantity of labor, have changed the face of the economic world in the last fifty years. The increase of population especially, but also of the sources from which savings can be made, was first made possible in large measure through the different employment of the then existing means.

The next step in our argument is also self-evident: command over means of production is necessary to the carrying out of new combinations. Procuring the means of production is one distinct problem for the established firms which work within the circular flow. For they *have* them already procured or else can procure them currently with the proceeds of previous production as was explained in the first chapter. There is no fundamental gap here between receipts and disbursements, which, on the contrary, necessarily correspond to one another just as both

新的组合必须从某些旧的组合中提取出必要的生产资料——我们已经提到过原因，为了使我们所认为的关键的轮廓线更加形象突出，我们假定新组合将总是这样做。因此，新组合的实施只是对经济系统中现存的生产资料的供给作不同的利用——这可能给出了我们所说的发展的第二个定义。包含在资本形成的传统理论中的，关于发展的纯粹经济学理论的最初要点总是只提到储蓄以及由储蓄而产生的每年小增长的投资额。在这一点上，它所主张的没有什么错，但是它对更加重要的东西忽视了。国家对生产资料和储蓄的不断增长的供给——这种供给是缓慢的，而且在时间上是连续的，显然对于解释多少个世纪以来经济历史的进程是一个重要的因素，但是它的重要性因这一事实而被完全遮掩因而显得逊色，这个事实就是，发展主要在于用不同的方法使用现有的资源，用现有的资源做新的事情，而不管这些资源是否增加。而且，在研究较短时期内的问题时，甚至从一种更加明确的效果上看这也是真实的。在过去的50年里，是不同的使用方法，而不是储蓄和可用劳动数量的增加，已经改变了经济世界的面貌。尤其是人口的增加，还有产生储蓄的来源的增加，它们通过对当时存在的生产工具采用不同的使用方法，首先使得大部分成为可能。

我们论证的第二步也是不言而喻的：控制生产手段对于实施新的组合是必要的。对于在循环流转过程中已经建立起来的从事活动的企业来说，购买生产手段是一个独特的问题。因为他们已经购入了这种生产资料，或者当前能用以前生产的收入去购买它们，就像我们在第一章中所说的。这里，在收入与支付之间没有根本的缺口，而是相反，两者必须相吻合，就像两者必须与供给

correspond to the means of production offered and to the products demanded. Once set in motion, this mechanism works automatically. Furthermore, the problem does not exist in a non-exchange economy even if new combinations are carried out in it; for the directing organ, for example a socialist economic ministry, is in a position to direct the productive resources of the society to new uses exactly as it can direct them to their previous employments. The new employment may, under certain circumstances, impose temporary sacrifices, privations, or increased efforts upon the members of the community; it may presuppose the solution of difficult problems, for example the question from which of the old combinations the necessary productive means should be withdrawn; but there is no question of procuring means of production not already at the disposal of the economic ministry. Finally, the problem also does not exist in a competitive economy in the case of the carrying out of new combinations, if those who carry them out have the necessary productive means or can get them in exchange for others which they have or for any other property which they may possess. This is not the privilege of the possession of property *per se*, but only the privilege of the possession of disposable property, that is such as is employable either immediately for carrying out the new combination or in exchange for the necessary goods and services. ① In the contrary case – and this is the rule as it is the fundamentally interesting case – the possessor of wealth, even if it is the greatest combine, must resort to credit if he wishes to carry out a new combination, which cannot like an established business be financed by returns from previous production. To provide this credit is dearly the function of that category of individuals which we call "capitalists." It is obvious that this is the characteristic method of the capitalist type of society – and important enough to serve as its *differentia specifica* – for forcing the economic system into new channels, for putting its means at the service of new ends,

① A privilege which the individual can also achieve through saving. In an economy of the handicraft type this element would have to be emphasised more. Manufacturers' "reserve funds" assume an existing development.

的生产工具和需求的产品相适应一样。一旦开动起来，这个机制将自动地运转。而且，这个问题并不存在于非交换经济中，即使新的组合在非交换经济中执行；因为领导机构，例如一个社会主义经济部，就处于能够引导社会资源到新的用途的地位，完全像它能将社会资源引向以前的用途一样。在某种情况下，新的使用方法可能使社会成员要承担暂时的牺牲，贫困，或者需要增加努力；它可能以某些困难问题的解决为前提，例如，要解决从哪一个旧的组合里能将必要的生产资料提取出来的问题；但是却没有购入那种并不在经济部控制之下的生产手段的问题。最后，就实现新的组合而言，这个问题也不会发生在竞争性经济里，如果实施它们的人有必要的生产工具，或者能够用他们已有的其他东西，或者用他们可能拥有的任何其他财产，去交换他们现在需要的这种必要的生产工具。这并不是拥有财产本身的特权，而是拥有可支配的财产的特权，那就是要么为执行新组合可以直接使用的，要么就是可以用来交换必要的货物和服务的财产。[①] 在相反的情况下——这才是一般的情况，因为这在根本上是人们感兴趣的情况——财富的所有者，即使它是最大的组合，如果他想要实施新的组合，他也必须求助于信用，这个新组合不像已经建立起来的企业那样，可以从先前生产所得的收益中获得资金。很清楚，提供这种信用是我们称为“资本家”的那一类人的职能。显然，这是资本主义社会为了迫使经济系统进入新的轨道，为了使它的生产工具服务于新的目的所采用的

① 个人也可以通过储蓄来获得这种特权。在一个手工业型的经济中，这一要素可能被更多的强调。制造业者的“储备基金”可以认为是当前的发展。

in contrast to the method of a nonexchange economy of the kind which simply consists in exercising the directing organ's power to command.

It does not appear to me possible to dispute in any way the fore going statement. Emphasis upon the significance of credit is to be found in every textbook. That the structure of modern industry could not have been erected without it, that it makes the individual to a certain extent independent of inherited possessions, that talent in economic life "rides to success on its debts," even the most conservative orthodoxy of the theorists cannot well deny. Nor is the connection established here between credit and the carrying out of innovations, a connection which will be worked out later, anything to take offence at. For it is as dear *a priori* as it is established historically that credit is primarily necessary to new combinations and that it is from these that it forces its way into the circular flow, on the one hand because it was originally necessary to the founding of what are now the old firms, on the other hand because its mechanism, once in existence, also seizes old combinations for obvious reasons.① First, *a priori*: we saw in the first chapter that borrowing is not a necessary element of production in the normal circular flow within accustomed channels, is not an element without which we could not understand the essential phenomena of the latter. On the other hand, in carrying out new combinations, "financing" as a special act is fundamentally necessary, in practice as in theory. Second, historically: those who lend and borrow for industrial purposes do not appear early in history. The pre-capitalistic lender provided money for other than business purposes. And we all remember the type of industrialist who felt he was losing caste by borrowing and who therefore shunned banks and bills of exchange. The capitalistic credit system has grown out of and thrived on the financing of new combinations in all countries, even though in a different way in each (the origin of German joint stock banking is especially characteristic).

① The most important of which is the appearance of productive interest, as we shall see in Chapter Ⅴ. As soon as interest emerges somewhere in the system, it expands over the whole of it.

独特的方法——这足够重要以至于成为这个社会的特色，这与那种仅仅由领导机构行使权利来命令的非交换经济是完全不同的。

在我看来，无论如何都不可能对上面的陈述提出怀疑。在每一本教科书里都能找到对信用重要性的强调。没有信用就没有现代工业结构的建立，信用在一定程度上使个人独立于继承的财产，经济生活中有才智的人因为信用“通过负债而走向成功”，即使是最保守的正统的理论家也不能否认这些。这里，在信用和实现创新之间建立的联系也是不可指责的，这种联系我们将在后面论述。因为，不论从推理看，还是从历史事实的证明来看，有一点是很清楚的，即，信用对于新的组合是首要的，正因此信用强行进入循环流转过程，一方面因为信用在我们现在所称的旧厂商的建立之初是必要的，另一方面是因为，信用机制一旦建立就有明显的理由①取代旧的组合。首先，从推理上看：我们在第一章已经看到，在正常的循环流转中，在习惯的轨道内，借入并不是必需的生产要素，也不是那种没有它我们就不能理解循环流转的主要现象的要素。另一方面，实现新的组合，“信贷”作为一种特别的行为，在实践上与在理论上一样都是在根本上必要的。第二，从历史上看：那些为了工业的目的贷出和借入的人，在历史上并没有很早地出现。前资本主义的贷款人不是为了商业的目的而提供资金。我们都记得这种类型的工业家，他们认为如果借钱就是身败名裂，因此他们回避银行和汇票。资本主义的信用制度在所有国家都是产生于并且繁荣于对新组合提供资金，尽管在不同的国家采用不同的方式（德国的联合股票银行的起源就具有这种特色）。

① 其中最重要的是生产利息的产生，就像我们将在第五章看到的。只要利息在系统的某个地方出现，它就会在整个系统内扩展。

Finally there can be no stumblingblock in our speaking of receiving credit in "money or money substitutes." We certainly do not assert-that one can produce with coins, notes, or bank balances, and do not deny that services of labor, raw materials, and tools are the things wanted. We are only speaking of a method of procuring them.

Nevertheless there is a point here in which, as has already been hinted, our theory diverges from the traditional view. The accepted theory sees a problem in the existence of the productive means, which are needed for new, or indeed any, productive processes, and this accumulation therefore becomes a distinct function or service. We do not recognize this problem at all; it appears to us to be created by faulty analysis. It does not exist in the circular flow, because the running of the latter presupposes given quantities of means of production. But neither does it exist for the carrying out of new combinations,① because the productive means required in the latter are drawn from the circular flow whether they already exist there in the shape wanted or have first to be produced by other means of production existing there Instead of this problem another exists for us: the problem of detaching productive means (already employed somewhere) from the circular flow and allotting them to new combinations. This is clone by credit, by means of which one who wishes to carry out new combinations outbids the producers in the circular flow in the market for the required means of production. And although the meaning and object of this process lies in a movement of goods from their old towards new employments, it cannot be described entirely in terms of goods

① Of course the productive means do not fall from heaven. In so far as they are not given by nature or non-economically, they were and are created at some time by the individual waves of development in our sense, and henceforth incorporated in the circular flow. But every individual wave of development and every individual new combination itself proceeds again from the supply of productive means of the existing circular flow – a case of the hen and the egg.

最后，在我们谈到以“货币或者货币的替代物”的形式接受信用时，也不会有什么绊脚石。当然我们决不会说，人们可以用硬币、纸币，或者银行存款来生产，而且我们也从不否认生产需要的东西是劳动的服务、原材料和工具。我们所谈的只是获得它们的一种方法。

然而这里有一点，正像我们已经暗示过的，即我们的理论与传统的观点有分歧。传统的理论在生产工具的存在性上发现一个问题，即，这种生产工具对于新的或者任何生产过程都是必需的，因此，它的积累就变成一种特殊的职能或者服务。我们根本不承认这个问题；在我们看来，它是由错误的分析产生的。它不存在于循环流转中，因为循环流转是以一定数量的生产工具为前提的。但是，它对于实现新的组合来说也是不存在的，① 因为，循环流转所需要的生产手段是从循环流转中提取的，而不管它们是已经以需要的形式存在在那里，还是首先必须利用那里存在的其他生产工具将其生产出来。对我们来说，存在的问题不是这一个，而是另一个问题：把生产方式（已经在某些地方被使用）从循环流转中提取出来，并且把它们分配到新的组合中的问题。这是由信用来完成的，通过这种方式，那些想要实现新组合的人可以比在循环流转中的生产者，在市场上对所需要的生产工具出更高的价。尽管这一过程的意义和目的在于使货物从它们旧的用途转向新的用途，但是如果我们完全用货物去描述它，就

① 当然，生产手段不是从天上掉下来的。只要它们不是自然赋予的或者非经济地得来的，它们过去是，现在也是，在某个时候由发展的各个波浪创造出来的，这里的发展是我们所说的意义上的发展，从而体现在循环流转中。但是每一个发展的波浪和每一个新组合本身又是从现有循环流转中的生产工具的供给中产生——这就像母鸡和鸡蛋的产生过程一样。

without overlooking something essential, which happens in the sphere of money and credit and upon which depends the explanation of important phenomena in the capitalist form of economic organisation, in contrast to other types.

Finally one more step in this direction: whence come the sums needed to purchase the means of production necessary for the new combinations if the individual concerned does not happen to have them? The conventional answer is simple: out of the annual growth of social savings plus that part of resources which may annually become free. Now the first quantity was indeed important enough before the war – it may perhaps be estimated as one-fifth of total private incomes in Europe and North America – so that together with the latter sum, which it is difficult to obtain statistically, it does not immediately give the lie quantitatively to this answer. At the same time a figure representing the range of all the business operations involved in carrying out new combinations is also not available at present. But we may not even start from total "savings." For its magnitude is explicable. only by the results of previous development. By far the greater part of it does not come from thrift in the strict sense, that is from abstaining from the consumption of part of one's regular income, butit consists of funds which are themselves the result of successful innovation and in which we shall later recognise entrepreneurial profit. In the circular flow there would be on the one hand no such rich source, out of which to save, and on the other hand essentially less incentive to save. The only big incomes known to it would be monopoly revenues and the rents of large landowners; while provision for misfortunes and old age, perhaps also irrational motives, would be the only incentives. The most important incentive, the chance of participating in the gains of development, would be absent. Hence, in such an economic system there could be no great reservoirs of free purchasing power, to which one who wished to form new combinations could turnand his own savings would only suffice in exceptional cases. All money would circulate, would be fixed in definite established channels.

会忽视某些关键性的东西，而这些东西是发生在货币和信用领域的，所以依靠它们才能对资本主义经济组织形式中的重要现象进行解释，与其他类型做对照。

最后，沿着这个方向第三步：如果有关的个人恰好手中没有钱，那么购买新组合所必要的生产工具的钱从哪里来呢？传统的回答很简单：从社会储蓄的年增长额加上每年可能变为自由处置的那部分资源中获得。第一种数量在大战前的确是非常重要的——在欧洲和北美的私人总收入中这个数据或许可能估计到五分之一——所以连同后者的总数（这在统计上是很难得到的），并不能在数量上立即揭示这一回答的虚伪性。同时，我们在当前也得不到有关实现新组合的代表所有商业经营范围的数据。但是，我们甚至可以不从总的“储蓄”开始。因为它的数量大小只能通过以前发展的结果来说明。其中的大部分并不是来自严格意义上的节省，也就是说，大部分不是来自个人经常性收入中用于消费部分的节省，而是由基金组成的，这些基金本身就是成功的创新的结果，在那里我们以后将能看到企业家的利润。在循环流转中，一方面没有这种可以用来储蓄的丰富的来源，另一方面主要是很少有刺激因素来促使储蓄。它唯一的巨大收入是垄断收益和大地主的地租；然而为灾难和老年作准备，或许也有些不合理的动机，这恐怕是唯一的刺激因素了。参与发展的盈利机会这个最重要的刺激因素，在这里不存在。因此，在这样一个经济系统里，不可能有自由购买力的大蓄水池，为想要实现新组合的人从这里获得——而他自己的储蓄只是满足在特殊情况之用。所有的货币都将流动，都会固定在已经建立起来的确定的轨迹中。

Even though the conventional answer to our question is not obviously absurd, yet there is another method of obtaining money for this purpose, which claims our attention, because it, unlike the one referred to, does not presuppose the existence of accumulated results of previous development, and hence may be considered as the only one which is available in strict logic. This method of obtaining money is the creation of purchasing power by banks. The form it takes is immaterial. The issue of bank-notes not fully covered by specie withdrawn from circulation is an obvious instance, but methods of deposit banking render the same service, where they increase the sum total of possible expenditure. Or we may think of bank acceptances in so far as they serve as money to make payments in wholesale trade. It is always a question, not of transforming purchasing power which already exists in someone's possession, but of the creation of new purchasing power out of nothing – out of nothing even if the credit contract by which the new purchasing power is created is supported by securities which are not themselves circulating media – which is added to the existing circulation. And this is the source from which new combinations are often financed, and from which they would have to be financed *always*, if results of previous development did not actually exist at any moment.

These credit means of payment, that is means of payment which are created for the purpose and by the act of giving credit, serve just as ready money in trade, partly directly, partly because they can be converted immediately into ready money for small payments or payments to the non-banking classes – in particular to wage-earners. With their help, those who carry out new combinations can gain access to the existing stocks of productive means, or, as the case may be, enable those from whom they buy productive services to gain immediate access to the market for consumption goods. There is never, in this nexus, granting of credit in the sense that someone

尽管用传统方式回答我们的问题不存在明显的荒谬之处，但还有另一种为这个目的而获得货币的方法值得我们关注，因为它不像我们已经提到的那种，它不是以先前发展的累积结果的存在为前提条件的，因此它可以被认为是在严格逻辑意义上可以获得的唯一的方法。这个获得货币的方法，是通过银行来创造购买力。它所采用的形式并不重要。发行银行券而不完全依靠从流通中提取的货币来保证就是一个明显的例子，但是在银行存款的方法也提供了同样的服务，它们增加了可支付的货币的总额。或者我们可以考虑银行承兑，因为这种承兑和货币的服务一样，可以作为批发贸易的支付手段。这不是一个转移已经存在于个人手中的购买力的问题，而总是从无到有的这么一个新购买力创造的问题——即使创造新购买力的信用合同由有价证券做保证，这个有价证券本身并不是流通媒介——它也是新添加到这个流通中来的。这也是新组合常常获得资金供给的一处来源，而且新的组合总是从这里获得资金的供给，如果先前发展的结果并不是在任何时候都实际的存在。

这种信用支付方式，也就是出于支付的目的并且通过给予信用这种行为而被创造出来的支付手段，就像贸易中现金所起的作用一样，部分地是直接起着这种作用，部分地是由于它们可以随时转换成现金进行小额支付，或者支付给非银行业阶层——尤其是支付给工薪阶级。借助于信用支付手段，实施新组合的人们可以获得现有的生产工具的存量，或者根据实际情况，使得那些他们从其手中购买生产性劳务的人，可以直接进入市场购买消费品。在这种关系中，从没有这种意义上的信用的给予，即，某些人

must wait for the equivalent of his service in goods, and content himself with a claim, thereby fulfilling a special function; not even in the sense that someone has to accumulate means of maintenance for laborers or land, owners, or produced means of production, all of which would only be paid for out of the final results of production. Economically, it is true, there is an essential difference between these means of payment, if they are created for new ends, and money or other means of payment of the circular flow. The latter may be conceived on the one hand as a kind of certificate for completed production and the increase in the social product effected through it, and on the other hand as a kind of order upon, or claim to, part of this social product. The former have not the first of these two characteristics. They too are orders, for which one can immediately procure consumption goods, but not certificates for previous production. Access to the national dividend is usually to be had only on condition of some productive service previously rendered or of some product previously sold. This condition is, in this case, not yet fulfilled. It will be fulfilled only after the successful completion of the new combinations. Hence this credit will in the meantime affect the price level.

The banker, therefore, is not so much primarily a middleman in the commodity "purchasing power" as a *producer* of this commodity. However, since all reserve funds and savings today usually flow to him, and the total demand for free purchasing power, whether existing or to be created, concentrates on him, he has either replaced private capitalists or become their agent; he has himself become the capitalist par excellence. He stands between those who wish to form new combinations and the possessors of productive means. He is essentially a phenomenon of development, though only when no central authority directs the social process. He makes possible the carrying out of new combinations, authorises people, in the name of society as it were, to form them. He is the ephor of the exchange economy.

必须等待用货物形式表现的他的劳务的等价物，他自己只得到一个请求权，因此完成一个特殊的职能；甚至也没有这种意义上的信用，就是某些人不得不为劳工或地主积累生活资料，或者积累生产出来的生产工具，所有这些都只能从生产的最终结果中得到支付。经济上，这种支付手段（如果它们是因新的目的而创造出来的）与货币或者循环流转中其他的支付手段之间的确存在本质的区别。后者可以被构想为：一方面，是对已经完成的生产以及因生产影响而产生的社会产品的增加的一种证明，另一方面，是对一部分这种社会产品的一种汇单或者索取权。而前者没有这两种特征中的第一个特征。它们也是汇单，人们可以直接用来购买消费品，但不是对以前生产的证明书。要了解国民总收入，通常只能以先前提供过的某种生产性服务为条件，或者以从前出售过的某种商品为条件。在这种情况下，这个条件没有得到满足。只有在新的组合被成功地完成之后，它才得到满足。因此，这种信用将同时影响着价格水平。

因此，银行家与其说主要是商品“购买力”的中介人，倒不如说是这种商品的生产者。然而，由于今天所有的储备基金和储蓄通常都流向他那里，所以，对自由购买力（不论是已经存在的还是需要创造出来的）的所有需求都集中到他那里，他要么已经替代了私人资本家，要么成了私人资本家的代理人；他已经使他自己成为一个典型的资本家。他处于想要实现新组合的人和拥有生产手段的人的中间的地位。本质上他属于一种发展的现象，尽管只有在没有中央权力机构支配社会过程的时候。他使实现新的组合成为可能，他似乎是以社会的名义授权人们去实现新的组合。他主宰着交换经济。

Ⅲ

We now come to the third of the elements with which our analysis works, namely the "new combination of means of production," and credit. Although all three elements form a whole, the third may be described as the fundamental phenomenon of economic development. The carrying out of new combinations we call "enterprise"; the individuals whose function it is to carry them out we call "entrepreneurs." These concepts are at once broader and narrower than the usual. Broader, because in the first place we call entrepreneurs not only those "independent" businessmen in an exchange economy who are usually so designated, but all who actually fulfil the function by which we define the concept, even if they are, as is becoming the rule, "dependent" employees of s company, like managers, members of boards of directors, and so forth, or even if their actual power to perform the entrepreneurial function has any other foundations, such as the control of s majority of shares. As it is the carrying out of new combinations that constitutes the entrepreneur, it is not necessary that he should be permanently connected with an individual firm; many "financiers," "promotors," and so forth are not, and still they may be entrepreneurs in our sense. On the other hand, our concept is narrower than the traditional one in that it does not indude all heads of firms or managers or industrialists who merely may operate an established business, but only those who actually perform that function. Nevertheless I maintain that the above definition does no more than formulate with greater precision what the traditional doctrine really means to convey. In the first place our definition agrees with the usual one on the fundamental point of distinguishing between "entrepreneurs" and "capitalists" – irrespective of whether the latter are regarded as owners of money, claims to money, or material goods. This distinction is common property today

Ⅲ

现在我们讲到了我们的分析所要用到的第三个要素，即“生产工具的新组合”和信用。尽管所有这三个要素形成一个整体，这第三个可以被描述为经济发展的最根本的现象。新组合的实现，我们称为“企业”；某个人的职能是实现这种新组合，我们就称他为“企业家”。这些概念比通常所说的要宽一些，同时又比通常的窄一些。宽泛是因为，首先，我们所称的企业家不仅仅是那些在交换经济中通常所称的“独立的”商人，而且还包括所有在实际上执行我们用来定义这个概念的那种职能的人，尽管他们是（现在已逐渐变成惯例）“依附”公司的雇员，像经理、董事会成员等，或者即使他们行使企业家职能的实际权利有任何其他的基础，例如对大部分股权的控制。因为是实施新的组合才构成一个企业家，因此，他不一定要永久地和某个别厂商有联系；许多“金融家”、“发起人”等就不是和某个别厂商有联系，但他们仍然是我们这里所说的企业家。另一方面，我们的企业家的概念比传统的要狭窄，它并不包括厂商里所有的领导者，或者经理，或者工业家们，他们只是可能经营一个已建立的企业，而这里只包括实际履行这种职能的人们。不过我认为，上面的定义只不过是更准确地表述了传统理论真正想要表达的意思。首先，在区别“企业家”和“资本家”两者的基本观点上，我们的定义与普遍的定义是一致的——不管“资本家”是否被看做是货币的所有者，货币索取权的所有者，还是物质财富的所有者。这个区别在今天是共同的特征，

and has been so for a considerable time. It also settles the question whether the ordinary shareholder as such is an entrepreneur, and disposes of the conception of the entrepreneur as risk bearer. ① Furthermore, the ordinary characterisation of the entrepreneur type by such expressions as "initiative," "authority," or "foresight" points entirely in our direction. For there is little scope for such qualities within the routine of the circular flow, and if this had been sharply separated from the occurrence of changes in this routine itself, the emphasis in the definition of the function of entrepreneurs would have been shifted automatically to the latter. Finally there are definitions which we could simply accept. There is in particular the well known one that goes back to J. B. Say: the entrepreneur's function is to combine the productive factors, to bring them together. Since this is a performance of a special kind only when the factors are combined for the first time – while it is merely routine work if done in the course of running a business – this definition coincides with ours. When Mataja (in Unternehmergewinn) defines the entrepreneur as one who receives profit, we have only to add the conclusion of the first chapter, that there is no profit in the circular flow, in order to trace this formulation

---

① Risk obviously always falls on the owner of the means of production or of the money-capital which was paid for them, hence never on the entrepreneur *as such* (see Chapter IV). A shareholder *may* be an entrepreneur. He may even owe to his holding a controlling interest the power to act as an entrepreneur. Shareholders *Per se*, however, are never entrepreneurs, but merely capitalists, who in consideration of their submitting to certain risks participate in profits, That this is no reason to look upon them as anything but capitalists is shown by the facts, first, that the average shareholder has normally no power to influence the management of his company, and secondly, that participation in profits is frequent in cases in which everyone recognises the presence of a loan contract. Compare, for example, the Graeco-Roman *foenus nauticum*. Surely this interpretation is more true to life than other one, which, following the lead of a faulty legal construction – which can only be explained historically – attributes functions to the average Shareholder which he hardly ever thinks of discharging.

并且在相当长的时间内已经称为共同特征了。其次，它还解决了这样一个问题：普通股东是不是企业家；它也驳倒了把企业家作为风险承担者的这个概念。① 此外，对企业家类型的特征的通常的描述，如“首创精神”、“权威”或者“远见”，与我们的方向是完全一致的。因为在循环流转的常规的事务中，没有这些品质存在的地方，而且如果这一点与常规事务本身变化的出现严格区分开来，那么，在企业家职能的定义中的重点将被自动的转移到循环流转的常规事务中。最后，有一些定义我们可以直接接受。尤其是一个大家都熟知的，可以追溯到 J. B. 萨伊的定义：企业家的职能是组合生产要素，把它们放在一起。因为只有当要素是第一次被组合到一起时，这才是一种特殊的行为——然而，如果是在经营一个企业的过程中去做，那它就只是一项常规的工作了——这个定义与我们的定义是一致的。当马塔雅在《企业家利润》中定义企业家是获得利润的人时，我们只需加上第一章的结论，即在循环流转中没有利润，这是为了避免把这个表述追溯到距我们的表

---

① 显然，风险总是落到生产工具的所有者或者为购买生产手段而支付货币资本的所有者的头上，因此，绝不会落到企业家这种人的身上（参阅第四章）。一个持有股票的人可能是一个企业家，他甚至就是因为掌握控股权，才如同一个企业家那样行动。然而，股票持有者，单凭持有股票，绝不是企业家，而只是资本家，他们考虑到要承担某种风险，所以参与利润的分配。有充足的理由把他们仅仅看做是资本家，这可以由以下事实来说明。第一，普通的股票持有者通常没有权力影响他们的公司的经营管理；第二，在每一个人都承认债务合同存在的情况下，参与利润分配才是常见的事；例如，比较希腊－罗马的海运利益。这种解释肯定比其他的解释更接近真实生活，后者跟随着一个错误的法律结构的领导——这只能由历史去解释——把职能归于普通股票持有者，而他几乎从没有想过去执行这种职能。

too back to ours. ① And this view is not foreign to traditional theory, as is shown by the construction of the *entrepreneur faisant ni bénéfice ni perte*, which has been worked out rigorously by Walras, but is the property of many other authors. The tendency is for the entrepreneur to make neither profit nor loss in the circular flow – that is he has no function of a special kind there, he simply does not exist; but in his stead, there are heads of firms or business managers of a different type which we had better not designate by the same term.

It is a prejudice to believe that the knowledge of the historical origin of an institution or of a type immediately shows us its sociological or economic nature. Such knowledge often leads us to understand it, but it does not directly yield a theory of it. Still more false is the belief that "primitive" forms of a type are also *ipso facto* the "simpler" or the "more original" in the sense that they show their nature more purely and with fewer complications than later ones. Very frequently the opposite is the case, amongst other reasons because increasing specialisation may allow functions and qualities to stand out sharply, which are more difficult to recognise in more primitive condifions when mixed with others. So it is in our case. In the general position of the chief of a primitive horde it is difficult to separate the entrepreneurial element from the others. For the same reason most economists up to the time of the younger Mill failed to keep capitalist and entrepreneur distinct because the manufacturer of a hundred years ago was both; and certainly the course of events since then has facilitated the making of this distinction,

① The definition of the entrepreneur in terms of entrepreneurial profit instead of in terms of the function the performance of which creates the entrepreneurial profit is obviously not brilliant. But we have still another objection to it: we shall see that entrepreneurial profit does not fall to the entrepreneur by "necessity" in the same sense as the marginal product of labor does to the worker.

述太远的地方。[①] 这个观点与传统理论是不违背的，这可以用这句话来表明，“企业家既不获利，也不损失”，它是由瓦尔拉严密推导出来的，但也是许多其他作者的成果。对企业家来说，循环流转中的趋势是既不获利也不损失，也就是说，他在那儿没有特殊的职能，他几乎就是不存在；但是替代他的是，一种不同类型的厂商头目或者企业经理，我们最好不要用企业家这个头衔去称呼他们。

认为一种制度或者一种类型的人，他们的有关历史起源的知识能够直接向我们表明它的社会的和经济的本质，这是一种偏见。这种知识通常引导我们去理解它，但它不能直接产生一个关于它的理论。更严重的错误是这样一种信念，即认为，一种类型的“原始”形式事实上也是“更简单的”或“更原始的”形式，也就是说，原始形式比后来的形式更纯粹的，并且用更少的复杂性来反映它本身的性质。然而，实际情况常常相反，除了其他原因以外，还因为不断增长的专门化可能使职能和性质鲜明地突出来，而这些在更原始的条件下，与其他的职能和性质混在一起，很难辨认。这种情况在我们的例子里也是这样。在一个原始游牧民族首领的一般位置上，是很难把企业家的要素同其他要素区分开来的。由于同样的原因，小穆勒时代以前的大部分经济学家都不能区分资本家和企业家的不同，因为一百年前的制造商既是资本家也是企业家；从那以后，事态的进程肯定促进了两者差异的产生，

① 根据企业家利润，而不是根据创造企业家利润而需行使的职能来定义企业家，显然是不高明的。但是我们还有一个反对它的理由：我们将会看到，企业家利润不像劳动的边际产品必然归于工人那样，它不是“必然”落到企业家的手中。

as the system of land tenure in England has facilitated the distinction between farmer and landowner, while on the Continent this distinction is still occasionally neglected, especially in the case of the peasant who tills his own soil. ① But in our case there are still more of such difficulties. The entrepreneur of earlier times was not only as a rule the capitalist too, he was also often – as he still is to-day in the case of small concerns – his own technical expert, in so far as a professional specialist was not called in for special cases. Likewise he was (and is) often his own buying and selling agent, the head of his office, his own personnel manager, and sometimes, even though as a rule he of course employed solicitors, his own legal adviser in current affairs. And it was performing some or all of these functions that regularly filled his days. The carrying out of new combinations can no more be a *vocation* than the making and execution of strategical decisions, although it is this function and not his routine work that characterises the military leader. Therefore the entrepreneur's essential function must always appear mixed up with other kinds of activity, which as a rule must be much more conspicuous than the essential one. Hence the Marshallian definition of the enterpreneur, which simply treats the entrepreneurial function as "management" in the widest meaning, will naturally appeal to most of us. We do not accept it, simply because it does not bring out what we confider to be the salient point and the only one which specifically distinguishes entrepreneurial from other activities.

Nevertheless there are types – the course of events has evolved them by degrees – which exhibit the entrepreneurial function with particular purity. The "promoter," to be sure, belongs to them only with qualifications. For, neglecting the associations relative to

---

① Only this neglect explains the attitude of many socialistic theorists towards peasant property. For smallness of the individual possession makes a difference only for the petit-bourgeois, not for the socialist. The criterion of the employment of labor other than that of the owner and his family is economically relevant only from the standpoint of a kind of exploitation theory which is hardly tenable any longer.

就像英国的土地占有制促进了农民与地主的区分，然而在欧洲大陆，这种区别仍然偶尔地被忽视，特别是在当一个农民在他自己的土地上耕种的场合下。① 在我们的案例中，仍然有很多这样的困难。早期的企业家，不仅照例也是资本家，他也经常是——就像今天，在小企业里，他仍然是——他自己的技术专家，只要是在特殊的场合下没有邀请职业专家。同样，他过去和现在常常是他自己的买卖代理人，他的办公室的领导，他自己的人事经理，有时，甚至在日常事务中他是自己的法律顾问，尽管通常他肯定也会雇用律师。正是因为承担一些或者全部这样的职责，这通常占用了他的时间。实施新组合作为一种职业，只不过是进行战略决策的制定和执行，虽然正是这一职能，而不是他的常规工作，形成了一个军事领袖的特征。因此，企业家的主要职能必然总是显得与其他各种活动混合在一起，而且其他的各种活动一般必然比主要的职能更显眼。因此，马歇尔关于企业家的定义，只是把企业家的职能当作是从最广义上说的“管理”，这自然使我们中的多数人表示赞同。我们不接受这个定义，只是因为它没有表达出我们所认为的重要点，这是明确区分企业家活动与其他活动的唯一要点。

然而有些类型——事态的进展逐步产生了这些类型——用特别纯粹的方式展现了企业家的职能。“发起人”的确属于这种人，不过需要一些限制条件。因为，我们暂且忽略属于这一类型的人有关

① 只有用这种忽视才能解释很多社会主义理论家对农民财产的态度。因为个人财产是微少的，只有从小资产阶级来看，才是有差异的，而从社会主义者来看是没有差异的。雇佣除土地所有者及其家属以外的人，这种劳动雇佣标准，只有从一种剥削理论的观点来看才是经济上相关的，而这种理论几乎不能在长时间站住脚。

social and moral status which are attached to this type, the promoter is frequently only an agent intervening on commission, who does the work of financial technique in floating the new enterprise. In this case he is not its creator nor the driving power in the process. However, he *may* be the latter also, and then heis something like an "entrepreneur by profession." But the modern type of "captain of industry"① corresponds more closely to what is meant here, especially if one recognises his identity on the one hand with, say, the commercial entrepreneur of twelfth – century Venice – or, among later types, with John Law – and on the other hand with the village potentate who combines with his agriculture and his cattle trade, say, a rural brewery, an hotel, and a store. But whatever the type, everyone is an entrepreneur only when he actually "carries out new combinations," and loses that character as soon as he has built up his business, when he settles down to running it as other people run their businesses. This is the rule, of course, and hence it is just as rare for anyone always to remain an entrepreneur throughout the decades of his active life as it is for a businessman never to have a moment in which he is an entrepreneur, to however modest a degree.

Because being an entrepreneur is not a profession and as a rule not a lasting condition, entrepreneurs do not form a social class in the technical sense, as, for example, landowners or capitalists or workmen do. Of course the entrepreneurial function will *lead* to certain class positions for the successful entrepreneur and his family. It can also put its stamp on an epoch of social history, can form a style of life, or systems of moral and aesthetic values;

① Cf. for example the good description in Wiedenfeld Das Persönliche im modernen Unternehmertum. Although it appeared in Schmoller's Jahrbuch in 1910 this work was not known to me when the first edition of this book was published.

社会和道德地位方面的联系，发起人常常只是接受佣金而参与工作的代理者，他们在融通资金，开办新企业过程中从事财务技术工作。在这种情况下，他既不是新企业的创办者，也不是这个过程的推动力量。然而，他也可能是后者，于是他就有点像一个“职业的企业家”。但是“工业领袖”① 的现代类型与这里所指的更能密切地适应，特别是如果人们在下面两方面看到他的存在。一方面，比如说，有 20 世纪威尼斯的商业企业家，或者在后来的类型中，有约翰·劳；另一方面有乡村的当权者，他把诸如农村酿酒厂、一家旅馆和一个商店与他的农业、他的牲畜贸易结合起来。但是不管是哪一种类型，只有当他实际地“实施新的组合”时，他才是一个企业家；而一旦他建立起自己的企业，也就是当他安定下来，如同其他人经营各自的企业那样，经营这个企业时，他就失去了这个特征。这当然是一条规则，因此，很少有任何人在他几十年的活动生涯中总是一个企业家，就像一个工商业者，说他从没有一个时刻是企业家，这是很少的，不管其程度是多么低。

由于成为一个企业家并不是一种职业，通常也不是一种持久的状况，所以企业家不能形成一种从专门意义上讲的社会阶级，比如说，像地主或资本家或工人这样的阶级。当然，对成功的企业家及其家人来说，企业家的职能将引领他们走向某种阶级地位。这种职能也能够在社会历史的某个时代打上它们的烙印，可以形成一种生活形态，或者形成道德的和美术的价值体制；

① 参阅，例如，威登菲尔德在《现代企业人物》里的出色的描述。尽管它刊登在施穆勒的《年鉴》（1910 年）中，但是在这本书第一版发行之前，我并不知道这篇文章。

but in itself it signifies a class position no more than it presupposes one. And the class position which may be attained is not as such an entrepreneurial position, but is characterised as landowning or capitalist, according to how the proceeds of the enterprise are used. Inheritance of the pecuniary result and of personal qualities may then both keep up this position for more than one generation and make further enterprise easier for descendants, but the function of the entrepreneur itself cannot be inherited, as is shown well enough by the history of manufacturing families. ①

But now the decisive question arises: why then is the carrying out of new combinations a special process and the object of a special kind of "function"? Every individual carries on his economic affairs as well as he can. To be sure, his own intentions are never realised with ideal perfection, but ultimately his behavior is moulded by the influence on him of the results of his conduct, so as to fit circumstances which do not as a rule change suddenly. If a business can never be absolutely perfect in any sense, yet it in time approaches a relative perfection having regard to the surrounding world, the social conditions, the knowledge of the time, and the horizon of each individual or each group. New possibilities are continuously being offered by the surrounding world, in particular new discoveries are continuously being added to the existing store of knowledge. Why should not the individual make just as much use of the new possibilities as of the old, and, according to the market position as he understands it, keep pigs instead of cows, or even choose a new crop rotation, if this can be seen to be more advantageous? And what kind of special new phenomena or problems, not to be found in the established circular flow, can arise there?

① On the nature of the entrepreneurial function also compare my statement in the article "Unternehmer" in the handwörterbuch der Staatswissenschaften.

但它本身并不表示一种阶级地位，也不以一种阶级地位为前提条件。而且它可能获得的阶级地位也不是一种企业家的地位，而是根据企业的收入如何使用，以拥有土地或者资本家为特征的。于是，对金钱财富和个人品质的继承，这两者都可以使不止一代的人保持这种地位，而且使子孙后代更加容易地从事进一步的企业开发，不过企业家的职能本身并不能继承，这一点已经由制造业家族的历史充分地表明了。①

但是现在，一个决定性的问题产生了：那么，为什么新组合的实现是一个特殊的过程，是一种特殊“职能”的目标呢？每一个人都尽其所能地从事他的经济事务。诚然，他自己的意愿从来没有完美地实现，但是最终，他的行为是由他的活动的结果对其影响而塑造成的，以适应通常不会突然变化的环境。尽管从任何意义上说一个企业不可能是绝对的完善，但就周围的世界、社会条件、时代知识，或者个人或一个团队的视野而言，它可能在某个时候接近于一个相对的完善。周围的世界不断地提供着新的可能性，尤其是新发现连续不断地被增加到现有的知识宝库中。为什么个人不能像利用旧的可能性那样尽可能地利用新的可能性呢？为什么他不根据他所理解的市场情况，去养猪而不是养牛，或者如果他认为选择一种新的种类更加有利，就去选择一种新的耕种作物？有哪一种特殊的新的现象或者问题不能在已经建立起来的循环流转中找到，而能在那里产生呢？

---

① 关于企业家职能的本质，还可以比较我在文章《企业家》中的说明，载《社会科学简明辞典》。

While in the accustomed circular flow every individual can act promptly and rationally because he is sure of his ground and is supported by the conduct, as adjusted to this circular flow, of all other individuals, who in turn expect the accustomed activity from him, he cannot simply do this when he is confronted by a new task. While in the accustomed channels his own ability and experience suffice for the normal individual, when confronted with innovations he needs guidance. While he swims with the stream in the circular flow which is familiar to him, he swims against the stream if he wishes to change its channel. What was formerly a help becomes a hindrance. What was a familiar datum becomes an unknown. Where the boundaries of routine stop, many people can go no further, and the rest can only do so in a highly variable manner. The assumption that conduct is prompt and rational is in all cases a fiction. But it proves to be sufficiently near to reality, if things have time to hammer logic into men. Where this has happened, and within the limits in which it has happened, one may rest content with this fiction and build theories upon it. It is then not true that habit or custom or noneconomic ways of thinking cause a hopeless difference between the individuals of different classes, times, or cultures, and that, for example, the "economics of the stock exchange" would be inapplicable say to the peasants of to-day or to the craftsmen of the Middle Ages. On the contrary the same theoretical picture[①] in its broadest contour lines fits the individuals of quite different cultures, whatever their degree of intelligence and of economic rationality, and we can depend upon it that the peasant sells his calf just

① The same *theoretical* picture, obviously not the same sociological, cultural, and so forth.

虽然每个人在习惯了的循环流转中能够迅速地而且合理地采取行动，因为他对他的行为根据有把握，而且被所有其他人的适应这一循环流转的行为所支持，这些人反过来也期望他采取符合习惯的行为，然而，一旦他面临一项新的任务，他就不能仅仅这样做了。虽然在习惯了的方法中，他自己的能力和经验对正常的人来说是足够的，但是当他面临创新时，他就需要指导。尽管他在自己所熟悉的循环流转中是顺着流向游，但是如果他想改变这种循环流转的途径，他就是逆着流向游泳。从前作为帮助的力量现在变成了阻力，过去熟知的资料现在变成未知的了。到达了例行事务的边界，许多人就不能再前进一步了，而其余的人只能采取一种高度变化的方式行动。认为行为是及时的和合理的，这种假设在所有的情况下都是一种虚构。但是如果有足够的时间迫使人们去理解客观事物的逻辑的话，这种假设可以变得足够地接近现实。在这种事情发生的地方，以及在它发生的限度内，人们可以承认这种虚构，并在此基础上建立理论。于是那种认为习惯或者惯例或者非经济的思维方式会在不同阶级，不同时代，或者不同文化的个人之间产生一种不可设想的差异，以及认为例如“股票交易经济学”对今天的农民或者中世纪的手工匠来说都是不适用的，等等，这些就都不是真实的了。相反，相同的理论的图景①在其最广阔的轮廓上与属于完全不同文化的人是相适合的，而不管他们的智慧和经济理性的程度如何；我们可以有把握地说，农民卖出他的小牛时也是一样的精明，并且考虑他自己的利益，

① 相同的理论的图景，显然不是相同的社会学的、文化的那样的图景。

as cunningly and egotistically as the stock exchange member his portfolio of shares. But this holds good only where precedents without number have formed conduct through decades and, in fundamentals, through hundreds and thousands of years, and have eliminated unadapted behavior. Outside of these limits our fiction loses its closeness to reality. ① To cling to it there also, the traditional theory does, is to hide an essential thing and to ignore a fact which, in contrast with other deviations of our assumptions from reality, is theoretically important and the source of the explanation of phenomena which would not exist without it.

Therefore, in describing the circular flow one must treat combinations of means of production (the production-functions) as data, like natural possibilities, and admit only small② variations at the margins, such as every individual can accomplish by adapting himself to changes in his economic environment, without materially deviating from familiar lines. Therefore, too, the carrying out of new combinations is a special function, and the privilege of a type of people who are much less numerous than all those who have the "objective" possibility of doing it. Therefore,

---

① How much this is the case is best seen to-day in the economic life of those nations, and within our civilisation in the economics of those individuals, whom the development of the last century has not yet completely drawn into its stream, for example, in the economy of the Central European peasant. This peasant "calcu - lates"; there is no deficiency of the "economic way of thinking" (Wirtschaftsge sinnung) in him. Yet he cannot take a step out of the beaten path; his economy has not changed at all for centuries, except perhaps through the exercise of external force trod influence. Why? Because the choice of new methods is not simply an element in the concept of rational economic action, nor a matter of course, but a distinct process which stands in need of special explanation.

② Small disturbances which may indeed, as mentioned earlier, in time add up to great amounts. The decisive point is that the businessman, if he makes them, never alters his routine. The usual case is one of small, the exception one of great (*uno actu greet*), disturbances. Only in this sense is emphasis put upon "smallness" here. The objection that there can be no difference in principle between small and large disturbances is not effective. For it is false in itself, in so far as it is based upon the disregard of the principle of the infinitesimal method, the essence of which lies in the fact that one can assert of "small quantities" under certain circumstances what one cannot assert of "large quantifies." But the reader who takes umbrage at the large-small contrast may, if he wishes, substitute for it the contrast adapting-spontaneous. Personally I am not willing to do this because the latter method of expression is much easier to misunderstand than the former and really would demand still longer explanations.

这与股票交易所的经纪人出售他的股票时所考虑的自己的利益完全一样。但是这一看法，只有在无数的先例经过几十年，或者根本上经过千百年，排除了不适合的行为，从而形成了这样的行动，这时才是真实的。在这个范围之外，我们的虚构就失去了它接近现实的可能性。[①] 像传统的理论那样，在那儿还紧紧地抓住它不放，就是掩盖一种实质性的东西而忽视了一个事实，即，比起我们的假设与现实之间的其他分歧，这个事实却不同，它在理论上是很重要的，而且它是对一些现象作出解释的源泉，这些现象没有它就不可能存在。

因此，在描述循环流动时，人们必须把生产工具的组合（生产函数）当做已有的资料，就像自然的可能性那样，只允许在边际上作很小的[②]变动，就像每一个人都能通过调整自己以适应所处的经济环境的变化所做的，而不需要很大的偏离熟悉的路径。因此，新组合的实现也是一个特殊的职能，它是一类人的特权，这类人在数量上比所有具有实现新组合的“客观”可能性的人要少得多。所以，最后我们认为

① 这种情况究竟有多大的可能性，今天可以从这些国家的经济生活中看得更清楚，在我们的文化范围之内则可以从这些个人的经济学中看，那就是，上个世纪的发展还没有把这些国家或者个人完全纳入它的洪流中，例如在中欧农民的经济生活中。这些农民也在“计算着”；他们并不缺乏“经济的思维方式”，但是他不能跨越常规一步；多少世纪以来，他们的经济从来没有变化过，除了可能通过外部的力量和影响的推动。为什么呢？因为新方法的选择不仅仅是理性经济行为这一概念中的一个要素，也不是理所当然的事情，而是一个独特的过程，它需要特殊的解释。

② 像早先提到的那样，很小的干扰确实可能及时地加总起来变成很大的数额。关键在于，如果是商人自己制造了这些干扰，就绝不会改变他的例行做法。通常是小干扰，大干扰是例外情况。只有在这个意义上，这里才强调“小”。反对意见认为，小干扰和大干扰之间原则上是没有什么差别的，这是没有说服力的。因为它本身就是错误的，它以忽视无限小方法的原理为基础，这一原理的实质在于，在某种情况下，人们对于不能断定是“大量”的东西，可以判断为“小量”。但是，对于大和小的矛盾感到不耐烦的读者，如果他愿意，可以用适应和自发的比较来代替它。我个人并不希望这样做，因为后者的表达方法比前者更容易产生误解，实际上需要做更长的解释。

finally, entrepreneurs axe a special type,① and their behavior a special

① In the first place it is a question of a type of *conduct* and of a type of *person* in so far as this conduct is accessible in very unequal measure and to relatively few people, so that it constitutes their outstanding characteristic. Because the exposition of the first edition was reproached with exaggerating and mistaking the peculiarity of this conduct, and with overlooking the fact that it is more or less open to every businessman, and because the exposition in a later paper ("Wellenbewegung des Wirtschaftslebens," Archly für Sozialwissenschaft) was charged with introducing an intermediate type ("half-static" businessmen), the following may be submitted. The conduct in question is peculiar in two ways. First, because it is directed towards something different and signifies doing something different from other conduct. One may indeed in this connection include it with the latter in a higher unity, but this does not alter the fact that a theoretically relevant difference exists between the two, and that only one of them is adequately described by traditional theory. Secondly, the type of conduct in question not only differs from the other in its object, "innovation" being peculiar to it, but also in that it presupposes aptitudes differing *in kind* and not only in degree from those of mere rational economic behavior.

Now these aptitudes are presumably distributed in an ethically homogeneous population just like others, that is the curve of their distribution has a maximum ordinate, deviations on either side of which become rarer the greater they are. Similarly we can assume that every healthy man can sing if he will. Perhaps half the individuals in an ethically homogeneous group have the capacity for it to an average degree, a quarter in progressively diminishing measure, and, let us say, a quarter in a measure above the average; and within this quarter, through a series of continually increasing singing ability and continually diminishing number of people who possess it, we come finally to the Carusos. Only in this quarter are we struck in general by the singing ability, and only in the supreme instances can it become the characterising mark of the person. Although practically all men can sing, singing ability does not cease to be a distinguishable characteristic and attribute of a minority, indeed not exactly of a type, because this characteristic – unlike ours – affects the total personality relatively little.

Let us apply this: Again, a quarter of the population may be so poor in those qualities, let us say here provisionally, of economic initiative that the deficiency makes itself felt by poverty of their moral personality, and they play a wretched part in the smallest affairs of private and professional life in which this element is called for. We recognise this type and know that many of the best clerks, distinguished by devotion to duty, expert knowledge, and exactitude, belong to it. Then comes the "half," the "normal." These prove themselves to be better in the things which even within the established channels cannot simply be "dispatched" (erledigen) but must also be "decided" (entscheiden) and "carried out" (durchsetzen). Practically all business people belong here, otherwise they would never have attained their positions; most represent a selection – individually or hereditarily tested. A textile manufacturer travels no "new" road when he goes to a wool auction. But the situations there are never the same, and the success of the business depends so much upon skill and initiative in buying wool that the fact that the textile industry has so far exhibited no trustification comparable with that in heavy manufacturing is undoubtedly partly explicable by the reluctance of the cleverer manufacturers to renounce the advantage of their own skill in buying wool From there, rising in the scale we come finally into the highest quarter, to people who are a type characterized by super-normal qualities of intellect and will. Within this type there are not only many varieties (merchants, manufacturers, financiers, etc.) but also a continuous variety of degrees of intensity in "initiative." In our argument types of every intensity occur. Many a one can steer a safe course, where no one has yet been; others follow where first another went before; still others only in the crowd, but in this among the first. So also the great political leader of every kind and time is a type, yet not a thing unique, but only the apex of a pyramid from which there is a continuous variation down to the average and from it to the sub-normal values. And yet not only is "leading" a special function, but the leader also something special, distinguishable – wherefore there is no sense in our case in asking: "Where does that type begin then?" and then to exclaim: "This is no type at all!"

企业家是一种特殊的类型,[①] 他们的行为是一个特殊的问题,是大

---

① 首先,它是一个行为的类型和人的类型的问题,由于这种行为只在非常不平等的程度上以及对相对较少的人才是可能的,因此这些行为构成了这些人的突出的特征。由于第一版的说明被谴责为扩大和误解了这种行为的独特性,并且被认为忽视了这样一个事实,即每一个商人都或多或少可以这样做;还因为后来的一篇文章"经济生活的波浪式运动"(载《社会科学档案》)中的说明被指责引用了一种中间类型("半静态的"商人),所以我们提出下面的陈述。这里所说的行为在两个方面有其特殊性。第一,因为它与其他行为不同,它指向某种不同的东西,并且表明做某种不同的事情。在这一点上,人们确实可以把它与后者都包括在一个更高的统一体中,但是,这并不能改变这样一个事实:在这两者之间存在一个理论上相对的差异,而且两者中只有一个被传统的理论充分地描述。第二,这里所说的这类行为不仅在目标上与其他行为不同,它以"创新"作为独特的目的,而且它们的先决条件也不同,它以不同于仅仅理性的经济行为的才能为先决条件,这两种才能不仅在程度上不同,而且在种类上也不同。

现在,这些才能就像其他才能一样被假定为分配在伦理上同质的人群中,也就是说,它的分配曲线有一个最大的纵坐标,两边的情况变得更稀少,偏离也越大。同样我们可以假定,每一个健康的人,如果他愿意,他都可以唱歌。在一个伦理上同质的团体中,可能有一半的人的唱歌能力能够达到平均水平,四分之一的人的能力逐渐降低,同时我们假定,另四分之一人的能力超过平均水平;在这后面的四分之一里,通过一系列连续不断地增加唱歌能力,同时随之减少拥有这样能力的人的数量,最后我们才遇到恩里科·卡鲁索这样的人。通常我们只有被这四分之一中的人的唱歌能力吸引,而且只有在这种极端的情况下,这种才能才成为个人的特征。尽管实际上所有的人都能唱歌,歌唱能力仍然是少数人的显著特色和天赋,但确切地说它不构成一个类型,因为这个特点——不像我们的——对总的个人特性的影响相对来说很小。

我们现在来用这一点。同样,我们在这里假定,四分之一的人对于经济首创精神这种品质如此缺乏,以至于通过这些人的道德人格的缺乏,使人们感觉到了这种首创精神的匮乏;在需要这种精神的私人生活和职业生活的极小的事务中,他们只起很可怜的作用。我们看到了这类人,知道有许多优秀的职员,因为忠于职守,有专业知识,一丝不苟而区别于他人,他们就属于这一类。然后就有那"一半人","正常的人"。这些人证明自己做这些事情做得更好,而这些事情即使在已经建立起来的途径中也不能仅仅"派遣"出去,而是必须被"决定"和"执行"。实际上所有的商人都属于这一类,否则他们也绝不会达到他们的地位;大多数人代表着一种选择——在个人或遗传方面经过了检验。当一个纺织业制造商走向羊毛拍卖场时,他并不是走上"新"路。但是那里的情况绝不相同,商业的成功在很大程度上依赖于购买羊毛的技巧和主动性,所以与重工业相比,纺织工业至今没有呈现那种托拉斯化,这一点毫无疑问可以部分地用以下现象说明,即,比较聪明的制造商不愿意放弃他们在购买羊毛时所拥有的技巧方面的有利条件。从那里,级别在逐渐上升,我们最后到达了最高的那四分之一人中间,这四分之一的一类人有着超乎正常的才智和意志的品质。在这一类型人当中,不仅有许多各种职业的人(商人、制造家、金融家等),而且他们在"首创精神"方面,强烈程度不一也存在连续的变化。在我们的论证中,每一种强度的类型都会出现。很多人能够在不曾被人走过的地方开辟出一条安全的航道;也有其他一些人沿着别人以前走过的路前进;还有一些人只是跟随大流前进,不过他们是在大流的前锋。所以,每一种类和每一时代的伟大的政治领袖也属于一种类型,但他们不是独一无二的,而只是金字塔的顶部,从这里往下走,就会有连续不断的差异,一直降到平均数,从平均数又降到正常以下的数值。然而,不仅"领导"是一种特殊的职能,领导者也有他的特殊性,从而区别于其他的人——因此,在我们的例子中就没有理由问:"那种类型是从哪里开始的?"然后解释道:"这根本不是一种类型!"

problem, the motive power of a great number of significant phenomena. Hence, our position may be characterised by three corresponding pairs of opposites. First, by the opposition of two real processes: the circular flow or the tendency towards equilibrium on the one hand, a change in the channels of economic routine or a spontaneous change in the economic data arising from within the system on the other. Secondly, by the opposition of two theoretical *apparatuses*: statics and dynamics. ① Thirdly, by the opposition of two types of conduct, which, following reality, we can picture as two types of individuals: mere managers and entrepreneurs. And therefore the "best method" of producing in the theoretical sense is to be conceived as "the most advantageous among the methods which have been empirically tested and become familiar."

---

① It has been objected against the first edition that it sometimes defines "statics" as a theoretical construction, sometimes as the picture of an actual state of economic life. I believe that the present exposition gives no ground for this opinion. "Static" theory does not assume a stationary economy; it also treats of the effects of changes in data. In itself, therefore, there is no necessary contortion between static theory and stationary reality. Only in so far as one can exhibit the fundamental form of the economic course of events with the maximum simplicity in an unchanging economy does this assumption recommend itself to theory. The stationary economy is for uncounted thousands of years, and also in historical times in many places for centuries, an incontrovertible fact, apart from the fact, moreover, which Sombart emphasised, that there is a tendency towards a stationary state in every period of depression. Hence it is readily understood how this historical fact and that constriction have allied themselves in a way which led to some confusion. The words "statics" and "dynamo" the author would not now use in the meaning they carry above, where they are simply short expressions for "theory of the circular flow" and "theory of development." One more thing: theory employs two methods of interpretation, which may perhaps make difficulties. If it is to be shown how all the elements of the economic system are determined in equilibrium by one another, this equilibrium system is considered as not yet existing and is built up before our eyes *abovo*. This does not mean that its coming into being is genetically explained thereby. Only its existence and functioning are made logically clear by mental dissection, And the experiences and habits of individuals are assumed as existing. How just these productive combinations have come about is not thereby explained. Further, if two contiguous equilibrium positions are to be investigated, then sometimes (not always), as in Pigou's Economics of Welfare, the "best" productive combination in the first is compared with the "best" in the second. And this again need not, but may, mean that the two combinations in the sense meant here differ not only by small variations in quantity but in their whole technical and commercial structure. Here too the coming into being of the second combination and the problems connected with it are not investigated, but only the functioning and the outcome of the already existing combination. Even though justified as far as it goes, this method of treatment passes over our problem. If the assertion were implied that this is also settled by it, it would be false.

量重要现象的推动力。因此，可以用三对相应的矛盾来描述我们的立场。第一，用两个真实过程的对立：一方面是循环流转或者走向均衡的趋势，另一方面是经济例行事务途径的变化，或者产生于经济系统内部的经济数据的自发变化。第二，用两个理论工具的对立：静态的和动态的。[①] 第三，用两类行为的对立，根据现实，我们可以刻画出两类人物：单纯的经理和企业家。因此，在理论意义上，生产的“最好方法”被认为是“通过经验验证并且已经成为人们熟悉的各种方法中的最有利的方法”。

---

① 有人对本书第一版提出反对意见，说它有时把“静态”定义为一种理论结构，有时把它说成是经济生活现实状况的图画。我相信，现在所做的说明不会给这种意见提供根据。“静态”理论并不假设有一种静止的经济；它也考虑数据变化的影响。因此，它本身认为：静态理论和静止的现实之间没有必然的联系。只有当人们能够在一个不变的经济中用最简单的方式呈现事物的经济过程的本质形式时，这个假设才能上升为理论。无可计数的千百年来，在历史的各个时代，很多地方的多少世纪中，静止的经济是一个无可争辩的事实；此外还有这样一个事实，即桑巴特所强调的，在每一个萧条时期都有一种走向静止状态的趋势。因此我们就很容易理解，这个历史事实与那个理论的结构是怎样发生联系而产生了某种混淆。现在作者不用“静态”和“动态”两词在上面所表达的含义了，在上面它们只不过是对“循环流转理论”和“发展理论”的简括。还有一点：在理论中使用两种方法来解释，这可能产生困难。如果要表明经济系统里所有要素在均衡中是如何相互决定的，那么这个均衡体系就被看做尚不存在，它将在我们眼前重新建立。但这并不意味着，它的形成就自然地解释了它产生的根源。这仅仅是通过思想上的解剖，使它的存在和发生作用在逻辑上变得清楚。个人的经验和习惯被假定为是已经存在的。然而，为什么只是这些生产性的组合产生了，却没有因此得到解释。进一步说，如果要研究两个相接近的均衡位置，那么有时候（并不总是这样），就像庇古在《福利经济学》中，把第一位的“最好”的生产组合与第二位的“最好”生产组合相比较。而这又不一定，但可能，意味着这里所说的两种组合，不仅在数量上有细微的差异，而且在它们的整个技术和商业结构上也有差异。在这里也没有对第二种组合的产生及其相关的问题进行研究，而只是对已经存在的组合的运行和结果进行了研究。即使这种做法是合理的，但是这种处理方式忽略了我们的问题。如果这个论断也说它包含了这个问题的解决，这是不对的。

But it is not the "best" of the methods "possible" at the time. If one does not make this distinction, the concept becomes meaningless and precisely those problems remain unsolved which our interpretation is meant to provide for.

Let us now formulate precisely the characteristic feature of the conduct and type under discussion. The smallest daily action embodies a huge mental effort. Every schoolboy would have to be a mental giant, if he himself had to create all he knows and uses by his own individual activity. And every man would have to be a giant of wisdom and will, if he had in every case to create anew all the rules by which he guides his everyday conduct. This is hue not only of those decisions and actions of individual and social life the principles of which are the product of tens of thousands of years, but also of those products of shorter periods and of a more special nature which constitute the particular instrument for performing vocational tasks. But precisely the things the performance of which according to this should involve a supreme effort, in general demand no special individual effort at all; those which should be especially difficult are in reality especially easy; what should demand superhuman capacity is accessible to the least gifted, given mental health. In particular within the ordinary routine there is no need for leadership. Of course it is still necessary to set people their tasks, to keep up discipline, and so forth; but this is easy and a function any normal person can learn to fulfil. Within the lines familiar to all, even the function of directing other people, though still necessary, is mere "work" like any other, comparable to the service of tending a machine. All people get to know, and are able to do, their daily tasks in the customary way and ordinarily perform them by themselves; the "director" has his routine as they have theirs;

但它并不是在当时“可能的”方法中的“最好的”方法。如果人们不做这种区分，那么这个概念就没有什么意义了，而我们的解释就是想为这些没有解决的问题做一点贡献。

现在，让我们精确地对所讨论的关于行为和类型的特征进行陈述。日常中哪怕是最小的行为，也体现着一种巨大的精神上的努力。如果每一个小学生必须通过他个人的努力去创造他所知道的东西，以及他所使用的东西，那他必须是一个思想智慧上的巨人。同样，如果每一个人在任何一种情况下都必须重新创造指导他日常行为的所有规则，那他就必须是一个智慧和意志的巨人。这一点是真实的，不仅对于个人和社会生活的那些决策和行为来说——这些决策和行为是以历经成千上万年的原则为依据的，而且对于较短时期的和具有更特殊性质的产品来说也是真实的，这些产品构成了从事职业化任务的特殊工具。而正是这些事情，根据这一点，它们的完成应该包含着最大的努力，可是通常它根本不需要个人做特殊的努力；那些看起来应该是特别困难的事情，实际上是相当容易做的；那些应当是需要有超人的能力才能做的事情，而被最没有才能的人做到了，只要他心理健康。特别的，在日常例行事务中不需要有领导。当然，还必须要给人们安排任务，保持纪律，等等；但这是很容易做的，任何一个正常的人都可以学会执行这个职能。在人们所熟悉的范围内，甚至是指挥别人的职能——尽管仍然是必要的——也不过是像其他人的工作一样的“工作”，可以和看管机器的工作相类比。所有的人都以习惯的方式去获悉他们日常的事务，从而能够去做，通常他们也是由自己去完成任务；“领导者”也像其他人一样有着自己的例行工作；

and his directivefunction serves merely to correct individual aberrations.

This is so because all knowledge and habit once acquired becomes as firmly rooted in ourselves as a railway embankment in the earth. It does not require to be continually renewed and consciously reproduced, but sinks into the strata of subconsciousness. It is normally transmitted almost without friction by inheritance, teaching, upbringing, pressure of environment. Everything we think, feel, or do often enough becomes automatic and our conscious life is unburdened of it. The enormous economy of force, in the race and the individual, here involved is not great enough, however, to make daily life a light burden and to prevent its demands from exhausting the average energy all the same. But it is great enough to make it possible to meet the ordinary claims. This holds good likewise for economic daily life. And from this it follows also for economic life that every step outside the boundary of routine has difficulties and involves a new element. It is this element that constitutes the phenomenon of leadership.

The nature of these difficulties may be focussed in the following three points. First, outside these accustomed channels the individual is without those data for his decisions and those rules of conduct which are usually very accurately known to him within them. Of course he must still foresee and estimate on the basis of his experience. But many things must remain uncertain, still others are only ascertainable within wide limits, some can perhaps only be "guessed." In particular this is true of those data which the individual strives to alter and of those which he wants to create. Now he must really to some extent do what tradition does for him in everyday life, viz. consciously plan his conduct in every particular. There will be much more conscious rationality in this than in customary action, which as such does not need to be reflected upon at all; but this plan must necessarily

而他的领导职能只是纠正那些个别偏离正常轨道的行为。

这是因为，所有的知识和习惯一旦被获得，就像一条铁路的路堤植根于地面上一样，它们也紧紧地深藏在我们心中。它不需要被连续不断地更新和有意识地再建，而是深藏于潜意识的底层。通常它几乎毫无阻力地通过遗传、教育、培养、环境的压力被传递下去。我们所想的、所感觉的、所做的每一件事情，经常完全是自动产生的，而我们的有意识的生活并不觉得它们是负担。然而，这里所涉及的在种族和个人中的大量的力量的节省，并不是足够大以至于使日常生活成为很轻的负担，并足以阻止它继续需要消耗同样的平均能力。但是它已经足够大能满足普通的要求。这同样对日常的经济生活也是适用的。从这一点，就经济生活来说，也可以得出：例行事务边界以外的每一步都是有困难的，它包含着新的要素。正是这个要素构成了领导这一现象。

可以从以下三点来集中说明这些困难的性质。第一，在这些已经习惯的途径之外，个人没有那些用来做决策的资料和采取行动的规则，而这些资料和规则在习惯的途径以内通常是为他们非常准确地知道的。当然，他仍然必须以他的经验为基础来预测和估计。但是，很多事情必然是不确定的，还有一些事情只是在大的范围之内才是可以确定的，更有一些事情只能“猜测”。尤其是那些个人力图改变的数据，以及他想创造的数据，都是这样。现在，在日常生活中，他必须在某种程度上真正地做那些传统为他所做的事，也就是在每一个细节上有意识地计划他的行为。这样做比在习惯的行为中将会有更多的有意识的合理性，习惯的行为根本不需要反映这种有意识的合理性；但是这个计划必然不仅在

be open not only to errors greater in degree, but also to other kinds of errors than those occurring in customary action. What has been done already has the sharp-edged reality of all the things which we have seen and experienced; the new is only the figment of our imagination. Carrying out a new plan and acting according to a customary one are things as different as making a road and walking along it.

How different a thing this is becomes dearer if one bears in mind the impossibility of surveying exhaustively all the effects and counter-effects of the projected enterprise. Even as many of them as could in theory be ascertained if one had unlimited time and means must practically remain in the dark. As military action must be taken in a given strategic position even if all the data potentially procurable are not available, so also in economic life action must be taken without working out all the details of what is to be done. Here the success of everything depends upon intuition, the capacity of seeing things in a way which afterwards proves to be true, even though it cannot be established at the moment, and of grasping the essential fact, discarding the unessential, even though one can give no account of the principles by which this is done. Thorough preparatory work, and special knowledge, breadth of intellectual understanding, talent for logical analysis, may under certain circumstances be sources of failure. The more accurately, however, we learn to know the natural and social world, the more perfect our control of facts becomes; and the greater the extent, with time and progressive rationalisation, within which things can be simply calculated, and indeed quickly and reliably calculated, the more the significance of this function decreases. Therefore the importance of the entrepreneur type must diminish just as the importance of the military commander has already diminished. Nevertheless a part of the very essence of each type is bound up with this function.

程度上容易犯更大的错误，而且容易犯其他的错误，这些错误是习惯行为中不会出现的。凡是已经做过的事情，都有着与所有我们曾经看到过和经历过的事情一样的鲜明的现实性；新的事情只是我们想象中虚构的。执行一个新的计划，和根据一个习惯的计划去行动，这两件事情的不同就像建造一条公路和沿着公路行走这两种行为的不同一样。

如果人们能铭记这一点：彻底地去调查计划中的企业的所有影响和反影响是不可能的，那么就会更加清楚这是一件多么不同的事情。即使如果人们有无限多的时间和资料，那些影响和反影响在理论上可以被确定，它们在实际中必然也还是处于未知的状态。就像采取军事行动，即使所有潜在的可获得的数据并没有获得，也必须从一定的战略位置上考虑一样，在经济生活中，即使没有制定出将要做的事的所有细节，也必须采取行动。在这里，每一件事情的成功都依靠直觉，依靠用某种方式预测事情的能力，这种方式即使在当时不能肯定，但在事后却被证明是正确的，同时还依靠能抓住事实的本质，摒弃非实质性的事实的能力，尽管他不能说明这样做的根据。充分的准备工作，以及专业知识、思想理解的广度、逻辑分析的能力，在某种情况下可能成为失败的根源。然而，我们越是学着准确地理解自然的和社会的世界，我们就越能完全地掌控事实；对事物进行计算，而且确实是迅速的和可信的计算的范围（时间和逐渐增加的合理性）越大，那么这个职能的重要性就越是下降。所以，企业家一类的人的重要性必然会降低，就像军事指挥者的重要性已经下降了一样。不过，每一种类型的人的最本质的那部分是和这个职能联系在一起的。

As this first point lies in the task, so the second lies in the psyche of the businessman himself. It is not only objectively more difficult to do something new than what is familiar and tested by experience, but the individual feels reluctance to it and would do so even if the objective difficulties did not exist. This is so in all fields. The history of science is one great confirmation of the fact that we find it exceedingly difficult to adopt a new scientific point of view or method. Thought turns again and again into the accustomed track even if it has become unsuitable and the more suitable innovation in itself presents no particular difficulties. The very nature of fixed habits of thinking, their energy-saving function, is founded upon the fact that they have become subconscious, that they yield their results automatically and are proof against criticism and even against contradiction by individual facts. But precisely because of this they become dragchains when they have outlived their usefulness. So it is also in the economic world. In the breast of one who wishes to do something new, the forces of habit rise up and bear witness against the embryonic project. A new and another kind of effort of will is therefore necessary in order to wrest, amidst the work and care of the daily round, scope and time for conceiving and working out the new combination and to bring oneself to look upon it as a real possibility and not merely as a day-dream. This mental freedom presupposes a great surplus force over the everyday demand and is something peculiar and by nature rare.

The third point consists in the reaction of the social environment against one who wishes to do something new. This reaction may manifest itself first of all in the existence of legal or political impediments. But neglecting this, any deviating conduct by a member of a social group is condemned, though in greatly varying degrees according as the social group is used to such conduct or not. Even a deviation from social custom in such things as dress

上面说的第一点属于任务方面，而这第二点属于工商业者本身的精神方面。做一件新的事情，不仅在客观上比做熟悉的事和已经由经验验证的事更困难，而且个人也会感到不愿意接受它，即使客观上的困难不存在，他也不愿意做。在所有的领域都是这样。科学史为下面一个事实提供了强大的证明，那就是，我们发现接受一个新的科学观点或方法是极其困难的。即使习惯的轨道已经变得不适合了，更适合的创新本身也没有呈现什么特殊的困难，但思想还是反反复复回到习惯的轨道。固定的思维习惯的性质，以及这些习惯节省精力的作用，是以下面的事实为基础而建立的，即，这些习惯已经成为下意识的，它们自动地产生结果，它们不怕受到批评，甚至不怕与个别事实发生矛盾。但是正是因为这一点，当它们已经丧失了它们的用处时，就会变成一种障碍。在经济世界也是如此。在想要做某种新事情的人的心中，习惯的力量上升，并且反对处于萌芽状态的规划。因此，有必要有一种新的和另一种意志上的努力，以便在日常领域、范围、时间内的工作和牵挂中，去为构思和制定新的组合而拼搏，并使自己相信它是真正可能的东西，而不只是白日梦。这种精神上的自由是以超出每天需求的巨大剩余力量为前提条件的，它是一种特殊的并且在性质上稀有的东西。

第三点在于社会对一个想要做一些新的事情的人的反应，或者叫反作用。这个反作用可能首先通过法律上或政治上的障碍来表现自己。但是，暂不考虑这一点，一个社会团体的成员的任何偏离常规的行为都会受到谴责，尽管在程度上有很大不同，这要根据社会团体是否习惯于这种行为。即使像在穿着或者礼貌

or manners arouses opposition, and of course all the more so in the graver cases. This opposition is stronger in primitive stages of culture than in others, but it is never absent. Even mere astonishment at the deviation, even merely noticing it, exercises a pressure on the individual. The manifestation of condemnation may at once bring noticeable consequences in its train. It may even come to social ostracism and finally to physical prevention or to direct attack. Neither the fact that progressive differentiation weakens this opposition – especially as the most important cause of the weakening is the very development which we wish to explain – nor the further fact that the social opposition operates under certain circumstances and upon many individuals as a stimulus, changes anything in principle in the significance of it. Surmounting this opposition is always a special kind of task which does not exist in the customary course of life, a task which also requires a special kind of conduct. In matters economic this resistance manifests itself first of all in the groups threatened by the innovation, then in the difficulty in finding the necessary cooperation, finally in the difficulty in winning over consumers. Even though these elements are still effective to-day, despite the fact that a period of turbulent development has accustomed us to the appearance and the carrying out of innovations, they can be best studied in the beginnings of capitalism. But they are so obvious there that it would be time lost for our purposes to dwell upon them.

There is leadership *only* for these reasons – leadership, that is, as a special kind of function and in contrast to a mere difference in rank, which would exist in every social body, in the smallest as in the largest, and in combination with which it generally appears. The facts alluded to create a boundary beyond which the majority of people do not function promptly by themselves and require help from a minority. If social life had in all respects the relative immutability of, for example, the astronomical world,

这些事情上，与社会习惯相偏离的行为也会激起反对，更不用说，在更严重的事情上肯定会受到反对。在文化的最初始阶段，这种反对比在其他阶段更强烈，但它从没有消失过。甚至只是对偏离的行为感到惊讶，或者仅仅注意到这种行为，也会对个人施加一种压力，表明了谴责就可能立即带来引人注目的后果。它甚至可能带来社会的排斥，最终导致身心障碍和直接攻击。不论是逐渐的分化削弱了这种反对这一事实——尤其是由于这种削弱的最重要的原因正是我们想要解释的发展，还是社会的反对是在一定的环境下发生，同时像一种刺激因素影响着许多个别人这一事实，都不能在原则上对反对的意义有任何改变。克服这种反对意见总是一种特殊的任务，它不存在于常规的生活进程中，它也是一种需要有特殊行为的任务。在经济事务中，这种抵制首先在受到创新威胁的团队中表现出来，然后表现为难于找到必要的合作者，最后表现为难于赢得消费者。虽然一个突飞猛进的发展时期已经使我们习惯于创新的出现和实施，这些反对要素在今天仍然起着作用，但是我们最好还是将这些要素放在资本主义初期研究。但是它们在那儿是如此明显，以至于如果我们去描述它们，就我们的目的来说就是浪费时间。

只是因为这些原因才产生领导——领导是一种特殊的职能，与仅仅是等级上的差别不同，它存在于每一个社会主体中，不论是最小的还是最大的，它的出现通常是和社会主体联系在一起的。上面提到的事实创造了一种界限，超过了这个界限，大多数人本身就不能迅速地发挥作用，而需要从少数人那里得到帮助。如果社会生活在所有方面都有某种相对的不变性，比如像天文世

or if mutable this mutability were yet incapable of being influenced by human action, or finally if capable of being so influenced this type of action were yet equally open to everyone, then there would be no special function of leadership as distinguished from routine work.

The specific problem of leadership arises and the leader type appears only where new possibilities present themselves. That is why it is so strongly marked among the Normans at the time of their conquests and so feebly among the Slavs in the centuries of their unchanging and relatively protected life in the marshes of the Pripet. Our three points characterise the nature of the *function* as well as the *conduct* or behavior which constitutes the leader type. It is no part of his function to "find" or to "create" new possibilities. They are always present, abundantly accumulated by all sorts of people. Often they are also generally known and being discussed by scientific or literary writers. In other cases, there is nothing to discover about them, because they are quite obvious. To take an example from political life, it was not at all difficult to see how the social and political conditions of France at the time of Louis XVI could have been improved so as to avoid a breakdown of the *ancien régime.* Plenty of people as a matter of fact did see it. But nobody was in a position to *do* it. Now, it is this "doing the thing," without which possibilities are dead, of which the leader's function consists. This holds good of all kinds of leadership, ephemeral as well as more enduring ones. The former may serve as an instance. What is to be done in a casual emergency is as a rule quite simple. Most or all people may see it, yet they want someone to speak out, to lead, and to organise. Even leadership which influences merely by example, as artistic or scientific leadership, does not consist simply in finding or creating the new thing but in so impressing the social group

界的相对不变性，或者如果可以改变，这种可变性也还不能受到人类行为的影响，或者最后，如果可能受到这种影响，这类行为也不是每一个人都能做的，那么，世界上就不会有这种区别于其他例行工作的特殊的领导职能。

只有在新的可能性出现的地方，领导的特殊问题才产生，领袖类型的人物才出现。这就是为什么，在诺尔曼人征服的年代，领导才能表现得如此显著，而在斯拉夫人多少世纪以来在普里皮亚特河流域沼泽地的不变的，相对受到保护的生活中，领导才能又表现得那样微弱。我们的三个观点，表现了构成领袖类型的职能和举止或行为的特性。他的职能并不包括去“寻找”或者“创造”新的可能性。这些可能性一直在那里，被各种各样的人大量的积累起来。通常它们也是为大家所知道的，而且被科学作家或者文学作家讨论。在其他场合，人们没有什么兴趣去发现这些可能性，因为它们已经是相当明显的。从政治生活中举一个例子，我们根本不难看出，在路易十六时代，法国的社会和政治情况是如何能被改善，从而避免了一场旧统治的崩溃的。事实上，很多人都看到了这一点。但是没有一个人处于做的位置。现在，领导者的职能就在于去“做这些事”，如果不去做，可能性就会消失。这对所有的领导都是如此，不管是短暂的还是持续较长的领导。可以用前者作一个例子。在一个偶然的紧急事件中应该做什么，通常是十分简单的。大多数或者所有的人都能看到这一事件，但是他们需要有一个人先讲出来，来领导大家，组织大家。甚至只通过榜样来产生影响的领导，就像艺术领导或者科学领导，也不仅在于找到或创造新的事物，而在于通过它给社会团体以深刻的印象，

with it as to draw it on in its wake. It is, therefore, more by will than by intellect that the leaders fulfil their function, more by "authority," "personal weight," and so forth than by original ideas.

Economic leadership in particular must hence be distinguished from "invention." As long as they are not carried into practice, inventions are economically irrelevant. And to carry any improvement into effect is a task entirely different from the inventing of it, and a task, moreover, requiring entirely different kinds of aptitudes. Although entrepreneurs of course *may* be inventors just as they may be capitalists, they are inventors not by nature of their function but by coincidence and vice versa. Besides, the innovations which it is the function of entrepreneurs to carry out need not necessarily be any inventions at all. It is, therefore, not advisable, and it may be downright misleading, to stress the element of invention as much as many writers do.

The entrepreneurial kind of leadership, as distinguished from other kinds of economic leadership such as we should expect to find in a primitive tribe or a communist society, is of course colored by the conditions peculiar to it. It has none of that glamour which characterises other kinds of leadership. It consists in fulfilling a very special task which only in rare cases appeals to the imagination of the public. For its success, keenness and vigor are not more essential than a certain narrowness which seizes the immediate chance and *nothing else*. "Personal weight" is, to be sure, not without importance. Yet the personality of the capitalistic entrepreneur need not, and generally does not, answer to the idea most of us have of what a "leader" looks like, so much so that there is some difficulty in realizing that he comes within the sociological category of leader at all. He "leads" the means of production into new channels. But this he does, not by convincing people of the desirability of carrying out his plan or by creat ing confidence in his leading in the manner of a political leader –

从而使社会团队跟在它后面走。因此，领导者完成他的职能，更多的是靠意志而不是靠智慧，更多的是用“权威”，“个人名望”等，而不是用初始的思想。

正因此，尤其是经济上的领导，必须区别于“发明”。只要发明还没有用于实践，那它在经济上就是不起作用的。而执行任何改善并使之有效却是一项完全不同于发明这项改善的任务，而且这项任务需要完全不同类型的才能。尽管企业家当然也可能是发明家，就像他可能是资本家一样，但是他们并不是因为他们职能的性质而成为发明家，而只是一种巧合，反之亦然。此外，付诸实施的创新是企业家的职能，它也根本没必要必须是任何一种发明。因此，如同许多作家那样强调发明这一要素是不恰当的，而且它可能就是十足的误导。

企业家式的领导，不同于其他各种经济上的领导（比如我们所期望在原始部落里或者共产主义社会里看到的），当然要带上它特有的条件的色彩。它丝毫没有像其他各种领导特征的魅力。它在于执行一件非常特殊的任务，这项任务只在稀少的情况下才会引起公众的想象。为了它的成功，与其说聪慧和精力充沛是更关键的，不如说是某种精细，这种精细抓住了及时的机会，再没有别的了。当然，“个人名望”不是不重要。不过资本主义的企业家的个人品质没必要，而且通常也不会，与我们大多数人对于“领导者”是个什么样子的看法相吻合，所以要认识到他竟然属于社会学所说的领袖那一类，确实有些困难。他“领导”生产方式进入新的轨道。但他这样做，并不是通过说服人们相信执行他的计划的必要性，也不是用一个政治领导者的方式

the only man he has to convince or to impress is the banker who is to finance him – but by buying them or their services, and then using them as he sees fit. He also leads in the sense that he draws other producers in his branch after him. But as they are his competitors, who first reduce and then annihilate his profit, this is, as it were, leadership against one's own will. Finally, he renders a service; the full appreciation of which takes a specialist's knowledge of the case. It is not so easily understood by the public at large as a politician's successful speech or a general's victory in the field, not to insist on the fact that he seems to act – and often harshly-in his individual interest alone. We shall understand, therefore, that we do not observe, in this case, the emergence of all those affective values which are the glory of all other kinds of social leadership. Add to this the precariousness of the economic position both of the individual entrepreneur and of entrepreneurs as a group, and the fact that when his economic success raises him socially he has no cultural tradition or attitude to fall back upon, but moves about in society as an upstart, whose ways are readily laughed at, and we shall understand why this type has never been popular, and why even scientific critique often makes short work of it. ①

---

① It may, therefore, not be superfluous to point out that our analysis of the röle of the entrepreneur does not involve any "glorification" of the type, as some readers of the first edition of this book seemed to think. We do hold that entrepreneurs *have* an economic function as distinguished from, say, robbers. But we neither style every entrepreneur a genius or a benefactor to humanity, nor do we wish to express any opinion about the comparative merits of the social organisation in which he plays his röle, or about the question whether what he does could not be effected more cheaply or efficiently in other ways.

通过创造对他的领导能力的信任——他唯一必须说服或者打动的人就是将要给他提供资金的银行家——而是通过购买生产工具或者它们的服务，然后按照他认为合适的方式去使用它们。他还从这种意义上，即吸引其他的生产者到他的部门跟随他这种方式来实施领导。但是，由于他们是他的竞争者，这些生产者首先减少，然后消耗掉他的利润，这样好像是一种违背他自己的意愿的领导。最后，他提供一种服务，而要充分了解这种服务就需要对这件事情具有专家的知识。这对一般的公众来说不是很容易理解的，不像一位政治家的成功的演讲或者一个将军在战场上的胜利容易被人理解，他还不坚持这样一个事实，即他看上去好像是为他个人的利益而行动——经常是很严厉的行动。因此，我们将明白，在这种领导中，我们不会观察到所有那些感情方面的价值的出现，而这些价值是所有其他各种社会领导所引以为荣的。另外再加上单个的企业家和企业家集团的经济地位的不稳定性，以及当他在经济上的成功提高了他的社会地位时，他也没有文化传统和态度可以依靠，而是像一个暴发户在社会上走动，他的行为方式受人嘲笑，所以我们将会懂得，为什么这类人从来不受人欢迎，为什么即使是科学的批评家也常常只是简短地概括他们。①

① 因此，指出这一点并不是多余的：我们对企业家作用的分析不包括对这类人的任何的“美化”，像本书第一版某些读者所想象的。我们的确认为，企业家具有一种经济职能，这不同于，比如说，强盗。但是我们既没有把每一位企业家都说成是天才或者人类的救星，同时我们也不想对他所在的并起作用的社会组织的比较优势，或者对他所做的事能否用其他方式更便宜或更有效地完成的问题表达任何观点。

We shall finally try to round off our picture of the entrepreneur in the same manner in which we always, in science as well as in practical life, try to understand human behavior, viz. by analysing the characteristic motives of his conduct. Any attempt to do this must of course meet with all those objections against the economist's intrusion into "psychology" which have been made familiar by a long series of writers. We cannot here enter into the fundamental question of the relation between psychology and economics. It is enough to state that those who on principle object to *any* psychological considerations in an economic argument may leave out what we are about to say without thereby losing contact with the argument of the following chapters. For none of the results to which our analysis is intended to lead stands or falls with our "psychology of the entrepreneur," or could be vitiated by any errors in it. Nowhere is there, as the reader will easily satisfy himself, any necessity for us to overstep the frontiers of observable behavior. Those who do not object to *all* psychology but only to the *kind* of psychology which we know from the traditional textbook, will see that we do not adopt any part of the timehonored picture of the motivation of the "economic man."

In the theory of the circular flow, the importance of examining motives is very much reduced by the fact that the equations of the system of equilibrium may be so interpreted as not to imply any psychic magnitudes at all, as shown by the analysis of Pareto and of Barone. This is the reason why even very defective psychology interferes much less with results than one would expect. There may be rational *conduct* even in the absence of rational *motive.* But as soon as we really wish to penetrate into motivation, the problem proves by no means simple. Within given social circumstances and habits, most of what people do every day will appear to them primarily from the point of view of duty carrying a social or a superhuman sanction. There is very little of conscious rationality, still less of hedonism

我们最后将试图用我们经常在科学中以及在实际生活中所用的相同的方式来完成我们对企业家的描绘，试图理解人们的行为，也就是，通过分析他的行为的特殊的动机。这样做的任何企图当然必定会遇到对经济学家侵入“心理学”领域的所有反对，这些反对已经通过许多作家而变得众所周知了。在这里，我们不能讨论心理学和经济学之间的关系这个重大问题。我们只是指出，那些在原则上反对在经济论证中作任何心理学考虑的人，可以省去我们将要说的话，而不会因此失去与下面各章论证的联系。指出这一点就足够了。因为我们分析想要得到的结果，没有一个会由于我们的“企业家心理学”而有所得失，或者因其中的任何错误而变得无说服力。读者将很容易让自己感到满意，没有什么必要让我们超越我们可观察到的行为的范围。那些不反对所有的心理学，只反对我们从传统的教科书中知道的那类心理学的人将会看到，我们不采用有着辉煌历史的“经济人”动机的图景的任何一部分。

在循环流转理论里，由于一个事实使考察动机的重要性被大大地削减，那就是，均衡系统中的等式可以被解释为根本不包含任何心理数值，正像帕累托和巴龙的分析所表明的。这就是为什么即使有严重缺陷的心理学，它对结果的干预也比人们预期的要少得多的原因。即使在缺乏理性动机的情况下，也会有合理的行为。但是当我们一旦真的想要深入研究动机时，问题就变得一点也不简单了。在一定的社会环境和习惯中，人们每天所做的大部分事情，对他们来说，主要是从职责的角度去做的，是执行社会或神的指令。很少是出于自觉的理性的原因去做的，更少是从享乐主

and of *individual* egoismabout it, and so much of it as may safely be said to exist is of comparatively recent growth. Nevertheless, as long as we confine ourselves to the great outlines of constantly repeated economic action, we may link it up with wants and the desire to satisfy them, on condition that we are careful to recognise that economic motive so defined varies in intensity very much in time; that it is society that shapes the particular desires we observe; that wants must be taken with reference to the group which the individual thinks of when deciding his course of action – the family or any other group, smaller or larger than the family; that action does not promptly follow upon desire but only more or less imperfectly corresponds to it; that the field of individual choice is always, though in very different ways and to very different degrees, fenced in by social habits or conventions and the like: it still remains broadly true that, within the circular flow, everyone adapts himself to his environment so as to satisfy certain *given* wants – of himself or others – as best he can. In *all* cases, the *meaning* of economic action is the satisfaction of wants in the sense that there would be no economic action if there were no wants. In the case of the circular flow, we may also think of satisfaction of wants as the normal *motive*.

The latter is not true for our type. In one sense, he may indeed be called the most rational and the most egotistical of all. For, as we have seen, conscious rationality enters much more into the carrying out of new plans, which themselves have to be worked out before they can be acted upon, than into the mere running of an established business, which is largely a matter of routine. And the typical entrepreneur is more self-centred than other types, because he relies less than they do on tradition and connection and because his characteristic task – theoretically as well as historically – consists precisely in breaking up old,

义和个人利己主义去做事的，即使可以有把握地说存在那么一点点，那也是新近才发展起来的。然而，只要我们把自己限制在反复重复的经济行为的庞大范围内，我们就可以把它和需求以及满足需求的欲望联系起来，这里的条件是，我们要小心承认，这样定义的动机随着时间的推移，其强度会有很大的变动；正是社会形成了我们所观察到的特殊的欲望；考虑需求就必须要涉及那种当个人在决定他的行动进程时所想到的集团或团队——比如家庭或者任何其他比家庭小一些或大一些的团队；行动并不能紧跟着欲望，而只是或多或少不完全地与它相适应；个人选择的领域总是——尽管在方式上以及在程度上非常不同——受限制于社会习惯或者习俗等；然而大体上这仍然是真实的：在循环流转中，每个人都使自己适应他所处的环境，以便尽其所能地最好地满足某种给定的需求——他自己的或者其他人的需求。在所有的场合，经济行为的意义就是满足需求，其含义就是，如果没有需求，就没有经济行为。就循环流转而言，我们也可以把需求的满足看做是一种正常的动机。

后者并不是我们所说的类型。从某种意义上说，他可能确实称得上是最理性并且是最以自我为中心的人。因为，正像我们已经看到的，执行新的计划比仅仅是经营一个已经建立起来的企业，需要注入更多的有意识的理性，因为新计划本身在其能够被执行以前必须制订出来，而经营旧企业大部分是例行的事务。典型的企业家比其他类型的人，更加以自我为中心，因为他与其他类型的人相比，对传统和社会关系的依靠少很多，而且因为他的特殊的任务——从理论上以及历史上讲——正是在于打破旧传统，

and creating new, tradition. Although this applies primarily to his economic action, it also extends to the moral, cultural, and social consequences of it. It is, of course, no mere coincidence that the period of the rise of the entrepreneur type also gave birth to Utilitarianism.

But his conduct and his motive are "rational" in no other sense. And in *no* sense is his characteristic motivation of the hedonist kind. If we define hedonist motive of action as the wish to satisfy one's wants, we may indeed make "wants" include any impulse whatsoever, just as we may define egoism so as to include all altruistic values too, on the strength of the fact that they also mean something in the way of self-gratification. But this would reduce our definition to tautology. If we wish to give it meaning, we must restrict it to such wants as are capable of being satisfied by the consumption of goods, and to that kind of satisfaction which is expected from it. Then it is no longer true that our type is acting on a wish to satisfy his wants.

For unless we assume that individuals of our type are driven along by an insatiable craving for hedonist satisfaction, the operations of Gossen's law would in the case of business leaders soon put a stop to further effort. Experience teaches, however, that typical entrepreneurs retire from the arena only when and because their strength is spent and they feel no longer equal to their task. This does not seem to verify the picture of the economic man, balancing probable results against disutility of effort and reaching in due course a point of equilibrium beyond which he is not willing to go. Effort, in our case, does not seem to weigh at all in the sense of being felt as a reason to stop. And activity of the entrepreneurial type is obviously an obstacle to hedonist enjoyment of those kinds of commodity which are usually

创造新传统。尽管这一点主要适用于他的经济行为，但它也可以扩展到经济行为的道德的、文化的和社会的结果。当然这也绝不仅是偶然：企业家类型的人物出现的时期也产生了功利主义。

但是企业家的行为和他的动机是“理性的”，除了上面所说的没有其他意义了。他的特殊的动机丝毫没有享乐主义那类含义。如果我们把行为的享乐主义动机定义为满足某个人的需要的愿望，那么我们就可以让“需求”包含任何一种冲动，就像我们可以把自我主义定义为也包含所有利他主义价值观念一样，这是基于这样一个事实，即，利他主义也含有自我满足方面的某种意义。但这会使我们的定义陷入同义反复。如果我们想赋予它某种意义，我们就必须限制它的需求，这种需求必须是能够用商品的消费达到满足的，同时限制在我们期望能从它得到的满足上。于是，我们所说的那一类型的人是基于满足他的需求的一种愿望而行动，这就不再真实了。

因为，除非我们假定我们所说类型的人被享乐主义以及无法知足的一种渴望所驱动，戈森定律的作用在商业领袖场合会使进一步的努力立即停下来。然而，经验告诉我们，典型的企业家只是在，并因为他们的精力已经耗尽、感到不能再胜任他的工作时，才退出舞台。这看起来似乎并不能证实对经济人的描绘，他把可能的结果与努力的反效用进行对比衡量，在适当的时候达到一个均衡点，超过这一点他将不愿意再前进了。在我们的例子中，努力被认为是停止前进的理由，它似乎根本没什么分量。企业家类型的人的活动显然是享乐主义的障碍，他们的享受通常是

acquired by incomes beyond a certain size, because their "consumption" presupposes leisure. Hedonistically, therefore, the conduct which we usually observe in individuals of our type would be irrational.

This would not, of course, prove the absence of hedonistic motive. Yet it points to another psychology of non-hedonist character, especially if we take into account the indifference to hedonist enjoyment which is often conspicuous in outstanding specimens of the type and which is not difficult to understand.

First of all, there is the dream and the will to found a private kingdom, usually, though not necessarily, also a dynasty. The modern world really does not know any such positions, but what may be attained by industrial or commercial success is still the nearest approach to medieval lordship possible to modern man. Its fascination is specially strong for people who have no other chance of achieving social distinction. The sensation of power and independence loses nothing by the fact that both are largely illusions. Closer analysis would lead to discovering an endless variety within this group of motives, from spiritual ambition down to mere snobbery. But this need not detain us. Let it suffice to point out that motives of this kind, although they stand nearest to consumers' satisfaction, do not coincide with it.

Then there is the will to conquer: the impulse to fight, to prove oneself superior to others, to succeed for the sake, not of the fruits of success, but of success itself. From this aspect, economic action becomes akin to sport – there are financial races, or rather boxing-matches. The financial result is a secondary consideration, or, at all events, mainly valued as an index of success and as a symptom of victory, the displaying of which very often is more important as a motive of large expenditure than the wish for the consumers' goods themselves. Again we should find countless nuances, some of which,

用超过一定数量的收入来购买的，因为他们的“消费”是以闲暇为前提条件。因此，从享乐主义来看，我们通常观察到的我们所说类型的个人的行为就是不理性的。

当然，这并不能证明享乐主义动机是不存在的。然而，它指出了另一种非享乐主义特征的心理学，尤其是如果我们考虑到冷漠地对待享乐主义，这种冷漠在这种类型的代表人物身上常常是很明显的，而且也不难理解。

首先，有一种梦想和意志要找到一个私人空间，通常，虽然不一定，它也是一个王朝。现代世界实际上并不知道有这种地位，但是通过工业或者商业上的成功所获得的地位可能仍然是现代人可能达到的最接近于中世纪贵族的那种地位。对于那些没有其他机会可以获得社会地位的人来说，它的诱惑力特别强烈。权力和独立的感觉不会因为它们两者都是一种幻觉而有任何损失。更进一步的分析将会发现在这一类动机中有着无尽的变化，从精神上的野心到仅仅是媚上欺下，但是这些不需要我们详细讨论。我们只要指出这一点就够了：这种动机尽管与消费者的满足最接近，但却不能与它相一致。

其次，有一种征服的意志：战斗的冲动，证明自己要胜过其他人的冲动，追求成功不是为了成功的果实，而是为了成功本身。从这方面看，经济行为变得与体育运动很相似——有财富上的竞赛，或者拳击比赛。财富比赛的结果是次要的考虑，或者不管怎样，只有作为成功的指标和胜利的象征才被重视，对财富的炫耀常常更重要的是作为大量开支的动机，而不是作为对消费者商品本身的渴望。同时我们又可以发现无数细微的差别，其中有一些，

like social ambition, shade into the first group of motives. And again we are faced with a motivation characteristically different from that of "satisfaction of wants" in the sense defined above, or from, to put the same thing into other words, "hedonistic adaptation."

Finally, there is the joy of creating, of getting things done, or simply of exercising one's energy and ingenuity. This is akin to a ubiquitous motive, but nowhere else does it stand out as an independent factor of behavior with anything like the dearness with which it obtrudes itself in our case. Our type seeks out difficulties, changes in order to change, delights in ventures. This group of motives is the most distinctly anti-hedonist of the three.

Only with the first groups of motives is private property as the result of entrepreneurial activity an essential factor in making it operative. With the other two it is not. Pecuniary gain is indeed a very accurate expression of success, especially of *relative* success, and from the standpoint of the man who strives for it, it has the additional advantage of being an objective fact and largely independent of the opinion of others. These and other peculiarities incident to the mechanism of "acquisitive" society make it very difficult to replace it as a motor of industrial development, even if we would discard the importance it has for creating a fund ready for investment. Nevertheless it is true that the second and third groups of entrepreneurial motives may in principle be taken care of by other social arrangements not involving private gain from economic innovation. What other stimuli could be provided, and how they could be made to work as well as the "capitalistic" ones do, are questions which are beyond our theme. They are taken too lightly by social reformers, and are altogether ignored by fiscal radicalism. But they are not insoluble, and may be answered by detailed observation of the psychology of entre preneurial activity, at least for given times and places.

比如，社会野心，将归于第一类动机。我们又面临一种与上面所定义的“需求的满足”有根本区别的动机，或者换句话说，它与“享乐主义的适应”有本质区别。

最后，存在创造的快乐，做成事情的快乐，或者只是展示某个人的能力和智慧的快乐。这与一种无处不在的动机相似，但它作为一种独立的行为要素，再没有其他任何地方比在我们的情况中能让它更清楚地强行表现出来。我们所说的类型的人寻找困难，为改变而变化，以冒险为乐趣。这类动机在三者中，是最突出的反享乐主义的。

只有第一类动机是企业家活动的结果的私人财产，是促使这种活动起作用的必要因素。而其他两类却不是。金钱上的收益确实是对成功的准确的表现，尤其是对相对的成功而言；而从为之奋斗的人的观点看，它还有另一个好处，即，它已经是一个客观事实，在很大程度上独立于其他人的意见。这些与其他伴随“贪图财富的”社会机制的特点，使得很难代替它作为工业发展的动力的地位，即使我们排除它在创造一笔随时可用于投资的资金中的重要性。尽管如此，这一点是真实的，即第二类和第三类企业家的动机在原则上可能被其他社会安排所处理，而不包括来自经济创新的私人收益。至于还能提供其他什么激励，怎样使它们工作得像“资本主义”所做的一样好，这些都是超出我们论题范围的问题。这些问题被社会改革家过于轻视了，同时也被财政上的激进主义完全忽视。但是它们不是不能被解决，至少在一定的时间和地点，通过对企业家活动的心理学详尽地观察，它们可以被解答。

CHAPTER III
Credit And Capital

The Nature And Function Of Credit[1]

The fundamental notion that the essence of economic development consists in a *different* employment of *existing* services of labor and land leads us to the statement that the carrying out of new combinations takes place through the withdrawal of services of labor and land from their previous employments. For every form of economy in which the leader has no direct power of disposal over these services, this again leads us to two heresies: first to the heresy that money, and then to the second heresy that also other means of payment, perform an essential function, hence that processes in terms of means of payment are not merely reflexes of processes in terms of goods.

---

① The line of thought that is expounded fundamentally unchanged in the following has in the meantime received valuable substantiation and improvement from the investigations of A. Hahn in his Volkswirtschaftliche Theorie des Bankkredits (1ed. 1920,2ed. 1926). The reader is expressly referred to this original and meritorious book, which has essentially advanced our knowledge of the problem. Also in many respects parallel is W. G. Langworthy Taylor in The Credit System. Perhaps the post-war phenomena and the discussions of the rôle of bank credit in boom and depression have removed from what I have to say much of the appearance of a paradox. To-day every theory of the business cycle considers the fact of "additional credit" in prosperity and takes account of the question, raised by Keynes, whether the cycle may be mitigated by being influenced from the money side. This does not yet mean the acceptance of my point of view. But it must lead to it. Cf. also my article "Kreditkontrolle" in the Archlv für Sozialwissenschaft und Sozialpolitik (1925). Recently Robertson, in Banking Policy and the Price Level, has arrived at similar results (cf. on this Pigou, Economic Journal, June, 1926).

第三章 信贷与资本

信贷的性质与作用①

就本质而言，经济发展在于对现有的劳力和土地的服务用不同的方式加以使用；这一基本概念使我们得出这样的结论：新组合的实施，是通过从原先的使用方式中把劳力和土地服务提取出来而实现的。对于每一种经济形态，其中的领导者没有直接处置劳力和土地服务的权利，从这些，我们又可以得出两点与众不同的观点：首先，货币起着一种基本作用，其次，其他的支付方式也起着这种基本作用，因此，以支付手段为表现形式的过程不只是以商品为表现形式的过程的反映。然而，众多的理论家，尽

① 下面所陈述的基本上没有改动的思想脉络，曾从对汉恩（A. Hahn）著的《银行信贷的国民经济理论》（1920年第一版，1926年第二版）一书的研究中获得宝贵的充实和改进。特别提请读者参考他的这本具有开创性的值得称赞的佳作，这本书从根本上推进了我们对这个问题的认识。兰沃斯·泰勒的《信贷制度》一书，在许多方面也同样有益。也许战后现象以及对在繁荣和萧条时期银行信贷的角色的讨论，已经消除了我们所要说的那些矛盾的表象。今天，每一个商业周期理论都在考虑繁荣时期"补充信贷"的事实，并思考由凯恩斯提出的这个问题，即，是否可以通过货币流向的影响来缓解周期问题。然而，这并不意味着接受我的观点。但是它一定会导向我的观点。参考我的论文《信贷控制》，载德文《社会科学与社会政策文献》（1925年）。最近，罗伯逊在其《银行政策与价格水平》一书中，也得出同样的结论（参阅1926年6月《经济学杂志》中庇古的文章）。

In every possible strain, withrare unanimity, even with impatience and moral and intellectualindignation, a very long line of theorists have assured us of theopposite.

Economics, almost since it became a science, has continuallyresisted the popular errors which cling to the phenomenon ofmoney-quite rightly. This has been one of its fundamentalservices. And whoever thinks through what has been said so far will easily be convinced that none of these errors is maintained in it. Of course if one were to say that money is only a medium for facilitating the circulation of goods and that no important phenomena can be connected with it, this would be false. If one would forge out of this an objection against our argument, then it would be at once refuted by our proof that in our case a different employment of the system ' s productive powers cannot be achieved otherwise than by a disturbance in the relative purchasing power of individuals. We saw that, in principle, a loan of the services of labor and land by workers and landlords is not possible. Nor can the entrepreneur himself borrow produced means of production. For in the circular flow there would be no idle stocks for the needs of the entrepreneur. If somewhere or other exactly such produced means of production as the entrepreneur needs happen to exist, then of course he can buy them; for this, however, he again needs purchasing power. But he cannot simply borrow them, for they are needed for the purposes for which they were produced, and the possessor cannot and will not wait for his return-which the entrepreneur could indeed reimburse him for, but only later-and also can and will bear no risk. If someonenevertheless does this, then two transactions occur, a purchaseand an extension of credit. Both-are not only two legally distinctparts of one and the same economic process, but two very differenteconomic processes, to each of which very different economic phenomena adhere, as will be seen later. Finally the entrepreneuralso cannot " advance" ① consumption goods to workers and land-lords, simply because

① The theoretical construction which this unreal conception has enforced sinceQuesnay ' s clay thus refutes itself. And it is so important that one may speak of" advances – economics" . cuvrs chussökonomie.

可能紧张的，带有很少的一致性，甚至用不耐烦的态度，以及道德和理智上的愤怒，要我们确信那种与此相反的观点。

经济学，几乎从它成为一门科学时起，就一直在与那些紧紧抓住货币现象的人的普遍的错误相抗争，这是很对的。这是经济学的基本贡献之一。任何人，只要他深思了我们以前的论述，他就不难相信，在我们的论述中没有一个这样的错误。当然，如果有人说货币只是一种为了让商品流通更便利的媒介，没有什么重要现象与它相关联，那是错误的。如果有人借此提出一种反对我们的论点的意见，那么它就会立刻被我们的论据所驳倒，那就是，在我们的案例中，对一定经济系统的生产力的不同利用方式，只有通过改变人们的相对购买力才能实现。我们已经看到，原则上，让工人把他们的劳动服务，地主把他们的土地借给别人使用，是不可能的。同样，企业家自己也借不到生产出来的生产手段。因为在循环流转中，没有闲置不用的存货供企业家的需要。如果在某个地方恰好存在企业家所需要的这种已经生产出来的生产工具，那么他当然可以购买，然而为了购买，他又必须有购买力。但是他不能随便把它们借来，因为它们被生产出来正是因为有人需要它们，而拥有生产工具的人，既不能也不愿等候企业家再把它们归还——企业家的确可以归还，但时间上要晚一些——同时拥有生产工具的人不能也不愿承担风险。然而如果有人这样做，那么会出现两笔交易，一笔是购买，一笔是信贷的扩大。这两者不仅在法律上是同一经济过程的两个不同部分，而且就像下面要说的，它们是两种很不同的经济过程，每一个都依附着不同的经济现象。最后，企业家也不能给工人和地主“预付”① 消费品，因为

① 自从魁奈的时代以来，这个不真实的概念所强加的理论结构就不攻自破了。这个理论太重要了，以至于人们可能称之为“预付经济学”。

he has none. If he buys them, then he needs purchasing power for *that* purpose. We cannot get over this point, since it is always a question of drawing goods out of the circular flow. With respect to the loan of consumption goods, the same holds true as for the loan of produced means of production. Thus we are asserting nothing mysterious or strange.

It is clear that there would be no sense in objecting that nothing essential "can" depend upon money. Actually purchasing power is the vehicle of an essential process; of this there can be no doubt. Moreover the objection cannot really be made at all, because everyone acknowledges the analogous phenomenon that changes in the quantity or distribution of money can have very far-reaching effects. But this observation has stood on a side-track so far. Yet the comparison is quite instructive. Here too there is not necessarily a change in the sphere of goods, a preceding cause on the commodity side, which could be resorted to for explanation. Goods behave quite passively in any case. Nevertheless their kind and quantity are, as everybody knows, very much influenced by such changes.

Our second heresy is also far from being as dangerous as it seems. It also rests, in the ultimate analysis, on a fact that is not merely demonstrable and even obvious but also generally acknowledged. Means of payment are created in the economic system which are, in their external form, it is true, represented as mere *claims* to money, but which differ essentially from claims to other goods in that they perform exactly the same service-at least temporarily-as the good in question itself, so that they may under certain circumstances take its place. ①
Not only is this recognised in the literature on money and banking,

---

① Although one may not in general add up claims to goods and the goods themselves-any more than the ear and the grains of corn-yet the matter is clearly somewhat different here. While I cannot ride on a claim to a horse, I can, under certain conditions, do exactly the same with claims to money as with money itself, namely buy.

他根本还没有消费品。如果他购买消费品，那么他也需要为了这个购买目的的购买力。我们不能忘记这一点，它始终是一个从循环流转中把商品抽取出来的问题。关于消费品的借贷是这样，对于已经生产出来的生产工具的借贷仍是这样。所以，我们正研究的问题既不神秘也不稀奇。

我们很清楚：没有什么重要的事物“能”取决于货币，反对这一说法是没有道理的。实际上，购买力是极其关键的过程的一个工具，这是不容怀疑的。此外，这种反对意见事实上根本不会产生，因为每一个人都承认，货币在数量和分配上的变化这类现象，可能产生很深远的影响。但是迄今为止，这种观察还处于事物的边缘。不过这种比较还是很有启发的。在这里，也不一定要有商品范围的变化，也就是上述商品方面的原因，它可以作为解释的一个原因。在任何情况下，商品的运动都是被动的。尽管如此，众所周知，商品的种类和数量在很大程度上受到这些变化的影响。

我们第二个有异议的观点，也远远不像看起来那么危险。归根结底，它也是以事实为基础的，这个事实不仅可以论证，甚至是显然的，而且是被人们普遍认同的。的确，从外在形式上看，经济系统创造了支付手段，这个支付手段只表现为对货币的索取权，但是这种对货币的索取权与对其他商品的索取权的本质区别在于它与货币起着完全相同的作用——至少暂时是这样——所以在一定情况下它可以取代货币。① 这一点不仅在有关货币和银行

① 尽管通常不能把对商品的索取权与商品本身加起来——就像不能把谷穗与谷粒相加一样——但是这里情况还是有些不同的。尽管我不能依靠着对一匹马的索取权，但在一定条件下，我可以像处理货币本身一样来处理对货币的索取权，那就是购买。

but also in theory in the narrower sense. This can be seen in any textbook. We have nothing to add to the observation, but only to the analysis. The problems the discussion of which had most to do with the recognition of the fact were the questions of the concept and value of money. When the quantity theory set up its formula for the value of money, the critics first seized upon the fact of other means of payment. It is well known too that the old question whether these means of payment, more especially bank credits, are money has been answered affirmatively by many of the best writers. But it is sufficient that it was put. In any case the fact with which we are concerned has been recognized without exception so far as I know, even by those writers who answered the question negatively. It was also always explained, in more or less detail, how and in what forms the matter is technically possible.

This implies recognising that the circulating media so created do not merely represent an equal quantity of metal money, but that they exist in such quantities that they could not possibly all be redeemed at once; and further, that they not only replace, for the sake of convenience, sums of money which previously circulated, but also appear newly created side by side with the existing sums. Likewise the point, by no means essential for us, but which we maintain for purposes of exposition, that this creation of means of payment centers in the banks and constitutes their fundamental function, we find agrees with the prevailing conception. The creation of money by the banks establishing claims against themselves, which is described by Adam Smith, and indeed by still earlier authors in a way quite free from popular errors, has become a commonplace to-day; whereupon I hasten to add that for our purposes it is all the same whether or not one regards the expression "creation of money" as theoretically correct. Our deductions are completely independent of the particulars of any monetary theory.

的文献中被承认，而且在更狭义上的理论中也被人们认识到了。在任何一本教科书中都可以看到这一点，我们不能再对这一看法作任何补充，只是想增加一点分析。在讨论的问题中，与对事实的认可关系最密切的是货币的概念与价值问题。当数量论为货币的价值建立起公式的时候，批评家们首先就抓住其他支付手段的事实不放。众所周知，像这样一些老问题，诸如这些支付手段，尤其是银行信贷是否就是货币，已经由许多最优秀的作家作了肯定的回答。有关这方面的讨论已经够多了。无论如何，我们所关心的事实，据我所知，已经毫无例外地被认可了，甚至那些对这个问题持否定态度的作家也承认这个事实。人们也曾详略不等地解释了，在技术上，支付手段是怎样并且以何种方式影响货币的价值。

这意味着承认这样产生的流通媒介不仅代表等量的金属货币，而且它们实际存在的数量是这样大，不可能立即全部兑换它们；而且由于方便的缘故，它们不仅取代了先前流通中的一笔笔货币，而且表现出新的流通手段与原来的支付手段同时存在着。同样，有一点对我们来说并不很重要，但是我们仍然认为这样，因为它与我们的表述很有关系，也就是：这种支付手段的产生集中于银行，并且构成银行的基本职能。我们发现这与通行的概念是一致的。由银行创造出来的货币又使银行承担了义务，这一论断由亚当·斯密以及更早的作家们以一种与众不同的正确方式提出来，今天已经成为常识了。在此，我急于补充的是，不管人们认为“货币的创造”这种表达在理论上是否正确，这对我们的论述目的而言都是一样的。我们的推论完全独立于任何货币理论的细节。

Finally, there can be no doubt that these circulating media come into being in the process of granting credit and are created especially-neglecting the cases in which it is only a question of avoiding the transport of metal money-for the *purpose* of granting credit. A bank is, according to Fetter (Principles of Economics, p. 462), "a business whose income is derived chiefly from lending its promises to pay."

So far I have said nothing controversial and so far I do not even see the possibility of a difference of opinion. No one can reproach me with offending against, say, Ricardo's statement that "banking operations" cannot increase a country's wealth, or with making myself guilty of, say, a "vapory speculation"① in Law's sense. Furthermore, who would deny the fact that, in some countries, perhaps three-quarters of bank deposits are simply credits,② and that the businessman as a rule first becomes the bank's debtor in order to become its creditor, that he first "borrows" what he *uno actu* "deposits," to say nothing of the fact that only a negligible fraction of all transactions are and can be effected by money in the strict sense. Therefore I shall not consider these things more closely. There is really no purpose in advancing explanations here which anyone to whom they offer anything new can find in every elementary book.

---

① Cf. J. S. Mill. Moreover, every economist will admit that Ricardo's statement is not quite correct, even if he is ever so conservative on this point. Cf. for example J. L. Langhlin, who says in his Principles of Money: "Credit does not increase capital (that is means of production) but mobilises it and makes it more efficient and thereby leads to an increase in product." We shall have something similar to say.

② Only a few banks show in their periodical statements what part of their deposits consists of real deposits. The above estimate is based upon English statements, which show it at least indirectly, and probably amounts to a *communis opinio*. This does not hold good for Germany, for example, because there it is not the practice simply to credit a customer with the amount of the loan. However, the essence of the theory is not on this account different. Strictly speaking, moreover, all bank deposits are based upon mere credits, as Hahn rightly emphasised-only that credits which arise out of "suns paid in" are covered in a special manner and do not increase the purchasing power of the depositors.

最后，不容怀疑的是，这些流通手段形成于提供信贷的过程，甚至就是——如果我们忽略纯粹为了避免金属货币的运输而产生这种手段的情况——为了提供信贷的目的而产生的。根据费特的观点（《经济学原理》，第462页），银行“主要是靠出借支付承诺来获取收入的企业”。至此，我所说的，没有什么争议性，甚至我也看不出有意见分歧的可能性。人们不能责备我，说我违背了，比如说，李嘉图说过的“银行业务”不会增加一个国家的财富的观点，人们也不能说我犯了罪，比如说，以银行家劳的意思，犯了“滥发钞票空头投机”罪。[①] 更有甚者，谁也不会否认这样的事实，即在某些国家，或许四分之三的银行存款只是信贷；[②] 通常，工商业者都是为了成为银行的债权人而首先变成它的债务人，他们首先借的实际上是他们要“存”的；更不用说，在所有的交易额中只有极微少的一部分，在严格意义上，是可以利用并且通过货币完成的。因此，我对这些问题不再作进一步的讨论。在这里作一些对于某些人来说是新鲜的但可以在任何一本基础读本里都能找

① 参阅J. S. 穆勒的著作。任何一个经济学家，即使他在这一点上是很保守的，也会认为，李嘉图的观点不是十分正确。例如，参阅劳弗林的著作，他在他的《货币原理》一书中写道：“信贷不能使资本（指生产手段）增长，但可以使资本活起来，使它更有效率，从而导致产品增加。”我们的观点与此大致相同。

② 只有少数银行在它们的定期报告中表明，他们的存款中有多少是真正的存款。上面的估计是根据英国的报告作出的，这些报告至少间接表明了这种情况，而且很可能达到了公认。但在德国情况不是这样，例如，在德国，银行业务中通常不把贷款额计入客户的贷方。不过理论上的本质并不因此而不同。此外，严格地说，正如汉正确地强调的那样，所有的银行存款都以纯粹的信贷为基础——只有以“银行收进的金额”为基础的信贷，才是一种以特殊方式保付的信贷，它不能增加存款户的购买力。

That all forms of credit, from the bank-note to book-credits, are essentially the same thing, and that in all these forms credit increases the means of payment, is also held to be uncontroversial. ①

So far only one point can be controversial. Most of these circulating media obviously cannot be created without a basis consisting of legal tender or commodities. I believe I do not err when I say that to the businessman as well as to the theorist the producer's bill of exchange appears as the typical example of such circulating media. The producer, after completing his production and selling the product, draws on his customers, in order to turn his claim into "money" immediately. Then these products serve as the "basis"-*in concreto* say bills of lading-and even if the bill is not backed by existing money, it is based instead upon existing goods and so still in a certain sense upon existing "purchasing power." The deposits mentioned above obviously also arise to a great extent from the discounting of commercial paper of this kind. This could well be considered as the normal case of granting credit or putting credit instruments into the channels of commerce, and every other case might be called abnormal. ②But even in those cases where there is no question of settling a normal commodity transaction, collateral is usually demanded, and therefore what we call "creation" would only be a question of the mobilisation of existing assets. At this point we should

---

① Of course there are always theorists who take the layman's standpoint, who regard with astonishment "the gigantic sums in the banks." It is more surprising that financial writers sometimes take a similar line too. As an example, see the otherwise very serviceable book of Clare, A Money Market Primer, which indeed does not accept this standpoint outright, but yet defines the sums available for granting credit as "other peoples' money," which is of course only true for a part, and even then only in a figurative sense.

② In this I am neglecting from the outset the case in which the regular business of an economic system is dispatched with credit means of payment and the producer receives a hill or other credit instrument from his customers and buys producers' goods with it immediately. Here there is no granting of credit at all in any relevant sense, and the case is not fundamentally different from cash transactions by means of metal currency. This case, of which we shall say no more here, was mentioned in the first chapter.

到的解释，的确是没有什么意义的。所有的信贷形式，从银行券到账面信贷，在本质上都是相同的事物，在所有这些形式里，信贷都增加了支付手段的数量，这是无可争议的。①

至此，只有一点可能是有争议的。显然，大多数这些流通手段，如果没有构成法币或商品的依据，是不会凭空产生的。我相信，当我对工商业者或者理论家说，生产者的票据就是这种流通手段的典型例子的时候，我并没有说错。生产者完成了他的生产并且售出了他的产品后，就给他的客户开出汇票，要求立即支付“货币”。于是，这些产品就起到了“依据”的作用——具体说就是提货单——即使没有现成的货币支持这些票据，它却有现存的商品作为依据，所以，从某种意义上说，它仍然是以现存的“购买力”为依据的。显然，前面所提到的存款，在很大程度上也是形成于这种商业票据的贴现。似乎可以把这种情况看成是提供信贷或者把信贷工具放入商业渠道的正常情况，而把其他情况看做是不正常的。② 但是即使在正常的商品交易的结算没有问题的情况下，通常也需要有附属担保品，因此我们所说的信贷“创造”只是一个把现有的资源整合利用起来的问题。因此，在这一点上，我

① 当然，一直有一些理论家用世俗的观点，对“银行里的巨额资金”惊讶不已。更让人惊奇的是，有些金融问题的作家有时也持相同的观点。比如，克莱尔写的《货币市场入门》一书，它在其他方面是很有益的，它确实也没有直接接受这个观点，但是却把提供信贷的金额定义为“其他人的钱”，这种说法当然只有部分是正确的，而且只能作为一种比喻。

② 关于这一点，我一开始就忽略了这种情况，即，在一个经济系统里，正规业务用信用支付手段结清，生产者从其客户那里收到票据或者其他信用工具，并且立即用它来购买生产资料。从任何有关的意义上说，这里与提供信用没有任何关系，而且从根本上说，它与用金属货币进行的现金交易没有什么区别。这种情况，我们在第一章已经谈到了，在这里不再重复。

therefore come back again to the traditional conception. In fact the latter seems to triumph, because then there would not only be no circulating media without a basis, but even money could be abstracted from and hence everything would be traced back to the exchange of commodities for commodities, that is, purely to processes in the sphere of goods. This interpretation also explains why it is generally believed that the "creation of money" is merely a technical matter, with no deeper significance for the general theory of economic life, which can safely be relegated to a chapter on banking methods.

We do not wholly agree with this. For the time being it need only be emphasized that what practice designates as "abnormal" is only the creation of circulating media which pretend to be the result of regular commodity transactions, without such being the case. Apart from this, finance bills are not simply something "abnormal." They are, it is true, not creations of credit for financing new combinations, but they frequently come to much the same thing. As regards the collateral, which in such cases cannot be existing products but only other things, its significance, in principle, is not that the assets constituting the collateral are "mobilized" by the granting of credit. This is not a good characterization of the nature of the thing. On the contrary we must distinguish two cases. First, the entrepreneur may have some kind of security which he can mortgage at the bank. ①This circumstance certainly makes it much easier for him in practice to obtain credit. But it does not belong to the nature of the thing in its purest form. The entrepreneurial function is not, in principle, connected with the possession of wealth, as analysis and experience equally teach, even though the accidental fact

---

① Moreover, if it is a question of things like land or shares, which do not circulate-or are not in the market for goods-then the creation of money has just the same effect in the sphere of commodities and upon prices as an uncovered issue. This is often overlooked. Cf. the analogous error in the case of government fiat money when this money is "based" upon land. The frequent foundation of this category of means of payment upon some kind of collateral only eliminates the in security which would otherwise exist, but does not alter the fact that there is no new supply of products corresponding to the new demand for products proceeding from it. Cf. Chapter II.

们应该再次回到传统的概念上。事实上，传统的概念似乎是胜利的，因为在那种情况下，不仅所有的流通手段都有其依据，而且甚至货币也可以从流通过程中抽走，从而所有交易都可以追溯到物物交换，也就是说，属于纯粹的商品范畴的过程。这种解释也说明了为什么人们通常认为“货币的创造”仅仅是一个技术上的问题，它对于经济生活的一般理论没有更深的意义，而只要在有关银行经营方式的一个章节说一下就可以了。

我们不完全赞同这个观点。目前只需要强调的是，那些被实践表明是“不正常”的，只是装扮成正规商品交易的结果的那种流通手段的再造，仅此而已。除此之外，金融票据不能简单视为“不正常的”。诚然，它们不是为了给新组合融资的信用产物，但是在很大程度上，它们频繁地起着相同的作用。至于附属担保品，在这种场合下，不可能是现有的产品，而是其他东西；从原则上说，它的重要性不在于构成附属担保品的资产因银行提供信贷而被“灵活运用”起来。这不是附属担保品本质的主要特征。相反，我们必须区分两种情况。第一，企业家可能拥有某种可以拿到银行作抵押的担保品。① 这种情况一定使他更容易获得信贷。但它不属于最纯粹形式下的事物的性质。分析和经验都告诉我们，在原则上，企业家的作用与拥有财富没有关系，尽管就偶然的情况而言，

① 此外，如果作抵押的是土地或者股票这类不能流通的东西——或者是不能在市场上交换商品的东西——那么货币的产生在商品领域的影响，以及其对价格的影响，与没有担保的货币发行就没有什么差别。这一点常被人们忽视。比较政府以土地为“依据”发行不兑现纸币的情况，就可以发现类似的错误。常常见到以某种担保品作为某种支付手段的基础，这不过是消除了如果不这样做就可能存在的不安全，但却没有改变这一事实，即，没有对应于新的产品需求而产生的新的产品供给。参阅第二章。

of the possession of wealth constitutes a practical advantage. In view of the cases in which the latter circumstance is absent, this interpretation can hardly be challenged, and it follows then that the statement that credit as it were "coins property" is not a sufficient formulation of the matter. Or secondly, the entrepreneur may mortgage goods, which he acquires with the borrowed purchasing power. The granting of credit comes first and collateral must be dispensed with, at least in principle, for however short an interval. From this case the conception of putting existing assets into circulation receives still less support than from the first. On the contrary it is perfectly clear that purchasing power is created to which in the first case no new goods correspond.

From this it follows, therefore, that in real life total credit must be greater than it could be if there were only fully covered credit. The credit structure projects not only beyond the existing gold basis, but also beyond the existing commodity basis. Again, this fact as such cannot very well be denied. Only its theoretical significance can be in doubt. The distinction between normal and abnormal credit is, however, important for us. Normal credit creates claims to the social dividend, which represent and may be thought of as certifying services rendered and previous delivery of existing goods. That kind of credit, which is designated by traditional opinion as abnormal, also creates claims to the social product, which, however, in the absence of past productive services could only be described as certificates of future services or of goods yet to be produced. Thus there is a fundamental difference between the two categories, in their nature as well as in their effects. Both serve the same purpose as means of payment and are externally indistinguishable. But the one embraces means of payment to which there is a corresponding contribution to the social product, the other means of payment to which so far nothing corresponds-at least no contribution to the social product, even though this deficiency is often made up by other things.

After these introductory remarks, the shortness of which it is hoped will cause no misunderstanding, I proceed to the theme of

拥有财富会构成一种现实的利益。如果不存在这种利益条件,我们的观点也经得住挑战。于是,把信贷说成是“货币财产”,并不是对事情的一种充分的表述。第二,企业家可能抵押商品,而这些商品是他用借来的购买力所获得的。于是,首先出现提供信贷,然后才有附属担保品,至少在原则上是这样,不管两者之间的间隙有多短。在这种情况下,把现有资产放入流通中的概念所得到的支持甚至比第一种情况下还要少。相反,这正好清楚地表明,在第一种情况下,当购买力被创造出来时,没有与之相对应的任何新商品。

因此可以说,在现实生活中,信贷总量必然大于有充分担保品所提供的信贷量。信贷结构显得不仅超过了现存的黄金基础,而且超过了现存的商品基础。这样的事实是很难被否认的。只能怀疑它在理论上的重要意义。然而,对我们来说,划分正常的与不正常的信贷才是重要的。正常的信贷创造了对社会收益的要求权,它代表着并可以被认为是对已经提供服务以及现存商品已经交付的证实。那种被传统观点认为是不正常的信贷,也创造了对社会产品的要求权,然而,由于缺少过去的生产性服务的基础,只能被看做是对未来的服务或者尚待生产的商品的证明。这样,在两个类型之间,它们的性质以及它们的效应上出现了根本的差异。两者作为支付手段从属于相同的目的,而且在外在形式上没有差别。但是其中一方所包含的支付手段对社会产品有相应的贡献,而另一方所包含的支付手段却没有作出相应的贡献——至少没有对社会产品作出相应的贡献,尽管这个欠缺经常由其他事物弥补。

这些介绍性的评述很简短,希望不会因此而产生误解,接下来,

this chapter. First we must prove the statement, so strange at first sight, that in principle no one other than the entrepreneur needs credit-or the corollary but at once much less strange statement that credit serves industrial development. It has already been established that the entrepreneur-in principle and as a rule-does need credit, in the sense of a temporary transfer to him of purchasing power, in order to produce at all, to be able to carry out his new combinations, to *become* an entrepreneur. And this purchasing power does not flow towards him automatically, as to the producer in the circular flow, by the sale of what he produced in preceding periods. If he does not happen to possess it and if he did then it would simply be the consequence of former development-he must borrow it. If he does not succeed, then obviously he cannot become an entrepreneur. In this there is nothing fictitious; it is merely the formulation of generally known facts. He can only become an entrepreneur by previously becoming a debtor. He becomes a debtor in consequence of the logic of the process of development, or, to put it in still another way, his becoming a debtor arises from the necessity of the case and is not something abnormal, an accidental event to be explained by particular circumstances. What he first wants is credit. Before he requires any goods whatever, he requires purchasing power. He is the typical debtor in capitalist society. ①

The argument must now be completed by the negative proof that the same cannot be said of any other type and that no one else is a debtor by the nature of his economic function. Of course there are in reality many other motives for borrowing or lending. But the point is that the granting of credit does not then

① The entrepreneur is also a debtor in a deeper sense, as may be emphasised here; he receives goods from the social stream-again in principle-before he has contributed anything to it. In this sense he is so to speak a debtor of society, Goods are transferred to him, to which he has not that claim which alone gives access to the national dividend in other cases. Cf. Chapter II.

我就要进入本章的主题。首先我们要证明一个乍看起来有些奇怪的说法，那就是，在原则上只有企业家才需要信贷——或者证明这一说法的不很奇怪的推论，即信贷服务于产业发展。已经被证明了，企业家在原则上并且通常都需要信贷，其意义是为了使企业家最终能够生产，暂时转让给他购买力，以实现他的新组合，进而成为一个企业家。但是这种购买力不会自动地流向企业家，这与在循环流转中生产者通过销售他前一期生产的产品而使购买力自动流向他是不同的。如果一个企业家碰巧没有购买力——如果他有购买力，但那只不过是先前发展的结果——那他就必须借入购买力。如果他没有借到，显然他就不会成为一个企业家。这里所说的没有虚构，只不过是对普遍接受的事实进行概括。要想成为企业家，只有首先成为债务人。由于发展进程的逻辑，企业家成为一个债务人，或者换一种说法，他成为债务人是情况的必然要求，不是什么不正常的事情，也不是用特殊情况来解释的偶然事件。他首先需要的就是信贷。在他需要任何商品之前，他需要有购买力。在资本主义社会，他是典型的债务人。①

现在我们必须用反证法来完成我们的论证，也就是证明上述企业家负债的情况与任何其他情况都不同，任何其他人都不会因为他的经济职能而成为债务人。当然，在现实生活中有许多其他动机是为了借与贷。但关键是，在那些情况下，提供信贷并不作为

① 从更深一层意义上说，企业家也还是债务人，在这里应该强调这一点，他从社会流转额中获得商品——同样，在原则上是这样——在他对社会流转额作出任何贡献之前。从这个意义上可以说他负了社会的债，商品转移到他手中，而他还没有因此获得在其他情况下对国民收入分配的要求权。参阅第二章。

appear as an essential element of the economic process. This holds good first of all for consumptive credit. Neglecting the fact that its significance can only be a limited one, it is not an element in the fundamental forms and necessities of industrial life. It is not part of the economic nature of any individual that he should contract consumptive loans or of the nature of any productive process that the participators should incur debts for the purposes of their consumption. Therefore the phenomenon of consumptive credit is of no further interest for us here, and in spite of all its practical importance we exclude it from our consideration. This involves no abstraction-we recognize it as a fact, only we have nothing particular to say about it. Exactly the same holds good for those cases in which a credit requirement arises solely for the maintenance of a business which has been disturbed, perhaps by misfortunes. These cases, which I embrace under the concept of "consumptive-productive credits," are also no part of the nature of an economic process in the sense that their treatment appertains to the understanding of the life of the economic organism. They too are of no further interest to us here.

Since every kind of extension of credit for purposes of "innovations" is by definition the granting of credit to the *entrepreneur*, and forms an element of economic development, then the only kind of granting of credit left for consideration here is credit for running a business in the circular flow (Betriebskredit). Our proof is achieved if we can explain it as "unessential" in our sense. What of it then?

We saw in the first chapter that it is not part of the nature of the circular flow that credit (Betriebskredit) is currently taken and given:①when the producer has finished his products, then accordingto our conception he sells them imme-and begins his production anew with

① It is to be hoped that the reader will not confuse *this* "current credit" (in the circular flow) with the sum which must also be supplied to the entrepreneur for "running" in contrast to founding the business, that is especially for the purpose of current wage payments.

经济过程的本质要素出现。这首先对于消费信贷就是这样。先忽略一个事实不谈,即消费信贷的重要性是很有限的，我们要说明消费信贷并不是产业生活基本形式和必要条件的一个要素。它不是任何个人经济性质的一部分，说他应该承担消费性债务；它也不是任何生产过程性质的一部分，规定生产过程的参与者为了自身的消费必须借债。因此，在这里，消费信贷现象对我们没有更多的意义，不管它在实际中有多么重要，我们对它不作考虑。这不包括抽象过程——我们承认它是事实，只是我们对此没有什么特别要说的。一个企业也许因为遭受灾难而深受困扰，纯粹为了维持局面而需举债，对于这种情况，我们同样不予考虑。这些情况，我把它们归于“消费性——生产性信贷”的概念之下，它们也不是经济过程本质的一部分，也就是说，不谈它们与对经济有机体的生命的理解有关。同样，它们在这里对我们没有更深的意义。

因为根据定义，每一种为“创新”目的而提供的信贷是给企业家提供的信贷，而且构成经济发展的一个要素，那么在这里，唯一留下来的我们需要考虑的信贷是为了在循环流转中商业运营而提供的信贷（经营信贷）。如果我们能够解释，在我们所规范的意义上，这种信贷是“非主要的”，我们的证明就完成了。那么如何来说明呢?

我们从第一章可以看出，目前接受经营信贷并不是循环流转本质的一部分①：当生产者完成了他的产品的生产，根据我们的概

① 希望读者不要把这个“流通信贷”（在循环流转中的）与相同数额必须提供给企业家以维持企业“运转”（非创建企业）的信贷，尤其是为了支付当前工资而需要的信贷相混淆。

diately the proceeds. To be sure, things do not always happen thus. It may be that he wishes to begin producing before he has delivered the products to his customer. But the decisive point is that we can, without overlooking anything essential, represent the process within the circular flow as if production were currently financed by receipts. Credit in the ordinary routine of established business owes its practical importance solely to the fact that there is development and that this development carries with it the possibility of employing sums of money which are temporarily idle. Hence every businessman will turn these receipts to account as promptly as possible and will then borrow what purchasing power he may require. If there were no development, then the sums of money necessary to carry out transactions would normally have to be actually kept in every firm and household, and during the time when they were not needed would have to lie idle. It is development that alters this. It soon sweeps away those types whose pride it was that they never took any credit. And when in the end all businesses-old as well as new ones-are drawn into the circle of the credit phenomenon, bankers will even prefer this kind of credit on account of the smaller risk it involves. Many banks, particularly of the "deposit" type and also almost all old-established houses, actually do this and restrict themselves more or less to such "current" credit. But this is only a consequence of development already in full swing.

This interpretation does not place us in opposition to the prevailing one as much as might be thought. ①On the contrary, we assert by it, in complete agreement with the usual view, that we can dispense with credit if we want to grasp the economic process of the circular flow. Only because the prevailing theory takes the same view, and like us sees

① Moreover, it is directly verified by the facts. For many centuries there was practically only consumptive credit. Then there was no more than credit for founding a business. And the circular flow went on without it. Current credit only attained its present importance in modern times. And since a modem factory differs economically from a medieval workshop in no other fundamental respect, the conclusion is reached that the former needs no credit in principle.

念，他立即出售它们，并利用所得开始他的新一轮的生产。当然，实际情况并不总是这样。有可能他在交货给客户之前就想开始生产了。但关键是我们能够在循环流转的领域中体现这个过程，如同那里的生产通常是以营业收入来提供资金的，而同时不忽略任何实质性的东西。在已建立企业的日常事务中，信贷之所以有实际的重要性完全在于发展，而发展就可能使暂时闲置的资金利用起来。因此，每一个工商业者都会尽快地利用收到的款项，然后借来他需要的购买力。如果没有发展，那么做生意所必需的资金按理就不得不由厂家或者住户保存起来，在这些资金没有派上用途时，它们就处于闲置的状态。正是发展改变了这种状况。发展把种种那些因从来不借债的自豪感完全否定了。最后当所有的企业——无论是老企业还是新企业——都被拉进信贷现象这个圈时，银行家们甚至仍然宁愿进行这种信贷，因为它所包含的风险更小。许多银行，尤其是“储蓄”型的，还有几乎所有早期建立的银行，事实上都这样做，而且或多或少限制在这种“流通”信贷中。而这只不过是已经全面发展的结果。

这种阐释，不像有的人可能想像的那样，会把我们置于流行说法的对立面。① 相反，我们的说法与通常的观点完全一致，我们认为，如果想要理解循环流转的经济过程，我们可以暂时略去信贷不提。只是因为通行理论采取与我们一样的观点，而且与我们同

① 而且，实际情况直接证实了这一点。过去的多少个世纪里，事实上只有消费信贷。那时只有为创立企业而提供的信贷，而没有它循环周转仍然进行。流通信贷只是到了现代才有当前这样的重要性。既然现代工厂与中世纪手工作坊在经济上没有其他根本差别，我们就可以得出结论：现代工厂在原则上也不需要信贷。

in the financing by credit of current commodity transactions nothing essential to the understanding of the matter, can it eliminate this proceeding from its treatment of the main features of the economic process. Only on this account can it restrict its view to the sphere of goods. Within the world of goods something like credit transactions may of course be found, but we have already come to an understanding on this. At all events the prevailing theory recognizes the necessity of creating new purchasing power at this point just as little as we do, and the fact that it also does not see such a necessity at any other point shows again that it is merely static.

This current credit can therefore be eliminated from our treatment with the same justification as consumptive credit. From the knowledge that it involves only a question of a technical expedient of exchange-in the circular flow, of course, because with development it would be something different for the reason mentioned-an expedient which has no further effect upon the economic process, we come to the following conclusion. In order to contrast current credit sharply with that credit which does play a fundamental role and without which complete understanding of the economic process is impossible, we shall assume in the case of the circular flow that all exchanges are effected by metal money which exists once for all in given quantities and with a given rapidity of circulation. Obviously the whole circulation of an economy without development may also consist of credit means of payment. Since these means of payment, however, would function just Iike metal money in that they are "certificates" for existing goods and past services, and since there is therefore no essential difference between them and metallic money, by using this expository device we merely indicate that what we regard as the essential dement in the credit phenomenon is not to be found in current credit within the circular flow.

By this we have both proved our thesis and precisely formulated the sense in which it is meant. Only the entrepreneur then, in principle,

样地认为，在当前商品性交易中依靠信贷来筹集资金，对理解这类事物没有什么本质关系，所以这种理论在对经济过程的主要特征进行论述时，可以略去这一过程。仅仅是这个原因，通行的理论才能将它的视角限制在商品的范围之内。在商品世界里，当然也可以找到像信贷交易这类事物，不过对此我们已经有所理解了。不管怎样，流行的理论认为在这一时刻创造新的购买力没有什么必要性，这与我们的观点是一致的。而在任何其他时候，流行的理论也看不到这种必要性，这个事实再一次表明了流行的理论只是静态的。

因此，这种流通性的信贷与消费信贷一样，理所当然地可以从我们的论述中略去不提。由于我们认为这种信贷只是一个为了方便交换的技术上的问题——当然，这只是在循环流转中，因为就发展而言，根据前述的理由，那就有所不同了——它是一种对经济过程没有深远影响的权宜措施，我们才能得出下面的结论。为了鲜明地对比这种流通性的信贷与那种起着根本性作用、没有它就不可能完全理解经济过程的信贷，我们假定，在循环流转情况下，所有的交换都受金属货币的影响，而且金属货币的数量是一定的，其流通速度也是一定的。显然，一个不包含发展的经济的整个流通中，也可能含有信用支付手段。然而，由于这些信用支付手段，在作为现有的商品和过去的服务的“证明”方面与金属货币起着相同的作用，因而，这些证明与金属货币没有本质区别，所以，我们用这种方式来解释，只是为了表明，我们所认为的信贷现象中的本质要素，在循环流通领域内，不可能在活期信贷中找到。

这样，我们既证明了我们的论点，也精确地规定了其中的含义。

needs credit; only for industrial development does it play a fundamental part that is a part the consideration of which is essential to an understanding of the whole process. Furthermore, it is seen at once from the arguments of the second chapter that the correlative of the thesis also holds good, namely the statement that where there is no direct power of disposal by leaders over means of production, development is in principle impossible without credit.

The essential function of credit in our sense consists in enabling the entrepreneur to withdraw the producers goods which he needs from their previous employments, by exercising a demand for them, and thereby to force the economic system into new channels. Our second thesis now runs: in so far as credit cannot be given out of the results of past enterprise or in general out of reservoirs of purchasing power created by past development, it can only consist of credit means of payment created ad hoc, which can be backed neither by money in the strict sense nor by products already in existence. It can indeed be covered by other assets than products, that is by any kind of property which the entrepreneur may happen to own. But this is in the first place not necessary and in the second place does not alter the nature of the process, which consists in creating a new demand for, without simultaneously creating, a new supply of goods. This thesis needs no further proof here, but follows from the arguments of the second chapter. It provides us with the connection between lending and credit means of payment, and leads us to what I regard as the nature of the credit phenomenon.

Since credit in the one case in which it is essential to the economic process can only be granted from such newly created means of payment (provided there are no results of previous development); and since, conversely, only in this one case does the creation of such credit means of payment play more than a merely technical role, then to this extent giving credit involves creating purchasing power, and newly created purchasing power is of use only in giving credit to the entrepreneur, is necessary for this purpose alone. This is the only case in which we cannot, without impairing the truth of our theoretical picture, substitute metal money for credit means of payment.

因此，在原则上，只有企业家需要信贷；只有就产业发展而言，信用才起着根本性的作用，考虑这种作用对于理解整个经济过程是极其重要的。此外，从第二章的论述中能立即看出与此论点相关的另一论点，即在领导者没有直接权利支配生产手段的情况下，在原则上，没有信用就不可能有发展。

我们所谈的信贷，其根本作用在于使企业家能够把他需要的生产者的产品从它们先前使用的地方抽取出来，按照需要加以利用，从而迫使经济系统进入新的轨道。我们第二个论点现在可以这样表述：只要不是以过去企业的成果为依据的信贷，或者一般来说，只要不是以过去发展所创造的购买力的储藏为依据的信贷，它就只能是特别创造的信用支付手段，它既没有严格意义上的以货币支持，也没有已经存在的产品来支持。这种信用的确可以由非产品的其他资产，也就是企业家碰巧可能拥有的任何其他财富来担保。但首先这是不必要的，其次它没有改变事物过程的性质，这个过程的本质在于为产品创造一种新的需求，而同时并未创造出一种新的供给。在这里无须对这一论题进一步证明，它只是第二章论证的延伸。它告诉我们借出与信用支付手段之间的联系，并引导我们走向我认为是信贷现象本质的东西。

因为这种在经济过程中极其重要的信用只能通过这些新创造的支付手段来支付（假设没有早期发展的成果）；同时，从反面来说，由于只有在这种情况下，新创造的这种信用支付手段才不仅仅在技术上起作用，在这个意义上，提供信贷就意味着创造购买力，而新创造出来的购买力如果起作用，就只限于把信用给予企业家，只有为了这个目的，新创造的购买力才是必需的。这是我们不能用金属货币替代信用支付手段的唯一情形，同时不损害

For we can assume that a certain quantity of metal money exists at any time, since nothing depends upon its absolute magnitude; but we cannot assume an increase of it to appear just at the right time and place. Therefore if we exclude from lending as well as from the creation of credit instruments those cases in which credit transactions and credit instruments play no essential part, then the two must coincide, if we neglect the results of previous development.

In this sense, therefore, we define the kernel of the credit phenomenon in the following manner: credit is essentially the creation of purchasing power for the purpose of transferring it to the entrepreneur, but not simply the transfer of existing purchasing power. The creation of purchasing power characterizes, in principle, the method by which development is carried out in a system with private property and division of labor. By credit, entrepreneurs are given access to the social stream of goods before they have acquired the normal claim to it. It temporarily substitutes, as it were, a fiction of this claim for the claim itself. Granting credit in this sense operates as an order on the economic system to accommodate itself to the purposes of the entrepreneur, as an order on the goods which he needs: it means entrusting him with productive forces. It is only thus that economic development could arise from the mere circular flow in perfect equilibrium. And this function constitutes the keystone of the modern credit structure.

Hence, while granting credit is not essential in the normal circular flow, because in it no necessary gap exists between products and means of production, and because it can be assumed there that all purchases of production goods by producers are cash transactions or that in general whoever is a buyer previously sold goods of the same money value, it is certain that there is such a gap to bridge in the carrying out of new combinations. To bridge it is thefunction of the lender, and he fulfils it by placing purchasing power created *ad hoc* at the disposal of the entrepreneur.

我们的理论的真实性。因为没有一个事物依存于它的金属货币量的绝对数额，我们可以假定，在任何时候都存在一定数量的金属货币；但我们不能假定，货币量的增长恰好出现在适当的时间和地点。因此，如果我们从贷款以及从信用工具的创造中，排除在那里信用交易和信用工具不起重要作用的情况，那么，贷款和信用工具的创造这两者必然相一致，当然在此我们不考虑先前发展的成果。

因此，在这个意义上，我们用下面的方式定义信贷现象的核心：信贷在本质上是为了把购买力转移给企业家而进行的购买力的创造，而不是单纯的转移现有的购买力。在原则上，购买力的创造标志着，在私有财产和劳动分工的制度下实现发展所采用的方法。凭借信用，企业家在还不具备对社会商品流的正式索取权时，就取得了分享社会商品流的机会。可以说，信贷以一种虚拟的要求权暂时替代了这种索取权本身。在这个意义上，提供信贷就像一道命令，要求经济系统来适应企业家的目的，也像是一道命令要求提供商品去满足企业家的需求：这意味着把生产要素都委托给企业家。只有这样，才可能在完全均衡的简单的循环流转中实现经济的发展。这种职能构成了现代信贷结构的基石。

因为在正常的循环流转中，产品和生产手段之间不一定存在距离，而且，因为可以假定在那里生产者购买所有生产物品都是现金交易，或者，一般来说，任何一个购买者都是先出售相同货币价值的商品然后再买进，所以，提供信贷在正常的循环流转中不是至关重要的。尽管如此，但在实施新的组合时，肯定会出现一个有待填充的缺口。填充这个缺口就是贷款者的职能，他通过把创造出来的购买力特地交给企业家支配来履行这个职能。于是，提供

Then those who supply production goods need not "wait" and yet the entrepreneur need advance them neither goods nor existing money. Thus the gap is closed which would otherwise make development extraordinarily difficult, if not impossible in an exchange economy where private property prevails. That the function of lenders lies in this is denied by no one. Differences of opinion exist only about the nature of the "bridge." I believe that our conception, far from being more audacious and foreign to reality than others, is nearest to reality and makes a whole network of fictions superfluous.

In the circular flow, from which we always start, the same products are produced every year in the same way. For every supply there waits somewhere in the economic system a corresponding demand, for every demand the corresponding supply. All goods are dealt in at determined prices with only insignificant oscillations, so that every unit of money may be considered as going the same way in every period. A given quantity of purchasing power is available at any moment to purchase the existing quantity of original productive services, in order then to pass into the hands of their owners and then again to be spent on consumption goods. There is no market for the bearers of the original productive services themselves, especially for land, and there is also no price for them within the normal circular flow. ①

If we neglect, as unessential, the value of the material of the monetary units, the purchasing power then really represents nothing but existing goods. Its total tells us nothing, but the shares of households and firms in this total do. If now credit means of payment, new purchasing power in our sense,

① Cf. the construction in Chapter I, from which it is clear why I do not mention produced means of production with the services of labor and land, although purchasing power is obviously applied to them too and not only to the services of labor and land.

生产品的人就不需要“等待”，而企业家也就既不需要用商品，也不用拿现金预付供货商。这样，缺口被弥合；否则，在私有财产制的交换经济中，实现发展，即使不是不可能的，也将特别困难。谁也不会否认，贷款者的职能就在于此。意见的分歧只存在于对这个弥补缺口的“桥梁”的性质的认识。我相信我们的概念，其他观点更不审慎，更脱离实际，而我们的是最接近事实的，并且用不着编造一套虚构的解释。

在我们一直以此为出发点的循环流转中，年复一年地以相同的方式生产着同样的产品。对于每一项供给，总有一个相应的需求在经济系统里的某个地方等着它；同样对于每一项需求，都有相应的供给。所有商品都按照一个确定的价格进行买卖，这个价格只可能有微小波动，所以每一单位货币可以被看做在每一时期起相同的作用。在任何时候，一定数量的购买力可以购买到最初生产性服务的现有数量，然后按此顺序，购买力转移到拥有生产性服务的人手中，继而又被花费到消费品上。对这些初始生产性服务的主体本身来说，尤其对土地来说，没有市场，而且在正常的循环流转中也不存在任何购买服务的价格。①

如果我们忽略货币单位的材料价值，因为它对根本问题不重要，那么购买力实际上就只代表现存的商品。购买力总量说明不了什么问题，但是在这个总量中，家庭和厂商所占的份额，对我们是很有意义的。如果现在信用支付手段，就是我们说的新的购买

---

① 参阅第一章的解释，就可以明白为什么我没有提及用劳动和土地服务生产出来的生产工具；尽管购买力显然也用来购买它们，而不只是购买劳动和土地的服务。

are created and placed at the entrepreneur's disposal, then he takes his place beside the previous producers and his purchasing power its place beside the total previously existing. Obviously this does not increase the quantity of productive services existing in the economic system. Yet "new demand" becomes possible in a very obvious sense. It causes a rise in the prices of productive services. From this ensues the "withdrawal of goods" from their previous use, to which we have referred, ①The process amounts to compressing②the existing purchasing power. In one sense no goods and certainly no new goods correspond to the newly created purchasing power. But room for it is squeezed out at the cost of previously existing purchasing power.

This explains the manner in which the creation of purchasing power works. The reader can see that there is nothing illogical or mystical in it. ③The external form of the credit instruments is

---

① On this point I differ from Spiethoff. His three articles: "Die ussere Ordnung des Kapita – lund Geldmarktes," "Das Verhaltnisvon Kapital, Geld, und Güterwelt," and "Der Kapitalmangel in seinem Verhaltnisse zur Güterwelt" in Schmollet's Jahrbuch (1909) (also independently under the title Kapital Geld und Güterwelt) have above all the merit of having attacked the problem. At a number of points they anticipated what is said in this chapter. The possibility of "creating new money substitutes" was also expressly emphasised (for example, in the second article, p. 85). But to this there is an "insurmountable economic limit, in the existing supply of goods. Only in so far as these artificial measures can put hitherto idle goods in circulation are they able to work." If this limit is exceeded prices rise. The latter is certainly correct-but the salient point for us is precisely here. Of course we agree that tightness of money cannot be eliminated by creating purchasing power-or at any rate can only be when it is a matter of a momentary panic.

② In the first place, the purchasing power of previous producers in the market for producers' goods will be compressed, then the purchasing power in the market for consumption goods of those people who receive no share or no adequate share in the increased money incomes resulting from the entrepreneur's demand. This explains rising prices in periods of boom. If I am not mistaken it was yon Mises who coined the extremely happy expression "forced saving" (erzwungenes Sparen) for this process.

③ Cf. also A. Hahn, the article "Kredit" in the Handwörterbuch der Staatswissenschaften.

力，被创造出来并交给企业家支配，那么企业家就会跻身于先前生产者的行列，并且他的购买力也与先前的购买力总量并存。显然，这没有增加经济系统里现有的生产性服务的数量。但是很明显，“新的需求”可能出现了。它将导致生产性服务的价格的提高。接着出现了物品从其原先的用途中“撤除商品”的现象，这一点我们已经提过。[①] 这一过程起到了压缩[②]现有购买力的作用。在某种意义上说，没有任何商品，而且肯定没有任何新的商品与这个新创造出来的购买力相适应。只有以牺牲先前存在的购买力为代价，才有这种新创造出来的购买力的容身之地。

以上解释了购买力的创造是如何起作用的。读者可以看出，其中没有任何非逻辑或者神秘的东西。[③] 信用工具的外在形式是

---

① 关于这一点，我与斯皮托夫有分歧。他发表在《施穆勒年鉴》(1909 年）的三篇文章：《资本市场和货币市场的外部秩序》、《资本、货币和商品世界的关系》和《资本缺乏及其对商品世界的关系》（这三篇文章也曾以《资本、货币和商品世界的关系》为书名单独出版过)，它们的主要功绩在于探索了这个问题。在若干方面，这三篇文章预见了本章所论述的问题。那里也曾明确强调过“创造新的货币替代品”的可能性（比如，在第二篇文章的第 85 页)。但在现有的商品供应的状况下，强调这个可能性，有一个“不可逾越的经济限制。只有当这些人为的措施能够把迄今为止闲置的商品放入流通中，它才能起作用”。如果超过这个限度，价格就会上涨。这一点肯定是正确的——这也正是值得我们关注的一点。当然，我们也认为银根紧不能靠创造购买力来消除——或者说，无论如何只有当银根紧只是暂时的恐慌情况下，才可能是这样。

② 首先，先前的生产者在生产品市场上的购买力会被压缩，接着一些人在消费品市场上的购买力被压缩，这些人不能分享由于企业家的需求而产生的货币收入的增加，或者说没有分享到足够的利益。这可以用来解释繁荣时期价格上涨的情况。如果我没有弄错的话，是冯·米塞斯曾把这个过程绝妙地概括为“强迫储蓄”。

③ 也可参阅 A. 汉恩写的《信贷》一文，载《政治学袖珍辞典》。

quite irrelevant. To be sure, the matter is seen most plainly in the case of the uncovered bank-note. But also a bill, which does not replace existing money, and which is not based upon goods already produced, is of the same character, if it actually circulates. Of course this is not true if it merely records the entrepreneur's obligation to his creditor or if it is merely discounted, but only when it is used in paying for goods. And all other forms of credit instruments, even simple credits in the books of a bank, may be considered from the same point of view. Just as when additional gas streams into a vessel the share of the space occupied by each molecule of the previously existing gas is diminished by compression, so the inflow of new purchasing power into the economic system will compress the old purchasing power. When the price changes which thus become necessary are completed, any givencommodities exchange for the new units of purchasing power on the same terms as for the old, only the units of purchasing power now existing are all smaller than those existing before and their distribution among individuals has been shifted.

This may be called credit inflation. But it is distinguished from credit inflation for consumptive purposes by a very essential element. In these cases also new purchasing power takes its place beside the old, prices rise, a withdrawal of goods results in favor of the credit receiver or of those to whom the latter pays out the borrowed sums. There the process breaks off: the goods withdrawn are consumed, the means of payment created remain in circulation, the credit must be continually renewed, and prices have risen permanently. It may be then that the loan is paid off out of the normal income stream-for example by an increase in taxation. But this is a new, special operation (deflation), which, proceeding in the well known way, again restores the health of the monetary system, which but for it would not return to its previous state.

In our case, however, the process goes *vi impressa* further. The entrepreneur must not only legally repay money to his banker, but

毫不相关的。当然，从无保证的银行券来看，事情最清楚不过了。但是，那种不能代替现存货币，并且不是以已经生产出的商品为基础的票据，如果它们在实际中流通，也会有相同的特征。当然，这里说的只是票据作为偿付货款的情况，如果票据只是用来偿付企业家对其贷款人的债务，或者仅仅是用来贴现，那么情况就不是这样了。信用工具的所有其他形式，甚至是银行账面上的简单信贷，也都可以从相同的观点来考虑。这就像当新的气流进入一个容器时，容器里先前存在的气体的每一分子所占的空间就会因挤压而缩小一样，当新的购买力注入经济系统时，也会压缩老的购买力。当价格变动结束时——这是必然的，任何一定数量的商品都可以按照交换购买力的老单位的相同的条件来交换购买力的新单位，只不过这时的购买力的单位比以前的都小一些，而且在每个个体当中购买力的分配也互相交换了。

这可以被称为信用膨胀。但是这种信用膨胀与以消费为目的的信用膨胀在某一本质问题上是不同的。在消费信用膨胀的情况下，新的购买力也与老的并存，价格也上涨，结果商品被抽取出来，信贷获得者或者从这种贷款的偿还中获得收入的人从中受益。这时老的流通过程断裂，抽取出来的商品被消费，而新创造出来的支付手段仍在流通，信用必须不断地更新，上涨的物价将继续上涨。这时可能发生用正常的收入流来偿付贷款的情况——比如增加赋税。但这是一个新的特殊的措施（通货紧缩），它以人们都知道的方式，又重新恢复货币体系的健康，除了它，没有能使货币体系回到原先状态的措施了。

然而，在我们的例子中，这个过程肯定会向前发展。企业家不仅一定会依法向银行家还款，而且在经济上，他也必然会把生

he must also economically repay commodities to the reservoir of goods-the equivalent of borrowed productive means; or, as we have expressed it, he must ultimately fulfill the condition upon which goods may normally be taken out of the social stream. The result of the borrowing enables him to fulfill this condition. After completing his business-in our conception, therefore, after a period at the end of which his products are on the market and his productive goods used up-he has, if everything has gone according to expectations, enriched the social stream with goods whose total price is greater than the credit received and than the total price of the goods directly and indirectly used up by him. Hence the equivalence between the money and commodity streams is more than restored, the credit inflation more than eliminated, the effect upon prices more than compensated for, ①so that it may be said that there is no credit inflation at all in this case-rather deflation-but only a non-synchronous appearance of purchasing power and of the commodities corresponding to it, which temporarily produces the semblance of inflation.

Furthermore, the entrepreneur can now repay his debt (amount credited plus interest) at his bank, and normally still retain a credit balance (= entrepreneurial profit) that is withdrawn from the purchasing-power fund of the circular flow. Only this profit and interest necessarily remain in circulation; the original bank credit has disappeared, so that the deflationary effect in itself and especially if new and bigger enterprises are not continually being financed-would be much more severe than that just indicated. It is true that in practice two reasons prevent the prompt disappearance of the newly created purchasing power: first the fact that most enterprises are not terminated in one period but in most cases only after a series of years. The essence of the matter is not

① This alone would explain falling prices in periods of depression and actually explains the secular fall in the price level in times when no other causes, for example gold discoveries, prevent it, as we shall see in Chapter VI.

产出来的产品归还到商品的储存地与借来的生产手段相等价；或者，像我们已经表述的那样，他最终必然履行他能够从社会流转中正常地获取商品的条件。借款的结果使他能够履行这个条件。因此，企业家在完成他的经营活动之后——在我们所定义的意义上，在他的产品已经上市，生产品已经用完，这样一个生产周期的终点时——如果所有的事都按照预期的发生，那他就以一批总价格高于他所得的信贷款，也大于他直接和间接用掉的商品的总价格的商品，增加了社会流转的财富。因此，货币流转额与商品流转额不仅达到了平衡，还有节余，信用膨胀被消除而有余，对价格的影响也已弥补且有余，[①] 因此可以说，在这种情况下，根本没有信用膨胀——倒可以说存在信用紧缩——只不过是购买力与其相应的商品不同时出现，这样就造成了暂时膨胀的假相。

进一步说，企业家现在可以偿还他欠银行的债务（贷款额加上利息），而且在正常情况下，仍然持有一个信贷余额（=企业家利润），这是从循环流转的购买力基金中提取出来的。只有这个利润和利息必然保留在流通中；初始的银行信贷已经消失了，所以，这种紧缩效应本身——尤其是，如果新的以及更大型的企业没有继续被要求提供资金——将比刚才所说的还要严重得多。诚然，在实际中有两个原因阻止了新创造的购买力的立即消失：第一个原因是，大多数企业不会在一个时期内就终止其生产经营，而是在多数情况下，它们要持续一些年份。事情的本质并不

---

① 这一点就足以解释经济萧条时期价格下跌的现象，事实上它也解释了价格水平下降的长期趋势，如果在那时没有其他原因，例如发现黄金，就阻止了这个趋势。我们在第六章可以看到这一点。

altered by this, but the newly created purchasing power remains longer in circulation and the "redemption" at the legal date then often takes the form of a "prolongation." In this case it is economically no redemption at all but a method of periodically testing the soundness of the enterprise. Economically this should really be called "presentation for audit" instead of "presentation for payment"-whether the thing to be redeemed is a bill or a personal loan. Moreover, if it is true that long-term enterprises are financed by short-term credit, every entrepreneur and every bank will try for obvious reasons to exchange this basis as soon as possible for a more permanent one, indeed will regard it as an achievement if the first stage can be completely jumped in an individual case. In practice this approximately coincides with replacing purchasing power created *ad hoc* by that existing already. And this generally happens in the case of development in full swing which has already accumulated reserves of purchasing power – thus for reasons which our theory itself explains and which do not argue against it-and indeed in two steps.

In the first place, shares or bonds are created and their amounts are credited to the enterprise, which means that banking resources still finance the enterprise. Then these shares and bonds are disposed of and gradually are paid for-not always at once, on the contrary the accounts of the subscribing customers are often only debited-by the subscribers out of existing supplies of purchasing power or reserves or savings. Thus, as it may be expressed, they are resorbed by the community's savings. The redemption of the credit instruments is thus accomplished and they are replaced by existing money. But this is not yet the final redemption of the entrepreneur's debt, the redemption in goods. The latter only comes later, even in this case.

Secondly, still another fact prevents the prompt disappearance of the new purchasing power. Credit instruments may disappear in the case of final success, they have so to say the tendency to do so automatically. But even if they do not disappear, no disturbance occurs either in the individual or in the social economy for now the commodities are there which constitute a counter-balance to

因此而改变，但是新创造的购买力要在流通中存在很久，信贷票据到法定日期的“偿还”常常采取“延期”的方式。在这种情况下，从经济上说，根本不是信贷的偿还，而是一种定期对企业健全性检查的方法。在经济上，这实际应该被称作“申请审核”，而不是“申请付款”，无论应偿还的是银行票据还是个人贷款。此外，如果生产周期长的企业是靠短期信贷来融资的，那么每一个企业家和每一家银行都会因明显的理由力图尽快地把这个信贷改为更长时期的；在个别情况下，如果完全可以越过这第一阶段，那么借贷双方都将把此看做一项成就。实际上，这就相当于用实际存在的购买力替代特地创造出来的购买力。通常这种情况发生在已经积累了购买力储备，充分自由的发展之中——我们的理论本身已经说明了其原因，这些原因与我们的理论并不相悖——实际上这有两个步骤：

第一，发行股票或者债券，并将数额记在企业的贷方，这意味着仍然是银行的资源帮助企业筹集资金。然后这些股票和债券被卖掉，并逐步由购买者用现存的购买力供给，或者储备基金，或者存款，来支付款项——当然通常不是立即支付，相反，只在往来账的借方记上认购者的姓名。这样，正如所说的，股票和债券又被社会的储蓄吸收了。信贷工具的偿还就这样完成了，并被现存的货币取代。但这还不是企业家对其债务的最后的偿还，那是要用商品来偿还。即使在这情况下，用商品偿还也会在稍迟才出现。

第二，还有另一个原因阻碍着新购买力的立即消失。在最终取得成功时，信用工具可能会消失，可以说这一趋势是自发的。但是即使信用工具不消失，对个人的经济或者社会经济也不会有什么干扰——因为这时商品已经生产出来，它与新购买力持平，

and the only really significant kind of "cover" for the new purchasing power, which is precisely what is always absent in the case of consumptive credit. And so the process of production can always be repeated anew with the help of renewal of credit, although this is no longer "new enterprise" within our meaning. The credit instruments thus not only have no further influence upon prices, but they even lose that which they originally exercised. Indeed, this is the most important of the ways in which bank credit forces its way into the circular flow, until it has so established itself there that analytical effort is necessary in order to recognize that its source is not there, if this were not so the received theory would not only be false-which it is in any case-but inexcusable and incomprehensible.

If the possibility of giving credit is therefore not limited by the quantity of liquid resources existing independently of creation for the very purpose of granting credit, nor by the existing-idle or total-quantity of goods, by what is it limited?

First as regards practice: let us assume that we have a free gold standard, that is redemption of bank-notes in gold upon demand, the obligation to purchase gold at a legal price, and free export of gold. Assume also that we have a banking system grouped around a central note-issuing bank, but that there are no other legal barriers and rules for the gestation of banking business – for example no note-reserve regulations and so on for the central bank or deposit-reserve regulations and so on for the other banks. This represents the leading case, the treatment of which is easily applicable to other cases. Then every new creation of purchasing power which precedes the appearance of the corresponding quantities of goods and hence raises prices will have the tendency to raise the value of the gold contained in gold coin above the value of the monetary unit. This will lead to a diminution of the quantity of gold in circulation, but above all to the presentation of bank means of payment for redemption, first bank-notes, then directly and indirectly all others, in another sense, for another purpose and for another reason

而且是新购买力的唯一真正重要的“保证”，这恰恰是消费性信贷情况下所没有的。所以生产过程借助于信贷展期而周而复始地进行，尽管这已不再是我们所说意义上的“新企业”了。于是，信用工具不仅不再对价格有影响，而且甚至失去了它们原先产生的影响。这的确是银行信贷跻身于循环流转所用的方式中最重要的一个方式，直到它在循环流转中的地位确立，必要的分析才认清它的本源并不存在于循环流转中。如果情况不是这样，那么被公认的理论就不仅是错误的——无论在什么情况下都是如此——而且是不容宽恕的以及不可理解的。

如果提供信贷的可能性，不受实际流动资金数额的限制，这个流动资金数额独立于专为提供信贷目的的创造，也不受现存商品数量（闲置的或者总量）的限制，那么是什么限制着提供信贷的可能性呢？

首先从实际来说，我们假定有一个自由金本位，也就是钞票可以随时从银行兑换黄金，必须以法定价格兑换黄金，黄金可以自由出口。我们还假定有一个以发行钞票的中央银行为中心的银行体系，但除此之外没有其他不利于酝酿银行业务的法律障碍和条款——比如，对中央银行没有钞票准备金发行之类的规定，对其他银行没有存款准备金之类的规定。这代表着一种主要情况，对它的论述可以很容易用到其他场合。于是，在相应数量的商品出现之前，每一次新的购买力的创造使得价格上涨，这样就有一个趋势：把包含在金币内的黄金的价值抬高到单位货币价值之上。这将导致流通中的黄金数量的减少，但最重要的是银行支付手段申请兑换黄金，首先是银行券要求兑现，然后所有其他支付手段直接或间接地要求兑现，在意义、目的和原因上都与

than that which we have just described. And if the solvency of the banking system in this sense is not to be endangered, the banks can only give credit in such a way that the resulting inflation is really temporary and moreover remains moderate. But it can only remain temporary if the commodity complement of the newly created purchasing power comes on the market at the right time, and if, in cases of failure where it does not appear on the market at all and in cases of lengthy production where it appears only after long years, the banker intervenes with purchasing power drawn from the circular flow, for example with money saved by other people. Hence the necessity of maintaining a reserve, which acts as a brake on the central bank as well as on the other banks. Competing with this nexus is the circumstance that all credits given are finally resolved into small sums in daily trade, and in order to serve in the latter must be changed into coin or small state notes-at least in most countries which cannot be created by the banks. Finally, the credit inflation must start an outflow of gold abroad-hence a further danger of insolvency. It may happen, however, and is indeed sometimes approximately realised, that the banks of all countries extend their credits almost simultaneously. Therefore, even if we cannot, in the nature of things, state the limit to the creation of purchasing power under the assumptions made as accurately as, say, the limit to the production of a commodity, and even if the limit must vary according to the mentality of the people, legislation, and so on, yet we can state that there is such a limit at any time and what circumstances normally guarantee its maintenance. Its existence neither excludes the creation of purchasing power in our sense nor alters its significance. But it makes its volume at any time an elastic, though nevertheless a definite, magnitude.

The fundamental question under consideration here is of course only very superficially answered by the above; just as the question regarding the reasons for a rate of exchange is answered superficially by saying it must lie between the gold points in the case of a universal free gold standard. However, just as we look at essentials in the latter case

我们已经描述的不同。而且如果这个银行体系在这个意义上的偿付能力没有什么危险，那么银行就只能用这种方式发放信贷，也就是它所引起的膨胀确实是暂时的，而且它的强度始终是温和的。但是只有当新创造的购买力所需补充的商品适时到达市场，膨胀才可能是暂时的；同时如果经营失败，使补充商品根本不能提供到市场，或者由于生产周期过长，补充商品只能在较长年份之后提供，那么银行家将用从循环流转中提取出来的购买力进行干预，比如，用别人的存款。因此，有必要维持一定量的储备，它对中央银行以及其他银行起着制动作用。与银行这种结构相对立的一种情况是：所有发放的信贷在日常买卖中最终都将化为很小的数额，而为此目的，必须将其换成硬币或者小面额的政府纸币——至少在大多数国家是这样——那不是银行所能创造的。最后，信用膨胀必然引起黄金外溢——因而将进一步带来无力偿付的危险。然而也有可能：所有国家的银行几乎同时扩张信贷，有时实际情况确实就是这样。因此，即使我们不能理所当然地在我们假设的情况下，如同表述某种商品生产的限度那样准确地表述创造购买力的限度，而且即使这种限度一定会根据人们心理状态及立法等等而发生变化，我们也还是可以说，在任何时候都存在着这种限度，而且也可以说明，是什么条件正常地保证着这个限度持续地起着作用。这个限度的存在既不排除我们所说的购买力的创造，也不改变它的重要性。但是，这个限度使得信贷量在任何时候都有一个弹性，尽管仍然是一个确定的量。

以上当然只是很肤浅地回答了这里我们提出的基本问题，就像把普遍实行自由金本位制度下确定外汇率的问题简单地回答为它必然处于黄金输送点之间一样。然而，就像我们看汇率问题，

if we omit the gold mechanism and look at the "commodity points" underneath, so in our case, by the same principle, we arrive at a more fundamental explanation of the fact that the creation of purchasing power has definite, even though elastic, limits if we consider a country with a paper standard or let us say outright with nothing but bank means of payment. Since the case of countries trading with one another offers nothing fundamentally new we leave the analysis of it to the reader. Here, then, the limit is given by the condition that credit inflation in favor of new enterprises should be only temporary, or that there should be no inflation at all in the sense of permanently raising the price level. And the brake which guarantees the maintenance of this limit is the fact that any other conduct in the face of the rush of entrepreneurs seeking credit would mean a loss for the bank concerned. This loss always occurs if the entrepreneur does not succeed in producing commodities at least equal in value to the credit plus interest. Only when he succeeds in so doing has the bank done good business-then and only then, however, is there also no inflation, as we have shown, that is no infraction of the limit. From this the rules may be derived which determine in individual cases the magnitude of the possible creation of purchasing power.

Only in one other case could the banking world, if it were released from the obligation of redeeming its means of payment in gold and if the regard for international exchange were suspended, start inflation and arbitrarily determine the price level, not only without loss but even with profit: namely, if it pumped credit means of payment into the circular flow either by making bad commitments good by a further creation of new circulating media or by giving credits which really serve consumptive ends. In general no single bank could do this. For while its issue of means of payment would not appreciably affect the price level, the bad commitment would remain bad and the consumptive credit

如果我们忽略黄金机制而去关注作为基础的“商品输送点”，就能看到这个问题的实质。所以在我们的信贷问题中，用同样的原理，如果我们考虑一个纸本位的国家，或者干脆考虑的是只有银行支付工具的国家，那么我们将得到一个对下面这一事实更基本的解释，这一事实即是：购买力的创造有确定的，尽管有弹性的限度。由于国家之间的贸易没有什么根本上新的东西，我们把这个问题的分析留给读者去做。于是，在这里，我们说，这个限度是由下面的条件产生的：即，为了使新企业受益所产生的信用膨胀应该只是暂时的，或者说根本不该有像物价水平持续上涨那样的膨胀。并且，保证这个限度起作用的制动器就是一个事实，即，面对企业家们追求银行信贷的冲击，任何其他行为都将对所涉及的银行造成损失。如果企业家不能成功地生产出至少与贷款额加利息之和等价值的商品，这种损失就会经常发生。只有当企业家成功地生产了足够的产品，银行做的才是有利的放贷——然而这时，而且只有这时，才没有我们前面所说的通货膨胀，才没有逾越上述的限度。从这里可以得出某种尺度，它决定了在各自的情况下可能创造购买力的数量。

只有在另一种情况下，即：如果银行取消了黄金作为支付手段的义务，如果暂停了国际兑换的责任，银行才可能引发膨胀，并且放任地决定价格水平，这不仅没有损失，反而还有利，也就是说，银行把新的信用支付手段注入循环流转中，或者由于进一步创造新的流通手段，而使不佳的偿还能力状况转好，或者使消费目的因提供信贷而真正得到满足。通常，没有任何银行能单独做到这一点。因为尽管它发放的支付手段不会对价格水平有显著的影响，但是偿债能力不佳的状况仍然不佳，而消费信贷，由于银

become bad if it did not lie within the limits in which it could be repaid by the debtor out of his income. But all banks together could do it. They could, under our assumptions, continually give additional credit and precisely through its effect upon prices make good that given previously. And that this is possible to a certain extent even outside these assumptions is the chief reason why special legal restrictions and special safety-valves are actually necessary in practice.

This last statement is really self-evident. Just as the state, under certain circumstances, can print notes without any assignable limit, so the banks could do likewise if the state-for it comes to this-were to transfer the right to them in their interest and for their purposes, and common sense did not prevent them from exercising it. But this has nothing to do with our case, viz. the case of granting credit and creating purchasing power for carrying out new combinations *which are remunerative at the existing level of prices*①-hence nothing to do with the meaning, nature, and origin of the creation of entrepreneurial purchasing power in general. I emphasize this expressly because the thesis concerning the unlimited power of the banks to create circulating media, after being repeatedly quoted, not only without the necessary qualifications, but also without the context in which it stands, ②has become a point of attack and a ground for rejecting the new theory of credit.

---

① Our theory has been interpreted to mean that credit creation facilitates the carrying out of new things by raising prices and thereby making remunerative what would not otherwise be so. This is *not* what it means.

② Cf. the otherwise excellent article by Hahn in the Handwörterbuch der Staatswissenschaften on "Kredit." Against his formulation it appears to me correct to say: although not by existing goods, the quantity of new purchasing power that it is possible to create is supported and limited by *future* goods, and, to repeat, by future goods at *present* prices.

行的债务人不能在限期内用其收入偿还债务，而变得不利。但是如果所有的银行一起行动，就可能实现。在我们的假设下，他们可以继续发放新的信贷，并通过对价格施加影响，使原先发放的信贷发生转机。在某种程度上，甚至在我们假设的范围之外，这种情况也是可能发生的，这正是为什么专门的法律限制和专门的安全调节阀门，在实际中确实是必需的主要原因。

上面最后一点的确是不言自明的。正像国家在某种情况下不需要任何规定的限制就可以印发钞票一样，银行也可以这样做，如果国家果真把印发钞票的权利转交给银行，使银行以自己的利益和目的照样去做，而且常识也不会阻止银行这样做。但这与我们讨论的问题无关，换句话说，我们讨论的问题是为了在现实的价格水平下可以获利的新组合的实现，而提供信贷和创造购买力①——因此，这与一般创造企业家的购买力的意义、性质和起源无关。我明确强调这一点是因为有关银行有无限权利创造流通手段的论点，被反复引用之后，不仅失去了必要的证实，而且也脱离了它所立论的上下文，② 结果变成了受攻击的对象，变成了拒绝新的信贷理论的一个基础。

---

① 我们的理论曾被解释为，信贷的创造通过提高价格使新事物得以实现，并因而使新事物获利，否则就不会获利。这并不是我们的本意。

② 参阅另一篇由汉恩写的极好的文章《信贷》，在《政治学袖珍辞典》中，但在有关这一点上有待商榷。我与他的观点不同，我认为正确的说法应该是：尽管没有现实的商品支持它，但是可能创造出来的新的购买力的数量却受到未来商品的支持与限制，重复一下，我所说的是用现行价格计算的未来商品。

CAPITAL

It is now time to give expression to a thought which has long been awaiting formulation and which is familiar to every businessman. That form of economic organisation in which the goods necessary for new production are withdrawn from their settled place in the circular flow by the intervention of purchasing power created *ad hoc* is the capitalist economy, while those forms of economy in which this happens through any kind of power of command or through agreement of all concerned represent noncapitalistic production. *Capital is nothing but the lever by which the entrepreneur subjects to his control the concrete goods which he needs, nothing but a means of diverting the factors of production to new uses, or of dictating a new direction to production.* This is the only function of capital, and by it the place of capital in the economic organism is completely characterised.

Now what is this lever, this means of control? It certainly does not consist of any definite category of goods, of any definable part of the existing supply of goods. It is generally recognized that we meet with capital in production and that it is useful in some way or other in the productive process. Hence we must also see it somewhere in operation in our case of carrying out new combinations. Now all the goods which the entrepreneur needs are on the same level from his standpoint. He wants the services of natural agents, of labor, of machinery, of raw material, all of them equally and in just the same sense, and nothing distinguishes one of these wants from the others. Of course this is not to say that there is no relevant difference at all between these categories of goods. On the contrary there are certainly differences, even though their significance was and still

资　本

现在正是我们就一个早就等待着被系统地说明，并且是所有工商业者都熟悉的观点，发表我们见解的时候了。在一个经济系统中，如果新的生产所必需的货物，是通过特别创造出来的购买力的干预，从循环流转中它原来放置的地方抽取出来的，那么这种经济组织的形式就是资本主义经济；而在另一种经济系统里，新的生产所必需的货物，是靠任何一种命令的权利或者靠所有有关方面的协议，从循环流转中抽取出来，这种经济组织的形式就是非资本主义生产。资本，只不过是一种杠杆，凭借它，企业家就可以控制他所需要的具体的商品；资本，只不过是一种将生产要素转到新的用途，或者将其引入一个新的生产方向的手段。这就是资本唯一的职能，凭借这个职能，资本在经济组织中的地位就被完全描绘出来。

那么，这个杠杆是什么，控制的手段是什么？它肯定不是由任何确定的商品种类构成，也不是由现有供应的商品的任何可确定的部分构成。通常人们认为，我们在生产中遇到资本，而且在生产过程中资本以不同的方式发挥作用。因此，在我们所说的实施新组合的场合下，我们也必然会在某个地方看到资本在起作用。现在，从企业家的视角看，他所需要的所有商品都处于相同的地位。他需要自然力、人力、机器、原材料，所有这些都同等重要，而且具有同样的意义，并且无法区分这些需要中哪一个更重要。当然这并不是说，这些类型的商品之间根本没有任何相应的区别。相反，肯定有差别，即使这些差别的重要性在过去和现在

is overestimated by many theorists. But it is clear that the entrepreneur's behavior is the same towards all these categories: he buys all of them for money, for which he calculates or pays interest, without distinction, whether they are tools or land or labor. They all play the same part, are equally necessary for him. In particular it is quite immaterial whether he begins his production as it were *ab ovo*, that is merely buys land and labor, or whether, he also acquires already existing intermediate products instead of producing them himself. Finally, if he should acquire consumption goods this would make no fundamental difference either. Nevertheless, it would look as if consumption goods had the first claim to be emphasized, especially if one accepted the theory that the entrepreneur "advances" consumption goods to the possessors of productive means, in the narrower sense of the word. In this case these goods would be characteristically different from other goods; they would play a special role, and indeed precisely the one which we assign to capital: From this it would follow that the entrepreneur would exchange productive services for consumption goods. Then we should have to say that capital consists of consumption goods. However, this possibility is already settled.

Setting aside this last interpretation, then, there is no reason for making any kind of distinction between all the goods which the entrepreneur buys, consequently no reason for including any group of them under the name capital. That capital defined so as to consist of goods belongs to every economic organization and hence is not suitable for characterising the capitalistic one, requires no argument. Furthermore, it is not true that if the businessman were asked wherein consists his capital, he would point to any of these categories of goods. If he mentions his factory he includes the ground on which it stands, and if he wishes to be complete he will not forget his working capital in which directly or indirectly purchases of labor services are included.

The capital of an enterprise, however, is also not the aggregate of *all* the goods serving its purposes. For capital *confronts the* world of goods. Goods are bought for capital-"capital is invested in goods"

都被许多理论家高估了。但是有一点是很清楚的，那就是，企业家对这些类型的商品所采取的行为是相同的：无论对工具、土地，还是劳力，他都要花钱，这些钱是他仔细计算，付了利息得来的，这一点没有任何区别。对企业家来说，这些商品起着同样的作用，而且都是必需的。特别有一点是不重要的，那就是，企业家是像开始创业那样，仅仅购买土地和劳力来开始生产，还是他也购买已经存在的中间产品，而不再自己生产它们。最后，如果他应该获得消费品，情况也不会有任何根本差别。尽管如此，获取消费品似乎是最有要求权的，应该被重视，尤其是，如果人们接受这一理论：企业家“预付”（就狭义的概念而言）消费品给生产手段的所有者，情况更是如此。在这种情况下，这些消费品不同于其他商品，它们有独特的地方；它们起着一种特殊的作用，这正是我们赋予资本的作用。由此，我们认为，企业家用生产性服务交换消费品。所以，我们不能不说，资本包含着消费品。然而，我们的论述已经解决了这种可能性。

于是，除了上面的论述，就没有理由再区分企业家所购买的所有商品了，因此也就没有理由把其中的任何一类商品包含在资本的名义中。把资本定义为是由商品构成的，这种定义适用于每一个经济组织，因此就不能作为资本主义经济组织的独有特征，这是没有争议的。此外，如果一个商人被人问起他的资本在哪里，他将举出这些商品中的任意一种作为他的资本，这是不正确的。如果他提到他的工厂，他就会把工厂所占的土地也包括在其中；如果他想说得全面一些，他将不会忘记包括他的流动资本，这些流动资本是直接或间接为购买劳动力服务的。

然而，一个企业的资本也不是服务于企业目的的所有商品的总和。因为资本对应于商品世界。购买商品来作为资本——“资本被投资于商品”

-but this very fact implies the recognition that its function is different from that of the goods acquired. The function of the goods consists in serving a productive purpose corresponding to their technical nature. The function of capital consists in procuring for the entrepreneur the means with which to produce. It stands as a third agent necessary to production in an exchange economy *between* the entrepreneur and the world of goods. It constitutes the bridge between them. It does not take part directly in production, it is not itself "worked up"; on the contrary it performs a task which must be done before technical production can begin.

The entrepreneur must have capital before he can think of providing himself with concrete goods. There is a time when he already has the necessary capital but not yet the production goods, and at this moment one can see more clearly than ever that capital is not something identical with concrete goods but is an independent agent. And its only purpose, the only reason why the entrepreneur needs capital-I appeal to obvious facts -is simply to serve as a fund out of which productive goods can be paid for. Furthermore, so long as this purchase is not completed, the capital has absolutely no relation to any definite goods at all. It exists of course-who could deny it? -but its characteristic quality is precisely that it does not come into consideration as a concrete category of goods, that it is not employed technically as a good, but as a means of providing those goods which are to be employed in production in the technical sense. But when this purchase is completed, does the entrepreneur's capital then consist of concrete goods-of all kinds of land bought as well as of tools bought, but still of goods? If one exclaims with Quesnay: "Parcourez les fermes et les ateliers, et... vous trouverez des bâtiments, des bestiaux, des semences, des matières premières, des meubles et des instruments de touteèesp ce"-from our point of view one must add further: services of land and labor and also consumption goods as well -is not this justified after the purchase? The capital has now fulfilled the function ascribed to it by us. If the necessary productive means, and, as we shall assume, also the necessary labor services, are bought, then

——但这个事实本身就意味着承认资本的功能与它所购买来的商品的功能是不同的。商品的功能在于服务相应于其技术性质的生产性目的。资本的功能在于为企业家获得用以生产的手段。在一种交换经济中，资本处于企业家与商品世界之间，是生产所必需的第三种要素。它为这两者构建了一座桥梁。它不直接参与生产，它本身不是“工作对象”；相反，它承担着一项在技术生产开始之前必须完成的任务。

企业家在考虑购买具体的商品之前，必须持有资本。在某个时期，当企业家已经拥有了必需的资本，但还没有开始生产商品时，正是在这个时候比其他时候，人们更清楚地看到资本并不是与具体商品相同的某种东西，而是一种独立的要素。资本的唯一目的，也就是企业家为什么需要资本的唯一原因——我求助于客观事实——只是作为购买生产品的一种基金。进一步说，只要这项购买还没有完成，资本就决不会与任何确定的商品有任何关系。资本当然存在——谁能否认呢？——但是它的特性恰好就是，不能把它看做某类具体的商品，它也不能在技术上作为商品来使用，而只是作为在技术的意义上用来提供将在生产中使用的商品的一种手段。但是当这项购买完成之后，企业家的资本是否就是由具体商品构成的——由他购买的各种土地以及各种工具构成，即仍然由商品构成了资本？如果有人对魁奈说：“当你走过一些农场和工场之后，……，你会继续看到房屋、牲口、种子、原料、家具等等这些工具”——从我们的观点看，还应该加上土地和劳动的服务，以及还有消费品——在购买完成之后，难道不是这样吗？这时，资本已经履行了我们赋予它的职能。让我们假定，如果必要的生产手段以及必要的劳动服务已经买来，那么企

the entrepreneur no longer has the capital which was placed at his disposal. He has surrendered it for productive means. It has been dissolved into incomes. The traditional conception at present is that his capital now consists of the goods acquired. Indeed it is a presupposition of this interpretation that the function of capital in procuring goods is completely ignored, and replaced by the unreal hypothesis that the very goods which he needs are lent to the entrepreneur. If one does not do this and if, following reality, one distinguishes the fund out of which production goods are paid for from these productive means themselves, there cannot in my opinion be the slightest doubt that it is to this fund that everything that one is accustomed to say of capital and all that we designate as capitalistic phenomena refer. If this is correct then it is furthermore clear that the entrepreneur no longer possesses this fund, because he has just paid it out, and that the parts of it in the hands of the sellers of productive means can be no different in character from the sums received from the sale of bread in the hands of the baker. The everyday method of expression frequently met with, which describes the productive means when purchased as "capital," proves nothing, all the more when the other expression goes with it, namely that capital is "embodied in these goods." The latter method of expression can only be correct in the sense in which it can also be said that coal is "embodied" in a steel raft, that is in the sense that the use of coal has led to the creation of the steel rail. But for all that, does not the entrepreneur still have his capital? And can he not at least "draw out" his capital from this "investment" again, while the same coal cannot be obtained again? I believe that these questions can be satisfactorily answered. No, the entrepreneur has spent his capital. In return for it, he has acquired goods which he will not employ as capital, that is as a fund in paying for other goods, but in technical production. However, if he changes his mind and wishes to part with these goods, there will usually be other people ready to buy them- and then he can again obtain possession of a greater or smaller amount of capital. From this point of view, since his productive means can serve not only as productive means

业家就不再有他能够支配的资本了。为了购买生产手段他已经把资本用出去了。资本已经被融入到收入中了。按照传统的概念，他的资本现在就是由他所获得的商品构成的。这种理解的前提其实是完全忽视了资本在购买商品过程中的职能，而代之以一个不真实的假说，即，企业家所需要的商品是由他借来的。如果人们不这样理解，并且如果人们实事求是地区分用来购买生产品的基金与这些生产工具本身，那么在我看来，毫无疑问，人们习惯上成为资本的东西以及我们认为是资本主义现象的标志的东西，都是指这个基金了。如果这是正确的，那么就更清楚了，因为企业家已经把资本支付出去而不再拥有它们，而生产工具的卖主手中获得了部分资本，这与面包师出售面包获得的收入相比，在性质上没有什么差别。几乎时时碰到这样的描述，把购买来的生产手段说成是“资本”，这什么都解释不了。与上述说法相类似的另一个说法是资本“体现于商品之中”，这更不能说明问题。如果要说后面一种说法是正确的，那就意味着可以说煤“体现于”铁轨中，因为煤的使用导致了铁轨的产生。但是这样一来，不就是说企业家仍然拥有资本？尽管相同的煤不能再从铁轨中抽取出来，难道企业家也不能至少从他的“投资”中再“抽取”他的资本吗？我相信这些问题能够被满意地回答。不过对这些问题的回答是否定的，因为企业家已经支出了他的资本。他所换来的商品将不能再当做资本使用，因为资本是为了购买其他商品的基金，而这些商品只能用于生产技术方面。然而，如果企业家改变主意，而希望把这些商品转手，那么通常将有其他一些人愿意购买这些商品——于是，企业家就可能再得到比原先更多或更少数量的资本。根据这个观点，由于他的生产手段不仅作为生产手段使用，

but also indirectly as capital-in so far as he can use them to obtain first purchasing power and then other productive means-he is right if he calls them elliptically his capital. Really they are the only source of purchasing power at his command if he should be in need of it before his production is completed. We shall come to still another reason for this interpretation. The second question is now also answered: the entrepreneur can obtain capital again by selling his production goods. He cannot of course get the identical capital again, in most cases not even the same amount. But since this does not matter, the plastic expression "to draw out his capital" has though only a figurative yet quite a sound meaning. It does not conflict with our interpretation.

What is capital then if it consists neither of a definite kind of goods nor of goods in general? By this time the answer is obvious enough: it is a fund of purchasing power. Only as such can it fulfill its essential function, the sole function for which capital is necessary in practice and for which alone the capital concept has a use in theory, which cannot be just as well replaced by enumerating categories of goods.

The question now arises as to what exactly constitutes this fund of purchasing power. This question seems to be very simple. Of what does my fund of purchasing power consist? Why, of money and of my other assets calculated in money. This answer would bring us practically to Menger's capital concept. Certainly I call this "my capital" innumerable times. Further, there are also no difficulties in distinguishing it as a "fund" from the "stream" of returns, so that here we take a step again in Irving Fisher's direction. Again, it might be said that I can embark upon an enterprise with this very sum or lend it to an entrepreneur.

However, this view, apparently so satisfactory at first sight, is unfortunately not completely adequate. It is not true that I can enter the ranks of entrepreneurs only with this sum.

而且还间接地作为资本——只要他首先能用它们获得购买力，然后再获得其他生产手段——如果他笼统地把它们称作自己的资本，他是没有错的。事实上，如果他在完成生产之前需要购买力，那么这些生产手段就是他能支配的用来购买生产力的唯一来源。我们将会谈到关于这种理解的其他理由。现在第二个问题也有了答复：企业家可以通过出售他的生产品重新获得资本。当然他不可能再获得与原来同样形式的资本，而且在多数情况下甚至数量也不一样。但是，因为这并不重要，所以“抽取他的资本”这种形象的表述尽管只是一种比拟，也是有合理意义的。它与我们的解释并不矛盾。

如果资本既不是由某种确定的商品构成，也不是由一般意义的商品构成，那么，资本究竟是什么呢？这时，答案是非常明显的：它是一笔购买力基金。只有这样，它才能履行它的基本职能，这是体现资本在实际中是必不可少的唯一职能，也是体现资本这个概念在理论上是有用的唯一职能，它不能仅靠列举商品的种类来代替。

现在这个问题上升为：这个购买力基金到底是由什么构成的呢？这个问题看起来非常简单。我的购买力基金是由什么构成的呢？不就是由钱以及折算成钱的我的其他资产构成的吗？这种回答实际上将把我们带到门格尔的资本概念。的确，我无数次把它称为“我的资本”。此外，要把它作为一笔“基金”相区别于收入“流”也没有任何困难，所以，在这里，我们向欧文·费希尔的方向又进了一步。因此可以说，运用这笔资金我可以创办一家企业，或者把它借给某个企业家。

然而，这个观点，初看起来似乎很令人满意，但不幸的是它并不全面。如果说我仅靠这笔资金就能跻身于企业家之列，这是不

If I can draw a bill that will be taken in payment, then I can also buy production goods for its amount. One might now say that I simply contract a debt thereby, which is far from increasing my capital. One might say further that the goods "bought" with the bill are just lent to me. Yet let us look more closely. If I am successful I shall be able to redeem the bill with money or counter-claims, which do not come out of my capital but out of the proceeds of my product. Thus I have increased my capital, or if there is any reluctance in granting this, I have done something that renders me just the same service as an increase of my capital, without incurring debts which would later decrease my capital again. It might be objected that my capital would have grown if I had not had to repay debts. However, these debts were paid out of a gain, which we cannot even be certain would have been added to my capital if it had accrued to me unimpaired. For I might use it to acquire consumption goods, in which case it would be contrary to every kind of usage to describe it as a part of capital. If it is correct that the function of capital only consists in assuring the entrepreneur control over production goods, then we cannot evade the conclusion that my capital would be increased by creating the bill. If the reader keeps in mind what was said earlier in combination with what follows, our result will lose much of its paradoxical appearance. It is true, I have not become richer by creating the bill. But the term "wealth" (vermögen) makes it possible to take account of this other aspect of the matter.

But it is also not true that expression in terms of money suffices to lend a capital character in our sense to property which is not itself held in the form of money. If one possesses some sort of goods it will not in general be possible to obtain by direct exchange the production goods which one needs. On the contrary one will always have to sell the goods one has and then employ the proceeds of the sale as capital, that is in obtaining the production goods required.

真实的。如果我能开出一张被别人接受并支付现款的票据，那么我也就能用它买到相同金额的生产品。这时有人可能会说，我只不过因此而承担了一项债务，而远不是增加了我的资本。有人还可能说，用这张票据“购买”来的商品，只不过是借给我的。那么让我们更加仔细地研究一下这个问题：如果我经营成功，那么我就能用来自我的产品的收益而不是来自我的资本的钱或等价的东西，来赎回这张票据。这样，我就增加了我的资本，如果有人不赞同这种说法，我也可以说，我这样做使我获得了一种服务，这种服务与增加我的资本产生同样的效果，而同时又不会招致在今后减少我的资本的债务。可能还有人反对说，如果我没有必须偿还的债务，那么我的资本本来就应该增长。但是这些债务是用收入来偿还的，如果这些所得毫无损失地都归我所有，它是否会增加我的资本，这也是不能确定的。因为我可能用所得去购买消费品，这种情况与所说的资本增加是完全相反的。如果说资本的作用仅仅在于保证企业家对生产品的控制，这种说法是对的，那么我们就不能回避这个结论，即，因为创造了票据，所以我的资本增加。如果读者还记得先前的论述，并将其与后来的论述结合起来，那我们的结论就远不至于显得那样难以理解了。当然，我并没有因为创造票据而变得更富有。然而“财富”一词，可能使我们考虑这个问题的另一面。

但是，如果认为能用货币形式表现，就足以给其本身并非货币形态的财富冠以我们所说的资本的性质，是不对的。如果某人拥有某种商品，一般来说，他不可能直接用这种商品去交换他所需要的生产品。相反，他将总是必须先卖掉他拥有的商品，然后，把出售所得的收入当做资本来使用，也就是用收入再获得他需要

Actually the conception under consideration recognizes this also in that it stresses the money value of the goods which anyone possesses. It is easy to see that it is only an elliptical or figurative method of expression when one describes these goods themselves as capital. The same is also true of purchased means of production, as already mentioned, which this conception also treats as capital.

So far our definition is on the one hand wider and on the other hand narrower than Menger's and others related to it. Only means of payment are capital, not merely "money" but circulating media in general, of whatever kind they may be; not all means of payment, however, but only those which actually fulfill the characteristic function with which we are concerned.

This limitation lies in the nature of the thing. If means of payment do not serve to provide an entrepreneur with production goods and to withdraw the latter from their previous employment for this purpose, then they are not capital. In an economic system without development there is therefore no "capital"; or, otherwise expressed, capital does not fulfill its characteristic function, it is not an independent agent. Or, still differently expressed, the various forms of general purchasing power do not constitute capital there; they are simply exchange media, technical means for carrying out the customary exchanges. With this, their rôle in the circular flow is complete-they have none except this technical rôle, so that they can be neglected without overlooking anything very essential. In the carrying out of new combinations, however, money and its substitutes become an essential factor, and we express this by describing them as capital. Thus, according to our point of view, capital is a concept of development to which nothing in the circular flow corresponds. *This concept embodies an aspect of the economic process which only the facts of development suggest to us.* I should like to draw the reader's attention to this statement. It contributes much to the understanding of the point of view here developed.

的生产品。实际上，我们所讨论的概念也意识到了这一点，因为它强调了任何人所拥有的商品的货币价值。很容易看出，当人们把这些商品本身看做是资本时，那只是一种简略的或者比喻的表述方法。同样，对于已经提到的，我们把它看做资本购入的生产手段，也适于这种说法。

至此，我们的定义与门格尔的概念以及相关的其他人的概念相比，一方面要更宽些，另一方面要更窄些。只有支付手段才是资本，这不仅只有“货币”是资本，一般流通媒介，不管它的种类，都是资本；然而，并不是所有的支付手段都是资本，只有那些实际履行我们所说的独特职能的支付手段才是资本。

这种限定在于事物的性质。如果支付手段并不能服务于为企业家提供生产品，并为这个目的把生产品从其原先的用途中抽取出来，那么它们就不是资本。因此，在一个没有发展的经济系统里，就没有“资本”；或者用另一种方式表述，资本不能履行其独特的职能，它就不是一种独立的要素。或者，还有不同的说法，一般购买力的各种变化的形式，在那里并不构成资本；它们只是交换媒介，是为执行传统交换的技术手段。这就是它们在循环流转中所起的全部作用——除了这个技术上的作用之外，它们就没有其他作用了，所以可以忽略它们而不影响对任何重要事物的理解。然而，在实施新组合的过程中，货币及其替代品变成了一种关键的要素，为了表明这种情况，我们把它们称为资本。这样，根据我们的观点，资本是一个发展的概念，而在循环流转中，没有与之相对应的东西。这个概念体现了经济过程的一个方面，只有发展的实际情况才使我们认识到这个方面。我希望提请读者注意上面这个论述。它对于理解我们在这里谈到的观点很有帮助。

If one speaks of capital with the connotation which the word has in practical life, then one always thinks not so much of things as of processes or of a certain aspect of things, namely of the possibility of entrepreneurial activity, of the possibility of control over productive means in general. This aspect is something common to many concepts of capital, and the efforts to bring it out explain, in my opinion, the "protean" qualities of the concrete definition. According to it nothing is really in itself capital, absolutely and by virtue of immanent qualities, but that which is designated as capital is so only to the extent that it satisfies certain conditions, or only from a certain point of view.

We shall define capital, then, as that sum of means of payment which is available at any moment for transference to entrepreneurs. At the moment when development starts from a circular flow in equilibrium, only a very small part of that sum of capital could, according to our interpretation, consist of money; on the contrary, it would have to consist of other means of payment newly created for the purpose, If development is once in motion or if capitalist development joins a non-capitalist or a transitional form, it will start with a supply of accumulated liquid resources. But in strict theory it could not do this. And even in reality it is always impossible when something really significant is to be clone for the first time.

Capital, then, is an agent in the exchange economy. A process of the exchange economy is given expression to in the capital aspect, namely the transfer of productive means to the entrepreneur. There is therefore in our sense really only private and no "social" capital. Means of payment can only perform their capital rôle in the hands of private individuals. Hence there would be little purpose in speaking of social capital with this meaning. Nevertheless, the sum of private capitals tells us something: it gives the magnitude of the fund that can be put at the disposal of entrepreneurs, the magnitude of the power of withdrawing means of production from their previous channels.

如果一个人在谈到资本时，用的是这个词在实际生活中的涵义，那么他对经济过程或者事情的某些方面考虑得总不会很充足，也就是对企业家活动的可能性，对一般生产手段控制的可能性考虑不足。对资本的许多概念来说，这是共性的方面；为了说明这个意义，人们所做的种种努力，在我看来，表明了这一具体定义的“变化莫测”的性质。由此看来，没有任何东西，因其不变的性质特征，因而就绝对地是资本，而那些被指明为资本的东西，之所以是资本，仅仅是因为它满足了某些条件，或者只是从某种观点来看是资本。

于是，我们将资本定义为：可以在任何时候可以转交给企业家的支付手段的数额。当从一个均衡状态的循环流转中开始发展的时候，依据我们的论述，只有很小一部分的资本量是由货币构成的；相反，它必然包括着为发展目的而新创造的其他支付手段。如果一旦开始发展，或者，如果资本主义发展与非资本主义形式或者一种过渡的形式结合在一起，发展将从已经积累起来的流动资金的供给开始，但是在严格的理论上并不是这样。甚至在实际中，如果某个真正重要的步骤要在第一次实施，通常是不可能做到的。

所以，资本是交换经济的一个要素。交换经济的一个过程表现在资本方面，就是生产手段转交给企业家。所以，在我们所说的意义上，确实只有私人资本而没有“社会”资本。支付手段只有在私人手中才能起到作为资本的作用。所以，在这个意义上谈论社会资本是没有意义的。尽管如此，私人资本的数量还告诉我们一些情况：它提供了能够交给企业家并由其支配的资金的数量，它表明了能够从原先的使用渠道中抽取出来的生产手段的能量

Therefore the concept of social capital is not meaningless,[①] even though there would be no such capital in a communist economy. Yet one thinks for the most part of a nation's stock of goods when one speaks of social capital, and only the real capital concepts have led to that of social capital.

THE MONEY MARKET

One more step remains to be taken. Capital is neither the whole nor a part of the means of production-original or produced. Nor is capital a stock of consumption goods. It is a special agent. As such it must have a market in that theoretical sense in which there is a market for consumption goods and for production goods. And to this theoretical market something similar must correspond in reality as in the case of these other two. We saw in the first chapter that there are markets for the services of labor and land and for consumption goods in which everything essential to the circular flow is settled, while the produced means of production, transitory, items, have no such independent market. In development, which introduces the new agent capital into the economic process, there must be still a third market in which something interesting happens, the capital market.

This does exist: reality shows it to us directly, much more directly than it shows us the markets for services and for consumption goods. It is much more concentrated, much better organised, much easier to observe than the other two. It is what the businessman calls the

① This is especially true if one measures every unit of capital by the amounts of production goods obtainable for it at any time. If one does this then one may also speak of "real" capital-but only in a figurative sense.

的大小。因此，社会资本的概念并不是没有任何意义，[①] 尽管在共产主义经济中也没有社会资本。不过，当人们谈论社会资本时，多数情况下考虑的是一个国家的商品储备量，而只有真实资本的概念才能产生出社会资本的概念。

货币市场

我们必须继续向前走一步。资本既不是生产手段的全部，也不是它的一部分——无论是初始的生产手段，还是生产出来的生产手段，都是如此。资本也不是消费品的储备量，它是一个特殊的要素。就像在理论上有一个消费品市场，一个生产品市场一样，必然存在一个资本市场。如同其他两个市场的情况，在实际生活中必然有某种类似的东西对应于理论上的这个资本市场。从第一章我们可以看到，存在着劳动和土地服务的市场以及消费品市场，在那里，循环流转所需要的重要的事物都具备，而生产出来的生产手段属于暂时项目，所以没有这样独立的市场。发展把新的要素资本引入经济过程，从而产生一个让人感兴趣的第三市场，即资本市场。

这个市场确实存在，现实生活直接向我们显示了这个市场，比显示服务市场和消费品市场还要直接得多。这个市场比另两个市场更加集中，组织得也更好，而且更容易观察。这就是商人

---

① 如果用每一单位资本在任何时候可以换得的生产品的数量来衡量单位资本，则情况更是如此。所以，如果有人这样做了，他也可以称之为“真实”资本——但只是作为比喻性的意义。

money market, that about which every newspaper reports daily under this title. From our standpoint the name is not wholly satisfactory: it is not simply money that is dealt in, and we might in part join the protest of economists against this conception of it. But we accept the name. In any case the capital market is the same as the phenomenon that practice describes as the money market. There is no other capital market. ① It would be an attractive and a profitable task to out- line a theory of the money market. As yet we have none. ②It would be especially interesting and profitable to collect and test the theoretical meaning of the practical rules of experience which determine the practical man's decisions and his judgment of particular situations. They are indeed for the most part strictly formulated, and guide every writer of money-market articles. These practical rules for economic forecasting are at present quite detached from theory, although the study of them leads deep into the understanding of modern economic life. We cannot go into this here. We shall only say what is necessary for our purposes. This can be done in a few words.

In an economy without development there would be no such money market. If it were highly organized and its transactions were settled with credit means of payment it would have a central settlement bureau, a kind of clearing house or bookkeeping centre for the economic system. In the transactions of this institution everything that happens in the economic system would be mirrored, for example the periodical payments of wages and taxes, the requirements for moving the harvest and for holidays.

---

① At the most one may with Spiethoff (loc. cit.) distinguish the capital market as the market for long-term purchasing power from the money market as the market for short loans. But purchasing power is the commodity in each.

② Cf., however, A. Hahn, "Zur Theorie des Geldmarkts," Archlv für Sozialwis- senschaft und Sozialpolitik (1923).

们所称的货币市场，报纸每天在这个标题下报道着它的情况。从我们的观点看，这个名称不能完全让人满意：因为它经营的不只是货币。有些经济学家也反对这个概念，我们部分地支持这些经济学家的观点。但是我们接受这个名称，无论怎么说，资本市场的现象与实际生活中所描述的货币市场的现象是完全一样的。此外没有任何其他资本市场了。[①] 如果要对货币市场理论拟写一个提纲，那将是一项很有吸引力且很有益的工作。但是目前我们还没有这样的著作。[②] 收集并检验那些决定人们的实际决策以及人们在特殊情况下的判断的实际经验规律的理论意义，是特别有趣且有益的事情。这些规律有大部分确实被严格规范化了，而且引导着每一位撰写货币市场文章的作家。尽管对这些实际规律的研究，引导人们深入地理解现代经济生活，但是这些有利于经济预测的实际规律，至今还是严重地偏离理论。我们不可能在这里研究这个问题。我们只谈对我们的目的是必要的东西。这不需要用过多的言语。

在没有发展的经济中，就不会有这种货币市场。如果货币市场高度组织化，而且它的交易都是通过信用支付手段来结清，那么它就需要一个中央结算机构，这是此经济系统的票据交换所或簿记中心。经济系统中发生的所有事情都将反映在这个机构的交易中，例如定期的支付工资和交纳税款，因搬运收获物和休假

① 对于斯皮托夫的观点，赞同最多的要数他对资本市场与货币市场的区分，他把资本市场看做是获取长期购买力的市场，把货币市场看做是为了获取短期贷款的市场，但是购买力在两个市场都是商品。

② 参阅汉恩的《货币市场理论》，刊登在《社会科学和社会政策文献》杂志（1923 年），德文。

But these would only be matters of accounting. Now these functions must also be performed if there is development. With development, moreover, there is always employment for purchasing power which is momentarily idle. And finally, with development, as already emphasized, bank-credit penetrates into the transactions of the circular flow. Thus it is, then, that these things become, in practice, dements of the function of the money market. They become a part of the organism of the money market. And so the requirements of the circular flow are added to the entrepreneur's demand in the money market on the one hand, and money from the circular flow increases the supply of money in the money market on the other. Hence we feel in every money-market article the pulse of the circular flow, hence we see that the demand for purchasing power increases at harvest-time, when taxes are due and so forth, while after these times the supply increases. But this must not prevent us from distinguishing the transactions in the money market which belong to the circular flow from others. Only the latter are fundamental; the former are added onto them, and the fact that they appear in the money market at all is merely a consequence of development. All the reciprocal effects which obviously bind the two together do not alter the fact that, even practically, they may be distinguished in every case and that in the money market it is always possible to say what belongs to the circular flow and what belongs to development.

The kernel of the matter lies in the credit requirements of new enterprises. Of course we must remember that the influence of the international relations in which every economic system finds itself, and of non-economic intervention, to which every economic system is exposed, are neglected here, in order to shorten and simplify the exposition. Hence the phenomena of the national balance of payments, of the bullion trade, and so on drop out of sight. With this proviso, only one fundamental thing happens on the money market, to which everything else is accessory: on the demand side appear entrepreneurs and on the supply side producers of and dealers in purchasing power, viz. bankers, both with their staffs of agents and middlemen. What takes place is simply

而产生的要求，但这些只是会计上的事。而现在，如果有发展，这些职能就必须得到发挥。此外，因为有发展，常常就会利用暂时闲置的购买力。最后，正像我们已经强调的，因为有发展，银行信贷才渗入循环流转的交易中。所以在实践中，正是这些东西成为货币市场职能的基本要素，它们成为货币市场有机体的一部分。所以，一方面循环流转的需要量被加到企业家在货币市场的需求量上；另一方面，循环流转中的货币量增加了货币市场上的货币供应量。因此，我们对每一个货币市场的事物都能感到循环流转的脉动，我们发现在收获季节，在税款到期等时节，对购买力的需求就增长，而过了这些时期，就出现购买力的供给增长。但这决不能阻止我们对货币市场上属于循环流转的交易与其他交易进行区分。只有后者是根本的，前者只是被附加到后者上，而前者终究出现在货币市场上这个事实，只是发展的一个结果。所有那些明显地把两者结合在一起的相互影响，并不能改变这个事实，即使在实际中，在任何一种情形下都可以区别它们；并且在货币市场上，总是可以说出，什么是属于循环流转的，什么是属于发展的。

事情的核心在于新企业的信贷要求。当然我们必须记住，在这里，那些每个经济系统都不能摆脱的国际关系的影响以及每个经济系统都要面对的非经济干预，都被我们给略去了，这是为了使我们的说明更加简短、易懂。因此国家收支平衡、贵金属贸易等等这些现象，我们都没有涉及。在这些条件下，货币市场上只发生一件根本性的事情，所有其他事情都从属于它：在需求一方出现了企业家，在供给一方出现了购买力的生产者和交易者，即银行家，双方都有他们的代理人和中间人。所发生的事情只是用当前

the exchange of present against future purchasing power. In the daily price struggle between the two parties the fate of new combinations is decided. In this price struggle the system of future values first appears in a practical, tangible form and in relation to the given conditions of the economic system. It would be wholly wrong to believe that the price of short-term credits is a matter of indifference for new undertakings since it is long-term credit that they want. On the contrary, the whole economic situation at every moment is nowhere so dearly expressed as in the price of short loans. The entrepreneur does not necessarily borrow for the whole period over which he needs credit, but as necessity arises and often almost from day to day. Moreover, speculators often hold shares, especially of new enterprises, with such short-term credit, which may be granted to-day and denied tomorrow. We may observe from day to day how the credit requirements of industry manifest themselves and how the banking world sometimes supports and encourages, sometimes curbs, the demand. While in other markets the demand as well as the supply exhibits a certain constancy, even in development, here surprisingly large fluctuations appear from day to day. We shall explain this by the special function of the money market. All plans and outlooks for the future in the economic system affect it, all conditions of the national life, all political, economic, and natural events. There is scarcely a piece of news that does not necessarily influence the decisions relative to the carrying out of new combinations or the money-market position and the opinions and intentions of entrepreneurs. The system of future values must be adapted to every new situation. This is of course not merely effected by variations in the price of purchasing power. Frequently, personal influence acts in addition to or in the place of the latter. But there is no need to go into these well known details.

The money market is always, as it were, the headquarters of the capitalist system, from which orders go out to its individual divisions, and that which is debated and decided there is always in essence the settlement of plans for further development. All kinds of credit requirements come to this market; all kinds of economic projects are first brought intorelation with one another, and contend for their realization in it;

的购买力交换未来的购买力。每天双方之间对价格的争论，决定了新组合的命运。未来的价格体系就是通过这一价格的斗争首先以实际的、可感知的形式出现，并且与给定的经济系统的条件相关。如果认为新企业想要的是长期信贷，因而短期的信贷价格与新企业无关，这种想法是完全错误的。相反，在任何时候，以短期信贷价格所表达的整个经济形式是最清楚的。企业家没必要把他在整个时期所需要的贷款都借来，而是随着需要来贷款，并且常常是每天贷款。此外，投机者们通常用这些短期信贷购买股票，尤其是购买新企业的股票，这种信贷可能今天给予，明天就拒绝了。我们通过每天的观察可以知道，产业的信贷要求是怎样提出来的，而银行又是怎样在有的时候支持和鼓励这种需求，在有的时候又抑制这种需求。尽管在其他市场上需求和供给表现出某种稳定性，甚至在发展中，但是在货币市场，每天都会出现惊人的大波动。我们将用货币市场的特殊职能来解释这个现象。经济体系中所有的计划以及对未来的展望，比如，国民生活的所有情况，所有政治、经济、自然事件，都影响着货币市场。几乎没有一条新闻不对实施新组合的决策或者货币市场的形式以及企业家的观点和目的产生必然影响。未来价值体系必须要适应每一个新形式。当然这不仅受到购买力价格变动的影响，常常个人的影响也同时起作用，或者代替了购买力价格变动的影响。但是没有必要探究这些人们都知道的细节了。

货币市场总是资本主义体系的指挥部，命令从这里下达到各个部门，而在那里所争论和决定的，实质上总是为进一步发展的计划的定案。各种信贷要求都来到这个市场；所有类型的经济项目都首先在这里彼此发生关系并为各自的实现相互竞争；各种购

all kinds of purchasing power, balances of every sort, flow to it to be sold. This gives rise to a number of arbitrage operations and intermediate manoeuvres which may easily veil the fundamental thing. Nevertheless, I believe that at bottom our conception need hardly fear contradiction.

Thus the main function of the money or capital market is trading in credit for the purpose of financing development. Development creates and nourishes this market. In the course of development it is assigned still another, that is a third, function: it becomes the market for sources of incomes themselves. We shall consider later the relation between the price of credit and the price of sources of permanent or temporary returns. Here so much is dear, that the sale of such sources of returns represents a method of acquiring capital, and their purchase a method of employing capital, consequently the dealing in sources of returns cannot be far removed from the money market. Tragic in land also belongs here, and only technical circumstances prevent it from appearing in practice as a part of money-market transactions; but there is no lack of causal connection between the two.

买力和资金余额都流到这里出售。这会产生一系列套利行为和间接牟利，而这些行为可能很容易地遮掩根本性的事物。不过，我相信，它们终究不会给我们的概念带来矛盾。

因此，可以说，货币或者资本市场的主要职能就是为发展筹措资金而进行的信贷交易。发展创造并滋养着这个市场。在发展的过程中，货币市场又被赋予了第三个职能：它成为收入本身来源的市场。我们将在以后讨论信贷价格与长、短期收益来源的价格之间的关系。这种收益来源的出售反映了获得资本的一种方法，而它们的买入则反映了利用资本的一种方式，因此，很难把收入来源的处置与货币市场相分离，这已经是很清楚的了。土地交易也属于这种情况，只不过因为技术上的原因，使土地交易看起来似乎在实际上不属于货币市场交易的一部分，但是在货币交易和土地交易之间并不缺乏因果关系。

[英 汉 对 照]

西方学术经典文库

经济发展理论

对利润、资本、信贷、利息和经济周期的探究

THE THEORY OF ECONOMIC DEVELOPMENT

AN INQUIRY INTO PROFITS, CAPITAL, CREDIT, INTEREST, AND THE BUSINESS CYCLE

[美] 约瑟夫·阿洛伊斯·熊彼特 著

叶 华 译

(二)

九 州 出 版 社
JIUZHOUPRESS

CHAPTER IV

Entrepreneurial Profit[①]

The first three chapters laid the foundation upon which rests all that is to follow. As a first fruit we arrive at an explanation of entrepreneurial profit, and indeed so easily and naturally that in order to keep this chapter short and simple I prefer to put some more difficult discussions, which really belong here, in the next chapter, where all the knotty problems may be dealt with as a whole.

Entrepreneurial profit is a surplus over costs. From the stand point of the entrepreneur, it is the difference between receipts and outlay in a business, as we have already been told by a long line of economists. Superficial as this definition is, it is sufficient as a starting point. By "outlay" we understand all the disbursements which the entrepreneur must make directly or indirectly in production. To this must be added an appropriate wage for labor performed by the entrepreneur, an appropriate rent for any land which may chance to belong to him, and finally a premium for risk. On the other hand I do not insist here that interest on capital should be excluded from these costs. In practice it is included in them, either visibly or, if the capital belongs to the entrepreneur himself,

① The most important theories of profits may be characterised by the following terms: friction theory, wages theory, risk theory, differential rent theory. I refer to the discussion of them in Wesen, bk. III, and shall not here enter into a critique of them. For history of the doctrine see Pierstorff and Mataja. At the same time J. B. Clark, whose theory is nearest to mine, may be cited here; cf. his Essentials of Economic Theory.

第四章　企业家利润①

前三章奠定了以后各章的基础。作为首次成果，现在我们可以解释企业家利润了，为了使本章简短易懂，我宁愿把本应属于这一章的某些难懂的讨论放在下一章，这是很自然并且容易办到的。在下一章，所有困难、纠纷的问题可以作为整体加以讨论。

企业家利润是超过成本的剩余。从企业家的角度看，它是一个企业收入与支出的差额，正像众多经济学家告诉我们的那样。这个定义下得如此肤浅，但足以作为讨论的出发点。所谓“支出”，我们理解为所有的在生产中企业家必须的直接或间接的支付。在此基础上，还必须加上企业家因付出劳动而应得的适当工资，以及企业家拥有的土地的租金，最后还要加上风险的保险金。另一方面，我并不坚持说资本的利息应排除在这些成本之外。实际上，资本成本应该包括在成本内，无论是以明显的方式支付利息，还是按照如同付给企业家工资（如果资本属于企业家自己），

① 最重要的利润理论可以用下述术语概括：摩擦理论、工资理论、风险理论、差额地租理论。在《本质》一书的第三章中有对它们的讨论，在这里我就不作评论了。关于利润的学说史，可以看皮埃斯多夫和马塔雅的书。同时我在这里还要提到克拉克的理论，它与我的理论很接近，参阅他的《经济理论基础》。

by the same accounting method as wages for his personal work or rent for his own land. This may suffice for the moment, all the more so since many theorists put interest on capital in the same category with wages and rent. I now leave it to the reader' s discretion in this chapter either to neglect the existence of interest on capital, in the sense of our interpretation, or to recognise it, in the sense of any theory of interest whatsoever, as a third "static" ranch of income and to include it in business costs. Its nature and its origin do not concern us here in any case.

Upon this definition of outlays it may appear doubtful whether there is any surplus at all as against costs. To prove that there is a surplus is therefore our first task. Our solution may be expressed briefly: in the circular flow the total receipts of a business-abstracting from monopoly-are just big enough to cover outlays. In it there are only producers who neither make profits nor suffer losses and whose income is sufficiently characterized by the phrase "wages of management." And since the new combinations which are carried out if there is "development" are necessarily more advantageous than the old, total receipts must in this case be greater than total costs.

In honor of Lauderdale,①who was the first to deal with our problem, I shall begin with the improvement of the productive process and indeed with the time-honored example of the power-loom, which is also commended by the fact that it has been subjected to a searching analysis by B hm-Bawerk. ②Very many ff not most of the achievements of the leaders of modem economic life are of this kind; in particular the new era of the eighteenth and nineteenth centuries exhibits efforts in this direction. It is true that in this period we find the several functions which are to be distinguished in the process of introducing

① Inquiry into the Nature and Origin of Public Wealth. It is true that he had an altogether different object in view, viz. the explanation of interest.

② In his Capital and Interest, VII, 3.

或者以租金的会计方式支付给他的土地的报酬。目前不妨就这样看待资本的利息，特别是因为许多理论家都把资本的利息与工资和租金归于同一类。在本章，我听任读者的选择，要么按照我们论述的意思，忽略资本利息的存在，要么承认它的存在，按照任何一种利息理论来理解，把它作为收入的第三种“静态”分支，将其包含在企业成本里。我们在这里完全不涉及它的性质与起源。

根据上面对支出所下的定义，究竟是否还有超出成本的剩余呢？这就显得可疑了。于是，证明有剩余存在就是我们的首要任务。我们的解答办法可以简短地表述如下：在循环流转中，一个企业的总收入——不包括垄断收入——恰好足够与支出相抵。在这种情况下，只有既不获得利润也没有遭受损失的生产者，他们的收入的特征可以用“管理的工资”这个短语来概括。如果有发展，就会实施新的组合，它必然比老的组合更有利，所以在这种情况下，总收入一定大于总成本。

为了纪念劳德代尔，[①] 他是第一个探讨我们正在讨论的这个问题的研究者，我将以生产过程的改进为起点，并且仍然用那个历时已久的动力织布机的例子，这个例子由于被庞巴维克[②]做过仔细地分析，所以值得引用。如果不是说绝大多数的，但也可以说是许多现代经济生活的领导者的成就属于这一类，尤其是在18、19世纪的新时代，显示了人们在这个方向的努力。我们确实发现在那个时期，在生产完善过程中应该加以区分的几种职能，

① 《对公共财富的性质与起源的探讨》。当然，他的研究目的完全不同，他以解释利息为目的。

② 参阅庞巴维克的《资本与利息》，第七章，第3节。

improvements in production even less separated than to-day. Men of the Arkwright type invented and at the same time put their inventions into Practice. They had not our modem credit system at their disposal. However, I hope I have taken the reader so far that I may make use of our analytic tools in their purest form without further explanations and repetitions.

The matter then appears as follows. If anyone in an economic system in which the textile industry produces only with hand labor sees the possibility of founding a business which uses power-looms, feels equal to the task of overcoming all the innumerable difficulties, and has made the final decision, then he, first of all, needs purchasing power. He borrows it from a bank and creates his business. It is absolutely immaterial whether he constructs the power-looms himself or has them constructed by another firm according to his directions in order to confine himself to employing them. If a worker with such a loom is now in a position to produce six times as much as a hand-worker in a day, it is obvious that given three conditions the business must yield a surplus over costs, a difference between receipts and outlay. First, the price of the product must not fall when the new supply[①] appears, or else not fall to such an extent that the greater product per worker brings no greater receipts now than the smaller product obtainable by hand labor did before. Secondly, the costs of the power-loom per day must either remain below the daily wages of the five workers dispensed with or else below the sum which remains after allowing for the possible fall in the price of the product and deducting the wage of the one worker required. The third condition supplements the other two. These two cover wages of the workers who attend to the looms, and wages and rent which go in payment for the looms.

① Here we depart from Lauderdale's example in order to remain true to our whole conception of the process and at the same time to reality.

甚至比今天更是互相结合在一起。像发明动力织布机的阿克赖特式的人物，不仅发明了新东西，同时将其发明用于实践中。而他们当时并没有像我们今天的现代信贷体系可以利用。然而，我希望我已经给读者陈述的足够多了，以至于我现在可以利用我们的分析工具的最纯粹的形式来分析，而不需要作进一步的解释与重复。

于是，事情就如下面所述：如果在一个纺织工业只用手工劳动来生产的经济系统里，有人发现了建立使用动力织布机的企业的可能性，他觉得足以克服创建新企业的种种困难，而且他最终下定决心这样做，那么他首先就需要有购买力。他从银行借款来创建他的企业。无论是他自己制造动力织布机，还是他让别的厂商按照他制定的规格来生产，然后由他使用，这完全是无关紧要的。如果现在，使用这种织布机的一个工人每天能生产的数量是手工工人日产量的 6 倍，那么显然，只要满足下面三个条件，这家企业就一定能获得超过成本的剩余，即收入大于支出的差额：第一，当出现新的供应[①]时，产品价格一定不下降，或者即使下降，但其跌价程度还不至于使现在每一个工人因较大产量所带来的收益还不如以往手工工人较小产量带来的收益。第二，动力织布机每天的成本必须要么低于所裁减的五名工人的工资，要么低于可能的产品价格的下降额和需要增加一名工人的工资额之和。第三个条件是对前两个的补充。前两个条件，包括照管织布机的工人的工资，以及为获得织布机而支付的工资和地租。至此，我

① 为了保证我们对这个过程的总的概念的一致性并符合实际，在这里我们撇开劳德代尔的例子。

So far I have taken the case in which these wages and rents are simply those which ruled before the entrepreneur hit upon his plan. If his demand is relatively small we can rest content with this. ①If not, however, then the prices of the services of labor and land rise because of the new demand. For the other textile businesses at first continue working and the necessary means of production need not be withdrawn directly from them, but from industry in general. This happens by means of an advance in prices. And therefore the businessman, who must anticipate and estimate the rise in prices in the market for production goods which follows his appearance, may not simply include the former wages and rents in his calculation, but must add an appropriate amount, so that yet a third item must be deducted. Only if the receipts exceed outlays after allowing for all three sets of changes is there a surplus over costs.

These three conditions have been fulfilled innumerable times in practice. This proves the possibility of a surplus over costs. ② However, they are obviously not always fulfilled, and when they are not, and the fact is foreseen, the new business is not organised; if this fact is not foreseen no surplus results but rather a loss. If the conditions are fulfilled, however, the surplus realised *is ipso facto* a net profit. For the looms produce a greater physical product than the services of labor and land contained in them could produce by the previous method, although in the case of constant prices of production goods and products this latter method

① This would be the case of completely free competition, to the concept of which it is necessary that no firm be strong enough perceptibly to influence prices by its own action on supply and demand.

② It should be noticed that in this statement there is not an appeal to the reality of a phenomenon yet to be explained, of the kind found respecting the fact of interest in many representatives of the productivity theory. For the rest, further substantiation comes later.

们假定这些工资和地租的情况处于企业家想出使用织布机计划之前的状态。如果他的需求相对较小，我们这样假定完全是可行的。[①] 但如果不是这样，那么，劳动和土地服务的价格就会上涨，因为有新的需求了。其他的纺织企业起初继续生产，所以必要的生产工具还不会直接地被削减，但对整个纺织工业来说，一般是会削减的，这是因为生产工具的价格上涨了。因此，实行创新的企业家必须预见并估计，在他出现以后，生产品市场价格的上涨。所以，在他的估算中或许不只包括原先的工资和地租，还必须加上一个适当的数额，所以在计算利润时还有一个第三项要减去。只有考虑了所有这三种变化，收入超过支出时，才有超出成本的剩余。

实际上，这三个条件已经实现过无数次。它证明了存在超过成本的剩余的可能性。[②] 然而，这三个条件显然不总是能够实现，当它们不能实现时，而这种情况又被预见到了，新企业就不会建立了；如果没有预见到这三个条件不能实现，那么新企业就不会有剩余，甚至还会有损失。相反，如果条件都满足了，这个剩余实际上就是一种净利润。因为织布机生产出更多的物质产品，与利用织布机所包含的同等的劳动和土地服务，并用原先的生产方法相比而言；虽然在生产品和产品的价格保持不变的情况下，用原先

① 这应该是完全自由竞争下的情况，关于这种情况的概念，必须满足以下要求：没有一个厂商足够的强大，以至于可以其自己的供求行为影响价格。

② 必须注意，这种表述并不是求助于一种尚未解释的现象的真实性，就像在许多有关生产力理论的代表著作中对利息这一事实所作的论述那样。对于其他各观点，我们将在后面进一步论证。

would also enable production to be carried on without loss. Furthermore, the looms are obviously available at cost to our entrepreneur-we neglect the possibility of patenting as being intelligible without further consideration. Hence there arises a difference between receipts, which are determined according to the prices which were equilibrium, that is cost, prices when hand labor alone was being used, and outlays, which are now essentially smaller per unit of product than for other businesses. And this difference need not be annihilated by the price changes brought about by the appearance of the individual in question on the demand and the supply side. This is so dear that we may forego a more rigorous formulation at this point.

But now comes the second act of the drama. The spell is broken and new businesses are continually arising under the impulse of the alluring profit. A complete reorganisation of the industry occurs, with its increases in production, its competitive struggle, its supersession of obsolete businesses, its possible dismissal of workers, and so forth. We shall consider this process more closely later. Only one thing interests us here: the final result must be a new equilibrium position, in which, with new data, the law of cost again rules, so that now the prices of the products are again equal to the wages and rents of the services of labor and land which are embodied in the looms plus the wages and rents of the services of labor and land which must still cooperate with the looms in order that the product may come into existence. The incentive to produce more and more products will not cease before this condition is arrived at, nor before price falls as a result of the growing supply.

Consequently, the surplus of the entrepreneur in question and of his immediate followers disappears. ①Not at once, it is true, but as a rule only after a longer or shorter period of progressive diminution. ② Nevertheless, the surplus is realised, it constitutes under given conditions

---

① Cf. Böhm-Bawerk, loc. cit., p. 174.

② However, for the sake of simplicity of exposition we confine the process in general to one economic period

的方法仍然能使生产继续进行，不发生损失。进一步说，只要我们的企业家付出代价，显然，织布机是可以获得的——我们忽略织布机取得专利的可能性，因为不进一步考虑这个问题将更容易理解。这样，在由均衡价格决定的收入与现在实质上更小了的支出之间就出现了差额。这个均衡价格是在原先只有手工劳动时的价格，也就是成本价格，这个支出，指的是现在使用动力织布机之后，每单位产品的支出比其他企业更小。这个差额不会因为有我们所说的企业家的出现，进而带来的在供求方面价格的变化而消失。这一点是很清楚的，我们不需要为此作更严密的说明。

但是现在来到了戏剧的第二幕。魔法被识破了，在诱人的利润的刺激下，新的企业不断出现。整个行业的全面重新组合发生了，伴随而来的是：产量增长，竞争加剧，过时企业被淘汰，工人更有可能被解雇，等等。我们在以后将更仔细地研究这个过程。在这里我们只对一件事情感兴趣，那就是这个过程的最终结果必然是一个新的均衡状态，在那里，有新的资料，成本规律又开始起作用，所以产品价格又等于体现在织布机中的为使用劳动力和土地服务应支付的工资和地租，加上为使用织布机生产产品而必须一起利用的劳力和土地服务应支付的工资和地租。在达到这个状态之前，刺激人们生产越来越多的产品的因素不会消失，在因为供给的增加而使价格下降之前，这种刺激因素也不会终止。

因此，我们所说的这位企业家以及他的直接跟随者的剩余就会消失。[①] 当然，不是立即消失，而总是在一个递减的或长或短的时期后消失。[②] 尽管如此，剩余还是实现了，在一定的条件下，这

① 参阅前面说的庞巴维克的著作，第174页。

② 不过，为了使说明简单化，我们一般把这个过程限制在一个经济时期内。

a definite amount of net returns even though only temporary. Now to whom does it fall? Obviously to the individuals who introduced the looms into the circular flow, not to the mere inventors, but also not to the mere producers or users of them. Those who produce them to order will only receive their cost price, those who employ them according to instructions will buy them so dearly at first that they will hardly receive any profit. The profit will fall to those individuals whose achievement it is to introduce the looms, whether they produce and use them, or whether they only produce or only use them. In our example the chief importance attaches to employment, but that is not essential. The introduction is achieved by founding new businesses, whether for production or for employment or for both. What have the individuals under consideration contributed to this? Only the will and the action: not concrete goods, for they bought these-either from others or from themselves; not the purchasing power with which they bought, for they borrowed this -from others or, if we also take account of acquisition in earlier periods, from themselves. And what have they done? They have not accumulated any kind of goods, they have created no original means of production, but have employed existing means of production differently, more appropriately, more advantageously. They have "carried out new combinations." They are entrepreneurs. And their profit, the surplus, to which no liability corresponds, is an entrepreneurial profit.

Just as the introduction of looms is a special case of the introduction of machinery in general, so the introduction of machinery is a special case of all changes in the productive process in the widest sense, the aim of

个剩余构成了一笔数额确定的净收益，尽管是暂时的。现在的问题是，这个剩余落入谁的手中了呢？显然落入到把织布机引入循环流转中的那些人手里，而不是落入纯粹的发明者手中，也不是落入单纯的制造者或使用者手中。那些按照订单生产织布机的人只得到他们的成本价格，那些按照说明书使用织布机的人，起初购买时花费了很大代价，他们几乎没有得到任何利润。利润将归于那些成功地把织布机引入产业的人们，不管他们是否制造并使用织布机，也不管他们是只制造或只使用，这都无关紧要。在我们所举的例子中，首要问题在于使用，但这并不是问题的实质。通过创建新的企业，动力织布机进入产业才得以实现，而不管创建新企业是为了生产织布机还是为了使用织布机，还是两者皆有。那么，我们所讨论的企业家创建新企业作了什么贡献呢？只有他的意志和行动。他们不以具体的商品作贡献，因为他们要购买商品——要么从其他企业购买，要么从他自己的企业购买；他们也不是以所拥有的购买织布机的购买力作贡献，因为他们的购买力是从别人那里借来的，或者如果我们考虑他前期所获得的收入，那么购买力就是从他自己那里借用来的。那么，他们究竟做了些什么呢？他们没有积累任何品种的商品，他们也没有创造任何独特的生产手段，而只是用与别人不同的、更恰当的、更有利的方式，使用现存的生产手段。他们“实现了新的组合”，他们就是企业家。而他们的利润，即剩余，对此没有承担什么相应的义务，这就是企业家的利润。

就像把织布机引进生产是把机器引入生产这种一般性的事件中的一个特殊案例一样，把机器引进生产也是最广义上的生产过程的各种变化中的一个特例，生产过程变革的目的是用更少的

which is to produce a unit of product with less expense and thus to create a discrepancy between their existing price and their new costs. Many innovations in business organisation and all innovations in commercial combinations are included in this. For all such cases, what has been said may be repeated word for word. Representative of the first group is the introduction of large-scale manufacturing businesses into an economic system in which they were previously unknown. In a large-scale business a more suitable arrangement and better utilisation of the factors of production are possible than in smaller businesses; and furthermore the choice of a more favorable location is possible. But the introduction of large-scale businesses is difficult. Under our assumptions all the necessary conditions are wanting-workers, trained personnel, the necessary market conditions. Innumerable resistances of a social and political character work against it. And the organisation itself, still unknown, requires special aptitude to set it up. However, if anyone has in him all that pertains to success under these circumstances, and if he can obtain the necessary credit, then he can put a unit of product on the market more cheaply, and, if our three conditions are realised, make a profit which remains in his pocket. But he has also triumphed for others, blazed the trail and created a model for them which they can copy. They can and will follow him, first individuals and then whole crowds. Again that process of reorganisation occurs which must result in the annihilation of the surplus over costs, when the new business form has become part of the circular flow. But previously profits were made. To repeat: these individuals have done nothing but employ existing goods to greater effect, they have carried out new combinations and are entrepreneurs in our sense. Their gain is an entrepreneurial profit.

As an example of the cases of commercial combinations, the choice of a new and cheaper source of supply for a means of production, perhaps a raw material may be cited. This source of supply did not exist previously for the economic system. No direct and regular connection existed with its country of origin-if overseas, for example, neither a steamship line nor foreign correspondents.

花费生产单位产品，从而在产品现有的价格和其新的成本之间创造一个差额。企业组织中的很多创新以及商业组合中的所有创新都属于这种情况。我们前面的论述，字字适用于所有的情况。代表第一组情况的是，把大规模的制造企业引进一个原先没有这种企业的经济系统里。与小企业相比，大企业可以进行更恰当的安排，对生产要素更好的利用；而且，还可以选择一个更有利的地点。但是，引进大规模企业也有困难。依据我们的假设，所有必要的条件都缺乏——工人，训练有素的职员，必要的市场条件。来自社会和政治因素的无数的阻力抵制着新企业的创建。而不为人所知的新机构本身，它需要有特殊才能的人来创建。但是，如果有人在这种情况下具备走向成功的所有才能，并且他能获得必要的贷款，那么，他就能更便宜的单位产品投放到市场上去；如果我们的三个条件都实现了，他就能把取得的利润放进自己的口袋。但他同时也为其他人树立了成功的典范，照明了路径，为别人创造了一种可以模仿的模型。别人能够并且愿意仿效他，起初是个别人，然后是成群的人。这样，再一次发生改组过程，这次改组的结果必然是：当新的企业形式成为循环流转的一部分时，超过成本的剩余消失。但在此之前，可以获得利润。重复一遍：这些人只不过是更有效地利用了现有的商品，他们实现了新组合，并且就是我们所说的企业家。他们的所得就是企业家利润。

作为商业组合方面的一个案例，可以选取这样的例子。为了某种生产手段，或许是为了某种原材料，选择一种新的和更便宜的供应来源。这个供应来源，原先并不存在于这个经济系统。与它的起源没有过直接的和正规的联系——比如，如果这个来源是在海外，那么就既没有轮船往来，也没有国外通讯人员。这种创

The innovation is hazardous, impossible for most producers. But if someone establishes a business having regard to this source of supply, and everything goes well, then he can pro- duce a unit of product more cheaply, while at first the existing prices substantially continue to exist. He then makes a profit. Again he has contributed nothing but will and action, has done nothing but recombine existing factors. Again he is an entrepreneur, his profit entrepreneurial profit. And again the latter, and also the entrepreneurial function as such, perish in the vortex of the competition which streams after them. The case of the choice of new trade routes belongs here.

Analogous to the cases of simply improving the process of production is the case of replacing one production or consumption good by another, which serves the same or approximately the same purpose, but is cheaper. Concrete examples are offered by the partial replacement of wool by cotton in the last quarter of the eighteenth century, and by all production of substitutes. These cases are to be treated exactly as those just mentioned. The difference, that the new products here will certainly not bring the same price as those previously produced in the industry under consideration, is only one of degree, as may easily be seen. For the rest, exactly the same holds good. Again it is immaterial whether the individuals concerned produce the new production or consumption good themselves or only employ or dispose of it as the case may be, and draw it for this purpose from its possible existing uses. Here also these individuals contribute neither goods nor purchasing power. Here also they nevertheless make a profit which is connected with the carrying out of new combinations. We recognise them accordingly as entrepreneurs. Here too the profit will not last long.

The creation of a new good which more adequately satisfies existing and previously satisfied needs is a somewhat different case. The production of improved musical instruments is an example. In this case the possibility of profit rests upon the fact that the higher price received for the better commodity surpasses its costs,

新是很危险的，对大多数生产者来说也是无法实现的。但如果有人已经看到这项供应来源，建立了一个企业，而且进展得很顺利，那么，他就能用更便宜的成本生产单位产品，然而起初，现有的价格根本保持不变。所以他获得了利润。同样，除了意志和行动，他没有作什么贡献；他除了对现有的要素进行重新组合之外，没有做任何事情。他同样也是企业家，他的利润是企业家利润。这种利润以及企业家的作用，也同样在其引进的竞争的漩涡中消失。这就是属于选择新的贸易途径的一个案例。

用服务于同一目的或者大致相同目的的一种生产品或消费品，代替另一种生产品或消费品，会更节省，这种情况类似于仅仅改进生产过程。具体的例子是，在 18 世纪的最后 25 年间，用棉花部分地代替羊毛，以及所有用替代品生产的情况。应该像对待刚才提到的那种情况完全一样的方式来对待这些情况。区别是，这时的新产品肯定不会带来与该种工业原先生产的产品一样的价格，但是很显然，区别只是程度上不同。至于其他的，我们的论述完全适用。而有关的人是自己生产新产品或消费品，还是根据具体情况只使用或处理这些生产品或消费品，并为了这一目的，把它们从可能的现实的用途中转向新的用途，同样，这都是无关紧要的。在这里，这些人也是既不贡献商品，又不贡献购买力。在这里，他们也不过是因为实现了新组合而获得利润。因此，我们认为他们是企业家。同样，这里的利润也不会持久。

一种新产品的诞生，能更充分地满足现有的需求以及以前已经满足了的需求，它多少是有些不同的情况。被改进的乐器的生产就是一个例子。在这种情况下，产生利润的可能性取决于这样一个事实，即，用较好的产品卖得的较高的价格要超过其成本，在

which are likewise higher in most cases. One can easily convince oneself of its existence. Furthermore, the adaptation of our three conditions to this case presents no difficulties and may be left to the reader. If a surplus exists and if, therefore, the introduction of better instruments occurs, then here also a tendency to reorganisation in the industry will set in, which will finally restore the rule of the law of cost. Hence, here also there is clearly a new combination of existing factors, an entrepreneurial act and an entrepreneurial profit, even though it is not permanent. A combination of the case of the better satisfaction of a need with the case of lower cost of the unit of product following the appearance of a very great increase in demand is presented by the example of railway and canal construction.

The search for new markets in which an article has not yet been made familiar and in which it is not produced is an extraordinarily rich, and in former times was a very lasting, source of entrepreneurial profit. Primitive trading profits belong here, and the sale of glass beads to a negro tribe may serve as an example. The principle of the matter is that a new commodity is valued by purchasers much as gifts of nature or pictures by old masters, that is its price is determined without regard to cost of production. Hence the possibility that it may sell above costs, including all the expenditure connected with overcoming the innumerable difficulties of the venture. At first only a few see the new enterprise and are able to carry it out. This also is an entrepreneurial act, the carrying out of a new combination; and it yields a profit, which remains in the entrepreneur's pocket. It is true, the source dries up sooner or later. To-day an appropriate organisation would soon come into existence and the trade in glass beads would very soon no longer yield a profit.

At the same time the above covers the case of the production of a completely new good. Such a good must first of all be forced on consumers, perhaps even given away gratis. A host of

多数情况下，这种产品的成本也同样较高。人们很容易理解这种情况是存在的。此外，把我们的三个条件用到这种场合也并不困难，这留给读者自己去做。因此，如果剩余是存在的，并且，如果引进更好的乐器也实现了，那么，在这个产业中，改组的趋势也将开始，这种改组最终将使成本规律重新起作用。因此，显然这里也会出现现有要素的新组合，出现企业家行为和企业家利润，尽管它们不是永久性的。铁路和运河建设的例子，代表了另一种情况。因为修建了铁路，开凿了运河，随之出现需求的极大增长，所以，一方面更好地满足了某些需求，另一方面又降低了单位产品的成本，这两种情况同时发生。

寻找新的市场以销售一种产品，这种产品是该市场所不熟悉的，而且这个市场也没有生产过这样的产品，那么这个市场是企业家利润的一个极其丰富的来源，而在更早的时期，它曾是一个非常持久的来源。原始的贸易利润就属于这一类，卖给黑人部落玻璃珠子可以看做其中的一个例子。这种事情的实质是，购买者把一种新的商品简直视为天赐或者是古代巨匠的杰作，所以它的价格完全不是由生产成本决定的，因此就有可能以超出成本的价格出售，这里的成本包括所有为了进行这项商业冒险，克服无数困难而产生的支出。起初，只有少数人看到这种新企业，并能够经营它。这也是一种企业家行为，实施了新的组合；它也产生了一种利润，属于企业家所有，诚然，这种来源迟早也是要枯竭的。今天，一种适当的组织很快就会诞生，而贩卖玻璃珠子的买卖很快就不再产生利润了。

同时，上面的论述也包括生产一种全新商品的情况。这种商品必须首先被强加给消费者，甚至可能是白给而不要钱。一系列的

obstacles arise. But when these are overcome and the consumers take to the commodity, there follows a period of price determination solely on the basis of direct valuation and without much regard to costs, which here also consist fundamentally of the hitherto prevailing prices of the necessary services of labor and land. Hence a surplus can exist which remains in the hands of the successful producers. These again are entrepreneurs who have only contributed will and action and have only carried out the new combination of existing productive factors. Again there is an entrepreneurial profit. And this disappears again when the new commodity becomes part of the circular flow and its price is put in the normal relation to costs.

These examples show us the nature of profit as the result of carrying out new combinations. They show too how the process must be thought of-essentially as the new employment of existing production goods. The entrepreneur does not save in order to obtain the means which he needs, nor does he accumulate any goods before beginning to produce. Furthermore, when a business is not established all at once in its definitive form but slowly develops, the matter is not as different as one would believe. If the entrepreneur's strength is not exhausted on one project and yet he continues to carry on the same business, then he proceeds to new changes which are always new enterprises according to our terminology, often with means which he draws from his past profits. The process then appears to be different, but its nature is the same.

The same is true if a new enterprise is started by a producer in the same industry and is connected with his previous production. This is by no means the rule; new enterprises are mostly founded by new men and the old businesses sink into insignificance. But even If an individual who previously carried on his business by annually repeating his part in the circular flow becomes an entrepreneur, no change takes place in the nature of the proceeding.

障碍会相继出现。但是，当这些困难被克服，消费者喜欢上了这种商品之后，就会出现一个这样的时期：在这个时期，价格的确定仅仅以直接估计为基础，而不需要过多地考虑成本，这时说的成本，基本上也是由在此之前生产这种商品所必需的劳力和土地服务的通行价格构成。因此，剩余就可能出现在成功的生产者手中。这些人也只不过是贡献意志与行动，只是对现有的生产要素进行新的组合，他们同样是企业家。这里又出现了企业家利润。当新的商品成为循环流转的一部分，并且它的价格与成本建立起正常的关系时，这些企业家利润又都将消失。

这些例子向我们表明了作为实施新组合的结果的利润的性质。它们也告诉我们应该怎样去思考这个过程——从根本上说就是用新的使用方式利用现有的生产品。企业家并不以储蓄来获得他需要的生产手段，他也不在开始生产之前积累任何商品。而且，如果一个企业不是迅速地以一种确定的形式建立起来，而是慢慢地发展起来，那么情况也并非像人们认为的那样不同。如果企业家的精力没有耗竭在一个目标上，而是在同一事业上继续发展，那么，他将继续推行新的变革，按照我们的定义，这些变革总是会产生新的企业，而变革所需要的工具，是从他过去的利润中抽出来的。于是，过程就显得有所不同，但是它们的本质是一样的。

如果是一个生产者在同一行业中创建一个新企业，这个新企业与他原先生产的产品有关系，这种情况也是一样的。这绝不是常规情况，多数情况下，新企业是由新人物创建的，而老企业变成不重要的了。但是，即使一个以前在循环流转中，每年都以重复的角色，经营着企业的人，变成一个企业家，这个过程的本质也不

The fact that in this case the entrepreneur himself already has the necessary means of production, wholly or in part, or, as the case may be, can pay for them out of existing resources of his business, does not change his function as an entrepreneur. It is true our conception does not then fit the facts in every detail. The new enterprise still coexists with the other businesses, which at first continue to operate in the customary manner, but it does not increase the demand for means of production nor does it necessarily supply new products. Yet we only so arranged our picture be- cause the practically more important case demands it and because it shows us the principle of the matter and especially the fact that the new business need not spring directly from the old. Appropriately interpreted, it also fits this case in essentials. Here also it is only a matter of carrying out new combinations and nothing else.

The entrepreneur is never the risk bearer. ①In our example this is quite dear. The one who gives credit comes to grief if the undertaking fails. For although any property possessed by the entrepreneur may be liable, yet such possession of wealth is not essential, even though advantageous. But even if the entrepreneur finances himself out of former profits, or if he contributes the means of production belonging to his "static" business, the risk falls on him as capitalist or as possessor of goods, not as entrepreneur. Risk-taking is in no case an element of the entrepreneurial function. Even though he may risk his reputation, the direct economic responsibility of failure never falls on him.

It may now be briefly observed that profit as here conceived is the main element of the phenomenon which is described as promoter's profit. Whatever promoter's profit may be in addition, its basis is the

① Cf. Chapter II, p. 74 ff.

会有什么变化。事实是，在这种情况下，企业家本人早已有了全部或者部分必要的生产手段，或者，依据实际情况，他已经能够用他企业现有的资源购买必要的生产手段了，这不会改变他作为企业家的职能。当然，在这种情况下，我们的概念就不适合于事实的每一个细节。这个新企业仍然与其他企业同时存在，这些老企业起初继续以传统的方式经营，而新企业并不扩大对生产手段的需求，也不一定供应新的产品。不过，我们这样描绘我们的图景，只是因为实际中更重要的情况要求这样安排，而且，只有这样才能向我们表明事物的原理，特别是只有这样才能揭示新企业未必从老企业直接产生的事实。加上适当的解释，它仍然可以解释这种情况的实质。在这里，关键仍然是实现新组合的问题，没有其他。

企业家从来都不是风险承担者。[①] 在我们的例子中，这是很清楚的。如果新企业经营失败，贷款给这个企业的债权人就会深受损失。因为，尽管企业家所拥有的任何财产都有偿债义务，但是，拥有这种财富并不重要，即使是有利的。如果企业家是用以前的利润来提供资金支持，或者如果他利用属于他的“静态”企业的生产手段来经营，那他也只是以资本家或者商品拥有者的身份承担风险，而不是以企业家的身份承担。在任何情况下，承担风险并不是企业家职能的一个要素。即使他可能冒名声的风险，但是经营失败的直接经济责任从来都不会由他承担。

现在可以简要地说，这里所讨论的利润是由开创者的利润所描述的现象的主要要素。不管还能在这个开创者的利润上再加

① 参阅第二章，第Ⅲ部分。

temporary surplus of receipts over cost of production in a new enterprise. The promoter may indeed be, as we saw, the purest type of the entrepreneur genus. He is then the entrepreneur who confines himself most strictly to the characteristic entrepreneurial function, the carrying out of new combinations. If, during the founding of a business, everything were to proceed correctly and with ideal perfection and foresight on all sides, the profit would be what remained in the founder's hands. Of course, in practice it is quite different. But this still gives the principle of the matter. It is true, this applies only to the real promoter and not to the agent who sometimes performs the technical work of forming a company and frequently also goes by this name. The latter only receives a remuneration which is of the character of wages. Finally, everything new that is created in a company is not in most cases perfected with the promotion of it. On the contrary, its leading men often continually embark upon new enterprises, whereby they then continue the rôle of the original promoter and are entrepreneurs, whatever their official position in the company may be. If we assume, however, that the company, once founded, is simply carried on, then the promoter is the only one who exercise's entrepreneurial activity in relation to this business. Let us assume that the prices of the means of production[①] are represented by bonds, that the capitalised higher return of the lasting sources of gain associated with the enterprise are represented by shares, and that there are also promoter's shares which were transferred to the promoter gratuitously. Then these promoter's shares will not yield a lasting income, but will only bring to the promoter that temporary surplus which exists before the enterprise is embodied in the economic system, and then they become worthless. In such a case profit would appear in its purest form.

---

① That is, strictly speaking, those prices of the means of production constituting the material investment, which correspond to their values in their hitherto prevailing employments without regard to the contemplated new one, even though in practice more would have to be paid in most cases.

上什么，它的基础都是，在一个新企业中收入超出成本的暂时的剩余。正如我们所看到的那样，这样的开创者可能的确是最纯正的一流的企业家。这样，他是最严格地将自己限制于企业家独特职能的企业家，即实现新组合。在创办新企业的过程中，如果每一件事情都进展得顺利无误，在所有方面都很完美并且具有远见，那么利润就会留在创建者手中。当然，实践中的情况却有很大不同。但是这样说仍能够揭示事情的原理。当然，这种表述只适用于真正的创业者，而不适用于那些有时从事创建企业的技术工作，也常常被称为创建者的代理人，他们只获得工资性质的报酬。最后，一个公司所创造的所有的新事物，在多数情况下，不会一下子就达到完善的状态。相反，它的领导者经常是继续从事新的事业，因而他们继续发挥着最先创业者的作用，所以，无论他们在公司里的公职是什么，他们都是企业家。然而，如果我们假定，公司一旦创建，就这样一直办下去，那么，创办者对于公司而言就是唯一对该公司从事企业家活动的人。让我们假定：生产手段的价格由债券表现，① 股票代表着与企业有关的被资本化的更高的回报，这种回报是持久收益来源，也有创办人的股票，它们都无偿地转归在开创者名下。于是，这些开创者的股票将不会产生持久的收入，而只会给开创人带来暂时的剩余，这些剩余存在于这个新企业被融入经济系统之前。以后，这些股票就变得没有价值了。利润在这种情况下表现为它的最纯粹的形式。

① 严格地说就是，构成投资实物内容的生产手段的价格，它们的价值与至此这些生产手段仍然流行的使用方式中的价值相适应，而与所考虑的新方式无关，即使在实践中，多数情况下，往往要支付更多。

This picture of profit must now be worked out. And this is done by our asking ourselves the question of what corresponds to this phenomenon in other than the capitalist form of society. The simple exchange economy, that is the kind of economic system in which there is exchange of products but in which the "capitalistic method" is unknown, gives us no new problem to solve. In the units of such a society there must be a different kind of power of disposal over means of production, in which respect the exchange economy can be dealt with as in the case which we are about to take up. For the rest, however, the same will hold true as for the capitalistic system. Therefore in order to avoid repetitions I shall turn to the simple non-exchange economy.

Here two types of organisation come into consideration. The first is that of an isolated manorial estate in which most means of production belong to the lord and all people are subject to him. The second is that of an isolated communist society in which a central organ disposes of all material goods and services of labor, and expresses all value judgments. At first both forms may be treated in common. In both *some* individuals have absolute control over the means of production. They expect neither cooperation in production nor the offer of possibilities of profit-making from other economic units. The world of prices does not exist and only that of values remains. Thus, when we pass from the consideration of our examples to the treatment of the non-exchange economy we begin the investigation of value phenomena which are at the bottom of profit.

We know that here too there is a circular flow, in which the law of cost strictly rules, in the sense of equality between value of products and value of means of production, and that here too economic development in our sense is only accomplished in the form of carrying out new combinations of existing goods. One might think that the accumulation of stocks of goods would here be necessary and would form a special function. The first is in part correct; not always, it is true, but frequently the accumulation of stocks is a step towards the end of carrying out new combinations. But it never constitutes a special function to which

这幅关于利润的图景现在必须被完成。为此，我们要问自己这样的问题：如果在非资本主义形式的社会里，什么情况与这种现象相对应呢？简单交换经济，它是一种存在产品交换，而不存在“资本主义方法”的经济系统，它没有向我们提出任何新的问题。在这种社会的经济单位中，必然存在一种不同的支配生产手段的权利，对于这种交换经济的这个方面，可以用我们下面将要说的情况来处理。而在其他方面，对待方式与在资本主义制度下一样。因此，为了避免重复，我将转为讨论简单的非交换经济。

在这里，有两种组织类型需要考虑。第一种类型是孤立的庄园，在那里，大多数生产工具属于庄园主，所有的人都顺从于他。第二种类型是孤立的共产主义社会，在那里，有一个中央机构，它处理所有的物质商品和劳动服务，并作出所有的价值判断。我们在一开始同等地看待这两种情况。在这两种情况下，某些个人绝对地控制着生产工具。他们既不期望与其他经济单位进行生产合作，也不期望从其他经济单位获得赚取利润的可能性。价格世界不存在，只有价值世界。这样，当我们从我们所考虑的例子转到非交换经济时，我们就开始了对价值现象的探索，价值现象是利润的根源。

我们知道，在这里也有一个循环流转，其中，成本规律严格地起着作用。这里的成本规律，其意义是产品价值与生产手段的价值相等；同样，这里的经济发展，按照我们的定义，也是通过对现有商品实施新的组合的形式完成的。人们可能认为，商品存量的积累在这里是必需的，这样就会形成一种特殊的职能。第一个观点部分是正确的；的确，虽然商品存量的积累不总是，但常常是最终实现新组合的一个步骤。但它从来不构成一种特殊的职能，因为特殊的职能需要

special value phenomena may be attached. A different employment of goods is simply prescribed by the leader or leading organ of the system. Whether the desired result, is reached directly or only indirectly through a preparatory stage of collecting stocks is completely immaterial. Whether all the participators individually agree with the new aims and are willing to undertake the collection of stocks is likewise immaterial. The leaders make no sacrifice and take no notice of a possible temporary sacrifice of those led-if and so long as the reins rest firmly in their hands. If the execution of far-reaching plans diminishes the present consumption of the people led-which is not necessary, but possible -the latter will oppose them, if they can. ①Their opposition may make these plans impossible. But neglecting this, they have no direct and economic influence on what shall happen; in particular a shrinkage of consumption and accumulation of stocks is not their voluntary service. Therefore this also involves no special function which should be inserted in our picture of the process of development. If the leader promises the people a premium it amounts to nothing more than when a general promises his soldiers some special remuneration; it is a gift intended to make the people more docile, but it is not part of the essence of the matter and forms no special, purely economic category. Hence the difference between the "lord" and the leader of a communist economy is only one of degree. The fact that according to the idea of a communist society the advantages accruing are to go to the whole community while the lord possibly has only his own interest in view, constitutes no fundamental difference.

---

① For they will have in view only the immediate loss, while the future gain may possibly have just as little reality as if it would never exist. This applies to all stages of civilisation of which we have any knowledge; throughout history the dement of force has never been absent when it has been a question of development which presupposes the cooperation of great masses. In many cases, it is true, no sacrifice at all was exacted from the people.

加上特殊的价值现象。商品的不同的使用方式完全取决于这个系统的领导者或者领导机构。所期望的结果是直接达到，还是要通过一个收集存货的准备阶段，这完全是不重要的。不管参与的个人是否都赞同新的目标，并愿意去收集存货，这同样也是不重要的。领导者不会有任何牺牲，而且也不会去关心属下的人可能要付出的暂时的牺牲——只要权利仍然紧紧地掌握在他们手中。如果执行了有深远影响的计划，因而减少了他们属下人的当前的消费——这不是必要的，但是可能的——如果可能，这些人将会反对这些计划。① 他们的反对可能使这些计划不能执行。但是如果忽略这种情况，那么，属下的人们对将要发生的事情就不会有任何直接的经济的影响，特别是压缩消费，积累存货，并不是他们自愿这样做的。因此，这里也不包括任何应纳入我们所描绘的发展过程图景的特殊职能。如果领导者向人们承诺将获得一笔额外补贴，这也不过像一位将军向他的士兵承诺他们将得到某种特殊的报酬。那只是为了让人们更顺从的一种赠与，而不是事情本质的一部分，也不形成特殊的、纯经济的某个类型。因此，“庄园主”和共产主义的领导者之间的区别，仅仅是程度上的一种差别。根据社会主义的观点，增长的利益属于整个社会，而在庄园主眼中可能只有他自己的利益，这一事实并不构成任何根本上的区别。

---

① 因为他们将只看到眼前的损失，而未来的收益可能只有小得几乎从来不存在的现实性。这一点适用于我们对其哪怕只有一点认识的所有文明阶段。纵观历史，就发展问题而言，力的因素从来都没有消失过，这里的发展以巨大的人群的合作为前提。的确，在许多情况下，牺牲不是强加于人民的。

From this it follows also that the element of time can have no independent influence here. It is true, leaders must compare the result of the contemplated combination not merely with the result that the same productive factors could produce in the same time in their previous method of employment, but also with the results of other new combinations which could alternatively be carried out with the same means. And if these latter require less time, the results of as many other combinations as could be carded out in the time saved must be allowed for in estimating the relative importance of the competing methods of employment. Therefore the time element will certainly appear in a non-exchange economy, while in the capitalist system its influence is expressed by the interest item, as we shall see later. This, however, is self- evident. Even here time plays no other rle; none, for example, that would make the necessity of waiting or the smaller desire for future enjoyments special factors. One only waits unwillingly because, and as long as, one can do something else in the mean- time. Future enjoyments only appear smaller because the further in the future their realisation lies, the greater become the deductions on account of "enjoyments realisable elsewhere."

Thus the leader of such a community, whatever his position may be, withdraws a certain quantity of means of production from their previous uses and with them carries out a new combination, for example the production of a new good or the production of a good already known by a better method. In the latter case it is quite immaterial whether he withdraws the necessary means of production from the branch of industry which hitherto manufactured the same commodity, or whether he allows existing firms to continue working in the habitual manner and begins to produce alongside of them with the new method and withdraws the necessary means of production from quite different branches of industry. The new products will be *ex hypothesi* of higher value than those produced previously by the same quantities of means of production-how ever valuations in such a society may be formed. How does the process of imputation proceed with respect to the new products?

从这里我们还可以得出，时间要素在这里不会独立地影响事情。诚然，领导者必须把已经深思熟虑的组合的结果，不仅与用同样的生产要素以它们先前的使用方式，在同样的时间内可能得到的结果相比较，还要把它与用同样的生产手段，在其他新的组合方式中可能产生的结果相比较。如果后者需要更少的时间，那么，就必须考虑其他可能实施的若干组合在节省的时间里可能产生的结果，以估计相互竞争的各种使用方式的相对重要性。因此，时间要素必将出现在非交换经济中，而在资本主义制度里，它的影响是由利息表现的，这一点我们将在后面看到。不过，这一点是很显然的。甚至在这里，时间也不起任何其他作用，例如，它决不会把等待的必要性，或者把对未来享受的欲望变得更小，成为某种特殊的因素。人们不愿意等待只是因为，人们可以在这个时期做其他的事。未来的享受变得更小，只是因为他们的享受在未来实现的越晚，按照“可以在其他地方实现这种享受”来说，应打的折扣就越大。

这样，这个社会的领导者，不管他的地位是什么，从原先的用途中把一定数量的生产工具抽取出来，并用它们实现一种新的组合，例如生产一种新产品，或者用一种更好的方法生产某种已有的产品。在后一种情况下，领导者是从一直制造同一种产品的工业分支中提取必要的生产工具，还是允许现有的厂商继续以习惯的方式生产，并同时与其一起开始采用新的方法进行生产，而从完全不同的工业分支中抽取必要的生产工具，这些都是不重要的。根据假设，新产品的价值要高于用原来的生产方式以同样数量的生产资料所生产的产品的价值——不管在这样的社会里，估价是怎样形成的。有关新产品的归属过程是怎样进行的呢？当

At the moment when the combination is completed and the products come into existence their value is determined. How will the values of the factors which have participated be formed? It is still better to choose the moment when the decision is made to carry out the new combination and to assume that everything happens exactly according to the decision.

First of all a valuation must be made by the producers: the value of the new products must be compared with the value of those products which the same means of production have been producing so far in the normal circular flow. Clearly this valuation is necessary in order to make any estimate of the advantage of the new combination, and without it no action would be possible. The central question for our problem is now, which of the two alternative values that may be produced by the means of production will be imputed to the latter. So much is clear: before the decision about carrying out the new combination is made, only that value which corresponds to the old employment. For there would be no sense in imputing beforehand the surplus value of the new combination to the means of production, since the carrying out of it would then no longer appear as an advantage and the basis for the necessary comparison of the values in the two uses would be lost. But how does the matter stand once the decision is made? Must not the whole gain in satisfaction be imputed in the Mengerian sense① to the means of production, just as in the circular flow, since they now realise the higher value; so that if everything functions with ideal perfection the whole value of the new products will be reflected in the means of production used?

I answer no; and assert that even here the services of labor and land are to be estimated at their old values; and in fact for the following two reasons. First, the old values are customary values. Long experience has determined them, and they are established in the consciousness of individuals. They are only altered in the course of time and under the pressure of further long experience. Their values are stable to a

① Cf. Wieser, Natürlicher Wert, p. 70 f.

新的组合已经完成，产品已经生产出来时，它们的价值就已经被决定了。那些参与新组合的要素的价值将是怎样形成的呢？我们最好还是选择决定实施新组合那个时刻，并假定所有的事情都按照决定的进行。

首先，生产者必须作出价值评估：必然要比较新产品的价值和在正常循环流转中用同样生产资料所生产出来的产品的价值。显然，为了评价新组合的优势，这种评估是必要的，如果没有这样的评估，就不会有后面的任何行为。现在，我们所研究的核心问题是，用同样的生产资料生产，可能产生的两种价值，哪一个将被归属于那些生产资料？这一点很清楚：在决定实施新组合之前，只有与旧的生产方法相适应的价值。因为如果事先把新组合的剩余价值列入生产手段，那是没有什么意义的，因为那样做的话，实施新组合就显得不再有利益了，也失去了比较新旧两种方法所得的价值的必要性的基础。但是，一旦新组合实施，情况会是怎么样的呢？难道因为这时生产手段实现了更高的价值，所得到的所有满足就不该像门格尔所说的那样，[①]就像在循环流转中那样，全部归于生产手段；从而，如果所有的事都完美地运行，那么新产品的全部价值将被反映在所使用的生产手段中？

我的回答是否定的。我甚至坚持认为，在这里，劳动和土地服务都应该用它们原来的价值来估计，这有以下两个理由：第一，原来的老的价值是人们习惯了的价值。长期的经验决定了这些价值，在人们的意识中，这些价值是确定的。它们只有在经过了一段时间并受到更长期的经验的压力，才会改变。这些价值是高

① 参阅维塞尔的《自然价值》，第70页。

high degree, all the more so since the services of labor and land themselves have not changed. The values of the new products on the contrary stand just as much outside the existing value system as the prices of new products in the capitalist system. They are not joined in continuity with the old values, but are separated discretely. Hence the justification of the method of interpretation① according to which any productive good is only assigned the value which it would realize in other than its actual employment. For only this value, that is in our case its hitherto prevailing value, is dependent upon the concrete means of production. If they ceased to exist they would be replaced by other units from these other employments. No unit of a commodity can be valued higher than another identical unit, if they exist simultaneously. Now the services of labor and land employed in the new combination are homogeneous with those simultaneously employed-if they were not there would indeed be a difference in value, but one easily explicable without affecting the principle-and therefore cannot have a different value from the latter. Even in the extreme case, if all productive powers in the economic system were put at the service of the new combination they would have to be invested at this stage with the values hitherto prevailing, which in case of failure they could realise again and upon which the magnitude of the losses would be based if they were completely annihilated. Therefore the successful carrying out of new combinations also results in a value surplus in the non-exchange economy, not only in the capitalistic; and in fact a value surplus in the sense of a quantity of value to which there is no corresponding claim of imputation by means of production, not merely a surplus of satisfaction as against the earlier position. As we may also put it, surplus value② in development is not only a private but also

① With which I do not agree in every respect; cf. Wesen, bk. II, and "Bemerkun- gen ber das Zurechnungsproblem," Zeitschrift für Volksw., Sozialp. und Verw. (1909).

② Only this surplus, which appears from the private economic standpoint as profit and interest on capital, can be described as surplus value in the Marxian sense.

度稳定的，特别是因为劳动和土地服务本身没有变化，所以它就更加稳定。与其相反，新产品的价值独立于现有的价值体系之外，就像资本主义制度下新产品的价格那样。新产品的价值与老的价值并不相连接，而是分别独立的。因此，任何生产品的价值只能按照它的其他使用方法所能实现的价值来估计，而不是根据它实际被用的方法产生的价值来估计，这种说法是有道理的。[①] 因为只有这个价值是我们所说的迄今最流行的价值，才是依赖于具体的生产手段的。如果它们不存在了，它们将被用其他使用方式所产生的其他单位所替代。如果这些价值同时存在，任何一单位商品的价值都不能高于同样的另一个单位的价值。现在，使用在新组合中的劳动和土地服务，与同时存在的其他组合中的劳动和土地服务是同质的——如果不是这样，将会出现价值差异，但我们也能容易地阐明其原因，同时不影响我们的原则——这样两者之间就没有价值差异了。甚至在极端的情况下，如果经济系统里所有的生产力都投入到新组合中，在这个阶段，它们也必须按迄今流行的价值来投资。即使新企业失败，这些生产力的价值还是可以再实现。如果生产力完全赔光，那么损失的数量也要以以前流行的价值为基础来衡量。因此，在非交换经济中，新组合的成功也会带来价值剩余，这不仅在资本主义制度下才有。事实上，价值的剩余是一定的价值量，生产手段没有相应的要求其归属的权利，价值的剩余不仅仅是超过以前状态的一种满足的剩余。我们还可以说，发展中的剩余价值[②]不仅是一个私人的现象，而且是

---

① 我并不在各方面都赞同这种说法；参阅《本质》第二章，以及《关于归属问题的评论》，载《政治经济学、社会政策与管理杂志》(1909 年)。

② 只有这种从私有经济的观点看是利润和资本利息的剩余，才能被马克思主义观点描述为剩余价值。

a social phenomenon, and so far is in every respect the same thing as the capitalistic entrepreneurial profit which we met before.

Secondly, the same result may be reached by another approach. The entrepreneurial activity of the leader, which is indeed a necessary condition of the realisation of the combination, may be conceived as a means of production. I do not so conceive it ordinarily, because more interest attaches to the contrast between entrepreneur and means of production. But here this method of consideration does good service. For the time being, therefore, let us constitute the leadership function a third original productive factor. Then it is clear that some part of the value of the new products must be imputed to it. But how much? Leader and means of production are equally necessary, and the whole surplus value of the new products depends upon the cooperation of both of them. This requires no further comment and does not contradict what was said in the preceding paragraph. The appropriate magnitudes of all value categories are only determined by the force of competition, whether of goods or of individuals. Since this second kind of competition does not exist in the non-exchange economy, and since in it the difference between what is and is not profit is also of much less significance than in an exchange economy (as we shall see immediately), its value would not always appear with the dearness that it does where this difference is very essential. But we can nevertheless specify for most cases how much is to be imputed to the entrepreneur's function. In most cases, as we have said, the means of production are replaceable, but not the leader. ①Hence the former will have imputed to them that value which will be lost in the event of replacement being necessary, and the leadership function will be assigned the remainder. To the leadership function is imputed the value of the new products minus the value which could be realized without it.

---

① Even if the activity of the leader competes with an irreplaceable means of production, a value surplus remains over in favor of the former. For, at the time of the introduction of the innovation, the latter is only to be assigned its hitherto prevailing value.

一种社会现象，它与我们在前面所说的资本主义企业家利润，在各方面都是相同的。

第二，用另一种方法可以得到相同的结果。领导者的企业家性质的活动，确实是实现新组合的一个必要条件，它可能被当做是一种生产手段。我通常不这样构想它，因为我对比较企业家活动与生产手段的不同更感兴趣，但是在这里，这样的构想是有帮助的。因此，暂且让我们把领导者的职能看做是第三种最初始的生产要素。那么，显然，新产品价值的一部分必须归于它的名下。但是，是多少呢？领导者和生产手段同样是必要的，新产品的全部剩余价值取决于这两者的合作。这不需要更多的评论，而且与我们在前段中所讨论的并不矛盾。所有价值范畴的适当数量仅仅取决于竞争力，不管是对商品来说还是对个人来说。因为在非交换经济中不存在这第二种竞争，同时由于在非交换经济中，什么是利润与什么不是利润之间的区别，并不像在交换经济中那么重要（我们很快就会看到这一点），所以，它的价值常常就不像在这种区别非常重要的交换经济中那样清楚。尽管如此，在大多数情况下，我们还是能够明确地说明，有多少价值应归于企业家的作用。正像我们已经论述过的，在多数情况下，生产手段是可以被替代的，但领导者不可以替代。[①] 因此，在有必要替代生产手段的情况下，将损失的那部分价值应该属于生产手段，余下的部分将归属于领导职能所起的作用。而归属于领导职能的价值，是新产品的价值减去在没有这种领导职能时可能实现的价值的差额。

---

① 即使领导者的活动与某种不可替代的生产手段相竞争，剩余价值仍然归于前者。因为，在引进创新之时，生产手段只能被赋予迄今流行的价值。

Hence, the surplus here corresponds to a special claim to imputation, and can therefore in no case swell the claim which originates in the means of production.

In this it must not be forgotten, however, that it would not be quite right if we were always to speak of the imputation of the hitherto prevailing value to the means of production. The marginal value in the previous uses indeed rises in consequence of the withdrawal of means of production from them. We observed the same phenomenon in the capitalistic system. The rise of prices of means of production in consequence of new demand by entrepreneurs in the capitalistic system corresponds exactly to this valuation process. Our method of expression must be corrected accordingly. However, nothing is changed in fundamentals. This rise in value must not be confused, of course, with the imputation of the value due to development to the means of production.

No one can assert that the valuation process described above is not real and that profit as a special value magnitude has no meaning in a non-exchange economy. Even a non-exchange economy must know clearly what it is doing, what advantage its new combinations yield and also to what this advantage is to be attributed. One might assert, however, that profit has no significance as a distributive category in a non-exchange economy. In a certain sense this is true. In the feudal type of non-exchange economy the lord can indeed dispose freely of the quantity of product corresponding to his "service," but in it the lord can dispose freely of all returns-he can give the workers more but also less than corresponds to their marginal productivity. In the communist type the profit falls entirely to the people as a whole-at least in theory. This in itself does not concern us. But can one not infer from it, especially for the communist type, that profit is absorbed in wages, that reality pushes the theory of value aside and that wages embrace the whole product? No, one must distinguish the economic nature of a return from what happens to it. The economic nature of a return rests upon a productive service. In this sense we call wages that return which is to be imputed to a labor service. Under free competition in an exchange economy

因此，剩余在这里与一种对价值归属的特殊要求权相对应，从而无论怎样都不能夸大产生于生产手段的要求权。

然而，这里也决不能忘记，如果我们总是谈论归属问题，把迄今流行的价值的归属问题归于生产手段，那不是很正确的。由于从原先的用途中抽取出生产工具，原先使用过程的边际价值确实提高了。我们在资本主义制度下可以观察到相同的现象。在资本主义制度下，由于企业家的新需求导致生产工具价格的上涨，这恰好符合这个价值变化过程，因而我们的表述方法必然要做相应修正。然而，根本没有任何改变。当然，决不能把这种价值的上涨与因生产手段的发展而导致的价值上升相混淆。

谁也不能说，上面描述的估价过程不真实，也不能说，利润作为一种特殊的价值量度，在非交换经济中没有任何意义。甚至是一个非交换经济，也必须清楚地知道它正在做什么，它的新组合会产生什么好处，还有，这些好处归因于什么。然而，人们可能会说，在非交换经济中，利润作为一个分配范畴，没有任何意义。从某种意义上说，这是对的。在封建式的非交换经济中，地主确实可以根据对他的“服务”，自由地支配产品数量，他可以自由地处置所有的收益——他可以给工人们高于或者低于他们的边际产量的报酬。在共产主义式的非交换经济中，利润完全归于全体人民——至少理论上是这样。这本身与我们的论述无关，但是难道我们不能推断说，尤其就社会主义类型来说，利润被工资吸收了，现实把价值理论推到一旁，而工资包含了全部产值？不可以，我们必须区分收益的经济本质和人们对它的处置。收益的经济本质以某种生产性服务为基础。在这个意义上，我们把工资称为应归于劳务的那部分收益。在交换经济的自由竞争下，这部分收

this return goes to the worker, but only because the principle of free competition is remuneration according to marginal significance. It is necessary only in the sense that in the capitalistic system precisely this wage calls forth the effort. If the effort were assured by another method-by the feeling of social duty or perhaps by compulsion-the worker might receive less; but his wages would nevertheless be determined by the marginal productivity of labor, and the amount by which his remuneration fell short of this should be classified as a deduction from his economic wage. This deduction would also be wages, quite on the same plane with the wage paid to the worker. In a communist society the leader would certainly not receive profit. And most decidedly it cannot be asserted that this would make development impossible. On the contrary, it is possible that the people in such an organization would in time think so differently that they would no more lay claim to profit than a statesman or a general would wish to keep the spoils of victory wholly or partly for himself. But the profit would remain profit. That it will not do to characterise it as the wages of labor may be seen by adapting the argument which Böhm-Bawerk formulated classically with respect to interest. ① It also applies to rent of land, in which likewise the nature and value of the productive contribution of land are to be distinguished from the revenue received by particular individuals. ②

As the wage of which workers would the profit be designated? Two answers to this question are conceivable. In the first place it may be said: as part of the wage of the workers who worked on the new product. Now this cannot be. For then these workers would *ex hypothesiget* higher wages than their fellows. The latter, however, perform no less work of no inferior quality, so that if we accept this possibility we come into conflict with

① Positive Theorie, final chapter.

② Cf. Wesen, bk. III.

益落到劳动者那里，但这仅仅是因为按照自由竞争的原则，根据边际重要性来获得报酬。这是必然的，仅仅是因为在资本主义制度下，正好是这种工资鼓励人们去努力。如果这种努力是通过另一种方法来保证的——比如通过社会责任感或者强制作用——那么，工人获得的报酬可能更少，尽管如此，他的工资仍然是由劳动者的边际生产力决定的。如果他的报酬比边际生产力少，那么，少的这部分应该被看做是对他的经济工资的一种扣除。这个扣除部分也是工资，与支付给工人的工资性质完全一样。在共产主义社会，领导者当然得不到利润。但是可以完全肯定地说，并不能因此就认为发展不可能。相反，在这样的组织中的人们可能很快会形成一种十分不同的思想，他们不再对利润提出要求，就像在这种社会里，一位政治家或者一位将军不会把战利品全部或者部分地归于他自己一样。但利润仍然是利润，不可以把利润看成是劳动者的工资，通过把庞巴维克关于利息的经典阐释用到这上面来，就可以明白了。[①] 他的阐释也适用于地租，同样，应该把土地的生产性贡献的本质和价值同某些特定个人所得的收入区别开来。[②]

那么，利润应该被认为是哪些工人的工资呢？对这个问题可以构想两种答案：第一个答案可以这样说，它是工作在新产品上的工人的工资的一部分。现在这种情况是不可能的，因为如果这样，那么根据我们的假设，这些工人所得的工资将比其同伴的工资高。然而，他们的同伴的工作丝毫不比他们少，劳动质量也不比他们的差，这样，如果我们接受这种可能性，我们就会与一个

---

① 见《资本实证论》最后一章。
② 参阅《本质》第三章。

a fundamental economic principle, that excludes different values for different parts of homogeneous goods. Quite apart from the injustice that would lie in such a measure, privileged workers would plainly be created by it. The arrangement is possible, but the surplus received by these workers would not be wages.

The other conceivable answer is: the values which we call profit and the amounts of product corresponding to them simply constitute a part of the national dividend and are to be allotted equally to all labor services contributed in the relevant economic period-assuming homogeneity of the services or, as the case may be, taking account of disparities in any recognised way. In this case the laborers who have not worked on the new products get more than the product of their labor. Never yet has an economic meaning been associated with a wage that is higher than the total value product. Therefore it will easily be conceded that in this case the workers get their share not wholly as an economic wage but partially under a non-economic title. To be sure, this arrangement is also possible, and many others equally so. The community must indeed dispose somehow of its "profit" as of all other returns. It must dispose of it in favor of the workers since there are no others entitled to shares. In this it can proceed according to the most varied principles; it can for example distribute according to intensity of need or promote general ends without distributing it. But this alters nothing in the economic categories. In the normal circular flow it is not possible for the workers, any more than land, to receive directly or indirectly more than their economic product, for more does not exist. If this is possible in our case it is solely because some other agent does not receive its product. If we so define the ambiguous expression "exploitation" that exploitation occurs when a necessary agent of production, or the possessor of it as the case may be, receives less than its product in the economic sense, then we can say that this extra payment to the workers is only possible by exploiting the leaders. If

基本的经济原理相冲突，即，同质商品的不同部分不该有不同的价值。暂且撇开这种说法的公正性不谈，但是它确实能产生一种享有优先权的工人。由此的某些安排是可能的，但是，这些工人所得到的剩余将不属于工资范畴。

构想的另一个答案是，我们称为利润的那部分价值，以及与其相对应的产品的数量只是构成了国民报酬的一部分，应该平均地分配给在相关经济时期内做贡献的所有劳动服务——假定服务是同质的，或者根据具体情况，考虑以任何可被识别的差异来分摊。在这种情况下，没有参与新产品生产的工人得到的将比他们的劳动产品多。然而，在经济学意义上还从没有说过，工资高于产品的总价值。因此，很容易看出，在这种情况下，工人们并不完全以经济学上的工资的名义获得他们的份额，而有一部分收入是非经济学意义的。的确，这种安排也是可能的，许多其他安排也同样可能。社会必然就像处理其他收益一样，以某种方式来处理它的“利润”。社会必须按照有利于工人的方式处理利润，因为没有其他人有资格来享有它。而在这时，人们可能按照极不相同的原则来行事，比如，人们可能按照对需求的程度来分配，或者为了促进总的目标而不进行分配。但这丝毫不能改变经济类型。在正常的循环流转中，工人们就像土地一样，所得的直接或间接收入不可能多于他们的经济产品，因为不存在超过的那部分。如果我们的案例中存在这种情况，那纯粹是因为某些其他要素没有得到它们的产品。如果我们定义“剥削”这个模糊的概念为：当某种必要的生产要素，或者根据情况是生产要素的所有者，所得的收益少于其在经济意义上的产品时，就是剥削。于是，我们可以说，工人们所得的额外的报酬，由于剥削了领导者才有可能。如果我

we confine the expression to the case in which some personal service is deprived of its product-in order to exclude the concept of exploitation from being applied to land, where, considering the non-existence of landlords in the communist society, it would be out of place-then we can still say that exploitation of the leaders occurs, to be sure, without wishing to pass any moral judgment.

Therefore profit does not become wages in the economic sense even if it goes wholly to the workers. It is practically important for a communist system to recognize this dearly and always to separate profit from wages. For the general understanding of its life as well as decisions about concrete questions manifestly depend upon such recognition. This whole consideration teaches us the independence of the phenomenon from the concrete form of economic organisation. And then there is the general truth: profit as a special and independent value phenomenon is fundamentally connected with the rôle of leadership in the economic system. If development required no direction and no force then profit would indeed exist; it would be a part of wages and rents, but it would not be a phenomenon *sui generis*. As long as this is not the case, that is as long as the bulk of the people have the slightest resemblance to the masses of all nations of whom we have any knowledge, so long the whole return cannot be imputed to the services of labor and land, even in the ideally perfect case of frictionless and timeless economic process. ①

---

① A word about the argument which is so often heard today: that the entrepreneur produces nothing, organisation everything; that no one's product is his own, but the product of the social whole. At the bottom of this is the truth that everyone is the product of his inherited and personal milieu and that no one can produce anything for which the conditions do not exist. But we can do nothing with this in the realm of theory, which is not concerned with the moulding of men but with men already formed. To the question whether individual initiative has a function, even the representatives of this interpretation would eagerly reply affirmatively. Further, it is precise and correct with respect to the secondary phenomena of development. For the rest, it is merely based upon the popular preconception that only physical work is really productive and upon the impression that all elements of development work harmoniously together and every phase of development is based upon preceding ones. This, however, is the result of development already set in motion and explains nothing. The principle of its mechanism is the main question.

们把这种表述局限于在某些人力服务被剥夺其产品的情况，目的是为了避免把剥削的概念应用到土地上，因为考虑共产主义社会不存在地主，如果应用到土地上那是不符合实际情况的，所以，我们仍然可以说，对领导者的剥削出现了。当然，我们并不希望超越任何道德上的判断。

因此，即使将利润全部分给工人，在经济意义上，它也不能成为工资。对共产主义制度来说，清楚地认识到这一点，并且总是区分利润与工资，这在实际上是很重要的。因为如果要一般地了解共产主义社会下的生活，以及决策具体的问题，显然都依赖于对这一点的认识。所有这些考虑告诉我们，这些现象是独立于经济组织的具体形式之外的。于是有一条一般真理：利润作为一种特殊的、独立的价值现象，它与经济制度中领导的职能有着根本的联系。如果发展不需要任何指导，不需要任何外力，那么，利润将确实存在，它将是工资和租金的一部分，但它不是一种独特的现象。只要情况不是这样，也就是说只要大多数人民，与我们对其有任何了解的所有民族的人民，哪怕只有极小的相似点，那么我们就不能把所有的收入归于劳动和土地服务，甚至是在没有任何摩擦，不考虑任何时间因素的极其完美的经济过程中，也是如此。①

① 当前，经常听到这样的说法：企业家不生产任何东西，而组织产生所有的东西，没有哪一个人的产品是他自己的，而是社会整体的产品。这种说法以下面的这个真理为基础，即，每个人都是他所继承的、他本人的社会环境的产物，如果条件不存在，没有人能生产出任何东西。但是在理论领域，我们不能用这个观点解决任何问题因为理论并不考虑人是如何被塑造的，而是探索已经形成的人类的问题。对于个人的首创精神是否是一种职能的问题，即使是上述观点的代表人物也会急切地作出肯定的回答。此外，对于发展的次要现象来说，这也是准确和恰当的。除此以外，这种说法仅仅是以一种流行的偏见为基础，即，只有体力劳动才是真正的生产性劳动，而且它也基于一种印象，即，发展的所有要素都是和谐地共同起作用，发展的每一阶段都基于前一阶段。然而，这是已经启动了的发展的结果，它不能解释任何东西。我们要研究的主要问题是发展机制的原理。

But also in the non-exchange economy profit does not live eternally. Here too, necessary changes appear which put an end to it. The new combination is carried out; its results are at hand, all doubts are silenced; the advantages, and at the same time the manner of obtaining them, are henceforth evident. There is further need, at the most, of a manager or foreman, but not of the creative power of a leader. It is only necessary to repeat what has been done before to acquire the equivalent advantages. And that can and will be done without a leader. Even if resistances from friction must still be overcome, the matter has become essentially different, and easier. The advantages have become realities to all members of the community, and the new products, uniformly distributed in time, are continually before their eyes; they free them, in the sense of what we said on this point in the first chapter, from every sacrifice or necessity of waiting for the completion of further products. The economic system is no longer expected to advance, but only to assure the continuity of the existing stream of goods. We can expect that of it.

Thus the new process of production will be repeated. And for this entrepreneurial activity is no longer necessary. If we conceive it again as a third productive factor, then we can say that in the mere repetition of the familiarised new combinations one of the factors of production, which were necessary to carrying them out initially, disappears. At the same time the claim to imputation associated with it is abolished and the values of the others, that is of the services of labor and land, will be increased until they exhaust the value product. Only these are necessary now, they alone create the product. Imputation is to them alone; in the first place to the services of labor and land which are actually used in the given production, but subsequently, in accordance with well known principles, equally to all. *The values of the former services of labor and land will first increase and then will diffuse themselves over all others.*

但是在非交换经济中，利润也不能永久地存在。在这里，也发生了必要的变化，它使利润消失。实施了新的组合；其成果指日可待，所有怀疑都已消失；新组合带来的利益，以及获得这些益处的方式，因此都是显而易见的。这时，充其量还需要一位经理或者一位监工，而不需要领导者的创造力了。于是，必要的事就是重复以前所做的事以得到同等的利益。要做到这些，能够而且也将不需要有领导者。即使仍然必须克服由于摩擦带来的阻力，但事情在本质上已不同，而且更容易了。对所有的社会成员来说，利益已成为现实，新产品总是及时一致地被分配，这已是经常发生的事了。他们不需要像本书第一章所说的那样，为进一步完成产品生产，需付出任何牺牲或者必要的等待。人们不再期望经济制度向前发展，而只是确保现有的产品流持续下去。我们可以料想到这些。

于是，新的生产过程将被重复。为此，企业家活动就不再是必要的了。如果我们仍然把企业家活动构想成第三种生产要素，那么，我们可以说，在纯粹的重复人们已熟悉的新组合的过程中，这种生产要素，在刚刚实行新组合时是必需的，现在则消失了。同时，与其相关联的价值归属的要求也没有了，而属于其他要素，即属于劳动和土地服务的价值将增长，直到包括全部产品价值。这时只有劳动和土地服务是必需的要素，只需这两个要素就可以创造产品。价值只属于它们，起初归属于劳动和土地服务，这些劳动和土地服务是在一定生产中实际使用的，但是后来，根据人们所熟悉的一般原则，价值就平均地归属于所有的劳动和土地服务。先前使用的劳动和土地的价值将首先增长，然后将扩展到所有其他的劳动和土地服务上。

Hence, the values of all services of labor and land will rise correspondingly. This rise, however, must be distinguished from that which appeared with the carrying out of the new combination, not only in degree but also in kind. It signifies no rise in their scale of values but only in their marginal utility in consequence of the fact that, because of the withdrawal of means of production from the hitherto prevailing uses, production cannot be carried as far as before, hence only needs of higher intensity than before can be satisfied. In the other case something quite different occurs, namely the entry of the value of the new products into the scale of values of means of production. This may also raise the marginal utility of the latter; but it raises their total value too, a difference which is of practical importance where the disposal of larger quantities of factors is concerned. Hence the values of the means of production now express the fact that the new increase in satisfaction depends upon them and them alone, that the product of labor and land has become greater. They will now no longer be assigned the values which they had in the former circular flow, but those which they realise in the new circular flow. At the time of the transformation there was no sense in imputing to them a value higher than their replacement value then. Now their replacement value already includes the value of the new employment. The rise in the value of the social product draws the values of the means of production after it and the new state of affairs will soon replace the old accustomed value by a new one, which will finally become the customary one, based upon the new marginal productivity. Thus the contact between value of product and value of means of production would be reestablished. There will be no more discrepancy between the two value categories in the new system than there was in the earlier. And if everything functions with ideal perfection then the communist society is now quite right if it considers all the resulting product as a permanent return to its labor and land and distributes it amongst its members for consumption.[①] The facts would not disavow it.

① As the capitalist system does too after its own fashion.

因此，所有的劳动和土地服务的价值将相应地上升。然而，这种价值上升必须区别于由于实施新组合而带来的价值增长，这种区别不仅表现在程度上，而且表现在种类上。这种增长并不表示价值规模的增长，而仅表明它们的边际效用的增长，这是因为从当前流行的用途中抽取出生产工具，生产就不能像以前那样进行，因此只有提高生产工具的利用强度才能达到满意的程度。在其他情况下，情况有很大不同，即，新产品的价值进入生产资料的价值规模中。这也可能使生产资料的边际效用上升，但它也提高了生产资料的总价值，当考虑所支配的生产要素的数量巨大时，这一差别有实际的重要性。因此，这时生产手段的价值表明一个事实，即，满意度的新增长依赖于这些生产手段，而且仅仅依赖于这些生产手段，劳动和土地的产量变得更大了。这时它们所赋予的价值将不再是在以前循环流转中它们被赋予的价值了，而是它们在新的循环流转中实现的价值。在这种转化的时候，把高于它们的重置价值的价值归属于它们，是没有意义的。这时它们的重置价值已经包括新的使用方式的价值了。社会产品价值的增长使生产手段的价值跟随其增长，事态的新形势将很快用一种新的价值替代旧的、已习惯了的价值，这个新的价值最终也会成为人们习惯的价值，它是以新的边际生产力为基础的。这样，产品价值与生产手段的价值之间的关联将重新建立。在新体系中的这两类价值之间，也像在前一阶段那样，没有差异。如果一切都以理想的状态完美地起着作用，那么共产主义社会这时如果把所有产生的产品看做是对它们的劳动和土地的永久性的回报，并把它们在其成员内分配以消费，那是十分合理的。[①] 上面的这些事实不会对此有任何异议。

① 正如资本主义制度也以它自己的方式来处理。

So far the elimination of profit in the non-exchange economy proceeds in a manner quite analogous to its elimination in the capitalistic system. But the other part of this process in the capitalist system, namely the forcing down of the price of the new product in consequence of the appearance of competing firms, must be absent in the non-exchange economy. It is true that here too the new products have to be incorporated in the circular flow, that here too their values must be brought into relation with the values of all other products. Theoretically we can still distinguish the carrying out of the innovation and the process of its embodiment in the circular flow as two different things. But it is easily seen that it makes a considerable difference practically whether both actually take place *uno actu* or not. In a non-exchange economy the demonstration of a surplus attributable to entrepreneurial activity is quite enough to solve our problem. In a capitalist system these surpluses can only find their way to the entrepreneur with the help of the mechanism of the market and can be wrested from him again only by means of this mechanism. Thus there is besides the simple value problem the further one of how it happens that the profit actually accrues to the entrepreneur. And this mechanism creates many phenomena which must be absent in a non-exchange economy.

In spite of this, not only is the innermost economic nature of profit the same in all forms of organisation, but so is the innermost nature of the process that eliminates it. In all cases the matter turns upon the elimination of the obstructions which prevent the whole value product from being imputed to the services of labor and land, or, as the case may be, their prices from being put on a level with the price of the product. The ruling principles are always that the economic process, if unobstructed, first does not tolerate value surpluses in the case of individual products, and secondly always forces the values of the means of production up to those of the products. These principles are valid immediately in a non-exchange economy, and they are realised through free competition in a capitalist system. In the latter the prices of the means of production must under free competition be such that they exhaust the price of the product.

于是，在非交换经济中利润的消失过程，与资本主义制度下利润的消失过程，是十分类似的。但是，资本主义制度下这个过程的另一部分，也就是由于竞争厂商的出现导致新产品价格的被迫下降，在非交换经济下必然是不存在的。当然，这里新产品也必须被纳入循环流转中，新产品的价值也必然与所有其他产品的价值有关系。理论上，我们仍然可以把创新的实现，与在循环流转中创新所体现的过程，有区别地看成是两种不同的事情。但是也很容易看出，实际上，这两者是否真的同时发生有着相当大的差别。在非交换经济中，能够证实一种剩余是归因于企业家活动，就足以解决我们所研究的问题。在资本主义制度下，这些剩余要到达企业家手中，只有借助于市场机制，而且只有通过这一机制，这些剩余才能再被剥夺掉。这样，除了单纯的价值问题，还有一个是利润如何在实际中落入企业家手中的问题。这个市场机制创造了许多在非交换经济中肯定不存在的现象。

尽管如此，在所有的组织形式中，不仅利润的最内在的经济本质是相同的，而且利润消失过程的最内在的性质也是相同的。在所有情况下，那些阻碍整个产品价值归属于劳动和土地服务的障碍，或者，根据具体情况，那些使劳动和土地价格与其产品价格不在相适应的水平上的障碍，终归是要被消除的。这个原则是：经济过程，如果不受阻碍的话，首先它不允许个人产品有价值剩余，其次，总是强制生产手段的价值上升到产品的价值水平，这一原则始终处于支配地位。这些原则在非交换经济中也直接有效，而在资本主义制度下，它们是通过自由竞争得以实现的。在后一种情况下，由于自由竞争，生产手段的价格必然要将产品的价格完

In so far as this is not possible the price of the product must correspondingly fall. If under these circumstances profit exists at all, it is only because the transition from one position in which there are no surpluses to another new position in which there are again none cannot happen without the help of the entrepreneur, and unless the further condition necessary in a capitalist system is also fulfilled, namely that the profit cannot be immediately wrested from him by competition.

Profit clings to the means of production in no other sense than does the effort of a poet to his partly finished manuscript. No part of the profit is imputed to them, nor is the possession and the furnishing of them the content of the entrepreneurial function. And above all, as we saw, profit is not to be sought in the permanent increase in value which the original means of production experience in consequence of the new employment. Let us consider the case of a slave economy in which land and workers belong to the entrepreneur who has bought them for the purpose of carrying out new combinations. One could say in this case, if anywhere, that a price will be paid for land and workers corresponding to their hitherto prevailing employments, and that profit is the amount by which land and workers now permanently produce more. But this would be wrong for two reasons. First, the receipts for the new products will reach a height from which competition must pull them down again, so that this conception would not allow for an element of profit. Secondly, the lasting surplus amount-in so far as it is not quasi-rent-is economically simply an increase of the wages of labor, which, it is true, accrues to the "owner of labor" here, not to the worker, and of rent of land. Slaves and land certainly have a higher value now for their proprietor, but he has become permanently richer as their proprietor and not as an entrepreneur, if one neglects occasional or temporary profit. Even if a natural agent of production first comes into existence in the new combination, for example a brook as water-power, the matter is in no way different. It is not the water-power that yields the profit. What it permanently yields is rent in our sense.

全耗尽。如果不是这样，那么产品的价格必然会相应地下降。如果在这些情况下，利润竟然还存在，这仅仅是因为，从一个没有剩余的状态过渡到另一个也没有剩余的状态，一定要借助于企业家，此外还要满足资本主义制度下的一个必要条件，即，企业家的利润不会因为有竞争就立刻被夺走。

利润依附于生产手段，就像一位诗人对他已完成部分的诗稿的尽力。此时没有哪一部分利润可以归属于生产手段，而且拥有和使用生产手段也不是企业家职能的内容。正如我们所看到的，最重要的是，利润也不是因为对原先的生产手段采用新的用途以后，所带来的价值的持续增长。让我们考虑在奴隶经济的情况，在那里，土地和劳动者属于企业家，企业家为了实施新的组合而购买土地和奴隶。人们可能会说，在这种情况下，支付给土地和劳动力的价格，将与迄今通行的雇佣情况相适应，如果存在这种雇佣的话；利润是土地和劳动力从现在直到永久生产的产品价值的超出值。但这是不正确的，有两个原因。首先，新产品收入将达到一个高度，但竞争必然又将它拉下来，因此，这种构想并不能估计利润要素。第二，持续的剩余量——只要它不是准地租——在经济意义上，只是劳动工资的增长（当然，在这里，它属于“劳动力的所有者”，而不属于工人）以及地租的增长。此时，奴隶和土地对于它们的所有者来说，当然有了一个更高的价值，但是如果忽略掉偶然的或者暂时的利润，这个所有者也只是作为奴隶和土地的所有者而成为永久的富人，而不是作为一个企业家变得更富有。即使一种自然生产要素第一次出现在新组合中，例如一条小川成为水力资源，问题也没有任何不同，并不是水力产生了利润，水力不断产生的是我们所说的租金。

Hence a part of what is in the first instance profit changes into rent. Thereby the economic nature of the quantity in question is changed. Let us assume that a planter who has previously cultivated sugar cane changes over to cotton-growing, which until recently was more lucrative than it is now. [1] This is a new combination; the man thereby becomes an entrepreneur and makes a profit. For the time being rent of land appears in the list of costs only at the amount appropriate to sugar cane cultivation. As has actually happened, we shall assume that competition sooner or later forces down the receipts. If a surplus still remains, however, how is that to be explained and what is it economically? Neglecting friction, it can only result because the land either is differentially suited to cotton-growing or the rent of land has risen in general as a result of the new employments-in principle it is always a consequence of both elements. This at once characterises that part of the increase in total return which is permanent as rent of land. The entrepreneurial function of this man disappears if he continues to grow cotton, and the whole return is henceforth imputed to the original factors of production.

A word about the relation of profit to monopoly revenue. Since the entrepreneur has no competitors when the new products first appear, the determination of their price proceeds wholly, or within certain limits, according to the principles of monopoly price. Thus there is a monopoly element in profit in a capitalist economy. Let us now assume that the new combination consists in establishing a permanent monopoly, perhaps in forming a trust which need fear absolutely no competing outsiders. Then profit is obviously to be considered simply as permanent monopoly revenue and monopoly revenue simply as profit. And yet two quite different economic phenomena exist. The carrying out of the monopolistic organisation is an entrepreneurial act and its "product" is expressed in profit. Once it is running smoothly the concern in this case goes on earning a surplus, which henceforth, however, must be imputed to those natural or social forces upon which the monopoly position rests-it

---

① Written in 1911.

因此，在第一个例子中一部分利润转变成地租，从而我们的问题中这个数量的经济性质就变化了。让我们假定一位种植园主开始种的是甘蔗，后来改种棉花，直到前不久种棉花还是比现在要更赚钱的。[①] 这是一种新组合；从而这位种植园主成为一名企业家并赚得了利润。现在，在成本清单上显示的地租还是与种甘蔗时的地租相符合。如果按照实际所发生的，我们应该假定竞争迟早会迫使收入下降。然而，如果仍然存在剩余，那么应该如何解释呢？这在经济学上又是什么意思呢？忽略摩擦因素，产生这个结果，要么是因为土地特别适于种棉花，要么是因为由于土地的新的用途而使地租普遍上涨——理论上，这通常是两个要素共同作用的结果。这一点立刻表现出总收益中增长部分的特点，即它总是地租。如果这个种植园主继续种棉花，那么他的企业家职能就消失了，从此全部收益就都归于原来的生产要素。

再谈一谈利润与垄断收益的关系。因为当新产品刚刚出现时，企业家还没有竞争对手，新产品价格的决定完全或者在一定范围内，根据垄断价格的原则。这样，在资本主义经济内，利润就包含有一种垄断因素。现在让我们假定，新的组合想要建立一种永久性的垄断，或者想形成一种完全不用担心外界竞争的托拉斯。这样，利润显然只被看做是永久的垄断收入，而垄断收入也就是利润了。然而，这里还存在两种截然不同的经济现象。实现垄断性组织是一种企业家行为，它的“成果”表现在利润中。这个组织一旦顺利地运行，企业就能持续地获得剩余，然而以后，这些剩余必然将归属于垄断地位所依靠的自然力和社会力——它已

① 这里的“现在”指当时写书时，是1911年。

has become a monopoly revenue. Profit from founding a business and permanent return are distinguished in practice; the former is the value of the monopoly, the latter is just the return from the monopoly condition.

These discussions cannot be continued further within the scope of this work. Perhaps they are too long already. But if I must reproach myself with having wearied the reader too much with these things, I still cannot spare myself the reproach that not all points are exhaustively explained and not all possible misunderstandings excluded. The fundamental aspects of the matter ought to be elucidated. A few more observations before we leave the subject.

Entrepreneurial profit is not a rent like the return to differential advantages in the permanent elements of a business; nor is it a return to capital, however one may define capital. So that there is no reason for speaking about a tendency towards equalisation of profits which does not exist at all in reality: for only the jumbling together of interest and profit explains why many authors contend for such a tendency,[①] although we can observe such extraordinarily different profits in one and the same place, at the same time and in the same industry. We want finally to emphasise that profit is also not wages, although the analogy is tempting. It is certainly not a simple residuum; it is the expression of the value of what the entrepreneur contributes to production in exactly the same sense that wages are the value expression of what the worker "produces." It is not a profit of exploitation any more than are wages. However, while wages are determined according to the marginal productivity of labor, profit is a striking exception to this law: the problem of profit lies precisely in the fact that the laws of cost and of marginal productivity seem to exclude it. And what the "marginal entrepreneur" receives is wholly a matter of indifference for the success of the others. Every rise in wages is diffused over all wages; one who has success as an entrepreneur has it alone at first.

---

① Others, as Lexis for example, dispute also the uniformity of the rate of interest. The problem, which made so many difficulties for Marx, disappears if our conclusion is accepted.

经是一种垄断收入。创建一个企业所得的利润与持续性的收入，在实际中是相区别的，前者是垄断价值，后者只是来自于垄断条件的收入。

鉴于本书的范围，这些讨论不能再继续展开，或者说已经谈的很多了。但是，即使我必须谴责自己用过多的言语使得读者疲倦，我仍然不能不责备自己没有把所有的论点都详尽地解释清楚，也没有排除所有可能的误解。这个问题的根本方面必须被阐明。在我们结束这个问题之前，还有几点意见。

企业家利润不像是对一个企业永久性要素的差别优势的回报那种租金；它也不是资本的回报，不管人们怎么定义资本。所以，没有理由去谈论利润的平均化趋势，这在现实中根本不存在。因为就是把利息和利润混在一起才使得许多作家对这个趋势问题展开争论，[①] 尽管我们能在同一地点，同一时间，同一行业中观察到如此异常不同的利润。最后我们想强调，利润也不是工资，尽管这样的类推是很吸引人的。它当然不是一种简单的余额，它是企业家对生产所做贡献的价值表现，正像工资是工人“生产”的价值表现。利润与工资一样，不是剥削。然而，尽管工资是按照劳动的边际生产力决定的，利润此时还是这条准则的显著的例外，利润问题恰好在于这样一个事实，即，成本规律和边际生产力规律似乎不包括利润。“边际企业家”所得到的，对于其他企业家的成功来说，完全是不相关的事。工资的每一次增长都扩展到所有工资上，作为一名已经成功的企业家，起初只有他得到了这个

① 其他人，比如累克西斯，也对利率的一致性提出异议。这个曾经使马克思也很为难的问题，如果接受我们的论述，就不存在了。

Wages are an element in price, profit is not in the same sense. The payment of wages is one of the brakes to production, profit is not. One might say of the latter, but with more right, what the classical economists asserted of rent of laud, namely that it does not enter into the price of the products. Wages are a permanent branch of income, profit is no branch of income at all if one counts the regular recurrence of a return as one of the characteristic features of income. It slips from the entrepreneur's grasp as soon as the entrepreneurial function is performed. It attaches to the creation of new things, to the realisation of the future value system. It is at the same time the child and the victim of development. ①

Without development there is no profit, without profit no development. For the capitalist system it must be added further that without profit there would be no accumulation of wealth. At least there would not be the great social phenomenon which we have in view-*this* is certainly a consequence of development and indeed of profit. If we neglect the capitalisation of rents and saving in the narrow sense of the word-to which we ascribe no very big rôle-and finally the gifts which development in its repercussions and chance throw in the lap of many individuals, which it is true are in themselves temporary but which may lead to the accumulation of wealth if they are not consumed, then by far the most important source of the accumulation of wealth still remains, from which most fortunes spring. The non-consumption of profit is not saving in the proper sense, for it is not an encroachment upon the customary standard of life. And so we may say that it is the entrepreneur's action that creates most fortunes. It seems to me that reality convincingly substantiates this derivation of the accumulation of wealth from profit.

Although I left the reader free in this chapter to put interest on capital beside wages and rent as a productive outlay, I have

① How very closely this corresponds to reality and how dearly it represents an unprejudiced view is seen in Adam Smith's observation-which any practical man might have made and actually does make in ordinary life-that new branches of production are more profitable than old.

收益。工资是价格的一个要素，利润却不是。支付工资是生产的制动因素之一，而利润不是。古典经济学家认为地租不能被纳入产品价格，对于利润，我们更应这样看。如果我们把某种收益的规律性的重复出现看做是收入的典型特征之一，那么，工资就是收入的一项永久性分支，利润却根本不是收入的一个分支。一旦企业家的职能已经完成，利润就从企业家的手中溜走了。利润依附于新事物的创造，依附于未来价值体系的实现。它既是发展的产物，也是发展的牺牲品。①

没有发展就没有利润，没有利润也没有发展。对于资本主义来说，还必须增加一句：没有利润就没有财富的积累。至少不会有我们所看到的这样伟大的社会现象——这当然是发展的结果，确切地说是利润的结果。如果我们忽略地租和狭义上的储蓄的资本化——我们认为这些没有很大的作用——最后，如果我们把发展在其影响和机遇中投入到许多个别人手中的意外财富（这些意外财物本身确实是暂时的，但是如果它们不被消费掉，也可能导致财富的积累）也忽略掉，那么，财富积累的最重要的来源将依然保存，由此又产生众多财富。未消费的利润在恰当的意义上并不是储蓄，因为它没有侵犯习惯了的生活标准。所以我们可以说，是企业家的行为创造了大部分财富。在我看来，实际生活让人信服地证实了是利润产生了财富的积累。

虽然在这一章我让读者自由地将资本的利息，与工资和地租

① 这种表述是如何符合现实，又是怎样清楚地表达一种无偏见的观点的，可以看亚当·斯密的观察——任何实事求是的人都会有这样的观察，事实上在日常生活中也作了这样的观察——亚当·斯密认为，新的生产部门比老的部门更能获利。

yet conducted the investigation as if the whole surplus over wages and rent passed to the entrepreneur. Actually he must still pay interest on capital. That I may not be reproached with designating a sum first as profit and then as interest, let it be expressly remarked that this point will be fully elucidated later.

The size of profit is not as definitely determined as the magnitude of incomes in the circular flow. In particular it cannot be said of it, as of the elements of cost in the latter, that it just suffices to call forth precisely the "quantity of entrepreneurial services required." Such a quantity, theoretically determinable, does not exist. And the total amount of profit actually obtained in a given time, as well as the profit realised by an individual entrepreneur, may be much greater than that necessary to call forth the entrepreneurial services which were actually operative. It is true that this total amount is frequently overestimated. ①It is true that it must be borne in mind that even obviously disproportionate individual success has its function, because the possibility of attaining it works as a stronger incentive than is rationally justified by its magnitude multiplied by the coefficient of probability. Such prospects also belong, as it were, to the "remuneration" of those entrepreneurs for whom they are not realised. Nevertheless it is quite clear that in very many cases smaller amounts and especially smaller total amounts would have the same result, as it is also clear that the connection between quality of service and private success is here much weaker than for example in the market for professional labor. This is not only important for the theory of taxation-even though the importance of this element in practice is limited by the need of taking account of "capital accumulation" in the sense of increasing the supply of produced means of production-but it also explains why the entrepreneur can be relatively so easily deprived of his profit and why the "salaried" entrepreneur, for example the industrial manager who frequently plays the entrepreneurial rôle,

① Cf. on this Stamp, Wealth and Taxable Capacity, p. 103 f.

放在一起视为生产性开支，但我在探索这个问题时，却把扣除工资和地租的整个剩余似乎都归于企业家了。事实上企业家仍然必须支付资本利息。可能不会因为我起初把一笔钱指为利润，然后又将其指为利息，就要责备我，但让我特别申明一下，在后面我将充分地阐述这一点。

利润的大小，不像循环流转中收入的度量那样可以明确地确定。特别地，不能说像循环流转中成本各要素那样，利润的度量恰好可以确切地引发“必需的企业家活动量”。这一数量，在理论上是可以确定的，但它不存在。在一定时期内实际获得的利润总量，以及个别企业家实现的利润，可能远大于必然引发的实际起作用的企业家活动量。的确，这个总量常常被高估。[①] 诚然，必须记住，甚至是明显的不相称的个人成就也有它的作用，因为获得这种成就的可能性发挥着一种更强大的激励作用，它比按理应用利润量乘以概率系数的积所表示的那个激励作用还大。对于那些没有实现这种成就的企业家而言，这种前景似乎也属于一种有吸引力的“报酬”。尽管如此，有几点是很清楚的，即，在许多场合，较小的利润量，尤其是较小的利润总量，将产生相同的结果。同样，企业家活动质量与个人成就之间的联系，在这里，比起例如在专业性劳动市场的情况要微弱得多。这一点不仅对于税收理论是重要的——即使这一因素的重要性在实际中仅限于考虑“资本积累”，从增长被生产出来的生产资料的供给这个意义来说——而且它也说明了为什么企业家能那么相对容易地被剥夺其利润，以及为什么“领薪水的”企业家，例如经常起企业家作用

① 参阅《印花税、财富及纳税能力》，第103页。

can generally be adequately remunerated with much less than the full amount of the profit. The more life becomes rationalised, levelled, democratised, and the more transient become the relations of the individual to concrete people (especially in the family circle) and to concrete things (to a concrete factory or to an ancestral home), the more many of the motives enumerated in the second chapter lose their importance and the more the entrepreneur's grip on profit loses its power.①To this process the progressive "automatisation" of development runs parallel, and it also tends to weaken the significance of the entrepreneurial function.

To-day, as well as in the epoch in which the beginnings of this social process were not yet known, the entrepreneurial function is not only the vehicle of continual reorganisation of the economic system but also the vehicle of continual changes in the elements which comprise the upper strata of society. The successful entrepreneur rises socially, and with him his family, who acquire from the fruits of his success a position not immediately dependent upon personal conduct. This represents the most important factor of rise in the social scale in the capitalist world. Because it proceeds by competitively destroying old businesses and hence the existences dependent upon them, there always corresponds to it a process of decline, of loss of caste, of elimination. This fate also threatens the entrepreneur whose powers are declining, or his heirs who have inherited his wealth without his ability. This is not only because all individual profits dry up, the competitive mechanism tolerating no permanent surplus values, but rather annihilating them by means of just this stimulus of the striving for profit which is the mechanism's driving force; but also because in the normal case things so happen that entrepreneurial success embodies itself in the ownership of a business; and this business is usually carried on further by the heirs on what soon become traditional lines until new entrepreneurs supplant it.

---

① Cf. on this my article, "Sozialistische Möglichkeiten von heute" in the Archiv für Sozialwissenschaft (1921).

的工厂经理，通常能够满足于远低于利润总量的报酬。生活越是合理化，平均化，民主化，个人与某些具体的人（尤其是在家庭范围），以及与具体的事物（比如一个具体的工厂或者一幢祖传的宅院）之间的关系就越是短暂，我们在第二章列举的许多动机就会越加丧失其重要性，而企业家也越来越丢失其对利润把握的权利。[①] 这一过程与发展的日益“自动化”是并行进行的，而它也有削弱企业家职能重要性的趋势。

今天，就像过去对这个社会过程的开端还不了解的时代一样，企业家的职能不仅是经济系统不断重组的工具，而且也是推动包括社会上层阶级在内的各要素不断变化的工具。成功的企业家，连同他的家人，其社会地位上升，他从他的成功的果实中获得不直接依赖于个人行为的某种地位。这是资本主义世界人们社会阶层上升的最重要的因素。因为它的进程是靠竞争性地摧毁旧企业，从而一切都在旧企业的基础上存在，所以，总是相应地有一个衰落、丧失社会地位、消亡的过程。这种命运也威胁着那些权利正在衰落的企业家，或者威胁着那些已经继承企业家的财富却不具备他的能力的后代。这不仅是因为竞争机制不容许有持续的剩余价值，从而所有的个人利润都会枯竭，甚至正是通过这个追求利润的激情（这种激情是竞争机制的推动力）消灭它；而且还因为，在正常情况下，事情总是按照将企业家的成功体现在他对企业的所有权上来发生；这个企业通常由他的继承人继续管理，很快也就成为因袭行业，直到被新的企业家代替。美国有一

① 参阅我的文章《今后社会主义的可能性》，载《社会科学文献》，1921 年。

An American adage expresses it: three generations from overalls to overalls. And so it may be.[①] Exceptions are rare, and are more than compensated for by cases in which the descent is still faster. Because there are always entrepreneurs and relatives and heirs of entrepreneurs, public opinion and also the phraseology of the social struggle readily overlook these facts. They constitute "the rich" a class of inheritors who are removed from life's battle. In fact, the upper strata of society are like hotels which are indeed always full of people, but people who are forever changing. They consist of persons who are recruited from below to a much greater extent than many of us are willing to admit. Whereupon a further host of problems is opened up, the solution of which alone will show us the true nature of the capitalist competitive system and of the structure of its society.

---

① We have only a few investigations into this fundamental phenomenon. Cf., however, for example, Chapman and Marquis: "The Recruiting of the Employing Classes from the Ranks of the Wage Earners," Journal of the Royal Statistical Society (1912).

句谚语：三代之内，兴而复衰，的确如此。[1] 例外的情况是很少的，而衰落得更快的情况多得足以抵补那些例外的情况还有余。因为总是有企业家、企业家的亲戚、企业家的继承者，而公众舆论以及关于社会斗争的措辞很容易忽视这些事实。这样，那些逃离社会斗争的继承者们构成了一个“富人”阶级。事实上，社会上层就像是旅馆，里面的确住满了人，但是里面的这些人永远在变化着。他们当中包括来自下层的人，这些人的数量很多，多到我们中的许多人都不愿接受的程度。于是我们又面临一个更进一步的问题，只有解决这个问题，我们才能看到资本主义竞争制度及其社会结构的真实性质。

① 我们只对这个基本现象做过很少的调查。但可以参阅，比如查普曼及马奎斯写的《从工资收入等级来招募新成员的情况》，载《皇家统计学会杂志》，1912 年。

CHAPTER V

Interest On Capital

Preliminary Remarks

After mature consideration I submit for the second time the theory of interest which I originally published in the first edition of this book, unaltered apart from quite unimportant verbal changes. To all objections which have come to my attention my only answer is to refer to the original text. They have merely induced me not to shorten it further. Otherwise I should have been glad to have done so. But since the things which seem to me most prolix and labored, and which impair the simplicity and cogency of the argument, anticipated correctly the most important objections, they have acquired a fight to existence which they perhaps did not have originally.

In particular the previous exposition made it so clear that I do not deny that interest is a normal element of the modem economy -which would indeed be absurd-but on the contrary try to explain it, that I can hardly understand the assertion that I denied it. Interest is a premium on present over future purchasing power. This premium has several causes. Many of them constitute no problem. Interest on consumptive loans is a case in point. That anyone in unexpected distress (for example, if fire destroys a business) or in expectation of a future increase in income (for example, if a student is heir to a well disposed aunt of tender health) values a hundred present more highly than a hundred future marks requires no explanation, and it is self-evident that interest may exist in such cases. All categories of government credit requirements

第五章　资本的利息

慎重考虑之后，我第二次提出最先曾在本书第一版中已发表的利息理论，除了对一些词句作了不重要的改动外，没有改动内容。对于所有引起我注意的异议，我唯一的答复就是请参阅第一版原文。这些异议竟促使我不要对原文作进一步缩短，而我原本乐意缩短原文的。因为在我看来，本来这是原文中最冗长、最难解，从而有损于论点的简明和说服力的部分，但是它们正确地预见到了这些最重要的异议，所以它们就有被保留的权利，起初它们可能并没有这种权利。

尤其是原先的解说清楚地表明了：我并不否认利息是现代经济的正常的要素——否认它的确是荒谬的——相反地，我试图解释它，我几乎不能理解那种说我曾否认过利息的观点。利息是现在购买力对未来购买力的一种溢价。这个溢价有几方面原因，其中许多原因是没有疑问的。消费性贷款的利息就是这样的一个例子。任何一个处在意外困境中（比如，火灾毁坏了一家企业）的人，或者处在预期未来收入会增加（比如，假设一个学生是其体弱而富有的姑妈的继承人）状况中的人，对当前一百马克的估价会高于对未来一百马克的估价，这不需要解释，在这种场合可能存在利息，这是不言自明的。各种政府信贷要求都属于这

belong here. There have always been such cases of interest, and obviously they could also exist in the circular flow in which there is no development. But they do not constitute the great social phenomenon that needs explaining. This consists of interest on productive loans (produktivzins). It is to be found *everywhere* in the capitalist system and not only where it originates, that is in new enterprises. I merely want to show that productive interest has its source in profits, that it is by nature an offshoot of the latter, and that it, like that which I call the "interest aspect" of returns, spreads from the profits incident to the successful carrying out of new combinations over the whole economic system and even forces its way into the sphere of old businesses, in whose life it would not be a necessary element if there were no development. This is all I mean by the statement: "the static' economy knows no productive interest"-which is certainly fundamental to our insight into the structure and workings of capitalism. And is it not almost self-evident in the last analysis? No one can deny that just as the business situation decides the movement of the rate of interest-and business situation means normally, that is to say, neglecting the effects of non-economic forces, simply the existing tempo of development-so the money required for innovations constitutes the chief factor in the industrial demand on the money market. Is it such a great step from this to the recognition that the chief real factor is also the fundamental theoretical factors, by which alone the other source of demand is brought into play, while the latter-that is the demand of the old businesses in the tested, continually repeated round-would normally not have to come into the money market at all, because old businesses are adequately financed by the current return from production. From this the rest follows-especially the theorem that interest attaches to money and not to goods.

I am concerned with the truth and not with the originality of my theory. In particular I willingly base it upon that of BöhmBawerk as much as possible-however decidedly the latter has declined all communion. From his point of view too it must be a question of purchasing power in the first place, even though he immediately passes to the premium on present *goods*.

种情况。常常有这种情况的利息，即使在没有发展的循环流转中，这种利息显然也存在。但是它们并不构成需要解释的重大社会现象，这是由生产性贷款的利息构成的。在资本主义制度下，到处可以发现这种利息，而它们不仅存在于新企业中。我只想表明生产性利息的源泉在利润，它本质上是利润的派生物，而且，就像我称为收益的“利息方面”的东西那样，生产性利息会从由于成功地实施了新组合而带来的利润，发展到整个经济系统，甚至跻身于旧企业的领域，在那里如果生活中没有发展，利息就不是一个必要的要素。这就是我所说的“‘静态’经济不知道有生产性利息”的全部含义——这当然是我们洞察资本主义结构与运行的基础。以上这些分析，难道不是几乎不言而喻的吗？没有人能否认，就像商业形势决定利息率的变动一样——商业形势通常仅指当前发展的速度，也就是说忽略非经济力量的影响——因此，创新所需要的货币就构成了货币市场产业需求的主要因素。从这一点到认识主要的真实因素，也是根本的理论因素，难道不是进了一大步吗？只有通过创新这个根本因素，才能使对货币需求的其他来源起作用，而后者——即处在不断循环重复运行中，被考验的旧企业，其对货币的需求——通常根本不必进入货币市场，因为旧企业从当前生产的收入中可以获得足够的资金。从这一点可以推导出其他理论——尤其是利息是依附于货币，而不是依附于商品的这条定理。

我关心的是真理，而不是我的理论的原创性。我特别希望尽可能地以庞巴维克的理论为基础建立我的理论——不管庞巴维克是怎样坚决地拒绝所有的交流。根据他的观点，即使他即刻转到利息是对当前商品的溢价，也必须首先承认它是一个购买力的

Actually, of the famous three reasons upon which he bases the value premium on present purchasing power, I reject only one: the "discounting" of future enjoyments, so far as Böhm-Bawerk asks us to accept it as a cause not itself requiring any explanation. On the other hand I could claim that reason which he calls the changing relation between wants and means of satisfaction, as a formula into which to fit my theory. And what of the third, the "roundabout methods of production"? If Böhm-Bawerk had kept strictly to his expression "*adoption* of roundabout methods of production" and if he had followed the indication which it contains, this would be an entrepreneurial act-one of the many subordinate cases of my concept of carrying out new combinations. He did not do this; and I believe it can be shown with the help of his own analysis that no net income would flow from the mere repetition of round- about methods of production which have already been carried out and incorporated in the circular flow. A point soon comes at which our explanation enters upon a fundamentally different course. However, our analysis fulfils the requirements of BöhmBawerk's theory of value throughout, and at no point is it exposed to any of Böhm-Bawerk's objections so far advanced. ①

1. Interest on capital, so experience teaches us, is a permanent net income that flows to a definite category of individuals. From where, and why? First there is the question of the source of this stream of goods: in order that it may flow, a value, out of which

① This must be emphasised so much because outside of a narrow circle of special- ists even the critical part of Böhm-Bawerk's contribution has not yet been fully absorbed. But I presuppose a knowledge of it. The following relates to it at all points, and whoever still maintains the self-evidence of interest and does not see the decisive problem must find the following unnecessarily tortuous, much of it incomprehensible, even false. In Böhm-Bawerk's work, however, the reader can find everything necessary and references to almost all the literature. General knowledge of it is necessary. Finally, I do not wish to repeat what I have already said: cf. Wesen, bk. III.

问题。实际上，在他据以为利息是当前购买力的价值溢价的三条著名的理由中，我只反对一条，即利息是未来享受的“贴现”。庞巴维克要求我们完全接受这一条，认为这本身不需要任何解释。另一方面，我可以要求他称之为欲望和满足手段之间的变动关系的一个原因，作为适应我的理论的一个公式。第三条理由，即“迂回的生产方法”，是什么含义呢？如果庞巴维克严格地坚持他说的“采用迂回的生产方法”，并遵循它所包含的意义，那么这就会成为一种企业家的行为——也就是从属于我所说的实施新组合的众多情景中的一个。他没有这样做；但我相信，借助于他自己的分析就可以表明，仅靠简单重复已经实施并已结合在循环流转中的迂回生产方法，决不会产生净收入。很快就到达了这一点，从这一点我们的解释就进入一条根本不同的路径。然而，我们的分析自始至终都满足了庞巴维克的价值理论的要求，而且没有一处招致迄今为止庞巴维克所提出的任何反对意见。①

1. 正像经验告诉我们的，资本的利息是一种流向某一确定类型的个人的永久性的净收入。它从哪里来？为什么是这样呢？首先，有一个这种商品流的来源问题：为了有这个商品流，首先必

① 这一点必须这样强调，因为除了一个狭小的专家圈子之外，甚至对庞巴维克的贡献的关键部分还没有完全吸收。但是我先假定大家已对他的理论有所了解了。下面的论述在各方面都与他的理论有关系，而且任何人，如果他仍然认为利息的存在是自然的，而看不到关键性的问题，那他必然会发现下面的分析不必要，太拐弯抹角，很多地方很难理解，甚至是错误的。然而，在庞巴维克的著作中，读者可以发现每一件东西都是必要的，而且提到了几乎所有的参考文献。有必要对庞巴维克的著作有一个一般性的了解。最后，我不愿再重复我已说过的话：参阅《本质》一书，第三章。

it may come, must first of all exist. [1] Secondly there is the question of the reason why this value becomes the spoils of these particular individuals: the question of the cause of this current in the world of goods. Finally there is by far the most difficult question, which may be described as the central problem of interest on capital: how does it happen that this stream of goods flows permanently, that interest is a net income which one may consume without impairing one's economic position?

The existence of interest constitutes a problem because we know that in the normal circular flow the whole value product must be imputed to the original productive factors, that is to the services of labor and land; hence the whole receipts from production must be divided between workers and landowners and there can be no permanent net income other than wages and rent. Competition on the one hand and imputation on the other must annihilate any surplus of receipts over outlays, any excess of the value of the product over the value of the services of labor and land embodied in it. The value of the original means of production must attach itself with the faithfulness of a shadow to the value of the product, and could not allow the slightest permanent gap between the two to exist. [2] But interest is a fact. What now?

This dilemma is difficult, much worse than the analogous one which was relatively easily overcome in the case of profits because there it was only a question of temporary, not of permanent, streams of goods, and consequently we did not come so sharply into conflict with the fundamental and undoubted facts of competition and imputation; on the contrary we could safely draw the conclusion that the services of labor and land are the only sources of income

---

① Cf. Böhm-Bawerk, for example on Say, I, 142, Böhm-Bawerk's method of expression is, however, already influenced there by the fact that he has a definite theory of interest in mind.

② Cf. Böhm-Bawerk, I, 230.

须存在一个能产生商品流的价值。[①] 其次，有一个为什么这个价值成为这些特定个人的战利品的原因的问题，也就是在商品世界中这个价值流的原因问题。最后，存在一个更困难的问题，这可能被看做是资本利息的核心问题，即这种商品流永久地流动下去，这是怎么发生的？利息是如何成为一个可以被消费而同时不损害人们的经济地位的净收入的呢？

利息的存在之所以成为一个问题，是因为我们知道在正常的循环流转中，全部的价值产品必须归属于原始的生产要素，也就是归于劳动和土地服务；因而从生产获得的全部收入必须在工人和土地拥有者之间进行分配，所以除了工资和地租之外，不可能有任何永久性的净收入。一方面有竞争，另一方面有归属，这必然会消灭任何收入超过支出的剩余部分，消灭任何产品价值超过体现在产品中的劳动和土地服务的价值的剩余。原始生产资料的价值必然紧密地与产品价值结合在一起，而且不允许这两者之间存在哪怕一点永久性的差距，[②] 但是存在利息却是事实。现在的问题是什么呢？

这种两难的境地是很困难的，比在利润中相对容易征服的类似问题要更难解决，因为在利润问题中，利润只是一个暂时的，非永久性的，涉及商品流的问题，因而我们不会遇到利润与竞争和归属这种根本的，毫无疑问的事实之间这种尖锐的冲突；相反，我们可以有把握地说：劳动和土地服务是收入的唯一来源，而由于

① 参阅庞巴维克，第一章，关于萨伊的例子，第 142 页。然而，庞巴维克的表述方法在那里已经受到他自己心中明确的利息理论的影响。

② 参阅庞巴维克，第一篇，第 230 页。

whose net return is not reduced to zero by those facts. In the face of this dilemma we may proceed in two different ways.

First, it may be accepted. It then appears that interest must be explained as a kind of wages or rent, and since the latter is not feasible, then as wages: as the spoliation of wage-earners (the theory of exploitation), as the wages of the labor of capitalists (labor theory in the literal meaning), or as the wages of the labor embodied in the instruments of production and raw materials (the conception for example of James Mill and McCulloch). All three efforts at explanation have been made. To Böhm-Bawerk's critique I have only to add that our analysis of the entrepreneur, especially his isolation from the means of production, also cuts part of the ground from under the feet of the first two variants.

Secondly, the theoretical conclusion which leads to the dilemma may be denied. Here again we may either extend the list of costs, that is assert that with wages and rent all necessary means of production are not yet paid, or search in the mechanism of imputation and competition for a hidden brake which permanently prevents the values of the services of labor and land from reaching the height of the value of the product, so that a permanent value surplus is left over.[①] I turn to the cursory discussion of these two possibilities.

Extending the list of costs means in this sense not merely asserting that interest represents a regular expenditure in the accounts of a business. This would be self-evident and would have no explanatory force. It means much more, namely conceiving interest as an element of cost in the narrower and special sense which was formulated in the first chapter. This is equivalent to constituting a third original productive factor, which bears interest as labor receives wages. If this were satisfactorily achieved, our three questions,

① Cf. the concluding considerations of Böhm-Bawerk, I, 606 f.

上述事实，劳动和土地服务的净收入是绝不会减少到零的。面对这种两难的困境，我们可以采用两种不同的方法。

第一，承认利息的存在。于是，利息必然被解释为一种工资或者租金，而由于把利息说成是租金不大可行，所以，我们就把它解释为工资：作为对工资收入者的掠夺（剥削理论），作为支付给资本家劳动的工资（这是字面意义上的劳动理论），或者作为支付给体现在生产工具和原材料中的劳动的工资（例如詹姆斯·穆勒和麦卡洛克所说的概念）。这三种解释方法都曾被人尝试过。对于庞巴维克的批评，我只要补充一句，即我们对企业家的分析，尤其是把企业家与生产资料相分离，使得前两个演变来的观点失去了部分立足的依据。

第二，可以否认产生这种尴尬境况的理论上的结论。在这里，我们也可以要么扩大成本项目，也就是坚持认为只有工资和地租还不能支付全部必要的生产资料，要么在归属和竞争机制中寻找一个制动力，它可以永久地阻止劳动和土地服务的价值到达产品价值的高度，这样就有了永久性的价值剩余。① 下面我对这两种可能性进行粗略地讨论。

在这个意义上，扩展成本项目不仅意味着坚持利息代表一个企业在会计账项中的正规的支出。这是很明白的道理，不需要说服力。它还意味着更多的含义，即把利息构想成一种成本要素，这个成本要素是第一章中所阐述的狭义的、有特殊意义的成本要素。这就相当于构成一个第三类原始生产要素，它能产生利息就像劳动获得工资一样。如果这一点能够满意地实现，那么我们的

① 参阅庞巴维克第一篇的结束语，第606页。

the question of the source, of the basis, and of the non-disappearance of interest, would obviously all be answered at once, and the dilemma would be escaped. Abstinence might be such a third factor. If it were an independent productive service all our requirements would be fulfilled in a manner free from objection, and the existence and source of a permanent net income as well as its assignment to definite individuals would be explained beyond doubt. Only it would still have to be proved that in reality interest does rest upon this element. But unfortunately this explanation is not satisfactory, because such an independent element does not exist, as has already been shown by BöhmBawerk, and need not be further discussed here.

Produced means of production might also be constituted a third productive factor independent of abstinence. With them it is the other way round. There can be no doubt about their productive effect. It is so dear, that the investigator's glance very soon fell upon it, and that today the fundamental proposition of the equality between the value of the product and of the services of labor and land still excites astonishment. It is so clear that even today it is still extremely difficult, as experience teaches, to divert even specialists from this wrong track. Yet it does not explain a permanent net income. To be sure, produced means of production have the capacity of serving in the production of goods. More goods may be produced with than without them. And these goods also have a higher value than those which could be produced without the produced means of production.[①] But this higher value must also lead to a higher value of these instruments of production, and this again to a higher value of the services of labor and land employed. No element of surplus value can remain permanently attached to these intermediate means of production. For, on the one hand, no discrepancy can exist permanently between the value of the products to be imputed to them and their own value.

① cf. Böhm-Bawerk, I, 132, on the concept of physical and value productivity of produced means of production.

三个问题：来源问题、基础问题以及利息的永久性问题，显然立即都被解答了，也避开了这个两难的境地。节俭可能就是这个第三种要素。如果它果真是一个独立的生产性服务，那么我们所有的要求都会毫无异议地实现，而且永久性的净收入的存在及来源，以及它归属于一定的个人，都会毫无疑问地得到解释。唯一尚需证明的是：在现实中，利息确实取决于节俭这个要素。然而不幸的是这个解答不能让人满意，因为这一独立的要素不存在，正像庞巴维克已经表明的那样，这里就没有必要进一步讨论了。

已经生产出来的生产资料也可能构成第三种生产要素，它独立于节俭。其实这是论证的另一种途径。不用怀疑，生产出来的生产资料有其生产性的影响。很清楚，调查者一眼就注视到产品价值与劳动和土地服务的价值相等这一根本命题，直到今天，这个命题仍然使人们感到惊奇。正像经验告诉我们的，这是如此清楚，以至于甚至在今天，即使是专家要远离这条错误的思路也极其困难，可是它没有解释永久性的净收入。诚然，被生产出来的生产手段有能力服务于商品的生产过程。用一定的生产手段比没有生产手段能生产出更多的商品；而且用生产出来的生产资料来生产商品，它的价值要比没有用这种生产资料所生产的商品的价值大。① 但是这种更高的价值必然也导致更高的生产工具的价值，而这又将导致所使用的劳动和土地服务的价值更高。没有一种剩余价值要素能永久地与这些中间生产资料保持联系。因为，一方面，在应当归属于生产手段的产品价值与生产手段本身的价

① 参阅庞巴维克，第一篇，关于被生产出来的生产资料的物质生产率和价值生产率的概念，第 132 页。

However many products a machine may help to produce, competition must always lower their price until equality is established. On the other hand, however much more than hand labor the machine may do, once introduced it does not continually save labor anew, so that it does not continually yield a new profit. The extra receipts due to it which are so conspicuous, the whole sum which the "user" is ready to pay for it, must be handed over to workers and landowners. In general it does not produce the value which it adds to the product, as is often naively[①] assumed, but the latter is only temporarily associated with it, as was argued in the previous chapter. A coat containing a bank-note has indeed, as long as this is the case, a correspondingly higher value for its owner, but it only received this higher value from outside and did not produce it. Similarly a machine has a value corresponding to its product, but has only Received[②] it from the services of labor and land which existed before it was created, to which the value has already been imputed as a whole. It is true that a stream of goods flows to the machine, but it also flows through it. At this point it is not dammed to form a reservoir for consumption. The possessor of the machine does not permanently get more than he must pay out, either by value or by price accounting. The machine itself is a product, and therefore just like a consumption good its value is conducted on to a reservoir, from which no interest can flow any more.

① Cf. Böhm-Bawerk's remarks, for example on Say and Roesler.

② To the machine, the value of its products is imputed; to the services of labor and land necessary to the production of the machine, the value of the latter is im puted. Consequently the services already have the value of the final product, and if they become a machine the latter simply takes their place. In this sense we say that the machine "receives" the value of the productive services. It is to be hoped that I am not misunderstood as deriving its value from its costs.

值之间不可能存在永久的偏差。无论一台机器能帮助生产多少产品，竞争必然总是压低产品价格直到出现彼此相等。另一方面，无论机器比手工生产能多生产多少产品，只要一旦采用机器，它就不能继续节约新的劳动力，从而，它就不能继续产生新的利润。由于采用机器而产生的额外的收入是如此引人注目，这也是“使用者”已经准备为购买机器所支付的全部金额，都必须交给工人和土地所有者。一般来说，机器不像人们常常天真地[①]想像的那样，能生产出价值增加到产品上去，不过，增加的价值只是暂时与机器联系在一起，就像前面一章所讨论的那样。只要在这种情况下，一件装有一张银行票据的上衣，对其所有者来说就确实有相应较高的价值，但是这件上衣只是从外界获得了这个较高的价值，并不是它自己创造的。同样，机器也有与其产品相对应的价值，但是它只是从劳动和土地服务中获得价值，[②] 而劳动和土地在机器被创造出来之前已经存在了，机器的全部价值已经归属于劳动和土地服务。的确，一系列商品流向机器，但它们通过机器也流走了，在这一点，机器并没有拦住商品流从而为消费形成一个储藏室。机器的拥有者不会永远是收入远大于支出，无论是从价值来说还是从价格的会计核算来说。机器本身也是产品，所以，就像一种消费品一样，它的价值被引入一个蓄水池，在那里任何利息

---

① 参阅庞巴维克对萨伊和鲁伊斯勒的评论。

② 对于机器来说，其产品的价值归属于它；对于生产机器所必须的劳动和土地服务来说，机器的价值又属于劳动和土地服务。因此，这些服务已经具有最终产品的价值，一旦这些服务转变成机器，机器就代替了它的价值。从这个意义上我们说，机器“接受”了生产性服务的价值。希望我没有让读者误解我支持价值来自成本的观点。

Hence on the basis of the arguments in the first and fourth chapters and of the reference to Böhm-Bawerk we can state that the above opens up no way out of the dilemma and that no source of value at all exists here for the payment of interest. At the most a difficulty occurs in the case of goods which are said to increase "automatically"-for example seed-corn or cattle used in breeding. Do not the latter ensure to their owner more corn or more cattle in the future, and must not the more corn and the more cattle be more valuable than the original seed-corn and cattle? Everyone to whom these ideas are familiar knows how firmly most people are convinced that they are proof of the existence of an increase in value. But seed-corn and breeding cattle do not increase "automatically"; on the contrary, well known items of expenditure must be deducted from their "return." However, it is decisive that even the residue left over after this deduction represents no gain in value-for the crop and the herds are certainly dependent upon seed-corn and breeding cattle, and the latter must therefore be valued according to the values of the former. If seed-corn and breeding cattle were sold, then (assuming no substitution is possible) the value of crop and herd, after deducting costs still to be incurred and making allowance for risk, would be fully expressed in their price. Their price would be equal to the price of the product imputed to them. And corn and animals would be employed in reproduction until their employment no longer yielded a profit and their price only just covered the necessary expenditure in wages and rent. The marginal utility of "their" product, that is of the share of the product imputed to them, would consequently tend towards zero.

2. Here I should like to observe that it is not correct, or rather not expedient-it means committing oneself to a definite view-to characterize the state of affairs represented in this stage of our argument as follows: "We cannot explain the gap between value of product and value of means of production in this way. But it actually exists. And we must try to explain it other wise." On the contrary I deny the fundamental existence of such a permanent gap. We are faced only with an

都不能再流动了。

因此，基于第一章和第四章的论述，以及参考庞巴维克的观点，我们可以说，以上的论述没有为解决两难的困境找到任何出路，并且在这里，根本不存在用于支付利息的价值源泉。至多只是说，在商品“自动”增长的情况下，困难才会发生——例如谷物的种子或者用于繁殖的牲畜。难道它们不能使它们的所有者确信未来将得到更多的谷物或者更多的牲畜，并且增加的谷物和牲畜必将比原来的谷种和牲畜价值更高吗？明白这些思想的人都知道大多数人是如何确信这就是存在价值增长的证据。但是，谷种和用来繁殖的牲畜不会“自动”增长；相反，必须从它们的“收益”中减去人们所熟悉的支出项目。然而，即使作了扣减以后，剩余的部分也没有表示价值的任何增加，这一点是肯定的——因为庄稼和牲畜一定依赖于谷种和繁殖的牲畜，所以，后者必然根据前者的价值来估价。如果卖掉谷种和用来繁殖的牲畜，那么（假设不存在替代）作物和牲畜的价值，在扣除了仍将发生的成本以及考虑风险因素之后，将以其价格充分表现出来。它们的价格将等于归属于它们的产品的价格。谷物和牲口将在再生产过程中被使用，直到对它们的使用不再产生利润，并且它们的价格恰好够支付工资和地租这些必要的费用。因此，“它们的”产品的边际效用，也就是应归属于它们的产品的份额将趋于零。

2. 在这里，如果把我们现阶段论述所反映的情况描述为：“我们不能用这种方式解释产品价值与生产资料价值之间的差额，但是，它确实存在。所以，我们必须试着用其他方式解释。”我认为这样看是不正确的，或者说是不明智的，因为它意味着自己有一定的成见。相反，我完全否认这种永久差异的存在。我们面对的

unanalyzed fact, and it should rather be suspected-as I believe a glance at reality teaches us-that it is a consequence of interest on capital, which is to be explained quite differently, than that it is a primary fact independently explaining interest. Individuals may value means of production less than products because they must pay interest on the way from the former to the latter, but they do not perforce pay interest because they value the former less than the latter on other grounds. This is very important. Here I only wish to draw attention to the fact that the difficulty against which the whole of my exposition must fight is especially great in the case of interest-the difficulty, namely, that outside of certain fundamentals we have become accustomed to simply accepting a series of unanalyzed facts, and instead of penetrating more deeply into the interior of things, to considering many things as elements which are complex combinations. Once this habit is acquired we proceed to further analysis only with reluctance; we are always inclined to point to such facts as to living objections. Abstinence is such a fact. The assertion that capital value is simply the capitalized value of the return is another. And because in making this assertion one always takes one ' s stand upon experience, the latter does not offer a sufficiently emphatic contradiction. For the time being, however, we must still retain this conception of the "gap."

A few remarks are now necessary to formulate precisely the process of computation (Einrechnun – gsvorgang). Hitherto we have always spoken of the process of imputation and have traced it back from its anchoring ground in the value of the product to the services of labor and land. It might now seem that the imputation could take still another step, that it might lead the value stream still further back, namely to the labor-power and to the land themselves. Since there is no reason in an exchange economy to become conscious of a value of labor – power as such, and since if there were the same would hold true of it as for land, we shall confine ourselves to the latter, and respecting labor-power merely emphasize again that it would only present a special problem if we regarded it (which we do not) as a product of the means

只是一个尚未分析的事实，我们宁可去怀疑它——因为我相信只要看一眼现实，我们就会明白——那是资本利息产生的结果，这应该用完全不同的方式解释，而不是被解释为：用来独立解释利息的一个基本事实。个人对生产资料的估价可能低于产品的价值，因为他们在生产资料转化为产品的过程中必须支付利息，但并不是因为他们以其他依据对生产资料的估价低于对产品的估价，就被迫支付利息，这一点很重要。在这里，我只想把注意力放在这个事实上，即我的全部解说所必须挑战的困难在利息这个问题上尤为严重——这个困难也就是，除了某些基本原理之外，我们已经习惯于简单地接受一系列尚未分析的事实，而不是更加深入地探析事物内部的本质；把许多复杂的综合体只看成是一些要素。一旦形成这种思维习惯，我们对事物作进一步分析也是很勉强的了；并且我们总是倾向于把这些事实当做生动的反对意见。节俭就是这样一个事实；认为资本价值只不过是资本化了的收入价值，也是一个事实。由于在表达这种主张时，人们总是以经验作为自己的立足点，而经验并不能提供充足有力的反驳理由。尽管如此，我们仍然必须保留“差额”这个概念。

现在为了精确地阐述计算过程，需要提出几点必要的评论。迄今为止，我们常常谈到归属的过程，从产品价值的落脚点追溯到劳动和土地服务。现在看来，归属问题还可以采用另一个步骤，它可能把价值流引导到更远的地方，即引导到劳动力和土地本身。由于在交换经济中人们不可能意识到劳动力这样的价值，如果人们能够意识到，那同样也应该能够意识到土地的价值，在这里，我们只谈土地的价值，关于劳动力，我们只需再强调一次，如果我们把劳动力看做（我们现在并不这样看）是劳动者及其家

of subsistence of the laborer and his family. Now, one might first of all conceive the services of land as the product of land and the latter itself as the true original means of production to which imputation must sweep the value of its product. This would be logically false. ①For land is not an independent commodity, separate from its own services, but merely a bundle of these services. Therefore it is better not to speak of imputation at all in this case. For imputation involves the transference of value to goods of continually higher orders. It so operates that nowhere is a piece of value left hanging, In determining the value of land, however, something else is involved, namely the derivation of its value from the given values of the elements of which it "consists" economically, which were determined by imputation. Here it is better to speak of computation (Einrechnung).

In the case of every good, whether a consumption or a production good, these two processes are to be distinguished. Only its services have definite values, determined②directly by the scale of wants or indirectly by imputation, from which its value must be derived. But while the latter process is extremely simple in the case of produced goods, and through the necessity of their reproduction, which arises sooner or later, is reduced to fixed and known rules, in the case of land it is complicated by the fact that an unlimited series of uses inhere in land,

---

① Cf. Böhm-Bawerk, Rechte und Verh ltnlsse vom Standpunkte der Volkswirtschaftlichen Güterlehre. Also his observations on the "use" theories of interest, which are likewise applicable to our case. At the same time I may observe that I exclude the fundamental idea of the use theory of interest from my consideration because I have nothing to add to Böhm-Bawerk's arguments.

② Strictly speaking this method of expression is suited only to the case of a non-exchange economy. In an exchange economy the value of means of production is nowhere felt as indirect use Value. Nevertheless, here also the conception of them as potential products gives the principle for the formation of their value. And a more correct method of expression only leads to the same result.

属维持生活资料的产品，那它只会表现一个特殊的问题。现在，人们可能首先把土地的服务设想为土地的产品，把土地本身看做是真正的原始生产资料，并且认为土地的产品的价值应全部归属于土地，这在逻辑上是荒谬的。[①] 因为土地不是一种独立的商品，它不能与自己的服务相分离，它仅仅是这些服务的总和。因此在这种情况下，最好不谈归属问题。因为归属问题包含价值不断地向更高层次的商品转移。这样下去，就不会有任何残余的价值悬在那里找不到来源。然而在决定土地价值时，还需要考虑其他因素，也就是从某些要素的特定价值中派生出来的价值，这些要素是在经济上“构成”土地的要素，它们的特定价值由归属决定。在这里最好称为计算。

对于每一种商品，不管是消费品还是生产品，都要区分这两个过程。只有商品的服务才有确定的价值，它要么直接由需求的规模决定，要么间接地由归属决定，[②] 从中一定能得出商品的价值。尽管已生产出来的商品的归属过程极其简单，并且通过它们再生产的必要性（再生产迟早会发生的），就变成固定的了，成为众人皆知的规则，但是对于土地，归属过程就变得复杂了，因为土地本身蕴涵着无限可能的用途，这些用途自动地而且原则上不需

---

① 参考庞巴维克的《法权与国民经济商品学观点的关系》。他对“使用”利息理论作的观察同样也适合我们的情况。同时，我发现我可以将这种使用利息理论的基本思想排除在我的思想之外，因为对于庞巴维克的论证，我没有什么要补充的。

② 严格地说，这种表述的方法只适合于非交换经济的情况。在交换经济中，生产资料的价值绝不会当做间接的使用价值。尽管如此，生产资料作为潜在产品这一概念，在这里仍然为商品价值的形成提供了基本原理。表述方法更准确，也得到相同的结果。

which reproduce themselves automatically and in principle without cost. [①]Hence the question arises, on account of which we have embarked upon this discussion: must not the value of land be infinitely great and so rent as a net income disappear through computation? I answer this question in a different way from Böhm-Bawerk. [②]

First, even if the value of land were infinitely great I should still describe rent as a net income. For the source of the return could not then be exhausted by consuming it and a continuous stream of goods to the landowner would be explained. The mere summation of net returns can never abrogate their character as net returns. Only imputation, never computation, annihilates a net return. Secondly, in real life, of course, the price of a piece of land is never infinitely great. However, my conception should not be reproached with leading to this infinite value, that is to an absurd result. It is not my conception that is false but the fundamental idea of the prevailing theory of capitalization, namely that the value of income-yielding property is formed merely by the summation of appropriately discounted returns. On the contrary the determination of this value is a special, fairly complicated problem, which will be studied in this chapter. In this as in every case of valuation it is necessary to look at the concrete purpose in view. There is no rigid rule of addition here, since value quantifies are mostly not simply additive. Within the normal course of the circular flow there is no reason at all to be aware of the value of land as such. It is different with a machine: every product must have a definite total value, since it is necessary in deciding the question of its reproduction.

---

① The case of self-reproduction of the services of land is distinguishable from the case of the increase of a herd of cattle by the fact that one can allow the latter to increase in such a way that the value of a beast finally falls to its cost in labor and land. The services of land reproduce themselves automatically only by the same amount in every economic period. They are, it is true, not incapable of increase, but their increase involves costs.

② Cf. Kapital und Kapitalzins, vol. II.

要成本就能再生产它们本身。[①] 因此，问题就产生了，为了说明这个问题，我们已经开始讨论：难道土地的价值没必要无限大，因而作为净收入的租金通过计算就应消失？我将用不同于庞巴维克的方式回答这个问题。[②]

首先，即使土地价值无限大，我仍然将租金看做一种净收入。因为这样，收益的源泉就不会因消费而枯竭，不断回到土地所有者手中的商品流也得到解释。仅仅把净收入相加，永远不会使其失去作为净收入的特征。只有归属才能消灭净收入，计算则永远不会使净收入消失。第二，在真实生活中，一块土地的价值当然从不会无限大。不过，不应该由于导致这个无限的价值（这也是一个荒谬的结论）而责备我的概念。并不是我的概念错了，而是盛行的资本化理论的基本思想错了，也就是认为产生收入的财产的价值只是对适当折扣的收入进行加总所得到的，这种观点是错误的。相反，这个价值的确定是一个相当复杂的问题，在本章我们将进行研究。评估这个价值就像对任何事物的评估一样，有必要看一看研究的具体目的。这里没有严格的相加规则，因为通常价值量是不能简单相加的。在正常的循环流转过程中，根本不需要知道土地价值本身。而机器则不同：每一种机器产品必须有一定的总价值，因为这对于决定它的再生产问题是必要的。而且，相

---

① 土地服务的自我再生产的情况，与一群牛的增加情况是不同的，因为人们可以通过把一头牲畜的价值最终归于它在劳动和土地上所花费的成本的方式来增加牲畜数量。而在每一经济周期里，土地服务只是以相同的数量自动地进行自我再生产。的确，土地服务不是不能增加，而是它们的增加需要花费成本。

② 参阅《资本和利息》，第二卷。

And the rule of addition applies here too. Competition enforces it. If a machine could be had for less than it produced, a profit would be made, which would necessarily raise the demand for and the price of machines; if it cost more than its employment yielded, a loss would result, which would lower the demand and the price. Land, on the other hand, is not sold in the normal circular flow, but only its uses. Therefore only their values and not the value of land as such are elements in economic planning. And the processes of the normal circular flow can teach us nothing about the determination of the value of land. Only development creates the value of land; it "capitalizes" rent, "mobilizes" land. In an economic system without development the value of land would not exist at all as a general economic phenomenon. A glance at reality confirms this. For the only occasion on which there is any sense in being aware of the value of land is upon the sale of it. And actually this hardly occurs at economic stages in which economic reality most nearly approaches the conception of the circular flow. The market for trading in land is a phenomenon of development, and can only be understood from the facts of development in which alone we can find a key to this problem. For the time being we still know nothing about it. Thus, so far, we can say that our conception does not lead to an infinite value but in general to no value, that the values of the services of land are not to be related to any other values and hence are net returns. In case it is objected that incentives to sale must nevertheless arise, it must be said that these incentives must necessarily be sporadic and that personal conditions, like distress, dissipation, non-economic aims, and the like, must be deciding. Nothing else can be stated at this juncture.

Wherever the rule of addition yields an infinite value we thus speak of a net income just as in the case of wages. For our sole concern here is that a permanent stream of goods flows to an individual and that he is not required to pass them on. And the computation

加的规则在这里也适用。竞争迫使这条规则执行。如果购买一台机器所花的钱少于它生产的产品的价值，那么就会赚得利润，这必然会使机器的需求量增加，机器的价格上升；如果购买机器花费的成本大于使用机器所得到的价值，就导致亏损，这将使机器的需求量下降，机器的价格也会降低。另一方面，在正常的循环流转中，土地不能卖，卖的只是它的用途。因此，只有土地的使用价值，而不是土地本身的价值，是经济计划中的要素。正常的循环流转过程不能告诉我们任何确定土地价值的方法。只有发展才能创造土地的价值；发展“资本化”地租，“动员起”土地。在一个没有发展的经济系统里，土地价值根本不会作为一般的经济现象存在。看一下现实，就可以证明这一点。因为能够意识到土地价值的唯一场合，就是在出卖土地的时候。事实上，在经济现实最接近循环流转这个概念的经济阶段，这种现象几乎是不会发生的。土地交易市场是一种发展现象，而且只有从发展的事实才能理解它，我们也只有在发展的事实中，才能找到解决这个问题的答案。目前，对于这个问题，我们仍然一无所知。于是，直到现在，我们可以说，我们的概念不是导致土地无限的价值，而是一般来说，导致土地没有价值；并且土地服务的价值不应与任何其他价值有关系，因而它是纯收益。如果有人反对说，尽管如此，必然还是会出现出售土地的激励因素，那么我们就只有说，这些刺激因素必然是偶然发生的，而且个人的情况，比如穷困、浪费、非经济目的等等，必然起决定作用。这样就没什么可说的了。

无论在哪里，只要附加规则产生了一种无限价值，我们就可以像谈论工资那样谈论纯收入。因为在这里，我们关心的唯一问题是一种永久的商品流流到个人手中，并且不需要他再把这些商

which yields an infinite result, far from excluding the possibility of such a stream of goods, is a symptom of its existence. This is in fact an essential element in understanding the theory of interest which is to be expounded.

3. There is still a second method of escaping the "dilemma of interest." The question of how a permanent surplus over the values of the services of labor and land is possible may also be answered by pointing to a brake on the latter. If there were such a brake then the possibility of a permanent value surplus would undoubtedly be proved, and to the circumstance which brings it about would have to be ascribed-at least from the "private" standpoint-value productivity in the fullest sense. It-or the commodity in which it is embodied - would yield a net income. A special and independent value surplus would occur in every economic process. Interest would then not be an element of cost in the real sense; it would owe its existence to a discrepancy between costs and the value or price of the product; it would be a real surplus over costs.

Such a case occurs in an exchange economy when a product is monopolised-monopolies of original productive factors do not interest us here because it is clear from the outset that interest cannot be based upon them. The monopoly position actually operates as a brake and brings the monopolist a permanent net income. We regard monopoly revenue as a net income with the same right and for the same reasons as we do rent. In this case too, the rule of addition would give an infinite result. And here also this would not deprive the revenue of the character of a net income. Why the value of the monopoly - say of a perpetual patent-is not infinite, however, does not interest us at this point; the answer will appear later. Finally, here too the determination of the value of the monopoly is a special problem, and in solving it we must not forget that in the normal circular flow no

品转给别人。产生一种无限价值的结果的计算，完全不排斥这种商品流的可能性，反而正是这种商品流存在的象征。事实上，这是理解将要论述的利息理论的关键要素。

3. 还有第二种方法可以避免“利息的困境”。超过劳动和土地服务价值的永久性的剩余是如何成为可能的，这个问题也可以通过谈劳动和土地服务的制动因素来回答。如果确实存在这种制动力，那么永久的价值剩余的可能性无疑是可以证明的，并且把产生这种可能性的环境归因于——至少从“私人的”观点看——最完全意义上的价值生产率。价值生产率——或者体现价值生产率的商品——将产生一种纯收入。在每一个经济过程中都会出现一种特殊的、独立的价值剩余。于是，利息就不是真正意义上的成本要素；利息的存在是因为在成本和产品价值或价格之间有差异；利息是超过成本的真正剩余。

在交换经济中，当某种产品被垄断时，就会发生这种情况——在这里我们对原始生产要素的垄断不感兴趣，因为从一开始讨论，我们就很清楚，利息的产生不会以对原始生产资料的垄断为依据。实际上，垄断地位所起的作用就像一种制动因素，它给垄断者带来一种永久性的净收入。我们把垄断收入看做是一种纯收入，就像我们有权并且有相同的理由把地租看做是纯收入一样。在这种情况下，附加规则也将产生一种无限价值的结果，而且在这种情况下，这种收入也不会被剥夺其纯收入的特征。然而为什么垄断价值——比如，永久性专利的垄断价值——并不是无限的，在这里，这个问题我们并不感兴趣，我们将在后面作出回答。最后，在这里决定垄断价值也是一个特殊的问题，在解决这个问题时，我们必须记住，在正常的循环流转中，不存在任何形成

motive to form such a value exists, hence the gain is not to be related to any other magnitude. However all this may be, the monopolist can at any rate never say: "I make no profit because I ascribe an extremely high value to my monopoly." This is sufficiently certain.

In discussing Lauderdale's theory of interest Böhm-Bawerk also comments upon the case in which a labor-saving and hence profit – yielding machine is monopolised. He emphasizes rightly that this machine will be so dear that no profit, or only the mini mum which will just induce people to purchase or hire it, will be connected with its employment. So much is certain. Yet a profit is undoubtedly connected with its production, which is as permanent as the patent. It might be said that the monopoly position is for the monopolist something analogous to a productive factor. Imputation takes place with reference to the "services" of this quasi-factor of production just as with reference to other factors. The machine as such is not a source of surplus value, nor are its means of production, but the monopoly makes it possible to obtain a surplus value with the machine or its means of production. Obviously nothing is changed if we allow producer and user to coincide in one person.

Hence we have a net income *sui generis.* If what is called interest were the same as this, all would be well. Our three questions would be satisfactorily answered. There would be a source of surplus value the existence of which would be explained by the theory of monopoly; there would also be a reason for the assignment of a return to monopolists; and finally the fact that neither imputation nor competition annihilates the return would be explained. However, such monopoly positions do not occur regularly and numerously enough for this explanation to be accepted, and moreover interest exists without them. ①

---

① Yet a very elaborate attempt has been made in this direction: cf. Otto Conrad, Lohn und Rente. All other suggestions of this kind of explanation of interest are not of the rank of an elaborated theory.

这种垄断价值的动力，因此，这种收益不应与任何数量存在关系。不管所有这些会怎样，垄断者从不会说："我不赚取利润，因为我已经赋予我的垄断以一个极高的价值。"这一点是肯定的。

庞巴维克在讨论劳德代尔的利息理论时，也评论过机器被垄断这种情况，这种机器节省了劳动力，从而能够产生利润。他合理地强调，使用这种机器是如此昂贵，所以没有任何利润，或者只有极其小的利润，仅足以引诱人们去购买它或者租用它，这是肯定的。然而，利润毫无疑问地会与机器的生产相联系，这就像专利一样永久。人们可能会说，对于垄断者而言，垄断地位类似于生产要素。当谈到这种准生产要素的"服务"，就像谈到其他要素一样，归属问题就产生了。机器本身并不是剩余价值的来源，机器的生产手段也不是剩余价值的来源，但是垄断作用通过使用机器或者机器的生产手段，有可能使得它们产生剩余价值。如果我们把机器的生产者和使用者合并为一人，显然结果没有任何改变。

因此，我们有一个特殊的纯收入。如果被称之为利息的东西也像这种纯收入，那就都好办了。我们的三个问题也将得到满意的答复。这里有一个可以由垄断理论来解释的剩余价值的来源；也有一种理由给垄断者分配收益。最后，不管是归属还是竞争都不会消灭收益，这个事实将得到解释。然而，这种垄断地位不会规则地、大量地出现，以使这种解释充分地为人们所接受，此外，即使没有垄断地位，利息仍然存在。①

---

① 然而，还是有人沿着这个方向作过艰苦的尝试：参阅奥托·康拉德的《工资与地租》。所有以这种方法解释利息的其他观点，都不能算作完善理论之列。

Another case in which one might speak of a permanent and regular lagging of the value of the services of labor and land behind the value of the product would exist if future goods were systematically and in principle valued less than present goods. The reader knows already that this is not accepted here, but it is necessary to mention the case once more. While in all the cases treated so far a permanent source of income resulted simply from a permanent and-at least from the "private" standpoint- productive service, this case would involve something different, namely a movement in values themselves. While previously the explanation lay in the determination of the value of some productive service *sui generis*, here it would lie in the determination of the value of the services of labor and land on the one hand and of consumption goods on the other hand. Here there would be a surplus of the value of the product above the value of the means of production, in a narrower and truer sense than in the case of monopoly. And "surplus over costs" would *ipso facto* signify a net return and surplus above the "capital value" of the produced means of production. Hence it would be proved *ipso facto* that the return would neither disappear nor be absorbed by the process of computation. For the full value of a future product cannot be imputed and computed if, at the moment when the imputation and the determination of the value of the means of production are to be undertaken, it appears not at its real magnitude but smaller. The possibility of a permanent stream of goods would thus undoubtedly be proved, whether or not it was the interest which we observe in real life. Our first question would be answered: a source of value from which interest can flow would exist. The second question, namely why the stream of goods flows to those particular individuals, would obviously not be difficult to answer. And the third, why the return does not disappear, by far the thorniest part of the interest problem, would be superfluous. Since the value surplus would have been explained by reason of non-imputation, there would be no sense in asking why it is not imputed.

还有另一种情况，在那里，如果对未来商品的估价系统地并在原则上要低于对现在商品的估价，那么，人们可能会说，劳动和土地服务的价值永久地并且经常地落在产品的价值之后的这种情况将存在。读者已经知道，在这里不会接受这种观点，但是还是有必要再次提到这种情况。在至今所论述的所有情况中，收入的持久性来源仅仅产生于永久性的——至少从“个人的”观点看是这样——和生产性的服务，这种情况将包含另一个问题，即价值本身的运动。原先，这种解释目的在于确定某些特殊的生产性服务的价值，然而在这里，它的目的一方面在于确定劳动和土地服务的价值，另一方面在于确定消费品的价值。从一个比垄断情况更狭窄、更真实的意义上说，这里将会存在产品价值超过生产资料价值的一种剩余。事实上，“超过成本的剩余”将表明一种净收入以及超过被生产出来的生产资料的“资本价值”的剩余。因此，这就在实际上证明了收益既不会消失，也不会因计算过程而被吸收。因为，未来产品的全部价值是不能归属和计算的，如果确实要采用归属，并且确定生产资料的价值，一旦这样，所表现出来的未来产品的价值就不是它们的真实价值量，而是较小的价值量。这样就证明了永久性商品流的可能性，而不管它是不是我们在实际生活中所观察到的利息。于是，我们的第一个问题就可以这样回答：能够产生利息的价值源泉是存在的。第二个问题，为什么商品流会流到那些特定的个人手中，这显然也不难回答。第三个问题，为什么这种收益不会消失，这是迄今为止利息问题中最棘手的部分，这将成为多余的问题。既然可以用非归属作为原因来解释价值剩余，那么再问为什么它没有用归属方法就没有任何意义了。

Hence if the mere passing of time had a primary effect upon valuation, and if what reality shows us to be its influence were not merely an unanalyzed fact which fundamentally rests in turn upon the existence of interest, which is again to be explained on other grounds, this line of argument would be in itself quite satisfactory, even though in my opinion it brings us into many a conflict with the actual course of the economic process. Purely logically it would be free from objections. But the passing of time has not this independent primary effect. And even the growth in the value of many goods in the course of time proves nothing. Since this fact is especially prominent and has played a certain r 1e in the literature of the subject, a few words may be devoted to it.

There are two kinds of such increase in value. First, the services-actual or potential-of a good may alter automatically in the course of time and the value of the good increase. A young forest and a stock of wine are examples frequently cited. What happens in such cases? Now both forest and wine certainly become more valuable goods by natural processes which demand time. However, they only grow into the higher value physically; economically this higher value already exists in the small trees of the young forest and in the wine newly cellared, because it depends upon them. These small trees and this wine must therefore so far-from the standpoint of the facts with which we are already acquainted-be exactly as valuable as the timber fit for felling and the matured wine. In so far as wood and wine may also be sold to consumers before they are quite ripe, their owners will ask themselves which of two alternatives will yield the greater return per economic period: allowing time for further ripening or selling now and producing anew. They will choose the alternative which yields the greater return, and they will value accordingly the trees and wine and the necessary services of labor and land from the very beginning. In reality this is not so. For the forest and wine continually increase in value *pari passu as* they approach maturity.

因此，如果仅仅时间的流逝对价值有首要的影响，并且如果现实向我们表明，时间的影响还只是尚未分析的事实，这个事实又根源于利息的存在，而利息又要由其他理由来解释；这种论证路线，就其本身而言是让人很满意的，尽管从我的观点看，它将把我们带到与经济过程的实际进程有许多冲突的地方。从纯逻辑上看，它不会受到反对，但是时间的流逝并没有这种独立的首要的影响作用。甚至在时间的发展过程中，众多商品价值的增长也不能证明任何问题。既然这个事实尤为突出，并且它在这个论题的相关文献中起过一定的作用，所以我们可以对此做几句说明。

这种价值增长有两种方式。第一，一种商品的服务——实际的或者潜在的——可能在时间的进程中自动地改变，并且该商品的价值会增长。未成林的森林以及窖存的酒，是常常被列举的例子。在这两种情况下发生了什么呢？森林和酒随着自然进程一定都会变得更有价值，这个自然进程是要有时间的。然而，它们只是在物质上变得有更高的价值；而在经济上，这种更高的价值早就存在于树的幼苗以及刚存储的酒中了，因为这种价值依赖于它们。所以，从我们已经熟悉的事实的观点看，这些幼苗以及新酒必然与适合砍伐的老树以及陈年的酒有完全相同的价值。既然木材和酒在它们完全成熟之前也可以卖给消费者，那么它们的所有者就会问自己，这两种选择中哪一种会在每一经济周期产生更大的收入：是随着时间等待它们进一步成熟呢，还是现在就把它们卖了，然后进行新的种植和生产？他们将选择能产生更大收益的方式，而且他们从一开始就会相应地对树木、酒以及必要的劳动和土地服务进行评价，而实际上并不是这样的：因为随着不断接近成熟，树木和酒的价值会不断地增长。我们不久就会发现，

This is due, however, fundamentally to material and personal risk, especially the risk of life, and to the fact that interest already exists, a fact which under certain conditions makes time an dement of cost, as we shall soon see. If it were not for these factors there would be no such increase in value. If it is decided to let the forest and wine ripen longer than was originally intended, that can only be because it has been discovered that it is more advantageous to do so. There then occurs a new method of employing the forest and the wine, which must obviously result at the time of the decision in a rise in value. But there is in general no real, continuous growth of value with the passing of time as a primary and independent phenomenon.

Secondly, it often happens that the services of a good remain absolutely the same physically but yet in the course of time increase in value. This can only be attributable to the appearance of a new demand, and is a phenomenon of development. It is easy to see how this case is to be regarded. If the increase in demand is not foreseen, then there is a gain, but not one which constitutes a permanent increase in value. If on the contrary it is foreseen, then it must be imputed from the very beginning to the good concerned, so that again there is no increase in value. If in reality it nevertheless appears that there is, we shall explain it in the same way as in the case of the improvement of physical qualities.

4. We have exhausted the most important lines of thought which might have led us out of the dilemma of interest, and with a negative result. Hence we find ourselves driven back again to those surplus values of which we have already spoken repeatedly and which we can consider as net surpluses with a dear conscience, namely surpluses of the value of products above the value of the quantities of production goods embodied in them. They owe their existence to some special circumstance which raises the value of products above the equilibrium value that the commodities in question would have in the circular flow. The character of such surpluses as a net return and as the source of a flow of goods

这在根本上是因为要冒物质的和个人的风险，尤其是个人的生命的风险，而且还由于存在利息这个事实，在一定条件下，利息的存在使时间变成一种成本要素。如果没有这些原因，就不会有这种价值的增加。如果人们决定延长原定的森林和酒的成熟期，那只是因为人们发现这样做会更有利。于是就会出现一种利用森林和酒的新方法，这种新方法在被决定采用时，显然必定能带来价值的增长。但是，通常随着时间的流逝这成为一种首要的和独立的现象，并不能产生真正的、持续的价值增长。

第二，常常有这样的情况，即某种商品的服务在物质上与原来完全一样，但是随着时间的发展，它的价值增加了。这只能归因于出现了新的需求，而且这是一种发展现象，很容易明白人们是怎么看待这种情况的。如果没有预见到需求会增加而产生了盈利，那这种收益就不会形成价值的持久增长。相反，如果预见到需求的增加，那么从一开始就会把这种收益归属于相关的商品，从而也没有价值的增长。尽管如此，如果在现实中还是出现了价值的增长，我们就将以和物质特性改善相同的方式来解释它。

4. 我们已经花费很大的代价来探讨这个最重要的思路，这个思路可能引导我们摆脱利息问题的困境，同时我们得到一个否定的结果。因此，我们发现我们又被迫回到剩余价值的问题上，这个问题我们已经反复谈到过，而且我们可以明确地把这些剩余价值看做是净剩余，也就是，产品价值超过体现在产品中的生产性商品的价值的剩余额。剩余价值的存在，是因为某种特殊的环境把产品的价值提高到这些产品在循环流转中的均衡价值之上。所以，这些作为净收益以及作为商品流的来源的剩余额的特征，

is thereby *ipso facto* established just as much as it would be in the case of systematic undervaluation of future goods.

Circumstances which raise the value of a product above that of its means of production, so that with the help of the latter a profit can be made, also occur in an economy without development. Errors and windfalls, unintentional and unexpected deviations of results from expectations, conditions of distress and accidental superabundance-these and many other circumstances may produce surpluses, but this kind of deviation of actual values from normal values, and at the same time from the values of the means of production used, is of little importance. We turn to those surplus values which owe their existence to development, and which are much more interesting. We have already divided them into two main groups. The one embraces those surplus values which development carries with it of necessity, in the creation of which development consists in a sense, and which are explained by the choice of new, more advantageous, uses of producers' goods, whose values were previously determined according to other, less advantageous, uses. The second group embraces those surplus values which are based upon repercussions of development, that is upon increases, actual or anticipated, of the demand for certain goods which development brings about.

To repeat, all these surplus values are-as Böhm-Bawerk would also admit-true and real surpluses in every conceivable sense, and have nothing to fear either from the Scylla of computation or from the Charybdis of the list of costs. All streams of goods which flow to individuals under any other title than wages, rent, and monopoly revenue must directly or indirectly be due to them. Let us recall, however, the proposition already derived, that competition and the working of the general laws of valuation tend to eliminate all surpluses above costs. ①For example, if a business suddenly and unexpectedly requires machines of a certain kind the value of the latter will rise and the possessor of such machines will be assured of the surplus value, in whole or in part. But if the new demand

① Cf. the argument of Chapter IV.

实际上就和系统地低估未来商品价值的情形一样。

使产品的价值高于它的生产资料的价值，从而借助于生产资料获得利润，这种环境或者条件在一个没有发展的经济中也会发生。差错和横财，偏离预期的无意识的意外结果，困境以及偶然的额外财富——这些以及许多其他情况都可能产生剩余，但是实际价值对正常价值的这种偏离，以及同时对所使用的生产资料价值的偏离，是不重要的。我们关注那些由于发展而产生的剩余价值，那些更有趣。我们已经把它们分成两个主要部分，一部分包括那些因发展必然会带来的剩余价值，从某种意义上说，发展就是为了创造这种剩余价值，而且，可以用选择生产品的新的、更有利的用途来解释这些剩余价值，这些生产品的价值原来是根据其他较为不利的用途所决定的。第二部分包括那些基于对发展的反映而产生的剩余价值，也就是根据发展所带来的对某些商品在实际上或者预期的需求的增长，而产生的剩余。

再重复一遍，所有这些剩余价值——正如庞巴维克也会承认的——在任何可以想像的意义上都是真实存在的剩余，不用担心由于计算或者成本项目而产生的两难困境。除了工资、地租和垄断收益之外，以任何其他名义流入个人手中的所有商品流，都必然直接或者间接地源自剩余价值。然而，让我们回想一下已经推导出来的命题：竞争和一般估价规律的作用，有消除超过成本的任何剩余的趋势。[①] 例如，如果一家企业突然地，意想不到地需求某种机器，那么这种机器的价值将会上升，而且拥有这种机器的人肯定会全部或者部分地获得剩余价值。但是如果这种新的需

① 参阅第四章的论点。

is foreseen then it must be assumed that more of such machines have already been produced and are now supplied by competing producers. Then either no special profit will be realized at all or, if production cannot be appropriately extended, the surplus will be imputed to the natural and original productive factors, and surrendered to their owners, in accordance with well known rules. Even if the new demand is not anticipated, the economic system will finally be adjusted to it, and no permanent surplus value will be associated with the machines.

5. We can now formulate five propositions of our theory of interest which follow almost automatically from the first elementary conclusion that interest is a value phenomenon and an element in price-we have this much in common with every scientific theory of interest-and which will have to be completed later by a sixth proposition.

First, interest flows essentially from the surplus values just considered. It can flow from nothing else since there are no other surpluses in the normal course of economic life. Of course this is only true for what we have called productive interest in the narrowest sense, which does not include "consumptive-productive interest."① For in so far as interest is only a parasite in the body of wages and rent it has clearly nothing to do directly with these surplus values. But the large, regularly flowing stream of goods on which the capitalist class lives and which flows to it in every economic period from the proceeds of production-this can only come from our surplus values. These points will be examined more closely later. Moreover, there is one surplus value which is not of this kind, namely monopoly revenue. Our thesis therefore assumes that the typical source of interest is not in monopoly revenue. This, however, as I have already said, should be sufficiently clear. Thus without development, with the qualifications mentioned,

① Cf. Wesen, bk. III, ch. iii; also Chapter III, Part I, in the present work. Example: if a factory is destroyed by accident and if it is rebuilt by means of a loan, then the interest on this loan is what we mean by "consumptive-productive."

求被预见到了，那么必然可以想像，已经生产出更多的这种机器，此时由相互竞争的生产者供应给市场。于是，根本不会实现任何特殊的利润，或者，如果生产不能相应地扩大，将有部分剩余归属于自然和原始的生产要素，并以众所周知的规则交给它们的所有者。即使新的需求没有被预料到，经济系统最终还是会适应这种需求，所以也就没有与机器相关联的任何永久性的剩余价值了。

5. 现在我们可以阐述我们关于利息理论的五个命题，这五个命题几乎是自动地产生于第一个基本结论，即利息是一个价值现象，是价格的一个要素——关于这一点，我们与任何一个科学的利息理论都一致——而且这一点将由第六个命题来完成论证。

首先，利息本质上来自于刚刚讨论过的剩余价值。由于在正常的经济生活进程中没有其他剩余，所以利息不可能来自于其他东西。当然这仅适用于我们在狭义上所称的生产性利息，它不包括“消费性—生产利息”。[①] 因为只要利息只作为工资和地租的寄生物，那么，很清楚，它与这些剩余价值就没有什么直接关系了。但是，资产阶级赖以生存的大量的、有规则的商品流，在每一经济时期都从生产过程流到资本家手中——这种商品流也只能来自于我们所说的剩余价值。这几点将在以后更详细地验证。此外，还有一种不同的剩余价值，即垄断收益，因此，我们的论题假设典型的利息来源不是垄断收益。然而，就像我已经说过的，这一点应该是十分清楚的。于是，如果没有发展，在上述限制条件下

① 参阅《本质》第三篇，第三章，以及本书第一部分，第三章。例如：假设一家工厂因突发事故而惨遭毁损，同时，它借款重建，那么这笔贷款的利息就是我们所说的“消费性—生产利息”。

there would be no interest; it is a part of the great waves which development causes in the sea of economic values. Our thesis rests first of all upon the negative proof that the determination of value in the circular flow excludes the phenomenon of interest; this proof in turn rests first upon direct knowledge of the process which determines values and secondly upon the untenableness of various attempts to establish decisive differences between the values of products and of means of production in an economy without development. Then we have added the positive proof that such a difference in value does occur in development. The thesis will lose much of its strangeness in the course of the following discussion. It may be emphasized here at once, however, that it is not nearly so far from an unprejudiced treatment of reality as it might seem, for industrial development is certainly at least the chief source of the interest form of income. ①

Secondly, surplus values in development fall, as we have seen, into two groups-entrepreneurial profit and those values which represent the "repercussions of development." It is dear that interest cannot attach itself to the latter. We can assert this so easily because the process of creating this kind of surplus is quite dear, so that we can see immediately what is and is not there. Let us consider the example of a tradesman who, in consequence of the establishment of factories in his village, receives more than equilibrium income for a time. Thus he makes a definite profit. This profit cannot itself be interest, for it is not permanent and is soon wiped out by competition. But neither does interest *flow* from it-assuming that the tradesman has done nothing more in the acquisition of it than simply stand in his shop and charge higher prices to his customers-for absolutely nothing further happens to it: the tradesman pockets it and uses it as he pleases. The whole process leaves no room for the phenomenon of interest.

---

① Only the regularity of interest supports the preconception that it must be explained "statically"; but we do account for this regularity.

就不会有利息；利息是在经济价值的海洋中由于发展而掀起的巨大波浪的一部分。我们的论题首先是根据一个反证，即在循环流转中价值的确定不包括利息现象；而这一反证首先依赖于我们对价值决定过程的直接了解，其次根据各种站不住脚的尝试：企图在一个没有发展的经济中，建立产品价值和生产资料之间的决定性差异。然后我们从正面证明，这种价值差异在发展中的确存在。这个论题在下面的讨论过程中，就不会显得奇怪了。然而，在这里我们可以即刻强调，这个论题并不像它看起来可能的那样远离我们对现实的无偏见的对待，因为工业发展至少确实是利息形式的收入的主要来源。①

第二，正如我们已经知道的，发展中的剩余价值分成两类——企业家利润和那些代表“对发展反应”的价值。显然利息不属于后者。我们可以这样轻松地断言，是因为创造这种剩余的过程十分清楚，因此我们可以立即看出其中有什么，没有什么。我们来看一个商人的例子，由于他在村庄里开办了一些工厂，所以他暂时获得了高于均衡收入的收益，这样他就得到了一定的利润。而这种利润本身并不是利息，因为它不是永久性的，而且很快就会被竞争所消灭。然而，利息也不是从这种利润中流出来的——假设商人为获得这个利润，也只不过是站在他的商店里，向顾客要更高的价格，并没有做其他事——因为对于这种利润根本不会再发生任何什么事：商人将把它们放入口袋，并且随心所欲地使用它们，整个过程没有为利息现象留下任何余地。所以

① 只有当利息是规则的才能支持这种必须解释为“静态”的偏见；但是我们正要对利息的规则性作说明。

Therefore interest must flow from entrepreneurial profit. This is an indirect conclusion to which I attach, of course, only secondary importance as compared with the other facts which support this thesis. Development, then-in some way-sweeps a part of profit to the capitalist. Interest acts as a tax upon profit.

Thirdly, however, it is obvious that neither the whole profit nor even a part of it can be directly and immediately interest, because it is only temporary. And analogously we see at once that interest does not adhere to any class of concrete goods. All surplus values adhering to concrete goods must be by nature temporary, and even though such surpluses constantly arise in an economic system in full development – so much so that it requires deeper analysis to recognize the ephemerality of any one of them-yet they cannot immediately form a permanent income. Since interest is permanent it cannot be understood simply as a surplus value from concrete goods. Although it flows from a definite class of surplus values no surplus value *per se* is interest.

These three propositions, that interest as a great social phenomenon is a product of development, ① that it flows from profit, and that it does not adhere to concrete goods, are the basis of our theory of interest. The admission of them puts an end to all the continually repeated attempts to find an dement of value in concrete goods corresponding to interest, ② and thereby concentrates work on the problem of interest within quite a small field.

---

① Cf. Wesen, bk. III, ch. iii.

② From this two practical results follow at once. First, the so-called primitive trading interest is not interest. In so far as it is not monopoly revenue or wages it must be entrepreneurial profit-also only temporary. Secondly, rental is not interest. Rental is partial purchase and can include no element of interest in the circular flow. The net income from a house could only be ground rent-and wages of "superintendence." How an element of interest can, in development, enter into the rental will be seen automatically from our argument. The fact that already existing interest on capital makes time an element of costs is especially important.

利息必然来自于企业家利润。当然，这是间接结论，而且与支持这个论题的其他事实相比，我只把它放在第二重要的位置。所以，发展——以某种方式——将一部分利润交给资本家。利息成为对利润的一种课税。

第三，很显然，全部利润，甚至是部分利润，都不可能直接地即刻成为利息，因为利润只是暂时的。类似地，我们立即就会明白，利息不依附于任何具体的商品。所有依附于具体商品的剩余价值在本质上必然是暂时的，即使这种剩余在一个充分发展的经济系统里能够不断地增长——以至于必须进行更深入地分析才能认识任何一种这样的剩余价值的暂时性——它们也不能立即形成一种永久性的收入。因为利息是永久性的，所以我们不能简单地将其理解为是来自于具体商品的剩余价值。尽管利息源自一定种类的剩余价值，但是没有一种剩余价值本身就是利息。

这三个命题表明，利息作为一个重大的社会现象，它是发展的产物；① 它来自于利润；并且利息不依附于具体商品，这些都是我们利息理论的根据。承认这些命题，就终止了所有在具体商品中寻找与利息相对应的价值要素的反复尝试，② 因此，我们集中精力在一个相当狭小的领域研究利息问题。

---

① 参阅《本质》第三篇第三章。

② 从这一点我们立即可以得到下面两个实际结果：第一，所谓原始交换利息并不是利息。只要它不是垄断收益或者工资，那它必定是企业家利润——而且仅仅是暂时的。第二，租金不是利息。租金只是部分收益，在循环流转中，它不可能包含任何利息要素。出租房屋所得到的净收入只是地租——和“监督”工资。在发展的经济中，利息要素是怎样进入租金的，这一点将从我们的论证中自然地看明白。早已存在的资本利息使时间成为一种成本要素，这个事实尤为重要。

6. It is now time to get the significant question more firmly in our grasp. The main question, the solution of which settles by far the most important point in the interest problem, now runs: *how is this permanent stream of interest, flowing always to the same capital, extracted from the transitory, ever-changing profits*? This statement of the question embodies the results so far attained and is independent of the direction in which we continue. If it is answered satisfactorily, then the interest problem is solved in a way that satisfies all the demands which Böhm-Bawerk's analysis has proved to be indispensable and-whatever its defects may other wise be-it is not exposed to the objections fatal to previous theories.

We proceed with our fourth thesis, which differs totally from the usual theories, with the exception of the exploitation theory, and which has the weight of the most competent authority against it: *in a communistic or non-exchange society in general there would be no interest as an independent value phenomenon.* Obviously no interest would be *paid*. Obviously there would still exist the value phenomena from which interest flows in an exchange economy. But as a special value phenomenon, as an economic quantity, even as a concept, interest would not exist there; it is dependent upon the organization of an exchange economy. Let us formulate this still more precisely. Wages and rent also would not be paid in a purely communist organization. But the services of labor and land would still exist there, they would be valued, and their values would be a fundamental element in the economic plan. Nothing of this holds good for interest. The agent for which interest is paid simply would not exist in a communist economy. Hence it could not be the object of a valuation. And consequently there could not be a net return corresponding to the interest form of income. Thus interest is indeed an economic category-not created directly by non-economic forces-but one which only arises in an exchange economy.

Why is there no interest in a communist society, although there is in an exchange economy? This question leads us to our fifth thesis. It opens to us a first view of the nature of the suction

6. 现在我们就应紧紧抓住重要问题了。这个主要问题的解决也是处理利息问题最重要的一点，现在这个主要问题是：这种总是流向同一资本的持久的利息流，是如何从暂时的、不断变化的利润中被提取出来的？问题的这种表述体现了至今我们研究所得的结果，而且它独立于我们继续研究的方面。如果这个问题能被满意地答复，那么利息问题也就可以解决了，并且满足已经被庞巴维克分析所证明的所有那些必不可少的要求——不论它在其他方面可能有什么缺陷——它不会遇到先前的理论所遭受的那种致命的反击。

我们继续进入我们的第四个命题，除剥削理论之外，第四个命题与通常的理论完全不同，而且它受到最有资格的权威理论的反对：在共产主义社会或者通常的非交换社会，不会存在任何作为独立价值现象的利息。显然，没有人愿意支付利息。显然，仍然会存在交换经济中产生利息的价值现象。但是，作为一种特殊的价值现象，作为一种经济数量，甚至作为某种概念，利息不会存在于那里；利息依存于交换经济组织。让我们对这个问题进行更精确地阐述。在一个完全的共产主义组织中，人们不会支付工资和地租。但是，那里仍然会存在劳动和土地服务，人们会对它们进行估价，并且它们的价值是经济计划的基本要素。然而，这些对利息都没有用。在共产主义经济中根本没有接受利息的人。因此，利息不可能成为估价的对象，因而也就不存在与收入的利息形式相对应的净收益。这样，利息的确是一个经济范畴——但它并不是由非经济势力直接创造——而只是在交换经济中才能产生。

为什么在共产主义社会没有利息，而在交换经济中就有利息呢？这个问题引出我们的第五个命题。它在我们面前首先展现

apparatus that draws a permanent stream of goods from profits. The capitalist certainly has something to do with production. And technically, production is always the same process under whatever organization it may occur. Technically it always requires goods and nothing but goods. Hence no difference can exist here. But elsewhere there is a difference. The entrepreneur's relation to his production goods in an exchange economy is essentially different from that of the central organ in a non-exchange community. The latter has the disposal of them directly, the former must first of all procure them by hire or purchase.

If entrepreneurs were in a position to commandeer the producers' goods which they need to carry their new plans into effect, there would still be entrepreneurs' profit, but no part of it would have to be paid out by them as interest. *Nor would there be any motive for them to consider part of it as interest on the "capital" they expend.* On the contrary, the whole of what they make over and above costs would be "profits" to them and nothing else. It is only because other people have command of the necessary producers' goods that entrepreneurs must call in the capitalist to help them to remove the obstacle which private property in means of production or the right to dispose freely of one's personal services puts in their way. No such help is wanted in producing within the circular flow, for firms already running can be, and in principle are, currently financed by previous receipts, which stream to them without the intervention of any distinct capitalistic agency. Hence nothing essential is obscured in the picture of the circular flow, if it is assumed that the means with which production is carried on consist of the products of preceding periods; but in the case of new combinations, entrepreneurs have no such products with which to procure means of production. Here, then, the function of capital comes in, and it becomes evident that nothing corresponding to it can exist either in a communist or even in a noncommunist but "stationary" society.

了一个吸引工具的性质，这个吸引工具能从利润中抽取永久的商品流。当然，资本家与生产有着某种关系。在技术上，无论组织形式可能是什么样，生产过程都是相同的。在技术上，它总是要求商品，而且也只要求商品，没有其他任何东西。因此，这里没有任何差别。但是在别处存在差异。在一个交换经济下，企业家与其生产品之间的关系，和在没有交换的社会里，中央机构与其生产品之间的关系，有着本质上的差别。因为中央机构有权直接处理生产品，而企业家必须首先通过雇佣或者购买才能获得生产品。

如果企业家有权征用他实现新的计划所必需的生产品，那么仍然会存在企业家利润，但是企业家不会把利润的任何一部分支付出去作为利息，而且企业家也没有任何动力想把利润的一部分作为利息支付在他们所花费的“资本”上。相反，他们所获得的超过成本的全部收入都属于他们的“利润”，而不是别的。这仅仅是因为，其他人支配着必要的生产品，所以企业家必须请求资本家帮助他们移开对其经营有影响的生产资料的私有制或自由处置个人劳务的权利这些障碍。在循环流转中，生产不需要任何这样的帮助，因为已经经营的厂商能够，而且在原则上也是，用以前的收入提供当前需要的生产资金，这些收入不需要任何特殊的资本主义机构的干预就可以流到企业家手中。因此，在循环流转中，任何本质上的东西都是明晰的。如果假定进行生产所用的生产资料是由前期的产品所构成，而在新组合的情况下，企业家没用这些产品来获得生产资料。于是这时，资本的职能就体现出来了，显然，无论是在共产主义社会，还是在非共产主义而又处于“静态”的社会中，都不可能存在相当于资本的任何东西。

7. I should like to direct the reader's attention to the fact that our conception of the interest problem involves something different from the usual conception. Although this is really obvious it will nevertheless not be superfluous to elucidate the point still more.

For this purpose I shall start from the usual distinction between interest on loans and "original" interest on capital. It reaches back to the beginning of investigations into the nature of interest, and has become one of the foundation stones of the theory. Speculation about the interest problem started as a matter of course with interest on consumptive loans. First of all, it is in the nature of things that it should start with interest on such loans because this stands out as an independent branch of income distinguished by many clear features. It is always easier to grasp conceptually a branch of income which is also externally distinguished than one which must first be cleared of an admixture of other elements-therefore rent was first clearly recognized in England where it not only existed but was also as a general rule paid separately. But interest on consumptive loans was also the starting point because it was the most important and best known form in ancient times and in the Middle Ages. Interest on productive loans was not wanting, it is true; but in classical antiquity it operated in a world which did not philosophise, while the world which did philosophise only observed economic things fleetingly and only paid attention to the interest which was to be observed in their sphere. And also later, the elements of a capitalist economy which existed were familiar only to a circle which was a world in itself and neither pondered nor wrote. The church father, the canonist, or the philosopher dependent upon the church and Aristotle-all of them only thought of interest on consumptive loans, which made itself noticeable within their horizon and indeed in a very unpleasant manner. From their contempt for the bleeding of the necessitous and the exploiting of the thoughtless or profligate, from their reaction against the pressure exerted by the usurer, arose their hostility to charging interest, and this explains the various prohibitions of interest.

7. 我想提请读者注意这个事实，那就是，我们关于利息问题的概念所包含的内容，有别于通常的概念。尽管这是很显然的，但是对这一点作进一步说明并不多余。

为此，我将从贷款利息和资本的“原始”利息之间的一般区别开始谈。这个区别追溯到我们对利息性质的最初的研究，并且它已经成为利息理论的基石之一。对于利息理论的思考，理所当然地是从消费贷款的利息开始的。首先，从这种贷款利息开始是符合事物的本质的，因为这种利息有许多明显的独特的特征，使它成为收入的一项独立的分支。如果一项收入能从外部特征上区别出来，那么从概念上把握这项收入要比对那些必须首先去除混合的其他要素的收入更容易些——因此在英格兰，人们首先清楚地认识了地租，在那里，地租不仅存在，而且按常规，它是单独支付的。不过消费性贷款的利息也是利息的起点，因为在古代以及中世纪，它是最重要并且众所周知的形式。生产性贷款的利息确实也是存在的；但是在古代，它只在不探讨哲学的领域起作用，而探讨哲学的人只是匆匆、飞快地观察经济事物，而且只关注他们生活圈子内可以观察到的利息现象。同样后来，对所出现的资本主义经济要素，也只有生活在其中的小圈子里的人熟悉，并且这些人既不思考也不写作。教堂的神父、宗教法规的学者，或者依赖教会的哲学家和亚里士多德——他们这些人都只考虑消费性贷款的利息，这种利息闯进他们的视线，引起了他们的注意，并且的确是以一种令人不快的方式。从他们对榨取穷人血汗者、对毫无顾及地剥削或者挥霍者的蔑视，从他们对高利贷者乘人之危压迫别人的反感来看，他们对索取利息是敌对的，这也解释了对利息的各种禁令。

Another conception grew up from observation of business life, as the capitalist economy gathered strength. It would be an exaggeration to say that interest on productive loans was positively a discovery of later authors. But in effect the emphasis upon this came to much the same as a discovery. It immediately made clear that the old conception simply ignored one part, and indeed what now was by far the most important part, of the phenomenon, and at the same time that the debtor by no means always becomes poorer by borrowing. This took the edge off the fundamental reason for the hostility to interest and led scientifically a step further. The whole English literature on interest up to Adam Smith's time is filled with the idea that a loan often leads the borrower to business profit. In the place of the weak debtor there appears in the mind of the theorist a strong debtor, in the place of the piteous crowds of distressed poor and thoughtless landowners there appears a figure of another breed, the entrepreneur-not quite clearly and boldly defined, it is true, but still plain enough. And this is the point which the theory here expounded takes up.

But productive interest is still interest on loans for this group of theorists. Entrepreneurial profit is recognized as its source. However, from this it no more follows that entrepreneurial profit is simply interest than it follows that the total receipts of production are wages because these total receipts are the source of wages. If anything definite at all can be said in view of the shortness of these writers' arguments about interest, it is that they did not confound interest and profit in the least or view them as identical in character. They perceived, on the contrary, as is seen from Hume,①the difference between the two, and were far from seeing in profit nothing more than interest on one's own capital. They explain profit in a manner which is not at all applicable to interest on loans as such, but only to another kind of profit which is the *source of*

① Petty, Locke, and Steuart might also be quoted.

另一个概念，随着资本主义经济的成熟，形成于对商业生活的观察。如果说生产性贷款的利息确实是后来的研究者所发现的，这可能有些夸大其词。而实际上强调这一点，也正如一种发现。我们立即就会明白，旧的概念完全忽视了这种现象的一部分，而这一部分现在的确是最重要的一部分；同时我们也明白了，债务人决不总是因借款而变得更穷。这就削弱了敌视利息的根本理由，并且在科学上更进了一步。在英国关于利息的全部文献，直到亚当·斯密时代，都充满着这种思想，即贷款常常使借款人得到商业利润。原来被认为是弱者的借款人，现在在理论家的心目中成为借款强者；原来被认为是一群可怜的穷困者或者粗心、愚笨的土地所有者，现在却成为另一类企业家——虽然对这个概念还不是十分清楚，没有明确地定义，但还是足以理解的。这就是我们在这里阐述理论所采用的观点。

但是对这一类理论家来说，生产性利息仍然是贷款利息。企业家利润被看做是产生它们的源泉。然而，从这里我们不能引申说企业家利润都是利息，这就像我们不能因所有收入是工资的来源，就引申说所有的生产性收入都是工资一样。如果要针对这些作家对利息的论证的不足之处，一定要说些他们值得肯定的地方，那就是至少他们没有混淆利息和利润，或者说他们没有在性质上把两者等同起来。相反，正如休谟所观察到的，[①] 这些作家注意到了利息和利润之间的差别，但是他们远没有看到利润只不过是他们自有资本的利息。他们用来解释利润的方式根本不适用于说明贷款利息，而只能用来解释另一种作为贷款利息的来源的

① 也可以引用配第、洛克和斯图亚特论证。

interest on loans.[1] All these authors traced interest back to business profit as its source, but did not say that the latter itself is again only a case and indeed the principal case of interest. Their "profit" may not be translated by interest even when it occurs in the phrase "profit of capital." They did not solve the interest problem. But it would not be correct to say that they merely traced back one derived form, interest on loans, to the original and real interest, without explaining the latter. They merely failed to prove why the creditor with his capital is in a position to exact this share of profit, why the capital market always decides in his favor. Furthermore, the central problem upon the solution of which insight into the interest phenomenon depends, certainly lies in business profit; not, however, because business profit is itself true interest, but because its existence is a prerequisite of the payment of productive interest. Finally, the entrepreneur is certainly the most important person in the whole matter; not, however, because he is the true, original, typical interest receiver, but because he is the typical interest payer.

In the case of Adam Smith we may still perceive a trace of the view according to which profit and interest do not simply coincide. Only with Ricardo and his epigoni are the two plainly synonymous. Not till then did theory come to see in business profit in general the only problem, and in fact the interest problem; not till then did the question, why does the entrepreneur obtain a business profit, become the interest problem; and finally not till then is the meaning of the English authors correctly rendered if their "profit" is translated by "profit on capital" (kapitalgewinn) or "primary interest" (ursprunglicher zins). This constitutes by no means merely the harmless substitution of interest on one's own capital for contractual interest on borrowed capital, but a new assertion, namely that the entrepreneur's profit is essentially interest on capital.

---

① This explains the disharmony actually exhibited upon a first glance into Locke's theory, as Bözhm-Bawerk emphasises. (Cf. Kapital und Kapitalzins, 2 ed., I 52.)

利润。[①] 所有这些作家把利息回溯到营业利润，以此作为利息的源泉，但是他们没有说明营业利润只是利息的一种来源，虽然它的确是利息的主要来源。或许不能用利息来说明他们的“利润”，即使利息出现在“资本利润”的术语中。他们没有解决利息问题。但是，如果说他们只是把一种派生形式的利息，即贷款利息，追溯到原始的、真实的利息，而没有对原始利息进行解释，这也是不正确的。他们只是没有证明为什么拥有资本的贷款者能够索取这份利润，为什么资本市场的决定总是对资本所有者有利。更进一步说，洞察利息现象所要解决的核心问题，当然在于营业利润；不过，这并不是因为营业利润本身就是真实的利息，而是因为营业利润的存在是支付生产性利息的先决条件。最后，当然企业家是整个事情中最重要的人物；不过这也并不是因为他是真正的、最初的、典型的利息接受者所致，而是因为他是典型的利息支付者。

谈到亚当·斯密，我们仍能够察觉到某种观点的痕迹，根据这个观点，利润和利息不能简单地相重合。只有李嘉图及其追随者认为这两者是简单的同义词。直到这时，理论界才开始注意到一般营业利润中的唯一问题，实际上是利息问题；直到这时，企业家为什么能获得营业利润这个问题才归结为利息问题；最后，也是到这时，如果把英国作家写的“利润”解释为“资本利润”或者“原始利润”，那么他们的意思才被正确地表达。这决不只是毫无损害地用自有资本的利息代替了借入资本的契约利息，而且它构成了一种新的主张，即企业家的利润在本质上就是资本的利息。

---

① 这解释了由于没有真正理解洛克理论而产生的不一致，正如庞巴维克所强调的那样。（参考《资本与利息》第二版，第一篇52页）。

The following facts must have contributed to what from our standpoint dearly appears as a deviation from the right path.

First of all, this statement of the question is extraordinarily obvious. Contractual agricultural rent is certainly only a consequence of the "original" phenomenon, namely of that part of the product which is "imputable" to land. It is nothing more than the latter itself, the net return of agriculture from the landlord's point of view. Contractual wages are only the consequence of the economic productivity of labor; they are simply the net return of production from the worker's point of view. Why should it be otherwise in the case of interest? Without special reason it will not be taken to be so. The conclusion, that corresponding to contractual interest there is an original interest and that the latter is just as much the typical income of the entrepreneur as rent is the typical income of the landlord, appears to be perfectly natural, almost self-evident. In practice the entrepreneur allows for interest on his own capital-this appears as an incontestable sanction if such is necessary at all.

The surplus of the value of products over their costs, then, is really the fundamental phenomenon upon which interest is also dependent. And it arises in the hands of the entrepreneur. Is it to be wondered at that only this problem was seen and that it was hoped that everything was settled with the solution of it? Economists had just wrested themselves free of mercantilist superficialities and become accustomed to looking at the concrete goods which lay behind the money veil. It was emphasized that capital consists of concrete goods, and the tendency was to constitute this capital a special productive factor. This standpoint, once taken up, leads directly to considering interest as an element in the price of stocks of goods, and hence it has simply been identified with what the entrepreneur obtains by means of these stocks. Because interest undoubtedly came from profit, and thus represented a part of profit, the latter or at any rate the better part of it became interest unawares, quite automatically at the moment when interest was connected with the concrete goods which the entrepreneur makes use of in production.

下面的事实一定有助于解释那种从我们的观点看显然是偏离正确路径的问题。

首先，这个问题的陈述是极其明了的。签订契约的农业地租当然只是“原始”现象的一个结果，也就是可以“归属于”土地的那部分产品的一个结果。地租只是这部分产品本身，从地主的角度看，地租是农业的净收益。契约工资只是劳动的经济生产率的结果；从工人的角度看，契约工资仅仅是生产的净收益。为什么一谈到利息，情况就是另一回事了呢？如果没有特殊的原因，绝不会是这样。如果我们总结说，与契约利息相对应的还有一种原始利息，而且这种原始利息就是典型的企业家收入，就像地租是地主的典型收入一样，这个结论看起来是十分自然的，几乎是不言而喻的。实际上，企业家容许自有资本取得利息——如果这样做确实是必要的，那么这就是不可争辩的认可条件。

于是，产品价值超过其成本的那部分剩余，才真正是利息赖以存在的基本现象。剩余产生于企业家之手。仅仅看到这个问题，并且希望所有的问题都会因这个问题的解决而迎刃而解，这难道还有什么奇怪的吗？经济学家们刚刚使自己挣脱了重商主义肤浅的表面性，而开始习惯于关注货币现象背后的具体商品。他们强调说资本由具体商品组成，并且倾向于把资本看做是一种特殊的生产要素。这个观点一旦形成，直接导致的结果是，把利息看做是商品存货价格的一个因素，从而人们就把利息与企业家通过这些商品存货所得到的利润等同起来。由于利息毫无疑问地来自于利润，并且代表一部分利润，所以，利润，或者无论利润中的多大一部分，不自觉地就成为利息，这种转变是自动发生的，尤其是当利息恰好与企业家用以生产的具体商品联系在一起时。

That wages do not similarly become interest, because interest may be paid out of them, is a reflection that is remoter than one would think.

The unsatisfactory analysis of the entrepreneurial function contributed powerfully to make this view general. It is perhaps not quite correct to say that entrepreneur and capitalist were simply lumped together. But in any case one started from the observation that the entrepreneur can only make his profit with the aid of capital in the sense of a stock of goods, and placed an emphasis upon this observation which it does not deserve. One saw-and this was quite natural-in the employment of capital the characteristic function of the entrepreneur and distinguished him by it from the worker. He was regarded in principle as the employer of capital, the user of production goods, just as the capitalist was regarded as the provider of some kind of goods. The above statement of the question then readily suggests itself; it must appear simply as a more precise and more profound statement of the question concerning interest on loans.

This must obviously have had grave consequences for the interest problem. There was interest on loans because there was original interest and the latter arose in the hands of entrepreneurs. Thereby the whole apparatus for the solution of the problem was focussed on the entrepreneur. Now this led to a great number of false scents. Many attempts at explanation like the exploitation theory and some labor theories-as explanations of interest – became possible for the first time. For only when interest is linked with the entrepreneur can the idea arise of explaining it by his labor service or by labor contained in production goods or by the price struggle between entrepreneur and workers. Other attempts, such for example as all productivity theories, even though not made possible were nevertheless made essentially more obvious by this way of formulating the interest problem. It made a sound theory of entrepreneurs and capitalists impossible; it made the recognition of a special entrepreneurial profit difficult, and ruined the explanation of it from the outset. But by far the worst consequence of this interpretation was the creation of a problem

利息也可以从工资中支付，但工资并不因此也同样地转变为利息，这是远超过人们所想的一种反映。

对企业家职能的令人不满意的分析，曾为上述观点的普遍性做了有力的贡献。把企业家与资本家简单地混为一谈，可能不是十分正确的。但是无论怎样，人们是从这种观点开始的，即企业家只有借助于商品存货这样意义的资本才能获得利润，人们所强调的这个观点其实并不值得强调。人们可以看到——这是很自然的——人们可以从资本的使用中看到企业家的特殊职能，并且据此把企业家与工人区别开来。在原则上，企业家被看做是资本的雇佣者，是生产品的使用者，就像资本家被看做是某种商品的提供者一样。于是，对以上问题的阐述，就很容易地表达了自身，并且它必然也是对贷款利息问题的更明确，更深刻的表述。

显然，这一定曾对利息问题产生过重大影响。存在贷款利息，是因为有原始利息，而原始利息又产生于企业家之手。因此，解决利息问题需要的所有工具都集中在企业家身上。这样又导致了许多虚假的迹象。许多人试图用一些理论，诸如剥削理论以及某些劳动理论——来解释利息——这些尝试第一次成为可能。因为只有把利息与企业家联系在一起，那种用企业家劳务，或者用包含在生产品中的劳动，或者用企业家与工人之间的价格斗争来解释利息的观点，才会产生。其他尝试，比如所有的生产力理论，尽管尝试用它们来解释利息没有成为可能，但由于这种对利息问题的阐述，基本上也变得更加明显。这种阐述利息的方法不可能建立一套合理的有关企业家和资本家的理论；也使我们很难识别某种特殊的企业家利润，从而一开始就摧毁了对利息的解释。但这种解释的最糟糕的结果在于它产生了一个问题，这个问

that became a kind of economic *perpetuum mobile*.

Interest is, as experience teaches, a permanent income. It originates in the hands of the entrepreneur. Consequently a permanent income *sui generis* originates in the hands of the entrepreneur. And the question confronting the traditional theory of interest is: from where does it come? For more than a century theorists have been attacking this impossible, indeed meaningless, question.

Our position is entirely different. If traditional theory links up contractual interest with entrepreneurs' profits, it only traces the problem to what it believes to be its fundamental case, and has, after having done so, still to perform the main part of the task. If we succeed in linking up interest with entrepreneurs' profits, we shall have solved the whole problem, because entrepreneurs' profits themselves are not another case of interest, but something different from it which has been explained already. The statement that "there is interest on loans because there is a business profit" is only valuable as a more precise statement of the question for the prevailing theory; while for us it already has explanatory value. The question, but whence comes the business profit? which contains for the prevailing theory a summons to do its chief work, is for us settled. For us there remains only the question: *how* does interest arise from entrepreneurial profit?

It was necessary to draw the reader's attention especially to this different and narrower statement of the question in our interest problem because the objection that nothing more is done here than the reduction of interest to business profits, which theory accomplished long ago, would be particularly annoying. Thus the repeated emphasis upon things which the reader might easily have said himself is well justified. Now we shall proceed to the sixth and last proposition in our theory of interest.

8. The surplus which forms the basis of interest, being a value surplus, can only emerge in a value expression. Therefore in an exchange economy it can only be expressed in the comparison of two money sums.

题成为经济永续运动中的永久问题。

经验告诉我们，利息是一种永久性的收入，它产生于企业家之手。因此我们说，企业家手中产生了一种特殊的永久性收入。于是传统利息理论所面临的问题是：利息是从哪里来的？一个多世纪以来，理论家一直在探讨这个无法解释，并且确实是毫无意义的问题。

我们的观点完全不同。如果传统理论把契约性利息与企业家的利润联系起来，那么它只是把利息问题追溯到它所认为的基本情况，而它完成这一步以后，还需要去做利息问题的主要工作。如果我们成功地把利息与企业家利润联系起来，那么我们就能解决全部的利息问题，因为企业家利润本身并不是利息的另一种情况，它不同于利息，这一点我们已经解释过了。“贷款需要付息是因为有营业利润”的这种表述，对于当前流行的理论来说，只有作为对问题的更准确的表述才有价值；而对我们来说，早已具有解释性的价值了。然而，营业利润从何而来呢？对于流行理论而言，这个问题是要求其解决的主要问题，而对我们来说，这个问题已经解决了。我们剩下的问题只是，利息是如何从企业利润中形成的？

由于有一种特别令人烦恼的反对意见，认为我们在这里所做的只不过是把利息变成营业利润，而这一理论很早以前就被论证了，所以我们有必要在这里提请读者特别注意我们在利息问题中不同的和较狭义的说明。这样，我们反复强调那些读者自己也可能很容易说清楚的事情，就是完全恰当的了。下面我们将要说明我们的利息理论的第六个命题，也是最后一个命题。

8. 形成利息基础的剩余，是一种价值剩余，只能以价值形式表现。因此，在交换经济中，只有通过比较两笔货币量才能表现

This is self-evident, and *prima facie* completely uncontroversial. In particular, no comparison of quantities of goods can in itself assert anything about the existence of a value surplus. Wherever quantities of goods are spoken of in such a connection, they appear only as symbols of values. In practice the value expression is used and interest is represented in the money form alone. In any case we must accept this fact, but we can interpret it very variously. We might come to the conclusion that this appearance of interest in the form of money is merely dependent upon the necessity of a standard of value, and has nothing to do with the nature of interest. This is the prevailing view. According to it, money serves as the form of expression and nothing else, while interest on the contrary arises in goods of some kind as a surplus of the goods themselves. We take this view too in the case of entrepreneurial profit. A measure of value is also necessary to express it, and the money representation is therefore made use of as a matter of expediency. But in spite of this the nature of entrepreneurial profit has nothing at all to do with money.

Unquestionably it is extraordinarily tempting in the case of interest also to try to turn away from the element of money as quickly as possible and to carry the explanation of interest into the region where values and returns arise, namely in the realm of the production of goods. However, we cannot turn aside. It is true that in every case, corresponding to money interest, that is to the premium on purchasing power, there is a premium on goods of some kind. It is true that goods and not "money" are needed to produce in the technical sense. But if we conclude from this that money is only an intermediate link, merely of technical importance, and set about substituting for it the goods which are obtained with it and for which therefore in the last analysis interest is paid, we at once lose the ground from under our feet. Or more correctly expressed: we can indeed take a step or even a few steps away from the money basis into the world of commodities. But the road suddenly ends because these premiums on commodities are not permanent – and then we see at once that this road was wrong, for an essential characteristic of interest is that it is permanent. Therefore it is impossible to pierce the money veil in order to get to the premiums on concrete goods.

出这个剩余。这一点是不言而喻的，显然也是完全没有争议的。尤其是，商品数量的比较，其本身对价值剩余的存在并不能说明任何问题。在这一方面，无论何处提到商品数量，都只是作为价值符号出现。实际上，价值表现以及利息都仅仅用货币形式来表示。在任何情况下，我们都应该承认这一事实，但是我们可以用不同的方式去解释它。我们或许还能得出这样的结论：这种货币形式的利息的出现一定依存于某一价值标准，而与利息的本质没有任何关系，这就是流行的观点。据此，货币就只有表现形式的作用了，而利息则不同，它作为商品本身的一种剩余，产生于该种商品。我们对企业家利润也持相同的观点。为了表示企业家利润，也需要价值衡量单位，因而用货币表示，作为权宜之计。但是尽管如此，企业家利润的本质与货币根本没有任何关系。

对于利息，试图尽快脱离货币要素，而把对利息的解释带到价值与收益的产生地，也就是带到商品的生产领域，这无疑是极其诱人的。然而，我们不能回避问题。的确，在任何情况下，与货币利息相对应，也就是与对购买力的升水或者溢价相对应，一定存在着对某种商品的升水。从技术意义上说，生产确实需要商品而不是“货币”。但是如果我们由此而得出结论说，货币只是一个中间联系物，只在技术上有其重要性，并且打算用货币所购买的，进而最终要支付利息的商品来替代货币，那么我们就会立即失去根基而站不住脚。或者更准确地说，我们的确可以离开货币基础一步，甚至是好几步，从而进入商品世界。但是，这条路会由于这些商品的溢价不持久而突然终止——于是我们立即就会发现这条路我们走错了，因为利息的一个本质特征就是它的永久性。因此不可能通过戳破货币的面纱来走进具体商品的溢价或者升水。

If one penetrates through it one penetrates into a void. ①

Thus we cannot move away from the money basis of interest. This constitutes an indirect proof that a second interpretation of the significance of the money form in which interest encounters us is to be preferred, namely the interpretation that this money form is not shell but kernel. Obviously such a proof alone would not justify far-reaching inferences. But it fits into our earlier arguments on the subject of credit and capital, by virtue of which we can understand the rô1e played by purchasing power here. Hence as a result we can now state our sixth proposition: *interest is an element in the price of purchasing power regarded as a means of control over production goods.*

This proposition of course does not ascribe to purchasing power any productive röle. Yet most people reject it a *limine* in spite of the fact that interest fluctuates in the money market with the supply of and demand for money, which undoubtedly points to our interpretation. ② Another point may be added at once. That one gets wet when it rains is no more self-evident to the businessman than that interest falls when credit facilities increase, other things being equal. In reality, if a government were to print paper money and to lend it to entrepreneurs, would not interest fall? And would not the state be able to receive interest for it? Does not the connection of interest with rates of exchange and gold movements speak plainly enough? It is an extremely wide and significant range of everyday observations that supports us here.

Nevertheless, only a few significant theorists introduced these facts into the discussion of the interest phenomenon. Sidgwick represents an interpretation in which I perceive, with BöhmBawerk,

① Here I shall not enter further into the expedients "stock of consumption goods" and "stock of accumulated services of labor and land."

② Cf. Marshall's remarks before the Commission on the Depression of Trade. In the discussion of the relation between the quantity of money and commodity prices he says, speaking of an increase in the quantity of money: "I should say it would act at once upon Lombard Street, and make people inclined to lend more; it would swell deposits and book credits and so enable people to increase their speculation..." One Who says this (and who could deny it?) cannot reject our interpretation lightly.

如果有人想穿透它，就相当于要穿透真空。①

因此，我们不能离开利息的货币基础。这也间接证明了对货币形式重要意义的第二种解释（利息就是以货币形式出现在我们面前），即货币形式不是外壳而是核心，这种解释是很恰当的。显然，仅有这一个证据，我们还不能作进一步推导。但是，它与我们前面对信用和资本的论证是相吻合的，由前面对信用和资本的论证，我们可以理解购买力在这里所起的作用。所以现在可以陈述我们的第六个命题：利息是购买力价格中的一个要素，而购买力又被看做是控制生产品的一个工具。

这个命题当然不会赋予购买力任何生产性作用。尽管利息在货币市场上随着货币供求的变化而波动——这无疑是支持了我们的解释，② 但是多数人还是否认它。所以这里必须加上另一点。假定其他条件不变，对商人来说，信用工具的增加会使利息下降，这和下雨就会使人淋湿一样，是十分明白的。实际上，如果一个政府打算印制纸币并借给企业家，难道利息不下降吗？难道政府不会因此而得到利息吗？难道利息与汇率以及黄金运动的联系还不足以清楚地说明这一点吗？正是这些日常观察的极其广泛和有意义的领域在此支持着我们的论点。

尽管如此，只有少数有影响的理论家在讨论利息现象时引入这些事实。西奇威克提出了一种解释，我和庞巴维克都认为它实

① 这里我不想对权宜之计“消费品存货”和“累积的劳动和土地服务的存货”作进一步讨论。

② 参阅马歇尔对贸易萧条委员会的评论。在讨论货币量和商品价格之间的关系时，他说，一谈到货币量的增长，“我认为它将立即影响隆巴德大街，而且使人们倾向于借出更多的钱；它将使存款和账面信贷膨胀，并使人们能够增加他们的投机……”说这些话的人（谁又能否认它呢?）不会轻易否认我们作的解释。

essentially an abstinence theory. But before the *sedes materiae*, the chapter on interest, he treats of interest in the chapter on the value of money, and here he brings it into relation with money and recognizes the influence of the creation of purchasing power upon interest in the statement: " ... We have to consider, that the banker to a great extent produces the money he lends ... and that he may easily afford to sell the use of this commodity at a price materially less than the rate of interest on capital generally. "[①] This statement contains several points over which we cannot rejoice. Furthermore, it provides no thoroughgoing foundation for the process. Finally, no further conclusions for the theory of interest are drawn. Yet it is a step in our direction, obviously made with reference to Macleod. Davenport applies himself much more to the subject; but his analysis also comes to nothing. He rides quite nicely and willingly up to the fence but then refuses to take it. The prevailing theories completely neglect the clement of money – they leave it to the financial writers as a technical matter without theoretical interest. This attitude is so general that it must rest upon an element of truth and in any case is in need of explanation.

Least may be said for the attempt to deny the statistical connection between the interest rate and the quantity of money. R. Georges Le' vy[②] has compared the interest rote with the production of gold and, as was to be expected, found that no significant correlation exists. Neglecting the fact that the statistical method employed was defective, it does not justify the conclusion that the quantity of money and the interest rate have nothing to do with one another. In the first place, an exact time correlation is not to be expected. Then the supply of gold, even of the banks, is not simply proportional to the volume of credit granted – and only the granting of credit is significant for the rate of interest.

---

① Principles of Political Economy, 3 ed., p. 251.

② Journal des Economistes (1899).

际上是一种节约理论。但是在引用资料的来源，即讨论利息的那一章之前，他在关于货币价值的那一章谈到了利息；在这里他把利息与货币联系起来，并且承认购买力的创造对利息的影响，他说："……我们必须考虑，在很大程度上，银行家可以制造他借出的货币……同时，一般来说，他可能很容易地以大大低于资本利息率的价格卖出这种商品的使用。"[①] 这种表述包含几个观点，我们对此并不感到高兴。此外，对于分析利息的发展过程，它没有提供任何彻底可靠的基础。最后，它没有对利息理论作出进一步的结论。但是，它还是朝着我们的方向进了一步，显然是参照麦克劳德作了这一步。达文波特在这个论题上花费了更多的精力，但他的分析也没有得到任何结果。他骑马骑得很好，并且如果骑的话情愿一直骑到栅栏，但他却拒绝骑马。流行理论完全忽略了货币这一要素——而把它作为一个毫无理论意义的技术问题留给金融作家。这种态度是相当普遍的，所以它必然以某些真理成分为基础，而且无论如何都要给予解释。

对于试图否认利息率与货币量之间的统计联系的看法，没有什么好说的。R. 乔治·勒维[②]曾对利息率和黄金的生产做过比较，正如他所料，他发现两者之间没有重要的相关性。暂且不说所用的统计方法存在缺陷——这是事实，也不能得出货币量与利息率彼此互不相关的结论。因为首先，不可能期望存在精确的时间相关。其次，黄金的供给，甚至是银行的黄金供给，并不简单地与贷出的信用量成比例——只有信用的贷出才对利息率是重要

① 《政治经济学原理》第三版，第251页。

② 《经济学杂志》(1899年)。

Finally, the whole production of gold does not flow to the entrepreneur.

Nor does the inductive refutation attempted by Irving Fisher (Rate of Interest, p. 319 ff.) affect our argument. Yearly averages prove absolutely nothing as against the observations which may be made in the details of everyday dealings in money. Also, he compared the circulation of money per capita with the interest rate and thereby made the comparison completely irrelevant.

But of course economists of the eighteenth century had every reason to emphasize that interest is ultimately paid for goods. They had to fight not only mercantilistic but all sorts of other errors, both of businessmen and philosophers, and in so doing they did in fact establish valuable truths and expose a long list of popular fallacies. Law, Locke, Montesquieu, and others were undoubtedly quite wrong in making the rate of interest simply depend on the quantity of money, and Adam Smith was right in pointing out① that an increase in the quantity of money will *caeteris paribus* raise prices, and that, at a higher level, the same relation between return and capital which ruled before will tend to reestablish itself. Even the immediate effect of an increase of *money in circulation* would be to raise the rate of interest rather than to reduce it. For anticipation of such an increase must have that effect,② and in any case the demand for credit will be stimulated by the rise in prices. But all this, while it explains and to some extent justifies the aversion which most of our highest authorities display against any "monetary" theory of interest, yet has nothing whatever to do with our proposition.

We can also discover other elements of truth in the point of view "hostile to monetary explanations."③ Businessmen

---

① Cf. his short and pregnant argument in bk. II, ch. iv, of the Wealth of Nations.

② Cf. Fisher, Rate of Interest, p. 78.

③ For example its justifiable scorn of the causal connection between interest and than quantity of money in the following form: if more money exists then the value of money falls-and for this less valuable money less interest is paid. In this, of course, there is no redeeming feature. I have not discussed this interpretation at all in the text, but I believe that it has contributed largely to frightening off economists once for all from this nexus between money and interest.

的。最后，并不是所有的黄金生产都流向企业家。

即使欧文·费希尔试图进行的归纳性反驳（《利息率》第319页及以下各页）也不影响我们的论证。年平均数绝对不能提供任何与我们对日常货币交易细节的观察相对立的证据。同时，他还比较了单位资本的货币流通量与利息率，从而使这种比较与论题完全无关。

然而，18世纪的经济学家一定有理由强调说，利息最终是付给商品的。他们不仅必须同重商主义，而且还要和来自商人、哲学家的各种其他错误作斗争；通过斗争，他们实际上建立了许多价值真理，揭露了一系列普遍的谬误。劳、洛克、孟德斯鸠以及其他人，认为利息率只是依赖于货币量，无疑这是错误的；而亚当·斯密则正确地指出，[①] 如果其他情况不变，货币数量的增加将使价格提高，并且，在较高的价格水平上，收益与以前也起作用的资本之间的相同的关系，也将逐渐重新建立。甚至，流通中货币量的增加的直接影响也会使利息率上升，而不是下降。因为，对这种增长的预期一定会产生那种影响，[②] 而且在任何情况下，价格的上升都会刺激对信贷的需求。尽管这种论述可以解释，而且在某种程度上证实了为什么我们大多数的最高权威对任何“货币”利息论的反感，但是这与我们的命题没有任何关系。

我们也可以从“与货币解释相敌对的”那种观点中[③]发现真理

---

① 参阅他在《国富论》第二篇第四章所作的简短而意义深远的论证。

② 参阅费希尔的《利息率》，第78页。

③ 例如，对利息与货币量之间因果关系的有理由的蔑视可以如下表述：如果存在越多的货币，那么货币的价值就会下降——因而支付给这些价值较低的货币的利息就越少。当然，在这里不存在赎回特征。我在本文中根本没有对这种解释进行讨论，但我相信，它曾对打击经济学家起了很大的作用，因为它使经济学家永远回避货币与利息的关系。

and financial writers often emphasize the importance of discount policy and the monetary system in a wrong way. The fact that the central banks can influence the interest rate no more proves that interest is the price of purchasing power than the fact that the state can fix prices proves that prices in general are explicable by governmental action. The interest rate can no doubt be influenced by the attention paid to the state of the currency, but the theoretical significance of this fact does not in itself go far. It is a case of influencing a price for motives which lie outside the market. The view that by the monetary system and by discount policy a country's interest rate can be kept lower than that of other countries, and that such a policy stimulates economic development, is nothing but a pre-scientific prejudice. The organization of a money market is of course just as capable of improvement as that of a labor market, but nothing in the fundamental processes can be altered by this.

9. Our problem now reduces to the simple question: what are the conditions for the emergence of a premium on present over future purchasing power? Why is it that if I lend a certain number of units of purchasing power, I can stipulate for the return of a greater number of such units at some future date?

This is obviously a market phenomenon. The market we have to study is the money market. And it is a price-determining process which we have to investigate. Every individual loan transaction is a real exchange. At first it seems strange, perhaps, that a commodity is as it were exchanged for itself. After Böhm-Bawerk's arguments on this point,①however, it is not necessary to go into it in detail: the exchange of present for future is no more an exchange of like for like, and therefore meaningless, than the exchange of something in one place for something in another place. Just as purchasing power in one place may be exchanged for that in another, so present can also be exchanged for future purchasing power.

① Cf. Kapital, vol. II.

的其他成分。商人和金融作家常常以一种错误的方式强调贴现政策以及货币体系的重要性。中央银行能够影响利息率，但这一事实能够证实利息是购买力的价格的程度，与政府能够控制价格这一事实来证实一般价格水平，可以由政府行为来解释的程度差不多。无疑，对通货状况的关注程度影响利息率，但是这一事实的理论意义本身并不很重要。这是市场之外的动机影响价格的一种情况。那种认为利用货币体系和贴现政策，一个国家就可以保持其利息率低于其他国家，进而这种政策可以刺激经济发展的观点，只不过是一种未经科学论证的偏见。一个货币市场组织，就像劳动市场的组织一样，当然也可能改进，但是在根本过程中的任何东西不会因此而改变。

9. 现在我们的论题可以归结为一个简单的问题：当前购买力超过未来购买力的额外费用，其产生条件是什么？如果我借出一定数量单位的购买力，为什么我可以规定在未来某一天收回更大的数目？

显然这是一个市场现象。我们必须研究货币市场，它是一个我们必须考察的价格决定过程。每一个体的贷款交易都是一个真实的交换。起初它看起来或许有些奇怪，因为商品竟然与其自身相交换。但自从庞巴维克对这一点论证以后，[①] 就没有必要再对下面命题进行详细论述了：当前与未来的交换，并不是相同事物之间的交换，因而是没有意义的；它像是某地的事物与另一地的事物相交换。正像某地的购买力可以用来交换另一地的购买力一样，当前的购买力也能交换未来的购买力。赊购交易与外汇

① 参阅《资本》第二卷。

The analogy between loan transactions and exchange arbitrage is obvious, and may be recommended to the reader's attention.

If we succeed in proving that under certain circumstances – let us say at once in the case of development-present purchasing power must regularly be at a premium over future purchasing power in the money market, then the possibility of a permanent flow of goods to the possessors of purchasing power is theoretically explained. The capitalist can then obtain a permanent income which behaves in every respect as if it arose in the circular flow, although its sources are individually not permanent and although they are the results of development. And no imputation or computation can alter anything in the character of this stream of goods as a net return.

We can now state directly how high the total value of an interminable annuity must be. It must be the sum which, if lent at interest, will yield a return equal to the annuity, for if it were less, lenders would compete to buy the annuity, and if it were more, potential buyers would rather lend their money at interest than buy it. This is the real rule of "capitalization" which already pre – supposes the existence of a rate of interest. From this it follows again that the valuation of permanent returns cannot take away the character of net incomes from them.

Therefore we answer all three questions of which the interest problem consists if we solve the problem of the premium on present purchasing power. The proof of a permanent flow of goods to capitalists, from which no deduction is to be made and which is not to be passed on to other individuals, completely settles the matter and explains *ipso facto* that this flow also represents a gain, that it is a net return. We shall now proceed to produce this proof and enfold step by step our explanation of the many sided problem of interest.

10. It has been said already that even in the circular flow cases may and will arise in which people will be ready to borrow even on the condition of having to pay back a larger sum than they receive. Whatever the

套利有明显的相似处，这一点请读者注意。

如果我们成功地证明了，在一定条件下——让我们就假定在发展的情况下——在货币市场上，当前购买力的价值按常规必然超过未来购买力额外费用部分，那么就从理论上解释了商品流永久地流向购买力持有者的可能性。于是，资本家可以得到永久性收入，这笔永久性收入在各方面看起来都好像是产生于循环流转中，尽管它的来源，单个来说并不是永久的，并且尽管它们都是发展的结果。任何归属和计算都不能改变这个作为净收益的商品流的特征。

我们现在可以直接说，一笔永续年金的总价值应该有多高。它应该是一笔总数，即，如果它以利息为目的而被借出去，将产生一笔相当于年金的收益，因为如果利息低于年金，出借者就会竞争购买年金，如果利息高于年金，潜在的年金购买者将宁愿贷款来获取利息，而不购买年金。这是“资本化”的真正原则，它已经预先假定存在一个利息率。从这一点，我们再说一遍，对永久性收益的估价不能脱离它们作为纯收入的特征。

因此，如果我们解决了当前购买力额外费用的问题，我们就回答了构成利息问题的所有这三个问题。证明存在流向资本家的永久商品流，对这种永久商品流不再作扣除，而且它也不会流向其他人，这个论证完全解决了问题，并且根据事实，它解释了这种流动也代表一种利得，也就是一种净收益。我们现在将进行这一论证，并且逐步完成对这个多方面的利息问题的说明。

10. 我们已经说过，甚至在循环流转中也可能发生而且确实将发生人们打算借款的情况，甚至在归还的数额将大于他们借到的数额的情况下，他们也会借款。不管出于什么动机——暂时的

motive-temporary distress, expectation of a future increase in income, weakness of will, or foresight-such people will be able to express their valuation of present purchasing power in terms of future purchasing power, which determines their demand curve for the former in the ordinary way. On the other hand, there may be, and generally will be, people ready to meet this demand provided they get a premium which more than compensates them for the disturbance which the lending of sums held for definite purposes must entail. Therefore we can also construct supply curves, and it is hardly necessary to show in detail how a price-a determined premium-will emerge in this market.

But transactions of this kind could not normally be of any great importance and, above all, *they would not be necessary elements in the conduct of business.* Lending and borrowing can become part of the normal routine of industry and commerce, and interest can economically and socially acquire the importance that it actually has, only if the control of present purchasing power means more future purchasing power to *the borrower.* As the prospect of business profit is the pivot on which the valuation of sums of present purchasing power actually turns, we shall now put aside for the moment all other factors which may give rise to interest even where there is no development.

Now within the circular flow and in a market which is in equilibrium it is impossible with a given money sum to obtain a greater money sum. However I employ a hundred monetary units' worth of resources (including management) within the generally known and customary possibilities, I can obtain no greater receipts from them than exactly a hundred monetary units. To whichever of the existing possibilities of production I may apply any hundred monetary units I shall always receive for the product not more- possibly less, however-than a hundred monetary units. For that is precisely the characteristic of the equilibrium position, that it represents the "best" combination-under the given conditions in the widest sense-of the productive forces. The value of the monetary unit is in this sense necessarily at par, for *ex hypothesi* all arbitrage gains have already been made and are therefore excluded. If I buy the services of labor and land with the hundred monetary units,

贫困、预期未来收入增长、意志薄弱，或者对未来的展望——这些人能够根据未来的购买力表达他们对当前购买力的估价，这就以通常的方式决定了他们对当前购买力的需求曲线。另一方面，可能会有，而且通常就会有人愿意满足这种需求，只要他们能得到一笔溢价，这笔溢价足以补偿他们因借出这笔原本为特定目的而保存的款项所带来的麻烦，而且补偿还有节余。因此，我们也可以构造供给曲线，至于详细说明那种价格——被决定的溢价——是如何在这个市场上出现的，几乎就是不必要的了。

但是，这种交易通常并不重要，而且，首先要注意，它们不是日常经营活动中的必要条件。只要对当前购买力的控制意味着在将来能给借款者带来更多的购买力，那么借和贷就能成为工商业日常事务的一部分，利息才能在经济上和社会上获得其实际的重要性。由于商业利润的前景是对当前实际表现的购买力进行估价的关键，所以我们现在暂且把那些甚至是在没有发展的情况下也可能产生利息的所有其他因素放在一边。

于是，在循环流转以及处于均衡状态的市场中，人们不可能用一定量的货币得到更大数目的货币。然而，在众人皆知以及习惯可能的范围内，我使用一百货币单位价值的资源（包括管理），从中我也只能刚好得到一百货币单位的收入，不会更多。无论我把一百货币单位用于当前哪一种可能的生产过程，我总是从该产品中仅得到一百货币单位，不会更多——倒有可能更少。因为这正是均衡状态的特征，它反映了各种生产力量的“最佳”组合——在一定的条件下，并从最广泛的意义上说。在这个意义上，货币单位的价值必然等于其票面价值，因为我们假定所有的套利收益已经得到了，所以应该排除这种情况。如果我用这一百货币单位

and with these carry out the most lucrative production,I shall find that I can market the product for exactly a hundred monetary units. It was precisely with regard to these most lucrative possibilities of employment that the values and prices of the means of production were established, and this most lucrative employment also determines the value of purchasing power in our sense.

Only in the course of development is the matter different. Only then can I obtain a higher return for my product,that is,if I carry out a new combination of the productive forces which I bought for a hundred monetary units and succeed in putting a new product of higher value on the market. For the prices of the means of production were not determined with regard to this employment,but only with regard to the previous uses. Here,then,the possession of a sum of money is the means of obtaining a bigger sum. On this account,and to this extent,a present sum will be normally valued more highly than a future sum. Therefore present sums of money-so to speak as potentially bigger sums-will have a value premium,which will also lead to a price premium. *And in this lies the explanation of interest.* In development the giving and taking of credit become an essential part of the economic process. There,the phenomena appear which have been described by the expressions "relative scarcity of capital" and "the lagging of the supply of capital behind the demand" and so forth. Only if and because the social stream of goods becomes broader and richer does interest stand out with such sharpness and bring us finally so vary much under its influence that long analytical effort is required to perceive that it does not always appear where men act economically.

11. Let us now look more closely into the process of the formation of interest. After what has been said this means that we shall examine more closely the method of determining the price of purchasing power. To this end let us confine ourselves first of all strictly to the case which we recognized as the fundamental one, and to which the argument of the earlier chapters was also directed, namely to the case of exchange between entrepreneurs and capitalists. Later we shall pursue the most important ramifications of the interest phenomenon.

购买劳动和土地服务，并用它们从事最有利的生产，我就会发现，用生产的产品在市场上恰好可以得到一百货币单位。正是根据这些最有利的、可行的使用方式，生产资料的价值和价格才被确立，这种最有利的使用方式还决定了我们所说的购买力的价值。

只有在发展的过程中，情况才有所不同。只有在那时，如果我用一百货币单位购买生产能力，对其实施新的组合，并成功地把具有较高价值的新产品投入市场，那么我才会从我的新产品中获得较高的收益。因为生产资料的价格不是根据这个新的用途，而是根据原先的用途来决定的。于是，在这里，拥有一笔钱是获得更大数目的货币的条件。因此，在这个程度上，人们通常认为当前的一笔钱比未来的这笔钱有更高的价值。所以，现在的钱数——也可以说是潜在的更多的钱数——将有一个价值升水，这也将导致价格升水。在这里可以找到对利息的解释。在发展中，提供信用以及取得信用已成为经济过程的重要的一部分。在那里，被描述为“资本的相对稀缺”、“资本供给滞后于需求”等等，这些表达的现象就会发生。只有，而且也因为，社会的商品流变得越来越宽，越来越丰富，利息才会如此鲜明突出地表现出来，并且最终这样有力地使我们深受其影响，以至于我们必须经过长期的努力分析才能觉察到，并不是在人们经济活动的任何地方都会出现利息。

11. 现在让我们更加仔细地研究利息的形成过程。经过以上的论述，这意味着我们将更加严密地考察购买力价格的决定方法。为此，我们首先严格地限定我们的研究情况，我们认为这种情况是基本的，并且在以前章节中也曾讨论过，也就是企业家与资本家之间的交易情况。后面我们将探索利息现象的最重要的

Under our present assumptions, the only people who have a higher estimation for present as against future purchasing power are the entrepreneurs. Only they are the bearers of that market movement in favor of present money, of that demand which raises the price of money above par as we define it.

Capitalists on the supply side confront entrepreneurs on the demand side. Let us start with the assumption that the necessary means of payment for carrying out new combinations must be withdrawn from the circular flow and that there is no creation of credit means of payment. Furthermore, since we are considering an economy without results of previous development, there are no great reservoirs of idle purchasing power, for these are, as was shown above, only created by development. A capitalist would thus be one who is ready under certain conditions to transfer a definite sum to the entrepreneur by withdrawing it from its customary uses, that is by restricting his expenditure either in production or in consumption. We still assume that the quantity of money in the system does not increase in any other way, for example through gold discoveries.

Exchange will develop between entrepreneurs and possessors of money and will proceed just as in any other case. We have definite demand and supply curves for all the exchanging individuals. The entrepreneur's demand is determined by the profit which he can make with the help of a certain money sum by exploiting the possibilities hovering before him. We shall follow the practice of assuming these demand curves to be continuous just as we do in the case of other goods, although a very small loan, say of a few monetary units, will be of little use to the entrepreneur, and at certain points, namely where important innovations become possible, the individual demand curves will in fact be discontinuous. Beyond a certain point, namely beyond the sum which is necessary to the carrying out of all the plans which the entrepreneur has thought of at all, his demand will fall sharply, perhaps absolutely to zero. However, in considering the whole economic process, that is in considering very many entrepreneurs, these circumstances lose much of their importance.

细节。

在我们现在的假设条件下，只有那些对当前购买力的估价高于未来购买力价值的人才是企业家。只有他们看好当前货币的市场运动，支持那种使货币价格提高到我们所说的票面价值之上的需求。

处于供给一方的资本家与处于需求一方的企业家相对立。让我们以下面的假设开始，即实施新组合所必需的支付手段一定要从循环流转中提取，并且没有创造信用支付手段。此外，由于我们所考虑的是一个不存在先前发展结果的经济体，所以也就没有庞大的闲置购买力的积存，如上所述，因而只有发展才会创造出这些购买力的蓄水池。所以，资本家就是这样一种人，在一定条件下，他愿意将一定金额从其通常的用途中抽出来，也就是从限制他的生产或者消费中抽出来，转移给企业家。我们还假定，系统中的货币量不会以其他方式增加，比如发现金矿。

企业家和货币所有者之间的交易将会发展，而且就像任何其他情况一样，会继续进行下去。我们已经为所有参与交换的个体确定了需求和供给曲线。企业家的需求是由他借助一定量的货币开拓萦绕在他面前的生产可能性，所取得的利润决定的。尽管一笔小的贷款，比如说很少的货币单位，对企业家来说没有什么用途，而且在那些可能形成重要创新的特定的位置上，个人的需求曲线实际上是不连续的，但我们还是像对待其他商品的需求曲线那样，假定这些需求曲线是连续的。超过了一定点，也就是超过了实施企业家曾经想到过的所有计划所必需的金额，他的需求就会急剧下降，也许会绝对地达到零。然而，在考虑经济过程整体时，也就是考虑众多的企业家时，这些情况会大大失去其重要性。

Therefore we shall imagine that the entrepreneur is able to attach determined quantities of entrepreneurial profit to the individual monetary units from zero to the limit for practical purposes, in the same way as every individual attaches certain values to the successive units of any good.

Any normal individual's valuation of his stock of money per economic period follows from the subjective exchange value of any unit, as was explained in the first chapter. The same rules are also valid for an increase in money beyond this accustomed stock. From this there results a definite utility curve for every individual, and from this again, according to well known principles, a definite curve of the potential supplies on the money market.① And now we have to describe the "price struggle" between entrepreneurs and potential suppliers of money.

Let us assume as a starting point that upon our money market, which might be regarded as similar to a stock exchange, someone offers a certain price for purchasing power by way of experiment. Under our present assumptions this price would have to be very high, since the lender would have to disturb severely all his private and business arrangements. Suppose then that this price of present purchasing power expressed in future purchasing power is 140 for one year. With a premium of 40 per cent only those entrepreneurs could exercise an effective demand who hoped to make an entrepreneurial profit of at least 40 per cent, or more correctly of over 40 per cent; all others would be excluded. Assume that a certain number of the former existed. According to the principle "better to exchange with small advantage than not to exchange at all,"② these entrepreneurs will really be ready to pay this interest rate for a certain quantity of purchasing power. On the other side of the market there will likewise be lenders who will not exchange even at this rate. Assuming again that a number of people considered this compensation to be adequate,

---

① Cf. for details Wesen, bk. II. Here we are not concerned with an elaborate ex-position of the theory of prices.

② Cf. Böhm-Bawerk, Kapital, vol. II.

因此，我们假设企业家能够从零到实际需要的最大金额之间，确定每货币单位所得到的企业家利润量，就像每个人都能对任何商品的各单位确定一定价值一样。

正如我们在第一章说明的那样，任何人对其在每一经济时期所拥有的货币存量的正常的估价，依赖于对每一单位货币的主观交换价值。这个规律也适用于超过常规存量的增加的货币量。由此，我们可以得到每个人的确定的效用曲线，还可以从这里，根据众所周知的原理，得到一条明确的货币市场的潜在供给曲线。① 现在，我们必须来描述企业家与潜在的货币供给者之间的“价格斗争”。

作为一个出发点，我们假定这里的货币市场，可以视同一个证券交易所，有人尝试对购买力提出一定的价格。在我们现有的假设下，这个价格一定非常高，因为借出者必然严重地打乱了所有他个人的以及业务的安排。于是假定，用未来购买力表示的当前购买力的价格是140，期限一年。在40%的升水下，只有那些有希望至少获得40%，或者更确切地说获得超过40%的企业利润的企业家，才能产生有效需求；其他人都不会产生有效需求。假设存在一定数量的这些人，根据“薄利多销比一点不交换要好”的原则，② 这些企业家真正愿意为获得一定量的购买力而按这个利息率支付。在市场的另一边，同样也存在着甚至不愿以这样的利率进行交换的借方。让我们再假定，有一些人认为这种补偿是合

① 详见《本质》第二篇。在这里，我们不打算对价格理论作详尽的说明。

② 参阅庞巴维克的《资本》第二卷。

they would ponder the question of how much they should lend. The 40 percent is only a sufficient compensation for a certain sum; for everyone there is a limit beyond which the magnitude of the sacrifice in the present economic period must exceed the magnitude of the increase in utility in the next. But the loan must also be actually so big that an increase would result in a surplus of disadvantage, for as long as it is smaller the lending of further monetary units at that rate would afford a surplus of advantage which, according to general principles, no individual can forego.

Supply and demand, therefore, are unequivocally determined in every such case of a "tentative" price. If they were by accident equally great, then the price would stand, in our case, a rate of interest of 40 percent. If the entrepreneurs, however, can use more money at this rate than is supplied, they will outbid one another, whereupon some will drop out and new lenders will appear until equilibrium is attained. If the entrepreneurs cannot use as much money as is supplied at this rate, then the lenders will underbid one another, whereupon some of them will drop out and new entrepreneurs will appear until equilibrium is attained. Thus in the exchange struggle on the money market a definite price for purchasing power will be established just as on any other market. And since, as a rule, both parties value present more highly than future money-the entrepreneur because present money signifies more future money for him, the lender because under our assumptions present money makes possible the orderly course of his economic activity while future money is merely added to his income —the price will practically always be above par.

The result of our discussion up to this point may be expressed in terms of the marginal theory, just as in the case of any price-determining process. On the one hand interest will be equal to the profit of the "last entrepreneur," who is simply the one who anticipates from carrying out his project a profit which just makes the interest payment possible. If we rank entrepreneurs- with due regard to

算的，他们考虑的问题是应该借入多少钱。40% 只是对一定范围内的金额才是足够的补偿，因为每一个人都有一个最高限度，超过这个限度，他在本经济时期内所做的牺牲必将超过下一时期可能增加的效用。但是实际上，贷款额一定还是会达到这个最高限度，再增加一点点都是得不偿失的；因为如果贷款额小于这个限额，那么以这个利率继续借出货币单位，将会得到一点盈余，根据一般原理，没有人会放弃借出货币。

因此，供给与需求确实是在这种“暂时的”价格下决定的。如果碰巧供需数量相等，那么在我们的例子里，这个价格就表示为 40% 的利息率。然而，如果以这个利率企业家需要的货币比所供给的货币多，企业家之间就会竞相抬高价格，这样某些企业家就会被挤出竞争，同时会出现新的借出者，直到供需均衡。如果在这个利率下，企业家所需要的货币量还不到所供给的货币量，那么贷款者之间就会竞相压低价格，这样其中的一些贷款者会被挤出，同时会出现新的企业家，直到供需均衡。所以，在货币市场的交易斗争中，会建立一个确定的购买力价格，就像在其他市场上一样。而且，通常由于双方对现值的估计要高于对未来货币的估价——这对于企业家来说，是因为现在的货币对他意味着更多的未来货币；而对于贷款者来说则是因为，在我们的假定下，当前的货币使他能够有条理地安排他的经济活动，而未来的货币只会增加他的收入——实际上价格总是高于票面价值。

我们讨论到这里的结果，就像其他任何价值决定过程一样，也可以用边际理论来表达。一方面，利息将等于“最后一个企业家”的利润，这个“最后一个企业家”预期从他实施的项目中所能得到的利润，恰好足以支付利息。如果我们给企业家进行排队

the element of variation in risk-in a row according to the size of the profits which they hope to make, so that the "borrowing capacity" of the entrepreneurs falls the further we advance in the row, and if we think of this array as continuous, then there must always be at least one entrepreneur whose profit exactly equals the interest and who stands between those who make bigger profits and those who are excluded from exchanging on the money market because their profit is smaller than the interest to be paid. In practice the "last" or "marginal" entrepreneur must also retain a small surplus, but there will be at times entrepreneurs for whom this surplus is so small that they can only exercise a demand for purchasing power at the actually ruling interest and not at a higher rate by however small an amount. These are in the position which corresponds to the theoretical marginal entrepreneur. We can say, then, that interest must in every case be equal to the smallest entrepreneurial profit that will be actually realized. With this statement we approach again the usual interpretation.

On the other hand interest must also be equal to the value estimate of a last or marginal capitalist for his money. The concept of such a marginal capitalist is attained *mutatis mutandis* in just the same way as that of the marginal entrepreneur. It can easily be seen that from this standpoint interest must be equal to the valuation of the last lender, and further, that the latter must also be equal to the valuation of the last entrepreneur. It is also obvious how this result could be developed further-it has already been done often in economic literature. Only one point must still be mentioned. The last lender's valuation rests upon the importance which he attaches to the habitual course of his economic life; and this may be expressed by saying that the loan involves a sacrifice, and indeed for the marginal capitalist a "marginal sacrifice," that corresponds to the valuation of the increase in income by the receipt of interest. Then interest is also equal to the greatest or marginal sacrifice that must be made in order to satisfy the existing demand for money at a given rate of interest.

——考虑风险的变化因素——根据企业家期望获得的利润大小来排队，使企业家的“借款能力”在队列中逐渐下降，同时，如果我们把这个排列看做是连续的，那么必然会有，至少有一个企业家，他的利润恰好等于利息，这个企业家正好处于那些能获得较大利润的企业家和被排除在货币市场交易之外的企业家中间，那些被排除在交易外的企业家，是因为他们的利润小于要支付的利息。实际上，“最后的”和“边际的”企业家也可能保留一个小的剩余，但有时会存在这样的企业家，对他们来说，这个小的剩余太小了，以至于他们只有按照实际流行的利率才能产生购买力需求，而利息率任何微小的上升都会使这个需求消失。这些企业家相当于理论上的边际企业家。于是，我们可以说，在任何情况下，利息必然等于实际中实现的最微小的企业家利润。通过这样表达，我们又接近通常的解释了。

另一方面，利息也必须等于最后一个或边际的资本家对其货币的估价。这种边际资本家的概念，可以用与得到边际企业家的概念相同的方法，经过必要的修改而得到。我们可以容易地看出，根据这个观点，利息必然等于最后一个贷款者的估价，进一步说，最后一个贷款者的估价必须等于最后一个企业家的估价。同样明显的是，这个结果是如何进一步发展的——这在经济学文献中经常做。还有一点必须提到：最后一个借出者对其货币的估价，依赖于他对习惯了的经济生活过程的重视程度；我们可以这样说来表达这个意思，即贷款包含一种牺牲，而且对于边际资本家来说，这确实是一种“边际的牺牲”，这个“边际的牺牲”相当于对利息收入所引起的收入增加的估价。所以利息也等于在给定的利息率下，为满足现有的货币需求所必须作出的最大或者边际

And with this we approach the method of expression of the abstinence theory.

12. Interest would have to be determined in this way if industrial development were actually financed with the resources of the circular flow. However, we observe that interest is also paid for purchasing power created *ad hoc*, namely for credit means of payment. This leads us back to the results which were developed in the second and third chapters of this book, and it is time to introduce them here. We saw there that in a capitalist society, industrial development could in principle be carried out solely with credit means of payment. We now adopt this conception. Let it be remembered once more that the great reservoirs of money which actually exist arise as a consequence of development and must therefore be left out of account at first.

By the introduction of this element our previous picture of reality is altered but is not made unusable in its main features. What we said about the demand side of the money market remains provisionally unaltered. Now as before, the demand comes from the entrepreneurs and indeed in the same way as in the case just considered. Only on the side of supply is there much alteration. Supply is now put upon another basis; a new source of purchasing power, of a different nature, appears, which does not exist in the circular flow. The supply also comes from different people now, from differently defined "capitalists," whom we call "bankers" in conformity with what was said earlier. The exchange, to which interest owes its origin in this case and which, according to our interpretation, is also typical of all other exchanges concerning money in modern society, takes place between entrepreneur and banker.

Hence we shall have grasped the fundamental case in the phenomenon of interest if we can give the conditions governing the supply of credit means of payment. We know already by what forces this supply is regulated: first with regard to possible failures by entrepreneurs, and secondly with regard to the possible depreciation of the credit means of payment. We can eliminate the first element from our consideration. For this purpose we only need to consider an addition for risk, which is known empirically, as included once for all

的牺牲。至此，我们接近表述节欲理论的方法了。

12．如果产业的发展确实是依靠循环流转中的资源来融资的，那么利息一定以上述方式决定。然而，我们也注意到，对特意创造出来的购买力，即信用支付工具，也要支付利息。这又把我们带回到本书第二章和第三章所得到的结果，现在正是介绍它们的时候了。我们知道，在资本主义社会，产业的发展在原则上可以仅仅依靠信用支付手段来实现。我们现在接受这个观点。让我们再一次记住，实际存在的巨大的货币蓄水池是发展的一个结果，所以必须首先不予考虑。

我们以前对现实的描绘，由于这种信用支付手段的介入而被改变，但它的主要方面还是有用的。我们对货币市场需求方面所说的话暂时不会改变。就像以前一样，现在的需求仍然来自企业家，而且的确以上述同样的方式。只有货币市场的另一方，即供给方，有较大的改变。现在供给处于另一基础之上，出现了一种新的、具有不同性质的购买力来源，这种购买力来源在循环流转中是不存在的。现在，供给也来自于不同的人，来自不同含义的“资本家”，遵照我们前面所说的，我们将其称为“银行家”。在这种情况下，作为利息起源的借贷交易，根据我们的解释，也具有现代社会所有有关货币的交易的典型特征，这发生在企业家与银行家之间。

因此，如果我们能够提供支配信用支付手段的条件，我们就将把握利息现象的根本情况。我们已经知道，凭借什么力量可以调节供给：首先要考虑企业家可能失败，其次要考虑信用支付手段可能会贬值。在这里我们可以不考虑第一个要素。为此，我们只需考虑加上风险因素，这是从经验中得知的，并且总是把它包括

in the "par price of the loan." This means that if it is known from experience that one percent of loans is irrecoverable then we shall say that the banker receives the same sum that he lent if he actually receives an additional 1.01 percent approximately from all debts which are not bad. And there is, of course, an element of wages for the professional activity of the banker, which we also neglect. The size of the supply will then only be determined by the second element, that is with regard to the necessity of avoiding a difference in value between the newly created and the existing purchasing power. We must show that the value-and price-determining process also creates a premium on the newly created purchasing power.

In the case previously treated it was not wholly impossible that negative interest should occur. It might possibly occur in that case if the demand for money for new enterprises were smaller than the offers by those people to whom a "favor would be done" in temporarily taking charge of their money. Here, however, this is excluded. The banker who received back less than he gave would suffer a loss; he would have to cover the deficiency, since he would not be able completely to meet the claims upon him. Therefore in this case interest cannot fall below zero. But it will in general be above zero, because entrepreneurs' demand for purchasing power is distinguished in one important respect from the ordinary demand for goods. Demand in the circular flow must always be supported by an actual supply of goods or else it is not "effective." The entrepreneur's demand for purchasing power, however, in contrast to his demand for the concrete goods which he needs, is not subject, to this condition.

On the contrary, it is only restricted by the much less stringent condition that the entrepreneur will be able later on to repay the loan with interest. Since, even if there were no interest, the entrepreneur would only demand credit in the event of his being able to make a profit with the help of the loan-for otherwise he would have no economic incentive to produce-we can also say that the entrepreneur's demand is subject to the condition or is effective upon the condition that he can make a profit with the loan.

在“贷款的票面价值”中。这意味着，如果我们从经验中得知，贷款的1%收不回来，那么，如果银行家从其所有可以收回的债务中实际获得了额外的大约1.01%的利息，我们就可以说，他收到了与其借出数额相等的收入。当然，其中还含有作为银行家的职业活动的工资成分，我们也将其忽略。所以供给的大小将只决定于第二个要素，也就是只要考虑避免新创造的购买力与现有购买力之间的价值差异。我们必须表明，价值和价格的决定过程也对新创造的购买力增加了额外费用。

在先前论述的情况下，出现负利息也不是完全不可能的。如果新事业的货币需求小于那些愿意提供货币的人所供给的货币量，提供货币的人认为哪怕暂时索要他们的钱也是给他们“带来好处”，那么负利息就可能出现。不过，这里排除这种情况。因为如果银行家收回的钱少于他借出去的钱，他就遭受了亏损；这样他就不能偿付其全部债务，他就不得不设法弥补这个亏损，因此，在这种情况下，利息不可能降到零以下。

然而一般情况下，利息率将高于零，因为企业家对购买力的需求有一个重要的方面，这不同于对普通商品的需求。在循环流转中，需求必然总是有实际的商品供给来支持，否则它就不是“有效需求”。然而，企业家对购买力的需求较其对具体商品的需求而言，前者不受这个条件的限制。

相反，它只受制于一个不很严格的条件，即企业家今后要有能力还本付息。由于企业家只有在借助于贷款就可以获利的情况下，才会对信贷产生需求（即使在利息为零时也是如此）——否则他就没有进行生产的经济刺激——所以我们也可以说，企业家的需求受制于一个条件，或者说在利用贷款就可以牟利的条件下，

This leads to the relation between supply and demand. In any kind of economic situation whatever, the number of possible innovations is practically unlimited, as was explained in the second chapter. Even the richest economic system is not absolutely perfect and cannot be so. Improvements can always be made, and the striving after improvements is always limited by the given conditions and not by the perfection of what exists. Every step forward opens new prospects. Every improvement leads further away from the appearance of absolute perfection. The possibility of profit, therefore, and with it the "potential demand," have no definite limit. Consequently the demand with interest at zero would always be greater than the supply, which is always limited.

However, these possibilities of profit are powerless and unreal if they are not supported by the entrepreneur's personality. So far we only know that profit-yielding innovations are "possible" in economic life; we do not even know whether they will always be taken up by concrete individuals in such measure that the demand for purchasing power with interest at zero is always greater than the supply. We may go still further. The fact that economic systems without development may exist teaches us that individuals who are capable and inclined to carry out such innovations may even not exist at all. May it not be concluded from this that such individuals may also possibly exist in such a small number that the supply of purchasing power is not exhausted, instead of being insufficient for the satisfaction of all? There would be no creation of purchasing power at all and the total supply of credit means of payment would simply disappear① if no demand for purchasing power, or only an insignificant one, existed.

---

① To avoid misunderstandings it may be remarked that it would be possible for exchanges in the Circular flow to be effected with the help of credit means of payment. These would circulate without interest and at par. But in order that there may be an incentive to create more credit means of payment interest is certainly necessary,

企业家的需求才是有效的。这又联系到供求关系，无论在哪一种经济形势下，可能的创新数目实际上是无限的，这一点在第二章已经说明了。即使是最富裕的经济系统也不会绝对地完善，而且也不可能如此。总是要不断地改进，而追求改进的这种努力总是要受到一定条件的限制，但不受到对现有条件完善的限制。每前进一步都将展现新的前景。每一项改进都会使经济系统远离看上去是绝对完美的状态。因此，产生利润的可能性，以及由此所产生的“潜在的需求”，就没有一个确定的限度。所以，如果利息为零，贷款的需求就总会大于供给，而供给总是有限的。

然而，如果没有企业家人格的支持，这些获得利润的可能性就是无力的和不真实的。直到这里，我们仅仅知道在经济生活里，产生利润的创新是“可能的”；我们甚至不知道，这些创新是否总是被具体的个人所利用，而且达到这种程度，也就是在利率为零时，他们对购买力的需求总是大于供给。我们还可以进一步讨论。可能存在没有发展的经济体系，这一事实告诉我们，有能力并且愿意实现这种创新的人甚至可能根本不存在。由此，我们是否可以说，这种可能存在的个体的数量是这样少，以至于购买力的供给不能被完全吸收，而不是供给不足以满足所有的需求。如果没有对购买力的需求，或者只有一个微不足道的需求，那么就根本不会有任何购买力的创造，而且所有供给的信用支付手段就会完全消失。[①] 但是只要还存在企业家对信用的需求，哪怕一点

① 为了避免误解，应该提请注意，在循环流转中借助于信用支付手段进行交易是可能的。这种交易可以在无利息并且以票面价值的情况下进行循环，但是，如果要刺激创造更多的信用支付手段，就一定需要有利息。

But if *any* entrepreneurs' demand for credit exists at all, then it is impossible for it to be smaller than the supply with interest at zero. For the appearance of one entrepreneur facilitates the appearance of others. In the sixth chapter it will be shown that the obstacles with which innovations are confronted become smaller the more a community gets accustomed to the appearance of such innovations, and that in particular the technical difficulties in founding new enterprises become smaller because connections with foreign markets, credit forms, and so on, when once created, benefit the epigoni of the pioneers. Therefore the greater the number of people who have already successfully founded new businesses, the less difficult it becomes to act as an entrepreneur. It is a matter of experience that successes in this sphere, as in all others, draw an ever-increasing number of people in their wake, hence that continually more people proceed to carry out new combinations. The demand for capital of itself continually engenders new demand. And there fore on the money market there is a limited effective supply, how ever big it may be, as against an effective demand which has no definite limit at all.

This must raise interest above zero. As soon as it comes into existence many entrepreneurs are eliminated, and as it rises more and more of them disappear. For although possibilities of profit are practically unlimited, they differ in size and most of them are of course only small. The appearance of interest again increases the supply which is not absolutely fixed, but interest must and will nevertheless continue to exist. A price struggle is started on the money market, which we shall not describe again, and under the influence of all elements of the economic system a definite price for purchasing power is established which must contain interest.

13. We have now to connect the empirical facts, which we have so far excluded, with the fundamental principle relating to interest. First we must enumerate all those sources of existing, in contrast to newly created, purchasing power which actually feed the great money-market reservoir; and secondly we must show how interest spreads from its quite narrow basis over the whole exchange economy, permeates as it were the whole economic system, so that

点，那么，在利息为零时，这个需求就不会小于供给。因为一个企业家的出现会促使出现其他企业家。我们在第六章将表明，随着一个社会对这种创新的出现越来越习惯，这种创新所面临的障碍就会变得越来越小，尤其是创建一个新企业在技术上的困难，将会因与国外市场、信贷形式等等的联系而变得越来越小，因为这种联系一旦建立，追随于前人的后人们将会受益。因此，已经成功地创办新企业的人数越多，作为一个企业家他所面临的困难就越少。经验告诉我们，在这个领域获得成功，就像在所有其他方面一样，会吸引越来越多的追随者，因此从事新组合的人会不断增加。对资本的需求，其本身就不断地产生新的需求。因此，在货币市场上，不论有效供给有多大，它都是有限的，与其相对应的是有效需求，而这是没有任何确定限制的。

这就必然把利率提高到零之上。只要存在大于零的利率，许多企业家就会被淘汰，而且利率越高，被淘汰的企业家就越多。因为，尽管获得利润的可能性实际上是无限的，但是这些可能性的大小不同，而且当然其中的大部分是很小的。利息的出现又一次使供给量增加，这不是绝对固定的，但是利息必定并且将继续存在。一场价格斗争会在货币市场上展开，我们不打算再对此描述，在经济系统的所有要素的影响下，对购买力的一个明确的价格就会确立，其中必然包含利息。

13. 现在我们必须把我们至此一直排除在外的经验事实与有关利息的基本原理联系起来。首先，我们必须列举所有现存的而不是新创造的购买力的来源，实际上是它们填充着巨大的货币市场的蓄水池；其次，我们必须表明，利息如何从其十分狭小的基础扩展到整个交换经济，好像也渗透到整个经济系统，以至于似乎

interest seems to occupy much more room than one would expect from our theory. Only if the whole area of the interest problem in. these two directions can be exhaustively explored from our point of view can we consider our problem as solved.

The first task presents no difficulty. First of all, every concrete phase of development begins, as was said before, with a heritage from earlier phases. A reservoir of purchasing power may already be formed by the elements which the pre-capitalist exchange economy has created, and hence there will always be greater or lesser quantities of purchasing power in the economic system which are at the disposal of new enterprises either permanently or for a certain time. Moreover, when the capitalist development is in motion an ever-increasing stream of disposable purchasing power flows to the money market. We shall distinguish three branches of it. First, by far the largest part of entrepreneurial profit is employed in this way; the profit will be "invested." Here it is in principle quite immaterial whether an entrepreneur invests his profit in his own business or whether the sum in question comes on the market. Secondly, in the case of the retirement of entrepreneurs or perhaps of their heirs from active business life, if this leads to the liquidation of the enterprise, greater or lesser sums then become free without other sums always and necessarily at the same time becoming tied up. Thirdly and finally, those profits which development so to speak sweeps to other people than entrepreneurs, and which are based upon "repercussions of development," will to a greater or lesser extent come directly or indirectly into the money market. Let us notice here that this process is accessory in still another sense than in the sense that this sum only owes its existence to development: it is the fact that interest exists, the possibility of receiving interest for this sum of money, that draws disposable purchasing power to the money market. The acquisition of interest is the only motive that leads its possessor to offer it-if there were no interest the purchasing power would be hoarded or spent on goods.

It is similar in the case of another element. We saw that the

利息所占据的地位比人们根据我们的理论所预期的地位更重要。只有当这两个方向的利息问题的所有领域，都用我们的观点淋漓尽致地探讨，我们才可以说我们的问题被解决了。

第一项任务没有什么困难。首先，正如我们前面所说的，发展的每一个具体阶段都是以继承前一阶段开始的。购买力的蓄水池可能通过前资本主义交换经济所创造的某些要素已经形成了，因此，在经济系统里，总会有较大或较小数量的购买力，它们可以由新企业永久地或者在一定时间内支配。此外，当资本主义正在发展时，一股不断增加的、可控的购买力会流向货币市场。我们将把这股购买力分为三个不同的分支。第一，企业家利润中的绝大部分是这样使用的，利润转变为“投资”。在这里，无论是企业家将其利润投资于自己的企业，还是这笔资金出现在市场上，原则上都是不重要的。第二，在企业家或者他们的继承人退出当前的企业生活时，如果这将导致企业的清算，那么一笔或大或小的款项就会成为自由流动的，而同时未必总有其他款项被冻结。第三，也是最后一个分支，那些所谓的由发展带给其他人而不是企业家的，并且基于“发展的反应”的利润，将在某种程度上直接或者间接地进入货币市场。这里我们需要注意，这个过程是附带的，不仅是因为这笔资金源于发展，还有一个原因，即利息存在这一事实，这笔钱可能得到利息收入，这就把可支配的购买力吸引到货币市场上来了。获取利息是购买力的所有者提供购买力的唯一动机——如果没有利息，购买力就会被储藏起来，或者用于购买商品。

另一个要素的情形是相似的。我们知道在一个没有发展的

significance of saving in an economic system without development[①] would be relatively very small, and that what is usually meant by the size of the savings of a modern nation is nothing but the sum of those profits from development which never become dements of income. Now the importance of saving in the real sense might not be large enough, even in a system with development, to play a decisive part for industrial requirements, but for the fact that a new kind of saving-and indeed of "real" saving -appears which is absent in a system without development. The fact that one may be assured of a permanent income by lending a sum of money acts as a new motive to saving. It is conceivable that, just because a sum saved increases automatically and consequently its marginal utility sinks, less will sometimes be saved than if no interest were received. For the most part, however, the existence of interest, which opens up a new method of employing the money saved, leads dearly to a considerable increase in saving activity-which of course does not mean that every *rise* in interest must result in a proportional increase or any increase at all in saving. From this it follows that the saving which is actually observable is in part a consequence of the existing interest; and here also there is an "accessory stream of purchasing power" coming into the money market.

A third source which supplies the money market is money which is idle for a longer or shorter time and which is also lent if interest can be obtained for it. It consists of momentarily disposable business capital and so forth. The banks collect these sums and a highly developed technique enables every monetary unit, even if it is held ready for an impending expenditure, to contribute to increasing the supply of purchasing power. Still another fact belongs here. We saw that the nature of credit means of payment and the explanation of their existence must not be sought in the effort to economise metal money. Of course, credit means of payment cause less metal money to be used than would have to be used if the same transactions had to be carried out with metal money alone.

---

① Cf. Chapter II.

经济系统[①]里，储蓄的重要性相对来说非常小，而通常所说的现代社会的储蓄规模，只不过是那些来自于发展，并且是从来没有成为收入要素的利润的货币总和。现在，甚至是在有发展的经济系统里，要是没有一种新型的储蓄——确实是“真实的”储蓄——它在没有发展的系统里是不存在的，那么，真正意义上的储蓄的重要性，可能并没有那么大，以至于可以对产业需求起决定性作用。一个人如果确信通过借出一笔钱就可以获得永久性收入，那么这就成为储蓄的新动机。可以想像，正因为一笔储蓄额的自动增加会导致它的边际效用下降，所以，有时储蓄额反而比没有利息时更少。然而，在大多数情况下，利息的存在，还是为使用节省下来的钱找到了新的方法，显然导致了储蓄活动的大幅度增加——当然这并不意味着利息的每一次增长都必然引起同比例的储蓄量的增长，或者总会有所增长。由此可见，实际中可以观察到的储蓄，其中的一部分是现有利息的一个结果；并且在这里，还有一个“附属的购买力流量”进入货币市场。

第三个供给货币市场的货币的来源是那些长期或短期闲置的资金，如果能获得利息，这些资金也会被借出。它包括暂时可以自由支配的企业资本等项目。银行聚集这些资金，运用高度发达的技术可以使每一货币单位都能为购买力供给的增加有所贡献，即使这个货币单位是为即将发生的支出准备的。这里还有一个事实需要说明。我们知道，信用支付手段的本质以及解释它的存在，并不是为了节约金属货币。当然，对于同一项交易，运用信用支付手段会使所需要的金属货币，比仅仅使用金属货币来交易所

① 参阅第二章。

But these transactions only arose with the help of credit means of payment, and as against the money requirement which would have developed in the same time if there had been no credit means of payment, no "economy" in money so far occurs. Yet we must now recognize that, apart from the credit means of payment which development brings into existence, further trans actions which were perhaps carried out previously by means of metal money are settled with credit by the banks under the pres sure of the desire to increase the quantity of interest-bearing purchasing power; that is, credit means of payment are likewise created by banking technique, consequently a still further in -crease in the disposable quantity of money results from this source.

All these elements increase the supply on the money market and lower interest far below the level at which it would be if they were not present. They would very soon reduce it to zero if development did not continually create new possibilities of employment. Whenever development stagnates, the banker hardly knows what to do with the disposable funds, and often it becomes doubtful whether the price of money contains more than the capital sum plus a premium for risk and compensation for labor, Then especially, and particularly on the money markets of very rich nations, the element of creation of purchasing power often recedes into the background, and the impression can easily be formed, so dear to economic theory as well as to banking practice, that the banker is nothing more than a middleman between borrowers and lenders. From this conception it is only a step simply to substitute for the lender's money the concrete goods which the entrepreneur needs, or even the concrete goods needed by those who transfer the necessary means of production to the entrepreneur.

It may be remarked further that there are cases, as BöhmBawerk has already emphasized, in which interest is only demanded and paid because it is possible to demand and pay it. Interest on bank balances is an example. No one transfers his purchasing power to the bank with the intention of investing his capital in this way. On the contrary, money is deposited only in so far as it is desirable to have a supply of purchasing power available for business or private reasons. This would happen even if

需占用的货币量少。但是这些交易只有借助于信用支付手段才会发生，如果不曾有过信用支付手段，对于那些同时也将发展起来的货币需求而言，就不会出现货币的“节约”。然而，我们现在必须承认，除去由发展带来的信用支付手段，那些以前可能由金属货币工具完成的其他交易，由于现在银行迫于急切增加生息购买力的压力，这些交易可以通过信贷来结算；也就是说，信用支付手段同样可以由银行业的经营技术创造出来，因此，由这个来源产生的可支配的货币量进一步增加。

所有这些要素使得货币市场上货币供给增加，也使得利息水平比在没有这些要素的情况下大大降低。如果发展不能持续创造新的就业可能性，这些要素将很快使利息降为零。一旦发展停滞了，银行家几乎就不知道该怎样使用这些可支配的资金，而且常常怀疑，除了资本本身加上风险溢价，以及对劳动的补偿，货币价格是否还包含其他什么。特别地，尤其是在非常富裕的国家的货币市场上，创造购买力这一要素常常并不重要，而且人们容易形成这样的印象：银行家只不过是借贷双方之间的中介，而这一点在经济理论以及金融实践上，其代价都是十分昂贵的。从这个观点来看，它只是这样一个步骤，即用企业家所必需的具体商品，或者用那些转移必要的生产资料给企业家的人所需要的具体商品，来替代贷款者的货币。

这里要进一步提请注意，正如庞巴维克曾经强调的，在有些情况下，人们要求利息和支付利息，只是因为有可能要求和支付利息。银行余额的利息就是一例。没有人想以这种方式进行投资，把他的购买力转移给银行。相反，货币被储存起来，只是因为这样有利于为企业经营或个人原因提供购买力。即使需要为此

something had to be paid for it. But actually the depositor receives, in most countries, a kind of share in the interest which the sums in question yield in the banker's hands. And when once this has become usual people will not be inclined to leave a balance at a bank which does not pay interest. Here interest accrues to the depositor without anything being done on his part. Now this phenomenon reaches very far into all economic life. The fact that every particle of purchasing power can obtain interest puts a premium on it, whatever purpose it may serve. Thus interest forces its way into the business of people who have not themselves anything to do with new combinations. Every unit of purchasing power has to fight as it were against the current that attempts to draw it into the money market. Furthermore, it is obvious that in all cases in which anyone needs credit for any reason at all, the loan transaction-state loans and so forth-will be linked with the fundamental phenomenon.

14. In this way the interest phenomenon extends gradually over the whole economic system, and therefore it presents a much wider front to the observer than one would suspect from its innermost nature. Hence, time itself becomes in a certain sense an element of cost, as has already been indicated. This consequent phenomenon, which the prevailing doctrine accepts as the fundamental fact, explains-and at the same time justifies-the discrepancy between it and our interpretation. But we have still a further step to take, namely to explain the fact that interest finally becomes a form of expression for all returns with the exception of wages.

In practice we speak of land as yielding interest, likewise of a patent or of any other good which yields a monopoly revenue. We even speak of interest-bearing in the case of a non-permanent return; we say, for example, that a sum of money employed in speculation, even a commodity employed in speculation, has yielded interest. Does not this contradict our interpretation? Does it not show that interest is an income from the possession of goods, that it is in an altogether different category than it would be according to our interpretation?

付出代价，也会把货币储存起来。但是实际上，在大多数国家，存款者获得的是我们所说的银行家利用该笔资金得到的利息中的一个份额。一旦这种情况成为寻常的事情，人们就不会在一家不付利息的银行保存一笔余额。这里，存款者本身不需要做任何事情就可以得到利息。现在这种现象已经深深地渗透到所有的经济生活。每一份很小的购买力都可以获得利息，这一事实使得这个购买力形成了一个溢价，而不管这个购买力用于什么目的。这样，利息就强行进入了那些本身与新的组合没有关系的人的经营事务中。于是，每一单位购买力都必须与那股企图将其吸引到货币市场的潮流作斗争。此外，显然在任何情况下，不论什么人以什么原因需要信贷，贷款交易、政府证券等等——都将与这个根本现象联系在一起。

14. 利息现象以这种方式逐渐地扩展到整个经济系统，因而它在观察者面前展现了一个比仅从利息内在性质出发而猜想的更广阔的前景。因此，在某种意义上，时间成为成本的一个要素，这一点我们已经指出。这个被流行学说认为是基本事实的现象，表明了——同时也证明了——为什么流行学说与我们的论述之间有差别。但是，我们仍然还有进一步的工作要做，即说明为什么利息最终成为一种除工资之外的所有收入的表现形式。

实际上，我们说土地产生了利息，同样，专利权或者其他任何可以产生垄断收益的商品也可以产生利息。我们甚至可以说，非永久性的收益也可能生息；例如，一笔用于投机的资金，甚至是一批用于投机的商品，产生了利息。这难道不是与我们的论述相矛盾了吗？这不是表明了利息是由于拥有商品而产生的一笔收入，是一种完全不同于我们的解释的概念吗？

This method of expressing returns has borne definite fruit in theory amongst American economists. The impetus came from Professor Clark. He called the return from concrete producers' goods rent; the same return conceived as a result of the enduring economic fund of productive power-which he calls "capital"-interest. Here, then, interest appears merely as a special aspect of the returns and no longer as an independent part of the national income stream. Professor Fetter has developed the same idea still more strongly and in a somewhat different way. But here we are interested most of all in Professor Fisher's theory, expounded in his work The Rate of Interest. Professor Fisher explains the fact of interest simply by the underestimation of the future satisfaction of wants; most recently① he has expressed his theory in the statement: "Interest is impatience crystallised into a market rate." Accordingly he connects interest with all goods separated in time from final consumption. And since all returns to the latter can be "capitalized," consequently expressed in the form of interest, interest is not a part but the whole of the income stream: wages are interest on human capital, rent is interest on capital in the form of land, and every other return is interest on produced capital. Every income is value product discounted according to the rate of the undervaluation of future satisfactions. It is clear that we cannot accept this theory because we do not even recognize the existence of the fundamental element in it. It is just as clear that for Fisher this element becomes a central factor in economic life, which must be brought in to explain nearly every economic phenomenon.

The fundamental principle that comes into consideration here, and that should lead us to understand the universal practice of expressing returns in the form of interest, is the following. According to our interpretation concrete goods are never capital. Yet anyone who possesses concrete goods can, in a system which is conceived to be in full development, obtain capital by selling them.

---

① Scientia, Rivista di Scienza (1911).

这种表达报酬的方法，在美国经济学家的理论中，已经产生了明确的成果。它的推动力来自于克拉克教授。他把来自具体生产资料的收益称为租金；把相同的来自生产力的持久的经济资金——他把这称作“资本”——的收益，称为利息。于是，在这里，利息只是作为收益的一个特殊方面出现，而不再是国民收入流中的独立部分。费特教授更为有力地发展了同样的观点，不过采用的方法有所不同。但是在这里，我们最感兴趣的是费希尔教授在他的《利息率》一书中论述的理论。费希尔教授只用人们低估了未来需求的满足来解释利息现象，最近[①]他这样表述他的理论：“利息是由于缺乏耐心而在市场上明朗的一种价格。”相应地，他把利息与各个时期脱离于最终消费的所有商品联系起来。由于后者所得到的全部收入可以“资本化”，所以它们可以用利息形式来表示，利息不是总收入流的一部分，而是全部：工资是人力资本的利息，地租是土地形式的资本的利息，等等，其他收入是被生产出来的资本的利息。每一种收入都是根据低估未来满足的某个比率贴现所得到的价值产品。很明显，我们不能接受这个理论，因为我们甚至连它其中的基本要素的存在都不认同。同样明显的是，对于费希尔教授来说，低估未来满足这一要素，将成为经济生活的中心因素，它必将用来解释几乎所有的经济现象。

这是需要考虑的基本原理，并且它将引导我们理解为什么人们普遍用利息形式表示收入，如下所示。根据我们的论述，具体的商品从来都不是资本。然而，任何一个拥有具体商品的人，在一个充分发展的系统里，都能够通过卖出他的商品而获得资本。

① 科学院，《科学评论》(1911 年)。

In this sense the concrete goods might be called "potential capital"; at least they are so from the standpoint of their possessor, who can exchange them for capital. In this connection, however, only land and monopoly positions[①] come into consideration, for two reasons. First, it is clear that one cannot sell one's labor-power as such, if we neglect the case of slavery. But there are no stocks of consumption goods and produced means of production in the sense asserted by the prevailing doctrine-so in principle we come back immediately to land and monopolies. And secondly, only land and monopoly positions are directly income-bearing. Since capital is also income-bearing, its owner would not exchange it for goods which yield no net income-or only if such a price reduction is conceded to him that he can realize a profit with the goods in the current economic period and then reinvest his capital uninjured; but in this case the seller would suffer a loss to which he would only make up his mind in abnormal conditions, especially in distress, as will be shown immediately.

The possessors of "natural agents" and monopolists thus have every reason, if there is development, to compare their income with the return on the capital which they could obtain by selling their natural agents or their monopoly, since such sale might possibly be advantageous. And capitalists have reason to compare their income from interest with the rent or permanent monopoly revenue which they can obtain with their capital. Now how high will be the price of such sources of income? No capitalist, in so far as he takes the acquisitive standpoint, can value a piece of land higher than the sum of money which yields as much interest as the former does rent. No capitalist can, with the same qualification,

① Though I use this method of expression I do not mean to cast doubt upon the fundamental fact that monopoly Positions are not "goods," as will easily be seen.

在这个意义上，具体商品也可以称为是“潜在的资本”；至少从它们的所有者的角度看是这样，因为他们可以用商品交换资本。不过，在这一点上，只有土地和垄断地位[①]需要考虑，这有两个原因：第一，如果我们不考虑奴隶制的情况，那么，很明显的是人们不可能这样卖掉自己的劳动力。但是也没有了消费品存货和流行学术所宣称的被制造出来的生产资料——因此，原则上，我们立刻回到土地和垄断上来。第二，只有土地和垄断地位直接产生了收入。既然资本也能产生收入，那么它的所有者就不会用它去交换那些不能产生净收入的商品——除非给他一个价格折扣，使他能够在本经济时期用这些商品实现利润，并且能够无损失地重新投资；但是如果这样，商品销售者就会遭受损失，这只有当销售者处于不正常的环境下，特别是在危难的情况下，才会作出这样的决定。正如我们下面就要说明的。

于是，如果存在发展，“自然生产要素”的所有者和垄断者就有充分的理由，将他们的收入与通过卖出他们的自然生产要素或者垄断地位得到的资本而可能产生的收入相比较，因为这种销售可能是有利的。资本家也有理由把他们从利息中得到的收益和地租或者永久的垄断收益作比较，地租和垄断收益是通过交换资本得来的。现在的问题是，这种收益来源的价格会有多高呢？只要他总是怀有“想获取”的观点，那么，没有一个资本家会把一块土地的价值估计得高于这样一笔钱，即这笔钱所能产生的利息与这块土地所产生的地租恰好相等。同样的道理，没有一个资本家

① 虽然我用这种表达方法，但这并不是说我怀疑垄断地位不是“商品”这个基本事实，这一点将会很容易看到。

value a piece of land any lower. If the piece of land cost more it would-neglecting obvious secondary elements-be unmarketable: no capitalist would buy it. If it cost less, competition would arise among the capitalists which would raise its price to that level. No landowner who is not in distress will be inclined to give up his land for a lesser sum than that which yields him as much in interest as his piece of land yields in pure rent. But he will also not be able to get a bigger sum for it, because a large quantity of land would immediately be offered to the capitalist who was ready to give it. Thus the "capital value" of permanent sources of income is Unequivocally determined. The well known circumstances which cause either more or less to be paid in most cases do not affect the principle.

In this solution of the problem of capitalization the central and fundamental factor is interest on purchasing power. The return to every other permanent source of income is compared with this, and according to it-as a consequence of the existence of interest its price is so fixed by the competitive mechanism that in conceiving the return of potential capital as real interest no practical error is made. In reality, therefore, every permanent return is connected with interest; but only externally, only in so far as the magnitude to which it is related is determined by the level of interest. It is not interest, the contrary method of expression in practice is merely brachylogy. And it is not directly dependent upon interest as would be the case if the nature of interest were correctly characterized by the expression "time discount."

Our result may also be extended to non-permanent net returns, for example to quasi-rents. It is not difficult to see that under free competition a temporary net return will be sold and bought for that sum of money which, if invested at interest at the moment of the conclusion of the business, would accumulate to the same sum by the time the net return ceased as all the net returns would if they were lent as they accrued. Here also in practice

会对这块土地估价得再低一些。如果对一块土地索价高了——不考虑那些明显的次级因素——那它就卖不出去，因为没有资本家愿意买它。如果索价较低，那么资本家之间就会展开竞争，这将把价格又抬到那个水平。除非是陷于困境，否则没有一个土地所有者会放弃他的土地，如果卖价能产生的利息还不如这块土地所能产生的纯租金。不过，他也不可能以更高的价格出售，否则立即就会有大量的土地供应给愿意出这个价格的资本家。这样，永久的收入来源的“资本价值”就被明确地确定下来。那些众所周知的、在多数场合下会引起多付或少付一点的情况，并不影响这个基本原理。

对资本化问题的这种解答，其核心的和基本的因素是购买力的利息。所有其他永久性收入来源的收益都与之相比较，而且以它为根据——这是因为存在利息——它的价格由竞争机制决定，所以把潜在资本的回报假设为真实的利息，实际上也不会产生什么错误。因此，在现实中，每一种永久性收入都与利息有关系，但这只是外在的，只是就这种收入的大小是由利息水平决定的而言。实际上，这种永久性收入不是利息；相反的表示方法只是简化的表示法。而且，如果利息的性质可以通过“时间贴现”被正确地表达，这种永久性收入并不像应该表现得那样，它们不直接依赖于利息。

我们的结论还可以扩展到非永久性净收益，例如准地租。不难看出，在自由竞争环境下，一笔暂时的净收益可以按这样一笔货币额进行买卖，即，如果在交易结束时把这笔货币进行投资以获取利息，那么在净收益停止时，所积累的利息额应该与如果把所有的净收益都借出去所能产生的累积利息相等。实际上，在这里，

the buyer's capital will be spoken of as yielding interest-and with the same right as in the case of permanent returns-although the buyer no longer has his capital, and has changed from a capitalist into a rent receiver. And what sum will the owner of say a blast furnace be able to obtain for it if it is *not* the bearer of a permanent – perhaps monopolistic-or temporary net return, but is a business of the circular flow, that is-abstracting from rent, which we shall neglect here-profitless? Now no capitalist will "invest" his capital in such a business. The transaction, if it is to take place at all, must yield him not only the replacement of his capital after the plant is worn out, but also a net return during its lifetime corresponding to the interest which he could otherwise draw. Consequently, if the buyer has no other design for the furnace than simply to collect its returns in the circular flow, that is if it is not called upon to play a part in a new combination, it must be sold at a price lower than cost. The seller must make up his mind to a loss, for only so could the buyer obtain a profit equal to the interest which he could otherwise obtain with the purchase money.

In all these cases the businessman's interpretation and expression are not correct. But in all these cases the incorrectness has no practical consequences, and it is quite dear why the businessman makes use of this inadequate interpretation. In the modern economic system the rate of interest is such a ruling factor, interest is so much the barometer of the whole economic situation, that regard to it is necessary in the case of practically every economic action and it enters into every economic deliberation. It leads to the phenomenon observed by theory from time immemorial, that all returns in the economic system, seen from a certain aspect, tend to equality.

15. The elliptical expression of the practical man, which is always implied in speaking of interest on concrete goods, has certainly led theory astray. But now I want to show that the theoretical error

购买者的资本被认为产生利息——并且与永久性收入有同样的权利——尽管购买者将不再拥有他的资本，并且从一个资本家变成租金的收入者。比如说，一座高炉不能产生永久性的——可能是垄断性的——或者暂时的净收益，而是一种循环流转的经营，也就是无利可图的经营——抽象掉我们在这里不加考虑的租金，那么，这座高炉的所有者会从中获得多少钱呢？现在，没有一个资本家愿意把其资本“投资”于这个业务。无论什么交易，只要它一旦发生，就必须不仅在工厂清算时使他能够收回资本，而且还必须在其经营期间，使他能够得到与如果把该项投资用于其他用途可能得到的利息相当的净收益。因此，如果购买者只是简单地希望从循环流转中积累高炉的收益，并没有其他打算，也就是说，如果没有打算把高炉用于新的组合，那么就必然以低于成本的价格卖掉高炉。卖方必然要下决心承受损失，因为只有这样，买方才能获得一笔利润，这笔利润与该笔购买款可能获得的利息相等。

在任何情况下，商人的解释和表达不都是正确的。但是，在所有这些情况下，这些不正确的表达实际上并没有什么影响，同时也十分清楚，为什么商人要使用这些不恰当的解释。在现代经济系统里，利息率已成为这样一种决定性的要素，而利息又是整个经济形式的晴雨表，所以，在每一实际的经济活动中，有必要对其关注，因而，它进入了每一项经济考虑之中。它导致了自古以来理论家们所观察到的现象，也就是，经济系统的所有收入，从某一方面来看，是趋于相等的。

15. 从事实际工作的人常常说到具体商品的利息，这种省略的表达当然会把理论引向歧途。但现在我想说明，那种常常把利

which always lies in this extension of the idea of interest beyond its real basis may also bring practical errors in its train.

The "interest aspect" of returns is a harmless view to take in the case of permanent returns, that is rents and permanent monopoly revenues, but not in other cases. Let us consider first of all our example of the furnace in order to show this. Under our assumptions the buyer of the furnace receives enough during its lifetime to recover his purchase money and interest besides – which we shall assume he spends as income. Now if all economic conditions remain unchanged, when it is worn out he can build another furnace,[①] of exactly the same kind as the old and at the same costs as the old. But if these costs are higher than originally, the individual in question must add something to his amortization fund in order to cover them. And henceforth the furnace would accordingly no longer yield him a net return. Now if the buyer of the furnace perceived these conditions dearly he would not undertake the construction, but would invest the sum recovered elsewhere. If he did not perceive them, if he allowed himself to be deceived by the interest aspect, then he would be the loser, although the seller on his part might also have been the loser and the buyer at the time rightly believed that he had made a good bargain. At first sight the case seems bewildering. But I shall not add another word of explanation because the matter must be clear to the reader who gives it the appropriate attention. Such cases are not rare in practice, and are consequences of the habit of attaching permanent net returns to goods which do not yield them. Of course other errors can also lead to such disappointments. On the other hand the disappointments may fail to materialize in consequence of particularly favorable circumstances.

---

① The reader will easily see that the argument is not changed if we assume that the buyer, who wishes to continue to work the furnace, does not let it perish and build it anew, but preserves it permanently by repairs.

息概念扩展到超出它的真实基础之外的理论上的错误，也可能带来实际工作的错误。

在永久性收益，也就是在租金和永久性垄断收益的情况下，而不是在其他情况下，收益的“利息方面”才是无害的观点，可以采用。为表明这一点，我们首先考虑前面提到的高炉的例子。在我们的假设下，高炉的购买者在高炉的使用期间获得的收入足以抵补他购买高炉的款项以及利息——这些我们假定他作为收入而花费掉。现在如果所有的经济条件保持不变，那么当高炉报废时，他可以用同样的成本建造另一座与以前完全相同的高炉。①但是如果这些成本高于以前的花费，那么购买者就必须在他提取的折旧的基础上增加一笔费用以补充重置费用。从这以后，高炉就不再给他带来净收益。现在，如果高炉的购买者清楚地观察到这些条件，他就不会重新建造高炉，而是把收回的资金投到其他地方。如果他没有意识到这些，如果他被利息的外表所蒙骗，那么他将是受损失者，尽管在他这一方的卖者也可能已经受损失，当时的购买者也合理地相信他已经做了一笔合算的买卖。乍看起来，这种情况似乎让人很迷惑。但我不打算对此作补充说明，因为只要读者对此适当地注意，问题就是很清楚的。在实际中这种情况也不少，这是因为人们习惯把永久性的净收入与并不产生这种收入的商品联系起来。当然，其他错误也会导致这种失望。另一方面，这种失望在特殊良好的环境下也可能不会成为现实。

① 读者将很容易看出，如果我们假定购买者希望继续使用以前的高炉，不让它报废，也不重建，而是通过维修使它持续地保存下来供使用，那么这个观点仍然适用。

But I believe that everyone must find sufficient proofs in his experience for what has been said.

The case is similar if net returns really exist but are not permanent, if for example a business still yields a few installments of entrepreneurial profit or temporary monopoly revenues or quasirents. If one nevertheless speaks of such things as interest-bearing it does no harm as long as one is aware of the temporary character of these returns. But at the moment when one explains them as interest the temptation is obvious to regard them as permanent; indeed, sometimes the expression is already a symptom of this error. And then of course one experiences the most unpleasant surprises. This interest has a way of diminishing obstinately, even of suddenly coming to an end. The businessman in this event complains of bad times, to be sure, and cries out for protective tariffs, government assistance, and so forth, or considers himself as the victim of a special misfortune or-with more reason-as the victim of new competition. Such occurrences are very frequent, and they substantiate our interpretation strikingly. Yet they obviously hark back to the fundamental error which leads in practice to false steps and bitter disappointments, in theory to those explanations of interest which we are criticizing.

The statement is often heard that somebody's business "yields" say 30 percent. Of course this is not simply interest. In most cases the result is arrived at by not counting the entrepreneur's activity as an outlay and consequently not including the payment for it under costs. If this is not the explanation then the return cannot be permanent. Business experience completely substantiates this conclusion of our interpretation. For what business "yields interest" permanently? It is true, the businessman often does not realize this temporary character of the return, and makes the most diverse hypotheses about its continual dwindling. And the buyer is very often lured by the expectation that such a return will be maintained – at the most he recognizes that the experience of the previous owner may have something to do with its size.

但是我相信，每个人必定会在实践中找到充分的证据验证上述情况。

如果净收益确实存在，但它不是永久性的，例如一家企业仍然分期获得少量企业家利润，或者获得临时的垄断收益，或者准地租，情况也是类似的。如果还是有人称这些情况是生息的，只要他意识到这些收益是暂时的，也就没有什么害处。但是一旦把它们解释为利息，人们就很容易把它们看做是永久性的，的确，在某些情况下利息这种表达就已经是错误的迹象。于是人们自然会感到最令人不快的惊讶。这种利息有一种难以抵挡的递减的趋势，甚至可能突然终止。遇到这种情况的商人，常常抱怨日子不好过，还有吵嚷着要实行保护关税，政府援助等等，或者认为他们自己是特殊不幸的牺牲者，或者——理由更充分——认为他们是新竞争下的牺牲者。这种情况经常发生，它们有力地证实了我们的解释。然而，显然它们又回到原来的基本错误上了，这些错误在实践中将导致错误的措施和更为痛苦的失望，在理论上将导致那些我们正在批判的有关利息的解释。

常常听到这样的说法，说某某人的生意“获利”30%。当然这不仅仅是利息。在多数情况下，得出这样的结论，是因为没有把企业家的行为作为一项支出来考虑，从而没有把支付给这种行为的报酬包括在成本之内。如果不这样解释，那么，收益就不会是永久性的。商业经验完全证实了我们解释的这个结论。为什么商业能够持久地“产生利息”呢？诚然，商人们常常不能认识收益的暂时性的特征，而且对收益的不断减少作了许多不同的假设。购买者也常常被期望所诱惑，以为这种收益会保持下去——至多他不过认识到以前的所有者的经验可能与收益的大小有关系。

Then he automatically applies the interest formula instead of the correct method of calculation. If he does this strictly, that is if he "capitalizes" the return at the current rate of interest, then failure will follow. The return of every business ceases after a time; every business, if it remains unchanged, soon falls into insignificance.

The individual industrial business is not a permanent source of any other income than wages and rent. The individual who is most inclined to overlook this in daily practice, and to suffer the unpleasant experience indicated above, is the typical shareholder. It might be thought that an objection against our theory of interest could be forged out of the "fact" that a shareholder may draw a permanent net income even without periodically changing his investment. According to our view the capitalist would first have to lend his capital to one entrepreneur and after a certain time to another, since the first cannot be permanently in the position to pay interest. Since we characterized the shareholders as mere contributors of money, and yet they draw a permanent income out of one and the same enterprise, the objection would seem to be very strong. But precisely the case of the shareholder —and of every creditor who throws in his lot permanently with an enterprise-shows how true our interpretation is to reality. For this "fact" is very doubtful. Do companies live eternally and do they pay dividends forever? Certainly there are such, but broadly only two groups of them. First there are branches of industry, some railways for example, which have, if not a perpetual, yet an assured monopoly for a long time. Here the shareholder simply receives monopoly revenue. Then there are kinds of enterprises which by nature and programme are continually doing new things and are really nothing but forms for continual new enterprises. Here the aims alter incessantly and the leading personalities also change, so that it is in the nature of the thing that people of considerable ability always appear in the leading positions. New profits are always arising, and if the shareholder loses his return this is not really necessary

于是，他自动地运用利息公式，而不是用正确的计算方法。如果他严格地这样做，按现行利率把收益“资本化”，那么失败会随之而来。每一个企业的收益在一段时间之后会消失；任何一家企业，如果它保持不变，很快也会失去其存在的意义。

个人经营的企业只是工资和租金收入的持久来源，不是其他收入的持久来源。那些在日常实践中最容易忽视这一点，并且遭受上面所说的不愉快经历的人，要算典型的股票持有者。也许有人认为，一个股东甚至不用定期变化他的投资就可以获得一笔永久性的净收入，这一“事实”所形成的观点完全反对我们所论述的利息理论。根据我们的观点，资本家必须首先把他们的资本借给一个企业家，然后，一段时间之后，再把资本借给另一个企业家，因为第一个企业家不可能永久地支付利息。由于我们认为股东的特点仅仅在于提供货币，然后从同一个企业获得一份永久性收入，那么这个反对观点似乎是十分有力的。但是，就是存在这种股东——以及每一个把自己的命运与一家企业永久地联系在一起的贷款者——表明我们的解释是多么真实，多么接近现实。因为这一“事实”是十分可疑的。公司能够永久地生存下去，并且能够永远支付股息吗？当然，这种情况有，但是一般只在两类情况下存在。第一，有些产业部门，比如铁路，即使没有永久的垄断权，但在一个较长时期内垄断权还是有保证的。在这种情况下，股东纯粹是坐享其垄断收益。第二，有这样一种企业，它们按照其性质和计划总是不断地创新，实际上，它们不是别的，而是连续的新企业形式。在这里，企业目标经常变化，企业领导人也在变化，所以事物的本质就是，让那些有能力的人总是处于领导地位。总是不断出现新的利润，如果股东失去其收益，这实际上不是必然的，

but just a misfortune to be explained by the individual case. But neglecting these two categories, that is if a company simply operates a definite business without a monopoly position, there is, at the most, rent of natural agents as a permanent income, and nothing more. Now experience confirms this strikingly, although in practice competition does not act promptly and hence enterprises remain in possession of surpluses for a considerable time. No industrial company of the type indicated gratifies its shareholders with a constant shower of gold; on the contrary it soon declines into a stage that has the most lamentable similarity with the drying up of a spring. Hence repayment of capital is frequently concealed in dividends, even though the wearing out of machines and so forth is ever so conscientiously taken care of by depreciation accounts. Quite rightly, therefore, much more than wear and tear is frequently written off and many companies strive to write off the whole capital as soon as possible. For the time comes for each when the business as such is really valueless, that is when its returns only just cover costs. So there is no such thing as a lasting income from interest out of one and the same business, as anyone who does not believe it and acts accordingly may learn to his cost. Hence the receipt of dividends by shareholders does not tell against our interpretation-quite the reverse!

16. How far this theory will prove an efficient instrument in the analysis of statistical material and in the investigation of the questions which arise in relation to interest still remains to be seen. It certainly seems to bring the facts of money, credit, and banking into closer touch with pure theory than other interpretations do. The author hopes to be able to submit the results of some work on these lines in a book to be published in the near future, in which such problems as, for example, the relation between gold reserves and interest, the influence of the monetary system upon interest, the differences between interest rates of different countries, and the correlation between rates of exchange and interest will be discussed.

Our argument should also explain the movement in time of the rate of interest. It is from this class of facts that verification of the fundamental idea might primarily be expected. If the interest of business life –

而只是因为出现了个别情况所导致的不幸。但是如果不谈这两类情况，也就是说，如果公司并不处于垄断地位，而只经营一种确定的业务，那它至多不过是获得自然要素的租金——这可以作为永久性收入，再没有其他的了。现在，实践经验有力地证实了这一点，尽管竞争在实际中并不立即起作用，因此，在相当长的时间内，企业可以保持着剩余。没有一个上述这种工业企业给其股东稳定持续地发放一笔金钱以满足股东；相反，它很快陷入这样一种可悲的困境，就像即将干涸的泉水。因此，资本的偿还总是隐藏于股息之中。尽管机器的磨损等等总是谨慎地被计入折旧账户。因此，实际摊消到成本中的数量往往比实际的磨损大得多，而且许多公司都设法尽快摊消掉其全部的资本，这是十分恰当的。因为，一旦到了一定时期，收益与成本恰好抵消，这种企业实际上就没有价值了。因此，不可能从同一家企业的利息中获得永久的收入，不相信这一点并如此行事的人，会从他的损失中明白过来。所以，股东获得股利，这并不与我们的解释相抵触——而正是相反！

16. 这一理论在多大程度上可以成为对统计资料的分析和有关利息问题的考察的有效工具，还有待观察。当然，与其他解释相比，它似乎更紧密地把货币、信用、银行业等方面的事实与纯理论结合起来。作者也希望在不远的将来，能把对这些方面研究的某些成果写成专著，其中对有些问题，比如黄金储备与利息的关系、货币制度对利息的影响、不同国家利率的差异，以及外汇汇率与利息的关系等等，将进行讨论。

我们的论证也应该能够解释利率的时间变动。主要还是基于这类事实，我们的基本思想才得以证实。如果经济生活中的利

what it is usual to call "productive interest"-has its roots in entrepreneurial profit, both should move closely together. As a matter of fact, this is true of short period fluctuations. In longer periods we may still observe some relation between the prevalence of new combinations and interest, but there are so many elements to be taken account of, and "other things" remain so imperfectly equal as soon as we go beyond the span of say a decade, that verification becomes extremely complicated. It is then not only necessary to allow for government borrowing, migration of capital, and movements of the general level of prices, but there are also more delicate questions, which cannot be entered upon here.

There is nothing in our theory to support the old view-which with many people from the classical economists onwards has acquired the force of a dogma-that interest must of necessity display a secular tendency to fall. It may be shown, however, that the impression to that effect, which seems so strongly to suggest itself, is largely due to the element of risk, which accounts for medieval figures; and that the *real* rate of interest does not display any dear secular trend, that its history rather verifies our interpretation than disavows it.

These remarks must suffice. However incomplete our arguments may be, and however much more precise formulation and however much modification they may require, I believe the reader will nevertheless find in them some of the elements for understanding that part of economic phenomena which has hitherto presented most difficulties. I have only one thing to add: I wished to explain the interest phenomenon but not to justify it. Interest is not, like profit for example, a direct fruit of development in the sense of a prize for its achievements. It is on the contrary rather a brake – in an exchange economy a necessary brake – on development, a kind of "tax on entrepreneurial profit." Certainly this is not sufficient to condemn it, even if one includes condemnation or approbation of things in the tasks of our science.

息——我们通常称为“生产利息”——其根源在于企业家利润，那么两者的变动就应该紧密联系在一起。事实上，短时期的波动是这样的。在较长时期内，我们仍然可以观察到新组合中普遍的利润与利息有某种关系，但其中需要考虑的因素太多，而且一旦我们超出一定的期间，比如说十年，所谓“其他情况”完全保持不变，要证明这些就变得极其复杂。因为那样不仅必须考虑政府举债、资本转移、一般物价水平的变动，而且还要考虑更为棘手的问题，这里不可能对此讨论。

在我们的理论中没有任何论据支持这样一种旧观点——这种观点对从古典经济学以来的许多人来说几乎已经是一种教条——它认为利息从长期来看必定表现下降的趋势。然而，这种观点看似有力地表明自己，给人强烈的印象，主要是因为风险因素，它说明了中世纪的利率数字；而真实的利率并没有表现出任何明显的长期趋势，所以，利息的历史不是否定我们的解释，而恰是证实了我们的解释。

关于这些评论已经说得足够多了。不管我们的论证可能有多么不完全，也不管它们是多么需要更精确的阐述和更好的修正，我相信，读者都将从其中找到有助于理解迄今为止经济现象中最难理解的那部分的某些要素。我只想补充一点：我的愿望是解释利息现象，而不是证明它的合理性。利息不同于利润，比如，它不像利润是发展的直接成果，如果就给予成就以奖赏这个意义来说。相反，不如说利息是一个对经济发展的制动因素——在交换经济是一个必要的制动因素——是一种“对企业家利润征收的税”。当然，这种说法并不足以谴责利息，尽管人们把对事物的谴责与赞同都包含在我们这门科学的任务之内。面对谴责性的判

Against the condemnatory verdict we can assert the importance of the function of this " ephor of the economic system," and we may conclude that interest only takes away something from the entrepreneur which would otherwise accrue to him, and not from other classes-neglecting the cases of consumptive and of " productive- consumptive credit. " Yet this fact, together with the fact that the interest phenomenon is not a necessary element in all economic organizations, will always result in the critic of social conditions finding more to object to in interest than in anything else. Therefore it is important to state that interest is only the consequence of a special method of carrying out new combinations, and that this method can be much more easily changed than the other fundamental institutions of the competitive system.

决，我们能够肯定这个“经济系统的‘监督官’”的重要职能，而且，我们可以得出结论：利息只是从企业家那里拿出来的东西（否则它就归企业家所有），而不是从其他阶级——忽略消费信贷和“生产—消费信贷”的情况。然而这一事实，即连同利息现象并不是所有经济组织的必要成分这个事实，将会使社会评论家在利息现象中比在其他任何事物中，能找到更多的反对的东西。因此，表明利息只是实施新组合的一种特殊方法的结果，这是很重要的，而且这个方法比竞争体系里其他基本制度或者惯例更容易改变。

CHAPTER VI
The Business Cycle

Preliminary Remarks

The following theory of crises, more correctly of recurrent business fluctuations, has still less claim to be considered a satisfactory representation of its subject-matter than the theories of the entrepreneurial function, of credit, capital, the money market, profit, and interest which have already been expounded. A satisfactory theory would require, today more than ever, a comprehensive treatment of the tremendously increased material, the working out of the numerous individual theories based upon different indices of business conditions and of their relation to one another. My work in this direction is a torso; the promise of exhaustive treatment has remained unfulfilled,[①] and according to my programme of work must long remain so.

---

① I have since published on the subject, apart from the article in the Zeitschrift für Volksw. Sozialpol. und Verw. (1910), the article "Die Wellenbewegung des Wirtschaftslebens," Archiv für Sozialwissenschaft und Sozialpolitik (1914). To this day my theory of crises is cited chiefly from this article. It was also expounded in 1914 in a lecture at Harvard University when in formulation and in the factual foundation-but without any essential change-a step beyond this chapter was taken. Furthermore, there is an article "Kreditkontrolle" (*ibidem*, 1925) which was primarily concerned with other things; and "Oude en nieuwe Bankpolitiek" in the Economisch-Statistischen Berichten (1925), which likewise barely touches the fundamental question. I expounded this in detail in a lecture at the Handelshochschule in Rotterdam in 1925. Finally, for a short exposition see "The Explanation of the Business Cycle," Economica (1928).

第六章　商业周期

初步评论

下面关于危机的理论，更准确地说是周期性的商业波动理论，它不像已经被详细说明了的关于企业家职能、信贷、资本、货币市场、利润、利息等理论那样，它甚至还没有一个令人比较满意的对其主题的陈述。一个令人满意的理论，在今天比过去，将更需要对大量的不断增多的资料进行综合处理，更需要以那些表明商业环境及其相互关系的不同指标为基础，制定出许多个别理论。在这方面，我的工作还只是一个不成形的框架；我所承诺的彻底研究还没有完成，[①] 而且按照我的工作计划，这种情况还将长

① 除了在《政治经济学、社会政策与管理杂志》（1910 年）上发表的论文以外，自此，关于这个主题，我还发表过《经济生活的波动》一文，载《社会科学与社会政策档案》（1914 年）。直到今天，我的关于危机的理论主要引自这篇论文。1914 年，在哈佛大学的一场演讲中，我详细说明了这篇论文，当时，在表述的系统性和事实依据方面——不过内容本质上没有任何变化——比本章更进了一步。此外，还有“信用控制”一文（刊载于与上同一本书，1925 年），它主要涉及的是其他事情；还有《银行政策》一文，载《经济-统计通讯杂志》（1925 年），同样，这篇文章也只是初步接触基本问题。1925 年，我在罗特达姆的高级商业学校一次演讲中详细论述了这个问题。最后，至于简短的说明，可以参考《商业周期解说》一文，载《经济学杂志》（1928 年）。

Nevertheless, I submit this chapter again without any alteration except in exposition, not only because it now has its place in the investigation of crises but also because I still hold it to be true; not only because I believe that it contains the contribution of the argument of this book to the topic but also because this contribution gives the essence of the matter. Hence I am ready to accept criticism on the basis of this chapter.

The study of the objections which have come to my notice has confirmed me in my conviction. I shall mention only two. First there is the criticism that my theory is merely a "psychology of crises." This objection has been made so urbanely by a most competent authority, and one most highly esteemed by me, that I myself must formulate its true content more sharply if the reader is to see what it really means. "Psychology of crises" means something quite definite, and is different from "psychology of value" for example: it means insisting on those tragi-comic aberrations of the frightened business world which we notice and specially *have* noticed in the past in every crisis. As a theory of crises, therefore, it would mean the basing of a scientific explanation either upon obvious accompanying and consequent phenomena (panic, pessimism, and so on) or, only a degree less bad, upon previous bullish tendencies, promotion fever, and so forth. Such a theory is barren; such an explanation explains nothing. But this is not my position. Not only do I always discuss external conduct, so that psychology can only be found in my argument in the sense in which it would be implied in every statement, even the most objective, about economic events, but I explain the phenomenon of business fluctuations-whether actually occurring now or not-solely by an objective chain of causation which runs its course automatically, that is by the effect of the appearance of new enterprises upon the conditions of the existing ones, a chain of causation which follows from the facts explained in the second chapter.

时间持续。尽管如此，我还是要提交这一章，除了在表述上，没有其他任何变化，这不仅是因为现在这一章对于考察危机有其一定地位，而且还因为我仍然坚信它是正确的；不仅是因为我相信这一章包含的内容有助于本书对这一主题的论证，而且还因为它对本书的贡献表达了事物的本质。因此，我愿意在这一章的基础上接受批评。

通过研究我所注意到的各种反对的意见，我更坚信我的信念。这里我只提两种意见：第一种意见，批评说我的理论只不过是一种“危机的心理”。这种反对意见是由一位最有才能的，也是我最尊重的权威者提出来的，意见表达得是这样文雅，所以为了让读者明白它的真实含义，我必须自己更加鲜明地阐述它的真实内容。“危机的心理”意味着某种十分明确的含义，它不同于“价值的心理”，比如，它意味着坚信那些令人害怕的商业世界的悲喜剧式的畸变，它们是我们在每一次危机中注意到的，特别是在过去已经注意到的。因此，作为一种危机理论，它意味着一种科学的解释要么依据显然是同时发生的以及相应产生的现象（恐慌、悲观主义，等等），要么，只在某种缓和的程度上，依据以前对股票看涨的趋势、促销热潮，等等。这种理论是很枯燥的；这种解释也没有说明任何问题，但这不是我的观点。不只是因为我总是讨论外在行为，因而在我的论述里，心理因素只能在对每一经济事件的陈述中找到，甚至是最客观的陈述，而且还因为我解释商业波动的现象——不管现在是否发生——仅仅用一串自动运行的客观的因果关系来解释，也就是用新企业的出现对现有企业所处的环境的影响来解释，这一连串的因果关系产生于第二章所解释的各种事实。

Then there is the objection formulated by Loewe: my theory does not explain the periodicity of crises. ①I do not understand this. Two things may be meant by periodicity. First, the mere fact that every boom is followed by a depression, every depression by a boom. But this my theory explains. Or secondly, the actual length of the cycle may be meant. But this no theory can explain numerically because it obviously depends upon the concrete data of the individual case. Yet my theory gives a general answer: the boom ends and the depression begins after the passage of the time which must elapse before the products of the new enterprises can appear on the market. And a new boom succeeds the depression when the process of resorption of the innovations is ended.

But Loewe means something else, which has been formulated as follows by Emil Lederer. ②My treatment is said to be "not satisfactory because it does not try at all to explain why the entrepreneurs appear periodically in swarms as it were, what the conditions are under which they can appear and whether they will always appear and why, if the conditions are favorable for them." Now one may assert that I have explained inconclusively the swarm-like appearance of entrepreneurs, which, with its consequential phenomena, constitutes the only cause of periods of boom. But that I have not tried at all to explain it-when my whole argument aimed at this-seems to me to be untenable. The conditions under which entrepreneurs may appear-neglecting the general economic and social conditions of the competitive economy-are shown in the second chapter and may be briefly and incompletely formulated as the existence of new possibilities more advantageous from the private economic standpoint-a condition which must always be fulfilled;

① In the Festschrift for Brentano, II, 351.

② Cf. his distinguished work, "Konjunktur und Krisen," in Grundriss der Sozialkonomik, vol. IV, pt, I, p. 368.

第二个反对意见由洛伊提出来，他说我的理论没有解释危机的周期性。[1] 对此我不理解。周期性可能有两种含义：第一，仅指每一次繁荣之后都有一次萧条，每一次萧条之后又跟着繁荣这个事实，而我的理论解释了这种现象。第二个含义，它指实际的周期长度。但是没有一个理论可以从数量上解释这一点，因为，显然它依赖于个别情况的具体数据。不过，我的理论对此作了一般性的回答：一段时间之后，繁荣结束，萧条开始，而在新企业的产品上市之前，这种现象必然会消失。当吸收创新的过程结束时，一种新的繁荣会战胜萧条，从而出现繁荣景象。

但是洛伊还有其他的含义，这些内容由埃米尔·莱德勒表述如下[2]：我的论证被说成是“令人不满意的，因为它根本没有试图说明为什么企业家实际上是周期性的大批的出现，他们可能出现的条件是什么，以及如果条件对他们有利，是否他们将会不断地出现，为什么会经常出现。”现在有人可能认为，我对企业家的成群或者大批出现（这是形成繁荣阶段的唯一原因）以及它所引起的现象的解释不能让人信服。但是如果说我根本不曾努力解释它——实际上，我的整个论证都在为了解释它——在我看来是没有根据的。企业家们得以出现的条件——不考虑竞争经济的一般的经济和社会条件——在第二章已经说明了，而且也可以简略地、不完全地表述为新的可能性的存在，这种新的可能性从私人经济的角度看是更有利的——这个条件必须被实现；由于人们主

① 参阅纪念布伦塔诺的文集第二篇，第351页。

② 参阅他的著作《周期变动和危机》，载《社会经济学大纲》第四卷，第一部分，第368页。

the limited accessibility of these possibilities because of the personal qualifications and external circumstances which are necessary;[①] and an economic situation which allows tolerably reliable calculation. Why the entrepreneurs appear under these conditions is no more problematical if one adheres to the assumptions implied in our entrepreneurial concept than the fact that anyone seizes a gain when it is immediately before his eyes.

I should now like, without any critical design and solely in order to allow the ideas to stand out more clearly, to compare my theory with by far the most thorough effort in this field, that of Spiethoff[②]-little as it is capable of comparison with the latter in thoroughness and perfection. The point of view-deriving from Juglar-according to which the wave-like fluctuation in business and not the crisis itself appears to be the fundamental thing to be explained, is common to both. We agree in the conception-which is established by me not in this chapter alone but also in the second-that the alternating situations (Wechsellagen-Spiethoff) are the form economic development takes in the era of capitalism. Hence we also agree in the view that completely developed capitalism is to be dated historically only from the time when such alternating situations first unmistakably occur (that is in England, according to Spiethoff, only from 1821, in Germany from the forties of the nineteenth century). Further, we agree that the figure for the *consumption* of iron is the best index of business conditions; that is, this index which Spiethoff discovered and worked out-I have no effort in this direction to exhibit-is also recognized by me as the right one from the standpoint of my theory. We agree that the causal nexus begins first of all with the means of production which are bought with capital and that

① The new formulation in Chapter II also dears up Loewe's objection, which he expresses with the concept of the "half-static" businessman.

② Cf. his more recent expositions, above all the article "Krisen" in the Hand wörterbuch der Staatswissenschaften, but also the exposition in the Hamburger Wirtschaftsdienst (1926), Heft I, and his lecture, "Moderne Konjunkturforschung," before the "Freunde und Förderer der Universität Bonn."

观意识的限制和必需的外界环境的影响，这些可能性也只能有限地实现；[①] 还要加上一个能够十分可靠地估算出来的经济形式。如果人们能坚持我们对企业家概念所做的假设条件，那么，为什么企业家会出现在这些条件下，就不是什么很难的问题了，就像人们一看到有利的机会就会伸手抓这个事实一样。

现在，我并不带有任何批评意图，只是为了更加清晰地展现这些观点，我打算比较我的理论与迄今为止在这个领域做过最充分论证的斯皮托夫的理论[②]——在彻底性和完备性方面很难与其比较。从尤格拉那里得来的观点——据此，商业中的波浪式波动，而不是危机本身，似乎是需要说明的基本问题，这个观点对两者是同样的。我们赞同这个观点——我不仅在本章，而且在第二章就确立了这个观点——即变换的状态（斯皮托夫称之为“Wechsellagen”）是资本主义时代经济发展所采用的形式。因此，我们也赞同这个观点，即充分发达的资本主义在历史上只能追溯到这种变换状态首次无误地出现的那个时代（根据斯皮托夫的观点，在英国就是，仅从1821年开始，在德国就是从19世纪40年代开始）。再者，我们赞同说钢铁消费数字是反映经营状况最好的指标；也就是说，斯皮托夫发现并计算出的这个指标——在这方面我没做任何努力——我承认也是我的理论认为是正确的指标。我同意这个因果关系首先开始于用资本购买的生产资料，而繁荣

① 本书第二章新的阐述也澄清了洛伊的反对意见，他的反对观点是用“半静态”商人的概念来表达的。

② 参阅他近期做的论述，首先是他在《政治科学袖珍词典》中的《危机》一文，还有在《汉堡经济通讯》（1926年）第一册中的论述，以及他在“波恩大学的朋友和资助者”面前做的演讲《现代经济变动考察》。

the boom materializes first of all in the production of industrial plant (factories, mines, ships, railways, and so forth). Finally, we agree with the conception that the boom arises, as Spiethoff puts it, because "more capital is invested," is fixed in new businesses, and that the impulse then spreads over the markets for raw materials, labor, equipment, and so forth. We also understand the same by capital in the sense which is here significant, with the exception that the creation of purchasing power plays a fundamental part in my argument which it does not in Spiethoff's. So far I should only have to add one thing, that capital investment is not distributed evenly in time but appears *en masse* at intervals. This is obviously a very fundamental fact, and for this I offer an explana tion not offered by Spiethoff. I accept Spiethoff's conception of the standard cycle. (Musterkreislauf)

The difference between us lies in the explanation of the circumstance which cuts short the boom and brings about the depression. For Spiethoff this circumstance is the overproduction of capital goods relative on the one hand to the existing capital and on the other hand to the effective demand. As a description of the actual facts I could also accept this. But while Spiethoff's theory stops at this element and tries to make us understand what circum stances induce the producers of factory equipment, of building materials, and so forth periodically to produce more than their markets are capable of absorbing at the time, my theory tries to explain the state of affairs in the manner to be found in this chapter, which may be summarized as follows. The effect of the appearance of new enterprises *en masse* upon the old firms and upon the established economic situation, having regard to the fact established in the second chapter that as a rule the new does not grow out of the old but appears alongside of it and eliminates it competitively, is so to change all the conditions that a special process of adaptation becomes necessary. This difference between us would be still further reduced by more detailed discussion.

It was impossible to keep my old exposition short and yet to make it invulnerable. Nevertheless I have cut it down still further in order to let the fundamental idea stand out more clearly.

首先实现于工业厂家（工厂、矿山、船舶、铁路，等等）的生产中。最后，我们同意这个观点，正如斯皮托夫所表述的，产生繁荣是因为“投入了更多的资本”，固定于新的企业中，接着这种冲击延伸到原材料、劳动、设备等等市场上。从在这里具有重要性这个意义来说，我们同样也可以理解资本，例外的情况是，在我的论述中购买力的创造起着根本性的作用，而在斯皮托夫的论述中则不是这样。至此，我只应该补充一点，即资本的投入不是随着时间均匀分布的，而是间隔着大批地出现的。显然，这是极其基本的事实，对此我提出了一种解释，这是斯皮托夫不曾提出的。我接受斯皮托夫关于标准周期的概念。

我与斯皮托夫的不同在于，我们对那种中断繁荣进而产生萧条的环境的解释不同。斯皮托夫认为这种环境就是资本品的生产过剩，一方面相对于现有的资本，另一方面相对于有效需求。作为对客观现实的描述，我也可以接受这个观点。然而，斯皮托夫的理论只停留在这一点上，还想使我们理解，是什么环境诱使那些设备、建筑材料等等的生产者，周期性地生产比当时的市场所能吸收的数量更多的这些产品，而我的理论试图解释这些事物，所采用的方式可以在本章中找到，也可以概括如下。考虑到第二章已经确认的情况，即，通常新企业并不是从老企业中产生，而是在它一旁出现，并以竞争形式消灭掉老企业，所以，新企业大量的出现，它对老企业以及对已经建立起来的经济形式的影响，就是要改变一切环境，从而一个特殊的适应过程就是必需的了。我们之间的这个区别，通过更详细的讨论，将会进一步缩小。

想把我原先的说明缩短而又无懈可击，这是不可能的。尽管如此，我还是对它做了进一步压缩，目的是为了更清晰地展现这

For the same reason I shall number the steps of the argument.

1. Our question is: does this whole development which we have been describing proceed in unbroken continuity, is it similar to the gradual organic growth of a tree? Experience answers in the negative. It is a fact that the economic system does not move along continually and smoothly. Counter-movements, setbacks, incidents of the most various kinds, occur which obstruct the path of development; there are breakdowns in the economic value system which interrupt it. Why is this? Here we meet with a new problem.

If these deviations of the economic system from a smooth line of development were rare, they would hardly constitute a problem with a special claim upon the theorist's attention. In an economy without development the individual may meet with misfortunes which are very serious for him without there being any reason for theory to go into such phenomena. Likewise, events which might perhaps destroy the economic development of a whole nation would require no general investigation if they were rare, if they could be conceived as isolated mishaps. But the counter movements and setbacks of which we are speaking here are frequent, so frequent that upon first consideration something like a necessary periodicity seems to suggest itself. This makes it impossible, practically at all events if not logically, to abstract from this class of phenomena.

Further, if it were the case that after such a setback is overcome the earlier development begins again at the point reached before it was interrupted, then the significance of the setback would not in principle be very great. We might say that we had taken account of all the fundamental facts of development even if we could not explain these disturbing incidents themselves or had simply abstracted from them. However, this is not the case. The countermovements do not merely obstruct development, they put an end to it. A great many values are annihilated; the fundamental conditions and presuppositions of the plans of the leading men in the economic system are changed. The economic system needs rallying before it can go forward again; its value system needs reorganizing. And the development which then starts again is a new one, not simply the continuation of the old.

个基本思想。出于同样的原因，我将给论述的步骤编号。

1. 我们的问题是：我们所描述的整个发展过程会不中断地持续下去吗？它与一棵树的渐进的有机成长相类似吗？经验的回答是否定的。的确，经济系统不是连续地、平稳地向前运动。多种不同的运动方式：逆运动、后退、事变，它们的出现阻碍了发展的道路；在经济价值体系里也有干扰发展的瓦解因素。为什么会是这样呢？这里我们遇到了新的问题。

如果经济系统从发展平稳的直线偏离出去的程度很小，那么，它们几乎就不构成是要求理论家特别关注的问题。在一个没有发展的经济里，个人可能会遇到对他非常严重的灾难，而理论又没有任何理由深入到这种现象中去。同样，那些很可能破坏整个国家经济发展的事件，如果很少，如果它们被认为是孤立的偶然遭遇，那么就不需要对此做全面的调查。但是，我们这里谈到的逆运动和后退是经常发生的，以至于一考虑到这个问题，似乎周期性就表现出来了。如果不是从逻辑上考虑，实际上，这表明，对这类现象进行抽象，无论在什么情况下都是不可能的。

此外，如果情况是这样：当克服了一种挫折之后，早期的发展又从它被中断的那一点重新开始，那么从原则上说，这个挫折的意义就不是很大了。或许我们可以说，我们已经考虑了所有有关发展的基本事实，即使我们不能说明这些干扰事件本身，或者干脆把它们抽象掉。然而，情况不是这样，逆运动不仅阻碍了发展，而且它结束了发展。大量价值被毁灭；经济体系中领导者计划的基本条件和前提被改变。经济系统在重新向前发展之前，必须振奋精神，恢复精力；其价值体系也需要重新组织。这时，再一次开始的发展是一个新的过程，而不是简单的旧过程的继续。

It is true, experience teaches that it will move more or less in a similar direction to the earlier, but the continuity of the "plan" is interrupted.[①] The new development proceeds from different conditions and in part from the action of different people; many old hopes and values are buried forever, wholly new ones arise. Empirically it may happen that the main lines of all these partial developments, which lie between the setbacks, coincide with the broad outlines of the total development, but theoretically we cannot merely consider the contours of the total. Entrepreneurs cannot skip the setback phase and carry their plans over intact into the next phase of development, and scientific explanation cannot do so either without completely losing touch with the facts.

We have now to investigate this class of phenomena, which stand out so sharply against, apparently in a certain opposition to, other phenomena of development. At the outset the following possibilities exist. First, crises may or may not be a uniform phenomenon. The peculiar breakdowns of development which we know from experience and describe as crises always appear even to the naive mind as forms of one and the same phenomenon. However, this homogeneity of crises certainly does not go far. On the contrary, it exists chiefly only in a similarity of the effects upon the economic system and upon individuals, and in the fact that certain events are in the habit of occurring in most crises. Such effects and such events, however, would appear with the most various external and internal disturbances of economic life and are not enough to prove that crises are always the same phenomenon. Actually, different kinds and causes of crises are distinguished. And nothing justifies us in assuming beforehand that crises have more in common with one another than the element from which we started, namely that they are all events which call a halt on the preceding economic development.

---

① Always less, of course, the more trustification progresses.

诚然，经验告诉我们，新的发展过程或多或少会朝着类似于早期的方向运动，但是这个“计划”的持续性被打断了。[①] 新的发展过程产生于不同的环境，部分地产生于不同人的行为；许多旧的愿望和价值被永远埋葬了，出现了全新的事物。从经验上看，存在于挫折之间的所有这些局部发展的主线，可能恰好与总体发展的粗略轮廓相吻合，但是，在理论上，我们不能仅仅考虑整个过程的轮廓。企业家不能逾越挫折阶段，把他们的计划原样地带入下一个发展阶段，而且科学的解释也不能这样做，除非它完全脱离实际。

现在，我们必须考察这一类现象，它与其他发展现象相比较，更鲜明突出，而且显然它处于某种与其他现象对立的位置。一开始就存在下面所说的可能性。第一，危机可能是也可能不是一种完全相同的现象。发展过程特殊的崩溃现象（我们从经验得知的并且描述为危机），甚至对于天真的人们，都总是显得是一个而且是相同的一个现象的各种形式。然而，危机的这种同一性肯定是不会持久的。相反，它主要存在于对经济系统和个人影响的相似性上，而且存在于这个事实中，就是某些事件总是习惯性地出现在大多数危机中。然而，这种影响和事件，倒是和经济生活中大多数外界的和内在的干扰一起出现，并且不足以证明危机总是同样的现象。实际上，危机的不同种类和起因是可以识别的。我们没有理由事先假定，危机相互之间的共同点，比我们作为开始的基本要素要多，也就是说，危机是所有那些使先前的经济发展过程停止的事件。

① 当然，托拉斯化越是发展，这种情况越少。

Secondly, whether homogeneous or heterogeneous phenomena, crises may or may not be capable of a purely economic explanation. Of course it cannot be doubted that crises belong essentially in the economic sphere. But it is by no means certain that they belong to the nature of the economic system or even to any one kind of system in the sense that they would necessarily result from the operation of economic factors left to themselves. On the contrary, it would be quite possible for the real causes of crises to exist outside the purely economic sphere, that is for them to be consequences of disturbances which act upon the latter from outside. The frequency and even the often asserted regularity of crises would be in itself no conclusive argument, since it can be readily conceived that such disturbances must often occur in practical life. A crisis would then simply be the process by which economic life adapts itself to new conditions.

As regards the first point we can at the outset say one thing. If we speak of crises wherever large disturbances are met with, then there is no general attribute beyond the fact of disturbance. For the moment, it is as well to conceive of crises in this broad sense. Economic processes are accordingly divisible into three different classes : into the processes of the circular flow, into those of development, and into those which impede the latter's undisturbed course. This arrangement is by no means remote from reality. We can dearly keep all three classes separate in real life. Only more detailed analysis will show whether one of them comes under one of the other two.

The absence of a general attribute in the disturbances is proved by the history of crises. Such disturbances have already broken out in every conceivable place in the economic body, and more-over in very different ways in different places. Sometimes they appear on the supply side, sometimes on the demand side: in the former case sometimes in technical production, sometimes in the market or in credit relations; in the latter case, sometimes through changes in the direction of demand (for example changes in fashion), sometimes through changes in the purchasing power of consumers. For the most part the various industrial groups do not suffer in the same way, but first one industry suffers more, then another. Sometimes the crisis is characterized by a breakdown of the credit system

第二，不管现象是同质的还是异质的，危机都不一定能作纯粹的经济解释。当然，危机本质上属于经济范畴，这是不容置疑的。但是，决不能断言说危机属于经济体系的本质，或者甚至说它们在这个意义上属于任何一种体系，即它们必然产生于经济因素本身的作用。相反，危机的真正原因很有可能存在于经济范畴之外，也就是说，危机是外界干扰经济领域的结果。危机发生的频率，甚至是人们常宣称的危机的规律性，本身都不是定论，因为很容易想像，这些干扰必定经常出现在实际生活中。所以，简单地说，危机是经济生活使其适应新环境的过程。

考虑到第一点，我们在开始就可以谈到一种情况。如果我们无论在哪儿遇到大的干扰就说是危机，那么除了干扰这个事实之外就没有其他一般性质了。目前，也可以在这个广义上构想危机。相应地，经济过程也可以分成三个不同的类型：循环流转过程、发展过程、阻碍发展不受干扰的过程。这种分类绝不是脱离现实的。在真实生活中，我们可以清楚地把这三类区分开来。只有更详细地分析才能表明其中的一类是否属于另两类中的某一类。

危机史已经证明了不存在干扰的普遍特征。这些干扰在经济实体每一个可以想像到的地方已经爆发了，甚至在不同的地方以不同的方式爆发。有时，它们出现在供给一方，有时出现在需求一方：在前一种情况下，有时出现在技术生产领域，有时出现在市场或者信贷关系方面；在后一种情况下，有时体现为需求方向的变化（例如时尚风格的变化），有时体现为消费者购买力的变化。对大多数工业集团来说，他们受的干扰不尽相同，但是第一个工业行业受到的干扰较多，然后才是其他的。有时危机以信用制度的崩溃

which especially affects capitalists, sometimes the workers or landowners suffer most. Entrepreneurs may also be involved in very different ways.

At first sight the attempt to seek the common element in crises in the form of their appearance seems to be more promising. Actually it is this element that has led to the popular and scientific conviction that crises are always one and the same phenomenon. However, it is easy to see that these external characteristics which may be seized upon superficially are neither common to nor essential for all crises in so far as they go beyond the one element of the disturbance of development. The element of panic, for example, is very obvious. It was a striking feature of earlier crises. But there are also panics without a crisis. And further there are crises without real panics. The intensity of the panic does not in any case bear a necessary relation to the importance of the crisis. Finally, panics are much more the consequences than the causes of the outbreak of crises. This is also true of catchwords like "speculative fever," "overproduction,"① and so forth. Once a crisis has broken out and changed the whole economic situation, a great deal of speculation may appear senseless and almost every quantity of goods produced too large, although both were perfectly appropriate to the state of affairs before the outbreak of the crisis. Similarly, the breakdown of individual concerns, the lack of the proper relation between the individual branches of production, the incongruence of production with consumption, and other such elements are effects rather than causes. That there is no satisfactory criterion of crises in this sense is indicated by the fact that although in the descriptive literature of the subject a certain number of crises invariably recur, yet beyond this the individual enumerations of crises do not agree with one another.

We now come to the other question, whether all crises are not at least purely economic phenomena, that is whether they and all their causes and effects are capable of being understood by explanatory

① By this we do not mean the elaborated overproduction theories but only the popular reference to this element.

为特征，尤其是对资本家影响的信用制度，有时工人或者土地所有者遭受最多的损失。企业家也以各种不同的方式被卷进来。

乍一看，试图在危机所表现的形式中寻找共同的成分，似乎更有希望。实际上，正是这种共同成分导致了一种流行的、科学的信念，即危机总是一个而且是同一个现象。然而，很容易看出，这些可以从表面获得的外在特征，除了是干扰发展的一种要素外，对于所有的危机来说，它们既不是共有的，也不是本质的。比如说，恐慌的要素就是非常明显的。它是早期危机的显著特征。但也存在这种情况，即，有恐慌但没有危机。进一步说，存在没有真正恐慌的危机。无论怎么说，恐慌的强度与危机的重要性之间，不存在必然的联系。最后，恐慌更多的是危机爆发的结果，而不是它的原因。这对诸如“投机热潮”、“生产过剩”[①] 等等流行口号也适用。一旦危机爆发并且改变了整个经济形式，那么大量的投机买卖就显得没有什么意义了，而且几乎生产出来的每一种商品的数量都显得过大，尽管在危机爆发之前这两者都与当时的状况完全适合。类似地，个别厂家的倒闭，生产的各个部门之间缺乏适当的联系，生产与消费的不一致，以及其他要素，基本上都是危机的结果，而不是原因。在这个意义上，没有令人满意的判断危机的标准，这一点可以由下面这个事实表明，即，尽管在有关这个主题的描述性文献中，必定重现了一定数量的危机，但除此以外，危机的个别细节彼此之间并不相符合。

现在我们来看另一个问题：是否所有的危机都是纯粹的经济现象，也就是说，是否危机以及所有的形成原因及其结果，都能从

① 我这样说，并不是指详尽的生产过剩理论，而只是关于这种要素的流行说法。

factors resulting from studying the economic System. It is clear that this is not always and not necessarily the case. It will be admitted at once that the outbreak of war, for example, may cause disturbances big enough for a crisis to be spoken of. To be sure, this is by no means the rule. The great wars of the nineteenth century, for example, did not for the most part lead immediately to crises. But the case is conceivable. Let us assume that an insular nation, which has an active trade with other nations and whose economic system may be conceived as in full development in our sense, is cut off from the outside world by an enemy fleet. Imports and exports alike are obstructed, the price and value system is shattered, obligations cannot be kept, the anchor chain of credit snaps-all this is conceivable, has actually occurred, and certainly represents a crisis. And this crisis is incapable of being explained purely economically since the cause, the war, is an element foreign to the economic system. By the operation of this foreign body in the economic sphere the crisis arose and is at the same time explained. Such external factors very frequently explain crises. [①] An important example is bad harvests, which may evidently evoke crises and, as is well known, have become even the basis of a general theory of crises.

But even circumstances which do not act from without on the economic system as strikingly as wars or meteorological conditions must be seen from the standpoint of pure theory as effects of external causes of disturbance and hence in principle as accidental. To take an example, the sudden abolishment of protective tariffs may cause a crisis. Such a commercial measure is certainly an economic event. But we can assert nothing accurate about its appearance; we can only investigate its effects. From the standpoint of the laws of economic life it is simply an influence from without.

---

① Not only do the crisis-like phenomena at the outbreak of the World War belong here, but also the post-war crises of all countries, the nature of which, moreover, is not exhaustively rendered by the catch-phrase "stabilisation crisis" or "deflation crisis" as the case may be.

对经济系统的研究所得到的解释因素中得以理解。很清楚，情况不总是这样，而且也不一定必然要这样。我们应该立即承认，比如说战争的爆发，它可能导致足够大的干扰，从而形成我们所说的危机。当然，这决不是规律，例如，19 世纪大规模的战争，大都没有立即导致危机。不过，那种情况是可以想像的，假设一个岛国，它积极地与其他国家进行贸易活动，而且它的经济体制是那种我们所说的达到了充分发展，假设它被敌国舰队切断了与外界的联系，进出口同样被阻碍，价格和价值体系被粉碎，债务不能保持，信用的链绳被切断——所有这些都是可以想像的，这些都已经实际出现，而且的确标志着一种危机。这种危机不能单纯从经济学来解释，因为战争的起因是经济制度以外的因素。由于这种外界实体在经济领域内的作用，便产生了危机，同时也解释了危机。这些外界的因素经常被用来解释危机，[①] 一个重要的例子就是糟糕的收成，显然它可能引发危机，而且众所周知，它甚至已经成为有关危机的一般理论的基础。

但是，即使环境不像战争或者气象条件那样明显地从外部作用于经济体系，但从纯理论角度看，它必须被看做是外界干扰原因的结果，因而在原则上它就是偶然的。举例来说，突然废止保护关税也可能引起一场危机，这种商业措施当然属于经济事件。但是我们不能精确断定它的外形；我们只能考察它的影响效果。从经济生活的规律来看，它只是外界的一种影响。这样，就存在

---

① 不仅在世界大战爆发时类似危机的现象属于此列，而且战后所有国家的危机都属于此列。此外，这些危机的性质，并没有像流行口号“稳定危机”或者“通货紧缩危机”所表述的那样，被详尽地描绘出来。

Thus, there are crises which are not purely economic phenomena in our sense. And because they are not, we can say nothing in general, from the purely economic standpoint, about their causes. With us, they must pass for unfortunate accidents.

The question now arises: are there any purely economic crises in our sense, crises which would appear without the outside impulses of which we have just given examples? In fact the view is conceivable, and has been actually held, that crises are always effects of external circumstances, And it is undoubtedly very plausible. If it is correct, then there is no real economic theory of crises, and we can do nothing but simply establish these facts or at most try to classify those external causes of crises.

Before we answer our question we must get rid of a special kind of crisis. If the industry of a country is financed by another country and if a wave of prosperity sweeps over the latter, which offers capital more profitable employment than it has found hitherto in the former country, then there will exist a tendency to withdraw capital from its previous investments. If this happens quickly and inconsiderately it can dearly result in a crisis in the first country. This example should show that purely economic causes in one economic area may give rise to crises in another. The phenomenon is frequent and generally recognized. Obviously this can happen not only between two different countries but also between different parts of one country and finally, under certain circumstances, within one economic area between the different branches of industry. When a crisis has once broken out in one place it usually involves other places. Now the question is, are such phenomena purely economic, of the kind we are seeking? The answer is in the negative. The economic conditions of other regions are data for any given economic system and can only play the part of non-economic elements in explaining phenomena within it. For the economic system under consideration they are accidents, and

这样一种危机，它不是我们所谓的纯经济现象。因为它们不是纯经济现象，所以从纯经济视角，我们通常说不出任何关于它们起因的东西。对我们来说，它们一定被当做不幸的偶然事件。

现在产生的问题是，在我们所说的意义上，是否存在纯粹的经济危机？是否存在没有我们刚才所列举的外界冲击而出现的危机？事实上，这种观点是可以理解的，而且实际上已经被接受：危机总是外界环境的影响结果。无疑，这又是似是而非的。如果它是正确的，那么就不会有真正的危机经济理论，我们也将无所作为，只能简单地证明这些事实，或者至多不过是试着对危机的那些外在原因进行分类。

在回答我们的问题之前，我们必须去掉一种特殊的危机。如果一个国家的工业是靠另一个国家来筹集资金的，如果繁荣的浪潮冲击着后者，而后者向资本提供的用途比前一个国家迄今为止所提供的用途更为有利，那么就会出现一种从先前的投资中抽出资本的趋势。如果这种行为迅速并且轻率地发生了，那么很清楚，会在前一个国家导致危机。这个例子应该表明，一个经济地区的纯粹的经济原因可能导致另一个地区产生危机。这种现象经常并且普遍地被认识到。显然，这不仅会在两个不同的国家之间发生，而且可能在同一个国家的不同地区之间发生，并且在一定的条件下，还可能在同一经济区域不同的工业部门之间发生。一旦危机在一个地方爆发，通常它将牵连到其他地方。现在的问题是，这种现象是我们在寻找的那种纯经济的吗？回答是否定的。其他地区的经济状况是任何给定经济系统的资料，并且在解释该系统内的现象时，只能作为非经济要素。对于正在考察的经济系统，它们是偶然事件，而且，如果试图为这种危机找到一

it would be idle to try to find a general law for such crises.

Finally, after discarding all extraneous causes of crises, we find still others which are of a purely economic character in the sense that they arise from within the economic system, but which nevertheless do not present a new theoretic problem. Every new combination, to use our old expression, is exposed to an obvious danger of turning out a failure. Although cases in which whole branches of industry commit fatal mistakes will be rare, yet they happen, and if the industry in question is of sufficient importance, most of the symptoms of a crisis may be produced by them. But again, events of this class are merely mishaps, to be individually explained in each case and not inherent in the economic process in the sense of being the result of any element or factor *essential to it.*

If we consider this list of possible causes of disturbance, it may well become doubtful whether there will be anything left if we abstract from all its items, and whether, therefore, anything more can be said about the causation of crises than that they happen if, in consequence of outside or inside accidents, anything of sufficient importance goes wrong. History would not contradict this theory. For there are in almost every historical case so very many "accidents," which may without any glaring absurdity be held responsible for the crisis actually occurring, that the necessity of any search for more general and fundamental causes is less obvious than some of us seem to believe. It may be remarked in passing that, however we may decide this question, the individual setting of most of the great crises in history is more important for the explanation of the actual happenings observed in each case than anything which enters into a general theory-supposing such theory to be possible-which can therefore never be expected to yield more than a *contribution* to either diagnosis or remedial policy in any actual case. If businessmen nearly always try to account for any crisis by circumstances special to the case in hand, they are not entirely wrong.

般规律，将是徒劳。

最后，摒弃了所有来自外界的危机的原因之后，我们还发现了其他纯经济特征的原因，也就是说，它们产生于经济体系内，但尽管如此，它们并不反映一个新的理论问题。用我们的老话说，每一种新的组合都有招致明显的失败的风险。尽管产业的各个部门犯致命性的错误的情况很少，但它们还是会发生，如果存在问题的这些产业相当重要，那么危机的大多数症状就可能产生于它们。但是，话说回来，这类事件只是小的意外，在每一种情况下都可以单独解释，而且，从经济过程的本质要素或因素的结果这个意义上说，它不是经济过程所固有的。

如果我们考虑这种干扰的一系列可能的原因，那么这就是值得怀疑的了：如果我们对所有的项目进行抽象，是否还会剩下什么，从而，如果由于内外部偶然事件的影响，任何足够重要的事情都出了差错，危机便发生了，我们是否可以对危机的因果关系比它这样实际发生的说得更多。历史并不与这个理论矛盾。因为，几乎在所有的历史情况下，都有许多“偶然事件”，这些偶然事件可能被认为应该对实际发生的危机负责，而这没有任何明显的荒唐之处，从而，探索更普遍的和更基本的原因的必要性就不像我们中的一些人所认为的那样明显。顺便应提到的是，尽管我们可以决定这个问题，但历史上大多数重大的危机，其个别背景，对于解释每一种情况下所观察到的实际发生的事，比一般理论中的内容更重要——假定这种理论是可能的——因而这种理论只能对实际情况下的诊断或补救政策有所贡献，而不期望它有任何其他作用。如果商人们总是试图用手中掌握的特殊情况来解释任何一种危机，他们也不完全是错误的。“经验主义者的”对试图构建

Nor is the "empiricist's" antagonism towards any attempt to construct a general theory without foundation-although it is not antagonism that is called for in this case but a dear distinction between two entirely different tasks.

The decisive discovery, which settled our question and at the same time shifted our problem onto somewhat different ground, consisted in establishing the fact that there is, at all events, one class of crises, which are *elements*, or at any rate regular if not necessary *incidents*, of a wave-like movement of alternating periods of prosperity and depression, which have pervaded economic life ever since the capitalist era began. ①This phenomenon, then, emerges from the mass of multifarious and heterogeneous facts which may account for setbacks or breakdowns of all sorts. These great peripeteias of economic life are what we have primarily to explain. As soon as we seize upon this problem we are, for the purposes of theoretic analysis, not only justified but forced to assume the absence of all the other-external and internal- disturbances to which industrial life is exposed, in order to isolate the only question interesting from the point of view of theory. In so doing, we must never forget, however, that what we discard is not on that account of inferior importance, and that our theory, if kept within the narrow limits of our question, must become in- commensurable with all analytic endeavors of wider scope which aim at providing an apparatus for the full understanding of the actual course of things.

That question may now be formulated as follows: why is it that economic development in our sense does not proceed evenly as a tree grows, but as it were jerkily; why does it display those characteristic ups and downs?

2. The answer cannot be short and precise enough: exclusively *because the new combinations are not, as one would expect according to general principles, of probability, evenly distributed through time*

① This discovery and the full perception of its consequences are due to Clement Juglar.

一种缺乏基础的一般理论的对抗态度也不完全是错的——尽管它不是这种情况所要求的对抗，而是这两种完全不同的事务之间的一种显然的区别。

这个决定性的发现，解决了我们的问题，同时把我们的问题转移到稍有不同的环境下，确立了这个事实，即在任何情况下都存在着一种危机，它是繁荣与萧条交替变化时期的波浪式运动的要素，或者，不论怎么说，它都是有规律的，如果不是必要的事变；这类危机自从资本主义时代开始就渗入经济生活。[①] 于是，这个现象从大量形形色色的和不同质的事实中产生，这些事实可以用来解释各种后退和崩溃的情况。经济生活的这些巨大的突变正是我们必须首先要解释的。我们一旦抓住了这个问题，为了进行理论分析，我们不仅有理由而且不得不假定：不存在所有其他——外部和内部的——工业生活可能招致的干扰，这是为了将理论研究上最有意义的问题独立开来。然而，这样做了，我们还必须牢牢记住，我们排除那些情况，并不是因为它们不重要。同时，如果我们的理论局限于我们所讨论的问题的狭窄范围内，那么它必定与所有更广阔领域的努力分析不相称，这种努力分析的目的是为全面理解事物的实际过程提供一种工具。

现在这个问题可以表述如下：为什么我们所说的经济发展不像树木的成长那样均匀地前进，而是跳跃式地前进？为什么它表现出特有的上升和下降？

2. 这个回答不可能简短，也不可能足够的精确：这完全是因为新的组合不像人们根据一般概率原理所期望的那样，在时间上

① 这个发现以及对它的结果的全面认识，都要归于克莱芒·尤格拉。

-in such a way that equal intervals of time could be chosen, in each of which the carrying out of one new combination would fall-but *appear, if at all, discontinuously in groups or swarms.*

This answer is now (*a*) to be interpreted, this appearance in groups is then (*b*) to be explained, whereupon (*c*) the consequences of this fact and the course of the causal nexus called forth by them are to be analyzed (in 3 of this chapter). The third point contains a new problem without the solution of which the theory would be incomplete. Although we accept Juglar's statement that "the only cause of the depression is prosperity"-which means that depression is nothing more than the economic system's reaction to the boom, or the adaptation to the situation into which the boom brings the system, so that its explanation is also rooted in the explanation of the boom-yet the manner in which the boom leads to the depression remains a thing by itself, as the reader can see at once in the difference on this point existing between Spiethoff and me. It will also be seen immediately that this question is answered-without difficulty and without the aid of new facts or theoretical instruments-by our argument.

(*a*) If the new enterprises in our sense were to appear independently of one another, there would be no boom and no depression as special, distinguishable, striking, regularly recurring phenomena. For their appearance would then be, in general, continuous; they would be evenly distributed in time and the changes which would be effected by them in the circular flow would each of them be relatively small, hence the disturbances would be of only local importance and easily overcome for the economic system as a whole. There would be no considerable disturbances of the circular flow and therefore no disturbances of growth at all. It should be noticed that this is true for any theory of crises with respect to that element which it considers as the cause, in particular for all disproportionality theories; the phenomenon is never made intelligible if it is not explained why the cause, whatever it may be, cannot act in such a way as to allow the consequences to

均匀分布——如果以这种方式，人们就可以选择等间隔的时间，在每一间隔里可以实施一种新的组合——而是，如果一旦出现，它就以不连续的方式成群或成组地出现。

现在，（a）解释这个回答，（b）解释这种成组方式的出现，（c）据此分析这一事实的结果以及它们所产生的因果关系的过程（看本章3.）。第三点包含一个新问题，如果不解决这个问题，那么这条理论就是不完全的。尽管我们接受尤格拉的观点："萧条的唯一原因是繁荣"——它意味着萧条只不过是经济系统对繁荣的一种反应，或者是为了适应繁荣给经济系统带来的新状况，所以，对萧条的解释也根源于对繁荣的解释——然而，从繁荣走向萧条本身就是一种独立的方式，就像读者能够立即看出斯皮托夫与我在这一点上存在的区别一样。人们也会立即看出，这个问题已经通过我们的论证解答了——没有任何困难，也没有借助新的事实或者理论工具。

（a）如果我们所指的新企业真是互相独立地出现，那么将没有像特殊的、可区别的、显著的、有规律性地发生那样的繁荣和萧条。因为它们的出现一般是连续的；它们将会按时间均匀地分布，而且在循环流转中，受它们影响而发生的变化，都相对很小，因此，这些干扰仅具有局部重要性，而且对于经济系统整体来说是很容易征服的。这样就不会有循环流转的重大干扰，所以也就根本不存在对增长的干扰。应该注意的是，这适用于把那种要素看做是危机的产生原因的所有危机理论，尤其是所有的"比例失调"理论；这个现象从来都是不容易理解的，不论它会是什么情况，如果它不能解释为什么其原因不是这样发挥作用，从而使其

be continuously and currently absorbed.[①]

Even then there would be good and bad times. Gold or other inflation would still hasten economic growth, deflation would obstruct it; political and social events and economic legislation would still exercise their influence. An event like the World War, for example, with the adjustment of the economic system to war requirements enforced by it, with the necessary liquidation after its conclusion, with its disturbance of all economic relations, its devastations and social upheavals, its destruction of important markets, its alteration of all data, would have taught men what crises and depressions are like even if they had not already known. But there would not be the kind of prosperity and depression which are here under consideration. Such events would not be regular, or necessary in the sense that they emerge from the working of the economic system itself, but would have to be explained by special external causes, as has already been sufficiently emphasized. One favorable circumstance, which always facilitates and partly explains a boom, must be particularly remembered, namely the state of affairs created by every period of depression. As is well known, there are generally masses of unemployed, accumulated stocks of raw materials, machines, buildings, and so forth offered below cost of production, and there is as a rule an abnormally low rate of interest. Indeed these facts play a part in nearly every investigation of the phenomenon, as for example with Spiethoff and Mitchell. But it is clear that we can never explain the phenomenon by these consequences of it if we wish to avoid first deriving the depression from the boom and then the latter from the depression. Therefore here, where it is only a question of the principle of the thing-and not of an exhaustive statement of the circumstances (bad harvests,[②] war

---

① By which I mean that this part of our argument must be simply taken for granted by every theory of crises. For even if otherwise free from objection, none explains precisely this circumstance.

② Good harvests, for example, facilitate and lengthen the boom, or alleviate and shorten the depression. They are often important in explaining an individual situation: so much H. L. Moore has certainly demonstrated. But they are never coordinate with our causal nexus; they only operate through it.

结果是连续的且容易被吸纳。[①]

即使这样，也还存在着繁荣与萧条。黄金或者其他通货膨胀仍将加剧经济增长，通货紧缩将阻碍经济增长；政治和社会事件以及经济立法仍将施加它们的影响。例如，像世界大战这样的事件，以及由于战争的需要而迫使经济系统作出的调整，战后必要的清理，对所有经济关系的干扰，战争劫后余迹及社会的动乱，对重要市场的毁灭，对所有资料的改变，等等都会告诉人们危机和萧条是什么样子，即使人们对此还不了解。但是这些都不是我们在这里所要探讨的那种繁荣和萧条。这些事件没有规律性，而且从产生于经济系统本身的运行这个意义来说，它们也不是必然的，而正如已经充分强调的那样，它们必须用特殊的外在原因来解释。我们尤其需要记住一种有利的情况，它总是促进并且部分地解释了繁荣，也就是每一时期萧条所导致的状态。众所周知，在这种情况下，通常总是存在大量的失业者，原材料、机器、房屋等等存品积压，以低于生产成本的价格待售，通常还存在不正常的低利率。的确，正如举例说明斯皮托夫和米切尔时那样，几乎在每一次对这些现象的考察中，这些事实都起着一定的作用。但是，如果我们不希望首先从繁荣中得出萧条，然后又从萧条中得出繁荣，那么，显然，我们就决不能用这些现象的结果来解释现象。因此这里只是一个讨论事物的原理的问题——而不是详细阐述在繁荣或危机中具体起作用的那些情况（不好的收成[②]、战争

---

① 由此，我认为，我们论证的这一部分应该完全被每一种危机理论接受。因为即使从反面说，也没有反对的意见，但也没有人能精确地解释这种情况。

② 例如，好的收成推动并延长繁荣，或者减轻并缩短萧条。它们对于解释个别情况通常是很重要的：穆尔确实对此作过论证。但是它们与我们的因果关系决不能等同；它们只是通过这种因果关系起作用。

rumors, and so forth) concretely operative in boom or crisis-we shall completely neglect these consequences.

Three circumstances increase the effect of the swarm-like appearance of new enterprises, yet without being real causes coordinate with it. First, our argument in the second chapter allows us to expect-and experience confirms it-that the vast majority of new combinations will not grow out of the old firms or immediately take their place, but appear side by side, and compete, with them. From the standpoint of our theory this is neither a new nor an independent element; nor is it essential to the existence of booms and depressions, although it is clearly very important in explaining the amplitude of the wave-like movement.

Secondly, the fact that entrepreneurial demand appears *en masse signifies* a very substantial increase in purchasing power all over the business sphere. This starts a secondary boom, which spreads over the whole economic system and is the vehicle of the phenomenon of general prosperity-which can only be completely understood in this way and cannot be satisfactorily explained otherwise. Only because new purchasing power goes in bulk from the hands of entrepreneurs to the owners of material means of production, to all producers of goods for "reproductive consumption" (Spiethoff), and to the workers, and then oozes into every economic channel, are all existing consumption goods finally sold at ever-rising prices. Retailers thereupon place bigger orders, manufacturers extend operations, and for this purpose increasingly more unfavorable and often already abandoned means of production come into use again. And only on this account do production and trade *everywhere* temporarily yield a profit, just as in a period of inflation, for example when war expenditure is financed with paper money. Many things float on this "secondary wave," without any new or direct impulse from the real driving force, and speculative anticipation in the end acquires a causal significance. The symptoms of prosperity themselves finally become, in the well known manner, a factor of prosperity. For the theory of business indices and the understanding of the business situation as a whole, this is of course most important. For our purpose, however, only the division between primary and secondary waves is essential, and it is enough to note that the latter can simply be traced back to the former and that in a theory elaborated

谣传，等等）的问题——我们将完全不考虑这些结果。

有三种情况增强了新企业成群出现的影响，但它们却不是与这个影响等同的真正原因。第一，在第二章的论证中，我们允许期望——这个期望也被经验所证明——大量新的组合将不是从原来的老厂商中产生，也不是立即替代老厂商，而是与老厂商并行出现，并与它们竞争。尽管在解释波浪式运动的幅度时，明显地，这很重要，但从我们的理论来看，这既不是新的也不是独立的要素；它对于繁荣与萧条的存在并不是关键性的。

第二，企业家的需求大批的出现，这一事实表明整个商业界购买力的巨大增长。这就开始了第二轮繁荣，它将延伸到整个经济系统，它是达到普遍繁荣的传播工具——只有这样才能充分理解它，用其他方式解释都不能让人满意。因为新的购买力大量的从企业家手中转移到生产资料所有者，转移到“再生产性消费”商品的生产者（斯皮托夫），转移到工人，然后渗入每一个经济环节，所以，所有现存的消费品最终以不断增长的价格出售。从而，零售商大量订货，制造商扩大经营，为此，越来越多不适宜的而且通常是已经被抛弃了的生产资料又重新被使用。仅仅出于这个原因，各个地方的生产和贸易短期获利，就像在通货膨胀时期，例如，用纸币开支战争费用，可以获得暂时利益。许多事物浮在“次级波”上，而没有来自真实驱动力的任何新的或者直接的冲击，最后，投机性期望形成了一种因果意义。繁荣迹象本身最后以人们所熟悉的方式成为繁荣的一个因素。对于商业指数理论，以及对于理解整个商业形式，这当然是极其重要的。然而，就我们的目的而言，唯一关键的是第一级波与次级波之间的区别，而且，我们还应注意，次级波可以径直追溯到第一级波，并且，根据以我们的

upon the basis of our principle everything that was ever observed in the cyclical movement would find its definite place. But in an exposition like the present, justice cannot be done to such things, hence an impression of remoteness from reality may arise which is actually not justified. ①

Thirdly, it follows from our argument that errors must play a considerable rôle at the beginning of the boom and during the course of the depression. Most theories of crises in fact use this element in one way or another. Errors, however, do not normally occur to the excessive extent required; production is entered upon by sane men only on the basis of more or less careful investigation of the facts. Although miscalculations may occur on a scale that may well endanger an individual business, in exceptional cases perhaps a whole industry, this is not as a rule enough to endanger the economic system as a whole. How can such general mistakes be made, then, that the whole system is affected, *and indeed as an independent cause and not merely as a consequence of the depression which is to be explained*? Once it has set in for other reasons, depression certainly upsets many plans which were previously quite reasonable and makes mistakes dangerous which would otherwise have been easily rectified. The initial mistakes require a special explanation, without which nothing is explained, Our analysis supplies this explanation. If the characteristic feature of a period of boom is not merely increased business activity as such, but the carrying out of new and untried combinations, then it is immediately clear, as has already been mentioned in Chapter II, that error

① In particular, all the circumstances which in other theories of crises act in the capacity of causes find their place within the framework of our theory, as the reader can easily see if he is inclined to think the matter through. In this book, of course, our explanation of the cycle always remains exposed to an objection similar to the one made against the theory of development in Chapter II, namely, that it emphasises one-sidedly and exaggeratedly one element out of many. This objection confuses the problem of explaining the nature and mechanism of the cycle with the problem of a theory of the concrete factors of individual cycles.

原理作为基础推导出来的一种理论，所有在周期运动中曾被观察到的事物都将找到它们明确的位置。但是在一种像当前这样的阐述中，不可能公正地对待这些事情，从而可能产生一种远离现实的印象，而这种印象实际上是没有道理的。①

第三，从我们的论证可以得出，在繁荣开始以及在萧条的过程中，过失必定起着相当重要的作用。大多数危机理论都以某种方式利用这个要素。不过，过失不会在超过所需要的程度上正常地出现；明智的或者神志正常的人，多少也是在对事实进行仔细考察的基础上才进入生产过程。尽管发生的错误估计其程度可能会达到危及个别企业的生存，在特殊情况下可能会危及整个产业，但通常它还不足以对整个经济系统构成威胁。那么，这种一般性的错误是如何产生的，从而影响到整个系统？如何解释它确实是萧条的一个独立的原因而不只是萧条的结果？一旦由其他原因产生了萧条，那么这自然就会扰乱许多原先十分合理的计划，并且使得这些错误变得很危险，而这些错误原先是很容易克服的。最初的错误需要一种特殊的解释，否则什么都不能解释。我们的分析可以提供这种解释。如果繁荣时期的特征不只是这样增加了企业活动，还有实现了新的和从未尝试过的组合，那么，我们立即就会清楚，就像第二章已经提到的那样，过失在那里承

① 特别地，如果读者深入思考这个问题，正如他能容易看到的那样，在其他危机理论中起着原因作用的所有情况，在我们的理论框架中都能找到它们的位置。当然，在本书中，我们对周期的解释总是会招来一种反对意见，它类似于反对第二章发展理论的意见，也就是，它片面地、夸大地强调众多要素中的某一种。这个反对意见混淆了对周期的性质与机制的解释问题与关于个别循环的具体因素的理论问题。

must play a special rôle there, qualitatively different from its rôle in the circular flow. Nevertheless, no "error theory" will be found here. On the contrary, in order to avoid any such impression we shall segregate this element. It is indeed a supporting and accentuating circumstance, but not a primary cause necessary to the understanding of the principle. There would still be cyclical movements-though in a milder form-even if no one ever did anything that could be described as "false" from his point of view; even if there were no technical or commercial "error," or "speculative fever," or groundless optimism and pessimism; and even if everyone were gifted with wide foresight. The objective situation which the boom necessarily creates explains exclusively the nature of the thing,[①] as will be seen.

(b) Why do entrepreneurs appear, not continuously, that is singly in every appropriately chosen interval, but in clusters? *Exclusively because the appearance of one or a few entrepreneurs facilitates the appearance of others, and these the appearance of more, in ever-increasing numbers.*

This means, first, that for the reasons explained in Chapter II the carrying out of new combinations is difficult and only accessible to people with certain qualities, as is best seen by visualizing an example from earlier times or the economic situation in the stage that most resembles an economy without development, viz. the stage of advanced stagnation. Only a few people have these qualities of leadership and only a few in such a situation, that is a situation which is not itself already a boom, can succeed in this direction. However, if one or a few have advanced with success

---

① Which of course does not mean that the practical importance of the element of error is denied, nor that of the elements which are usually designated by speculative fever, fraud, etc. -in which category overproduction also belongs. We assert only that all these things are in part consequential and that even in so far as this is not the case the nature of the phenomenon cannot be understood from them.

担着特殊的角色，其作用在本质上与在循环流转中的作用不同。尽管如此，在这里并不存在“过失理论”。相反，为了避免产生这种印象，我们将隔离这个要素。它的确是一种支持和加强的因素，但却不是理解这个原理的必要的基本原因。即使没有一个人曾经做过任何他自己认为可以说成是“错误”的事；即使没有任何技术或商业上的“过失”，或者“投机热潮”，或者毫无依据的乐观与悲观；即使每个人都有长远的预见的天赋，但仍然会有周期性的运动——尽管以一种温和的方式。繁荣所必然创造的客观情况独有地或者唯一地解释了事物的本质，① 正如我们将要看到的那样。

(b) 为什么企业家不是连续地出现，也就是，为什么只是在每一适当的间隔内出现，而且是成群地出现？唯一的原因是，一个或者几个企业家的出现促进了其他企业家的出现，这样使得企业家以递增的数量出现。

首先，这意味着，根据第二章所解释的原因，实施一种新的组合是很困难的，而且只有具有某种特殊品质的人才能达到它，对于这个问题，最好是设想一个较早时期的例子，或者设想一种经济状况，它类似于处在经济尚未发展阶段的情况，也就是处于高度停滞阶段的状态。只有少数人具备这种领导品质，而且只有少数人处于这种状况，这种状况本身还没有进入繁荣，少数的人能够沿着这个方向获得成功。然而，如果有一个或几个企业家成功

① 当然这并不是说，要否认过失这一要素的实际重要性，也不是否认那些通常被称为投机热、欺骗等等要素的重要性——生产过剩也属于这一类。我们只是断言，所有这些现象都是部分地互为因果，甚至如果情况不是这样，也不能从其中理解现象的本质。

many of the difficulties disappear. Others can then follow these pioneers, as they will dearly do under the stimulus of the success now attainable. Their success again makes it easier, through the increasingly complete removal of the obstacles analyzed in the second chapter, for more people to follow suit, until finally the innovation becomes familiar and the acceptance of it a matter of free choice.

Secondly, since as we have seen the entrepreneurial qualification is something which, like many other qualities, is distributed in an ethnically homogeneous group according to the law of error, the number of individuals who satisfy progressively diminishing standards in this respect continually increases. Hence, neglecting exceptional cases-of which the existence of a few Europeans in a negro population would be an example-with the progressive lightening of the task continually more people can and will become entrepreneurs, wherefore the successful appearance of an entrepreneur is followed by the appearance not simply of some others, but of ever greater numbers, though progressively less qualified, This is how it is in practice, the testimony of which we merely interpret. In industries in which there is still competition and a large number of independent people we see first of all the single appearance of an innovation- overwhelmingly in businesses created *ad hoc*-and then we see how the existing businesses grasp it with varying rapidity and completeness, first a few, then continually more. We have already come across this phenomenon in connection with the process of eliminating entrepreneurial profit. Here it comes into consideration again, though from another standpoint. ①

Thirdly, this explains the appearance of entrepreneurs in clusters and indeed up to the point of eliminating entrepreneurial profit, first of all in the branch of industry in which the pioneers appear. Reality also discloses that every normal boom starts in one or a few branches of industry

① For the elimination-mostly foreseen-of entrepreneurial profit is not "the" cause in our theory of crises. Cf. 3, second paragraph.

地前进了，那么许多困难就会消失。接着，其他人就可能跟随这些先驱者，就像此刻在获得成功的激励下，他们会明确地那样做一样。通过逐渐克服第二章所分析的那些障碍，他们的成功将使这个新组合的过程更加容易，因为有更多的人跟上来，直到最后，创新成为人们普遍熟悉的，并且成为人们自由选择的事情。

第二，由于正像我们所看到的那样，企业家的资质，也像其他品质一样，按照过失法则在同质种族的群体内被区分，所以，在这方面满足递减标准的个体的数目不断增加。因此，不考虑例外情况——例如，黑人人口中存在少数欧洲人——随着连续不断地减轻这项工作，越来越多的人能够并且将会成为企业家，从而，在一个企业家成功地出现之后，紧随着的不仅是简单的其他企业家的出现，而且甚至是更大数量的企业家出现，但这些人的资质更不符合企业家的要求。这就是实际情况，我们只是对其证据加以解释。在仍然存在竞争以及大量独立的个人这样的企业中，我们首先只看到创新的出现——其势不可挡地在企业中被独特地创造出来——然后我们会看到现有的企业是如何以敏捷的变化和不同的完整度来把握它，起初是少量单位，然后逐渐增多。我们已经遇到过这种与消除企业家利润过程有关的现象。这里我们再一次考虑这种情况，不过是从另一个视角。①

第三，这解释了企业家成群出现的现象，并且的确达到了消除企业家利润的境地，这首先发生在出现创业者的工业部门。现实情况也揭示了每一个正常的繁荣都开始于一个或几个工业部

① 因为企业家利润的消除——大多数人已经预见到——不是我们的危机理论的“某个”原因。参阅本章 3. 第二段。

(railway building, electrical, and chemical industries, and so forth), and that it derives its character from the innovations in the industry where it begins. But the pioneers remove the obstacles for the others not only in the branch of production in which they first appear, but, owing to the nature of these obstacles, *ipso facto* in other branches too. Many things may be copied by the latter; the example as such also acts upon them; and many achievements directly serve other branches too, as for example the opening up of a foreign market, quite apart from the circumstances of secondary importance which soon appear-rising prices and so on. Hence the first leaders are effective beyond their immediate sphere of action and so the group of entrepreneurs increases still further and the economic system is drawn more rapidly and more completely than would otherwise be the case into the process of technological and commercial reorganization which constitutes the meaning of periods of boom.

Fourthly, the more the process of development becomes familiar and a mere matter of calculation to all concerned, and the weaker the obstacles become in the course of time, the less the "leadership" that will be needed to call forth innovations. Hence the less pronounced will become the swarm-like appearance of entrepreneurs and the milder the cyclical movement. And dearly this consequence of our interpretation is also strikingly confirmed by reality. The progressive trustification of economic life acts in the same direction, even though today a great combine with its sales and its financial requirements is still so dependent upon the market situation, which is to a considerable extent determined competitively, that the universally advantageous postponement of its innovations, and especially of construction, to periods of depression-as exemplified in the policy of American railways-is only possible sporadically. In so far as it operates, however, this element also confirms our interpretation.

Fifthly, the swarm-like appearance of new combinations easily and necessarily explains the fundamental features of periods of boom. It explains why increasing capital investment is the very first symptom of the coming boom, why industries producing means of production are the first to show supernormal stimulation, above all why the consumption of iron increases. It explains

门（铁路建设、电力、化学工业等等），而且繁荣的特征形成于其产生产业的创新活动。但是，先驱者不仅在他们首次出现的生产部门为其他人消除了障碍，而且，由于这些障碍的性质，实际上也在其他部门消除了障碍。后来的跟随者可以模仿很多事情；这种事例也对他们起作用；许多成果或者成就也适用于其他部门，例如国外市场的开发，暂不说很快就要出现的次重要的情况——上升的价格等等。因此，第一批领导者的影响力超越了他们直接活动的范围，从而企业家团体将进一步增加，经济系统与在相反的情况下相比，将更迅速、更完全地被引入技术的和商业的重组过程，这一过程构成了繁荣时期的意义。

第四，发展的过程越为人们所熟悉，且发展的过程对所有涉及的方面变得越只是计算的问题，障碍随着时间的进程变得越微弱，那么，引发创新所必需的“领导才能”就越少。因此，企业家成群的出现就变得越不显著，同时周期运动也变得越温和。很清楚，我们解释的这个结果也明显地被事实所证实。经济生活的日益托拉斯化在同一方向上起作用，即使在今天，它与其销售以及金融需求大规模的联合仍然如此地依赖于市场形式，这个市场形式在相当大的程度上决定于竞争，以至于创新带来的普遍益处延迟到萧条时期，尤其在建筑业——比如像美国铁路政策的例子——偶尔也可能发生。然而，只要能起作用，这个要素也就能证实我们的解释。

第五，新组合的成群出现，很容易并且必然地解释了繁荣时期的基本特征。它说明了为什么不断增长的资本投入是即将到来的繁荣的首要征兆，为什么生产生产资料的产业首先表现出超乎寻常的激励，更重要的是，为什么铁的消费增加。它能够解释

the appearance of new purchasing power in bulk,[1]thereby the characteristic rise in prices during booms, which obviously no reference to increased need or increased costs alone can explain. Further, it explains the decline of unemployment and the rise of wages,[2]the rise in the interest rate, the increase in freight, the increasing strain on bank balances and bank reserves, and so forth, and, as we have said, the release of secondary waves-the spread of prosperity over the whole economic system.

3. (c) The swarm-like appearance of entrepreneurs, which is the only cause of the boom, has a qualitatively different effect upon the economic system from that of a continuous appearance evenly distributed in time, in so far as it does not, like the latter, mean a continuous, and even imperceptible, disturbance of the equilibrium position but a jerky disturbance, a disturbance of a different order of magnitude. While the disturbances caused by a continuous appearance of entrepreneurs could be continuously absorbed, the swarm-like appearance necessitates a special and distinguishable process of absorption, of incorporating the new things and of adapting the economic system to them, a process of liquidation or, as I used to say, an approach to a new static state (Statisierung). This process is the essence of periodic depressions, which may therefore be defined from our standpoint as the economic system's struggling towards a new equilibrium position, its adaptation to the data as altered by the disturbance of the boom. The essence of the matter does not lie in the fact that the individual entrepreneur, interested only in planning his own enterprise, takes no account of the swarm-like following of others, and so

---

① Hence it hardly needs to be emphasised that our theory does not belong to those which seek the cause of the cycle in the money and credit system, however important the element of the creation of purchasing power is in our interpretation. Nevertheless, we do not deny that cyclical movements could be influenced and even prevented by credit policy-with them, indeed, also this kind of economic devel-opment in general.

② In principle rents must also rise. But where land is let on a long lease they cannot do so, and in addition many circumstances prevent the prompt rise of this branch of income.

新的购买力的大量出现,[1] 从而解释繁荣时期价格的特征性上涨，显然，这些问题，仅靠需求的增加或成本的上升是不能解释的。进一步说，它解释了失业的下降以及工资的上升,[2] 利率的上升，货运的增加，对银行收支和银行储备的日益紧缩等等，并且正如我们已经说的，它还解释了次级波的释放——使得繁荣遍及整个经济系统。

3.（c）企业家成群的出现是繁荣产生的唯一原因，它对经济系统的影响，与如果企业家按时间分布均匀地连续出现所带来的影响在本质上不同，只要它不像后者那样，即连续地出现，甚至是不可察觉的，对均衡状态干扰，而是一种跳跃式的干扰，一种有着不同重要性顺序的干扰。尽管由企业家连续出现所引起的干扰可以被连续吸收，而企业家成批出现则必需一种特殊的、可识别的吸收过程，并且这个过程能够合并新事物，能够使其适应经济系统，它是一种清理的过程，或者就像我过去说的，它是一种达到新的静止状态的途径。这个过程就是周期性萧条的本质，因此，根据我们的观点，它可以被定义为朝向新的均衡状态的经济系统内的斗争，它适应了因繁荣的干扰而改变了的环境。

这个问题的本质不在于这一事实：仅仅关心制定本企业计划的单个企业家，完全不考虑其他企业家成群地跟随来，从而会遭

---

① 因此，几乎不必强调，我们的理论不属于那些在货币和信用制度中寻找周期原因的理论，无论创造购买力的要素在我们的解释中有多么重要。不过，我们不否认，周期运动会受到信用政策的影响，甚至被信用政策所阻碍——的确，这类经济发展通常也受到它们共同的影响。

② 在原则上，租金也必然上升。但是，如果土地以长期租约租出去，他们就不能这样做，此外，有很多情况阻碍这一部分收入的迅速上升。

comes to grief. It is certainly true that conduct which is correct from the standpoint of the individual business may be mulcted of its fruits by the general effect of the similar conduct of many. We recognized the most important example of this when we explained how producers, in their very striving for the maximum profit, set the mechanism in motion which tends to eliminate surplus value in the system. Similarly, here also the general effect may render false what was correct for the individual, and this element will actually play a part in most crises, for although the swarming after the entrepreneur is known beforehand to the latter and cannot take him unawares, the magnitude and tempo may frequently be estimated wrongly. However, the essence of the disturbance caused by the boom does not lie in the fact that it often upsets entrepreneurs' calculations,[①] but in the following three circumstances.

First, the new entrepreneur's demand for means of production, which is based upon new purchasing power-the well known "race for means of production" (Lederer) in a period of prosperity- drives up the prices of these. In reality this tendency is weakened by the fact that at least some of the new enterprises do not appear side by side with the old, but grow out of them, and that the old businesses do not simply work without profit, but may still earn some quasi-rent. We can best elucidate the nature of the operation, however, if we assume that all innovations are embodied in newly established businesses, are financed solely by newly created purchasing power, and take their place beside businesses which belong strictly to the circular flow and work without profit, and which, therefore, in consequence of the increase in their costs, begin to produce at a loss. Reality contradicts this construction less than one would imagine. Actually, only the atmosphere which hangs over the period of boom hides the fact that very soon after its beginning, and as long as it is

① Nor in the fact that the consequent general extension of production proves to be wrong.

到失败。从个别企业的角度看是正确的行为，它的成果可能因许多类似行为的普遍影响而被剥夺，这当然是真实的。当我们解释了生产者是如何在他们努力寻求最大利润的过程中，发动趋于消除整个经济系统剩余价值的机制的时候，我们就能理解这方面最重要的这个例子。同样，普遍作用在这里也可能导致错误，而这种作用对个人来说可能是正确的，实际上，这个因素在大多数危机中都起着作用，因为尽管企业家已经事先知道其后会有大批的跟随者，并且也不能使企业家攻其不备，但是对情况的规模以及发展速度可能常常估错。然而，因繁荣所引起的干扰，其本质并不在于它常常扰乱企业家对未来的估计，[①]而是在于下面三种情况。

第一，新的企业家基于新的购买力对生产资料的需求——著名的在繁荣时期的“争夺生产资料的竞争”（引自莱德勒的话）——抬高了这些生产资料的价格。实际上，这个趋势被这一事实所削弱：至少某些新的企业并不是与老企业并行存在的，而是产生于老企业，同时老企业也不是只生产而没有利润，而是仍然可以获得部分准地租。不过，我们能够对这种经营的性质作最好的说明，如果我们假设所有的创新都体现在新近建立的企业中，所需的资金都只通过新创造的购买力来筹集，并且创新都发生在这些企业身旁：它们严格属于循环流转范畴，并且经营无利润，从而，由于企业成本的增加开始亏本生产。现实与我们的构想相矛盾的情况，比人们想像的要少。实际上，仅仅弥漫于繁荣时期的状况就可以掩盖这一事实，即在繁荣开始后不久，只要它

① 也不在于这个事实：生产普遍扩张的结果被证明是错误的。

expressed simply in the increased demand, the boom means distress for many producers, although it is diminished again when the rise in the prices of their products sets in. This distress is a form of the process by which means of production are withdrawn from the old businesses and made available for the new purposes, as explained in Chapter II.

Secondly, the new products come on the market after a few years or sooner and compete with the old; the commodity complement of the previously created purchasing power-theoretically more than counterbalancing the latter-enters into the circular flow. Again the consequences of this process are practically moderated by the causes mentioned in the preceding section, and further by the fact that because some investments are remote from finished products this complement appears only gradually. But this does not touch the nature of the process. At the beginning of the boom costs rise in the old businesses; later their receipts are reduced, first in those businesses with which the innovation competes, but then in all old businesses, in so far as consumers' demand changes in favor of the innovation. Apart from the possibility of profiting-secondarily-from the innovation, their working at a loss is only checked by the buffer quasi-rent, which is merely temporarily effective. And it is only because old businesses are mostly well established and appear as especially deserving of credit that this working at a loss does not lead at once to collapse. Their partial breakdown affects the success of the new undertakings. The breakdown is moderated by the fact, which fits so well into the framework of our interpretation, that the boom is never general at first, but centres in one branch or a few branches of industry, leaving the other areas undisturbed, and subsequently only affects the latter in a different, and secondary, manner. Just as entrepreneurs appear *en masse*, so do their products, because the former do not do different but very similar things, and hence their products appear on the market almost simultaneously. The average time[①] which must elapse before the new products appear-though of course actually dependent upon

① This time is determined first technically, then by the tempo in which the multitude follow the leaders.

仅表现为增加的需求，那么这种繁荣对于许多生产者来说就意味着不幸，尽管当其产品价格开始上升时它又将减轻。这种不幸是使生产资料从老企业中撤出并用于新目的的过程的一种形式，就像在第二章中说明的那样。

第二，新产品在几年之后或者不久就上市，并与老产品相竞争，对先前创造的购买力的商品补充——理论上看能抵消购买力而有多余——进入了循环流转。另一方面，这个过程的结果实际上被前一节所提到的原因缓和，而且由于被缓和，即某些投资在过程中距离最终产品很远，所以这种补充只能渐进地出现，但这还没有涉及到过程的实质。在繁荣的初期，老行业的成本上升，后来它们的收益下降，这首先出现在与创新竞争的行业——只要消费者的需求变得有利于创新，然后才是所有的老行业收入下降。暂且不说创新带来盈利的可能性如何——盈利是次要的，他们亏本生产只受到起缓冲作用的准地租的抑制，这个准地租也只是短期有效。正因为老行业大多基础雄厚，看起来似乎尤其值得享受信用待遇，所以，虽然亏本生产也不会立刻导致崩溃。他们部分的破产会影响新行业的成功。企业的破产因这一事实而得到缓和，这个事实极符合我们的解释框架，即：繁荣。首先从来都不是普遍的，而是集中于工业的某一个或几个部门，不干扰其他领域，而且后来也只是以一种不同的且次要的方式影响其他领域。正像企业家大批出现一样，他们的产品也会成批出现，因为企业家们并不是做着各不相同的事情，而是非常相似的事情，因此他们的产品几乎同时上市。在出现新产品之前必须经过那段平均时间[①]——尽管在实际上，这当然还

① 这个平均时间首先由技术因素决定，然后决定于大量商品跟随于前锋商品的速度。

many other elements-fundamentally explains the length of the boom. This appearance of the new products causes the fall in prices,[①]which on its part terminates the boom, *may* lead to a crisis, *must* lead to a depression, and starts all the rest.

Thirdly, the appearance of the results of the new enterprises leads to a credit deflation, because entrepreneurs are now in the position-and have every incentive-to pay off their debts; and since no other borrowers step into their place this leads to a disappearance of the recently created purchasing power just when its complement in goods emerges, and which can henceforth be repeatedly produced in the manner of the circular flow. This thesis requires careful safeguarding. In the first place this deflation must be distinguished from two other kinds. The appearance of the new products must result in deflation, not only as against the price level of the boom period, but theoretically also as against that of the preceding period of depression, even if absolutely no means of payment disappeared in debt repayment by entrepreneurs, for the sum of the prices of the new products must obviously be normally greater than the amount of these debts. This would have the same effect as the liquidation of debts, only to a smaller extent; but we are now thinking of the effect of debt reduction. Deflation also occurs in a depression which is already in being or is expected by the banking world, because the banks endeavor on their own initiative to restrict their credits. This factor is practically very important and frequently starts a real crisis; but it is accessory and not inherent in the process. Here we are not thinking of this factor either, though we deny neither its existence nor its importance, but only its primary causal rôle. [②]Then, further, our

---

① This fall in prices is in practice generally postponed through many circumstances. Cf. *infra* on this. However, the underlying state of affairs is only accentuated, not eliminated, by the postponement of the fall in prices. The only thing eliminated by it is the serviceableness of price indices as symptoms of the cycle.

② Primary causal rôle, because the credit restriction initiated by the banks is certainly the " cause" of further occurrences which would not otherwise be expected.

依赖于很多其他因素——从根本上解释了繁荣时期的时间跨度。新产品的出现引起了价格下降，[①] 这一下降从它本身来看结束了繁荣，还可能导致危机，必然导致萧条，所有其他情况会相继发生。

第三，新企业这种结果的出现导致信贷紧缩，因为现在企业家处于偿还债务的地位——而且还有充分的积极性；同时因为没有其他借方干涉他所处的状况，这就导致了新近创造的购买力的消失，而且恰好就在这种购买力的商品补充物出现时，从而它能以循环流转的方式重复地进行生产。这个论点需要仔细地证实。首先，这种通货紧缩必须与其他两种情况相区别。新产品的出现必然导致通货紧缩，这不仅与繁荣时期的物价水平相对立，而且在理论上也与前段萧条时期的物价水平相逆，即使在企业家偿还债务的过程中，支付工具完全没有消失，因为显然，新产品的价格总和在正常情况下必定大于这些债务的总和。这本应该与债务的清偿有同样的效果，尽管只是在很小的程度上，但是我们现在只考虑债务减少的影响。通货紧缩也会出现在已经存在的萧条中或者出现在银行界预期的萧条中，因为银行主动努力地限制他们的信贷。实际上这个因素是非常重要的，而且常常因此而产生真正的危机；但它只是附属的，而不是这个过程内在的。这里我们也不考虑这个因素，尽管我们既不否认它的存在，也不否认它的重要性，而只考虑它基本的因果作用。[②] 于是，进一步说，我们的

① 实际上，这种价格的下降通常因许多环境因素而延迟。参阅下面对这个问题的论述。然而，事情的根本状况却因价格下降的延迟而得到加强，而不是被其消除。被它消除的唯一的东西是作为周期征兆的物价指数的可用性。

② 之所以称为“基本的因果作用”，是因为银行主动对信贷的限制当然是事物进一步出现的“原因”，否则它们就无法预料。

formulation contains two abstractions which will make the essentials stand out clearly, but which exclude moderating influences of great practical importance. First, it neglects the fact that the new products generally contain only small quotas for depreciation of the investments made in producing them, hence that only a part, mostly only a small part, of the total expenditure in the period of boom comes on the market in saleable form when the new enterprises are ready to produce; therefore the newly created purchasing power only gradually goes out of circulation, in part only when later periods of boom have brought more credit seekers into the money market. The resorption of the new purchasing power by savings alters nothing in this deflationary process-but the fact that many states, municipalities, and agricultural mortgage banks step into the place of the dwindling entrepreneurial demand does make a difference. Apart from this only gradual disappearance of entrepreneurs' debts, it must be borne in mind that, in the modem economic system in which interest has penetrated even into the circular flow, credit may even remain permanently in circulation, in so far as there are now goods produced year after year corresponding to it-which is the second factor moderating the process still further. But the deflationary tendency is operative, for all that, and liquidation of debts by successful enterprises takes place-so that deflation, even though in ever so mild a form, must always appear automatically out of the logic of the *objective situation*, when the boom has gone on far enough. A noteworthy verification of this theory, which leads to the conclusion that in the course of development the "secular" price level must fall, is in fact given by the history of prices in the nineteenth century. The two periods which were not disturbed by revolutionary monetary changes, that is the period from the Napoleonic Wars to the Californian gold discoveries, and the period 1873-1895, actually exhibit the feature which we should expect from our theory, namely that every periodic trough is deeper than the preceding and that a price curve eliminating cyclical fluctuations moves downwards.

Finally, it must still be explained why other entrepreneurs seeking credit do not always step into the place of those liquidating their indebtedness. There are two reasons, to which in practice others are added

公式包含两个抽象概念，它们将使事情的实质清晰地表现出来，但它们排除了具有重大现实意义的缓冲影响。首先，它忽略了这个事实：新产品通常只包含生产过程中投资折旧额的小份额，因此，当新企业准备生产时，在繁荣时期的总支出中，只有一部分，而且大都是很小的一部分可以在市场上销售。因此新创造的购买力只能逐渐地从流通中转移出来，部分只是在繁荣的后期当更多的信贷寻求者被带入货币市场才离开流通。通过储蓄对新购买力的再吸收，在这个通货紧缩过程中不改变任何东西——但是许多国家、自治区、农业抵押银行一旦遇到不断减少的企业需求，情况就不同了。除了企业家债务的逐渐消失，我们还必须牢记，在现代经济体系内，如果利息已经渗入循环流转，信贷甚至可能永久地存在于循环流转中，只要现在开始，年复一年地有生产的商品与之相对应——这是进一步缓和这个过程的第二个因素。但是，由于所有那些因素，通货紧缩的趋势仍然起作用，并且成功的企业清偿了债务——所以，当繁荣已经进入很完善的状态，通货紧缩，即使它以一种非常温和的形式，也必定会自动地遵循客观情况的逻辑出现。这个理论导致了这样一个结论：在发展的过程中，“长期”物价水平必定下跌，事实上，19 世纪的物价历史对此已经作出了值得注意的证明。有两个时期，没有被革命性的货币制度的变动所干扰，即从拿破仑战争到加利福尼亚发现金矿时期，以及 1873 ~ 1895 年这一时期，这两个时期实际上展现了我们从理论上应该可以预料到的特征，也就是，每一商业周期的低潮都比前一期更低，并且，消除了周期性波动的价格曲线向下倾斜移动。

最后，还必须解释，为什么其他寻求信贷的企业家不总是遇到清理债务的情况。有两个原因，实际上还可以加上其他原因，

which can be described either as consequences of the elements which we call fundamental, or as accidental, or as influences operating from outside, and in this sense as secondary, unessential, or accessory. In the first place, if, under the stimulus of success in the industry in which the boom occurs, so many new enterprises spring up that they would produce, when in full swing, a quantity of product which, through the fall in prices and rise in costs-which occur of course even if the industry in question obeys the so-called law of increasing returns-would eliminate entrepreneurial profit, then the impulse to further advance in this direction is exhausted. In practice, even in a competitive society, the elimination of profit is only approximate and the process excludes neither the survival of some profit nor the immediate realization of losses. The limit to which the appearance of entrepreneurs in other industries and the phenomena created by secondary waves of development can go is determined analogously. When it is reached, the impulse of this boom is exhausted. The second reason explains why a new boom does not simply follow on: because the action of the group of entrepreneurs has in the meanwhile altered the data of the system, upset its equilibrium, and thus started an apparently irregular movement in the economic system, which we conceive as a struggle towards a new equilibrium position. This makes accurate calculation impossible in general, but especially for the planning of new enterprises. In practice only the latter element-the characteristic uncertainty which results from the new creations of the boom-is always immediately observable; the first-named limit shows itself mostly only at individual points. Both of them, however, are obscured, first, by consequential phenomena which the foresight of many individuals anticipates. Some individuals begin to feel sooner than others either the strain, as is true of the banks, or the rise in costs and other elements, as in the case of many old businesses, and react accordingly-in most cases too late, it is true, but when they do, in panic-stricken fashion, especially the weaker ones. Secondly, they are obscured by fortuitous events, which always occur but

这些其他原因可以描述为我们所说的基本要素的结果，或者说是偶然的，或者说是外界产生的影响，在这个意义上，它也是次要的、非本质的、附属的。第一个原因，在出现繁荣的工业所获得的成功的激励下，如果涌现出许多新的企业，以至于在充分发挥作用时，他们将生产大量的产品，通过价格下降，成本上升——即使在我们所讨论的产业服从所谓的收益递减规律的情况下，这种上升和下降也还会出现——这些大量的产品将消除企业家的利润，然后，进一步朝着这个方向发展的冲力就会耗尽。实际上，即使在一个竞争的社会里，消除利润也只是近似地消除，并且这个过程既不排除还存在某些利润，也不排斥损失的立即出现。限制企业家在其他产业出现，以及限制发展的次级波所产生的现象，这些可以类似地加以确定。当达到了限制，这种繁荣的冲击力就耗尽了。第二个原因解释了为什么新的繁荣不直接随之而来：因为企业家团体的行为同时改变了经济系统的情况，打破了均衡，这样，在经济系统内开始了一种显然是不规则的运动，我们把它想像是朝着一种新均衡状态的斗争。这样，一般就不可能进行精确计算，而尤其是对于规划新的企业。实际上，只有后一要素——产生于繁荣的新创造而特有的不确定性——常常可以立即观察到，首先提到的那个限制大都只是表现在个别方面。然而，他们两者，第一，被许多个人所预料的应运而生的现象弄得含糊不清。某些人较其他人更快地感觉到紧张，比如银行；某些人更快地感觉到成本及其他要素上涨，比如在许多老企业中就是这样，从而他们作出相应的反应——然而在多数情况下，反应确实太迟了，但当时，他们的反应的确是深感恐慌的，尤其是弱者。第二，他们因偶然发生的事件而弄得含糊不清，这些事件总是会出现，但

which acquire an importance from the uncertainty created by the boom such as they did not have before. This explains why the practical man in almost every crisis thinks he can adduce fortuitous events, unfavorable political rumors for example, as causes, and why the impetus in fact frequently proceeds from these. Thirdly, they are obscured by acts of intervention from without, of which a conscious pull on the reins by the central bank is usually the most important.

4. If the reader thinks through what has been said, and tests it on any factual material or on the arguments of any theory of crises and the business cycle, he must understand how the boom (which is now explained) creates out of itself an *objective situation*, which, even neglecting all accessory and fortuitous elements, makes an end of the boom, leads *easily* to a crisis, *necessarily* to a depression, and hence to a temporary position of relative steadiness and absence of development. The depression as such we may call the "normal" process of resorption and liquidation; the course of events characterized by the outbreak of a crisis-panic, breakdown of the credit system, epidemics of bankruptcies, and its further consequences-we may call the "abnormal process of liquidation." In completion and in repetition of some points we now have a few more things to say about this process, but only about the normal, since the abnormal presents no fundamental problems.

What has been said leads directly to the understanding of all primary and secondary features of the period of depression, which now appear as parts of a single causal nexus. The boom itself of necessity causes many businesses to run at a loss, causes a fall in prices apart from that due to deflation, and in addition causes deflation through credit contraction-phenomena which all increase secondarily in the course of events. Further, the diminution of capital investment[①] and entrepreneurial activity,

---

① The phenomenon now under discussion is to be distinguished from the dimin ished investment involved in the contraction of credit by debt liquidation. The investment for additional new purposes is meant here. And the statistics of the issue of stocks and bonds, which are in practice such a good business index (Spiethoff), reflect mainly, though not only, a third element: the consolidating of bank credit by means of savings.

它们是从繁荣所产生的以前从没有过的不确定性中获得其重要性的。这就解释了为什么有经验的人，几乎在每一次危机中，都认为他能引证偶然事件，例如，把不利的政治谣传作为原因；并且解释了为什么在实际中推动力常常产生于这些。第三，他们被来自外界的干涉行为弄得模糊不清，通常，干涉行为中最重要的是中央银行对这根缰绳的有意识的拉动。

4. 如果读者通过所说的内容进行思考，并且基于实际资料或者基于任何有关危机和商业周期的理论的论述，加以检验，那么他必定会明白繁荣（正被解释的）是如何从自身创造一种客观的状态，这种客观状态，即使忽略所有附带的和偶然的因素，也会结束繁荣，很容易地导致危机，必然产生萧条，从而导致一个暂时相对稳定的和没有发展的状态。这种萧条，我们称为再吸收和清理的“正常”过程，以危机的爆发为特征的一系列事件——恐慌、信用制度的崩溃、破产的扩散以及更进一步的结果——我们称为“清理的不正常过程”。为了完成和重复某些观点，现在我们对这个过程有几点要说明，但这只是对正常过程而言，因为不正常过程不能表现任何根本性的问题。

我们的论述直接导致了对萧条时期主要和次要特征的理解，现在这些特征成为一种单项因果联系的组成部分。繁荣本身必然导致许多行业经营亏损，导致除通货膨胀之外的价格下降，此外，通过信用收缩引起通货紧缩——这是在事件发展进程中不断增加的处于次级的现象。进一步说，资本投资①和企业家活动

① 现在所讨论的现象，应该与清理债务而引起的信用收缩其包含的投资减少区别开来。出于新的目的进行投资，在此是有意义的。对股票和债券发行的统计，实际上是一种很好的商业指数（斯皮托夫），它主要，但不是唯一地反映了第三个要素：通过储蓄加强对银行信贷的控制。

and hence stagnation in the industries producing means of production, and the fall in the Spiethoff index (iron consumption) and similar barometers, such as the unfilled orders of the United States Steel Corporation, are all explained. With the fall in the demand for means of production, the rate of interest-if the coefficient of risk is removed-and the volume of employment also fall. With the fall in money incomes, which is causally traceable to the deflation, even though it is increased by bankruptcies and so forth, the demand for all other commodities finally falls, and the process has then penetrated the whole economic system. The picture of the depression is complete.

Two reasons, however, prevent these characteristics from appearing in the order in time which would correspond to their position in the causal nexus. First is the fact that they are not only anticipated by the conduct of individuals, but also anticipated in very unequal degrees. This happens especially in markets where professional speculation plays a great part. Thus the stock market sometimes exhibits speculative preliminary crises long before a real turning point arrives, which are then overcome and make room for a further upward movement, which still belongs to the same boom (thus 1873 and 1907). But something else is much more important. Just as in practice the rise in the price of a product often anticipates the increase in costs which is nevertheless its cause, so a similar phenomenon appears here. The decrease in capital investment in the sense just indicated, the parallel decrease in entrepreneurial activity, and the stagnation in the industries for producers' goods, for example, may occur, as far as the logic of the process is concerned, before the boom has attained its external culmination; but it is not necessary that they should. On the contrary, if these symptoms do regularly occur before the end of the boom, it is because they are under the influence of factors which anticipate relatively promptly what is coming. Secondly, however, various circumstances bring it about that in the actual course of events secondary elements often stand out more prominently than the primary. The anxiety of lenders, for example, expresses itself in a rise in the rate of interest, and only late in the depression does the effect appear which in the very nature of things would appear quite early in the normal course of events.

的减少，因而，生产生产资料的工厂停滞，斯皮托夫指数（钢铁消费）以及类似指标的下降，比如美国钢铁公司未满额的订单，都可以从这里得到解释。随着对生产资料需求的下降，利率——如果消除了风险系数——以及就业量也会下降。随着货币收入的下降（这种下降从原因上可以追溯到通货紧缩），即使这种需求会因破产等等而又增加，但对所有其他商品的需求最终还是下降，这样，这个过程就渗透到整个经济系统。萧条的情景就完成了。

然而，有两个原因阻止这些特征按照它们在因果关系中的地位以时间顺序出现。第一个原因是这一事实：这些特征不仅被个人行为所预料，而且以极不对等的程度被预料。这尤其发生在专业投机占据重要地位的市场上。这样，股票市场在一个真正的转折点到来之前很久，有时就已表现出投机的初期的危机，于是克服这个危机，并为进一步向前运动创造空间，这都仍然属于同一个繁荣时期（1873 年和 1907 年）。但是还有其他一些情况更重要。就像在现实中，一种产品的价格上升常常预期着成本的增加——这不过是价格上升的原因，所以在这里，出现了相类似的情况。只要在繁荣达到其外部顶点之前，考虑到这个过程的必然结果，那么，刚才所说的那些投资减少，企业家活动同时减少，以及比如说生产生产品的工业停滞，都可能出现；但是不一定它们就应该如此。相反，如果这些迹象在繁荣结束之前确实规律地出现，那是因为它们受到这些因素的影响，这些因素能相对迅速地预期将要发生什么。不过，第二个原因是，各种情形的影响将导致在事情的实际发展过程中，次要因素常常显得比主要因素更突出。例如，借出者对利率的上升表现出的忧虑，然而只有到萧条的晚期，那种作为事物的最本质的并且在事情正常发展过程中早

The reduction in the demand for labor should be a very early symptom of the change, but just as wages do not rise immediately in prosperity because as a rule there are unemployed workers, so wages and the amount of employment do not usually fall as promptly as one would expect because a series of well known obstacles stands in the way. The business world tries to defend itself against a fall in prices, and where competition is not completely "free"-as is practically nowhere the case-and when the banks lend their support, it resists with temporary success, so that the maximum price level is often later than the turning point. It is a fundamental task of the investigation of crises to establish all these things. But here it is sufficient to state, without further substantiation, that all this no more alters the essence of the matter than the analogous phenomena in other fields, to which I referred above, support objections against the theory of prices.

The course of events in periods of depression presents s picture of uncertainty and irregularity which we interpret from the point of view of a search for a new equilibrium, or of adaptation to a general situation which has been changed relatively quickly and considerably. The uncertainty and irregularity are quite comprehensible. The customary data are altered for every business. The extent and nature of the change, however, can only be learned from experience. There are new competitors; old customers and dealers fail to appear; the right attitude towards new economic facts has to be found; incalculable events-unsuspected refusals of credit-may occur at any moment. The "mere businessman" faces problems which lie outside his routine, problems to which he is not accustomed and in the face of which he makes mistakes which then become an important secondary cause of further trouble. Speculation is a further cause, through the distress in which it involves speculators as well as through the fact that the latter anticipate a further fall in prices, so that all these well known elements mutually increase one another. Nowhere is the final result dearly in sight; weak points, which in themselves have nothing to do with the crisis, may come to light anywhere.

就表现出来的影响，才会表现出来。对劳动需求的减少应该是这种变化的一个极早的征兆，但是就像工资在繁荣时期不会立即上涨，因为通常总存在着失业工人那样，工资和就业人数通常也不会像人们所料想的那样迅速下降，因为存在一系列人们了解的障碍。所以企业就会努力保护自己，防止价格下跌，而且在不是完全“自由”竞争的地方——实际上这种完全自由竞争根本不存在——当银行提供资金支持时，它抵制暂时的成功，所以最高的价格水平点通常要迟于转折点。确立所有这些要点是考察危机的基本任务。但是不需要进一步的证实，这里已足以说明：所有这些不会改变事情的本质，只不过是我上面提到的在其他领域发生的类似现象，会支持反对危机理论。

在萧条时期，事态的发展过程表现出一种不确定和无规律的景象，这是我们从寻求一种新的均衡的角度，或者从适应已经相对迅速变化并且相当可观的一般状况的角度，来解释的。这种不确定性以及无规律性是很容易理解的。不同的行业有不同的惯例资料，然而，变化的程度及性质只能从经验中了解。这时有了新的竞争情况：老客户和商人没有出现；必须找到对新的经济事实的正确认识；不可估计的事件——对信贷毫无疑问的拒绝——这些可能在任何时候出现。“纯工商业者”面对存在于常规事务之外的问题，面对他并不习惯做的问题，面对这些问题他会出错，而这些错误又会成为引起进一步麻烦的次等重要的原因。投机是产生进一步麻烦的一个原因，通过投机者所遇到的不幸，以及通过投机者会预见到价格进一步下跌这个事实，于是，所有这些为人熟知的要素相互激发而增长。没有一个地方能够看清楚最终的结果；而那些本身与危机并没有关系的弱点可能会出现在任何地

Business contraction or business extension may finally prove to be the correct type of reaction without its being possible at the moment to advance trustworthy reasons for the one or the other. This complication and lack of clarity in the situation, of which theory in my opinion makes an unwarranted use in explaining the causes of depression, really becomes an important factor in the actual events.

The uncertainty of the data and values involved in the new adjustment, the losses which apparently occur irregularly and incalculably, create the characteristic atmosphere of periods of depression. Those speculative elements which make up stock exchange opinion and are commercially and socially so noticeable in prosperity suffer especially. To many people, particularly the speculative class and the producers of luxury goods who are partly dependent on its demand, conditions appear essentially worse than they are-to them the end of all things seems to have come. Subjectively, the turning point appears to producers, especially if they resist the unavoidable fall in prices, as an outbreak of hitherto latent overproduction, and the depression as its consequence. The unsaleableness of commodities already produced, still more of those producible, at prices which cover costs calls forth the well known further phenomenon of the tightness of money, possibly insolvency, which is so typical that every theory of the business cycle must be in a position to explain it. Ours does so, as the reader can see, but it does not employ this typical fact as a primary and independent cause. ①The overproduction is accentuated by that skewness of the boom which we have already noticed and explained.

---

① Every theory of crises in which overproduction plays the part of one, or even the primary, cause seems to me to be exposed to the objection of reasoning in a circle (quite apart from the objection already formulated by Say), even if it does not assert "general overproduction." From this judgment I must exclude Spiethoff's theory. The very short arguments with which he tries to substantiate the periodical over production of goods for reproductive consumption allow no final judgment. Moreover, it is to be observed that Spiethoff's aim is a penetrating analysis of all the details of the subject. For such an analysis, the dements governing the external picture-the stagnation in industries producing means of production certainly belongs here-are really much more important in relation to the primary causes than for an exposition such as this. Finally, there is in the emphasis upon industries producing means of production a reference to the factors which in my opinion constitute the nature of the problem, so that it is by no means correct to describe Spiethoff's analysis as simply an overproduction theory; a mote detailed exposition of his theory would perhaps show still more far-reaching agreement than I now suspect.

方。企业收缩或者企业扩张，最终会证明是反应的正确方式，而不可能是在当时为这一问题或那一问题所提出的值得信任的理由。形势的这种复杂性以及不清晰性，在我看来，理论毫无根据地利用它们来解释萧条的原因，它们将真正成为实际发生的事件的重要因素。

包括在新的调整过程中的数据和价值的不确定性，以及明显会出现的无规律和不可估计的损失，形成了萧条时期独特的氛围。那些产生股票交易思想以及繁荣时期在商业和社会上十分显著的投机要素，尤其会遭受不幸。对许多人来说，尤其是投机阶层以及部分地依赖奢侈品需求的奢侈品生产者，情况在实质上比其表现出来的更糟糕——对他们来说，似乎所有的事物都已走到了尽头。从主观上看，转折点出现在生产者面前，尤其是，如果生产者抵制不可避免的价格下跌，就像爆发迄今为止潜在的生产过剩以及由此产生的萧条那样。已经生产出来的商品无法销售出去，严重的是那些将要被生产出来的商品更无法销售，以恰好偿付成本的价格出售会导致人们熟悉的银根紧缩现象，甚至可能导致无力偿付，这些现象是非常典型的，所以每一种关于商业周期的理论都必须恰当地对它作出解释。正如读者看到的，我们的理论也是如此，但它并不把这种典型的事实作为基本的和独立的原因加以运用。① 生产过剩被那种我们已经注意到并且解释了

① 把生产过剩作为一个原因，或者，甚至作为主要原因的每一种危机理论，在我看来，都会招致循环推论的反驳（且不说已经被萨伊系统阐述的反对观点），即使它没有坚持“一般生产过剩”的观点。根据这个论断，我必须排斥斯皮托夫的理论。他用非常简短的论点试图具体说明为再生产消费的商品的周期性生产过剩，而他的这一论述得不到任何最终判断。此外，还要注意，斯皮托夫的目的是对这一主题的所有细节作透彻的分析。对于这种分析，涉及外部情况的要素——制造生产资料的工业的停滞当然属于这一类——在与主要原因的关系上，确实比这种说明更加重要。最后，为了强调制造生产资料的工业，还要提到一些因素，在我看来，这些因素构成了问题的本质，所以，仅仅把斯皮托夫的理论描述为一种生产过剩理论，绝不是正确的；对他的理论作更详细的说明，可能会显示出比我现在所猜想的更深远的一致性。

This circumstance on the one hand, and the discrepancy between effective supply and effective demand which must occur in many industries during the depression on the other, make it possible to describe the external form of depressions in the language of the various disproportionality theories. The gist of every such theory lies in the manner in which it tries to explain the appearance of the disproportionality, and in the particular quantities between which disproportionality is held to exist. For us, the disproportionality between quantities and prices of goods, which results at many points because of the loss of equilibrium in the economic system, is an intermediate phenomenon just like overproduction and is not a primary cause. Connected with it there may be disproportionality between incomes in individual industries, but not between the incomes of different economic classes, for entrepreneurial profits bear no normal proportion to the incomes of other people which could be disturbed, and the other incomes, with the exception of those fixed in terms of money, have the tendency to move *pari passu* and to gain or lose ground at the cost or to the advantage of the fixed incomes, leaving the total consumers' demand undisturbed.

The skewness of the boom has the consequence, amongst others, that strain and danger in the situation are not equally great for all branches of industry. Experience teaches also, as Aftalion① has already shown, that many branches are hardly disturbed at all, others only relatively little. Within every industry new enterprises are generally implicated considerably more than established businesses, which seems to contradict our interpretation. This is to be explained as follows: an old business has the buffer quasirent, and, what is more important, generally accumulated reserves. It is embedded in protecting relationships, often effectively supported by banking connections of many years' standing. It may be losing ground for years without its creditors

① Les crises périodiques de surproduction, livre I. To be sure, the other fact, different from the one we have in view here, that the cyclical movement is always particularly strongly marked in the industries producing new plant, stands out much more clearly. It is likewise intelligible from our standpoint. Of course this does not contradict the interpretation here presented, rather the contrary.

的扭曲的繁荣加重了。一方面，这种环境，另一方面，在萧条时期的许多工业中必定出现的有效供给与有效需求之间的缺口，就有可能用不恰当的理论术语来描述萧条的外部形式。每一种这样的理论，其主旨在于试图解释不协调的出现，以及解释那些认为存在不协调的特殊的数量。对我们而言，商品数量与其价格之间的不协调——许多情况是因为经济系统丧失了均衡而产生的——就像生产过剩那样，是一种中间现象，而不是基本原因。与此相关的，各个产业收入之间也可能有不协调，但在不同的经济等级的收入之间不存在这种不协调，因为企业家利润与他人可能受到干扰的收入之间不存在正常的比例关系；除了那些货币形式的固定收入，其他收入都有以同一速度移动的趋势，并且有损于或者有利于固定收入而相应获利或损失，同时，总的消费者需求不受干扰。

扭曲的繁荣在其他情况下也有这样的结果：形势的紧张与危险并不是对所有的工业部门都同等的重大。经验也告诉我们，正如阿弗达农[①]已经表明的，许多部门几乎根本不受干扰，有些部门只是受到相对很小的干扰。在每一产业内，新企业一般受牵连的程度比老企业更大，这似乎与我们的解释相矛盾。对这一点的解释如下：老企业有缓冲工具“准地租”，而且更重要的是，他们普遍拥有累积储备金。它被置于保护关系中，而且常常得到经多年确立的银行关系的有效支持。它有可能若干年失利，但其债权人

① 参考《生产过剩的周期性危机》，第一册。肯定地说，不同于我们在这里考虑的另一个事实是，周期性运动总是特别强烈地带有生产新设备的工业的标记，而且越来越清晰。根据我们的观点，这同样是易于理解的。当然，这并不与此处陈述的解释相矛盾，而恰好相反。

becoming uneasy. Therefore it holds out much longer than a new enterprise, which is strictly and suspiciously scrutinised, which has no reserves but at best only overdraft facilities, and which only needs to give a sign of embarrassment to be considered as a bad debtor. Hence, the reaction of the change in all conditions upon new enterprises may become visible earlier and more strikingly than that upon old businesses. And therefore in the former it leads much more easily to the final consequence, bankruptcy, than in the latter, in which it rather initiates a slow decay. This distorts the picture of reality, and is also the reason why a selective process in crises may be spoken of only with an important qualification; for that firm which is well supported, and not the one that is most perfect in itself, has the best chance of surviving a crisis. But this does not affect the nature of the phenomenon.

5. Although it stands to reason that the process of adjustment and resorption which makes up the period of depression causes discomfort to the most vigorous elements in the economic system, those which do most to create the *mood* of the business world, and although it necessarily annihilates many values and existences even if everything occurs with ideal perfection, yet its nature and effects would be inadequately grasped if it were seen only from the aspect of the cessation of the impulse to prosperity or described merely by negative characteristics. There are more cheerful sides to it which are much more characteristic of it than the things just indicated.

First, the depression leads, as stated already, to a new equilibrium position. To convince ourselves that all that happens in it is really to be understood from this point of view and is only apparently meaningless and unregulated, let us consider once more the behavior of individuals in a period of depression. They must adapt themselves to the disturbance caused by the boom, that is by the swarm-like appearance of new combinations and their products, by the appearance of them alongside of the old businesses and by the one-sidedness of their appearance. The old businesses -that is, theoretically, all existing ones with the exception of those formed in the boom,

却并不感到忧虑。从而，老企业比新企业能更长时间地维持下去，而新企业总是受到严格地并且是被怀疑地审查，它没有准备金，至多只有透支工具，而且只要它表现出一点困境的迹象，就会被认为是即将破产的债务者。因此，所有情况的变化带来的反应，对新企业比对老企业，可能表现得更早并且更惊人。所以，在新企业比在老企业，它更容易导致最终的结果：破产，而在老企业则形成一种缓慢的衰败。这就歪曲了现实情景，这也是为什么危机中一个选定的过程仅仅以一种重要的限制条件来描述原因。因为，只有受到大力支持的厂商，而不是本身最完善的厂商，拥有在危机中生存的最好机会。但这并不影响现象的本质。

5. 尽管我们有理由说，产生萧条周期的调整和再吸收过程，引起经济体系中最有活力的要素的不安，那些要素对创造商业氛围贡献最大；而且尽管，即使所有的事情都以理想的完美形式出现，它也必定会消灭许多价值和现存的实体。然而，如果仅从对繁荣的冲动的终止方面来看，或者仅仅用消极的特征来描述，那么，也就不可能对萧条的性质和结果进行充分地把握。对于萧条，还有更多令人高兴的一方面，这比刚才提出的情况更能反映萧条的特征。

第一，就像已经陈述的那样，萧条将引向一个新的均衡状态。为了使我们自己相信，萧条下发生的所有情况确实可以从这个观点加以理解，而且所发生的显然是无意义和未加控制的，我们再一次考虑萧条时期的个人行为。他们必须调整自己以适应由繁荣引起的干扰，也就是因新组合及其产品成群地出现而产生的干扰，因他们与老企业的同时存在以及他们单方出现而产生的干扰。老企业——理论上，也就是除形成于繁荣时期的企业之外的

and with the further exception in practice of those removed from danger by a monopoly position, the possession of peculiar advantages, or lastingly superior technique -are faced by three possibilities: to decay if they are unadaptable for objective or personal reasons; to take in sail and try to survive in a more modest position; finally, with their own resources or with outside help either to change to another industry or to adopt other technical or commercial methods which amount to extending production at lower cost per unit. The new businesses have to undergo their first test, a much more difficult one than they would have to undergo if they appeared continuously and not in swarms. Once established, they must be properly incorporated in the circular flow, and, even if no mistake was made when they were founded, there must in many respects be much to revise. Even though from different, secondary, causes, problems and possibilities confront them similar to those confronting the old businesses; and, as mentioned above, they are in many respects less equal to cope with them than are the old. The characteristic conduct of businessmen in depression consists of measures, correction of measures, and further measures to solve this problem; all the phenomena, apart from panics unfounded in fact and the consequences of errors-which characterize the abnormal course of events in a crisis-may be included in this conception of the situation crested by the boom and of businessmen ' s conduct enforced by it, of the disturbance in equilibrium and the reaction to it, of the change in data and the successful or abortive adaptation to it.

Just as the struggle towards a new equilibrium position, which will embody the innovations and give expression to their effects upon the old firms, is the real meaning of a period of depression as we know it from experience, so it may likewise be shown that this struggle must actually lead to a close approach to an equilibrium position: on the one hand, the driving impulse of the process of depression cannot theoretically stop until it has done its work, has really brought about the equilibrium position; on the other hand, no new disturbance in the form of a new boom can arise out of the economic system itself until then.

所有现存企业，以及进一步排除那些因垄断地位、拥有特殊优势，或者持久优越的技术，从而实际上已经远离危险的企业——面临三种可能：如果他们因客观或个人原因而不能适应，就将衰败下去；开始收敛，并且试图在一种更稳当的状态下生存；最后，依靠他们自己的资源或者借助于外力，要么向另一种行业转变，要么采取其他技术性或商业性手段，以实现用较低的单位成本扩大生产。新企业不得不经受他们的第一次考验，这是一种比如果他们陆续出现而不是成群出现所需经受的更困难的考验。一旦确立，他们必然会适当地参与到循环流转中，而且，即使当他们建立时没有出错，在许多方面也必定会存在需要修改的地方。即使从不同的、次要的原因出发，他们所面临的问题和可能的选择也与老企业所面临的问题相类似；而且，如上所述，他们在许多方面应付问题的能力比老企业要差。在萧条时期，商人们特征性的行为包括采取一些措施，对措施的更正，以及为解决这一问题采取的进一步措施。所有这些现象，除了没有事实根据的恐慌和错误的结果——这是危机中事件非正常发展过程的特征——都可能归属于这种由繁荣所造成的情形的概念，也就是包含在商人被迫采取的行为，均衡受到的干扰并对此作出的反应，以及资料的改变和对它的成功或失败的适应这些概念中。

就像朝着新均衡状态的努力斗争——它将使创新具体化，并对老企业产生影响，它是萧条时期的真正意义，这是我们从经验中得知的，同样也可以表明，这种斗争在实际上必然会导致更接近均衡位置：一方面，萧条过程起推动作用的冲力，在理论上它不会停止，直到它发挥作用并且真正带来了均衡状态；另一方面，除非达到均衡，否则没有以新的繁荣形式出现的新干扰从经济系

Businessmen's conduct in the period of depression is clearly ruled by the element of actual or impending loss. But losses occur or are imminent-not necessarily in the whole economic system but in the parts exposed to danger-as long as all businesses, and hence the system as a whole, are not in stable equilibrium, which is as much as to say in practice until they again produce at prices approximately covering costs. Consequently there is, theoretically, depression as long as no such equilibrium is approximately attained. Nor will this process be interrupted by a new boom before it has done its work in this sense. For until then, there is necessarily uncertainty about what the new data will be, which makes the calculation of new combinations impossible and makes it difficult to obtain the cooperation of the requisite factors. Both conclusions fit the facts if the following qualifications are kept in view. A knowledge of the cyclical movement and its mechanism, which is peculiar to the modem business world, allows businessmen, whenever the worst is over, to anticipate the coming boom and especially its secondary phenomena; the adaptation of many individuals and hence of many values to the new equilibrium is frequently retarded or prevented by the expectation that if they can only hold out-which it is often in the interest of their creditors to facilitate-they will be able to liquidate on favorable terms in the next boom or will not find it necessary to liquidate at all-which is especially important in predominantly prosperous epochs and saves many firms really not fit to live as well as many that are, but in any case retards or prevents the attainment of a settled equilibrium position.

The progressive trustification of economic life facilitates the permanent continuance of maladjustments in the great combines themselves and hence outside of them, for practically there can only be complete equilibrium if there is free competition in all branches of production. Furthermore, in

统本身出现。在萧条时期，工商业者的行为，显然被实际的或者即将来临的损失所控制。但是，损失发生或者即将到来——在整个经济系统内并不是必然的，只是部分可能招致危险——只要所有的企业，以至整个经济系统，不是处于稳定的均衡位置，这实际上就相当于说，直到他们再次以与成本相当的价格生产为止。因此，在理论上，只要这种均衡没有完全达到就总存在萧条。在这个意义上，这一过程在它发挥了它的作用之前，就不会被新的繁荣打断。因为直到那时，必然存在对于未来新情况的不确定性，这就使得不可能去估计新的组合，而且获得必要因素的协作也很困难。如果遵循下面的限制条件，那么这两个结论都是符合事实的。对现代商业界特有的周期运动及其机制的认识，能使工商业者预测即将到来的繁荣，尤其是它的次级现象，只要当最坏的情况过去了。许多个人对新均衡的适应，从而许多价值对新均衡的适应，常常被一种期望延缓或者阻碍，这种期望即是，如果他们还能坚持——这通常是根据他们债权人的利益而进行的——那么他们就能在下一个繁荣时期以有利的条件进行清算，或者发现根本没有清算的必要——这在占有优势的繁荣时代尤为重要，并且挽救了许多实际上不能适应生存的厂商，使他们与其他适应者一样生存下来。但尽管如此，它还是延缓或者阻碍了到达稳定、均衡状态的过程。

经济生活趋于托拉斯化，这在大型联合企业内部以及它们的外部，形成了永久的并且是连续的失调；因为，如果在所有的生产部门都存在自由竞争，那么，实际上这只能是完全均衡了。此外，由于某些厂商，尤其是老厂商，他们有一定的财政力量，所以调整并不总是十分迫切的，它也不是与生死存亡密切相关的问题。

consequence of the financial strength of some firms, especially the older ones, the adjustment is not always very urgent, not an immediate question of life or death. There is also the practice of outside support being extended to firms or whole industries in difficulties, for example government subsidies, given upon the *bona* or *mala fide* assumption that the difficulty is only a temporary one, created by extraneous circumstances. In times of depression there is also frequently an outcry for protective duties. All this acts in the same way as the financial strength of old businesses; Further more, there is the element of chance-for example a good harvest occurring at the right moment. Finally, abnormalities in the course of the depression sometimes have the effect of producing over-compensations; if, for example, an unjustified panic has unduly depreciated the shares of a business and in consequence a corrective upward movement in them begins, this upward movement may in its turn overshoot the mark, maintain the shares at a quotation which is inappropriately high, and lead to a small pseudo-boom which may last under certain circumstances until a real one begins.

Of course the position reached in the end never completely corresponds to the theoretical picture of a system without development, in which there would no longer be income in the form of interest. The relatively short duration of depressions alone prevents this. Nevertheless, an approximation to a position without development always occurs, and this, being relatively steady, may again be a starting point for the carrying out of new combinations. In this sense, therefore, we come to the conclusion that according to our theory there must always be a process of absorption between two booms, ending in a position approaching equilibrium, the bringing about of which is its function. This is important for us, not only because such an intermediate position actually exists and the explanation of it is incumbent upon every theory of the cycle, but also because only the proof of the necessity of such a periodic quasi-equilibrium position completes our argument. For we started from such a position, out of which the wave of development first arises-without regard to whether or when this was the case historically. We might even merely assume an initial "static" state in order to let the nature of the wave stand out clearly.

而且，外界还有一种做法，支持处于困境中的厂商或者整个工业，例如政府补助金，它的发放基于这样一种善意的或者说虚假的假设，即困难只是暂时的，且困难是由外界环境造成的。在萧条时期，常常也有对实行保护关税的要求。所有这些都与老企业的财政力量一样，以同样的方式发挥作用，而且还存在机遇因素——例如出现在关键时刻的好收成。最后，萧条过程中的非正常情况有时候会产生过渡补偿的影响，例如，如果一种未经证实的恐慌不恰当地贬低了某家企业的股票，因而开始了一种纠正性的上升运动，那么这种上升运动就可能反过来进行得过于激烈，以一种不相称的高价维持该股票行情，并可能导致小规模的虚假繁荣，这可能在一定条件下持续下去，直到出现真实的繁荣。

当然，最终达到的状态决不会与一个没有发展的系统的理论情景完全一致，在这种理论情景中将不再有利息形式的收入。相对短暂的萧条时期独自就阻止了这个现象的发生。尽管如此，总会出现接近无发展状况的现象，而且这种状况，由于相对稳定，可能又是实施新组合的起点。因此，在这个意义上，我们得出结论：根据我们的理论，在两个繁荣之间必定会存在一个吸收过程，它最终会到达接近均衡的位置，而产生均衡就是它的功能。这对于我们是重要的，不仅因为这种中间状态确实存在，并且对其解释是每一种周期理论义不容辞的责任，而且因为只有证明了这种周期性的准均衡状态的必要性，我们才完成了我们的论证。因为我们从这个状态出发，而发展的波动首先就是从这里产生——不管这种情况在历史上是否或者什么时候出现过。我们甚至可以仅仅假设一种初始的“静止”状态，以清楚地突出波动的性质。但就

But for our theory to explain the essence of the phenomenon it is not enough that a trough *actually* follows every crest of the wave: it must do so *necessarily*-which cannot be simply assumed, nor may a proof be replaced by pointing to the fact. For this reason a certain amount of pedantry seemed to be required in this section.

Secondly, apart from the digestion of the innovations which has just occupied our attention, the period of depression does something else, which indeed comes less to the fore than those phenomena to which it owes its name: it fulfils what the boom promised. And this effect is lasting, while the phenomena felt to be unpleasant are temporary. The stream of goods is enriched, production is partly reorganized, costs of production are diminished,① and what at first appears as entrepreneurial profit finally increases the permanent real incomes of other classes.

This conclusion which emerges from our theory (cf. also the fourth chapter) is justified, in spite of the various obstacles which these effects meet with at first, by the fact that the economic picture of a *normal* period of depression② is throughout not so black as the mood pervading it would lead one to suspect. Apart from the fact that a great part of economic life

① We have twice spoken of the boom's effects in increasing costs: first entrepreneurs' demand drives up the prices of production goods, then the following demand of all people who ride on the secondary waves of development do so still further. These increasing costs have nothing to do with the secular rise asserted by the classical economists on the basis of their assumption of the progressive outstripping of the possibilities of producing means of subsistence by the increase in population. Now the decreasing costs in question above are not the complement of these increasing costs in money. They are the consequence of the productive progress realised by the boom, and signify a fall in real costs per unit of product, first in the new enterprises as against the old, then also in the latter, since they must either adapt themselves-for example by reducing their output and confining themselves to the best possibilities-or disappear. After every boom the economic system as such produces the unit of product with less expenditure of labor or land.

② Of course the post-war depression was not normal. In my opinion it is a mistake to try to read general results of the business cycle theory into the post-war material. But it is a mistake often made. Thus, many a judgment of the modem therapeutists of crises by means of credit policy is explicable by the fact that they assert of the normal cyclical movement what is only true for the post-war crisis.

我们用来解释现象本质的这个理论而言，仅仅说商业周期的波谷事实上是跟随着每一个波峰，这是不够的：还必须说明它是必然的——这不能被简单地假定，也不能用指出这个事实而代替对它的证明。由此，一定量的学究行为在这部分似乎还是需要的。

第二，除了对刚刚引起我们注意的创新的消化，萧条时期还有其他一些作用，这种作用确实不如那些它得以获得名气的现象那样重要：它完成了繁荣所容许的情况。同时这种影响是持续的，而让人感到不愉快的现象是暂时的。商品流被充实或者说被丰富，生产被部分地重组，生产成本被缩减，[①] 起初作为企业家利润出现的东西最终增加了其他阶层永久性的真实收入。

尽管这些作用一开始就遇到各种障碍，但由我们的理论得出的这个结论（请参考第四章），却被这个事实证实了，即，正常过程的萧条时期的[②]经济状况，在整个过程中，并不像渗透于其中的情绪将使人产生怀疑那么沉闷。除了这个事实，即经济生活的大部

① 我们两次谈到繁荣对增加成本的影响：首先，企业家的需求促进了生产品价格的上涨，然后接下来所有的人的需求也将进一步增加，这些人是指处于发展的次级波上的人。这些不断增加的成本，与古典经济学家以他们的假定：人口的增长有可能会逐渐超过生活资料的生产，以这种假定为基础而断言的那种长期增长，没有什么关系。现在，上述问题中不断下降的成本，也不是对货币形式逐渐增长的成本的补充。它们是因繁荣而实现的生产进步的结果，并且标志着每单位产品真实成本的下降，这种下降首先发生在与老企业对峙的新企业中，然后也出现在老企业中，因为他们必然要么是使自己适应——例如削减产量，将自己限制在最佳可能状态——要么是消亡。每一次繁荣过后，这种经济系统就以更少的劳动和土地支出来生产单位产品。

② 当然战后的萧条是不正常的。在我看来，试图把商业周期理论的一般结果用于战后资料，这是错误的。但这是经常犯的错误。这样，现代危机诊疗学家借助信贷政策的许多判断，可以由这个事实得到解释：他们坚决维护正常的周期运动，而这仅仅适用于战后危机。

remains almost untouched as a rule, the physical volume of total transactions in most cases falls only insignificantly. How exaggerated the popular conceptions of the ravages caused by a depression are, is shown by any official investigation of crises. [①]This is true not only of analysis in terms of goods but also of that in terms of money, in spite of the fact that the cyclical movement, with its inflation in prosperity and deflation in depression, must be especially strongly marked in the money expression. Total incomes rise in the boom and fall in the depression not more than 8 to 12 percent as compared with the figures for average years, even in America (Mitchell), where the intensity of development presumably makes the fluctuations more strongly marked than in Europe. Aftalion has already shown that the fall in prices during depression only constitutes a low percentage on the average, and that really great fluctuations have their causes in the special conditions of the individual articles and have little to do with the cyclical movement. The same thing may be shown for all really large general movements, as for example the post-war period. When the phenomena of the abnormal course of events (panics, epidemics of bankruptcies, and so forth), which are continually becoming weaker, and with them anxiety about incalculable danger, disappear, public opinion will also judge of depressions differently.

We see the true character of a period of depression if we consider what it brings to and takes from different categories of individuals-always abstracting from the phenomena of the abnormal course of events,

---

① Cf., for example, those of the Verein für Sozialpolitik, or the English reports in the time of predominant depressions before 1895, say the famous Third Report on the Depression of Trade. Accurate investigations are only of more recent date, as for example in the Special Memorandum No. 8 of the London and Cambridge Economic Service (by J. W. F. Rowe), or, for America, the data and estimates in the Report of a Committee of the President' s Conference on Unemployment. An interesting method, which leads to the same result for the year i921, although this was not simply a year of depression (cf. the preceding note), is due to C. Snyder (in Administration, May, 1923).

分通常几乎不被干扰，于是，在多数情况下，总交易的实物数量只是微不足道地有所下降。萧条造成的荒废残迹这个流行的概念是如何被夸大的，这一点可以通过任何对危机的官方调查[①]来表明。尽管周期运动，它在繁荣时期出现的通货膨胀以及在萧条时期出现的通货紧缩，必然特别强烈地以货币形式表现，但这不仅适用于根据商品作的分析，而且适用于根据货币作的分析。与平均年份数字相比，总收入在繁荣时期的上升以及在萧条时期的下降，不会超过8%到12%，甚至在美国也是如此（参考米切尔的论述），在美国，发展的强度可能比在欧洲使这个波动更加显著。阿弗达农已经表明，萧条时期价格的下跌，平均上只构成一个低的百分比，并且真正大的波动是在个别物品的特殊条件下产生的，它与周期运动没有什么关系。对于所有大规模的一般性的运动，比如战后时期，这些同样可以说明。当那些事件（恐慌、破产的蔓延等等）的非正常过程且不断变弱的现象，以及由此产生的对不可预测危险的焦虑都消失的时候，公众意见也会对萧条作出不同的判断。

如果我们考虑到萧条会给不同类型的个人带来什么，以及从他们那里取得什么——这些总是从事件的非正常过程的现象中

① 例如，“社会政策协会”作的调查，或者1895年之前显著大萧条时期的英文导报，比如说，著名的《贸易萧条的第三次报告》。精确的调查只是近期的，比如，在《伦敦和剑桥经济服务部第8号特别备忘录》（由罗提出）中，或者，美国的《总统议会委员会对失业问题的报告》中的资料和估计。一个有趣的方法，它产生与1921年相同的结果，尽管1921年不是萧条的年份（参阅前面的注释），这个方法的提出归因于斯奈德（《管理》杂志，1923年5月）。

which is of no concern here. From entrepreneurs and all their followers, especially from those who fortuitously or speculatively enjoy the fruits of the rise in prices during the boom, it takes away the possibility of profit-which especially in the case of speculation is only very imperfectly replaced by bear possibilities which appear in the slump. The entrepreneur has in the normal case made his profit and embodied it in the now established and adjusted business; but he makes no further profits, on the contrary he is threatened with losses. In the general case his entrepreneurial profit would dry up, his other entrepreneurial income would be at a minimum, even in the ideal course of events. In the real course of events many adverse influences supervene, although mitigated by some factors already mentioned. The existences connected with the old businesses, which are now being competitively vanquished, of course suffer. People with fixed money incomes or incomes only alterable after a long time, such as pensioners, rentiers, officials, and landlords who have rented their land for a long term, are the typical beneficiaries of the depression. The commodity content of their money incomes, which is compressed in prosperity, now expands, and indeed in principle it must expand more than it was compressed before, as has already been shown (cf. above, 3, "thirdly"). Capitalists with short-term investments gain from the increased purchasing power of the unit of income and capital, and lose by the lower interest rate; theoretically, they must lose more than they gain, but numerous secondary circumstances-on the one hand danger of loss, on the other hand high risk premiums and panic demand-deprive this theorem of its practical importance. Those landowners whose rents are not fixed in money by long term contracts-hence above all the landowning farmer-are fundamentally in exactly the same position as workers,

提取出来的，并且在这里我们对此并不涉及，那么，我们就能看到萧条时期的真实特征。它使企业家及其所有的跟随者，尤其是那些偶然幸运地或者投机性地享受到繁荣期间价格上涨带来的成果的人们，失去了获得利润的可能性——尤其在投机的场合下，这就极不完善地被暴跌中出现的看跌的可能性所代替。在正常情况下企业家已经获得利润，而且已经将其包括在现已建立起来且经过调整的企业中。但他不再进一步产生利润，而相反，他会受到亏损的威胁。一般情况下，即使在事件的理想过程中，他的企业家利润将枯竭，他的其他作为企业家收入的部分也将达到最小值。在事件的真实过程中，许多不利的影响，尽管被已经提及的一些因素所减弱，但还是会发生。与老企业有关联的现存事物，它们正竞争性地被征服，当然会遭遇到困难。拥有固定货币收入或者其收入只是在一个较长时间之后才会变化，这些人，比如领取养老金的人、收取租金的人、政府官员，以及长期出借土地的地主，都是萧条时期的典型受益者。他们货币收入的商品内涵，在繁荣时期已经被压缩，而现在却扩展了，而且，在原则上，确实它现在扩展的程度一定比过去被压缩的程度更大，这一点已经说明过了（参阅前面 3. 中的“第三”）。进行短期投资的资本家，从单位收入和资本的已经增长的购买力中获利，而由于更低的利息率受到损失。理论上，他们的损失必定大于收益，但是众多的次要情况——一方面是损失的危险，另一方面是高的风险补充和恐慌的需求——使这个原理失去了它实际的重要意义。那些没有用长期合约把地租以货币形式固定下来的土地所有者——从而首先是拥有土地的农民——他们在根本上与工人所处的地位完全一样，

so that what is now to be argued of the workers is also true of them. The practically important, theoretically inconsiderable, differences are so generally familiar that we shall not go into them. ①

In the boom wages must rise. For the new demand, first of entrepreneurs and then of all those who extend operations as the secondary wave rises, is, directly and indirectly, chiefly a demand for labor. Therefore employment must first increase and with it the sum total of wages of labor, then the rate of pay and with it the income of the individual worker. It is from this rise in wages that the increased demand for consumption goods proceeds which results in the rise in the general price level. And because part of the incomes of landowners, who are theoretically coordinate (Chapter I) with the workers, does not rise with wages for the reasons mentioned, and fixed incomes do not increase at all, the rise in total wages is not merely nominal, but is equivalent to a greater real income of labor, and this again to a greater share in the socialproduct which has not as yet increased. This is a special case of a general truth: no inflation can be immediately prejudicial to the workers' interests if, and in so far as, the newly created purchasing power must first operate upon wages before it can affect the prices of consumption goods. Only in so far as this is not the case or as the rise in wages meets external obstacles (as for example in the World War)

① Likewise it is not necessary here to go into the different degrees in which the depression affects different industries-for example luxury industries more than those producing foodstuffs. What there is of theoretical interest in this has already been touched upon in various places in this chapter.

所以，现在对有关工人问题的论述也适用于他们。在实践中很重要，而在理论上不值得考虑，人们对这种差别通常太熟悉了，所以我们不打算对此论述。①

在繁荣时期，工资必然会上涨。因为当次级波上升时，那些新需求主要是对劳动的需求，首先是企业家，然后是那些扩大经营活动的人，直接和间接地对劳动的新需求。因此，就业量必然首先增长，同时劳动工资的总数量也随之增加，然后是工资率以及随之的个别工人的收入的增加。正是由于工资的上涨，引起了对消费品需求的增长，这又导致了一般物价水平的上升。由于那些在理论上与工人同等重要的土地所有者（第一章），其一部分收入因上面提到的原因没有随工资的上涨而上升，而固定收入根本不会增加，所以，工资总额的上涨不仅只是名义上的，而且相当于更大的真实劳动收入，同时也相当于尚未增加的社会产品中的更大的份额。这是普遍真理的特殊情况：如果并且只要新创造的购买力在对消费品价格产生影响之前必定首先对工资产生影响，那么，通货膨胀就不会立即损害工人的利益。只要情况不是这样，或者工资的上升遇到外界障碍（比如，世界大战），那么工资就会以经常说到的方式滞后

① 同样，在这里也没有必要去讨论萧条对不同行业影响的不同程度——例如，对奢侈品工业的影响要大于食品生产的工业。对于这一点，哪些具有理论意义，已经在本章各处都有涉及。

can wages lag behind[1] in the manner so frequently depicted. If, indeed, the inflation is the vehicle of an excess in consumption, as for example if a war is financed by inflation, the consequent impoverishment[2] of the economic system must also react upon the workers' position, even though not so severely as upon the position of other groups of individuals. But in our case clearly the opposite happens.

In a depression the purchasing power of the unit of wages rises. On the other hand the money expression of the effective demand for labor falls in consequence of the automatic deflation which the boom starts.

---

① The statistical verification of this theory encounters various difficulties. First of all our data on the retail prices of the articles consumed by the workers do not go far enough back with the desirable completeness-and the mere movement of money wages of course means nothing; it would substantiate our thesis, it is true, if one were to be content with it. The measurement of the extent of employment is still less satisfactory, and yet we cannot do without it. As far as I know it was not possible to measure short-time work at all before the war, and complete unemployment only with the help of trade-union data and occasional censuses. To-day the attempt would be more successful, but for reasons already mentioned only pre-war figures come into consideration for our purposes. We now have a work which tries to find just what we need, namely that by G. H. Wood, "Real Wages and the Standard of Comfort since 1850," Journal of the Roy. Stat. Soc. (March, 1909). It extends to 1902 and confirms our expectation. However, at the turn of the century that noncyclical and in this sense secular price movement appeared which distorts the picture, and also involves an aberration of the lines of the cyclical movement. According to Professor Bowley's continuation of Wood's work and also according to the work of Mrs. Wood in "The Course of Real Wages in London 1900-1912," J. Roy. star. Soc. (December, 1913), and to A. H. Hansen in "Factors Affecting the Trend of Peal Wages," Amer. Econ. Review (March, 1925), which are not, it is true, concerned with the extent of employment, the theory does not fit the facts. But it is easy to see that our conclusion would be verified if the secular rise in prices were eliminated. Upon the question of the connection between gold-production and wage level cf. Pigou in the Econ. Journal (June, 1923).

The argument which now follows in the text is adequately supported by the figures. Real wages regularly fall in depression, yet only by a part of the amount which they had gained in the boom. This is exactly what we should expect.

② Impoverishment and its consequences and hence also, in the case of an approxi- mately constant quantity of means of payment, *relative* inflation would appear even without the employment of inflationary financial methods. The text refers to that intensification of the effects which paper money or credit inflation carries with it.

于物价。[①] 如果通货膨胀确实是消费中产生过剩的工具，比如说，如果战争是靠通货膨胀来融资的，那么因此造成的经济系统的贫困[②]也必然会对工人的地位作出反应，即使这种反应不像对其他群体的地位所产生的反应那样严重。但在我们这种情况下，显然出现了相反的现象。

在萧条时期，每单位工资的购买力上升了。另一方面，对劳动的有效需求的货币表现，因繁荣产生的自动通货紧缩的结果而

---

① 对这个理论的统计上的验证遇到了各种困难。首先，我们对工人所消费商品的零售价格的资料，远没有达到我们所期望的那种完整的程度——这样，单纯货币工资的运动当然就没有什么意义了，这倒真的证实了我们的观点，如果人们对此满意的话。对就业程度的测量仍然不能使人很满意，但我们又不能不用它。就我所知，在战前根本不可能测量短期的工作量，而且只有借助于工会资料和偶然的人口普查来衡量完全失业。今天，这种尝试将会更成功，但是因为已经提到的一些原因，从我们的目的出发，我们只考虑战前的数据。现在我们有一篇著作，它正好试图寻找我们需要的东西，它是由伍德写的《1850 年以来实际工资和满足标准》，刊登在 1909 年 3 月的《皇家统计协会杂志》上。它的论述延伸到 1902 年，并且证实了我们的预期。然而，在两个世纪之交，出现了非周期性的，并且在这个意义上是长期的价格运动，它歪曲了整个情景，而且也包含着偏离周期运动界限的越轨行为。根据鲍利教授对伍德论证的继续，同时也根据伍德夫人的文章：《1900 ~ 1912 年伦敦实际工资的进程》（发表在《皇家统计协会杂志》1913 年 12 月）中所作的研究，以及汉森在 1925 年 3 月发表在《美国经济评论》中的《影响实际工资趋势的因素》一文，这些文章与就业程度无关，我们可以确切地说这个理论不符合这些事实。但是很容易看出，如果价格的长期上涨趋势被消除，我们的结论就会被证实。关于黄金生产和工资水平之间关系的问题可以参阅庇古在 1923 年 6 月《经济杂志》中的论述。

本文接下来的论述有充足的数据支持。在萧条时期，实际工资有规律地下降，而这只是他们在繁荣时期获得的利益中的一部分。这正是我们应该期望的。

② 由于贫困及其结果，以及由此产生的问题，在支付工具的数量大致固定不变的情况下，即使不采用膨胀的金融方法，也会出现相对的通货膨胀。本文还提到了纸币或者信贷膨胀带来的影响程度的加剧。

In so far as only this occurs, the effective real demand[①]for labor could remain undisturbed. The real income of labor would then still be higher, not only than in the previous approximate equilibrium position, but also than in the boom. For what was previously entrepreneurial profit flows-theoretically and according to our conception wholly, but practically only gradually and incompletely to the services of labor and land, in so far as it is not absorbed by the fall in the price of the product (Chapter IV). But the following circumstances prevent this temporarily and cause the temporary fall in real income which is actually shown by statistics, while the rise finally to be expected in conformity with our theory is usually overshadowed in reality by the appearance of the next boom.

(a) First, the facts which we have called the uncertainty and apparent irregularity of the data and events in the period of depression, still more the panics and errors of the abnormal course of events, upset many firms and reduce others to idleness for a time. This must result amongst other things in unemployment, the essentially temporary character of which does not alter the fact that it is a great and under certain circumstances annihilating misfortune for those concerned, and that the fear of it-simply because of the incalculableness of its occurrence-contributes substantially to the atmosphere of depression. This unemployment is typical of periods of depression and the source of panic offers of labor, thus resulting in the loss of much ground previously gained by trade-union action and sometimes, though not necessarily, in a severe pressure on wages, the effect of which may be greater than might be thought from the number unemployed.

---

① This new concept means here simply demand expressed in units of an ideal standard which undergoes no cyclical changes of the kind due to changes in the quantity of circulating media; hence it only indicates real changes in the total demand for labor and not those which are merely nominal.

有所下降。只要仅出现这种情况，那么对劳动的有效真实需求①将保持不受干扰。于是，劳动的真实收入将继续变得更高，不仅高于原先接近均衡状态的收入，而且高于繁荣时期的收入。因为，原先的企业家利润，会流向——理论上并且根据我们的概念会全部流向，但实际上只是逐渐地并且是不完全地流向——劳动和土地服务，只要它没有被产品价格的下降所吞并（第四章）。但是下面这些情况在短期内阻碍了这种事情的发生，并且引起实际由统计所显示的真实收入的暂时下降，而最终期望收入的上升，这与我们的理论相一致，通常在现实中被下一个繁荣的出现所掩盖。

（a）首先，曾被我们称为萧条时期数据和事件的不确定性和明显的无规则，还有更多的非正常过程的恐慌和错误，这些事实使许多厂商受到困惑，并且使其他厂商在一段时间内无所事事。这必然导致失业等等事情的发生，但它本质上是暂时的，这一特征不会改变这个事实，即它是一个重大事件，而且在特定情况下可以消除有关的遭遇，以及对它的恐惧——仅仅因为它的发生是不可预测的——实质上它有助于反映萧条时的情景。这种失业是萧条时期的典型特征，是劳动急剧过剩供应的来源，这样就导致原先由工会活动所获得的利益的大量损失，有时，虽然不是必然的，但也会导致对工资的严重压力，而它的影响可能比从失业数据中所想像的结果还要大。

① 这里，这个新概念的含义仅指以一种理想的标准单位表达的需求，这种理想标准单位并不因流通媒介数量的变化而经历周期性变化；因此，它仅仅指对劳动的总需求的真实变化，而不是那种单纯的名义变化。

(*b*) From these things we must distinguish the fact that the new enterprises either completely eliminate the old businesses or else force them to restrict their operations. As against the unemployment so caused there is, to be sure, the new demand for the labor which is to carry on the new businesses. How much this demand often outweighs the unemployment created is shown by the example of the railway and the stage-coach. But this is not necessarily so, and even if it is so there may be difficulties and frictions which, with the incomplete functioning of the labor market, weigh disproportionately heavily in the balance.

(*c*) The new demand for labor mentioned above which springs up when prosperity is under way also loses in importance because of the fact that the entrepreneurs' demand for the labor which has created the new investments eventually ceases.

(*d*) As a rule the boom finally means a step in the direction of mechanising the productive process and hence necessarily a diminution of the labor required per unit of product; and often, though not necessarily, it also involves a diminution of the quantity of labor demanded in the industry in question in spite of the extension of production which occurs. Technological unemployment is thus shown to be a component part of cyclical unemployment, and should not be contrasted with it as if it had nothing to do with the cycle.

This element of practically every depression spells great and painful, but in the main only transitory, difficnlties. ①For the total real demand for labor cannot in general permanently fall, be - cause, neglecting all compensating and all secondary elements, the expenditure of that part of entrepreneurial profit which is not annihilated by the fall in prices necessarily more than prevents any lasting shrinkage. Even if it were expended solely on consumption

① Cf. on this my article "Das Grundprinzip der Verteilungslehre," Archiv für Sozialw. und Sczialp. (Bd. 42).

（b）由此，我们必须分清楚这两种情况：新企业要么完全消灭老企业，要么迫使老企业限制他们的经营活动。为了抵制由此而引起的失业，新企业的持续经营肯定会引起对劳动的新需求。究竟这种新需求的数量能超出所产生的失业数多少，可以通过铁路和公共马车的例子来说明。但并非必然如此，而且即使是这样，也可能会有困难和摩擦，同时由于劳动市场运行的不完全，可能在两者平衡中，困难与失业不相称的还偏重一些。

（c）由于企业家对劳动的需求——这曾经创造了新的投资——最终停止了，上面提到的因繁荣的到来而产生的对劳动的新需求也会失去其重要性。

（d）通常，繁荣最终意味着进一步使生产过程机械化，因而必然减少生产单位产品所需要的劳动量；而且经常，虽然不是必然，它也包含着所讨论的工业对劳动需求量的减少，尽管会出现生产的扩张。这样，技术性失业就表现为周期性失业的一个组成部分，而且不应该与周期性失业相对立，好像与周期性失业无关一样。

实际上，每一次萧条的这种要素都是巨大的而且让人感到痛苦，但它主要还是暂时的困难。① 因为一般来说，对劳动的总的真实需求不会持久地下降，这是因为，忽略掉所有补充的以及所有次要因素，企业家利润中那部分未被价格下跌而消除的支出必然超过阻止任何永久性收缩所需要的量。即使它仅仅花费在消费上，

① 关于这一点，请参阅我的论文：《分配学说的基本原理》，载于《社会经济与社会政策文献》（第二卷）。

it must be resolved into wages-and rents, for I repeat that everything said here holds good theoretically for them too. When, and to the extent that, it is invested, an increase in the real demand for labor takes place.

(*e*) The boom, directly or in its effects, can permanently lower the real demand for labor in only one way: if in the new combinations it shifts the relative marginal significance of labor and land which obtained in the old productive combinations sufficiently to the disadvantage of labor. Then not only the share of labor in the social product but also the absolute amount of its real income may permanently fall. Practically more important than this case-but again not necessarily of a permanent nature-is a shift in the demand in favor of produced means of production already in existence.

With this qualification, then, we return to our conclusion that the economic nature of depression lies in the diffusion of the achievements of the boom over the whole economic system through the mechanism of the struggle for equilibrium; and that only temporary reactions, which are only in part necessary to the system, overshadow this fundamental feature and produce the atmosphere expressed in the word depression as well as the repercussion which even those indices exhibit which do not (or not exclusively) appertain to the sphere of money, credit, and prices, and do not simply reflect the automatic deflation characteristic of periods of depression.

6. The outbreak of a crisis initiates an abnormal course of events or that which is abnormal in the course of the events. As has been mentioned, it raises no new theoretical question. Our analysis shows us that panics, bankruptcies, breakdowns in the credit system, and so on *need* not but *may* easily appear at the point where prosperity turns into depression. The danger persists for some time, but

它也必定要分解为工资——以及租金，因为我反复强调，这里所说的每一个问题，在理论上都适用于它们。一旦它们被投资，在某种程度上，就会发生对劳动的真实需求的增加。

（e）繁荣，不论是直接地还是以其影响，只可能以一种方式使对劳动的真实需求永久地降低：如果在生产要素的新组合中，繁荣会转变劳动和土地的相对边际重要性，这个边际重要性原先产生于对劳动极不利的老生产组合。于是，不仅社会产品中劳动所占的份额，而且劳动实际收入的绝对数量都可能永久地下降。在实际中，比这种情况更重要的——但也不一定属于永久性质——是一种转变，这种转变有利于已经存在的被生产出来的生产资料的需求。

于是，根据这个限制条件，我们回到我们的结论：萧条时期的经济本质在于，通过努力争取均衡的机制，把繁荣带来的成果扩散到整个经济系统；同时，那些对于整个系统不是完全必要的暂时的反应，遮掩了这个基本特征，并且制造了一种表达为“萧条”的气氛，还产生了一种反响：甚至那些指数所表现的形式不属于（或者不完全属于）货币、信贷，以及价格范畴，而且不仅仅反映萧条时期自动的通货紧缩的特征。

6. 危机的爆发就发动了事件的非正常过程，或者就形成了那些在事件进程中不正常的事物。正如已经提到的，它并没有提出新的理论问题。我们的分析表明，恐慌、破产倒闭、信贷制度的崩溃等等，这些非必然的但是可能的现象，很容易在繁荣转向衰退的转折点出现。这种危险会持续一段时间，但是只要萧条过程更

it is smaller the more thoroughly the process of depression has done its work. ①If panics occur, then errors, which are first made in such a situation or are merely thrown into relief by it, states of public opinion, and so forth become independent causes, which they could not have been in the normal course of events; they become causes of a depression which exhibits different features and leads to different final results from the normal. The equilibrium that is finally established here is not the same as that which would otherwise have been established. The blunders and destruction cannot in general be corrected and repaired again, and they create situations which in turn have further effects, which must work themselves out; they mean new disturbances, and enforce processes of adaptation which would otherwise be superfluous. This distinction between the normal and abnormal course of events is very important, not only for the understanding of the nature of the thing, but also for the theoretical and practical questions connected with it.

We have seen-in contrast to the doctrine which sees in the business

① As the depression continues, the danger of a collapse of the economic system and of its credit structure becomes continually slighter. This statement is compat ible with the fact that most bankruptcies do not occur exactly at or near the turning point but only later, sometimes only when the danger to the economic system is past. For even the mortal wounding of a firm does not necessarily cause immediate flight to the bankruptcy court. On the contrary, everyone resists it as long as possible. And most firms can for a longer or shorter time. They themselves hope-and with them their creditors-for more favorable times. They deliberate, resort to shifts, seek new supports, sometimes with success, sometimes at least with such success that liquidation by consent is possible-more frequently, it is true, without success, but even then the death struggle results in postponing the bankruptcy or reorganisation, often into the next upward movement so that the drowning takes place in sight of dry land. This is not the result of new disasters, the danger of which actually falls progressively, but is the final consequence of those which happened long ago. Here, as elsewhere, we have to do with primary causes and the characteristic feature of the explanation, not with the question of when causes become visible. This creates an apparent discrepancy between our theory and observation. But every such discrepancy can only become an objection if it is shown that it is not satisfactorily explained.

加彻底地发挥其作用，它们就会变得更小。① 如果出现恐慌，那么一些首先产生于这种情况的失误或者只是因恐慌而急待解除的失误，以及公众舆论等等，就会成为独立的原因，而它们在事情的正常发展过程中本不会发生的。这样，它们就成为萧条的原因，这种萧条表现为不同特征并且导致各种最终结果偏离正常过程。这里最终确立的均衡，不同于在相反情况下建立的均衡。一般，重大的错误和破坏不能被改正和重新修复，它们所造成的局面反过来又产生进一步影响，这样它们必然自己寻找解决的出路；它们意味着新的干扰，而且意味着要强制实施这个适应过程，否则，这个适应性过程就是多余的。事态的正常与非正常过程之间的区别是很重要的，这不仅对与理解事物的本质，而且对于理解与这种事物相关的理论和实践问题都很重要。

我们已经看到——上面的观点与以下这个学说形成鲜明的

① 随着萧条的继续，经济系统及其信贷结构崩溃的危险就会逐渐减轻。这种论述与这个事实相符合，即大多数破产情形并不是恰好发生在转折点或者其附近，而是出现在转折点稍后，有时候只是在经济系统的危险过去之后才发生。因为，甚至一家厂商经历致命的打击后也不一定立即导致破产。相反，每个人都尽可能长时间地抵制破产。大多数厂商都可能在或长或短的时间里做到这一点。他们自己希望——同时他们的债权人也希望——拥有更有利的时机。他们仔细考虑，借助一定的手段、办法，寻找新的支持，有时候他们获得成功，有时候他们至少获得同意债务清理的成功——当然，更多时候，他们没有成功，但甚至就是在这个时候，垂死挣扎也会延迟破产或者重组，常常延迟到下一个上升过程，这样就起死回生。这并不是新的灾难带来的结果——实际上，新的灾难带来的危险已渐进地降临，这是很早以前发生的灾难的最终结果。这里，与别处一样，我们只考虑基本原因以及所解释的特征，而不关心什么时候原因才是明显可见的。这就产生了我们的理论与观察之间明显的不一致。但是，如果这些不一致表现出来了而没有得到满意的解释，那么每一种这样的不一致就会成为相对立的观点。

cycle essentially a monetary phenomenon or one which has its root in bank credit, and which is to - day especially associated with the names of Keynes, Fisher, and Hawtrey and with the policy of the Federal Reserve Board—that neither profits in a boom nor losses in a depression are meaningless and functionless. On the contrary, where the private entrepreneur in competition with his equals still plays a part, they are essential elements of the mechanism of economic development and cannot be eliminated without crippling the latter. This economic system cannot do without the *ultima ratio* of the complete destruction of those existences which are irretrievably associated with the hopelessly unadapted. But the losses and destruction which accompany the abnormal course of events are *really* meaningless and functionless. Justification of the various proposals for a prophylaxis and therapy of crises chiefly rests with them. The other sound starting point for remedial policy is the fact that even the normal-still more the abnormal-depression implicates individuals who have nothing to do with the cause and the meaning of the cycle, above all the workers.

The most important remedy *à la longue*, and the only one which is exposed to no objections, is the improvement of business cycle prognosis. The ever-increasing familiarity of businessmen with the cycle is, together with progressive trustification, the chief reason why the real crisis phenomena-events like the World War and times like the post-war period do not belong here-are becoming weaker. ① The postponement of new construction by government enterprises

① Increasing foresight also weakens the normal cyclical movement. It cannot prevent it, however, as will be recognised if our argument is scrutinised from this point of view. Therefore T. S. Adams goes too far when he states: "To anticipate the cycle is to neutralise it." It is different with the element mentioned earlier (2, b, "fourthly") that in the course of time economic development becomes continually more a "matter of calculation" (Rechenstift). This element is something different from the familiarity and foresight of which we are now speaking. It also mitigates the cyclical movement, but for another reason: it tends to eliminate the fundamental cause of the boom and therefore acts much more slowly, but in tendency much more completely, than the mere anticipation of the course of the cyclical movement-which as long as the cause exists is nevertheless unavoidable. It is different again with trustification: this mitigates the normal and abnormal course of events for the same reasons.

对照，这个学说在商业周期中看到的主要是货币现象，或者是一种植根于银行信贷的现象，而且这种学说在今天特别地与凯恩斯、费希尔、霍特里的名字以及联邦储备局的政策联系在一起——无论是繁荣时期产生的利润还是萧条时期发生的损失，都不是没有意义和不起作用的。相反，在与其对手相竞争的私营企业家仍然起着作用的地方，它们是经济发展机制的关键要素，而且它们不会被消除，否则经济发展机制就会瘫痪。如果不对那些不可避免地与没有希望适应的那种事物有关联的现存实体进行最后彻底破坏的斗争，那么这个经济系统就不能发挥作用。但是伴随着事情非正常过程的损失和毁坏确实是没有意义和不起作用的。对预防和整治危机的各种建议的论证，主要就依靠它们。其他合理的关于整治危机政策的出发点是这个事实：甚至是正常的过程——这仍然比非正常情况更多——萧条也牵涉到那些与周期的原因和意义没有关系的个人，首先是工人。

最重要的长期治疗，也是唯一的不会招致反对意见的做法，是对商业周期预测方法的改进。工商业者对商业周期的了解不断增加，同时托拉斯形式逐渐形成，于是，这就成为为什么真实的危机现象——像世界大战这样的事件，以及像战后那段时期，都不属于这一类——变得越来越微弱的主要原因。[①] 由国营企业或

① 不断增加的预见也削弱了正常的周期运动。然而，这不能阻止它，如果从这个观点来检查我们的论点，那么这一点就会得到认可。因此，当亚当斯说："预测周期就是使其失效"，这未免走得太远。这与前面提到的要素（2. b 中的"第四"）不同，即在时间发展过程中，经济发展不断更多地成为一种"计算问题"。这个要素与我们正讨论的熟悉程度和预见性有所不同。它也缓和了周期运动，但是因为另一个原因：它趋于消除产生繁荣的根本原因，因此它的运行速度比单纯对周期运动进程预测的速度更加缓慢，但在趋势上它更加完整——只要原因存在，这些怎么都是不可避免的。这也不同与托拉斯：出于同样的原因，它缓和了事件的正常与非正常过程。

or by great combines to periods of depression appears from our standpoint as a moderation of the consequences of the swarm-like appearance of new combinations and as an attenuation of the inflation of the boom and the deflation of the depression, hence as an effective means of alleviating the cyclical movement and the danger of crises. An indiscriminate and general increase in credit facilities means simply inflation, just as does a régime of government paper money. It may possibly obstruct completely the normal as well as the abnormal process. And it encounters not only the anti-inflationary argument in general, but also the argument that it destroys that measure of selection which can still be ascribed to the depression, and burdens the economic system with the unadapted and with those firms which are unfit to live. In contrast with this, credit restriction, which is usually undertaken by the banks unsystematically and without much foresight, appears in the light of a policy which is at least open to discussion, the policy of curing the evil by letting its acute consequences run their course. This procedure could be supplemented by other measures which would make it difficult for individual producers to resist the necessary fall in prices. But a credit policy is also conceivable-on the part of the individual banks as such, hut still more on the part of central banks with their influence upon the private banking world-which would differentiate between the phenomena of the normal process of the depression, which have an economic function, and the phenomena of the abnormal process, which destroy without function. It is true, such a policy would lead far into a special variety of economic planning which would infinitely increase the influence of political factors upon the fate of individuals and groups. But this involves a political judgment which does not concern us here. The technical prerequisites for such a policy, a comprehensive insight into the facts and possibilities of economic and cultural life, although theoretically obtainable in time, are at present undoubtedly not available. But theoretically, it is of interest to establish that such a policy is not impossible and is not simply to be classed with chimeras or with measures which are by nature unsuited to attain their ends, or finally with measures the reactions to which necessarily more than compensate for their direct effects.

者大型联合企业进行的新的建设推迟到萧条时期，从我们的观点来看，这似乎缓和了新组合成群出现的结果，也似乎减弱了繁荣时期的通货膨胀和萧条时期的通货紧缩，因而似乎这是减轻周期运动和危机威胁的一种有效手段。不加区别的以及普遍增加的信用工具简直就意味着通货膨胀，就像政府纸币的支配作用一样。它可能完全阻碍正常的过程，也可能完全阻碍非正常过程。它不仅遇到反通货膨胀的一般争论，而且还遇到了破坏那种仍可以归因于萧条的选择性措施的论点，它使经济系统负担着那些不能适应以及不适于生存的厂商。与此相比较，信贷限制——通常由银行无系统性地并且没有预见性地实施——却出现在至少可以公开讨论的政策面前，而这种医治灾难的政策却任其严重的结果自行地发展下去。这个程序可以用其他措施来补充，而这些其他措施可能使个别生产者很难抵制价格的必然下降。但是也可以构想出一种信贷政策——在那些银行本身方面，而更多的是对私营银行产生影响的中央银行方面——这种信贷政策能将具有经济作用的萧条其正常过程中的现象，与只有破坏作用而无经济作用的非正常过程中的现象区别开来。这种政策肯定会导致一种特殊的经济计划，这种计划将使政治因素对个人和团体命运的影响无限地增加，但这也包含着一种政治判断，在这里我们并不关心这个政治判断。这种政策在技术上的前提条件，以及对经济和文化生活的事实和可能性的全面洞察，尽管这些在理论上可以及时地得到，但无疑，在目前却得不到。但在理论上，确立下面的事实引起了人们的注意，即这种政策不是不可能的，也不能简单地把它归于幻想，或者归于那些本质上就不适于用作达到目的的手段，或者最终归于其得到的反作用必然大于其直接影响的那些

The phenomena of the normal and of the abnormal course of events are not merely distinguishable conceptually. They are in reality different things; and with a sufficiently deep insight, concrete cases even to-day may generally be recognized immediately as belonging to the one or the other. Such a policy would have to distinguish, within the mass of businesses threatened by disaster in any given depression, those made technically or commercially obsolete by the boom from those which appeared to be endangered by secondary circumstances, reactions, and accidents; it would leave the former alone, and support the latter by granting credit. And it might be successful in the same sense as that in which a conscious policy of racial hygiene might lead to successes unobtainable as long as things are left to work out automatically. In any case, however, crises will disappear earlier than the capitalist system, whose children they are.

But no therapy can permanently obstruct the great economic and social process by which businesses, individual positions, forms of life, cultural values and ideals, sink in the social scale and finally disappear. In a society with private property and competition, this process is the necessary complement of the continual emergence of new economic and social forms and of continually rising real incomes of all social strata. The process would be milder if there were no cyclical fluctuations, but it is not wholly due to the latter and it is completed independently of them. These changes are theoretically and practically, economically and culturally, much more important than the economic stability upon which all analytical attention has been concentrated for so long. And in their special way both the rise and the fall of families and firms are much more characteristic of the capitalist economic system, of its culture and its results, than any of the things that can be observed in a society which is stationary in the sense that its processes reproduce themselves at a constant rate.

措施。事件的正常与非正常过程中的现象不能单纯从概念上来区分。在现实中它们是不同的事物，随着充分深入地研究，甚至是今天发生的具体情况也可能立即被普遍地认为是属于其中的这一种或另一种。在大量深受任何特定萧条时期灾害威胁的企业中，这种政策应该区别出那些由于繁荣而在技术上或商业上过时的企业，和那些因为次要情况、反作用以及偶然事件而面临危险的企业；这种政策将不去管前一种情况的企业，而对于后者将给予信贷支持。这种政策可能会成功，出于同样的道理，正如一种有意制定的种族卫生政策可能会成功，而只要听任事情自动地去完成，这种成功就是不能实现的。然而，无论情况会是怎样，作为资本主义制度产物的危机，将先于资本主义制度消亡。

但是没有一种整治方法能永久地阻挠大规模的经济和社会发展过程，在这个过程中，企业、个人地位、生活方式、文化价值和理想等等，将沉没于社会的大规模之中，并且最终消失。在一个存在私人财产和竞争的社会里，这个过程是对不断出现的新的经济和社会形态的必要补充，也是对所有社会阶层逐渐上涨的实际收入的必要补充。如果没有周期性的波动，这个过程会更缓和，但这也不完全归因于周期性波动，并且这个过程的完成是独立于周期性波动的。在理论上和实际上，经济上和文化上，这些变化要比经济的稳定性更重要，而长期以来所有分析的注意力都被集中在稳定性上。而且家庭和厂商的兴衰，在它们特殊的变动方式中，比在以固定比率进行自我再生产过程的这种静态社会中所观察到的任何事物，具有更多的资本主义经济制度特征，包括它的文化和影响效果方面的特征。

译者后记

本书作者约瑟夫·阿洛伊斯·熊彼特，1883 年出生于奥匈帝国摩拉维亚省一个织布厂主的家庭，后入美国籍，是著名的经济学家。《经济发展理论》是他早期的成名著作，在这本书中他首先提出了“创新理论”，他也因此成为创新理论的创始人。这本著作最先以德文发表，后被雷德弗斯·奥佩翻译成英文，本书就是在此英译本的基础上翻译的。

熊彼特早年就读于一所贵族中学，1901 ~ 1906 年在维也纳大学攻读法律和经济专业，是奥地利学派主要代表人物庞巴维克的弟子；曾在德国从事社会工作，1925 年回到学术界，任德国波恩大学教授；1932 年迁居美国，任哈佛大学经济学教授，直到 1950 年逝世。他在学术上担任的职务有：1937 ~ 1941 年任“经济计量学会”会长，1948 ~ 1949 年任“美国经济学会”会长。他的著作《经济发展理论》在后来的经济学界以及实践中产生了深远的影响，有评价称它是“西方经济学界第一本用‘创新’理论来解释和阐述资本主义的产生和发展的专著”。

这本著作最突出的地方是创新理论思想。全书分六章，前两章所占篇幅较大，也尤为重要。第一章，作者阐述了在特定环境下，经济实体的流转过程。用生产力的组合来解释生产过程，同时将生产要素分成不同的级别，重点考察土地和劳动这两个原始生产要素；进而论述了“归属理论”；并用效用指数和边际效用的概念来表明各种生产要素的贡献；对成本概念有了新的认识，在论述中已经蕴涵着机会成本的内容；通过对价值创造的分析，把归属过程回归到原始生产资料；在第一章还考虑了时间因素，这样就把风险价值也包括了；此外，它还分析了交换经济的方式，对货物流和货币流之间的关系进行了阐述。第二章，作者主要针对经济发展的本质现象进行讨论与分析。归纳起来有，经济发展过程如其他过程一样，每一阶段的情况都要依赖于前一阶段的结果，它是动态的；经济发展的动态过程不是没有规律的，而是由一个均衡走向另一个均衡，这个过程就是生产要素重新组合的过程，也就是创新的过程；经济发展离不开“企业家”这个创新的开拓者，这里，作者详细说明了企业家在经济发展中的职能。

第三、四、五章分别从信贷与资本、利润、利息这几种经济现象说明经济发展过程。第三章中，作者写到，信贷是为了企业家的创新行为而产生的，它是一种支付手段，也是经济发展的一种要素；资本，是一种杠杆，它可以将生产要素用于新用途，而且它被企业家所掌握；作者进一步说明了资本市场的主要职能是用信贷交易筹措资金。在第四章，作者围绕利润的产生、利润与工资的区别，以及利润在交换经济与非交换经济中由于竞争而最终消失，详细地论述了利润的特征，其产生与消亡过程，以及利润转变成地租。第五章，主要阐述了利息的存在，比较不同的经济形态下利息的存在问题，以及利息产生的源泉，作者认为利息是一种价值剩余。在最后一章，作者对商业周期进行了初步探讨。首先从危机谈起，认为危机的发生有其周期性，危机是经济繁荣与衰退交替波浪式运动的要素；接下来，作者详细论述了繁荣如何产生，繁荣带来的后果有哪些，由繁荣到萧条，再到繁荣，是由一个均衡到另一个均衡的过程，在这些过程中，对不同的企业带来不同的影响，有的企业将退出，有的企业通过前面所说的信贷，或者结构调整，可能获得重生。

熊彼特的《经济发展理论》是以早期发达资本主义国家为研究对象的，他的经济发展理论也可以称为“创新理论”，没有谈到生产关系和生产力在经济发展中的作用，他站在资本主义国家的角度谈经济的发展，谈企业家利润以及利息，所以有他的局限性；但他在提倡技术创新，强调企业家在经济发展中的作用等方面，提出了新的思想，对我们今天的企业改革，提高生产效率，鼓励创新有重要的理论借鉴意义。

这个英译本曾在上个世纪 90 年代初由商务印书馆翻译发行，本次翻译，借鉴其中的优良方法，忠实原著，希望在其基础上能有新的进步。

叶　华

2006 年 10 月

《西方学术经典文库》(第一辑)

功利主义	[英]约翰·斯图亚特·穆勒
诗学·诗艺	[古希腊]亚里士多德 [古罗马]贺拉斯
经济发展理论	[美]约瑟夫·阿洛伊斯·熊彼特
经济学原理	[英]阿尔弗雷德·马歇尔
国民财富的性质与原理	[英]亚当·斯密
联邦党人文集	[美]亚历山大·汉密尔顿
就业、利息和货币通论	[英]约翰·梅纳德·凯恩斯
尼各马可伦理学	[古希腊]亚里士多德
道德情操论	[英]亚当·斯密
君主论	[意]尼科洛·马基雅弗利
新教伦理与资本主义精神	[德]马克斯·韦伯
古代法	[英]亨利·萨姆奈·梅因
第一哲学沉思集	[法]勒内·笛卡儿
查拉图斯特拉如是说	[德]弗里德里希·威廉·尼采
哲学研究	[英]路德维希·维特根斯坦
实践理性批判	[德]伊曼努尔·康德
社会契约论	[法]让·雅克·卢梭
理想国	[古希腊]柏拉图
心理学原理	[美]威廉·詹姆斯
精神现象学	[德]威廉·弗里德里希·黑格尔
神圣者的观念	[德]鲁道夫·奥托
小逻辑	[德]威廉·弗里德里希·黑格尔

论人类不平等的起源	[法]让·雅克·卢梭
道德形而上学基础	[德]伊曼努尔·康德
人性论	[英]戴维·休谟
政府论	[英]约翰·洛克
论法的精神	[法]查尔斯·路易斯·孟德斯鸠
代议制政府	[英]约翰·斯图亚特·穆勒
英国法与文艺复兴	[英]弗雷德里克·威廉·梅特兰
法律社会学基本原理	[奥]尤根·埃利希
论美国民主	[法]夏尔·阿列克西·德·托克维尔
原始社会的结构和功能	[英]A. R. 拉德克利夫-布朗
政治学	[古希腊]亚里士多德
罗马帝国编年史	[古罗马]科尔涅里乌斯·塔西佗
普通语言学教程	[瑞士]费尔迪南·德·索绪尔
货币哲学	[德]格奥尔格·西梅尔
法理学讲演录	[英]约翰·奥斯丁
思想录	[法]布莱兹·帕斯卡
利维坦	[英]托马斯·霍布斯
意识形态与乌托邦	[德]卡尔·曼海姆
忏悔录	[古罗马]圣·奥古斯丁
西太平洋上的航海者	[英]布罗尼斯拉夫·马林诺夫斯基
历史学:理论和实际	[意]贝内德托·克罗齐
逻辑哲学论	[英]路得维希·维特根斯坦